UNDERSTANDING RESEARCH FOR SOCIAL POLICY AND SOCIAL WORK

THEMES, METHODS AND APPROACHES

Second edition

Edited by Saul Becker, Alan Bryman and Harry Ferguson

Editorial Assistant: Rebecca Swift

First published published in Great Britain in 2012 by
The Policy Press
University of Bristol
Fourth Floor, Beacon House
Queen's Road
Bristol BS8 1QU
UK
t: +44 (0)117 331 4054
f: +44 (0)117 331 4093
tpp-info@bristol.ac.uk
www.policypress.co.uk

North American office:
The Policy Press
c/o The University of Chicago Press
1427 East 60th Street
Chicago, IL 60637, USA
t: +1 773 702 7700
f: +1 773-702-9756
e:sales@press.uchicago.edu
www.press.uchicago.edu

British Library Cataloguing in Publication Data
A catalogue record for this book is available from the British Library.

Library of Congress Cataloging-in-Publication Data
A catalog record for this book has been requested.

ISBN 978 1 84742 815 8 paperback
ISBN 978 1 84742 816 5 hardcover

Cover design by Qube Design Associates, Bristol
Front cover: photograph kindly supplied by www.alamy.com
Printed and bound in Great Britain by Hobbs, Southampton
The Policy Press uses environmentally responsible print partners

UNDERSTANDING RESEARCH FOR SOCIAL POLICY AND SOCIAL WORK

Also available in the series

Understanding 'race' and ethnicity
Theory, history, policy, practice
Gary Craig, Karl Atkin, Sangeeta Chattoo and Ronny Flynn

"The title of this text belies the far reaching challenge it poses to the discipline, research base and practice of social policy. Its argument that mainstream social policy has consistently marginalised the issue of 'race' and minority ethnic concerns is well founded when judged against the historical record, the evidence base and contemporary shortfalls in policy and practice. This is a deep exploration of the complexities of diversity and difference that speaks to contemporary concerns about substantive citizenship and social justice." Professor Charlotte Williams, OBE, Keele University.
PB £22.99 (US$38.95) **ISBN** 978 1 84742 770 0 **HB** £65.00 (US$85.00) **ISBN** 978 1 84742 771 7
336 pages February 2012
INSPECTION COPY AVAILABLE

Understanding disability policy
Alan Roulstone and Simon Prideaux

"Disability policy has changed dramatically over the last fifty years and especially so since the turn of the 21st century. Roulstone and Prideaux have produced a comprehensive and accessible analysis of these changes that will prove to be an invaluable text for students, researchers and policy analysts across a range of disciplines: highly recommended." Colin Barnes, University of Leeds
PB £21.99 (US$36.95) **ISBN** 978 1 84742 738 0 **HB** £65.00 (US$89.95) **ISBN** 978 1 84742 739 7
256 pages January 2012
INSPECTION COPY AVAILABLE

Understanding housing policy (Second edition)
Brian Lund

"An excellent historical and theoretical review of housing policy: thoughtful, well informed, critical and up to date." Chris Paris, Professor of Housing Studies, University of Ulster, Northern Ireland
PB £22.99 (US$34.95) **ISBN** 978 1 84742 631 4 **HB** £65.00 (US$85.00) **ISBN** 978 1 84742 632 1
352 pages April 2011
INSPECTION COPY AVAILABLE

Understanding the environment and social policy
Tony Fitzpatrick

"The intersection of social policy and environmental policy is strategically and morally vital yet has remained a strangely neglected area. No longer. This comprehensive book covers real world challenges, sustainable ethics, a host of applied policy issues, and some bigger questions about the possibility of a green welfare state." Ian Gough, Emeritus Professor, University of Bath
PB £21.99 (US$36.95) **ISBN** 978 1 84742 379 5 **HB** £65.00 (US$85.00) **ISBN** 978 1 84742 380 1
384 pages February 2011
INSPECTION COPY AVAILABLE

For a full listing of all titles in the series visit www.policypress.co.uk

www.policypress.co.uk

INSPECTION COPIES AND ORDERS AVAILABLE FROM:
Marston Book Services • PO BOX 269 • Abingdon • Oxon OX14 4YN UK
INSPECTION COPIES
Tel: +44 (0) 1235 465500 • Fax: +44 (0) 1235 465556 • Email: inspections@marston.co.uk
ORDERS
Tel: +44 (0) 1235 465500 • Fax: +44 (0) 1235 465556 • Email: direct.orders@marston.co.uk

To Jane (SB), Sue, Sarah and Darren (AB)
and Claire (HF)

Contents

List of contributors

[*Publishers' note:* we have endeavoured to ensure that these details were correct at the time of going to print.]

Pete Alcock, Professor of Social Policy and Administration, Director of the Third Sector Research Centre (TSRC), School of Social Policy, University of Birmingham

Charles Antaki, Professor of Language and Social Psychology, Department of Social Sciences, Loughborough University

Karl Ashworth, Principal Methodologist, Office for National Statistics

Mary Baginsky, Assistant Director, Children's Workforce Development Council

Matt Barnard, Head of Evaluation, NSPCC

Sarah Banks, Professor in the School of Applied Social Sciences, Durham University

Fiona Becker, Senior Consultant, NSPCC

Saul Becker, Professor of Social Policy and Social Care, Head of School, School of Sociology and Social Policy, The University of Nottingham

Peter Beresford, Director of the Centre for Citizen Participation, School of Health Sciences and Social Care, Brunel University

Nigel Bilsbrough, Former Finance and Resources Manager, Centre for Research in Social Policy, Department of Social Sciences, Loughborough University

Annette Boaz, Lecturer in Translational Research, Division of Health and Social Care Research, King's College London

Joanna Bornat, Emeritus Professor, Faculty of Health and Social Care, The Open University

Jonathan Bradshaw, Professor of Social Policy and Social Work, Department of Social Policy and Social Work, University of York

John D. Brewer, Sixth Century Professor, Department of Sociology, University of Aberdeen

Alan Bryman, Professor of Organisational and Social Research, University of Leicester

Emma Carmel, Lecturer in Social Policy, Department of Social and Policy Sciences, University of Bath

Patrick Carmichael, Professor of Educational Research, Faculty of Education, Community and Leisure, Liverpool John Moores University

Anne Corden, Senior Research Fellow, Social Policy Research Unit, University of York

Louise Corti, Associate Director, UK Data Archive, University of Essex

Gary Craig, Professor of Community Development and Social Justice, School of Applied Social Sciences, Durham University

Duncan Cramer, Professor of Psychological Health, Department of Social Sciences, Loughborough University

Christopher Day, Professor of Education, School of Education, The University of Nottingham

David Deacon, Professor of Communication and Media Analysis, Department of Social Sciences, Loughborough University

David de Vaus, Executive Dean, Faculty of Social and Behavioural Sciences, University of Queensland, Australia

Mary Dixon-Woods, Professor of Medical Sociology, Department of Health Sciences, University of Leicester

Harry Ferguson, Professor of Social Work, Director of the Centre for Social Work, School of Sociology and Social Policy, The University of Nottingham

Ben Fincham, Lecturer in Sociology, Centre for Gender Studies, University of Sussex

Jerry Floersch, Associate Professor, Rutgers University School of Social Work, New Jersey, USA

Lynn Froggett, Professor of Psychosocial Welfare and Director of Psychosocial Research Unit, International School of Communities, Rights and Inclusion, University of Central Lancashire

Rachel Fyson, Associate Professor in Social Work, Centre for Social Work, School of Sociology and Social Policy, The University of Nottingham

Graham R. Gibbs, Reader in Research Methods, Human and Health Sciences, University of Huddersfield

David Gordon, Professorial Research Fellow, Centre for the Study of Poverty and Social Justice, and Director of the Townsend Centre for International Poverty Research, University of Bristol

Hilary Graham, Professor of Health Sciences, Department of Health Sciences, University of York

Martyn Hammersley, Professor in Educational and Social Research, Centre for Childhood, Development and Learning, The Open University

Mark Hardy, Lecturer in Social Work, Department of Social Policy and Social Work, University of York

Alexa Hepburn, Lecturer in Social Psychology, Department of Social Sciences, Loughborough University

Michael Hirst, Former Research Fellow, Social Policy Research Unit, University of York

Lesley Hoggart, Principal Research Fellow, School of Health and Social Care, University of Greenwich

Lisa Holmes, Assistant Director, Centre for Child and Family Research, Department of Social Sciences, Loughborough University

Sally Holland, Senior Lecturer in Social Work, Cardiff School of Social Sciences, Cardiff University

Annie Irvine, Research Fellow, Social Policy Research Unit, University of York

Stephen Joseph, Professor of Psychology, Health and Social Care, School of Sociology and Social Policy, The University of Nottingham

Savita Katbamna, Visiting Research Fellow, Department of Health Sciences, University of Leicester

Ravi K.S. Kohli, Professor of Child Welfare, Head of Applied Social Studies, Department of Applied Social Studies, University of Bedfordshire

Jane Lewis, Professor of Social Policy, Department of Social Policy, London School of Economics and Political Science

Pranee Liamputtong, Personal Chair in Public Health, School of Public Health, La Trobe University, Australia

Jeffrey Longhofer, Associate Professor, Rutgers University of School of Social Work, New Jersey, USA

Stephen McKay, Professor of Social Research, Institute of Applied Social Studies, University of Birmingham

Clare Madge, Reader, Department of Geography, University of Leicester

Reima Ana Maglajlic, Senior Lecturer, School of Human and Health Sciences, Swansea University

Nicholas Mays, Professor of Health Policy, Department of Health Sciences Research and Policy, London School of Hygiene and Tropical Medicine

Bren Neale, Professor of Life Course and Family Research, Sociology and Social Policy, University of Leeds

Carolyn Noble, Professor in Social Work, Department of Social Sciences and Psychology, Victoria University, Melbourne, Australia

Henrietta O'Connor, Senior Lecturer, Centre for Labour Market Studies, University of Leicester

Stewart Page, Professor of Psychology, Department of Psychology, University of Windsor, Canada

Jan Pahl, Emeritus Professor of Social Policy, School of Social Policy, Sociology and Social Research, University of Kent

Alison Park, Research Director, National Centre for Social Research

Elizabeth Peel, Senior Lecturer in Psychology, School of Life and Health Sciences, Aston University

Cassandra Phoenix, Lecturer, Sport and Health Sciences, University of Exeter

Robert Pinker, Emeritus Professor of Social Administration, London School of Economics and Political Science

Jennie Popay, Professor of Sociology and Public Health, School of Health and Medicine, Lancaster University

Catherine Pope, Professor of Medical Sociology, Faculty of Health Sciences, University of Southampton

Jonathan Potter, Professor of Discourse Analysis, Department of Social Sciences, Loughborough University

Stephen Potter, Professor of Transport Strategy, The Design Group, The Open University

Colin Robson, Emeritus Professor, School of Human and Health Sciences, University of Huddersfield

Karen Rowlingson, Professor of Social Policy, Institute of Applied Social Studies, University of Birmingham

Roy Sainsbury, Professor and Research Director, Welfare and Employment Team, Social Policy Research Unit, University of York

Jonathan Scourfield, Professor of Social Work, Cardiff School of Social Sciences, Cardiff University

Clive Seale, Professor of Medical Sociology, Institute of Health Sciences Education, Queen Mary University of London

Joe Sempik, Special Lecturer, School of Sociology and Social Policy, The University of Nottingham

Elaine Sharland, Senior Lecturer in Social Work and Social Care, Department of Social Work and Social Care, University of Sussex

Ian F. Shaw, Professor of Social Work, Department of Social Policy and Social Work, University of York

Janet Smithson, Research Fellow, School of Psychology, University of Exeter

William Solesbury, Associate Director of the Economic and Social Research Council (ESRC) UK Centre for Evidence-Based Policy

Bruce Stafford, Professor of Public Policy, School of Sociology and Social Policy, The University of Nottingham

Patricia Thomson, Professor of Education, School of Education, The University of Nottingham

Peter Townsend, Former Professor of International Social Policy, London School of Economics and Political Science, and Emeritus Professor of Social Policy, University of Bristol

Harriet Ward, Professor of Child and Family Research and Director of the Centre for Child and Family Research, Department of Social Sciences, Loughborough University

Samantha Warren, Professor in Management, Essex Business School, University of Essex

David Westlake, Research Associate, Centre for Child and Family Research, Department of Social Sciences, Loughborough University

Sue White, Professor of Social Work (Children and Families), Institute of Applied Social Studies, University of Birmingham

Sharon Witherspoon, Deputy Director, The Nuffield Foundation

Ruth Wodak, Distinguished Professor of Discourse Studies, Department of Linguistics and English Language, Lancaster University

Acknowledgements

This is the second edition of *Understanding research for social policy and practice*, but with a new title and 42 new contributors joining the 41 who also contributed to the first edition. Our intended audience has also expanded. This volume has been specifically designed for those studying and working in *social work* as well as those concerned with *social policy*. Thus, many of our new contributors are social work academics as well as others who are social policy experts, and the volume contains numerous new worked examples drawn from social work alongside the many dozens from social policy.

While the basic structure of the volume is similar to the first edition, effectively it is almost an entirely new book. With half of our contributors being new to this volume, we have also included a new chapter on ethics along with 21 new main sections and 38 new boxes. All other sections and boxes have been updated, often extensively, to take account of new thinking and developments in social research. We are grateful to our panel of 83 contributors who gave their time and expertise to make this volume possible.

Thanks also to Joe Sempik at The University of Nottingham who helped with the proofreading. Our special thanks must go to Rebecca Swift, also of The University of Nottingham, who was our Editorial Assistant and who was instrumental in helping with commissioning and putting together the typescript. We could not have coped without her! Thanks also to Alison Shaw at The Policy Press for persuading us to compile this volume, and her colleagues – Jo Morton, Charlotte Skelton, Laura Vickers, Kathryn King, Dave Worth, Emily Watt – for their fantastic support, super efficiency and abundance of patience.

Saul Becker, Alan Bryman and Harry Ferguson
Nottingham
October 2011

Introduction

Audiences

This book has been produced in order to meet the needs of several different audiences. One audience is made up of **undergraduate** and **postgraduate students** undertaking modules in research methods and conducting small-scale research projects as part of their degrees. The book will provide students with the knowledge and skills for critically appraising the research they read, and a springboard for undertaking and writing up their own investigations.

A second audience includes **researchers** in the broad areas of social policy and social work research. Researchers will benefit from the insights gleaned from an overview of the methodological issues and choices that relate to social policy and social work research that have been written by leading authorities in social research methods generally and in social policy and social work specifically. Some of the sections, particularly the ones on dissemination and knowledge transfer, have been written with this audience in mind.

The third audience for the book includes **practitioners** (including social workers, health workers and the many others) with an interest or engagement in the broad areas of social policy implementation and social work practice. Many of these practitioners are in a position where they need to evaluate or synthesise existing research, or to produce their own investigations. For this group, the insights from the book should be invaluable. Some of the sections will introduce practitioners to cutting-edge innovations in methodology and approaches that will be of particular significance to them and how they might go about conducting their own studies. For example, sections on user involvement in research, action research, practitioner research, psychosocial research and evaluation research have been included with this group in mind. Additionally, discussions of the nature of evidence, what counts as evidence and how research evidence can inform or influence policy and practice, will be of particular interest to practitioners 'in the field'.

Aims

The overall aims of the book are to:

- help the reader to understand better the policy-making process (including how policy is made, delivered and implemented at the 'front line' by social workers and others) (Chapter One);
- help the reader to understand the critical role that 'good' research plays within this process, and how it can be used to inform policy making and professional practice (Chapter One);
- equip the reader with a knowledge of ethics, approaches, issues, research designs and methods so that they are able to 'read' existing research on social policy and social work in a more critical and informed manner, and are able to conduct and manage their own studies (Chapters Two, Three, Four, Five and Six);

- provide an understanding of how research can be disseminated effectively, to increase the likelihood of trustworthy and reliable evidence being used by policy makers and practitioners to inform their work and practice (Chapter Seven);
- convey something of the breadth and excitement of social policy and social work research. We have drawn research examples and illustrations from a wide range of fields, utilising a diversity of methodological and other approaches. In so doing, we want to show how broad and dynamic social policy and social work research can be, how challenging are the debates and issues that researchers must face, and how important are the research findings for the welfare and well-being of millions of citizens – be they on the 'receiving end' of social policies or social work interventions, or those charged with formulating or implementing policy and practice.

Structure

Chapter One provides much of the background to the book and should be read first as a foundation for the subsequent chapters. It deals with the questions of what we mean by social policy and social work research and related terms, and what kinds of factors are conventionally associated with 'good research' in these areas. The chapter addresses the nature of the processes of policy making and implementation and the role that research can usefully play in relation to these activities and social work practice. The chapter recognises that in fields like social policy and social work, issues to do with values and politics frequently come into play, and explores the significance of this fact. It also explores why we need research at all, and why there has been a trend in recent years to *evidence-based (or evidence-informed) policy and practice*. The latter is very much at the heart of issues with which this book is concerned, namely, why we need *research-based* evidence in order to inform social policy and social work practice. Finally in this chapter, a model of the research process is presented which seeks to show how many of the different elements of social policy and social work research explored in this book are interconnected.

An important indicator of quality in research is attention to issues of ethics and ethical conduct. These issues lie at the heart of **Chapter Two**. Here, the rigour and ethical conduct of social policy and social work research is construed in terms of: the following of ethical principles and ethical codes; the systematic management of all stages of the research process; ensuring the safety of both researchers and research participants; and managing confidentiality and protecting data collected from participants. These issues are especially important given that so much social policy and social work research is concerned with sensitive topics and vulnerable groups, also discussed in the chapter. A key point of this chapter is to suggest that 'good' research is not just to do with technical issues such as how well a sample is designed, the quality of a questionnaire or how well the data are analysed. Ethical conduct looms large in considerations of the *quality* and *rigour* of research.

In this book, we emphasise how social policy and social work research is and should be driven by research ideas and specific research questions. These form the primary focus of **Chapter Three** where the issues of what research questions are and where they come from are examined. An important consideration here is the role that the existing published literature on a topic of inquiry has in helping the researcher to formulate research questions. The chapter emphasises the importance of conducting a literature review and the factors that need to be borne in mind when devising one. The budget and resources that a researcher has available also inform the question(s) to some extent, and this is also considered. A related issue is what part *theory* plays in relation to social policy and social work research. Theory can be used as a background and rationale to the research questions that are asked but equally research can inform theory. The nature of the interaction between theory and research figures prominently in the discussion.

The fields of social policy and social work research are beset with a diversity of methodological approaches and debates. **Chapter Four** provides a route through these issues. It begins by considering the well-known debate about the relative merits and significance of *quantitative* and *qualitative* research, and then considers the growing interest and use of *mixed methods* approaches. It then explores a diversity of different approaches to social policy and social work research, including the role of feminism, issues around 'race', the degree to which policy recipients and service users can be involved in the research process, action research, the evaluation of policies, programmes and practices, and doing research cross-nationally. Unobtrusive methods are also considered. The discussion then moves on to explore issues to do with the examination and synthesis of existing data and published research. As such, issues concerned with reviewing existing research and with the archiving and analysis of other researchers' data are emphasised.

Chapter Five is concerned with the tools of *quantitative* research. It begins by examining the criteria quantitative researchers employ for assessing the quality of investigations with this research strategy. It then moves on to a consideration of the main types of research design that are employed by quantitative researchers. This entails an examination of four types of research design: the experiment; the cross-sectional design; the longitudinal design; and the case study. Research questions continue to loom large here too because a research design is presented as a framework that will allow a research question to be answered. There then follows a discussion of sampling in quantitative research, which includes a consideration of what it means to seek a representative sample from which generalisations can be forged and the factors that promote and detract from the ability to generate such a sample from different approaches to sampling. The chapter considers the main research methods associated with the collection of data and how data are coded to facilitate analysis. In this section, the following are examined: structured interviews and questionnaires in survey research; internet surveys; content analysis; structured observation; and the use of official statistics. Finally, the chapter contains a discussion of the main ingredients of quantitative data analysis.

Chapter Six forms a parallel chapter to Chapter Five. Thus, it begins with an examination of the criteria *qualitative* researchers employ for assessing the quality of investigations with this research strategy. There is then an examination of the main research designs in social policy and social work research, which entails a primary focus on the case study, cross-sectional and longitudinal designs. The chapter then moves on to a consideration of issues to do with sampling. Here we find that the importance placed on generating a representative sample is less pronounced than in the context of quantitative research. There is then an examination of the main methods and sources of qualitative data. These include: semi-structured and unstructured interviewing; telephone interviewing; ethnography; focus groups; documents; and the use of the internet for the collection of qualitative data. Finally, there is an examination of some different approaches to the analysis of qualitative data, such as grounded theory, coding and computer-assisted analysis, discourse analysis, conversation analysis and narrative analysis. There is also a discussion of the use of verbatim quotes when writing up qualitative research.

Research is likely to be of little use to anyone unless it is disseminated and the knowledge gained from studies is made available to relevant audiences, and this is the main concern of **Chapter Seven**. In this chapter, the reader is introduced to what is meant by dissemination and knowledge transfer, and the different forms that these might take. Practical advice is offered on how to write a report and how to plan a strategy for disseminating findings and for knowledge transfer. The degree to which research really can inform and influence policy and practice – how it can make an impact – is also addressed.

Special features

In presenting discussions of these issues and topics, we make frequent use of a number of features to aid the reader's understanding:

- *Illustrative boxes:* many of the main expositions are embellished with boxed text that provides an example of the issue or method being discussed. In some cases, a box is used to describe a particular facet of the main topic, for example, a box on visual ethnography in conjunction with the main exposition of ethnography.
- *Questions for discussion:* these can be used as the basis for individual revision, or in class-based discussions, to check out learning and as a catalyst for further work and discussions.
- *Further reading:* most sections and boxes are accompanied by further reading to guide the reader in examining an issue in greater depth.
- *Relevant organisations:* many sections and boxes are supplemented with information about organisations that are relevant to the topic. These include organisations concerned with methodological issues and ones with specific policy or practice-related interests.
- *Website resources:* where appropriate, websites are given of relevant organisations or where further information relating to a research method or approach can be gleaned from a website.

one

Research for social policy and social work

Detailed contents

1.1 Introduction

This chapter provides the context for the rest of the book, and should therefore be read first. The overall aims of the book are to:

- help the reader to understand better the *policy-making process* (including how policy is made, delivered and implemented at the 'front line' by social workers and other professional groups) (Chapter One);
- help the reader to understand the *role that 'good' research plays* within this process, and how it can be used to inform policy making and social work practice (Chapter One);
- equip the reader with a knowledge of *ethics* and *ethical procedures, approaches, issues, research methods and designs* so that they are able to 'read' existing research on social policy and social work in a more critical and informed manner, and are able to conduct and manage their own studies in an ethically appropriate manner (Chapters Two, Three, Four, Five and Six);
- provide an understanding of *how research can be disseminated and how knowledge can be communicated effectively*, to increase the likelihood of trustworthy and reliable evidence being used by policy makers, social workers and other professionals to inform their work (Chapter Seven);
- convey something of the *breadth and excitement of social policy and social work research*. We have drawn research examples and illustrations from a wide range of fields, utilising a diversity of methodological and other approaches. In so doing, we want to show how broad and dynamic social work and social policy research can be, how challenging the debates and issues are that researchers must face, and the importance of research findings for the welfare and well-being of millions of citizens – be they on the 'receiving end' of social policies or social work intervention, or those charged with formulating or implementing them.

In this chapter we focus on the first two aims. We discuss:

- what is meant by terms such as *social policy, social work, research* and *good research*;
- how research can inform policy making and its implementation;
- the role that politics and ideology play in this process;
- how research evidence is an important *way of knowing* about the social world, and why it might be more reliable than, for example, personal beliefs or other sources of evidence;
- why there is a shift towards a greater emphasis on *evidence-based policy and practice* – in its various forms – and what the limits might be to this development.

Finally, we provide a *model of the research process* that helps readers to understand the relationships between research, policy making and professional practice, and signposts how all the chapters in the volume 'fit' with the model and how they relate to each other.

1.2 Social policy and social work
Pete Alcock and Harry Ferguson

What is social policy?

'Social policy' is an academic subject, studied by students in higher education as a discrete subject or as part of a broader social science programme. It is also incorporated into the professional training programmes for many public service professionals, such as social workers and nurses. Furthermore, it is the focus of research activity by academics who explore how and why policies have developed and how they operate within the social world.

Social policy is also the term used to refer to the practice of social intervention aimed at securing social change to promote the welfare and well-being of citizens. Social policies are pursued by governments, and by non-governmental organisations (NGOs), in order to promote well-being by improving individual life chances and social relations – for instance, through the provision of social security benefits, education, health and social care, public housing, and such like. Social policy refers both to the practice of, and to the academic study of, policy action. Most public service professionals, including social workers, therefore need to study social policy. It also means that social policy research is carried out not just by academics but also by policy makers, social workers and other practitioners – and by academics *for* policy makers and practitioners.

Policy, implementation and practice

This *relationship between analysis and practice* is thus right at the heart of social policy, and in particular it structures the way research on social policy is developed and carried out. Most (if not all) social policy research is linked directly or indirectly to the current or future development and implementation of social policies – for instance, social policy researchers work to monitor and evaluate the policy programmes implemented by government, and others. Social policy researchers, and social policy students, must therefore address this interface of theory and practice. More pertinently perhaps, most social policy researchers and students *want* to do this. It is in order to understand, and then to influence, the policy process that most people are attracted to study and research in social policy. And the evidence is that this study and research have often had a significant impact on the policy process – for instance, a famous study of the continuing problem of poverty in Britain by Brian Abel-Smith and Peter Townsend (1965), despite the welfare reforms of the post-war era, forced the government to admit that poverty was still a social problem and to develop new policy measures to respond to this (albeit not the measures that the authors might have been proposing at the time). Peter Townsend describes this research and its significance to social policy in *Box 1a*.

Box 1a: National Assistance and the rediscovery of poverty: *The poor and the poorest*
Peter Townsend

The idea for *The poor and the poorest* (Abel-Smith and Townsend, 1965) grew out of the long tradition of research in the UK on poverty. Booth, Rowntree, Bowley, Llewellyn-Smith and many more had pioneered surveys in various parts of Britain for the previous 100 years. But by the 1950s there was an air of complacency. It was widely believed, partly because of the Rowntree–Lavers report of 1951, that the post-war welfare state in the UK had virtually eliminated poverty (Rowntree and Lavers, 1951). Brian Abel-Smith and I had already set to work on the subject and believed that this conclusion was wrong and that a clear break from the traditional approaches to research had to be made to reach reliable conclusions. More convincing scientific investigation of low income and need, based on painstaking objective observations of social conditions and of personal and institutional behaviour, rather than on 'expert' or middle-class values, had to be organised. The values of social elites, and political entrepreneurs like Beveridge, continued to shape empirical enquiries – 'desert' was implicit in both the attitudes of investigators and the 'measures' believed to be appropriate. As a consequence poverty was minimised.

Two plans were devised. One was to undertake a new nationally representative survey of an unprecedently ambitious kind to develop objective, subjective and conventional institutional approaches to the investigation of poverty (see Chapter Five of this volume for a full discussion of survey methodology and sampling techniques). This was a programme of research approved and funded from 1964 by the Joseph Rowntree Memorial Trust. Inevitably, it would take some years to complete. The programme resulted in a series of reports in the late 1960s and through the 1970s – on unemployment, disability, large families and lone-parent families – and later, the final comprehensive report that also included an analysis of the four poorest areas in the UK, *Poverty in the United Kingdom* (Townsend, 1979).

The second plan was to quickly draw together in a short book the best estimates that could be made from existing data of trends in the extent of poverty. In 1965, *The poor and the poorest* (preceded, as it happens, by papers to the British Sociological Association in 1962) was to form the centrepiece of the newly founded Child Poverty Action Group's (CPAG) campaign to mobilise effective anti-poverty action. The Prime Minister at the time, Harold Wilson, welcomed the authors to Downing Street in December. The book was based on a new idea; its authority, based on government data, was difficult to deny, and it quickly gained wide public and specialist support. The reaction to the publication 'marked not only the campaign for what became child benefit, but also the arrival of the modern single-issue pressure group in British politics' (Timmins, 1995, p 257).

Because Sir William (later Lord) Beveridge had defined poverty as income insufficient to purchase the necessities of life, and intended to match National Insurance benefits with that 'subsistence standard' of living, we hit on the idea of comparing the levels of benefits put in place after the Second World War with information about the distribution of income – collected for other purposes by the government. The method allowed some answer to be given to the questions: how many people's incomes fall below the government's standards of benefit? How adequate are the different benefits to lift people out of poverty?

We took advantage of a new Ministry of Labour survey of 13,000 households in 1953-54 (published in 1957) about the distribution of income and expenditure to rework the data they had collected to reveal how many in the population had lower income than the rates of National Assistance at the time. These rates can be regarded as 'institutionalised' measures of need rather than as measures that can be scientifically justified. The Ministry of Labour wanted to construct a more reliable cost-of-living index rather than review need and low income, and from 1957 conducted a smaller annual survey, the *Family Expenditure Survey*. With the Ministry's generous help, visits were paid to their offices in London and Watford – where completed questionnaires and schedules could be examined and checked individually to extract specific household income and expenditure and social information. To reduce costs a subsample of 25% of the 1953-54 households, numbering 3,225, formed the basis for comparison with the full sample of 3,540 in 1960. For reasons discussed in the book, expenditure was the criterion for a low level of living in 1953-54 and income in 1960. Supplementary research with subsamples on both income and expenditure helped to establish reliable conclusions about trends in low living standards.

A poverty 'line' was then constructed from the 'official' operational definition of the minimum level of living allowed in the National Assistance rates. In reaching conclusions about the numbers (including those in wage-earning households) who were in need, careful account had to be taken of types of income and capital ordinarily disregarded by the National Assistance Board in dealing with applications, as well as allowances added to the basic rates for special needs. The outcome was that in addition to the numbers found to have smaller incomes than the 'basic' National Assistance rates, there were others, generally in the range of income up to 40% above the basic rates, who would also be, in practice, within the government's standard of need. This explains the title of the book, *The poor and the poorest*. With certain expressed technical qualifications, we found that between 1953-54 and 1960 there was a distinct increase in the number and percentage of the population living below or just above the National Assistance 'standard' of poverty.

Question for discussion
- In reopening the public debate about poverty, was *The poor and the poorest* innovative? Explain your answer.

References
Abel-Smith, B. and Townsend, P. (1965) *The poor and the poorest*, London: Bell.
Rowntree, S. and Lavers, G.R. (1951) *Poverty and the welfare state*, London: Longmans Green.
Timmins, N. (1995) *The five giants: A biography of the welfare state*, London: Harper Collins.
Townsend, P. (1979) *Poverty in the United Kingdom*, Harmondsworth: Penguin Books.

Further reading
Banting, K. (1979) *Poverty, politics and policy: Britain in the 1960s*, London: Macmillan.

Website resources
Child Poverty Action Group (CPAG): www.cpag.org.uk
Disability Alliance: www.disabilityalliance.org

Low Pay Commission: www.lowpay.gov.uk
National Pensioners Convention: www.npcuk.org
UK National Statistics: www.statistics.gov.uk

Social policy is thus the study of policy practice in order to contribute to policy reform. It is not only a *descriptive* subject but also a *prescriptive* one. This is what makes the subject attractive to those who study it. However, it is also what makes research and practice in the field so complex, as the other contributions to this volume reveal.

In the early development of social policy the links between academic study and policy practice were evident at the London School of Economics and Political Science (LSE) where the subject first developed. Clement Attlee, one of its first lecturers, became Prime Minister in the post-war Labour government which introduced much of the welfare state reform of the last century, and William Beveridge, one-time Director of the LSE, became the architect of the post-war social security reforms. In 1950 the LSE appointed the first Professor of Social Policy, Richard Titmuss, who went on to become not only the subject's leading scholar, but also an active member of advisory bodies and policy committees in the UK and abroad (see Alcock et al, 2001). Social policy is now studied across the university sector in the UK and abroad, and its leading researchers are frequently actively involved in the development and evaluation of policy programmes.

Social policy has also moved beyond the relatively narrow concern with the development and implementation of UK public welfare services, which concerned the early Fabians. Theoretical debate has developed within the subject to embrace a more pluralistic concern, not only with what should be done through policy intervention, but also with why and where policy intervention might be justified (or not) and how its (sometimes contradictory) outcomes might be understood and explained. This broadening of approach was recognised symbolically by a change in the name of the subject from *social administration* to *social policy*, suggesting a move within study and research, from a concern with *how* things were done, to *why* they were done – or *whether* they should be done at all.

What is more, study and research in social policy have moved beyond a focus only on the policy programmes of the UK and its government. Within an increasingly global economic and social environment, and with the growing influence of supranational agencies (most notably in the UK the European Union [EU]), it is no longer possible to confine the understanding of social policy to one national context. Policies in the UK are affected by international influences, and social policy students and researchers must embrace the need for comparative analysis to engage with the ideas and forces at work internationally (see Section 4.11 and ***Box 4m*** for a discussion of comparative and cross-national approaches in social policy research). Furthermore, much social policy within the UK has now been devolved to the separate administrations in Scotland, Wales and Northern Ireland. So, in areas such as health, social care and education there are now four distinct policy regimes, with significant differences in policy and practice on some key issues.

Social policy in the 21st century has, therefore, extended beyond its Fabian roots to become theoretically pluralist and internationally focused, and all current scholars and researchers now seek to embrace these broader influences in their work. Nevertheless, the theory and practice interface remains at the core of modern social policy, just as it did in the days of Attlee and Beveridge. What drives scholarship and research is the commitment not just to understand policy, but also to change it – and this prescriptive dimension informs the work of all the contributors to this volume.

What is social work?

Social work began as a discipline in the second half of the 19th century. In the early years it was led by philanthropists and delivered by voluntary organisations, within hospitals and casework organisations such as the National Society for the Prevention of Cruelty to Children (NSPCC). Since the establishment of the welfare state after the Second World War social work services have been primarily provided by the state. The voluntary/independent sectors still play a valuable role, but provision of children's and adult social care services is the statutory responsibility of local authorities. The language used to describe those whom social workers work with has changed in recent years from the traditional term 'client' to 'service users' or 'people who use services'. 'Service users' is regarded as more respectful and as doing better justice to what the recipient of the service brings to the encounter. Some argue that we need to go even further in adequately accounting for service users' knowledge by adopting the term 'experts by experience' (Preston-Shoot, 2007).

Social work is both an academic subject and a profession. Education to become a social worker is based in higher education institutions, at undergraduate and postgraduate studies levels. Courses provide classroom-based learning in theory and skills, while learning for professional development and how to work with service users continues into placements in agencies. Students study the law, social policy, human growth and development through the life course, social work theories and methods of intervention, sociology and issues of power and the politics of welfare and social work. The acquisition of knowledge about what is needed to practice in ethical ways is crucial. Codes of conduct insist that professional relationships do not permit becoming a personal friend or having sexual relationships with service users. People must be treated with respect and their confidentiality maintained, unless there are grounds to pass on information that suggests someone may be at risk.

Social work services tend to be focused on people who are living in poverty and socially disadvantaged in terms of poor housing, unemployment and/or educational disadvantage. There is a strong emphasis on values and the need for social work to promote relations of equality and to avoid being oppressive in responding to people who are suffering for personal and/or social reasons (Dalrymple and Burke, 2006). A key and increasingly popular concept that is relevant here is **reflective practice**, which refers to the need for practitioners to reflect on their assumptions, values and feelings when in direct contact with service users (Taylor and White, 2000). It also incorporates attention to the need for supervision to provide opportunities for reflection on actions that have been taken to ensure that good practice has been followed.

Debates in social work

It is not possible to provide a single overarching definition of what social work is. This is because it is not a fixed entity but changes over time according to how it is shaped by political, economic, social and professional influences. It is delivered in many different ways and diverging views exist among academics, policy makers and practitioners about what its purpose is or should be. There would, however, probably be agreement that social work is fundamentally concerned with intervening into the lives of people who are vulnerable, in need, at risk or traumatised, as well as those who constitute a risk to others.

Research and commentary have given considerable attention to how social work has developed historically and what it has become. Prior to the 1970s the dominant approach was 'social casework', a model that involved the practitioner working with individual 'clients', whether as children, adults or with families. Social work defined itself in therapeutic terms and drew heavily on ideas from psychoanalysis and counselling. In the 1970s a 'radical social work' movement emerged which drew on sociology, economics and politics rather than psychology to offer a new political vision of social work which linked it to social class divisions, gender, disability and ethnicity (Bailey and Brake, 1975; Ferguson and Woodward, 2009). Social casework was now criticised by radicals as being too focused on the individual to the neglect of socially produced inequalities. Since the 1970s social work has been deeply influenced by high profile media reporting of cases involving the deaths of children who were known to a range of professionals. Media criticism of social work in particular for not protecting vulnerable children has been fierce. Similar kinds of system failures have occurred in mental health services. One consequence is that the profession and practices like child protection have become increasingly defined in terms of risk (Webb, 2006). This refers not only to trying to protect children at risk but also seeking to avert the risk of practitioners and professional systems failing to protect children (Ferguson, 2004). Inquiries into the reasons for the deaths found that agencies did not communicate effectively with one another about risks that were known, and effective protective action was not taken. A policy shift occurred to creating greater integration of social work with health and education as a way of improving interagency communication and coordination of interventions.

Social work today has become more about assessment, planning and case management and less about the practitioner delivering long-term casework. Social workers are now expected to be much more accountable and their performance is micro-managed through them being expected to follow guidance and complete standardised assessments of risk/ cases within set time limits. The amount of computerised 'paperwork' on their cases has increased. This means that social workers now spend a lot of time in the office, doing bureaucratic work, making it difficult to find enough time to do direct face-to-face work with service users (Broadhurst, et al, 2010).

This does not mean that social workers today never have relationships or do quality work with service users. Social workers still have some discretion about how they choose to respond to vulnerable people. Most of the direct face-to-face work goes on not in the office but in service users' homes which means that it is out of sight of managers (Ferguson, 2011). Social work remains, in Pithouse's words, an 'invisible trade' (Pithouse, 1998). There is growing interest in academic social work and in practice in developing a **relationship-based** perspective (Ruch, 2005), where a high value is placed on maximising the amount and quality of direct contact with service users. This focuses on the individual or the family in a person-centred way, drawing on theories from counselling psychology to promote understanding of how therapeutic relationships enable people to change, the dynamics of interactions and the importance, for instance, of showing empathy. Psychoanalysis is drawn on to provide insights into both the uniqueness of each individual and the complexities of human beings and the role of the unconscious in relationships (Froggett, 2002; Cooper and Lousada, 2005).

Relationship-based practice does not necessarily ignore social problems and issues of power but prioritises the relationship as the key way to help vulnerable people (Healy, 2005).

Research has become increasingly important to social work in recognition of the need to make what it does visible and to provide evidence that can demonstrate what produces good outcomes for service users and what constitutes effective practice. The fact that several different perspectives exist about the nature of social work shows the richness of debate and the need for research to inform understandings of what social work is and its impact on and value to service users.

Questions for discussion

- Why is social policy sometimes described as a 'prescriptive' discipline?
- How might research promote better understanding of the role of social work in modern society?

References

Abel-Smith, B. and Townsend, P. (1965) *The poor and the poorest*, London: Bell.

Alcock, P., Glennerster, H., Oakley, A. and Sinfield, A. (eds) (2001) *Welfare and wellbeing: Richard Titmuss's contribution to social policy*, Bristol: The Policy Press.

Bailey, R. and Brake, M. (1975) *Radical social work*, London: Edward Arnold.

Broadhurst, K., Wastell, D., White, S., Hall, C., Peckover, S., Thompson, K., Pithouse, A. and Davey, D. (2010) 'Performing "initial assessment": identifying the latent conditions for error at the front-door of local authority children's services', *British Journal of Social Work*, vol 40, no 2, pp 352-70.

Cooper, A. and Lousada, J. (2005) *Borderline welfare: Feeling and fear of feeling in modern welfare*, London: Karnac.

Dalrymple, J. and Burke, B. (2006) *Anti-oppressive practice: Social care and the law*, Buckingham: Open University Press.

Ferguson, H. (2004) *Protecting children in time: Child abuse, child protection and the promotion of welfare*, Basingstoke: Palgrave Macmillan.

Ferguson, H. (2011) *Child protection practice*, Basingstoke: Palgrave.

Ferguson, I. and Woodward, R. (2009) *Radical social work in practice*, Bristol: The Policy Press.

Froggett, L. (2002) *Love, hate and welfare: Psychosocial approaches to policy and practice*, Bristol: The Policy Press.

Healy, K. (2005) *Social work theories in context: Creating frameworks for practice*, Basingstoke: Palgrave Macmillan.

Pithouse, A. (1998) *Social work: The social organisation of an invisible trade*, Aldershot: Ashgate.

Preston-Shoot, M. (2007) 'Whose lives and whose learning? Whose narratives and whose writing? Taking the next research and literature steps with experts by experience', *Evidence & Policy*, vol 3, no 3, pp 343-59.

Ruch, G. (2005) 'Relationship-based practice and reflective practice: holistic approaches to contemporary child care social work', *Child and Family Social Work*, vol 10, no 2, pp 111-23.

Taylor, C. and White, S. (2000), *Practising reflexivity in health and welfare: Making knowledge*, Buckingham: Open University Press.

Webb, S. (2006) *Social work in a risk society*, Basingstoke: Palgrave.

Further reading

Alcock, P. (2008) *Social policy in Britain* (3rd edn), Basingstoke: Palgrave.

Alcock, P., May, M. and Wright, S. (eds) (2011) *The student's companion to social policy* (4th edn), Oxford: Blackwell.

Baldock J., Manning, N. and Vickerstaff, S. (eds) (2007) *Social policy* (3rd edn), Oxford: Oxford University Press.

Ferguson, H. (2011) *Child protection practice*, Basingstoke: Palgrave Macmillan.

Ferguson, I. and Woodward, R. (2009) *Radical social work in practice*, Bristol: The Policy Press.

Gray, M. and Webb, S. (2009) *Social work theories and methods*, London: Sage Publications.

Howe, D. (2009) *A brief introduction to social work theory*, Basingstoke: Palgrave Macmillan.

Ruch, G., Turney, A. and Ward, A. (2010) *Relationship-based social work*, London: Jessica Kingsley Publishers.

Smith, R. (2009) *Doing social work research*, Maidenhead: Open University Press.

Relevant organisation

The major organisation representing academics and researchers working in social policy is the *Social Policy Association* (SPA). It is a membership organisation and all staff and postgraduate students working in social policy can join. For more details see www.social-policy.com

The College of Social Work aims to set out standards of good practice and be a voice for it: www.collegeofsocialwork.org

The British Association of Social Workers is a professional association for social workers in the UK: www.basw.co.uk

Website resources

This website, 'An introduction to social policy', was developed and is maintained by Professor Paul Spicker at the Robert Gordon University in Aberdeen. It contains general material on the subject of social policy as well as some discussion of a range of policy issues: www2.rgu.ac.uk/publicpolicy/INTRODUCTION/index.htm

The Social Care Institute for Excellence (SCIE) gathers and analyses knowledge about social work and research and its website contains a wealth of information: www.scie.org.uk

1.3 Policy research
Saul Becker and Alan Bryman

In understanding what we mean by 'policy research' we must first break down the term into its constituent parts: policy and research.

What is policy?

Levin (1997) suggests that when politicians and officials refer to **policy** they are referring to policy in a number of ways: 'a stated intention to take a particular action', an 'organisational practice' or as some other form of activity/intervention. *Figure 1a* summarises what is meant by policy and identifies some of its key attributes and characteristics. It is these attributes, and particularly a commitment to some form of action, which help us to recognise when something is a policy. As we have seen in Section 1.2, **social policy** refers to the practice of social intervention aimed at securing social change to promote the welfare and well-being of citizens. Many organisations and agencies, and the people who work in or for them, are involved in formulating and implementing social policies.

Figure 1a: 'Policy' and the attributes of policy

What is policy?
- *'Policy' as a stated intention:* policy is a stated intention to take a particular action, or bring about a particular situation, in the future. This is found in, for example, the manifestos of political parties, in white papers, and so on.
- *'Policy' as a current or past action:* in other words, the government's policy is what the government is currently doing (or has done in the past).
- *'Policy' as an organisational practice:* policy is often used to denote the established practices of an organisation, the rules and regulations, the ways in which things are customarily done or attitudes that are customarily taken.
- *'Policy' as an indicator of the formal or claimed status of a past, present or proposed course of action:* a course of action is often described as a policy in a context where the term appears to denote a claim for status of some kind; for example, if a policy can successfully be labelled 'government policy' in the allocation of money or scarce resources, that policy will have a valid claim to priority over others not so labelled.

Attributes of policy
- *'Policy' denotes belongingness:* a policy belongs to someone, or some body (for example, the government's policy, departmental policy, and so on).
- *'Policy'* denotes commitment: a policy carries commitment on the part of those to whom it belongs. A stated intention, for example, is not just a proposal, it is a proposal to which the government/department or organisation is committed.
- The description of a proposal or current course of action as 'policy' may also denote that it has, or is claimed to have, a certain status, possibly conferred on it by a prior event

of some kind (for example, a public announcement), or by being acted on even though no agreement to that effect has been reached.

- *A policy also possesses the attribute of 'specificity':* some stated intentions are quite specific, others less so. The less specific a policy, the more options it leaves open when it comes to translating the policy into action. The more specific it is, the closer it is to being a single blueprint for action. A policy must have at least some degree of specificity for it to be distinguishable from other policies.

Source: Adapted from Levin (1997, pp 15-19)

What is research?

Research in social policy, and research conducted by professionals employed in related spheres (for example, social workers, health workers, advice workers, and so on), is concerned with *understanding* social issues and social problems, policies and interventions, and the social world more generally. Policy research also aims to provide *answers* and *evidence* that can contribute to the *improvement* of 'policy' and policy making, can lead to better practice and interventions, the reduction of social problems and social distress, and the promotion of welfare and well-being. Finally, not only is policy research concerned to find answers to policy problems and improve policy action, but it is also concerned to identify the right *questions* to ask in the first place (Clarke, 2001, p 38).

Figure 1b shows that to 'count' as research the enquiry must be done in a systematic, disciplined and rigorous way, making use of the most appropriate research methods and designs to answer specific research questions.

Figure 1b: Five views of what constitutes 'research'

When we want to know something and there is no authority, or the authorities disagree, or we are just not ready to accept without question what the authority has told us, then we do research. When the existing literature on a subject does not answer the question we are asking, or we are dissatisfied with the answer, then we do research.... Research is a disciplined way to go about answering questions. This distinguishes research from other ways of answering questions. The fact that research is a disciplined process means that the answers are more reliable. (Bouma and Atkinson, 1995, pp 6-13)

Research starts as an extension of common sense – finding out about things, looking for information about them, trying to make sense of them in the light of evidence and working out what evidence is needed. (Abbott and Sapsford, 1998, p 3)

Research is a systematic investigation to find answers to a problem. (Burns, 2000, p 3)

Research and experimental development (R&D) comprise creative work undertaken on a systematic basis in order to increase the stock of knowledge, including knowledge of people, culture and society, and the use of this stock of knowledge to devise new applications. There are three forms of research:

- *Basic research* is experimental or theoretical work undertaken primarily to acquire new knowledge of the underlying foundation of phenomena and observable facts, without any particular application or use in view.
- *Applied research* is also original investigation undertaken in order to acquire new knowledge. It is, however, directed primarily towards a specific practical aim or objective.
- *Experimental development* is systematic work, drawing on existing knowledge gained from research and/or practical experience, which is directed to producing new materials, products or devices, to installing new processes, systems and services, or to improving substantially those already produced or installed. (OECD, 2002)

For the purposes of the REF [Research Excellence Framework], research will be defined as "a process of investigation leading to new insights effectively shared". (HEFCE, 2009)

The term **policy-oriented research** has been used to refer to research designed to inform or understand one or more aspects of the public and social policy process, including decision making and policy formulation, implementation and evaluation (Becker, 2004). A distinction can be made between research *for* policy and research *of* policy:

- Research *for* policy is concerned to inform the various stages of the policy process (before the formation of policy through to its implementation).
- Research *of* policy is concerned with how problems are defined, agendas set, policy formulated, decisions made and how policy is implemented, evaluated and changed (Nutley and Webb, 2000, p 15).

Policy-oriented research (or 'policy research', as we often refer to it in this volume) can simultaneously be research *for*, and research *of*, policy (Becker, 2004).

Methods and approaches in policy research

Policy research can serve several functions and can have a diverse range of audiences. It provides a *specialist* function of informing and influencing the policy process and the understanding of how policy works and 'what works', for target audiences of policy makers, policy networks and communities, research-aware professionals and service users, and academics; and a *democratic* or *enlightenment* function, where research findings contribute to the development of an informed and knowledge-based society as well as to the broader democratic process (Becker, 2004). Here the 'users' of research will include organised groups with vested interests, people whose lives are influenced by the policy and the public as a whole.

Policy research (like social work research; see Section 1.4) draws from the full range of research designs, methods and approaches outlined in this volume. Depending on the specific research question(s) to be addressed, in some cases just one method will be used. Chapter Five of this volume, for example, provides a discussion of quantitative research methods that can be employed in policy and social work research, while Chapter Six focuses on qualitative ones. In other cases, there may be an integration of different methods ('mixed methods') either within a single piece of research or as part of a wider programme of research being conducted across multiple sites or cross-nationally (see Chapter Four). Each method and design has its own strengths and limitations, as will be seen in later sections of this volume.

Ann Oakley, for example, has argued that policy research needs to make greater use of experimental designs and trial methodology, rather than rejecting these as inappropriate or part of an outdated positivist mentality. Experiments can contribute to the kinds of knowledge that academics, policy makers, social workers and other professionals, and the public, are interested in. Indeed, 'reliable information about the effectiveness of public policy and social interventions is hard to come by using any other means' (Oakley, 2000, p 323) because true experiments offer the most robust design for assessing cause and effect (see also Section 5.3 in Chapter Five).

How an issue is perceived, and the policies in place (or not in place) to respond or to deal with it, will also influence how it is researched – the type of questions, the nature of the enquiries and the methodologies and approaches used. For example, where policies already exist to respond to the unique needs of lone mothers (for example, New Deals designed to 'encourage' them back into the paid labour market, or specific cash benefits or childcare strategies) then these can be *evaluated* using a number of approaches and research methods described in Chapter Four and throughout this volume. Where an issue has not yet been defined as a social issue or as a social problem (for example, 'young adult carers'; see **Box 7e** in Chapter Seven), then other research approaches will need to be used, to highlight the issue for the first time and to bring knowledge of it to a wider audience, including policy makers and social workers. Qualitative studies (Chapter Six) are useful here, in that they can raise the profile of an issue, drawing on a limited number of cases, because at an early stage it may be difficult or impossible to do large-scale surveys. In the example of *The poor and the poorest* (**Box 1a**), secondary analysis of large-scale government datasets enabled poverty to be reconceptualised and its extent to be measured.

Attributes of 'good' policy research

Abbott and Sapsford (1998, p 180) suggest that 'Good research is the product of clear analysis of problems, clear specification of goals, careful design of fieldwork and thoughtful analysis and exposition afterwards'. Cutting across these issues is the need for selecting the appropriate research method and design by reference to the precise research question(s), and the need to contribute to knowledge creation in a reliable, trustworthy and transparent way. This is as much the case for social work research (Section 1.4) as it is for policy research. Ann Oakley has suggested: 'considerations of trustworthiness apply to all forms of research.... We need to examine all methods from the viewpoint of the same questions about trustworthiness, to consider how best to match methods to research questions, and to find ways of integrating a range of methods in carrying out socially useful inquiries' (Oakley, 1999, pp 165-6). Oakley also suggests that:

> ... the distinguishing mark of all "good" research is the awareness and acknowledgement of error, and that what flows from this is the necessity of establishing procedures which will minimize the effect such errors may have on what counts as knowledge. (Oakley, 2000, p 72)

However, the notion of error is a contested concept for many qualitative researchers, as will be seen in Chapter Six.

In reviewing what researchers themselves understand to be 'good' social research, Denscombe (2002, 2010) has identified certain ground rules that help to define the attributes of good social research (*Figure 1c*). These guidelines are relevant to both social policy and social work enquiries.

Figure 1c: Denscombe's ground rules for good social research

- Research should have clearly stated aims and questions.
- Research should be related to existing knowledge and needs.
- Research should be tailored to fit the resources available.
- Researchers need to protect the interests of participants.
- Researchers need to be open-minded and self-reflective.
- Research designs should be coherent and fit for purpose.
- Research should be aware of its underlying philosophical foundations.
- Research should produce valid data using reliable methods.
- Research should include an explicit description and justification of the methodology.
- Research should produce findings from which generalizations can be made.
- Research should contribute something new to knowledge.
- Researchers need to be cautious about claims based on their findings.

Source: Denscombe (2010)

In Section 1.4 we focus on the characteristics of social work research. There are significant overlaps between policy research and social work research, especially in what contributes to 'good' research (for example, the linking of method[s] to research questions etc), but there are also some important differences in emphasis. *Box 1b* illustrates the overlap between social policy and social work research, with a focus on child abuse as a social problem.

Question for discussion

- What do you think are the key characteristics of 'good' policy research? Why?

References

Abbott, P. and Sapsford, R. (1998) *Research methods for nurses and the caring professions* (2nd edn), Buckingham: Open University Press.

Becker, S. (2004) 'Policy-oriented research', in M. Lewis-Beck, A. Bryman and T. Futing Liao (eds) *The SAGE encyclopaedia of social science research methods*, Thousand Oaks, CA: Sage Publications, pp 830-1.

Bouma, G. and Atkinson, G.B.J. (1995) *A handbook of social science research: A comprehensive and practical guide for students* (2nd edn), Oxford: Oxford University Press.

Burns, R.B. (2000) *Introduction to research methods*, London: Sage Publications.

Clarke, A. (2001) 'Research and the policy-making process', in N. Gilbert (ed) *Researching social life* (2nd edn), London: Sage Publications, pp 28-42.

Denscombe, M. (2002) *Ground rules for good research: A 10 point guide for social researchers*, Buckingham: Open University Press.

Denscombe, M. (2010) *Ground rules for social research: Guidelines for good practice*, Maidenhead: Open University Press.

HEFCE (Higher Education Funding Council for England) (2009) *Research Excellence Framework: Second consultation on the assessment and funding of research*, Bristol: HEFCE.

Levin, P. (1997) *Making social policy: The mechanisms of government and politics, and how to investigate them*, Buckingham: Open University Press.

Nutley, S. and Webb, J. (2000) 'Evidence and the policy process', in H. Davies, S. Nutley and P. Smith (eds) *What works? Evidence-based policy and practice in public services*, Bristol: The Policy Press, pp 13-41.

OECD (Organisation for Economic Co-operation and Development) (2002) *Frascati manual: Proposed standard practice for surveys on research and experimental development*, Paris: OECD.

Oakley, A. (1999) 'People's way of knowing: gender and methodology', in S. Hood, B. Mayall and S. Oliver (eds) *Critical issues in social research: Power and prejudice*, Buckingham: Open University Press, pp 154-70.

Oakley, A. (2000) *Experiments in knowing: Gender and method in the social sciences*, Cambridge: Polity Press.

Further reading

Evidence & Policy (2011) vol 7, no 2 (special edition on 'The practice of policy making').

Hudson, J. and Lowe, S. (2009) *Understanding the policy process: Analysing welfare policy and practice*, Bristol: The Policy Press.

1.4 Social work research
Ian F. Shaw

Social work research is identifiable through a set of features, none of which exclusively or exhaustively defines it, but which typify its scope and character. Like policy research (see Section 1.3) these general features include a broad range of research methods, and recurring but diverse linkages between research method and research questions. Social work research is underpinned by a quest for both usefulness and theoretical contributions so that research is not categorised as only 'pure' or 'applied'. It is also marked by a pervasive, if variously understood, concern with social inclusion, justice and change.

An alternative way of capturing the nature and field of social work research is to see it as possessing two general identifiers – for example, as addressing characteristic *substantive* fields, and doing so with one or more characteristic *problem foci* (Shaw and Norton, 2007). Examples of *substantive fields* include adult offenders/victims as a category of service users/carers; people as members of communities or as citizens; and social work practitioners/managers, in their capacity as members of professional or policy communities. Examples of *problem foci* include:

- Understanding/explaining issues related to equality, diversity, poverty and social exclusion.
- Understanding/developing/assessing/evaluating social work practices, methods or interventions.
- Understanding/promoting learning and teaching about social work or related professions.

Box 1b uses the case of child abuse to illustrate both the overlap and interface between social work and social policy research, and the interplay between *substantive fields* and *problem foci*.

It is helpful to ask four questions (Shaw et al, 2010). What is the role and *purpose* of social work research? What *contexts* shape the practice and purpose of social work research? How can we maximise the quality of the *practice and method* of social work research? How can the aims of social work in its varied *domains* be met through social work research? The first question is a helpful starting point. While there is no unanimity on the best balance of purposes, they will typically include one or more of the following, each of which is sufficient for a career's endeavours:

- Generating or enhancing theory and knowledge about social work and social care.
- Providing impartial evidence about and for decision making.
- Instrumentally improving practice and organisational learning.
- Highlighting the quality of lived experience and advancing practical wisdom.
- Promoting justice, social change and social inclusion.

Box 1b: Child abuse research in social work and social policy
Harry Ferguson

A good example of the relationship between social policy, social work practice and the influence of research is child abuse and child protection. In 1963, an American pediatrician, Henry Kempe, headed up a team of clinicians and researchers who published a paper referring to what they called the 'battered child syndrome' (Kempe et al, 1962). The research team studied a sample of cases in which children had died from injuries by examining their medical histories and hospital records and X-rays and found that the children had previous injuries, including healed bone fractures, that had not previously been recognised. They looked at the backgrounds of the parents and found many to have been abused in their own childhoods. Few policies existed to promote awareness of child maltreatment and guide how professionals should respond. Kempe argued that serious and fatal child abuse was denied because it was too painful to contemplate that parents seriously harmed and even killed their children. The emotive terminology 'battered child' was deliberately coined by him to draw attention to how children were seriously harmed and killed by their parents, to try and shock policy makers, practitioners and the public into responding.

In the UK the policy response remained limited until the case of Maria Colwell hit the headlines. Maria died in January 1973 aged seven, having been murdered by her stepfather at her home in East Sussex, England. She was one of nine children and had spent the first five years of her life in the foster care of her aunt, but was returned to her mother and stepfather at the age of six years and eight months, being placed on a Supervision Order to the local authority. The then Conservative government called a public inquiry into why Maria had not been protected by social workers and other services. This led to the case gaining national media attention and child abuse becoming a major concern of politicians and public policy. By the late 1970s the term 'battered child' was replaced in policy and practice by 'non-accidental injury to children' (NAI) and new policies were brought in to facilitate better communication between professionals when abuse was suspected (Parton, 1985). Repeated disclosures that children have died from horrendous abuse in cases where they were known to social workers and other professionals – as exemplified in the 'Baby Peter' Connelly case in late 2008 (Haringey, 2008, 2009) – has been the most powerful factor that has driven child welfare and protection policy and practice since the 1970s (Ferguson, 2004). In response, policy makers have introduced more and more laws, procedures and guidelines to try and direct and micro-manage practitioners in how to work to keep children safe.

In the early 1990s the Department of Health funded a large-scale research programme into how professionals were responding to child welfare concerns. The findings from the various research studies were summarised in *Messages from research* (DH, 1995). It concluded that practice had shifted to focusing on investigations into child abuse to an extent that was viewed as too one-dimensional. Investigations were being focused on incidents of alleged abuse to an extent that practitioners were not gaining an understanding of the wider history and social context of children and families' experiences and needs. Where no evidence of incidents of abuse were found, too many families were left without services and feeling aggrieved, even where it was clear they had needs that social work and other services could assist with. The conclusion was that a focus on child protection was preventing a wider concept of child welfare and prevention from applying in practice. Attempts followed to 'refocus' policy and practice towards family support and a broader concept of need and the 'whole child'. The key policy outcome from these research findings was the *Framework for the assessment of children in need and their families* which was introduced in England and Wales in 2000 (DH, 2000). It directed practitioners to gather information on the child's developmental needs, parenting capacity and family and environmental factors. The intention was not just to enquire into a particular event or incident but to reach as deep as possible an understanding of the child's world (Horwath, 2010).

Recent policy developments have further consolidated this shift to a broader concept of child well-being. By the mid-2000s the language of policy and practice were changed to that of 'safeguarding', a term intending to capture the wider goals of promoting child well-being, of which protection was just one (Parton, 2006). The Children Act 2004 in England placed statutory obligations on agencies to cooperate in 'safeguarding' children and the hugely influential policy of *Every Child Matters* enshrined five outcomes for state intervention, one of which was 'being safe'. Notably, however, following on from the public outcry following 'Baby Peter' and other such cases, the concept of 'child protection' is reappearing in policy documents and language to reflect the need for social workers to use authority, especially in work with parents and carers who are resistant and hostile to receiving help and support, but which social workers must insist on providing in order to try and keep children safe (Ferguson, 2011).

Other research, funded not by the government, but by independent sources such as the Economic and Social Research Council (ESRC), has shown that the direct regulation of social workers' practice through procedures and intense management oversight has had the effect of practitioners having to spend too much time at their computers completing standardised forms and case records in which they have to account for what they have done with families. As a consequence, not enough time is spent doing quality work with children and their carers (Broadhurst et al, 2010). This reveals how policies can have unintended consequences, in this instance, by helping to create an over bureaucratised system which contributes to diminishing the time and capacity social workers have to develop the kinds of close, therapeutic and supportive relationships with children that can best keep them safe (see also *Box 7f*). Those research findings have been important in contributing to a momentum where attempts are now being made to redirect policy towards freeing up social work to use its expertise more confidently in working directly with children and families (Munro, 2011). Research will need to go on playing a key role in the policy process and shaping practice by providing vital evidence of how effective social work and other professions are able to be in protecting children.

References

Broadhurst, K., Wastell, D., White, S., Hall, C., Peckover, S., Thompson, K., Pithouse, A. and Davey, D. (2010) 'Performing "initial assessment": identifying the latent conditions for error at the front-door of local authority children's services', *British Journal of Social Work*, vol 40, no 2, pp 352-70.

DH (Department of Health) (1995) *Messages from research*, London: HMSO.

DH (2000) *Framework for the assessment of children in need and their families*, London: The Stationery Office.

Ferguson, H. (2004) *Protecting children in time: Child abuse, child protection and the consequences of modernity*, Basingstoke: Palgrave Macmillan.

Ferguson, H. (2011) *Child protection practice*, Basingstoke: Palgrave Macmillan.

Haringey (2008) *Serious case review, Child 'A', Executive summary*, Haringey Local Safeguarding Board, November (www.//media.education.gov/assets/files/pdf/s/) (first serious case review overview relating to Peter Connelly dated November 2008).

Haringey (2009) *Serious case review, Executive summary*, Haringey Local Safeguarding Board, March (www.haringeylscb.org/executive_summary_peter_final.pdf).

Horwath, J. (ed) (2010) *The child's world: The comprehensive guide to assessing children in need*, London: Jessica Kingsley Publishers.

Kempe, C.H., Silverman, F.N., Steel, B.F. et al (1962) 'The battered child syndrome', *Journal of the American Medical Association*, vol 181, pp 17-24.

Munro, E. (2011) *The Munro review of child protection: Final report – A child-centred system*, London: Department for Education.

Parton, N. (1985) *The politics of child abuse*, Basingstoke: Macmillan.

Parton, N. (2006) *Safeguarding childhood: Early intervention and surveillance in a late modern society*, Basingstoke: Palgrave Macmillan.

The field is marked by numerous debates and developments (and for a contrasting exposition, see Tripodi and Lalayants, 2008):

1. Social work as *evidence-based practice*. It is hard to generalise about this extensive and diverse debate. Being simultaneously 'scientific' and 'caring' have often been uneasy bedfellows throughout the history of social work research. How far can and should social workers be scientific in their practice? What are the best ways of understanding the relationship between practice and research? Bruce Thyer in the US and Geraldine Macdonald in the UK have been among the most articulate advocates for **evidence-based social work** (see also Section 1.6). Developments in systematic synthesising and reviewing research (Section 4.18) have also been stimulated by the movement for evidence-based practice, as has interest in practitioner research (Section 4.13).

2. *Methods and methodology*. Greene rightly asserts that 'epistemological integrity does get meaningful research done right' (Greene, 1990, p 229), although this is a less prevalent position than 30 years ago. In UK social work there has been a recent enthusiasm for mixed methods research (see Section 4.4), but also for improved quantitative methodology. Yet, without adopting the view that methodological choices are direct reflections of paradigm positions, it is unwise to dissolve contrasting commitments – for example, to qualitative or quantitative, to rigour or emancipatory research.

3. Research implications of *information and communication technologies* (ICT). There is a rich literature on internet research (see, for example, Sections 5.7 and 6.14), virtual ethnography and the sociology of technology. However, this is an area where limited work has been done hitherto by social work writers.

4. The role and challenge of *user research*. UK social work, alongside the older Commonwealth countries, has been a world leader in exploring and practising user-engaged research. This has been particularly evident in the fields of mental health, disability and learning disabilities. The impetus comes in part from the user movement and in part from the relatively open stance adopted by major UK research charities and NGOs. Concerns are beginning to be expressed about the risk that the user critique will be incorporated and weakened.

5. *Culture and international research*. A single global definition of social work research may not be helpful. This is not in the interests of fuzzy thinking, but more from a fear that such statements are likely to prove bland and unduly rounded, and dumb down important inter-cultural differences. Ideas of policy transfer, culturally competent social work research, comparative research and the significance of research context have played a part in this area of debate.

6. What does a commitment to research have to say about *social work history*? Rapid growth in the availability of digitally scanned documents from the 100 year-plus history of social work will continue to open new resources and research opportunities. How one sees the relationship between social work and other disciplines is closely linked to questions of how one interprets social work history.

7. Finally, an underlying, but rarely discussed, question is how one should understand the *limits of social work research*.

None of these developments and debates is easily resolved, and they demand of us that we should be 'long thinkers'. However, social work and social work research will be poorer if we over-emphasise their distinctiveness. On most occasions the right question to ask is not what makes social work research distinctive, but what might make it *distinctively good*? Distinctively good social work research will:

- at all times aim for methodological excellence;
- engage in social work inquiry marked by rigour, range, variety, depth and progression;
- sustain an active conversation with the social science community;
- achieve a thoroughgoing consistency with broader social work purposes;
- give serious attention to aspects of the research enterprise that are close to social work, while also aiming to unsettle our preconceptions by taking seriously aspects of the research enterprise that seem on the face of it far from social work (Shaw, 2007).

Question for discussion

- In what ways is social work research similar to or different from social research done by social policy researchers? Does your answer matter?

References

Greene, J. (1990) 'Three views on the nature and role of knowledge in social science', in E. Guba (ed) *The paradigm dialog*, Newbury Park: Sage Publications, pp 227-45.

Shaw, I. (2007) 'Is social work research distinctive?', *Social Work Education*, vol 26, no 7, pp 659-69.

Shaw, I., Briar-Lawson, K., Orme, J. and Ruckdeschel, R. (2010) *Sage handbook of social work research*, London: Sage Publications.

Shaw, I. and Norton, M. (2007) *Kinds and quality of social work research in higher education*, London: Social Care Institute for Excellence.

Tripodi, T. and Lalayants, M. (2008) 'Research: an overview', in T. Mizrahi and L.E. Davis (eds) *Encyclopedia of social work*, Washington, DC and New York: NASW Press and Oxford University Press.

Further reading

Kirk, S.A. and Reid, W.J. (2002) *Science and social work: A critical appraisal*, New York: Columbia University Press.

McLaughlin, H. (2007) *Understanding social work research*, London: Sage Publications.

Shaw, I., Briar-Lawson, K., Orme, J. and Ruckdeschel, R. (2010) *Sage handbook of social work research*, London: Sage Publications.

Website resources

Social Care Institute for Excellence (SCIE): www.scie.org.uk

European Conference for Social Work Research: www.ecswr.org

'A social work research strategy in higher education 2006-2020': www.swap.ac.uk/docs/strategy_JUCSWEC.pdf

1.5. 'Evidence' and other 'ways of knowing'
Saul Becker and Alan Bryman

'Evidence'

Research produces 'findings' which contribute to knowledge. Whether research findings *count* as 'evidence' (or 'reliable evidence'), and whether this evidence then informs or influences social policy and social work or other professional practice, are quite separate issues and depend on many factors, not just the rigour and trustworthiness of the research itself (see Section 1.6).

The dictionary defines **evidence** in various ways: 'means of proving an unknown or disputed fact', 'support for a belief', 'an indication', 'information in a law case', 'testimony' and 'witness or witnesses collectively' (Davies et al, 2000, p 2). Davies and colleagues observe:

> At one extreme, it might be argued that all evidence must conform to certain scientific rules of proof (the first definition). In other circumstances, any observation on an issue (whether informed or not) might be considered evidence (the last definition). However, perhaps the unifying theme in all the definitions is that the evidence (however construed) can be independently observed and verified, and that there is a broad consensus as to its contents (if not its interpretation). (Davies et al, 2000, p 2)

In addition to evidence from research there are other forms of evidence. For example, the legal structure and case law forms evidence that policy makers and social workers must take account of in their decision making. Nutley and Webb (2000) also identify a number of other sources of what counts as evidence, including evidence generated through experience of 'doing the job', and evidence and knowledge from people who use services on a daily basis and who have become experts through experience:

> The raw ingredient of evidence is information. Good quality policy making depends on high quality information, derived from a variety of sources – expert knowledge; existing domestic and international research; existing statistics; stakeholder consultation; evaluation of previous policies; new research, if appropriate; or secondary sources, including the internet. Evidence can also include analysis of the outcome of consultation, costings of policy options and the results of economic or statistical modelling.

There is a tendency to think of evidence as something that is only generated by major pieces of research. In any policy area there is a great deal of critical evidence held in the minds of both front-line staff in departments, agencies and local authorities and those to whom the policy is directed. (Nutley and Webb, 2000, p 23)

Additionally, there is evidence that contributes to knowledge drawn from organisational sources (such as the Social Care Institute for Excellence [SCIE]). Indeed, evidence is sometimes considered to be the interaction of information, ideologies and interests within the context of institutions (Weiss, 1995).

These different sources of evidence, including research evidence, contribute to knowledge – what we know about things in general and on specific matters. These different forms of evidence are also different *ways of knowing* about the world.

'Ways of knowing' and knowledge

In some areas of knowledge there is far less 'requirement' for any evidence at all. For example, people's knowledge (or more accurately perhaps, their *interpretation*) of religion, of art and beauty, are less reliant on evidence and are far more matters of *faith* and *belief*. Where knowledge is challenged or contested, we usually refer to it as 'beliefs'. This way of knowing can be termed the *method of tenacity* (see **Figure 1d**). In policy terms, the method of tenacity is closely related to political ideologies, or ideologies of welfare. These ideologies often rest not on evidence to prove their claim to truth or authority, but on beliefs about the world, about individuals and about society, on rational logic and matters of judgement – not necessarily 'hard facts or evidence' (Denscombe, 2002, p 198). As **Figure 1d** also shows, a further way of knowing can be termed the *method of authority* – where the claim to truth rests on the *authority* of the person making the claim, not on the basis of the evidence itself. For example, where a prime minister, or the head of a respected organisation, claims that there is evidence for a particular policy or approach, they may be more likely to be believed by the public than other people with less authority (even though these other groups could have direct experience of the policy itself).

Figure 1d: Methods and ways of knowing

Method of tenacity: people hold on to the truth because they know it to be true. This method of knowing rests on strong beliefs, which may not be moved even in the light of contrary evidence.

Method of authority: a thing must be true, for example, if it is in the Bible, Koran (and so on), or if we are told it by our leaders, teachers or others in authority.

Theoretical knowing: where policy makers and practitioners recognise different theoretical frameworks for thinking and responding to a problem or issue. This is often used intuitively and informally.

Experiential knowing: where craft and tacit knowledge build up over many years of experience. This can be very hard to make explicit.

Empirical knowing: where policy makers or practitioners may know how to respond on the basis of available research evidence. This is the most explicit form of knowing. It is the only way of knowing which allows self-correction through further research that can check and verify the knowledge base.

Source: Based on Brechin and Sidell (2000, p 4) and Burns (2000, p 5)

It is only *empirical knowing* that provides any systematic procedure for establishing the reliability and trustworthiness of the knowledge base and for assessing the superiority of one claim over another. It is for this reason that policy makers, professionals and researchers often privilege evidence from research as the *foundation* for policy and practice – the notion of 'evidence-based policy and practice' (see Section 1.6).

The phrase 'research evidence' is used throughout this volume to refer *to the results or findings of systematic, robust and trustworthy empirical enquiry* – what has been referred to in **Figure 1d** as *empirical knowing*. Policy makers and social work and other professionals have expressed a commitment to draw on this research evidence to inform their policy or practice choices. Indeed, the term 'evidence-based policy and practice' (Section 1.6) is widely used across the whole range of social policy-related spheres. Those conducting policy and social work research are involved in the process of knowledge creation to inform understanding, policy and practice. Research findings, and the conclusions reached, need to be based on the careful application of research designs, methods and analysis – some of the main hallmarks of 'good' social research (see Section 1.3). The outcomes of this process (the data, findings and conclusions) can count as evidence for policy and practice if they are suitably substantial and have been collected in a rigorous, systematic and accountable way (Denscombe, 2002, 2010).

Evidence, 'proof' and the provisional nature of knowledge

Unlike political ideology or religious beliefs, proof is not a matter of faith; nor is it a matter of logic or the rationality of an argument alone. It requires corroboration by *empirical evidence* collected, analysed and reported to the highest standards: 'What qualifies as evidence might vary between styles of research, but the need for research to verify its claims with reference to empirical evidence remains constant' (Denscombe, 2002, p 197). Thus, systematic reviews (see Section 4.17) are a favoured form of evidence by those in medicine and healthcare as they summarise, using a distinctive methodology, selected research evidence in a tightly defined area. They are also being used increasingly in social care research.

Proof, based on evidence, can either *verify* or *refute* existing knowledge and understanding. It can confirm what we already know about a social issue or social problem, or it can offer an alternative explanation – a competing form of knowledge or 'way of knowing'. In *The logic of scientific discovery*, Karl Popper (1959) argued that research evidence can support knowledge, but it can never prove it absolutely because new evidence may be found at a later date that will contradict or refute what we already know. He suggested that all knowledge, all theory, all evidence, must therefore remain *provisional* – the best available at the time – but always open to refutation by new evidence at a later date (see also Section 3.4).

In this context, research should actively seek to test existing knowledge and theories in circumstances where they are most likely to be refuted. Rather than trying to prove existing knowledge and evidence as 'right', research should try to prove them 'wrong' (the notion of *falsification*). Where research (conducted to the highest standards of enquiry) cannot prove (through empirical evidence) that what we know already about something is wrong, then that knowledge base can be considered to be stronger and more robust than before. The amount of confidence and trust that can be placed in a theory or knowledge depends on its ability to withstand concerted efforts to refute it

(Denscombe, 2002, pp 198-200; see also May, 2001, pp 30-4). While this approach to understanding knowledge creation is not universally accepted (see, for example, Kuhn, 1970, on the nature of scientific revolutions), it does raise important challenges for evidence-based policy and practice, and these are outlined in *Figure 1e*.

For research evidence to *refute* existing knowledge this would require more than one incidence of contra-evidence. It would also require contra-evidence to be genuine and based on high standards of research practice; to occur repeatedly and be produced regularly and consistently by a variety of researchers; and not to be susceptible to accommodation within existing knowledge or theory. Refutation requires the *accumulation of a body of evidence* that the existing theory or way of knowing does not work (Denscombe, 2002, p 202).

Figure 1e: 'Falsification' and the challenges for evidence-based policy and practice

- Research to support evidence-based policy and practice should be directed at trying to prove existing evidence *wrong* as much as proving it *right*. This would lead to a more robust, reliable and trustworthy evidence base *for* policy and practice. So, for example, while it is important to generate evidence on 'what works' in the various fields of social policy, this evidence will be more trustworthy and reliable if it withstands concerted research attempts to disprove it. In reality, little, if any, research is primarily directed at proving existing evidence to be wrong.
- Research, and the evidence it produces either to support or to refute existing knowledge, needs to be considered as *provisional*, rather than as absolute, proof.
- Regarding the notion of 'what works', *whether* something works is the question of greatest interest to many practitioners and policy makers. *How* and *why* something works, *when* and for *whom* (the 'realist' approach) and theories or models that might underpin the relationships between interventions and outcomes, are also important questions.
- Given the provisional nature of evidence, proof and knowledge, the need for research to be robust, rigorous and conducted to the highest standards – and open to verification or falsification – becomes even more necessary.

From a 'hierarchy' to a 'continuum' of evidence

Rather than adopting the influential medical and health approach which ranks different research methods and designs in a *hierarchy* of evidence (with several systematic reviews of randomised controlled trials [RCTs] at the top – see *Figure 1f*), it would perhaps be more useful for those involved in evidence-based policy and practice in social policy and social work to acknowledge the varying strengths and weaknesses of different research methods and designs and to consider them as a *continuum* rather than as a hierarchy.

Figure 1f: The traditional hierarchy of evidence in medical and health research

1. Several systematic reviews of RCTs or meta-analyses
2. Systematic review of RCTs
3. RCTs

4.   Quasi-experimental trials
5.   Case control and cohort studies
6.   Expert consensus opinion
7.   Individual opinion

Under the continuum approach, it would be acknowledged, for example, that systematic reviews, RCTs and other experimental designs (see Section 5.3) provide the most appropriate form of evidence on 'cause and effect', while ethnography and other qualitative methods provide the most appropriate forms of evidence on 'experiences and processes' – especially as understood by research participants themselves. This approach, which is also increasingly being recognised within the NHS Service Delivery and Organisation R&D Programme, allows the researcher to draw on the most appropriate method and design to answer specific research question(s). It also facilitates the integration of methods, breaking down the paradigm wars between quantitative and qualitative methods. Thus, the choice of method(s) to be used, and whether and how they may be combined, will depend largely on the research question(s):

> ... it is a question of carefully examining the research question, beginning with whether it has been asked and answered before, whether it makes sense to the people who might be asked to take part in the research, and identifying the other 'stakeholders' (including policy-makers); moving on to consider whether it is a question about evaluating the effect of something or about describing processes or events; whether it points to the generation of theory and/or the production of widely applicable findings, and so on. All research takes place within the context of cost and funding and 'political' constraints; these will inevitably feed into decisions about what methods to use. (Oakley, 2000, p 305)

In this context, just as the debate between rational and incremental policy making can be seen to be artificial (Smith and May, 1980), so too can the paradigm wars between quantitative and qualitative methods. This is a theme we return to in Chapter Three.

Question for discussion

- In your view, what should count as evidence for policy making and for social work practice? Would you privilege research evidence above other sources? Justify your answer.

References

Brechin, A. and Sidell, M. (2000) 'Ways of knowing', in R. Gomm and C. Davies (eds) *Using evidence in health and social care*, London: Sage Publications, pp 3-25.

Burns, R.B. (2000) *Introduction to research methods*, London: Sage Publications.

Davies, H.T.O., Nutley, S.M. and Smith, P. (2000) 'Introducing evidence-based policy and practice in public services', in H.T.O. Davies, S.M. Nutley and P. Smith (eds) *What works? Evidence-based policy and practice in public services*, Bristol: The Policy Press, pp 1-11.

Denscombe, M. (2002) *Ground rules for good research: A 10 point guide for social researchers*, Buckingham: Open University Press.

Denscombe, M. (2010) *Ground rules for social research: Guidelines for good practice*, Maidenhead: Open University Press.

Kuhn, T.S. (1970) *The structure of scientific revolutions* (2nd edn), Chicago, IL: University of Chicago Press.

May, T. (2001) *Social research: Issues, methods and process* (3rd edn), Buckingham: Open University Press.

Nutley, S.M. and Webb, J. (2000) 'Evidence and the policy process', in H.T.O. Davies, S.M. Nutley and P. Smith (eds) *What works? Evidence-based policy and practice in public services*, Bristol: The Policy Press, pp 13-41.

Oakley, A. (2000) *Experiments in knowing: Gender and method in the social sciences*, Cambridge: Polity Press.

Popper, K. (1959) *The logic of scientific discovery*, London: Hutchinson.

Smith, G. and May, D. (1980) 'The artificial debate between rationalist and incrementalist models of decision making', *Policy & Politics*, no 8, pp 147-61, reproduced in M. Hill (ed) (1993) *The policy process: A reader*, Hemel Hempstead: Harvester Wheatsheaf, pp 163-74.

Weiss, C. (1995) 'The four "Is" of school reform: how interests, ideology, information and institution affect teachers and principals', *Harvard Educational Review*, vol 65, no 4, pp 571-92.

Further reading

Evans, T. and Hardy, M. (2010) *Evidence and knowledge for practice*, Cambridge: Polity Press.

Oakley, A. (2007) 'Evidence-informed policy and practice: challenges for social science', in M. Hammersley (ed) *Educational research and evidence-based practice*, London: Sage Publications, pp 91-105.

Pawson, R. (2006) *Evidence-based policy: A realist perspective*, London: Sage Publications.

Website resources

NHS Service Delivery and Organisation R&D Programme: www.sdo.lshtm.ac.uk
Social Care Institute for Excellence (SCIE): www.scie.org.uk

1.6 Evidence-based policy and practice
Saul Becker and Alan Bryman

'Evidence-based everything'?

Evidence-based policy and practice are not new – there has been a long-term move in advanced industrialised countries towards using research and evaluation to guide the decisions and behaviour of policy makers and professionals. In the UK, since the early 1960s, government ministries have had their own research, statistics and evaluation departments which review research and commission their own studies, although in the current austere economic climate there is far less of this. In 2001, the UK Centre for Evidence-Based Policy and Practice was established by the ESRC (see **Box 1c**). The belief that policy and professional practice *should* be informed by research evidence has accelerated in recent years, perhaps more so in difficult economic times where

Box 1c: The UK Centre for Evidence-Based Policy and Practice and the Evidence Network
Annette Boaz and William Solesbury

Established by the ESRC in 2001, the UK Centre for Evidence-Based Policy and Practice has focused on the diverse ways in which evidence – including scientific, social scientific and other research, enquiry and debate – is used in public policy. To that end it has undertaken a programme of research, training, consultancy, networking and resource provision:

- *Research* projects have been concerned with the public debate about genetically modified (GM) crops and foods; the nature and uses of evidence in the audit, inspection and scrutiny functions of government; the conduct of research reviews; the development of a new 'realist' approach to the synthesis of evidence; the nature and quality of knowledge within social care; the assessment of research quality; the contribution to the work of government departments of officials and board members from outside the civil service; and the role of strategic thinking in government.
- *Training* has been provided for clients including the National School of Government, the National Audit Office (NAO) and SCIE and for researchers and postgraduate students supported by the ESRC (through a Research Development Initiative training programme and an annual PhD summer school).
- *Consultancy* clients have included the Parliamentary Office of Science and Technology (POST), the Learning and Skills Development Agency (LSDA) and the National Centre for Social Research (NatCen).
- The Centre has functioned as a *resource centre* through its website which includes a guide to many databases of published research and other resources for evidence-based policy and practice and an extensive searchable bibliography of publication on evidence-based policy (www.kcl.ac.uk/schools/sspp/interdisciplinary/evidence/).
- *Networking* has played a central role in the Centre's efforts to promote evidence-based policy. The Evidence Network includes associates from across the world in a wide range of disciplines including social care, education, public health and criminal justice.
- The Centre launched and edits the journal *Evidence & Policy: A journal of research, debate and practice*, published by The Policy Press.

Alongside the Centre, the ESRC funded a set of research programmes exploring the role of evidence in policy in different disciplinary areas, including housing and child health (for more information see the ESRC Society Today website at www.esrcsocietytoday.ac.uk). In addition to discipline-specific programmes, a research centre was set up conducting research on research utilisation (www.ruru.ac.uk).

Although the term 'evidence-based policy' has gained currency in recent years (and is reflected in the title given to the Centre by the ESRC in 2000), experience suggests that it misrepresents the relationships between evidence and policy (Boaz et al, 2008). 'Evidence-informed policy' is nearer to reality. Research conducted in the Centre on the role of strategy in government (Boaz and Solesbury, 2007) reveals the continuing interplay between 'facts' and 'values' that characterises policy activities. In our training work we find that the 'Four I's' framework (Weiss, 1995) helps practitioners to place evidence appropriately. It states that policy is the outcome of the interaction of Ideologies, Interests and Information (that is, evidence) within the context of Institutions.

Although the ESRC-funded programme of work has come to an end, efforts have been made to sustain some of its core activities under the new title of the Centre for Evidence and Policy. The Evidence Network continues to provide a focal point for evidence-based policy and practice in a wide range of disciplines. Through an associates programme, it has a membership of over 1,350 researchers, practitioners and policy makers in more than 34 countries. The Network addresses the needs of people who provide public services, and those who provide the research base for evaluation and development. The Centre website continues to provide searchable bibliographies and details of news, training programmes and events relevant to evidence and policy. The journal *Evidence & Policy* provides an international, multidisciplinary forum for research and debate relevant to evidence and policy. Now in its sixth year, it recently published a special issue exploring European perspectives on evidence and policy (Nutley et al, 2010). There continues to be an active academic and practitioner interest in exploring, understanding and improving the relationship between evidence and policy.

This box draws on a memorandum submitted to the Science and Technology Select Committee on Scientific Advice, Risk and Evidence-Based Policy Making: www.publications. parliament.uk/pa/cm200506/cmselect/cmsctech/900/900we23.htm

Question for discussion
• To what extent can or should policy be evidence-based?

References

Boaz, A. and Solesbury, W. (2007) 'Strategy and politics: the example of the United Kingdom', in T. Fischer, G.P. Schmitz and P. Seberich (eds) *The strategy of politics: Results of a comparative study*, Bertelsmanns Stiftung: Guterslow.

Boaz, A., Grayson, L., Levitt, R. and Solesbury, W. (2008) 'Does evidence-based policy work? Learning from the UK experience', *Evidence & Policy*, vol 4, no 2, pp 233-53.

Nutley, S.M., Morton, S., Jung, T. and Boaz, A. (2010) 'Evidence and policy in six European countries: diverse approaches and common challenges', *Evidence & Policy*, vol 6, no 2, pp 131-44.

Weiss, C. (1995) 'The four "I's" of school reform: how interests, ideology, information and institution affect teachers and principals', *Harvard Educational Review*, vol 65, no 4, pp 571-92.

Further reading

Nutley, S.M., Walter, I. and Davies, H.T.O. (2007) *Using evidence: How can research inform public services?*, Bristol: The Policy Press.

Scientific Advice, Risk and Evidence-Based Policy Making (2006) *Science and Technology Select Committee*, London: The Stationery Office Limited.

Website resources

ESRC Society Today: www.esrcsocietytoday.ac.uk

The Evidence Network: www.kcl.ac.uk/schools/sspp/interdisciplinary/evidence/

Research Unit for Research Utilisation (RURU): www.ruru.ac.uk

resources are tight and value for money and effectiveness are often stated goals for both policy *and* practice. This is associated with the slogan 'what works' as a justification for public policy action. 'What works' suggests that unless we can be confident of success we should not waste public funds on new initiatives. Evidence-based policy, as part of the performance ethic within the 'new public management', argues that effective and efficient public policy – and good returns to investment for taxpayers – requires that we understand what works before we spend.

This interest in evidence-based policy and practice has been heavily influenced by a parallel set of concerns in the fields of medicine and healthcare, which have developed systems for determining 'what counts as evidence' and what counts as the *most important* and trustworthy form of evidence (Harrison, 2004). This approach favours certain (quantitative) methods and methodologies – for example, experiments using quasi-experimental methods or preferably random assignment; and meta-analyses and systematic reviews following traditions drawn from drug trials in medical research (see *Figure 1f* in Section 1.5, and also *Box 1e* for a critique). However, whether this so-called 'hierarchy' can be taken and applied to other areas of social policy and social work is open to debate. As we have suggested (see Section 1.5), a 'continuum' approach may be more appropriate in social policy and social work.

In the late 20th century, the emergence of the Campbell Collaboration (modelled on medicine's Cochrane Collaboration but concerned with social policies) and the UK's post-1997 New Labour governments, with their *Modernising government* agenda, propelled the growth of the evidence-based policy movement. Both the Campbell and Cochrane Collaborations 'recommend making policy decisions on the basis of reliable evidence; both caution against the dangers of professional arrogance.... Campbell's conception of the social scientist's role in helping society towards his utopian vision was primarily that of the social scientist as methodological servant, giving policy-makers the tools with which to assess what *has* been done as a guide to decisions about what *might* be done in the future' (Oakley, 2000, p 321; original emphasis).

In most cases of policy formulation, development and policy change, it is, however, difficult to be precise about the nature and degree of influence that research plays, if any, in informing policy and practice. Research can make a contribution to both policy and professional practice, even if it is not linear or direct. For example, **instrumental utilisation** of research can be said to have taken place when there is evidence of policy makers and social workers *acting on* the findings of specific research studies. **Conceptual utilisation** occurs when research *influences* how policy makers and social workers *interpret* and *think* about a social issue or problem – where, for example, it provides alternative ways of understanding and informs their action strategies (Clarke, 2001, p 35). The flip side of research utilisation is **'making an impact'**. Researchers often want their research to make an impact on policy and practice, and to do this, research enquiries and findings need to be utilised in some way by policy makers and practitioners.

The extent to which research can make an impact and inform policy, social work and other professional practice is dependent on many factors, discussed later in this section. For example, research that does not come to the attention of policy makers or professionals cannot make an impact on their decision making in any explicit or transparent way. How research is *disseminated* and *communicated* to target audiences, and what target audiences make or do with it – not just how research is 'done' and its 'trustworthiness' – are therefore critical to whether research can have an impact on policy and practice (see Chapter Seven).

302111

In many discussions of the impact or influence that research can have on policy and practice, there is an assumption that *both* policy and practice are influenced in the same ways (and in the same direction). However, the connection between research and policy, and between research and professional practice, can be different (Bullock et al, 1998, p 11), and are thus considered separately here. However, it must also be remembered that the distinction between policy (and policy makers), and practice (and professionals/ practitioners) is not as clear-cut as might be inferred, as we shall see below where social workers, for example, could be considered to be *making* policy through their daily actions and interventions as street-level bureaucrats or practitioners.

Research and policy making

Models of policy making

In order to understand the relationship between research and policy making we must first have some knowledge of the policy-making process. *Figure 1g* summarises two of the main models of the policy process: *rational* and *incremental* policy making.

Figure 1g: Rational and incremental models of policy making

Rational policy making

Rational, or top-down, theory is built on the assumption that 'given the correct forms of implementation process – guidance, procedures, organisation, training and (especially in the past twenty years) management – policy implementation will proceed as intended by implementers at the top of organisations or Government' (Baldwin, 2000, p 15). The 'intended' policy itself will be determined through rational decision making, a process with a logical sequence, from problem awareness, to goal setting, to the formulation of clear objectives, to the selection from alternative strategies of the best means to accomplish the objectives, and finally, to the evaluation of outcomes (Smith and May, 1980, p 164).

Incremental policy making

In contrast to rational approaches is the incremental model of policy making, or what is often referred to as the 'bottom-up' approach. The writings of Charles Lindblom and Michael Lipsky are critical here. Lindblom (1959) argues that the pressures on policy decision makers are such that rationalism is unattainable in the policy process, that means and ends are often chosen simultaneously, and many decisions are incremental, involving 'successive limited comparisons' to what has been done before (Hill, 1993, p 159). Policy makers start not with ideal goals but with policies currently in force. 'Decision making entails considering only incremental change, or changes at the margins. Only a rather restricted number of policy alternatives is reviewed and only a limited number of consequences is envisaged and evaluated for any given alternative' (Smith and May, 1980, p 166).

There are many criticisms of the rational model of policy making and the assumptions that underpin it (for a thorough review, see Smith and May, 1980). Given that the assumptions behind the model (that policy, following the consideration of all possibilities and options, can be defined rationally and unambiguously, with clear goals, aims and means, which are acceptable to, and accepted by, all parties and players) have been so challenged, it is perhaps surprising that the model still commands such respect among policy analysts. The reasons for its continuing importance lie not in its usefulness for understanding how policy *is* made, but in helping us to understand how policy *ought* to be made. Gordon et al (1977, p 7) suggest that 'The main explanation for its [the rational model's] continuing existence must lie in its status as a normative model and as a "dignified" myth which is often shared by the policy-makers themselves'. Baldwin concurs: 'This is a prescriptive and normative approach designed to assist those interested in implementation to understand the best way to proceed' (Baldwin, 2000, p 15). Thus, the rational approach offers a model for 'ideal decision making procedures' (Smith and May, 1980, p 170).

Lindblom's (1959) 'science of muddling through' provides a critique of rationalist theory, noting that there is seldom such a thing as a 'new' policy. The incremental, bottom-up, model helps us understand why pro-inertia and anti-innovation are powerful characteristics of all human organisations and the policy-making process. In a later refinement of his thesis, Lindblom (1980) argues that disjointed incrementalism is a model that not only explains *how* policy is made in the real world, but, in his view, it is also a model that illuminates how policy *ought* to be made.

Lindblom's importance is not just in his analysis of 'disjointed incrementalism'. He sees policy making as a process of political and social interaction involving negotiation and bargaining among groups promoting and protecting differing and competing interests and values – what Lindblom terms 'partisan mutual adjustment'. This political process is, in Lindblom's view, essential to policy making, and is in contrast with the centralised information-based decision making of rational approaches, which can ignore the voices of important stakeholders (see Gregory, 1989, for a full discussion of the Lindblomian paradigm). Indeed, Gregory suggests that Lindblom's enduring message is not about incrementalism in policy making, but rather that 'public policy making has to be understood essentially as a political process, rather than an analytical, problem-solving, one' (Gregory, 1989, p 186).

Smith and May, however, suggest that the debate between rational and incremental models of policy making is an artificial one for two reasons:

> Firstly, the relationship between "is" and "ought" is confused and there are good grounds for suggesting that whereas incrementalist models may perform an explanatory function, rationalist models are largely confined to a prescriptive role. Secondly the debate does not consider seriously the issue of what it takes to act in accord with any set of decision making rules and thus neglects the way in which policy makers and administrators may use 'decision making' as a gloss for a range of practices. (Smith and May, 1980, p 172)

Research and professional practice

Social workers and other professionals are charged with implementing policy as well as working to the law, their own professional codes, principles, values and purposes (see Section 1.2). In this context, what do we mean by professions' responsibilities for the implementation of policy? Minogue (1983, p 17) suggests that it is 'the crucial business of translating decisions into events: of "getting things done".... Implementation relates to "specified objectives", the translation into practice of the policies that emerge from the complex process of decision making'. Hill suggests that implementation should not be seen as somehow separate from the policy-making process: 'Rather, implementation must be seen as part of policy-making' (Hill, 1993, p 213).

A model of implementation

The work of Michael Lipsky offers insights into how the implementation of policy actually works in social work and other professional practice. He focuses on the behaviour and actions of key implementers – what he refers to as 'street-level bureaucrats' – and their role in *creating policy through their practice*. As Hudson contends, 'If we wish to understand policy implementation, we must understand the street-level bureaucrat' (Hudson, 1989, p 397).

Lipsky argues 'that the decisions of street-level bureaucrats, the routines they establish and the devices they invent to cope with uncertainties and work pressures, effectively becomes the public policies they carry out' (Lipsky, 1980, p xii) – in other words, their day-to-day practice actually *constructs* policy. In response to organisational and workload pressures, street-level bureaucrats, like social workers, childcare workers and other social policy-related professionals, develop working practices which maximise their use of discretion. Discretion enables procedures to be adapted to the client or service user and the service user to be adapted to the procedures (Baldwin, 2000, p 83; see also **Box 1d** for a discussion of discretion as it relates to social work).

Box 1d: Evidence-based practice and social work
Mark Hardy

Evidence-based practice (EBP) is controversial in social work. Partly, this reflects the enduringly contested relationship between policy and practice, which arguably has an intrinsic top-down character which lends itself to the priorities of policy makers rather than the needs of 'street-level' practitioners and those they serve (Schon, 1983). Equally, positions in debates concerning its advantages and disadvantages reflect alternative perspectives regarding how best to *understand* and *undertake* social work, which very broadly can be characterised as 'artistic' and 'scientific'. Divisions between advocates and opponents of EBP reflect alternative paradigmatic affiliations. Supporters are generally associated with a positivistic worldview (Newman et al, 2005) and opponents with interpretive and critical traditions, often affiliated with an emancipatory view of social work (D'Cruz and Jones, 2003; Humphries, 2008).

For advocates, EBP represents a means of enabling social work to address a profound loss of trust and legitimacy resulting from high profile service 'failures'. It offers potential to equip practitioners to better achieve their objectives by basing practice on knowledge generated via 'robust' methodological strategies. Opponents, however, regard EBP itself as a threat to social work, because it entails limits on professional discretion. There is also little acknowledgement that practitioners must make judgements in conditions of inherent uncertainty and will need to do so on a subjective rather than objective basis (Taylor and White, 2000). Additionally, in its emphasis on 'what works', EBP is driven by pragmatic priorities that threaten social work as a value-driven endeavour. Consequently, the principal obstacles to the achievement of EBP reside with practitioners themselves – Sheldon et al (2005, p 8) regard 'the curse of Carl Rogers' as significant in the view that 'science' undermines the humanistic, relationship based 'art' of social work (England, 1986).

Against such a backdrop, the Social Care Institute for Excellence (SCIE) was established with a brief to accumulate and disseminate evidence of 'what works'. SCIE sought to steer a midway between competing paradigmatic positions, advocating a 'framework, rather than a straightjacket' (Fisher, 2005 p 167). Pawson et al (2003) developed a typology of 'forms' of knowledge whereby the value of a hierarchy of knowledge is acknowledged, but there is equal emphasis on tacit practitioner knowledge and service user perspectives. Criteria for evaluating the quality of knowledge claims, depending on their particular 'source', were developed, and have been influential in subsequent attempts to broaden out the basis for EBP. Despite this, ongoing efforts to operationalise EBP have met with scepticism, often on the basis of paradigmatic affiliation (Smith, 2005) and assumed links with technical–rational rather than practical–moral forms of practice (Fook and Gardner, 2007). Additionally, EBP has been characterised as a mechanism via which social work is utilised to achieve wider neoliberal policy objectives which conflict with its heritage, strengths and values (Webb, 2001).

Undoubtedly, the aims of 'strong' advocates of evidence-based practice were unrealistic. The idea that social workers would have the time or inclination to engage in the systematic but routine appraisal of research findings before deciding how to intervene is dependent on an idealised view of practitioners and the contexts within which they work. Consequently, there has been a notable shift in social work education towards the more achievable goal of enabling practitioners to counter 'commonplace complexity' (Evans and Hardy, 2010) via 'research mindedness'. Social workers are now trained to assess the relevance and utility of evidence according to both the general conventions of social science but also criteria of 'practice validity' (Sheppard, 1998, 2004), embedded within everyday processes of reflection and critical thinking. There are also ongoing efforts to promote the accumulation of research knowledge to inform practice, but in awareness that it is unlikely that this will ever be able to be applied in a proscriptive fashion. The assumption here is that the differences between alternative paradigmatic positions are generally overstated (Munro, 1998). Consequently, there are clear benefits in a framework that acknowledges the contested status of social problems but nevertheless utilises 'truth' as an orientating device (Shaw and Gould, 2001; Kirk and Reid, 2002). In particular, the merits of realism as a research framework that potentially transcends the distinctions between 'art' and 'science' have come to the fore (Houston, 2001, 2005). This entails a methodological focus on unique 'context-mechanism-outcome' configurations (Pawson and Tilley, 1997) in accounting for 'what works for whom in what circumstances and why', and, in practice, a parallel emphasis on the benefits of combining analytic and intuitive approaches (Munro, 2008) so as to minimise inaccuracy in judgement and decision making. At the same time, realism problematises the relationship between knowledge, research and practice. It acknowledges the complexity entailed in generating evidence that is straightforwardly applicable beyond the context in which it was produced, and thus the pitfalls of engaging in large-scale attempts to instrumentalise knowledge in practice, such as EBP.

Question for discussion

• What is distinctive about the nature of the issues that social workers must deal with which means that it might be problematic to generalise knowledge generated in one particular scenario – a setting or case – to alternative scenarios?

References

D'Cruz, H. and Jones, M. (2003) *Social work research: Ethical and political contexts*, London: Sage Publications.

England, H. (1986) *Social work as art: Making sense for good practice*, London: Allen & Unwin.

Evans, T. and Hardy, M. (2010) *Evidence and knowledge for practice*, Cambridge: Polity Press.

Fisher, M. (2005) 'The Social Care Institute of Excellence: the role of a national institute in developing knowledge and practice in social care', in A. Bilson (ed) *Evidence-based practice in social work*, London: Whiting and Birch, pp 141-75.

Fook, J. and Gardner, F. (2007) *Practising critical reflection: A resource handbook*, Maidenhead: Open University Press.

Houston, S. (2001) 'Beyond social constructionism: critical realism and social work', *British Journal of Social Work*, vol 31, pp 845-61.

Houston, S. (2005) 'Philosophy, theory and method in social work: challenging empiricism's claim on evidence based practice', *Journal of Social Work*, vol 5, pp 7-20.

Humphries, B. (2008) *Social work research and social justice*, Basingstoke: Palgrave Macmillan.

Kirk, S. and Reid, W. (2002) *Science and social work: A critical appraisal*, New York: Columbia University Press.

Munro, E. (1998) *Understanding social work: An empirical approach*, London: Athlone Press.

Munro, E. (2008) *Effective child protection* (2nd edition), London: Sage Publications.

Newman, T., Moseley, A., Tierney, S. and Ellis, A. (2005) *Evidence-based social work: A guide for the perplexed*, Lyme Regis: Russell House.

Pawson, R. and Tilley, N. (1997) *Realistic evaluation*, London: Sage Publications.

Pawson, R., Boaz, A., Grayson, L., Long, A. and Barnes, C. (2003) *Types and quality of knowledge in social care*, London: Social Care Institute for Excellence.

Schon, D. (1983) *The reflective practitioner: How professionals think in action*, New York: Basic Books.

Shaw, I. and Gould, N. (2001) *Qualitative research in social work*, London: Sage Publications.

Sheldon, B., Chilvers, R., Ellis, A, Moseley, A. and Tierney, S. (2005) 'A pre-post empirical study of obstacles to, and opportunities for, evidence based practice in social care', in A. Bilson (ed) *Evidence-based practice in social work*, London: Whiting and Birch, pp 11-50.

Sheppard, M. (1998) 'Practice validity, reflexivity and knowledge for social work', *British Journal of Social Work*, vol 28, pp 763-83.

Sheppard, M. (2004) *Appraising and using social research in the human services: An introduction for social work and health practitioners*, London: Jessica Kingsley Publishers.

Smith, D. (2005) 'The limits of positivism revisited', in A. Bilson (ed) *Evidence-based practice in social work*, London: Whiting and Birch, p 111-23.

Taylor, C. and White, S. (2000) *Practising reflexivity in health and welfare: Making knowledge*, Buckingham: Open University Press.

Webb, S. (2001) 'Some considerations on the validity of evidence-based practice', *British Journal of Social Work*, vol 31, pp 51-79.

Further reading
Evans, T. and Hardy, M. (2010) *Evidence and knowledge for practice*, Cambridge: Polity Press.
Orme, J. and Shemmings, D. (2010) *Developing research-based social work practice*, Basingstoke: Palgrave Macmillan.
Pawson, R. (2006) *Evidence based policy: A realist perspective*, London: Sage Publications.

Website resource
Social Care Institute for Excellence (SCIE): www.scie.org.uk

Lipsky's work is important in helping us to understand how policy is constructed through the practice of street-level implementers. Discretion (often referred to as 'professional judgement') is inevitable at the street level and thus policy making can never be truly 'rational', nor can implementation of policy ever be 'perfect' (Hogwood and Gunn, 1984). Nonetheless, the lessons for *improving* the implementation process, for making it less imperfect and perhaps more rational, do need to be learned. The 10 major 'blocks' to perfect implementation (Hogwood and Gunn, 1984) centre around organisational deficiencies in cooperation and communication, in defining objectives, and so on. An understanding of these organisational deficiencies helps explain the 'implementation deficits' that exist in all policy making, and particularly in complex and wide-ranging social policies that require implementation by many different organisations and professional groups from a range of sectors (statutory, private, voluntary, charitable and informal), with competing objectives and agendas, and working within predetermined budgets and, often, confusing political messages.

Politics and ideology

Politics is important on so many levels. Some argue that the research process is itself a 'political activity' (Mayall et al, 1999, p 5), where all aspects of research are constructed and reconstructed through the intersections of three sets of interests: those of the researchers; those of the researched (particularly disadvantaged individuals and groups); and those of socially dominant political structures, organisations, social groups and individuals (including policy makers, politicians, social workers, and so on). Researchers must manage these conflicting interests, and the demands and priorities of their organisations, funding bodies, and so on, as well as their own values, agendas, purposes and time constraints. In this context, research is political with a small 'p', and not some 'neutral' exercise in knowledge and evidence creation.

On another level, any intention by researchers to inform or influence policy or practice ('make an impact') is, by definition, a political activity. As we have already seen, social policy and social work research combines a number of aims and these include contributing to knowledge and understanding while also trying to *improve* the policy process or professional practice and outcomes.

Additionally, the political *climate* of the time (not just which party is in power, but their ideologies and values, particularly their 'ideologies of welfare' – see George and Wilding, 1994) are important in determining, in part, the impact that research can have on policy *ideas* as well as on policy making and implementation. Where research findings are consistent with government values and ideologies, there is some chance that the findings will be applauded and promoted, will 'count' as 'evidence', and may be used to justify a current policy approach or to usher in an 'evidence-based' change of direction. Where findings challenge the current approach of policy or practice, they may be 'welcomed' (in the spirit of enlightenment and democratic governance), but there is also a very good chance that the research will be ignored, or seen as irrelevant, or even dangerous. *Boxes 7d* and *7f* (Chapter Seven) provide examples of this.

Politics, and ideology, can also lead to the reframing of social issues and social problems, so that they are understood, and researched, in different ways. For example, Abel-Smith and Townsend's research on poverty, contained in *The poor and the poorest* (*Box 1a* in Section 1.2), helped to define poverty *and* inequality as major *social problems* requiring widespread and concerted collective action. The Labour government of the time was responsive to the evidence and committed to some form of intervention. However, just nine years after its publication, Sir Keith Joseph – a Conservative politician whose influence on 'Thatcherism' is widely acknowledged – reframed the social problem of poverty into something quite different. He proposed that poverty was not *the* problem, but rather the issue was to do with a 'cycle of deprivation', whereby deprivation was transmitted across generations through problem-creating parenting practices. This perspective, drawing on a different set of beliefs and ideologies of welfare, namely that post-war collectivism had failed to make a better society, and that poverty was more to do with the poor themselves rather than with the social and economic structures around them, was a precursor to the Thatcher values that were to dominate government social and economic policy from the mid-1970s to the end of the 20th century (Becker, 1997). These views helped to challenge the relatively new 'rediscovery' of poverty knowledge, by offering an alternative, more individualistic, way of understanding the issues. This reconceptualisation, from poverty to 'transmitted deprivation', led to a raft of research studies, first under the Conservative and then under New Labour governments (Deacon, 2004). New Labour's own responsiveness to this research evidence was consistent with its political objectives of tackling poverty and social exclusion and promoting opportunities for all. Today, there is some distance – conceptually and ideologically – between the current political concerns with the 'underclass' and 'benefit scroungers' of some in the Coalition government, and the spur to collective anti-poverty action generated by *The poor and the poorest* almost five decades earlier. *Figure 1h* summarises why issues of politics and ideology are important in the context of social policy and social work research.

Figure 1h: **Why politics and ideology matter**

- Politics and ideologies of welfare are important in determining the responsiveness of governments, organisations, policy makers and professionals to research evidence.
- Politics and ideological priorities can lead to some research questions (and answers) being ignored or suppressed, while others can be elevated and lead to extensions or new programmes of research and enquiry.
- Political ideologies help to determine what will be defined as a 'social issue' or as a 'social problem', and, over time, social problems can be reframed or redefined as something else (for example, 'personal' or 'private troubles'). The reframing of social problems as 'non-problems', or private troubles as social problems, will have major implications for policy and social work practice.
- The nature of 'evidence' (and what 'counts' as evidence) is largely a political, ideological and social construct as well as a research and methodological issue. Research methods (the procedures for collecting research data and forming evidence) are themselves

socially constructed, and represent particular views about the social world and about knowledge.
- Finally, the values, ideologies and political agendas of individual researchers and research units/think tanks influence how they define social issues and how they go about defining research questions, and answering them.

The impact of research on policy and practice

The relationship between a specific piece of research or body of research, and a particular policy or aspect of practice/social work intervention, is most transparent when those responsible for policy or practice actually cite the research 'evidence' that informs or influences their thinking and decisions. This would indicate that the research has 'made an impact' on policy, practice or both. The 'rediscovery of poverty', as we have already seen, was informed directly by the work of Brian Abel-Smith and Peter Townsend (**Box 1a** in Section 1.2). Their research drew on secondary analysis of government datasets to say new things about the meaning and extent of poverty, thus challenging accepted 'knowledge' and understanding of that time. There is a clear, and acknowledged, link between the Abel-Smith and Townsend research and a growing awareness and concern with poverty, the development of social policies and the growth of anti-poverty action – evidence of both *instrumental* and *conceptual utilisation* of their research. Sometimes research can take many years to permeate through the policy making and political processes and be utilised, and have an impact; at other times this can be relatively quick. The Abel-Smith and Townsend study illustrates the impact of research on both rational and incremental models of the policy process. In this case, research was utilised by the then Labour government and by others (for example, CPAG) to inform their policy options and strategies, thus combining 'top-down' and 'bottom-up' elements.

While the rational model of policy making outlined above sees research findings feeding into the process of specifying goals and objectives and identifying consequences (Nutley and Webb, 2000, pp 25-6), the incremental model of policy making and implementation sees research evidence feeding into the policy and practice process at many different points of time and being targeted at, and used by, different stakeholders in their negotiations, political interactions, decision making and interventions. Irrespective of which model is used to help us understand more clearly the workings of the policy process (and there are other models which can be referred to here – see Hill, 1993 and Hudson and Lowe, 2009), what most of these models share is the value placed on *research knowledge informing policy and practice decisions and choices* – the notion of *evidence-based policy and practice*.

However, there are limits to the influence that research by itself can have on rational or incremental forms of policy making. In some cases, the impact of a *specific* piece of research is not particularly apparent, but policy has changed gradually as a consequence of growing social and political awareness, growing evidence of injustice or need, and as different policy networks have evolved, engaged with and utilised, research findings. On other occasions, research fails to have any, or has very little, impact on policy making even though the 'quality' of the research is not itself in doubt (see also Chapter Seven).

There are a number of ways, then, in which we might understand the relationships between research evidence and policy making (**Figure 1i**).

Figure 1i: Models of the relationship between research and policy

- A 'knowledge-driven model' assumes that research (conducted by 'experts') *leads* policy.
- A 'problem-solving model' assumes that research *follows* policy, and that policy issues shape research priorities. Thus, research supplies the empirical evidence on which policy makers can base their decisions and choices.
- An 'interactive model' portrays research and policy as mutually influential.
- A 'political/tactical model' sees policy as the outcome of a political process, where the research agenda is politically driven. Here, research can become political ammunition or it can be ignored if it does not coincide with the answers that politicians want to see. Sometimes, the very fact that research is taking place is important for political and tactical purposes, rather than the findings themselves.
- An 'enlightenment model' sees research as serving policy in indirect ways, addressing the context within which decisions are made and providing a broader frame for understanding and explaining policy.

Source: Young et al (2002); see also Nutley and Webb (2000, pp 29-31); Clarke (2001, pp 35-27)

Abel-Smith and Townsend's research (**Box 1a** in Section 1.2) falls largely within the knowledge-driven model, where anti-poverty policy and action developed out of robust research evidence. However, as we saw earlier, the *political and ideological climate* of the time is also critical in determining the responsiveness of government and others to research evidence, and what they might do about, or with, research findings.

Figure 1j shows the circumstances that are favourable to research having an impact on *both* policy and practice. So, for example (and quite understandably), greater attention is paid to research findings when research is conducted by a trusted and authoritative source, or where research is timely and addresses an issue that is relevant with a methodology that is rigorously applied.

In a study on how local authorities use research, the authors found that having an effective structure for commissioning, undertaking and disseminating research within the authority was a necessary (but not sufficient) condition for research to have an impact on policy and practice. A centrally located, rather than devolved, research capacity results in more effective research, dissemination and adoption (Percy-Smith et al, 2002).

Figure 1j: Circumstances favourable to research having an impact on policy and practice

Greater attention is paid to research findings when:

- Policy makers and practitioners understand and believe in the benefits of using evidence, and are clear of its relative merits vis-à-vis expert opinion.
- Research is fully integrated into policy-making processes, practice training and delivery systems.
- Users of research are partners in the process of evidence generation.
- Research is produced by a trusted and authoritative source.
- Research is timely and addresses an issue that is relevant with a methodology that is relatively uncontested.

- Results support existing political ideologies, are convenient and relatively uncontentious, and do not represent a major challenge to existing policy.
- Results are reported with low degrees of uncertainty, have clear implications for action and can be implemented without incurring high costs if the decision needs to be reversed.
- Researchers, senior personnel and other key users seek implementation with skilful advocacy and great stamina.
- Research outputs reach the right people in the right form at the right time, and these people have the requisite skills and motivation to interpret and apply the findings of research in their own context.
- Research findings complement and confirm other 'ways of knowing', including theoretical and experiential knowing. (See also **Figure 1d** in Section 1.5.)

Source: Drawn from Davies et al (2000, p 359) and Percy-Smith et al (2002, pp 43-5)

Closing the gap between research and practice would also need practitioners to understand the relative strengths and weaknesses of different research methods and designs and how they answer, or provide evidence on, different questions. Practitioners (and policy makers) need to recognise that there are differences between the types of data generated by research studies of different designs and methodologies. As **Figure 1k** shows, there are also other factors that need to be in place if the gap between research and practice is to be narrowed. These include the need for practitioners to appraise evidence critically and to contribute to systematic reviews of research findings (Macdonald, 2000, p 130).

Figure 1k: Factors required for the development of evidence-based practice

- The generation of good quality data concerning effectiveness.
- A workforce critically able to appraise evidence and contribute to the process of systematic reviews of research findings.
- The dissemination of data and/or research syntheses in a readily accessible form to professionals, managers, policy makers and to service users – this is a methodological, as well as a technical, challenge.
- A work and policy environment that facilitates, rather than impedes, the development of practices that reflect 'best evidence'.

Source: Drawn from Macdonald (2000, p 130)

The issue of *how research is communicated* to policy makers and professionals, and its *accessibility*, are key issues here. Are professionals more likely to be informed and influenced by full, detailed research reports, or are short summaries of key findings a better vehicle for communicating research? Are *systematic* reviews of the literature more likely to be effective in influencing what professionals do in practice, than, say, a single research-based article (which would more likely be read by a few academics)? These are questions that we return to in Chapter Seven when we discuss in more detail issues around *dissemination* and *knowledge transfer*.

When research findings *do* reach the right audience and are actually read by policy makers and professionals, there is evidence, unfortunately, to suggest that these studies are not always sufficiently accessible to be understood and valued, and that some professionals do not have the time or skills to know what is relevant for *their* work (Needham, 2000, pp 135-6). How knowledge is diffused or transferred, and utilised by professionals, is one concern, but for practitioners to take any notice and *use* evidence as the base for policy or practice also requires them to be committed to the *ideology of evidence-based policy and practice* itself (Nutley and Davies, 2000, p 331). As **Box 1d** shows, the ideology of evidence-based practice in social work is far from universally accepted, and **Box 1e** provides a critique of the ideology *and* practice of 'evidence-based everything'.

Finally, as **Box 1d** also reminds us in the context of social work, it must be remembered that research evidence is only one source of knowledge that influences policy and practice. Other influences include the legal structure determining policy, practice and interventions; practitioners' knowledge gained through experience ('tacit knowledge' and 'craft routines'); values and principles; the views of service users and other sources of knowledge; organisational structures and norms; and resources, to name but a few (Nutley and Davies, 2000). For research to have an impact on policy and practice, researchers themselves must understand better and engage with the processes that influence decision making and interventions at the institutional, organisational and individual levels, and policy makers and practitioners must 'use' the research to inform their thinking and actions.

Limits to evidence-based policy and practice

Evidence-based policy and practice has become contested terrain in social work (**Box 1d**) and more widely. **Box 1e** provides a forceful and detailed critique of the evidence-based policy and practice movement and its claims to knowledge and evidence. There are debates about method that mirror wider methodological and theory of knowledge debates: is there a hierarchy of evidence and is random assignment the 'gold standard'? There are disagreements about the generalisability of 'evidence' across different contexts: is there a single truth that can be designated as 'best practice' across all or many contexts? There are debates about values and interpretation: what criteria – or *whose* criteria – are used to judge the 'truth' or reliability of evidence? And perhaps most importantly there are debates about the messy realities of politics: when evidence comes up against political mandates and expediency, which triumphs? There is now awareness that evidence itself is mustered selectively and the extent to which it shapes policy or practice is contingent on factors that are not simply about the rigour with which data are collected or analysed. There are, however, signs that the more simplistic approaches to what Ann Oakley (2000, p 318) once termed 'social science and evidence-based everything' are now losing ground to better-informed, more pluralistic and pragmatic approaches, concerned less with evidence-based policy than with developing the *evidence base for policy*. But realising even this more modest aim of strengthening the social science evidence base may require challenging some near-sacred assumptions about the value of established practices and research methods, and, for example, the relative value of different publication modes (for example, publication in peer review journals versus professional magazines). It may require more of a partnership between research producers (those who 'do' the research) and the user community (those who need to make use of research to inform their policy or practice, and 'service' users themselves), so that the evidence base for policy is both robust, methodologically sound, undertaken and managed to high standards, and is relevant to a wide range of stakeholders. It was to address these long-term strategic issues that the ESRC launched its 'Evidence-based Policy' initiative in December 2000 (see **Box 1c**).

Box 1e: Criticism of the evidence-based policy and practice movement
Martyn Hammersley

Who would deny that policy making and practice should be based on evidence? In broad terms, the desirability of this is obvious. However, the issue is not quite so simple.

In the 1990s the notion of evidence-based practice and policy making spread from health, where it had originated as evidence-based medicine, into other fields, notably social policy, education, social work and criminology. In these fields we can distinguish between an initial, rather strict model of evidence-based practice and later liberalised versions. According to the strict model, RCTs are the ideal research method, and can provide evidence about which treatments (policies or practices) work, and about their side effects. Systematic reviews (SRs) of the results of RCTs can then supply reliable specifications of which policies are effective and what is good and bad practice on the part of practitioners.

There has been much criticism of the various components of this strict model, as regards both the kind of research evidence required *and* its relationship to policy making and practice. The main points of this criticism are summarised here.

Randomised controlled trials
RCTs are, in principle and sometimes in practice, an extremely effective means of determining the effects of a treatment or intervention. However, as with any other research method, they have weaknesses, and also limits to their application (see Worrall, 2002; Cartwright, 2007).

A first point is that, even with double blinding (where neither those administering nor those receiving the treatments are aware of who is getting which one), RCTs do not rule out *all* sources of confounding error. There is always a chance that the treatment and control groups are not sufficiently similar in relevant respects; there may be unplanned variation in the ways the groups are treated, especially given the practicalities of administering randomisation in large trials (Gueron, 2002); and erosion of their membership may introduce bias. Moreover, like most other methods, RCTs face measurement problems. When the focus is on differential death rates over a short period of time, measurement of outcomes is not usually a significant issue. However, it gets more serious when we are concerned, for example, with quality of life over many years, the severity of various side effects, and so on. And outside the field of medicine, problems with measurement are frequently severe (Hammersley, 2010).

A second problem is that there is usually a trade-off between internal and external validity. In the field of health, it is common practice to exclude from the study any patients who suffer from other illnesses apart from the one for which the treatment is appropriate, thereby increasing the chances of detecting any treatment effect. However, when the treatment is subsequently applied to the wider population, it will be given to people who have other ailments and receive other treatments, and the findings may not tell us accurately how successful (or dangerous) the treatment is likely to be for them. This has sometimes led to the use of so-called pragmatic trials that are designed to measure external validity at the expense of internal validity – testing out the effect of treatments on more 'realistic' populations (Hotopf, 2002).

Equally important, there are severe restrictions on the applicability of the RCT method. It requires that the treatment being assessed is relatively specific and standardised in character. Generally speaking, only if what is applied to each case in the treatment category is more or less the same will any clear and reliable results emerge from the trial. Yet, even in some areas of health (such as psychiatry), and in most areas of social work, social policy, education and criminology, what is involved can rarely be a specific standardised treatment, since it involves processes of social interaction between professionals and those with whom they work. Furthermore, blinding is often impossible in these fields, so that it is not possible to control the effects of participants' expectations.

Systematic reviews

Advocates of SRs have sometimes been very dismissive of traditional reviews, for instance: 'Most literature reviews in social science are selective, opinionated and discursive rampages through literature which the reviewer happens to know about or can easily lay his or her hands on' (Oakley, 2007, p 96). There are undoubtedly some advantages in being 'systematic' in carrying out reviews, but it is important that any comparison with more traditional types of review focuses on good practice in each case, rather than comparing an idealised version of one with poor examples of the other.

Moreover, there are problems with aspects of SRs. Up to some point, the attempt to achieve exhaustiveness is of value, since it should ensure that important studies that are relevant are not overlooked. However, there are arguments for more theoretically directed searches of the literature (Pawson, 2006). Another point is that the more time spent searching for potentially relevant studies, and the more studies found, the less time will be available, other things being equal, for careful reading and assessment of each study (MacLure, 2005). Moreover, much depends on how synthesis is conceptualised. In its original strict form, where statistical meta-analysis is the model, synthesis is viewed as a process of aggregating data, or combining findings, from a range of studies; a strategy that is underpinned by the idea that the larger the 'sample' of data that can be employed the more likely it is that the conclusions of a systematic review will be sound. However, there are problems with the assumption that synthesis can be a matter of calculation for it necessarily involves interpretation and judgement. Furthermore, the concept of SRs tends to assume that all the studies are aimed at answering the same question in comparable ways, overlooking the variety of respects in which studies may complement one another (Hammersley, 2001, 2006).

Finally, while explicitness about the criteria of relevance and likely validity employed in a review can be of value, such judgement always depends on tacit knowledge, and, therefore, can never be made fully explicit. And attempts to make the criteria fully explicit can displace attention away from what is to be judged, on to filling out a tick-list of features, a process that cannot substitute for sound judgement.

The relationship between research and policy making or practice

In its original, strict form the notion of evidence-based practice gave the impression that conclusions about 'what works' can be derived by demonstrative calculation from research evidence; in other words, that what policies and practices should be adopted can be determined by scientific means, minimising or eliminating reliance on interpretation and judgement on the part of policy makers and practitioners. However, this is a misconception, for several reasons. First, scientific research cannot tell us what is *wrong* or what *ought to be* done; it can only provide factual information about the effects of an intervention. 'What works' is a misleading phrase in this respect, since in much usage it conflates the factual with the normative. Moreover, as we have seen, even as regards factual evidence, RCTs and systematic reviews, like all other methods, are open to threats to validity, in principle and even more in practice, so that the results of particular studies, and of reviews, must always be assessed for reliability by policy makers and practitioners. Perhaps most important of all, knowing what would be the likely outcome of a treatment for an average case within a population does not tell us what would be the likely outcome of a treatment for any particular case that happens to belong to that population. Even within a RCT where a strong positive effect has been discovered, there will often be members of the treatment group who do not show any improvement or do so only to a negligible degree, as well as some who suffer from severe side effects that could outweigh the value of the treatment. So, even after all the research evidence is in, practitioners must exercise judgement in evaluating it, and they need to combine it with other information, before making a decision in any particular case, a process that will require the exercise of practical wisdom (Dunne, 1997).

It is important to recognise that the rise of the notion of evidence-based practice has been closely associated with a particular conception of the role of policy in relation to professional practice, often referred to as 'the new public management' or 'managerialism' (Pollitt, 1990; Power, 1997). This arose from distrust of the claims to expertise made by professionals, and suspicion of their exercise of autonomy in pursuing their work, these feeding a demand for 'transparent' accountability. Making explicit the evidence base on which professionals operate was seen as essential to this process (see Oakley, 2000).

Liberalisation

More recent advocacy of evidence-based practice has generally involved a liberalised version of the strict model. Here, the fact that RCTs and SRs have limitations is acknowledged, and (to some degree and in particular ways) other kinds of research and reviewing are treated as legitimate. Also, the relationship between research evidence and what practitioners should do in particular situations is recognised to be weaker and more uncertain than the strict model assumes, and it is noted that decisions in particular cases necessarily rely on practitioner judgement.

There is much to be said in favour of this liberalisation: it may involve acceptance that there is no single hierarchy of research or reviewing methods, that trade-off decisions have to be made among them, and that research can never tell us on its own what should be done. At the same time, liberalisation downgrades the decisive role that the strict model assigned to research evidence. One result is that the dramatic novelty of the call for 'evidence-based practice' is lost: it becomes the much weaker, indeed uncontentious, requirement that research should 'influence' policy and practice. Furthermore, liberalisation effectively downgrades the criticisms made of other kinds of research than the RCT and other forms of reviewing than SRs, yet these raise important methodological issues that ought to be tackled. It is also important to note that, in practice, there is often a flip-flopping between the strict model and more liberal versions in an effort to retain the newsworthiness of 'evidence-based practice' while apparently acknowledging its limitations and complexities.

We should consider why the notion of evidence-based practice spread so successfully within the health field and beyond: why did it appeal, in one form or another, to some researchers and many policy makers, practitioners and others? For researchers, presumably, it seemed to open up the prospect of increasing the 'impact' of their research on policy and practice, giving them a direct role in processes of social improvement. For policy makers, it fitted with the notion of the new public management, apparently offering a means of subjecting professions to transparent accountability. For practitioners it promised solutions to the difficult practical problems they faced. As with many innovations, the idea was partly myth, but we can learn a great deal from it.

References

Cartwright, N.D. (2007) 'Are RCTs the Gold Standard?', *Biosocieties*, vol 2, pp 11-20 (http://personal.lse.ac.uk/cartwrig/Papers%20on%20Evidence.htm).

Dunne, J. (1997) *Back to the rough ground: Practical judgment and the lure of technique*, Notre Dame, IN: Notre Dame University Press.

Gueron, J. (2002) 'The politics of random assignment: implementing studies and affecting policy', in F. Mosteller and R.F. Boruch (eds) *Evidence matters: Randomized trials in education research*, Washington, DC: Brookings Institution Press.

Hammersley, M. (2001) 'On "systematic" reviews of research literatures: a "narrative" reply to Evans and Benefield', *British Educational Research Journal*, vol 27, no 5, pp 543-54.

Hammersley, M. (2006) 'Systematic or unsystematic, is that the question? Reflections on the science, art, and politics of reviewing research evidence', in A. Killoran, C. Swann and M. Kelly (eds) *Public health evidence: Changing the health of the public*, Oxford: Oxford University Press.

Hammersley, M. (2010) 'Is social measurement possible, or desirable?', in E. Tucker and G. Walford (eds) *The handbook of measurement: How social scientists generate, modify, and validate indicators and scales*, London: Sage Publications.

Hotopf, M. (2002) 'The pragmatic randomized controlled trial', *Advances in Psychiatric Treatment*, vol 8, pp 326-33.

MacLure, M. (2005) '"Clarity bordering on stupidity": where's the quality in systematic review?', *Journal of Education Policy*, vol 20, no 4, pp 393-416.

Oakley, A. (2000) *Experiments in knowing: Gender and method in the social sciences*, Cambridge: Polity Press.

Oakley, A. (2007) 'Evidence-informed policy and practice: challenges for social science', in M. Hammersley (ed) *Educational research and evidence-based practice*, London: Sage Publications, pp 91-105. [First published by Manchester Statistical Society, Manchester UK, 13 February 2001.]

Pawson, R. (2006) *Evidence-based policy: A realist perspective*, London: Sage Publications.

Pollitt, C. (1990) *Managerialism and the public services*, Oxford: Blackwell.

Power, M. (1997) *The audit society: Rituals of verification*, Oxford: Oxford University Press.

Worrall, J. (2002) 'What evidence in evidence-based medicine?', *Philosophy of Science*, vol 69, pp S316-S330.

What counts as the evidence base that should inform policy and practice will become a key issue for policy makers and professionals over the coming years. The advent of SCIE, to help identify the evidence base for social care policy and practice, mirrors the earlier advent of the National Institute for Health and Clinical Excellence (NICE) in the medical/healthcare domain. This is important because, as Macdonald has observed, 'Within social care, political ideology plays a major role in shaping policy and practice. The volatility inherent in the way that social problems are conceived, and therefore how they are responded to, also impacts on the shape and nature of social care provision' (Macdonald, 2000, p 118).

It has been argued that evidence-based policy and practice is likely to be the exception rather than the rule because of the many 'enemies' of a more evidence-based approach. These enemies include:

- *bureaucratic logic* – the logic that says things are right because they have always been done that way;
- *politics* – the art of the possible rather than what is rational or what might work best; and
- *crime* – there is scarcely room to think never mind time to think about evidence-based policy and practice (Nutley and Webb, 2000).

And:

- The methodological and other criticisms relating to the ideology and practice of evidence-based policy, specifically to do with *RCTs, systematic reviews* and *liberalisation*, as discussed in **Box 1e**.

Research, particularly where it is trustworthy and robust, can and should be a key *source* of evidence for both policy *and* practice.

In our review of 'evidence-based everything', it is possible to conceptualise at least three levels or strengths of evidence-based policy and practice (*Figure 1l*).

Figure 1l: Three levels of evidence-based policy and practice

1. Research *determining* policy and practice (the 'pure' ideological and implemented form of evidence-based policy and practice).
2. Research *informing* policy and practice (there is instrumental and/or conceptual utilisation of research, but other factors and evidence from diverse sources also play a role in informing policy and practice).
3. Research *influencing* policy and practice (the weakest form of evidence-based policy and practice, where the nature and intensity of any influence of research are rarely defined or articulated with any degree of specificity).

From the perspective of researchers themselves, if their research is utilised at any of the three levels as outlined in **Figure 1l**, then their work could be considered to have 'made an impact'. Many social researchers are increasingly having to think about how their research *might* make an impact on policy, practice or other aspects of social and economic life. Research Councils and some other funding organisations are increasingly requiring researchers to provide an 'impact statement' in their research proposals, and the measurement of 'impact' now features in national exercises and audits to measure the quality of all research conducted within British universities, with the assumption that making an impact is a good thing and an indicator of quality. However, within academic circles, and outside, this is a highly contested area.

It must be remembered that research is only one source, only one way of knowing about the social world, and that political imperatives, service user and professionals' views, resources and other considerations also need to be taken into account by policy makers, social workers and others: 'Rather, research evidence is just one influence on the policy process and, while the research community is free to argue that it should receive greater attention, it would be anti-democratic to insist that research evidence should be the prime consideration' (Walker, 2000, p 163).

A final note of caution. The discussion so far on policy and practice has assumed that there are strong advantages for both policy making and professional interventions where and when research impacts on these activities. However, some writers, such as Bulmer 20 years ago, have suggested that the close links between researchers and policy makers, while influencing policy, may divert attention from academic goals such as the improvement of the analytical procedures used to study social issues and processes: 'To that extent, they contribute to the methodological weakness characteristic of much British social-policy research. Research carried out for explicitly political reasons is not necessarily the most objective or fruitful in its outcome' (Bulmer, 1991, p 162). Today, the same note of caution should apply to research that is *specifically* conducted to 'make an impact'.

Questions for discussion

- What are the relationships between research, policy, implementation and practice?
- How can you explain why research sometimes influences social policy and professional practice, while at other times it may have little impact?

References

Baldwin, M. (2000) *Care management and community care: Social work discretion and the construction of policy*, Aldershot: Ashgate.

Becker, S. (1997) *Responding to poverty: The politics of cash and care*, Harlow: Longman.

Bullock, R., Gooch, D., Little, M. and Mount, K. (1998) *Research in practice: Experiments in development and information design*, Aldershot: Ashgate.

Bulmer, M. (1991) 'National contexts for the development of social-policy research: British and American research on poverty and social welfare compared', in P. Wagner, C.H. Weiss, B. Wittrock and H. Woolman (eds) *Social sciences and modern states: National experiences and theoretical crossroads*, Cambridge: Cambridge University Press, pp 148-67.

Clarke, A. (2001) 'Research and the policy-making process', in N. Gilbert, *Researching social life* (2nd edn), London: Sage Publications, pp 28-42.

Davies, H.T.O., Nutley, S.M. and Smith, P. (2000) 'Learning from the past, prospects for the future', in H.T.O. Davies, S.M. Nutley and P. Smith (eds) *What works? Evidence-based policy and practice in public services*, Bristol: The Policy Press, pp 351-66.

Deacon, A. (2004) 'Transmitted deprivation research', in S. Becker and A. Bryman (eds) *Understanding research for social policy and practice: Themes, methods and approaches*, Bristol: The Policy Press, pp 31-3.

George, V. and Wilding, P. (1994) *Welfare and ideology*, Hemel Hempstead: Harvester Wheatsheaf.

Gordon, I., Lewis, J. and Young, K. (1977) 'Perspectives on policy analysis', *Public Administration Bulletin*, vol 25, pp 26-30, reproduced in M. Hill (ed) (1993) *The policy process: A reader*, Hemel Hempstead: Harvester Wheatsheaf, pp 5-9.

Gregory, R. (1989) 'Political rationality or incrementalism?', *Policy & Politics*, no 17, pp 139-53, reproduced in M. Hill (ed) (1993) *The policy process: A reader*, Hemel Hempstead: Harvester Wheatsheaf, pp 175-91.

Harrison, S. (2004) 'Evidence-based healthcare as public policy', in S. Becker and A. Bryman (eds) *Understanding research for social policy and practice: Themes, methods and approaches*, Bristol: The Policy Press, pp 43-7.

Hill, M. (ed) (1993) *The policy process: A reader*, Hemel Hempstead: Harvester Wheatsheaf.

Hogwood, B.W. and Gunn, L. (1984) *Policy analysis for the real world*, Oxford: Oxford University Press.

Hudson, B. (1989) 'Michael Lipsky and street level bureaucracy: a neglected perspective', in L. Barton (ed) *Disability and dependency*, Lewes: Falmer Press, pp 23-41.

Hudson, J. and Lowe, S. (2009) *Understanding the policy process: Analysing welfare policy and practice*, Bristol: The Policy Press.

Lindblom, C. (1959) 'The science of muddling through', *Public Administration Review*, vol 19, no 2, pp 79-88.

Lindblom, C. (1980) *The policy making process* (2nd edn), Englewood Cliffs, NJ: Prentice Hall.

Lipsky, M. (1980) *Street-level bureaucracy: Dilemmas of the individual in public services*, New York, NY: Russell Sage Foundation.

Macdonald, G. (2000) 'Social care: rhetoric and reality', in H. Davies, S. Nutley and P. Smith (eds) *What works? Evidence-based policy and practice in public services*, Bristol: The Policy Press, pp 117-40.

Mayall, B., Hood, S. and Oliver, S. (1999) 'Introduction', in S. Hood, B. Mayall and S. Oliver (eds) *Critical issues in social research: Power and prejudice*, Buckingham: Open University Press, pp 1-9.

Minogue, M. (1983) 'Theory and practice in public policy and administration', *Policy & Politics*, no 11, pp 63-85, reproduced in M. Hill (ed) (1993) *The policy process: A reader*, Hemel Hempstead: Harvester Wheatsheaf, pp 10-29.

Needham, G. (2000) 'Research and practice: making a difference', in R. Gomm and C. Davies (eds) *Using evidence in health and social care*, London: Sage Publications, pp 131-51.

Nutley, S.M. and Davies, H.T.O. (2000) 'Making a reality of evidence-based practice', in H.T.O. Davies, S.M. Nutley and P. Smith (eds) *What works? Evidence-based policy and practice in public services*, Bristol: The Policy Press, pp 317-50.

Nutley, S.M. and Webb, J. (2000) 'Evidence and the policy process', in H.T.O. Davies, S.M. Nutley and P. Smith (eds) *What works? Evidence-based policy and practice in public services*, Bristol: The Policy Press, pp 13-41.

Oakley, A. (2000) *Experiments in knowing: Gender and method in the social sciences*, Cambridge: Polity Press.

Percy-Smith, J. with Burden, T., Darlow, A., Dowson, L., Hawtin, M. and Ladi, S. (2002) *Promoting change through research: The impact of research in local government*, York: Joseph Rowntree Foundation/York Publishing Services.

Smith, G. and May, D. (1980) 'The artificial debate between rationalist and incrementalist models of decision making', *Policy & Politics*, no 8, pp 147-61, reproduced in M. Hill (ed) (1993) *The policy process: A reader*, Hemel Hempstead: Harvester Wheatsheaf, pp 163-74.

Walker, R. (2000) 'Welfare policy: tendering for evidence', in H. Davies, S. Nutley and P. Smith (eds) *What works? Evidence-based policy and practice in public services*, Bristol: The Policy Press, pp 141-66.

Young, K., Ashby, D., Boaz, A. and Grayson, L. (2002) 'Social science and the evidence-based policy movement', *Social Policy and Society*, vol 1, no 3, pp 215-24.

Further reading

Boaz, A., Grayson, L., Levitt, R. and Solesbury, W. (2008) 'Does evidence-based policy work? Learning from the UK experience', *Evidence & Policy*, vol 4, no 2, pp 233-53.

Bogenschneider, K. and Corbett, T.J. (2010) *Evidence-based policymaking: Insights from policy-minded researchers and research-minded policymakers*, New York: Routledge.

Davies, H., Nutley, S. and Smith, P. (eds) (2000) *What works? Evidence-based policy and practice in public services*, Bristol: The Policy Press.

Evidence & Policy (2011) vol 7, no 2 (special edition on 'The practice of policy making').

Nutley, S.M., Walter, I. and Davies, H.T.O. (2007) *Using evidence: How can research inform public services?*, Bristol: The Policy Press.

1.7 Modelling the research process

Saul Becker and Alan Bryman

A dynamic research process

As we have seen from the preceding sections, social policy and social work research contributes to knowledge and can impact on policy making and practice as part of a dynamic process. The links between policy, practice and research are complex and rarely transparent or linear. The evidence-based policy and practice movement has tried to maximise the extent to which research evidence (or some types of research data) should be and are used to *determine* policy and practice – what we have referred to in *Figure 1l* (Section 1.6) as the 'level 1' or 'pure' form of evidence-based policy and practice. However, as we have also seen there are considerable criticisms and critiques of evidence-based policy and practice, as it relates specifically to social work (*Box 1d* in Section 1.6), and as it relates to broader issues of methodology, quality criteria and ideology (*Box 1e* in Section 1.6). Weaker forms of evidence-based policy and practice have emerged over recent years, with less of an imperative for research to *determine* policy and practice, and more of an aspiration that research should *inform* (level 2) or *influence* (level 3) policy and practice.

Either way, it is possible to conceive of this process as a research cycle, moving from identifying and defining what we want or need to research, to conducting a literature review (see Chapter Three), to undertaking that research, to actively promoting and disseminating the findings for knowledge transfer, to impacting on policy and practice, to change in the original situation, to ongoing monitoring and evaluation, and so on. While this model, as presented here, has a starting point (identifying a social issue to research), this may not always be the starting point for every piece of research. Some people, for example, may be advocating or lobbying for a change of policy or practice and then decide that research would be valuable to give them 'political ammunition' or 'evidence' to support their claim, or to identify more precisely what needs changing, why and how. Others will be involved in evaluating policy and practice that is ongoing – with no obvious start or finishing point.

Irrespective of where the so-called 'starting point' for research occurs, it is possible to understand the research process (and its relationship with policy and practice) as a dynamic and ongoing cycle, which is made more complex and uncertain by a range of external factors – such as politics, ideologies, organisational structures, practitioners' training and skills, and so on – the very things that have been referred to throughout this chapter.

Here we present a model of the research cycle. The model is an attempt to simplify complex processes into some understandable and stylised form; to inform understanding of the relationship between research, policy making and professional practice; and to show how the remaining chapters of this volume (and, indeed, the preceding sections) 'fit' with the model.

A model of the research cycle

The research cycle in social policy and social work can be understood as being made up of four phases:

- a cognitive phase;
- 'doing' research;
- dissemination and knowledge transfer;
- research adoption, utilisation and change.

While these phases are distinct from one another, they also merge into each other and it does not always follow that, for each piece of research, the cycle will start with a cognitive phase. Additionally, the cognitive – or thinking – phase extends throughout the others, while the dissemination and knowledge transfer (KT) phase extends some distance into the adoption, utilisation and change phase. The point of making a distinction between the four phases is that, at each phase, a particular activity ('thinking', 'doing', 'KT' or 'changing') is more dominant than the others. For example (and rather obviously), we do not stop thinking when we are disseminating or conducting KT activities, but our main purpose at these later phases is to disseminate and promote the research findings rather than defining what it is that needs to be researched in the first place. The phases of the research cycle are illustrated in *Figure 1m*.

Figure 1m: **The research cycle**

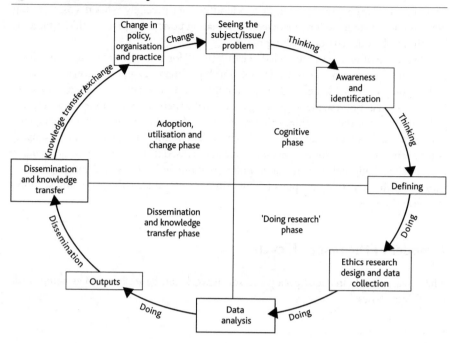

Stages of the research cycle

Cognitive phase

In this phase of the research cycle, researchers, research funders and others involved in the policy process or concerned with practice (including professionals, service users, and so on), are involved in thinking about the issues or problems that confront them. They will need to move beyond seeing that there is an issue, to refining their thinking and becoming more precise and specific about what needs to be researched, why and how. Within this phase, therefore, there are at least three stages: seeing, awareness and identification, and defining.

Seeing: policy researchers, policy makers, social workers and other professionals observe things that concern them or that they may wish to change. These may be social issues (the impact of community care changes on people with disabilities, the experiences of young carers, the practice of social workers in child protection cases to name a few), or social problems (poverty, deprivation, poor housing). We need to 'see' these as issues or problems before we can start to work out how to investigate them. **Some of the themes raised in Section 1.2, and** *Boxes 1a* **and** *1b* **(Section 1.4) are pertinent here.**

Awareness and identification: here, researchers need a heightened awareness that an issue needs further exploration. Is this an example of an injustice? Why is it coming to light now? These are just a few of the things that need thinking about. **Some of the issues discussed in Sections 1.2 and 1.3 are relevant here.**

Defining: having identified the issue/problem and a need for research, there is a need to define clearly and precisely what it is that requires investigation, why and how to go about it. What is already known about this issue? What literature and research already exist? Chapter Three shows that it is critical that *before* we embark on any new research we should conduct a thorough (and perhaps systematic) review of the existing sources of research and other knowledge on the topic. Do we actually need new research on this topic? **The issues and themes discussed in Sections 1.3, 1.4 and 1.5, and especially in Chapters Three and Four, will need to be considered here.**

'Doing' research

In this phase, the focus is on applying preparatory thinking to the actual mechanics of doing and managing research. Decisions will need to be taken about the most appropriate research design and method(s) to be used or integrated, how the fieldwork is to be conducted, the data collected and analysed. This whole process needs to be conducted and managed to the highest standards if the research, and findings, are to be trustworthy. **All the issues and themes discussed in Section 1.3, and Chapters Two, Three, Four, Five and Six, are central to this phase of the research cycle.**

Dissemination and knowledge transfer

Having conducted the research and analysis to the highest standards, the dissemination and KT phase is initially concerned with 'outputs' (the type of report, article or presentation that reports the findings), and then moves into how the outputs can be disseminated and communicated to appropriate audiences. **The issues discussed in Chapter Seven are central here.** As we show in Chapter Seven, dissemination of research results can also take place *throughout* the research cycle, particularly in cases of action research and user participatory research. Here, interim findings can be shared and disseminated well before the formal end of the project and KT activities (for example, consultancy, external lectures, networking, conference papers etc) will continue to take place perhaps long after the project has formally finished.

Research adoption, utilisation and change: 'making an impact'

Here, the focus is on the utilisation of research evidence, and its adoption by individuals and organisations, to either determine, inform or influence their thinking, decisions, policy and practice. As we have seen in Section 1.6, this is sometimes referred to as research 'making an impact'. It is also linked to the three levels of evidence-based policy and practice outlined in *Figure 1l*. Utilisation of research can work at various levels, from the more 'pure' form where research determines policy and practice, to the more fluid and poorly defined level of research 'having an influence'. **All the issues raised in Sections 1.5 and 1.6 are central here.**

The chapters that follow provide details of the issues, themes and debates that need to be considered when thinking about, conducting and disseminating research for the benefit of social policy and social work practice, and for the benefit of the people who are on the receiving end of these interventions.

Questions for discussion

- Why can it be useful to have a model of the research cycle and its relationship with policy and practice?
- To what extent do you think the model reflects accurately the relationship between research, policy and practice? Can you identify any specific strengths and weaknesses?

Ethical conduct and research practice

Detailed contents

2.1 Introduction

To make a judgement as to whether any piece of social policy or social work research has been conducted and managed *rigorously* requires us to know about how that research was designed and carried out, how data were collected and analysed and how the conclusions were reached. For us to know whether a study has been conducted and managed *ethically* requires us to know whether research participants were harmed or put in any danger, were deceived about the nature of the research or whether they had given informed consent, whether they received 'payment' or were promised other forms of reward(s) for particular types of answers, whether their accounts were treated respectfully and in confidence, and so on.

It would be hard to conceive of a piece of social policy or social work research that was not concerned with either a sensitive topic or a vulnerable group. How these inquiries are handled and managed, and how data are collected, analysed and interpreted, requires great care, sophistication and sensitivity.

In this section we want to add another indicator of *good* social policy and social work research to those discussed in the previous chapter – *the quality of the ethical conduct and practice of research*. In addition to those mentioned above, how the research process safeguards the safety and integrity of both researchers and participants, and how research is conducted and managed to high ethical standards, are important indicators of 'quality'. There are many aspects of the *research cycle* outlined in Section 1.7 and **Figure 1m** that require effective *ethical conduct* and *management*. These include the need to consider:

- what we understand by 'ethics' and what are the properties of ethical conduct;
- the ethical context for planning, conducting and managing research (which includes *codes of ethics*, *research governance*, *informed consent* and *managerial requirements*);
- particular issues around researching *sensitive topics* and *vulnerable groups*;
- matters of *safety* for researchers and participants;
- *confidentiality* issues; and
- the protection of participants and the data collected about them.

In this chapter we focus on each of these areas and offer some guidance. Good ethical conduct is an indicator of *quality* and *rigour* in research practice.

2.2 The conduct and management of research: ethics and rigour

Saul Becker and Alan Bryman

How a piece of social policy or social work research has been conducted and managed is an important indicator of the overall *quality* and *rigour* of that research. Just as research-based texts need to have a discussion of methodological and design issues, and of data collection and analysis techniques, they also need to refer explicitly to specific issues about the ways in which the research has been conducted and managed to *ethical standards* (including issues of *informed consent*, *confidentiality* and so on), how researchers (and participants) have been kept *safe* from harm, how *data are protected*, and so on. These are the concerns of this chapter.

Being systematic

In Chapter One we saw that to count as research an enquiry must be carried out in a systematic and rigorous way and conducted to the highest ethical and procedural standards within the limitations imposed through time, money and opportunity. Arber (1993, p 33) reminds us that 'You need to adopt a systematic and logical approach to research, the key to which is the planning and management of your time'. Planning and managing time and resources, and anticipating the next stages of the research process (and potential difficulties), are key to managing the 'doing' stage of research (see *Figure 1m* in Section 1.7). It is critical to plan ahead, to establish the procedures and working practices necessary to ensure that the research progresses smoothly and systematically, both to plan and to budget, and within an ethical framework that respects the integrity of both respondents and researchers, that keeps them safe, and that keeps the information collected secure and confidential, adhering to any legal requirements and ethical frameworks.

All stages of the research process modelled in *Figure 1m* need systematic and effective management, from the *cognitive phase* through to *dissemination, knowledge transfer* (KT) and *change*. Careful planning, ongoing monitoring of progress against a research plan and budget, and always anticipating and preparing in advance for the next phase of the research cycle, are central to effective and rigorous conduct and management of research practice. This management function can be overseen by a project manager, principal investigator or director of research who may take an instrumental lead, but it is also a function which needs to be undertaken by *all* those working on a research project – including researchers and those involved in administrative and technical support (for example, secretarial staff, data coders, transcribers, computer staff, and so on). This requires each person involved in an investigation not only to plan and monitor their own work, but also to work together to ensure that all aspects of the project 'fit' together, and that each phase of the study progresses according to intention and to plan, and to agreed ethical principles and practices. Additionally, staff must be kept safe, motivated and supervised adequately; researchers must ensure that data are collected, analysed and stored in ways which are safe, secure and confidential; all staff must be mindful of their legal responsibilities. The whole project must be conducted to ethical codes designed to protect and safeguard the integrity of all parties – participants, researchers, research organisations, funders and users of research, including policy makers and professionals.

Until research management is given a higher priority in published research methods texts it is unlikely that the research reported in books and journals will include a full discussion of *which* aspects of the research process were managed, and *how*. An absence of this discussion in published research raises an important issue concerning the *reading* of these texts, and the *interpretation* of whether a particular study has been conducted to rigorous methodological, ethical and procedural standards. Put simply, how can we know that a study has been conducted to high standards of ethical conduct if we are not given the necessary information on which to make that judgement? Moreover, can we say that a study is robust and sound when there is little, if any, evidence that it was conducted and managed effectively to high ethical and procedural standards (for example, where there appears to be no informed consent by participants to take part in the study, or where the safety of researchers and respondents was severely compromised, or where data were poorly protected)? Should we value the *findings* of research above all else – regardless of the *process* or *quality* by which that research was conducted and managed? In the sections that follow we focus on a number of aspects of research practice that require rigorous, effective and ethical conduct and management. These are meant to be illustrative rather than exhaustive. In focusing on the specific issues covered here, we hope to alert the reader to the need to manage the research process effectively in order for that research to be ethical, rigorous, robust and trustworthy, and especially where the research may be used as *evidence* to determine, inform or influence policy and practice, as discussed in the previous chapter.

Questions for discussion

- Why is it important that research should be conducted and managed in an ethical way?
- How would you judge a research project that gave no information about ethical, safety and confidentiality issues, but which, nonetheless, delivered research findings on time?

Reference

Arber, S. (1993) 'The research process', in N. Gilbert (ed) *Researching social life*, London: Sage Publications, pp 32-50.

2.3 Ethics
Sarah Banks

Ethics is about matters of right and wrong conduct, good and bad qualities of character and responsibilities attached to relationships. Although the subject matter of ethics is often said to be human welfare, the bigger picture also includes the flourishing of animals and the whole ecosystem.

There is a tendency to associate ethics in research with procedures for gaining institutional approval before commencing empirical studies involving human or animal participants. This is both too narrow (restricting ethics to fulfilling the requirements of the approval process) and too broad (as the approval process covers other elements of research governance, including practicality, scientific validity, reliability, risk assessment and safety). These aspects of research do have ethical implications (research of dubious validity wastes valuable resources); however, the main ethical considerations in social research, as outlined in the statements produced by professional bodies (see Section 2.4), include:

1. *Respect for research participants:* enabling participants or their representatives to make considered choices about whether and how to engage, treating them respectfully throughout the research process.
2. *Protection of research participants:* ensuring participants are not harmed, and/or minimising the risk of harm during the research.

3. *Public and professional responsibility of researchers:* being clear about what information gained during research may be disclosed to third parties; being prepared to act on serious matters relating to the welfare or safety of participants or the public.
4. *Honesty in communication:* being as open as possible about the purpose of research, and honest in analysis, presentation and publication of findings.

Respect

Respecting participants' choices about taking part in research, and withdrawing or withholding information is often implemented through seeking informed consent as described in ***Box 2b*** in Section 2.4. This is not straightforward and should not be regarded as a guarantee of ethical research. There may be issues about whether people are competent to understand the information or give meaningful consent; whether proxies (people authorised to act for others) should be consulted; how much information is sufficient; and whether researchers can predict how the research will develop. If features of the research change, strictly speaking consent should be sought again. Respect also entails agreeing when and how to discuss findings and how to acknowledge people's contributions. In participatory, feminist or other emancipatory approaches (see Chapter Four), where academic researchers may be working in partnership with community researchers, the distinction between researchers and researched may be unclear, and particular attention needs to be paid to agreements on how to work together and share power.

Protection

Researchers should consider what physical/psychological harm the research might directly or indirectly cause, and how this can be prevented or minimised. In research with human participants, this often involves concealing their identities and offering anonymity in written accounts. Participants may be given copies of interview transcripts or reports and asked if there are sections they wish to change or remove. When writing up, researchers have to consider carefully how to ensure anonymity. For example, if job titles are used, it may be possible for colleagues to recognise individuals (such as 'chief executive', where there is only one person of that description in the organisation being studied). If interviewing or conducting focus groups on sensitive topics (see Section 2.5), it may be important to ensure follow-up support is available (for example, when asking people about experiences of rape or asylum-seeking). However, researchers also need to bear in mind that some participants may wish to be named, and an overly protectionist approach may actually be disrespectful.

Public and professional responsibility

As citizens or professional practitioners (in the case of practitioner research; see Section 4.13), it is important to be clear what information cannot be kept confidential. Often promises of confidentiality are misconceived. If all information received from research participants was kept confidential, then researchers would have very little to write about.

What is usually promised is protection of the identity of the source of the information (anonymity). Occasionally, however, researchers may judge that they are ethically and/ or legally obliged to reveal information (which may have been discovered accidentally or observed, rather than given by participants), along with the identities of people or organisations concerned. There are no straightforward rules about this, as it depends on the status of the researcher, the promises made in advance and the seriousness of the issues at stake. A researcher undertaking an ethnographic study of drug users would probably agree not to report information about drug dealers to the police. However, if this researcher witnessed a knife attack, following which someone was seriously injured, they might decide they had a duty to contact the police. Researchers are also citizens, and sometimes citizens' responsibilities override researchers' promises or the desire to continue a piece of research. Similarly, if social work practitioners or students gain information about suspected child abuse in the course of research, they would be professionally obliged to act on this information.

Honesty

As in everyday life, so in research, while honesty is expected and valued, there is also scope for being economical with the truth. Respect for research participants entails being as honest as possible in dealings with them. However, sometimes if researchers reveal precisely what they are studying, they may fear that people will change their behaviour. If researchers say they are studying racial discrimination in the job selection process, job selectors may take greater care in decision making in relation to minority ethnic applicants. If researchers simply say they are studying the process of job selection, there may be less danger of specific behaviour change. The question of whether it is ever justified to undertake covert research (to conceal one's identity as a researcher) is a vexed one. 'Covert' research in public places may be acceptable (for example, observing behaviour in a shopping centre). However, taking a job in a residential care home secretly to research abusive working practices is more controversial. It is sometimes argued that such research is justifiable if it exposes bad practice (see also Section 4.15). However, there may be other methods, including seeking permission to observe and conduct interviews, which might reveal similar information.

Honesty in the analysis, interpretation, writing up and publication of research is important. Falsification of data, manipulation of findings and plagiarising the ideas of others are serious breaches of researchers' integrity and damaging to the reputation of social research. Sometimes it may be unclear whether researchers have 'manipulated' data with intention to deceive, or appropriated ideas of others deliberately or inadvertently. The Research Integrity Office and Committee on Publication Ethics provide helpful guidance (see 'Website resources' at the end of this section).

Developing ethical competence

Researchers need to think through ethical issues, discuss with supervisors and colleagues and decide what is acceptable and why. In addition to completing ethical approval forms or acting in accordance with published ethical codes and guidance, researchers need to cultivate moral qualities such as:

- *Ethical awareness:* to identify ethical challenges, anticipate potential harms and notice discomfort in participants.
- *Moral integrity/honesty:* to consider whether covert research is really necessary; when, if ever, it is right to lie or be economical with the truth; and how much of researchers' personal lives to share.
- *Moral courage:* to turn down funding from compromising sources; report allegations of abuse; publish controversial findings; and act according to researchers' responsibilities as citizens.
- *Professional wisdom:* to make sound judgements when faced with complex ethical dilemmas, for which principles and rules in codes of ethics give no clear answers.

The development of researchers' ethical competence is just as important as their knowledge and skills in research methods.

Question for discussion

- What are some of the main ethical considerations that should be taken into account when planning a piece of research and how would you build these into your research design?

Further reading

Banks, S. (2006) *Ethics and values in social work* (3rd edn), Basingstoke: Palgrave Macmillan.
Israel, M. and Hay, I. (2006) *Research ethics for social scientists*, London: Sage Publications.
Long, T. and Johnson, M. (2006) *Research ethics in the real world: Issues and solutions for health and social care professionals*, Edinburgh: Churchill Livingstone.
Oliver, P. (2003) *The student's guide to research ethics*, Maidenhead: Open University Press/ McGraw-Hill Education.

Website resources

British Association of Social Workers (BASW) (2002) *The code of ethics for social work*, see Section 4.4.4 on research: www.basw.co.uk/about/code-of-ethics/
Committee on Publication Ethics (COPE): http://publicationethics.org/
Office of Research Integrity (ORI) (USA): http://ori.dhhs.gov
The Social Research Association (2003) *Ethical guidelines*: www.the-sra.org.uk/guidelines. htm
UK Research Integrity Office (UK RIO): www.ukrio.org

2.4 Codes of ethics
Alan Bryman and Saul Becker

Many professional and occupational groups in society have *codes of ethics* that are meant to influence the behaviour of their members in a way that is consistent with ethically acceptable practices. As such, these codes would not seem to be contentious but in fact they may be so: some members of a profession may feel that having been trained in the ethos of their profession it should be taken as a matter of trust that they will behave ethically – they have absorbed and accepted their professional obligations and do not need to be dictated to. In an academic context, ethical codes could be construed as being inconsistent with the principle of academic autonomy. On the other hand, ethical codes may be deemed to be helpful to practitioners and the professions themselves. For the former, ethical codes may provide a source for helping to resolve ethical dilemmas and uncertainties, and, therefore, as a means of rationalising how they are resolved; for the profession, a code can represent a way of demonstrating to society at large its credibility and good intentions. The Department of Health's *Research governance framework for health and social care* identifies key principles and defines the responsibilities of the various parties involved in health and social care research (see ***Box 2a***). Research governance is concerned with the regulations and standards that need to be observed when research is carried out. Codes of ethics provide the ethical and moral context for that research.

Box 2a: Research governance framework for health and social care
Jan Pahl

The term 'research governance' means the regulations, safeguards and standards that surround the research process. More specifically, it refers to the *Research governance framework for health and social care*, published by the Department of Health in 2001 and modified several times (DH, 2010).

The *Research governance framework* provides a set of principles and defines the responsibilities of different parties. Its aims are to improve the standards of research, to reduce bad practice and to increase public confidence in research. These aims are to be secured by meeting key standards in the following domains:

- *Ethics:* ensuring the dignity, rights, safety and well-being of research participants.
- *Science:* ensuring that the design and conduct of the research, and the nature of its findings, are subject to independent review by relevant experts.
- *Information:* providing full and free public access to information on the research and its findings, but protecting intellectual property rights and the confidentiality of data about individuals.
- *Health and safety:* ensuring at all times the safety of participants, research workers and other staff involved in the research.
- *Finance:* ensuring financial probity and compliance with the law and compensation for those suffering harm.

Implementing the *Research governance framework* took place through the establishment of the National Research Ethics Service (NRES). The aim of NRES is to protect the dignity, rights, safety and well-being of research participants; and to facilitate and promote ethical research that is of potential benefit to participants, science and society. It coordinates a system of Research Ethics Committees.

When it was first introduced, the expectation was that the *Research governance framework* would apply to all research carried out within the National Health Service (NHS) and local authority Councils with Social Services Responsibilities (CSSRs). However, it was soon recognised that there are crucial differences between research in the NHS and research within CSSRs. These differences relate to the scale, volume and funding of research, the context in which research takes place, the mix of stakeholders and the multiplicity of academic disciplines.

Debates about the relevance of the *Research governance framework* to social care led to the formation of the Social Care Research Ethics Committee (SCREC) and of a system of ethics review committees within CSSRs. The SCREC is based at the Social Care Institute for Excellence (SCIE), where it is responsible for reviewing proposals for research on adult social care in England. It is part of the NRES and is funded by the Department of Health, but its membership, expertise and procedures have been developed to reflect the social care context.

Where should researchers go to get their proposal approved by an Ethics Committee? There are three main sources of ethics approval:

- *NHS/NRES:* if the proposed study involves NHS patients and carers or NHS staff, then the proposal should go to a committee within the NRES structure. Applications to the central NRES office are allocated to committees according to the nature and location of the study.
- *CSSRs/SCREC:* if the proposed study involves adults looked after by a CSSR, the proposal should go either to the SCREC or to a Research Ethics Committee in a CSSR. This also applies to research on people living in other settings, such as private care homes, but whose care is funded by a CSSR.
- *Universities:* university staff and students can seek approval for studies from a university-based Research Ethics Committee. These were set up following recommendations from the ESRC in its original *Research ethics framework*, now called the *Framework for research ethics*.

There are continuing problems with the system. Researchers may have to seek governance approval as well as ethics approval; they may have to apply to more than one ethics review body; and there may be delays that compromise the research. A planning group bringing together the relevant bodies set out five principles for ethics review:

- *Reciprocity:* there should be mutual respect between sources of ethics review.
- *Avoidance of double handling:* only one approval is required for each project.
- *Proportionality:* the intensity of the review should be proportionate to the risk.
- *Independence:* the review body should be independent of the researchers.
- *Researcher-led:* researchers are responsible for securing approval.

Good research governance aims to promote a research culture that is characterised by the promotion of excellence; by high standards of personal and scientific integrity; and by respect for diversity and for those who take part in research. Making the system work is likely to be a continuing issue.

Questions for discussion
- What are the key domains within the *Research governance framework*?
- Choose a research study known to you and consider how well it meets the standards in each domain of the *Research governance framework*.

Reference

DH (Department of Health) (2010) *Research governance framework for health and social care*, London: DH.

Further reading

Iphofen, R. (2009) *Ethical decision making in social research*, Basingstoke: Palgrave Macmillan.

Smyth, M. and Williamson, E. (2004) *Researchers and their 'subjects': Ethics, power, knowledge and consent*, Bristol: The Policy Press.

Website resources

The Department of Health's *Research governance framework* can be found at: www.dh.gov.uk/prod_consum_dh/groups/dh_digitalassets/@dh/@en/documents/digitalasset/dh_4122427.pdf

The Economic and Social Research Council's (ESRC) *Framework for research ethics* can be found at: www.esrc.ac.uk/about-esrc/information/research-ethics.aspx

National Research Ethics Service, National Patient Safety Agency: www.nres.npsa.nhs.uk/

Social Care Research Ethics Committee (SCREC): www.screc.org.uk/

The Social Research Association: www.the-sra.org.uk/

Many of the main disciplines in the social sciences have ethical codes that are meant to influence how research is conducted. The first code of ethics for social scientists was that of the American Psychological Association in 1953 (Sieber, 2004). The Social Policy Association (SPA), one of the professional groups closest to the field covered in this volume, published online *Guidelines* in 2009.

Ethical codes are meant to provide guidelines concerning proper ethical practice. They tend to be fairly general so that they can be relevant to a wide range of situations. They also tend to be reviewed fairly regularly, since changes in social values or the arrival of new technologies may require a revision of the recommendations. Ethical codes help to protect both the researcher and the researched. Researchers are protected, for example, because they can fall back on a code of ethics if they are asked to do research they judge to be ethically unjustifiable or if they are accused of acting unethically when in fact they have followed ethical guidelines. Research respondents are protected because codes invariably make reference to core principles, such as protecting privacy, ensuring research participants are given the opportunity for informed consent (see also **Box 2b**) and making sure that no harm comes to them. Issues such as these are covered in the SPA *Guidelines* that outline a social policy researcher's obligations under four headings: to society; to research participants; to research sponsors/funders; and to the subject and to colleagues. Under obligations to research participants, the *Guidelines* refer to some common motifs in ethical codes, such as protecting research participants from harm, providing informed consent, treating information from participants confidentially and protecting their rights (for example, privacy). There are also some guidelines that are particularly tailored to the social policy research context, such as giving special consideration to vulnerable groups, providing participants with advice on support services if they find the research process distressing and giving consideration to involving service users in the research (while recognising that the researcher must bear final responsibility for the research). Like most ethical codes, the SPA *Guidelines* are negative about *covert* methods of research, such as covert observation, since they cannot involve informed consent and are likely to involve invasions of privacy. On the other hand, as Bryman (2012) observes in relation to the British Sociological Association (BSA) *Statement*, they do not entirely close the door on covert research:

> Where research is carried out using a method which makes obtaining informed consent difficult – for example, covert research or secondary data analysis – researchers should take particular care to ensure the prevention of harm to participants and the protection of their anonymity. (BSA, 2000, p 5)

Box 2b: Gaining informed consent
Elizabeth Peel

As we have seen in previous sections, getting informed consent from research participants is ethically important. Researchers have a responsibility to explain to the people taking part in the research what the study is about, the risks and benefits of taking part, and should obtain their consent before involving them in the research. This is known as the *informed consent process*.

In a research project about patients' experiences of diabetes service provision, informed consent was gained to interview people newly diagnosed with diabetes three times over the course of a year (Peel et al, 2004, 2005), and then, at the end of the three interviews, consent was sought to retain participants' contact details so that they could be re-contacted in the future for a follow-up interview (Peel et al, 2007; Lawton et al, 2008). Forty people consented to take part in the original study and 20 took part in the longitudinal follow-up. Potential participants had a diagnosis of type 2 diabetes within the previous six months and were adults mentally able to understand what the research was about, and therefore were able to give their consent to taking part.

An information sheet was given to potential participants that provided details about the study as straightforward answers to the following questions: what is this study about? Why have you been chosen? What will the study require of you? Do you have to take part? And, Your rights? After participants had had an opportunity to read and digest this information, and I had clearly described the research, emphasising confidentiality and anonymity – I gave participants a *consent form*. Participants were asked to initial each of the three statements on the example consent form below and also to sign and date it. I also signed the consent form as the researcher; one copy was given to the participant and another retained by the research team.

Gaining *informed* consent is not always straightforward, however, and it can become a 'thorny issue' if participants physically deteriorate during the data collection period (Lawton, 2001), or are experiencing degenerative brain disease such as dementia (Sachs, 1998), or have learning disabilities (Stalker, 1998).

Consent form
Title of project: Diabetes service provision: a qualitative study of patients' experiences

1. I confirm that I have read and understood the information sheet for the above study and have had the opportunity to ask questions.

2. I understand that my participation is voluntary and that I am free to withdraw at any time, without giving any reason, without my medical care or legal rights being affected.
3. I agree to take part in the above study.

Question for discussion

- What is informed consent, and how would you ensure you gained informed consent from your research participants?

References

Lawton, J. (2001) 'Gaining and maintaining consent: ethical concerns raised in a study of dying patients', *Qualitative Health Research*, vol 11, no 5, pp 693-705.

Lawton, J., Peel, E., Douglas, M. and Parry, O. (2008) 'Shifting accountability: a longitudinal qualitative study of diabetes causation accounts', *Social Science & Medicine*, vol 67, no 1, pp 47-56.

Peel, E., Douglas, M. and Lawton, J. (2007) 'Self-monitoring of blood glucose in type 2 diabetes: longitudinal qualitative study of patients' perspectives', *British Medical Journal*, vol 335, pp 493-98.

Peel, E., Parry, O., Douglas, M. and Lawton, J. (2004) 'Diagnosis of type 2 diabetes: a qualitative analysis of patients' emotional reactions and views about information provision', *Patient Education and Counseling*, vol 53, pp 269-75.

Peel, E., Parry, O., Douglas, M. and Lawton, J. (2005) 'Taking the biscuit? A discursive approach to managing diet in type 2 diabetes', *Journal of Health Psychology*, vol 10, no 6, pp 779-91.

Sachs, G. (1998) 'Informed consent for research on human subjects with dementia', *Journal of the American Geriatrics Society*, vol 46, pp 8602-14.

Stalker, K. (1998) 'Some ethical issues and methodological issues in research with people with learning difficulties', *Disability & Society*, vol 13, no 1, pp 5-19.

Further reading

Miller, T. and Bell, L. (2002) 'Consenting to what? Issues of access, gate-keeping and "informed" consent', in M. Mauthner, M. Birch, M.J. Jessop and T. Miller (eds) *Ethics in qualitative research*, London: Sage Publications, pp 53-69.

Oliver, P. (2003) *The student's guide to research ethics*, Maidenhead: Open University Press.

Peel, E., Parry, O., Douglas, M. and Lawton, J. (2006) '"It's no skin off my nose": why people take part in qualitative research', *Qualitative Health Research*, vol 16, no 10, pp 1335-49.

Website resources

The British Psychological Society provides detailed professional guidelines about obtaining consent in the *Code of ethics and conduct*, 2009: www.bps.org.uk

The British Sociological Association provides a *Statement of ethical practice*: www.britsoc.co.uk

The Royal College of Nursing provides a document discussing informed consent in health and social care research, 2005: www.rcn.org.uk

Very often ethical codes recognise that covert research may solve problems of highly restricted access to certain groups or organisations. However, in social care and healthcare research it is likely to prove difficult to get permission to conduct covert research given the requirement for research proposals to go before ethical review committees, and the governance framework outlined in **Box 2a** (see also Section 4.15). Ethical codes, therefore, are not entirely unambiguous in their advice.

A further entrant into the ethical terrain is the Economic and Social Research Council (ESRC) which produced in 2010 a *Framework for research ethics*, formally called the *Research ethics framework* when it was first published in 2005. The *Framework* outlines the ethical practices that it expects will be applied to research that it funds but it has also been written in anticipation of influencing ethically informed social research more generally. It outlines six principles of ethical research: it must be of high quality; the purpose, methods and prospective uses of research must be fully disclosed to research workers and participants; information gleaned must be treated in confidence and participants' anonymity should be protected; the basis of a research participant's involvement must be voluntary; participants must be protected from harm arising from research; and the independence of the research must be transparent. The ESRC expects institutions whose members of staff apply for funding to have Research Ethics Committees to review applications if significant and troubling ethical issues are raised. Examples given in the *Framework* of such research are: when vulnerable groups are involved; when deception or lack of full informed consent is involved; when the research topic is sensitive; and when online data collection is employed, especially if images or sensitive topics are involved. If research does not raise significant ethical concerns, it can be subjected to an 'expedited review', as the ESRC calls it.

Ethical guidelines and codes do not have the force of law, although it is conceivable that severe transgressions might result in censure, such as expulsion from a learned society or even difficulty in obtaining a job. However, these forms of censure could feasibly ensue without a code of ethics, although the rationale for expulsion might be difficult to justify without such a code. It is also important to realise that if someone is doing social policy or social work research under the auspices of an institution, such as a university, it too may well have its own code of ethics. These are usually strongly influenced by professional associations' codes. Indeed, in many cases researchers may not be able to do research on humans (or perhaps certain kinds of research) without approval by a committee or review board to which a proposal for research must be sent for ethical clearance. Flagrantly ignoring codes of ethics at this institutional level could plausibly result in concrete forms of censure, such as termination of employment or a studentship. Consequently, social policy and social work researchers need to be attuned to institutional ethics codes, discipline-based codes and wider over-arching codes such as the ESRC *Framework* and the *Research governance framework*. Researchers intending to conduct research in a health milieu will also have to submit their intentions to ethical review by a Research Ethics Committee that represents the interests of the NHS and its patients (see **Box 2a**). The fact that there are so many levels of ethical guidelines nowadays might seem to suggest that there is the potential for them to be inconsistent and therefore to offer divergent guidelines. In reality, the different ethical codes draw on similar principles, but it is definitely worth paying attention to subtle differences.

Questions for discussion

- What part should codes of ethics play in influencing the conduct of social policy and social work research?
- Look at the codes of ethics of a number of organisations, including the Social Policy Association (SPA) and British Sociological Association (BSA). What do they have in common? How do they differ? (The websites for these organisations can be found below.)

References

Bryman, A. (2012) *Social research methods* (4th edn), Oxford: Oxford University Press.

Sieber, J. (2004) 'Ethical codes', in M. Lewis-Beck, A. Bryman and T. Futing Liao (eds) *The SAGE encyclopaedia of social science research methods*, Thousand Oaks, CA: Sage Publications, pp 321-2.

Further reading

BPS (British Psychological Society) (2000) *Code of conduct, ethical principles and guidelines*, Leicester: BPS.

Brown, L. (1997) 'Ethics in psychology: cui bono?', in D. Fox and I. Prilleltensky (eds) *Critical psychology: An introduction*, London: Sage Publications, pp 51-67.

Bryman, A. (2012) *Social research methods* (4th edn), Oxford: Oxford University Press, Chapter 6.

BSA (British Sociological Association) (2000) *Statement of ethical practice*, Durham: BSA.

Butler, I. (2002) 'Critical commentary: a code of ethics for social work and social care research', *British Journal of Social Work*, vol 32, no 2, pp 239-48.

Glendinning, C. and McKie, L. (2003) 'BSA working in partnership with SPA: ethics in social research', *Network: Newsletter of the British Sociological Association*, no 85, pp 15-16.

Lewis, J. (2002) 'Research and development in social care: governance and good practice', *Research, Policy and Planning*, vol 20, no 1, pp 3-10.

Website resources

British Association of Social Workers (BASW) (2002) *The code of ethics for social work*, see Section 4.4.4 on Research: www.basw.co.uk/about/code-of-ethics/

The British Sociological Association (BSA) *Statement of ethical practice* can be found at: www.britsoc.co.uk/NR/rdonlyres/801B9A62-5CD3-4BC2-93E1-FF470FF10256/0/StatementofEthicalPractice.pdf

Another relevant code of ethics for social policy researchers is that of The Social Research Association: www.the-sra.org.uk/documents/pdfs/ethics03.pdf

The following website contains, and has links with, many useful discussions of codes of ethics, as well as including many professional statements: www.iit.edu/departments/csep/PublicWWW/codes/codes.html

The Department of Health's *Research governance framework*: www.dh.gov.uk/prod_consum_dh/groups/dh_digitalassets/@dh/@en/documents/digitalasset/dh_4122427.pdf

The Social Policy Association's Guidelines on research ethics can be found at: www.social-policy.org.uk/downloads/SPA_code_ethics_jan09.pdf

The Economic and Social Research Council's (ESRC) *Framework for research ethics* can be found at: www.esrc.ac.uk/about-esrc/information/research-ethics.aspx
Useful advice on research ethics can be found at: www.ethicsguidebook.ac.uk

2.5 Researching sensitive topics
John D. Brewer

There is an increasing tendency to use 'sensitive' as an adjective, such as 'gender-sensitive', 'culture-sensitive' or 'time-sensitive' research, meaning to undertake research sensitive to – with an eye to – whatever prefixes the term, such as 'gender-sensitive research' on the impact of communal violence on women (for example, Callamard, 1999). This is not what is meant by sensitive research in the methodology literature, which describes, instead, research that is impacted by, and has an impact on, the social context in which the research takes place.

A concern with ethics has always been a feature of social research because it involves human subjects. But discussions of ethical practice tended to be formulaic, focusing on the autonomy of the researcher and their obligations to protect subjects. Ethical debates thus became associated with issues like confidentiality (Section 2.8) and informed consent (***Box 2b***) on the one hand, and academic freedom on the other. However, reading the disclosures they made of their research (for example, Bell and Newby, 1977; Bell and Roberts, 1984), it was clear that social researchers were struggling with other issues too, only unsatisfactorily subsumed under ethics (for example, Rainwater and Pittman, 1966): issues like handling the controversy surrounding their findings, the danger to themselves or their subjects during the research, and the difficulties in trying to get people to participate or talk about a certain topic, or of working with one group or set of people (see Punch, 1989, for difficulties in researching police corruption). By the early 1990s these sorts of concerns became codified under the name 'sensitive research', first addressed in a special issue of *American Behavioral Scientist* in 1990 and published later as an extended edited collection (see Renzetti and Lee, 1993). Topics included research on the Royal Ulster Constabulary, child abuse, cults, the informal economy and AIDS. Since then, the literature has been extended by Lee's codification of both sensitive research (Lee, 1994) and dangerous fieldwork (Lee, 1995), and further collections of case studies on sensitive topics (Lee-Treweek and Linkogle, 2000). ***Box 2c*** provides an illustration of research on the sensitive topic of suicide cases.

Box 2c: Working with distressing research material: coroners' files on suicide cases
Jonathan Scourfield and Ben Fincham

It is not really surprising that reading about suicide cases in the course of a research project can be upsetting. Suicides tend to shock, even when the deceased is not someone close to us, perhaps because the non-suicidal majority, who put considerable effort into living, find it very hard to understand the desire to end life and perhaps, too, because stories of suicides remind us of our own frailty.

Our study was a sociological autopsy of individual suicide cases. It was a qualitatively driven mixed methods study that involved three researchers reading 100 suicide case files in a coroner's office. These files comprised of a diverse range of sources, including witness statements from people who found the body, and from relatives and friends, suicide notes, mobile phone records, pathologists' reports, psychiatric reports and photographs of the corpse (Fincham et al, 2008; Scourfield et al, 2010).

Unlike many who are affected by a suicide, for us the act of self-destruction in these people's stories did not come as any surprise. It was, after all, the reason we were reading the files. We had not become emotionally hardened to the material, however, at least not at first, so details of the stories could nonetheless move or shock us. There is much discussion of the role of emotion in the interpretation of qualitative research. Our view was that our emotional reactions revealed something about the wider social and cultural context of death and gave us a small insight into the aftermath of a suicide. If we, whose job it was to read about these suicide cases, found the stories upsetting, how much more traumatic must be the unexpected loss of a loved one to suicide? Whereas we thought there were wider sociological lessons to be learned from our emotional reactions in general, we did not believe that individual reactions to particular cases were productive for data analysis, as this would be to prioritise our own concerns over the data. In this regard we would part company with some qualitative researchers.

It is important to put in place some kind of system of mutual support in teams of researchers working on potentially distressing material. This does not have to be elaborate. Flexibility and supportive relationships are most important. We made sure we had the opportunity to de-brief after a session of working with the case files and would often all go for a coffee and talk about the cases that had stayed with us. Even with this support in place, it is likely that researchers will remember some stories long after the research project has finished.

Question for discussion
- Should a researcher's emotional reaction to his or her data have an impact on his or her conclusions about the phenomenon being studied?

References
Fincham, B., Scourfield, J. and Langer, S. (2008) 'The impact of working with disturbing secondary data: reading suicide files in a coroner's office', *Qualitative Health Research*, vol 18, pp 853-62.
Scourfield, J., Fincham, B., Langer, S. and Shiner, M. (2010) 'Sociological autopsy: an integrated method for the study of suicide in men', *Social Science & Medicine*, doi:10.1016/j.socscimed.2010.01.054.

Further reading
Hubbard, G., Backett-Milburn, K. and Kemmer, D. (2001) 'Working with emotion: issues for the researcher in fieldwork and teamwork', *International Journal of Social Research Methodology*, vol 4, no 2, pp 119-37.
Kleinman, S. and Copp, M.A. (1993) *Emotions and fieldwork*, Newbury Park, CA: Sage Publications.

Website resources
International Association for Suicide Prevention (IASP): www.iasp.info/
National Centre for Research Methods commissioned inquiry into risk to the well-being of
    researchers in qualitative research: www.cardiff.ac.uk/socsi/qualiti/publications.html

In psychology and medical research, where social constructionist ideas are slowly diluting the heavy emphasis on experimental methods, there is now reference to what is called 'socially sensitive research', meaning research that has ethical implications beyond the research situation because it affects people and groups in wider society. This development owes much to social science discussions of sensitivity and is a measure of the influence of this field of literature. This growing focus on sensitivity fits two developments in modern social science: the recognition of risk as a feature of contemporary life, including risk behaviour in social research; and the injunction on modern researchers, particularly qualitative ones, to be reflexive and identify the contingencies that bore on their practice and helped to shape the extant data.

Sensitive research can be described as research that has potential implications for society or key social groups, and is potentially threatening to the researcher or subjects in bringing economic, social, political or physical costs. Sometimes these implications derive from the topic because of its controversy; from the status or behaviour of the subjects that brings risks to them or the researcher from the study; or the biographical features or conduct of the researcher and the problems arising from the general context within which the research is undertaken. Sensitivity is, therefore, often highly situational, depending on the topic, local circumstances and the people involved as subjects and researchers. What in one case may be unproblematic will be sensitive in another. It is for this reason that researchers often give considerable thought in the planning and design stage to what might be sensitive about their research, since it affects all stages, from identifying a topic and sample, negotiating access, data collection and publication of the results. The reflexive researcher, when writing up the results, will comment on how issues around sensitivity, among other things, affected their conduct and the data (see, for example, Brewer, 1991, pp 16–30, 1993).

Research on sensitive topics is best suited to qualitative methods (see Chapter Six). While questionnaire design can address these topics, often using the technique of funnelling where respondents are led slowly through a series of increasingly more personal and revealing questions, 'closed questions', where respondents select from pre-determined answers, are particularly inappropriate for the complexity and subtlety of people's responses or where evasion might be anticipated. Qualitative research often entails a more sustained contact with the respondent, developed gradually over time so that rapport is established. This helps with the management of sensitivity by putting respondents at ease, thus permitting risks and fears about the researcher or the topic to be assuaged, controversial topics to be raised in the context of trust, and provides an opportunity for maximising the potential for truthful answers. Some of the data collection techniques used in qualitative research are particularly suitable in this regard, such as in-depth interviewing, ethnography and unobtrusive methods like personal documents and records (see Lee, 2000). The use of vignettes, for example, is particularly popular in work with sensitive groups such as children (MacAuley, 1996; Barter and Renold, 1999; Brewer, 2000, pp 74–6) and drug users (Hughes, 1998). Indeed, some of the areas where sensitivity can be most anticipated is in research on socially disadvantaged and powerless groups, for example, children, women, abused groups such as survivors of domestic violence, elderly people, gay men and lesbians, non–able-bodied people and those from minority ethnic groups. These are respondents who are relevant to policy-related research by mostly being defined in policy terms as problem or target groups (see Hood et al, 1999). Sensitive research is also associated with topics that are difficult for subjects to talk about, such as personal health and medical-related topics (for example, Dickson-Swift et al, 2010). But the context of the research can make it sensitive beyond the obvious influence of the topic or the people involved, for the physical location, political and economic context and broad media agenda, among other things, can make all research controversial and thus, in retrospect, sensitive.

Question for discussion

- Is research on some topics or with some groups or in some contexts best ruled out because of its sensitivity? If not, how can these problems be managed?

References

Barter, C. and Renold, E. (1999) 'The use of vignettes in qualitative research', *Social Research Update*, no 25.

Bell, C. and Newby, H. (1977) *Doing sociological research*, London: Allen & Unwin.

Bell, C. and Roberts, H. (1984) *Social researching*, London: Routledge.

Brewer, J.D. (1991) *Inside the RUC: Routine policing in a divided society*, Oxford: Clarendon Press.

Brewer, J.D. (1993) 'Sensitivity as a problem in field research: a study of routine policing in Northern Ireland', in C. Renzetti and R. Lee (eds) *Researching sensitive topics*, London: Sage Publications, pp 125-45.

Brewer, J.D. (2000) *Ethnography*, Buckingham: Open University Press.

Callamard, A. (1999) *A methodology for gender sensitive research*, Montreal: Amnesty International.

Dickson-Swift, V., James, E.L. and Liamputtong, P. (2010) *Undertaking sensitive research in the health and social sciences*, Cambridge: Cambridge University Press.

Hood, S., Mayall, B. and Oliver, S. (1999) *Critical issues in social research*, Buckingham: Open University Press.

Hughes, J. (1998) 'Considering the vignette technique and its application to drug injecting and HIV risk and safer behaviour', *Sociology of Health and Illness*, vol 20, pp 381-400.

Lee, R. (1994) *Doing sensitive research*, London: Sage Publications.

Lee, R. (1995) *Dangerous fieldwork*, London: Sage Publications.

Lee, R. (2000) *Unobtrusive methods in social research*, Buckingham: Open University Press.

Lee-Treweek, G. and Linkogle, S. (2000) *Danger in the field*, London: Routledge.

MacAuley, C. (1996) *Children in long term foster care*, Aldershot: Avebury.

Punch, M. (1989) 'Researching police deviance', *British Journal of Sociology*, vol 40, pp 177-204.

Rainwater, L. and Pittman, D. (1966) 'Ethical problems in studying a politically sensitive and deviant community', *Social Problems*, vol 14, pp 357-66.

Renzetti, C. and Lee, R. (1993) *Research-sensitive topics*, London: Sage Publications.

Further reading

Dickson-Swift, V., James, E.L. and Liamputtong, P. (2010) *Undertaking sensitive research in the health and social sciences*, Cambridge: Cambridge University Press.
Lee, R. (1994) *Doing sensitive research*, London: Sage Publications.
Renzetti, C. and Lee, R. (eds) (1993) *Researching sensitive topics*, London: Sage Publications.
Lee-Treweek, G. and Linkogle, S. (eds) (2000) *Danger in the field*, London: Routledge.

Website resource

The British Sociological Association's statement of research ethics: www.britsoc.co.uk/
equality/Statement+Ethical+Practice.htm

2.6 Researching vulnerable groups
Pranee Liamputtong

Within the global crisis that we are now experiencing, it is inevitable that social workers will have to work with many 'vulnerable' people in their everyday life. It is likely that these population groups will be confronted with more problems in their private and public lives as well as with their health and well-being.

Who are the vulnerable?

A vulnerable person is an individual who experiences 'diminished autonomy due to physiological/psychological factors or status inequalities' (Silva, 1995, p 15). These vulnerable people will include those who are 'impoverished, disenfranchised, and/ or subject to discrimination, intolerance, subordination, and stigma' (Nyamathi, 1998, p 65). Based on these descriptions, we may include children, young people, older people, people from minority ethnic groups, immigrants, sex workers, the homeless, gay men and lesbians, and women. The term 'vulnerable' has also been used to refer to people with 'social vulnerability' (Quest and Marco, 2003, p 1297). Some population groups, including children, the unemployed, the homeless, drug-addicted people, sex workers and ethnic and religious minority groups, face particular social vulnerability. Often, the term 'vulnerable' is used interchangeably with such words as 'sensitive', the 'hard-to-reach' and 'hidden populations' (Liamputtong, 2007).

There are a number of salient issues that researchers must take into account in their attempts to conduct research with vulnerable people.

Accessibility to vulnerable groups

Locating vulnerable groups is a challenging task and often problematic. The level of distrust keeps many people in hard-to-reach or transient populations from interacting with researchers. It becomes more difficult when the research issues are sensitive or threatening since these people have a greater need to hide their identities and involvement (Dickson-Swift et al, 2008).

However, there are successful methods that can be used to gain access to these potential participants. The **snowball sampling** method has been extensively adopted in researching the 'vulnerable' or difficult-to-reach populations. Umaña-Taylor and Bámaca (2004, p 267) and Madriz (1998) refer to this approach as the 'word-of-mouth' technique. It is extremely useful in research with people from minority ethnic groups as potential participants are more likely to take part if someone they know is also participating. The snowball sampling technique is an essential technique used to locate hard-to-reach populations. Members of such populations may also be involved in deviant activities, such as taking drugs or selling sex. Accessing these hidden groups can best be done by referrals from their acquaintances or peers rather than by using other more formal methods of identification such as the use of existing lists or screening (Atkinson and Flint, 2001).

Reciprocity and respect for the participants

When working with vulnerable people, reciprocity and respect is essential. Ethical responsibility towards vulnerable groups needs to go beyond the protection of individuals' rights. It needs to include an emphasis on reciprocity and respect, which may mean what the participants can gain (Eder and Fingerson, 2002). By giving something in return for receiving information, researchers show their respect towards the participants. This can reduce the power inequality between themselves and the researched. Researchers must put efforts into making a positive difference in the lives of the participants or the group (Warr, 2004).

Compensation and incentive: a form of respect

Compensation or payment for participating in a research project is a controversial issue. Some may argue that payment is not appropriate as it may influence the participants' responses. Payment can also be seen as 'coercion' if researchers work with extremely poor people, the homeless or drug users. However, others assert that the contribution, knowledge and skills of the participants should be valued and payment should be provided to them, particularly if they have little or no money (Umaña-Taylor and Bámaca, 2004). Payment can be seen as equalising the relationship or exchanging the research fund – money, for participant time (Hollway and Jefferson, 2000). Based on this argument, compensation for the participants' time is crucial and should be seen as a symbol of the researchers' respect for the input of these people. This stance is applicable to researching the 'vulnerable', as most of these groups tend to be poor and money may assist them with their daily living (Madriz, 1998; Cook and Nunkoosing, 2008). Compensation from participating in a research study may be used to improve their life circumstances (Beauchamp et al, 2002).

Moral concerns

There are some debates about moral issues when researching vulnerable people. Should researchers carry out investigative work with some extremely vulnerable populations such as frail elderly people suffering from mental illness, or those who have experienced extreme loss and grief (see **Box 2d**), or who are homeless or terminally ill? These people are already vulnerable in many ways.

Morally speaking, the benefits of undertaking the research need to be measured against the risks of being involved in the research. Studies of vulnerable groups should be focused first on benefiting the group (Hall and Kulig, 2004). Harm to an individual, their relationship with others, their community and political implications with regards to the group due to research need to be considered at the beginning of the research process. The moral challenge for researchers is to develop inquiries that do not make individual participants suffer further. It is also imperative that the researchers are cautious and aware that the study may potentially reinforce stereotyping and contribute to discrimination against the group.

In conclusion, undertaking research with vulnerable people presents unique and often difficult challenges. Because of these challenges, many researchers have excluded vulnerable people from their research endeavours. Hence, the needs and concerns of vulnerable people are often ignored in the scientific literature. This will make these people even more vulnerable. Some research questions and evidence can only be answered by vulnerable individuals or groups. This necessitates researchers to initiate their research with them. As social researchers, we need to find ways to bring the voices of these vulnerable people to the fore. Giving voice to vulnerable people can contribute to attempts to empower them and create better opportunities to enhance their lives and health.

Question for discussion

- What key issues need to be taken into account when planning and conducting research into the lives of vulnerable people?

References

Atkinson, R. and Flint, J. (2001) 'Accessing hidden and hard-to-reach populations: snowball research strategies', *Social Research Update*, vol 33, pp 1-7 (www.soc.surrey.ac.uk/sru/SRU33.html).

Beauchamp, T.L., Jennings, B., Kinney, E.D. and Levine, R.J. (2002) 'Pharmaceutical research involving the homeless', *Journal of Medicine and Philosophy*, vol 27, no 5, pp 547-64.

Cook, K. and Nunkoosing, K. (2008) 'Maintaining dignity and managing stigma in the interview encounter: the challenge of paid-for participation', *Qualitative Health Research*, vol 18, no 3, pp 418-27.

Dickson-Swift, V., James, E. and Liamputtong, P. (2008) *Undertaking sensitive research in the health and social sciences: Managing boundaries, emotions and risks*, Cambridge: Cambridge University Press.

Eder, D. and Fingerson, L. (2002) 'Interviewing children and adolescents', in J.F. Gubrium and J.A. Holstein (eds) *Handbook of interview research: Context and method*, Thousand Oaks, CA: Sage Publications, pp 181-201.

Hall, B.L. and Kulig, J.C. (2004) 'Kanadier mennonites: a case study examining research challenges among religious groups', *Qualitative Health Research*, vol 14, no 3, pp 359-68.

Hollway, W. and Jefferson, T. (2000) *Doing qualitative research differently*, London: Sage Publications.

Liamputtong, P. (2007) *Researching the vulnerable: A guide to sensitive research methods*, London: Sage Publications.

Madriz, E.L. (1998) 'Using focus groups with lower socioeconomic status Latina women', *Qualitative Inquiry*, vol 4, no 1, pp 114-29.

Nyamathi, A. (1998) 'Vulnerable populations: a continuing nursing focus', *Nursing Research*, vol 47, no 2, pp 65-6.

Quest, T. and Marco, C.A. (2003) 'Ethics seminars: vulnerable populations in emergency medicine research', *Academic Emergency Medicine*, vol 10, no 11, pp 1294-8.

Silva, M.C. (1995) *Ethical guidelines in the conduct, dissemination, and implementation of nursing research*, Washington, DC: American Nurses Publishing.

Umaña-Taylor, A.J. and Bámaca, M.Y. (2004) 'Conducting focus groups with Latino populations: lessons from the field', *Family Relations*, vol 53, pp 261-72.

Warr, D.J. (2004) 'Stories in the flesh and voices in the head: reflections on the context and impact of research with disadvantaged populations', *Qualitative Health Research*, vol 14, no 4, pp 578-87.

Further reading

Booth, S. (1999) 'Researching health and homelessness: methodological challenges for researchers working with a vulnerable, hard-to-reach, transient population', *Australian Journal of Primary Health*, vol 5, no 3, pp 76-81.

Liamputtong, P. (2007) *Researching the vulnerable: A guide to sensitive research methods*, London: Sage Publications.

Liamputtong, P. (2010) *Performing qualitative cross-cultural research*, Cambridge: Cambridge University Press.

Morse, J.M. (2002) 'Interviewing the ill', in J.F. Gubrium and J.A. Holstein (eds) *Handbook of interview research: Context and method*, Thousand Oaks, CA: Sage Publications, pp 317-28.

Russell, C. (1999) 'Interviewing vulnerable old people: ethical and methodological implications of imagining our subjects', *Journal of Aging Studies*, vol 13, no 4, pp 403-17.

Stone, T.H. (2003) 'The invisible vulnerable: the economically and educationally disadvantaged subjects of clinical research', *The Journal of Law, Medicine & Ethics*, vol 31, no 1, pp 149-53.

Umaña-Taylor, A.J. and Bámaca, M.Y. (2004) 'Conducting focus groups with Latino populations: lessons from the field', *Family Relations*, vol 53, pp 261-72.

Warr, D.J. (2004) 'Stories in the flesh and voices in the head: reflections on the context and impact of research with disadvantaged populations', *Qualitative Health Research*, vol 14, no 4, pp 578-87.

Relevant organisations

Centre for Vulnerable Children and Families: www.cvcf.arts.uwa.edu.au

Alfred Felton Research Program: Promoting Safety and Well-being of Children, Young People and Families Social Work: www.socialwork.unimelb.edu.au/research/research_units/alfred_felton_research_program

Australian Council of Social Service (ACOS): www.acoss.org.au/

Brotherhood of St Laurence: www.bsl.org.au

St Vincent de Paul Society: www.vinnies.org.au/about-vinnies-national?link=9

Social Policy Research Centre: www.sprc.unsw.edu.au/

Website resources

This website is about a research project exploring the use and benefits of social and therapeutic horticulture for vulnerable adults in the community, undertaken by the Centre for Child and Family Research (CCFR) at Loughborough University: www.lboro.ac.uk/research/ccfr/growing_together/

This website provides information about a number of research projects undertaken by the National Foundation for Educational Research (NFER), including into the lives of children in public care, children with medical needs, Gypsy/Traveller children, asylum-seeker and refugee children, young carers, school refusers, teenage parents, young offenders and young people who are not in education, employment or training. It is argued that vulnerable children need additional educational support to ensure they are able to achieve their potential: www.nfer.ac.uk/nfer/index.cfm

---

Box 2d: Research with recently bereaved parents
Anne Corden

The Social Policy Research Unit (SPRU) was approached by a children's hospice in 1999 to undertake a small-scale study of the financial implications of the death of a child (Corden et al, 2001). There was little other literature or research that linked money matters and childhood death, areas of great sensitivity requiring care throughout. Three senior experienced researchers shared responsibility for all stages of the work, working closely with senior staff at the children's hospice. First, approval was sought from the relevant NHS Local Research Ethics Committee, which was given.

It was considered important to learn from other people's knowledge and experience, and this was approached in two ways. A project advisory group was recruited, including bereaved parents and staff from children's hospices and parents' support services, and this was particularly helpful in the early stages of the work. By joining the Bereavement Research Forum (BRF), a group of academics and practitioners meeting regularly to discuss issues around bereavement, the researchers learned from and shared experiences with others conducting bereavement research.

Sensitivities of both subjects and researchers had to be addressed. The research involved in-depth interviews with recently bereaved parents in touch with the children's hospice. The researchers followed normal good practice in research, paying particular attention to the way in which parents were approached (taking advice from the advisory group), language used in letters and interviews and the timing of interviews. Taking advice from hospice

---

staff, researchers did not approach families around the anniversary of their child's birthday or death, and there was a break in recruitment and fieldwork in the run-up to Christmas.

The researchers took cues from parents as to how much they wanted to talk about the child who had died, and whether, and how, brothers and sisters of the child who had died were drawn in. As the work proceeded some parents initially not selected for the research asked to take part, and the researchers responded positively.

What was talked about was very sad, but it proved possible to discuss money matters with recently bereaved parents (Corden et al, 2002). Hospice staff were ready to discuss these interviews with any parents who wanted this, at any stage. The researchers' letters thanking parents provided opportunities for sending other contact addresses which might be helpful, for example, employment advisers.

When a summary of research findings was available, the researchers checked before mailing whether parents still wanted these. Some parents decided not to receive a summary, after all, a further indication of the particular care needed when researching such sensitive topics.

Interviews about sensitive subjects make particular demands on researchers as well as subjects, and the research funder (the Joseph Rowntree Foundation) agreed to fund access to some professional support. Meeting a group psychotherapist before starting fieldwork to consider what personal impact and effect there might be helped the team prepare positively. At the end of the project, a further group meeting enabled discussion of the experience. This way of supporting researchers working in areas that might be risky to emotional health was considered useful (Corden et al, 2005).

Question for discussion
* At what stage in a research project should you pay attention to possible sensitivities in the area of study?

References
Corden, A., Sainsbury, R. and Sloper, P. (2001) *Financial implications of the death of a child*, London: Family Policy Studies Centre.

Corden, A., Sainsbury, R. and Sloper, P. (2002) 'When a child dies: money matters', *Illness, Crisis and Loss*, vol 7, no 4, pp 125-37.

Corden, A., Sainsbury, R., Sloper, P. and Ward, B. (2005) 'Using a model of group psychotherapy to support social research on sensitive topics', *International Journal of Social Research Methodology*, vol 8, pp 151-60.

Further reading
Gilbert, K. (ed) (2001) *The emotional nature of qualitative research*, Washington, DC: CRC Press.

Stebbins, J. and Batrouney, T. (2007) *Beyond the death of a child: Social impacts and economic costs of the death of a child*, Canterbury, Australia: The Compassionate Friends Victoria Inc. Also published on www.compassionatefriendsvictoria.org.au

Stroebe, M.S., Hansson, R.O., Schut, H. and Stroebe, W. (2008) *Handbook of bereavement research and practice: Advances in theory and intervention*, Washington, DC: American Psychological Association.

Website resources
Bereavement Research Forum (BRF): www.brforum.org.uk
The Social Research Association: www.the-sra.org.uk

2.7 Keeping safe
Gary Craig

Safety is an issue of growing importance for many people, both individually and professionally, as the disappearance of the estate agent Suzie Lamplugh (Suzie Lamplugh Trust, 1999), the continuing disappearance of many young people and the 100 or so racist murders of black and minority ethnic (BME) people since the death of Stephen Lawrence all demonstrate. Issues of community safety (Alcock et al, 1999) have achieved prominence through anti-poverty work and through Neighbourhood Watch schemes. Professions which require individuals to be alone in the normal course of their duties, such as social workers and social security officials, have codes of guidance and protective measures to help staff avoid dangerous or compromising situations. In the case of social work and education, such guidance also tries to address members' fears of having allegations of abuse made against them.

Social policy and social work research often also requires researchers to work on their own, and qualitative social research with individual respondents in particular characteristically involves one-to-one relationships, typically conducted in situations of privacy. Despite small-scale initiatives, and a limited literature on the subject (Arksey and Knight, 1999; Paterson et al, 1999), there was no consolidated guidance for the safety of social researchers until about 2000.

Safety is an increasingly pressing issue for research units, research managers and for the researchers themselves, who are frequently sent alone into potentially dangerous situations; studies on forced labour, human trafficking and child exploitation are examples of the kinds of potentially dangerous situations in which researchers may now find themselves. The initial exploration of the safety issue in 2000 identified quite unpredictable events – such as the case of a lone researcher visiting a bedridden respondent who drew a revolver on him – and suggested that the issue of safety was shared by cognate professional groupings such as general practitioners (GPs), other health professionals (Sandell, 1998) and others whose members work alone, such as political party canvassers. It also demonstrated that the scope of safety issues was very wide, going way beyond ensuring the personal safety of individual researchers conducting fieldwork. Evidence from this and from more recent events indicates that the boundary between safety and ethics is, at times, a blurred one, and that the boundaries of 'safety' itself need to be thought of flexibly. One researcher, for example, conducted a study with respondents about subjects potentially distressing for both respondents and researchers. This study provided counselling support for researchers, the mental health of the researcher being regarded as a legitimate aspect of their general safety (see also **Box 2c** on working with distressing research material).

The interest generated by this exploration led to a code of safety for social researchers being developed for The Social Research Association (SRA), and this has been picked up by other organisations since (for example, Nacro) to guide their own workers' behaviour and by workers in other related forms of research such as nursing research (Hughes, 2004). The following section briefly raises the key issues elaborated within this code.

The main focus of safety in relation to a social researcher might be thought to be with the researcher's own needs. However, there are other parties for whom researcher safety is important. Researchers are, generally, employees, and employers (usually universities or research institutes), under both UK and European legislation, have a general 'duty of care' to employees. There are, nevertheless, situations arising in the context of social research where this responsibility might be contested. How far does this duty of care extend to a researcher conducting interviews on the street at night in a 'foreign' town, or staying in a hotel or guesthouse, on his/her own? What might be regarded as reasonable precautions? Who should be responsible for taking them?

Although a university human resources office might legally stand as the employer, this duty of care would normally revert to the research manager – the head of a unit or a particular budget holder. However, despite the existence of a code of safety, brought to the attention of a researcher as part of the contractual framework within which they work (see also *Box 2e*), how much control can a manager reasonably exercise over a researcher during fieldwork? Where do contractual liabilities cease? For example, for a fieldworker having to stay overnight in a hotel, who chooses these hotels and on what basis? Managers can put safety provisos in place, for example, clear procedures for ongoing reporting back, monitoring incidents, written guidelines and the provision of safety aids, but they cannot be on the 'fieldwork spot' all the time. And when does fieldwork start and finish? Many universities appear not to have insurance policies which cover the use of private cars travelling to and from work, yet the use of a private car may be the only transport option – or the only safe one – open to researchers in remote or potentially dangerous contexts. Who, then, is responsible for meeting the costs of damage in the event of an accident or of violence done to the vehicle? And, are researchers insured for personal injury in all situations related to the conduct of fieldwork?

These issues become more critical where researchers are studying phenomena on or beyond the boundaries of criminality, working with higher risk groups such as ex-offenders or those with a history of psychological disturbance, or exploring issues where the threat of violence is greater – for example, working across sectarian divides, studying homophobic violence or exploring situations of extreme exploitation. The effects of actual or threatened violence on a researcher may be traumatic. Is it the responsibility of employers to ensure that suitable debriefing or therapeutic help should be available after such incidents? How many research units have access to such professional help?

It is equally necessary to consider safety from the perspective of research respondents. Ethical guidelines developed by professional bodies (see Section 2.4) remind researchers of the need to protect respondents' interests through respecting their privacy, the confidentiality of data collection (Section 2.8), ensuring informed consent is given (*Box 2b*) and by being alert to the possibilities of harm or discomfort (Section 2.3). Ethical considerations, however, often emerge in complicated ways. One study with children of lone parents might have prompted revelations about undisclosed child abuse. Researchers here would have needed, through an appropriate protocol, both to protect their own situation but also to make it clear to children that they would act if 'they thought anyone was in danger'. Section 2.8 expands on these issues of confidentiality. There are, however, no firm safeguards preventing research participants from exploitation by researchers.

Box 2e: Managing research practice and ethical conduct
Bruce Stafford

It is critical that all researchers, whether they are working by themselves or in an organisation or team, know about and understand the ethical and other procedural requirements of conducting high quality research. This of course means that they must know about and work to the ethical codes that relate to their areas of enquiry (see Section 2.4), and the relevant governance frameworks (see *Box 2a*). It also means that systems of management and support are built into the conduct of research, including debriefings when researchers are involved in distressing research with vulnerable groups (Section 2.6), or on sensitive topics that may affect the researchers themselves (Section 2.5 and *Boxes 2c* and *2d*).

Research managers seek to manage staff effectively and efficiently through following 'best practice' in human resource management, and to also deliver ethical conduct in research. Having explicit policies on recruitment and selection, staff review and development, disciplinary procedures, and so on is essential to assure employers and sponsors of the delivery of high quality and ethical research outputs, and staff of the fairness and transparency of working practices. Managers also need to provide leadership and to motivate staff. This is all part of ensuring good governance and rigorous processes.

Recruitment and selection procedures must comply with relevant legislation and guidance on equal opportunities; in the UK this framework is provided by the *Equality Act 2010*. Each post should have a detailed and written job description and person specification. Newly recruited staff should receive an induction package that includes guidance on how the organisation works (the 'staff handbook') and a mentor. The mentor aids the integration of the recruit into the community of the institution, and, most importantly, provides advice and 'on-the-job' training as and when required, and acts as a representative for the person if work-related problems arise.

Many research organisations operate some form of *performance or job appraisal* system. Managers will agree work tasks and goals with the individual, and (probably annually) review progress. For managers, there is a delicate balance to be struck between managing performance and offering career development advice. Managers will need to consider the competence of the individual, where they are in their career trajectory, and their personal ambitions as well as the organisation's culture and reward system, when striking this balance.

Staff will need to renew their *intellectual capital* and acquire new skills and knowledge in order to effectively, efficiently and ethically perform their duties. This cannot be left to chance or done in an ad hoc way. Various staff development schemes and procedures are available and managers must adopt and tailor those that are most suited to the ethos of their organisation. Typically, staff development systems will involve a competency-based assessment of training needs and regular reviews. Staff development procedures must also apply to managers and to senior researchers.

Research organisations can adopt a *team approach* to doing research. Managers must select project leaders and team members on the basis of staff:

- competencies and confidence levels;
- past experience in the specific research area and of working for a particular sponsor; and
- seniority.

Managers must provide intellectual and project *leadership* and motivate staff once a team is established. This involves encouraging people's intellectual curiosity; setting a timetable with milestones and monitoring work performance; sharing knowledge; providing on-the-job training, personal support and encouragement; and ensuring ethical, health and safety, and confidentiality requirements are met (for a full discussion of the need to ensure the safety of researchers and the confidentiality of data, see Sections 2.7 and 2.8). Motivating staff can entail highlighting the intellectual issues underpinning a project, the principal challenges of the research design, the significance of the study in terms of its potential impact on policy and practice and/or disciplinary knowledge. Different staff will be motivated by different factors.

Managers will want to *retain* committed and productive researchers. Fixed-term contracts (whereby a person's employment is tied to a specific research project for a limited period of time) mean that staff, concerned about their job prospects, may leave a study before it is completed, often to the detriment of the investigation. Job retention can be fostered by adopting progressive family-friendly policies and, when appropriate, managers being proactive in encouraging staff to seek promotion, accelerated increments and lump-sum payments.

However, there are occasions when *disciplinary procedures* have to be invoked. If performance-related, they could escalate through informal meetings to formal oral, then written warnings and, even, dismissal. A serious breach of conduct might justify jumping some stages. Managers should involve, if available, human resources services at an early stage and a written record of all actions and documents must be kept.

The above discussion focuses on research staff, but in a research centre, complementary policies and practices are required for secretarial and administrative staff. Similarly, the discussion assumes that the researchers are in the managers' own organisations. However, sometimes research is conducted by consortia, which involve subcontracts. Having clear lines of accountability for the management of staff, both within and across organisations, is vital if timely, high quality, ethical and rigorous research is to be achieved.

The management of research and support staff is not an optional extra. The social research community needs research-led organisations to manage researchers to the highest ethical, methodological and procedural standards.

Question for discussion
- What would you say to a researcher whose standard of work or ethical conduct was unsatisfactory?

Reference
Equality Act 2010 (www.opsi.gov.uk/acts/acts2010/pdf/ukpga_20100015_en.pdf).

Further reading

Careers Research and Advisory Centre (2008) *Vitae briefing for managers of researchers* (www.vitae.ac.uk/CMS/files/upload/Vitae_brief_Managers%20of%20researchers.pdf).

Research Concordat Revision Working Group (2007) *The Concordat to support the career development of researchers* (www.researchconcordat.ac.uk/documents/concordat.pdf).

Website resources

Association of Research Centres in the Social Sciences (ARCISS): www.arciss.ac.uk/

Association of Research Managers and Administrators UK (ARMA UK): www.arma.ac.uk/

Chartered Institute of Personnel and Development (CIPD): www.cipd.co.uk

Equality Challenge Unit: www.ecu.ac.uk/

Equality and Human Rights Commission: www.equalityhumanrights.com/advice-and-guidance/information-for-employers/

Investors in People in Higher Education: www.investorsinpeople.co.uk/Pages/Home.aspx/

Leadership Development for Principal Investigators: www.le.ac.uk/researchleader/index.html

Leadership Foundation for Higher Education: www.lfhe.ac.uk

Researcher Development Initiative (RDI): www.rdi.ac.uk/

Vitae: www.vitae.ac.uk/

Issues of 'race', culture and gender may impact significantly on the safety of researchers, particularly in violently divided societies. Lone female researchers are generally more vulnerable than lone male researchers. Even where the threat of physical violence is not pressing, some cultures may react with hostility to the presence of female researchers. Certain racialised contexts may make the conduct of non-ethnically matched interviewing fraught. Male researchers are increasingly anxious about the risks to themselves in interviewing children alone.

There are more subtle issues, including the use of body language, the way researchers dress and the acceptability or not of physical contact, where researchers may inadvertently increase risks to themselves. Sitting on a bed is an obvious example; even going into a bed-sitting room may be another. GPs constitute one professional group that has been given advice as to what constitutes 'unsafe' territory, but there are many nuanced situations where researchers are left to rely on their own intuition as to when an interview should be terminated. Should a door in the interview locale always be left open (even if this compromises confidentiality)? Should interviews only be conducted in rooms where there is a clear exit route should researchers need to leave in a hurry? The quality of social research frequently depends on establishing the appropriate distance – neither over-familiar nor too detached – between researcher and interviewee, but that distance will vary. Both too much intimacy and too little rapport may send out the wrong signals.

Some research funders now acknowledge that they have to address the resource implications of research which is both ethically robust and carried out in safety, recognising that its quality suffers if researchers feel vulnerable and frightened. Proposals are beginning to include a budget line covering the use of mobile phones, the carrying of personal alarms and phone cards, the use of hire cars or taxis and appropriately priced and located overnight accommodation (see ***Box 3a*** in Section 3.2 on establishing and researching within a budget). There are, however, more significant safety costs, particularly where it is inappropriate for researchers to visit participants alone. More costly strategies open to research managers include having researchers work in pairs, with non-researcher friends who are paid simply to wait while interviews are conducted, or to conduct interviews only in public places (for example, community centres). What is now clear is that an effective safety strategy for social policy and social work research requires employers, researchers and funders to work collaboratively.

Question for discussion

- What are the key aspects of safety that a researcher working alone needs to think about? Do these aspects have gender and 'race' dimensions?

References

Alcock, P., Barnes, C., Craig, G., Harvey, A. and Pearson, S. (1999) *What counts? What works? The evaluation and monitoring of local government anti-poverty work*, London: Improvement and Development Agency.

Arksey, H. and Knight, P. (1999) *Interviewing for social scientists*, London: Sage Publications.

Hughes, R. (2004) 'Safety in nursing social research', *International Journal of Nursing Studies*, vol 41, no 8, pp 933-40.

Paterson, B., Gregory, D. and Thorne, S. (1999) 'A protocol for researcher safety', *Qualitative Health Research*, vol 9, no 2, pp 259-69.

Sandell, A. (1998) *Oxford handbook of patients' welfare: A doctor's guide to benefits and services*, Oxford: Oxford University Press.

Suzie Lamplugh Trust (1999) *Personal safety at work: Guidance for all employees*, London: Suzie Lamplugh Trust.

Further reading

Arksey, H. and Knight, P. (1999) *Interviewing for social scientists*, London: Sage Publications.

Paterson, B., Gregory, D. and Thorne, S. (1999) 'A protocol for researcher safety', *Qualitative Health Research*, vol 9, no 2, pp 259-69.

Website resource

The code of safety and code of ethics for social researchers published by The Social Research Association is available at: www.the-sra.org.uk/guidelines.htm#safe

2.8 Managing confidentiality
Harriet Ward and David Westlake

Social policy and social work research often involves the collection and analysis of empirical data which, when gathered or explored at the individual level, can be extremely sensitive. Nobody wants it to be publicly known that information about them was used in a study of the treatment of offenders or the perpetrators of child abuse. Yet, without access to empirical data from individuals, either held on records or given at interview, it is virtually impossible to generate the findings that allow for the construction of evidence-based policy and practice (see also Sections 1.6, and Sections 7.4 and 7.5). *Confidentiality* is, therefore, a major issue in social policy and social work research, and needs to be addressed at all stages of the process, including access to potential subjects and to records held by professional agencies, collection and storage of data and the analysis and reporting of findings. Researchers need to be aware of the provisions of the Data Protection Act 1998 and the Human Rights Act 1998 (see *Figure 2a* for details), as well as of protocols set by some funding bodies, such as the Department of Health's *Research governance framework* (2010; see also *Box 2a*). Healthcare researchers will also need to be mindful of Section 251 of the National Health Service Act 2006, and the Health and Social Care Act 2008 (*Figure 2a*).

Figure 2a: The Data Protection Act 1998, the Human Rights Act 1998 and the Health and Social Care Act 2008

The **Data Protection Act 1998** sets out eight principles for the protection of personal data. Some relate to the collection and processing of data: it must be processed fairly and lawfully, and only with the consent of the data subject; it must be adequate, relevant and not excessive; it must be accurate and kept up to date; it must be processed according to the rights of data subjects. Others relate to the storage of data: it shall not be kept for longer than is necessary; appropriate technical and organisational measures shall be taken against unauthorised or unlawful processing, and against accidental loss, destruction or damage; it shall not be transferred outside the European Economic Area unless there is an adequate level of protection. Finally, the Act lays down principles for its use: personal data cannot be processed in any manner that is incompatible with the purposes for which it was obtained (see Data Protection Act, Schedule 1 [Part 1]; Schedule 2 [1] and Schedule 3 [2]).

Under Section 33 of the Act, the storage and handling of data for research purposes is exempt from some of these principles, provided that it is not used to support measures or decisions concerning particular individuals, and as long as it is not processed in such a way that substantial damage or distress is, or is likely to be, caused to any data subject (see Data Protection Act Part IV, Section 33). This section of the Act is interpreted differently by the various organisations that hold personal data about vulnerable people. In one study, for instance, three local authorities agreed to researchers examining files of children who had been in care 20 years ago to see whether it might be possible to trace them, while a fourth refused on the grounds that it would be contrary to the provisions of the Act to do this without first obtaining their consent.

The **Human Rights Act 1998** incorporates the European Convention on Human Rights into UK law. Article 8 of the Convention states that 'everyone has the right to respect for his private and family life, his home and his correspondence'. This right can be deemed to have been violated if, for instance, personal data are not kept private (see Wadham and Mountfield, 1999).

The **Health and Social Care Act 2008** established the National Information Governance Board (NIGB). This is a statutory body with the purpose of monitoring the practice followed by researchers and other relevant bodies in relation to the processing of information held by the NHS. This includes the administration of applications under Section 251 of the NHS Act 2006 that regulates the control of patient information and allows the common law duty of confidentiality to be set aside in specific circumstances.

It is difficult to invite users of public services directly to participate in research which relates closely to their experiences: advertisements are likely to produce a biased sample group, particularly if the service received can be interpreted as stigmatising, such as apprehension by the police, or support from social services or a benefits-related agency. Service users are therefore more usually approached indirectly, through negotiation with those agencies to which they are already known, and whose interpretation and implementation of policy is being evaluated. The need to adopt this indirect approach is one of the major reasons why issues of confidentiality and consent can become thorny problems if not adequately addressed.

Agencies have a duty to protect the identities of service users, to safeguard information that is given to them in confidence and to ensure that it is not inappropriately used. However, despite the legislation, agencies hold varying views as to what information can be made available to researchers when the consent of service users cannot be obtained, and as to what may constitute a consent to pass on information that makes it possible to arrange interviews (see **Box 2b**). At times, their duty of confidentiality can appear to conflict with the researcher's responsibility to gather information and to meet research deadlines. These and other pressures may tempt researchers to cut corners, but to do so is counterproductive. Research of this nature can only be successfully conducted if all parties are confident that the work will be undertaken within a strict ethical framework.

Researchers, therefore, have to go through what are often lengthy and time-consuming procedures in order to obtain access to confidential information, not only because they are required to do so by the Data Protection Act, but also because they need to demonstrate to the agencies with which they work that they will respect the rights of service users. Recent evidence suggests that this process is becoming increasingly complex and prolonged (Munro, 2008). There may be some attempt to reduce the complexities, following research by Boddy and Oliver (2010) into some of the ways in which the Department of Health (2010) *Research governance framework for health and social care* has been misinterpreted, but at present researchers who undertake studies of vulnerable children will need ethical approval from a wide range of bodies. For instance, the recent study of very young children at risk of significant harm, illustrated in **Box 2f**, required approval from: the university Research Ethics Committee, each of the participating departments of children's services, the Central Office for Research Ethics Committees (COREC, now NRES), the Ministry of Justice and the Children and Family Court Advisory and Support Service (Cafcass). Different paperwork had to be completed for each of these participating agencies, and the research timetable had to accommodate often lengthy gaps between the various committee meetings. Access cannot be obtained without ethical approval, and the time taken to obtain this should, therefore, be built into every research timetable.

While researchers may make every effort to preserve confidentiality, errors frequently arise. These need to be dealt with openly and not concealed, for unless agencies and service users have full confidence in the research team, the type of problem shown in the second study illustrated in **Box 2f** can irrevocably damage the relationship and lead to withdrawal from the project. It is helpful for research teams to draw up contracts with participating agencies, stating explicitly how confidential data will be accessed, stored and used. Some agencies, particularly children's social care departments, now require research teams to be police-checked before allowing access. Issues concerning confidentiality should also be spelled out at the start of each interview with service users; the way in which the information will be used should be explained and consent formally obtained (**Box 2b**).

Box 2f: Confidentiality in practice
Harriet Ward and David Westlake

A research team was contracted to undertake a prospective, longitudinal study which involved recruiting a sample of very young children who had been identified as being at risk of significant harm before their first birthdays, and following them until they were three. Data would be collected from information held on children's social services case files and records held by health visitors; case-specific interviews would be held with birth parents and carers, as well as a number of professionals including social workers, their managers, health visitors and children's guardians.

In the event, the research team experienced exceptional difficulties in recruiting the sample and in accessing case file data and arranging interviews with some professionals; these were largely a result of issues surrounding confidentiality. Because this was such a sensitive study, all the participating agencies required an 'opt in' approach whereby only those children whose parents had given their informed consent could be recruited. However, obtaining this proved problematic as the researchers could not be given direct access to parents' details, their names and addresses. Initial arrangements for practitioners to pass on invitations to participate to parents whose children met the criteria yielded only a minimal response. A year into the study, revised promotional materials were produced and distributed by post by administrators. This proved more successful and a sample was eventually recruited but, despite heavy investment into the recruitment process, it was much smaller than originally anticipated. Comparison data can give a valuable insight into the proportion of the total eligible population researchers have accessed, and the extent to which the study sample is skewed. In this study only around 4% of eligible parents agreed to participate (a proportion consistent across all 10 participating local authorities) and the sample was biased towards the more high risk cases.

Difficulties were also experienced with gate-keeping procedures within local authorities and with individual professionals, some of whom considered the case material too sensitive for the researchers to access, despite their ethical clearance. Protracted negotiations over access to documents, which lasted over two years in some cases, resulted in some case files being archived by the time the researchers were able to look at them. This type of scenario can have serious consequences in terms of resources and timescales, and it is therefore prudent for researchers to consider this during the design and planning stage of any project.

In another study, the research team made considerable efforts to ensure that all data were anonymised and stored in locked cabinets, and that identifying codes were kept separately. In principle, identifying information was never held on computer. However, although this was adhered to with the datasets, a research assistant was in the process of writing letters to the authorities when she was mugged and her laptop computer was stolen (in this respect, it is worth considering issues concerned with keeping researchers safe, as outlined in Section 2.7). Children's names had, by then, been given to the research team and were included as a necessary part of the letter. Addresses had not been held on the laptop and so the chances of the information being useful to third parties were minimal. However, the computer had not been password protected and the letters were not encrypted. The research team immediately informed the authorities, some of which were extremely concerned about the incident. Their worries were openly discussed and security increased.

Researchers also need to ensure that information of a sensitive and personal nature is collected and stored in such a way that confidentiality is preserved. It is a relatively simple task to anonymise all data by replacing names and addresses with research codes and by keeping any identifying information separate from the main dataset; it is also relatively easy to password protect and/or to encrypt data held on a computer. However, anonymising data can itself lead to difficulties – and not only when the computer password or the keys to the filing cabinet are mislaid. If too little identifying data are held, or too little thought has gone into the way in which it is coded, valuable information can be lost. For instance, in one study the aim was to record the frequent changes of household that were experienced by very young children in need. Identifying data were only recorded where absolutely necessary and held separately; names and addresses of successive foster carers who were identified numerically on the dataset were not regarded as essential and therefore not recorded. However, carers were coded in such a way that it later proved impossible to identify those who had looked after more than one child in the sample, and an important issue could not be explored. *Box 2g* provides some practical guidance on how to ensure confidentiality and data protection.

Box 2g: Guidance for ensuring confidentiality and the protection of data
Lisa Holmes

Data stored on hard drives
- Research participants' names and addresses should not be stored on the hard drive of either laptop or desktop computers.
- All participants should be identified on data files saved to the hard drive by research and authority identifier codes.
- These data files (including Access databases, Excel spreadsheets and SPSS files) should all be encrypted using, for example, *Cryptainer*, or an equivalent package.
- A corresponding paper list containing names along with identifier codes should be stored separately in a locked filing cabinet; alternatively, an electronic (encrypted) version of the document should be saved onto a USB memory stick that is also stored separately in a locked filing cabinet.

Correspondence by email with local authorities and other agencies
- As far as possible, there should be an agreement with local authorities and other agencies that research participants, especially children, will not be referred to by name in emails, the only exception being when there is prior agreement with a specific individual working within the organisation.
- Participants should only be identifiable by either their research ID or local authority ID.

Correspondence by letter
- Copies of letters sent to research participants should not be saved to the hard drive of laptop or desktop computers.
- A copy of the letter containing the participant's name and address should either be saved onto a USB memory stick or a copy of the letter printed.

- Both the USB memory stick and copies of letters should be stored in locked filing cabinets.
- All letters to research participants should be sent by special delivery.

Data collection
- When gathering data in a local authority or other agency office, information should be transferred from the case files to an *Access* (or other) database on the researcher's laptop. All of these databases should be encrypted.
- Participants' names should not be recorded on the database; they should be identified only by research or authority IDs.
- An encrypted version of the database should be saved onto a USB memory stick at the end of every day. The USB memory stick should then be stored and transported in a separate bag to the laptop.
- To assist with locating relevant case files, the researcher may use a paper list containing both names and the corresponding research/authority identifier codes.
- This list should be stored securely at the authority office at the end of the day.

Interviews
- All information gathered during interviews should be recorded by research ID only; participants' names should not be recorded on the interview schedules.
- The exceptions to this are the consent form and, where appropriate, the gift voucher receipt that the parent, young person or other participant has to sign.
- The use of gift vouchers should be negotiated with research funders. If gift vouchers are given these are as a 'thank you' for participation and should not be seen as an incentive.
- These informed consent forms should be stored in a separate locked filing cabinet.
- If possible all interviews should be recorded (following consent by the participant). All digital recordings should be encrypted.

Transcription
- All transcribers should be asked to sign a letter stating that they will abide by the Data Protection Act 1998, including an agreement that all transcriptions of interviews should not be stored on the hard drive of their computer.
- The transcripts should not contain participants' or children's names; all names mentioned in the interview should be translated into initials only.
- All tapes sent to transcribers should be sent by special delivery. All digital recordings should either be sent as encrypted files or sent via specialist password protected websites, such as *YouSentIt*. All transcribed interviews should be returned by special delivery.

Paper copies of interview schedules and transcriptions
- All copies of interview schedules and transcriptions for current research projects should be stored in locked filing cabinets.
- These documents should be stored separately to any records of names and addresses.

Travelling
- Travelling to and from an authority or organisation can present a risk to the security of information. As much care as possible must be taken to ensure that breaches of security do not occur. For example, if travelling by train confidential information should not be left unattended.

> **Risk**
> - It is not feasible to take computers and briefcases everywhere and at times they do have to be left. However, as much care as possible should be taken.
> - If computers do have to be left unattended, they should be locked using the 'Ctrl, Alt, Delete' function. Rooms should always be locked and research materials should always be packed away rather than left spread out.

Question for discussion

- Under what circumstances can the need to preserve the confidentiality of research subjects and participating organisations conflict with the researcher's need to gather data, analyse findings and produce a report within a fixed timescale? How can such conflicting demands be reconciled?

References

Boddy, J. and Oliver, C. (2010) *Research governance in children's services: Scoping to inform the development of guidance. Report to the Department for Education*, London: Institute of Education.

DH (Department of Health) (2010) *Research governance framework for health and social care* (2nd edn), London: DH.

Munro, E.R. (2008) 'Research governance, ethics and access: a case study illustrating the new challenges facing social researchers', *International Journal of Social Research Methodology*, vol 11, no 5, pp 429-40.

Wadham, J. and Mountfield, H. (1999) *Blackstone's guide to the Human Rights Act 1998*, London: Blackstone Press.

Further reading

Boddy, J. and Oliver, C. (2010) *Research governance in children's services: Scoping to inform the development of guidance. Report to the Department for Education*, London: Institute of Education.

Munro, E.R. (2008) 'Research governance, ethics and access: a case study illustrating the new challenges facing social researchers', *International Journal of Social Research Methodology*, vol 11, no 5, pp 429-40.

Munro, E.R., Holmes, L. and Ward, H. (2005) 'Researching vulnerable groups: ethical issues and the effective conduct of research in local authorities', *British Journal of Social Work*, vol 35, no 7, pp 1023-38.

Ward, H., Brown, R., Westlake, D. and Munro, E. (2010) *Very young children at risk of significant harm: A prospective, longitudinal study*, Report to the Department for Education, Loughborough: Centre for Child and Family Research, Loughborough University.

Website resources

Data Protection Act (1998): www.legislation.gov.uk/ukpga/1998/29/contents
Human Rights Act (1998): www.legislation.gov.uk/ukpga/1998/42/contents
Health and Social Care Act (2008): www.legislation.gov.uk/ukpga/2008/14/contents
National Health Service Act (2006), Section 251: www.legislation.gov.uk/ukpga/2006/41/
  contents

Formulating research ideas and questions

Detailed contents

3.1 Introduction

The main goal of this chapter is to encourage readers to consider what research questions are, where they come from and the role of existing knowledge – often referred to by the shorthand term 'the literature' – in formulating research questions. The ideas that derive from the **literature** are often referred to as existing **theory** and an important consideration is the relationship between theory and research in the overall research process: is it something that drives the formulation of research ideas and the collection and analysis of data, is it better thought of as an outcome of the collection of data or is it better to think of the relationship between theory and research as having elements of both of these facets? These issues are contested, not least in social work and social policy research, and indeed, *between* social policy and social work, as this chapter shows.

At the very least, examining what is already known in connection with a research question should guard against the disconcerting possibility that when we complete a research project, we find or someone points out to us that the answers to the research question are already known.

In this chapter we discuss:

- how *research questions* are formulated and why they are important;
- how *budgets* and resources can impact on the formulation of research questions and the whole research approach;
- the role of the existing *literature* in formulating research questions;
- the significance of a *literature review* and what kinds of considerations might be borne in mind when writing one;
- the role of *theory* in relation to both social policy and social work research.

3.2 Formulating research ideas
Alan Bryman and Saul Becker

Where do research topics and research questions come from? This is one of the most difficult areas for students and researchers to get to grips with, yet it is also fundamental. It connects with the issue of why we study the things that we do, in fact, study. There are, of course, several sources of research topics, issues and questions, but before addressing the matter of sources it is worth spending a moment on our understanding of the terms used so far: *research topic, research issue* and *research question*. Inevitably, these terms overlap but it is valuable to consider what lines we can draw between them.

Research topics, issues and questions

A research **topic** may be thought of as a fairly general focus. It might be something like Incapacity Benefit claimants. As a focus for research, it provides few (and arguably no) guidelines as to what should be studied and who should be included in any sample of people from which data might be collected. For example, is the research supposed to be on people who claim benefits, on the experiences of those who administer the benefits, or should it be on attitudes among the general population to claimants, or on some other facet of the topic? Simply saying that the focus is on the topic of Incapacity Benefit claimants tells us next to nothing.

A research **issue** begins to narrow the focus considerably. The issue may be something like how far there are social and demographic differences in patterns of Incapacity Benefit claiming. This narrows the issue down to the understanding that it is about the backgrounds of Incapacity Benefit claimants. At this point we are beginning to get a good idea of what the research is about and why it is being done.

A research **question** takes things even further and will provide a guide to our enquiry. It specifies in much more precise terms what the research is about by specifying a question or series of related questions. A research question is essentially a question that is put to the social world. Thus, for their research on Incapacity Benefit claimants, Kemp and Davidson (2009), having noted a paucity of research on female claimants, essentially asked whether there were important gender differences in the route to claiming (see *Figure 3a*). The importance of a research question is that it acts as a route map for research: it helps to guide the literature to be examined, who the focus of the inquiry should be, what kinds of questions might most usefully be asked in the research instruments (for example, an interview schedule or a questionnaire) and how the data should be analysed and interpreted.

A research question is not the same as a **hypothesis**. Hypotheses are better thought of as kinds of research questions, namely, ones that postulate a possible relationship between two variables. A hypothesis might be something like: the more affluent a household, the less likely they are to rely on informal (unpaid) family carers. Such a hypothesis stipulates a relationship between two variables: household wealth and reliance on informal family care. It is a form of research question, because it is asking whether there is a relationship between the two variables. However, not all research questions take this form, especially those emanating from qualitative research (see Chapter Six), where they tend to be less specific and less inclined to use the language of variables that is a particular feature of quantitative research. This issue of the distinction between quantitative and qualitative research is an important one that will be outlined in greater detail in Chapter Four.

Figure 3a: Research topics, issues and questions

Research topic: Incapacity Benefit claimants.

↓

Research issue: sociodemographic differences among Incapacity Benefit claimants (especially gender differences).

↓

Research question: are the pathways to Incapacity Benefit claiming different between men and women?

But to repeat the question posed at the outset, where do research topics and research questions come from? In social policy and social work research, two sources stand out, although it is crucial not to drive a wedge between them in drawing this distinction for reasons that will hopefully become apparent. One source is that **events** in the social policy/social work field may stimulate research ideas. New legislation, such as a new Act or a noticeable trend (such as an increase in the number of Incapacity Benefit claimants), is an example of the kind of event that may have this kind of impact. Equally, a growing awareness of a social issue or social problem in society may prompt researchers to conduct an investigation (see, for example, *Box 1b* in Section 1.4 on child abuse research).

A second source of research questions is **existing theory** in the field. This issue is addressed more fully in Sections 3.4 (theory in social policy) and 3.5 (theory in social work) and *Box 3d* (Section 3.4) on the role of theory in health inequalities research. The term 'theory' is a vague one and need not refer to the abstract ideas and concepts with which theories are often associated. Instead, 'theory' frequently refers to our existing knowledge and understanding surrounding an issue – what do we know about the issue? In the case of the research by Kemp and Davidson (2009), the identification of a significant gap in our knowledge about Incapacity Benefit claimants (that is, gender differences) was a motivating factor.

However, in conducting research connected with the former kind of context – issues that present themselves in the social policy and social work fields – it is crucial to realise that it is still important to assess existing knowledge that is concerned with that issue. Research is never conducted in a vacuum. Even topics and issues that burst onto the scene as apparently unresearched areas still need to be assessed in terms of what we already know because it will almost certainly be the case that there will be cognate topics and issues that have been researched and the findings of which will help to illuminate our understanding of our object of inquiry. This means that we need to conduct a *literature review* (see Section 3.3). Nor is research 'cost free'. Research is always conducted within a defined budget and in the context of other resource constraints (*Box 3a*), and these constraints can affect the design and conduct of research.

Question for discussion

- What are research questions and why are they important?

Reference

Kemp, P.A. and Davidson, J. (2009) 'Gender differences among new claimants of incapacity benefit', *Journal of Social Policy*, vol 38, pp 589-606.

Further reading

Bryman, A. (2012) *Social research methods* (4th edn), Oxford: Oxford University Press, Chapter 4.

Box 3a: Researching within a budget
Nigel Bilsbrough

In this section we are concerned with managing budgets in a social policy and social work research context, and how budgetary restraints can impact on the formulation of research questions and the conduct of the research itself. Keeping within predetermined cost is affected by a number of factors, not least the need to deliver results to a deadline and to the requisite standard. It is recognised that these issues may not be of immediate interest to some readers of this book, perhaps those who are students. However, an appreciation of budgetary issues is important nonetheless since students need to understand that research is always conducted within a budget and within other resource constraints, and established researchers may appreciate some guidance in this area, particularly if they are involved in costing out a new research proposal.

However, before looking at managing budgets and budgetary constraints in more detail we need to consider what is meant by a *budget* and what constraints may be imposed. A *budget* is defined as *a plan of expenditure*, but in the area of social policy and social work research this has come to mean *an allocation of financial resources within which a particular research project is to be undertaken*. In some cases (for example, where a lone researcher or student is working on a study which has no funding source), there may not be an explicit or planned budget per se, although even here the researcher will still be conscious of the real costs of time and other resources utilised.

In many other cases, research will be funded in some way. When devising a budget for a research project, the researcher or research organisation will need to take various factors into account, not least of which are the often proscriptive requirements of the particular sponsor concerned. Any expenditure included in the budget must be *eligible*, that is, appropriate to the needs of the research as well as being allowable under the funding guidelines of the particular sponsor (see, for example, the Economic and Social Research Council [ESRC] website at www.esrcsocietytoday.ac.uk, or the Joseph Rowntree Foundation site www.jrf. org.uk/funding; also see 'Research costs' in the Glossary).

It is also important to determine whether the project is to be undertaken for a fixed price, as is often the case with government-funded projects, where the sponsor will pay a set sum of money in return for a specified outcome. In this case payments are usually triggered by events such as completion of data collection, analysis and writing, submission of draft then final reports, and so on. In other instances the researcher will be required to submit claims to the sponsor justifying the expenditure incurred. If the budget is under-spent then the money will effectively be lost.

In either case it is worth noting that any project expenditure may be audited by the sponsor, and in the case of European Union (EU) funding this can take place several years after the completion of the project, so it is important that appropriate evidence of expenditure is retained.

Since publication of the first edition of this book the funding of research in higher education institutions (HEIs) underwent a major overhaul with the introduction of full economic costing (fEC) in 2005. This was effectively driven by government concerns that HEIs were not charging the full costs of the research they were undertaking, nor indeed did they have the mechanisms in place to determine these costs, and it was feared that the research infrastructure was suffering from long-term neglect. This was obviously not sustainable.

So, as well as allowing for the directly incurred costs of undertaking a research project, for example, salary costs, consumables, travel and equipment, HEIs now use an agreed formula known as TRAC (transparent approach to costing) to calculate directly allocated costs and indirect costs. These are worked out as a sum charged per full-time equivalent (FTE) researcher working on a project per annum. For more information on fEC and TRAC see, for example, www.rcuk.ac.uk/aboutrcs/funding/dual/fec.htm and www.hefce.ac.uk/finance/fundinghe/trac/

However the story doesn't end there as different sponsors treat their responsibility for paying fEC rates differently. Currently the UK Research Councils will only pay 80% of the total fEC cost of a project, leaving the beneficiary institution to find the 20% shortfall. UK charities will only pay the directly incurred costs of any project whereas UK government departments and industry are expected to pay the fEC.

Many other points will need to be considered when preparing a project budget, and some of the key ones are outlined in *Figure 3b*.

Figure 3b: Issues to consider when preparing a research project budget

- The *level* of staff employed. For example, Research Councils will specify the maximum grade of staff they would normally consider funding.
- Can nationally agreed *pay awards* be included or will the budget be inflation-linked?
- Can the costs of *recruiting* staff be included?
- Can the costs of *support staff* be included, or are these to be treated as part of the directly allocated costs?
- Is any specialist *equipment* required to undertake the project? In social work and social policy research the costs of equipment are often neglected but there may be a need for a high quality recording machine to undertake interviews or a transcribing machine.
- Can *office costs* and *consumables* be included, or are these considered to be part of the directly allocated costs?
- Other *directly incurred costs* (see 'research costs' in the Glossary) will need to be considered, such as:
  - travel and subsistence (which should not be underestimated);
  - recruitment of respondents;
  - payment of expenses to respondents;
  - transcription of interviews;
  - preparation and printing of questionnaires;
  - telephone and postal costs and costs of follow-ups.

Figure 3b is by no means an exhaustive list, but it is hoped that this will provide some guidance. Above all, it needs to be remembered that very few research proposals will fail on the grounds of cost alone, although obviously in these austere times value for money is a major consideration. Most sponsors will be prepared to negotiate the costs, invariably downwards, if they are otherwise happy with the proposal, but it is almost impossible to increase costs at a later stage.

Once a budget for a research proposal is finalised and agreed, it is important that it is adhered to. It may seem an obvious point to make but many researchers will continue to try and produce for the sponsor everything that was included in the original proposal, and often more as enthusiasm for the work takes hold, ignoring the fact that the funding may have been cut. It is therefore imperative that a project plan is devised for the project and that fully costed resources are allocated to it.

In addition, the project plan must be monitored on a regular basis to ensure that the appropriate resources are being utilised in a timely manner and that agreed milestones are being met. The project plan may require periodic adjustment.

The very nature of research means that the outcomes are not necessarily predictable. Problems and attendant delays may be encountered along the way. But at least if regular reviews of the work in progress are undertaken potential pitfalls can be identified at an early stage and remedial action can be taken. This is preferable to the sickening realisation that a project is rapidly coming to a close, that all available resources have been consumed, but yet the final output (in whatever form it may take) is still nowhere near completion.

Questions for discussion
- Why is it important to have a fully costed and adequate budget for any piece of social policy or social work research?
- Why was the introduction of full economic costing (fEC) important for sustaining the long-term health of research capacity in the UK?

3.3 Conducting a literature review
Alan Bryman and Saul Becker

Why conduct a literature review?

A literature review is an assessment of existing knowledge – both empirical and theoretical – relating to a research topic, issue or question. There are several reasons for needing to conduct one:

- Someone else might have carried out research relating to a research issue or research question. There is no point in going over the same ground unless you can add to what is already known. This may mean taking a different slant on what is already known by perhaps collecting data from groups who have been marginalised in previous research, or by accessing and developing information from published sources. Every experienced researcher at some time will have had the experience of thinking that he or she has suddenly uncovered a focus that has not been studied previously, only to find when looking at the literature that it has, in fact, already been covered. A literature review means that the researcher will not be in a position of making incorrect claims about the 'unresearched' nature of his or her area of interest.

• Doing a literature review will help researchers to appreciate what gaps there are in existing knowledge about the phenomenon of interest. These gaps can be usefully mined to provide their own particular slant on the topic. In the case of the research by Kemp and Davidson (2009), it was precisely the relative lack of research on female Incapacity Benefit claimants (in spite of the fact that they constitute 40% of all claimants) that led them to focus on gender differences in pathways to claiming.

• A literature review will help to identify concepts and ideas that have been used to illuminate the area of interest. These may be helpful in giving researchers ideas about the kinds of data that need to be collected and also how to interpret the data that are collected.

• A literature review can give researchers ideas about who should be the focus of the enquiry, how they can be sampled, what kinds of lists are available for sampling them and what is already known about them from surveys or from qualitative interview studies.

• A literature review is extremely useful for an appreciation of the research methods and research designs that have been used to examine this or related areas of interest. This kind of information in itself might be useful in formulating a research question because it might suggest that a particular topic or research question would benefit from a different data collection strategy from the ones that have been used up to that point.

• At a later stage, a literature review will help researchers with the interpretation of data and the formulation of conclusions. A literature review is helpful for providing 'pegs' on which to hang data. There are invariably numerous ways that researchers can interpret and analyse the data. An understanding of the literature can provide some clues about which aspects of the data to emphasise because researchers will be able to, and should, relate their own data to aspects of the literature (see also **Box 7c** in Section 7.3).

A useful aid to collecting materials for a literature review is to make use of computer software, such as a database. The potential of such software is described in **Box 3b**.

Box 3b: Managing references
Joe Sempik

Prior to the introduction of personal computers (PCs) one of the more tedious (and frequently neglected) tasks of managing a research project was the management of references and the bibliography. This required a boxful of index cards and an accurate transcription of author, title, journal and so on by hand. It is not surprising that this task was often neglected or often performed inaccurately.

However, with the advent of PCs and specialist applications called 'reference managers' the job of organising a bibliography has become considerably easier. But, surprisingly, many researchers (even experienced ones) do not use them and instead rely on copying and pasting references from other documents or type them manually. This is slow and inefficient.

Reference managers are computer applications specifically designed to hold and manipulate details of references and the bibliography. A reference manager also simplifies the task of writing papers and reports as it can be used directly with applications such as Word to insert references into the text while writing a paper.

Reference managers can:

- store references and bibliographical data;
- import references directly from online databases during literature searches;
- store and organise local copies of articles and images (for example, graphs and figures);
- add references directly to a Word (or other word processor) document;
- create a bibliography in a specific format for a particular journal;
- export a bibliography to another application;
- store users' comments;
- store details of online searches;
- enable sharing of references between users.

However, not all reference managers can handle all of the above tasks and some may require the installation of additional program components (add-ins).

There are many different examples of reference managers but two widely used ones are *EndNote* and *RefWorks*. These illustrate two different approaches to storing data. *Endnote* stores its 'library' of references directly on a local computer, while *RefWorks* is web-based and stores its bibliography on a host server. There are advantages and disadvantages of each of these two approaches. Having all of your references on one computer may seem convenient, but if there is a disk crash or the computer is stolen then all of the bibliography is lost. However, a web-based reference manager is not susceptible to a computer crash or loss and can be accessed from any computer but it does require an internet connection. The current trend is for reference managers to use a web-based system and there is now an online application based on *EndNote* (*EndNote Web*).

Both *EndNote* and *RefWorks* and many similar applications require a user licence that can be costly, but the researcher's university or institution may have a subscription for one of these. Distributors often provide free demonstration copies that perform all of the functions of the real thing but are time-limited. It is, therefore, possible to browse before committing to any particular one. Also, there are free applications available, for example, *Zotero*, which is an add-on to the *Firefox* browser and *BiblioExpress*, which is a 'lite' version of the *Biblioscape* software. This is a developing area and there are likely to be more products to choose from in the future.

An alternative approach is for researchers to build their own reference database using an application such as *Microsoft Access*. The advantage of this method is that in the course of preparation a great deal can be learned about how databases are constructed and managed and how to use them. The construction and use of databases is an important element of many research projects. For example, *Access* can be used very efficiently to carry out qualitative analysis (see Hahn, 2008). The disadvantage of creating a personal bibliographic database is that it takes time and some effort. However, a custom-made reference database can be used to analyse and classify the content of published material in exactly the way that is wanted.

Researchers can also import data from online databases and other applications (although they will probably need to save them first as text files before importing into *Access*).

Whichever reference manager is chosen, while it may take a while to master it and at first it may seem slow, it will soon save the researcher both time and effort.

Question for discussion
• Why do I need a reference manager?

Reference
Hahn, C. (2008) *Doing qualitative research using your computer: A practical guide*, London: Sage Publications.

Further reading
Agrawal, A. (2009) *EndNote 1 – 2 – 3 easy! Reference management for the professional*, Dordrecht: Springer.

Website resources
EndNote: www.endnote.com
RefWorks: www.refworks.com
Biblioscape: www.biblioscape.com
Zotero: www.zotero.org

Evaluating sources for a literature review

When reviewing the literature it is important to realise that researchers will be dealing with a variety of materials that will have different purposes and statuses. **Articles in academic refereed journals** such as the *British Journal of Social Work*, *Journal of Social Policy*, *Social Policy & Administration*, *Social Policy and Society*, are often regarded as 'higher status' outlets for the kinds of material researchers are likely to read for a literature review. The articles that appear in these journals are only a small proportion of those that are submitted. Many are rejected because they are not felt to be 'good' enough to be published in that journal or because the editors believe that the articles are outside the journal's brief. In addition to being read by an editor, all articles are also read by two, three and sometimes more referees who are authorities in the area covered by the articles. The refereeing process is 'blind', meaning that the referees do not know who the articles were written by, so that the possible 'halo effects' of being a big name author are eliminated. Thus, articles appearing in such journals are the outcome of a set of rigorous quality control procedures, often requiring authors to go through one or more revisions of their articles before final acceptance. This is often referred to as 'peer review'. **Books** by academic authors are also highly regarded, but not all publishers make substantial use of referees and, in any case, blind refereeing is usually not possible. Therefore, while some of the most important contributions to the field have been through books, it is also important to bear in mind that books have sometimes not gone through the same process as articles in refereed journals.

   Professional periodicals are valuable for a literature review because they give a good sense of how practitioners are approaching issues in fields such as community care or social work. They often provide useful reviews of policies and also give a sense of what is and what is not working in a particular field. The articles in such outlets rarely have the same status as articles in academic journals and books, however, partly because the refereeing process is rarely as rigorous and partly because the periodicals rarely address academic research concerns.

Another source researchers are likely to include in a review is reports from various **official and unofficial agencies**. For example, the Joseph Rowntree Foundation regularly provides reports of research it has commissioned and these can be very valuable in finding out about current findings in a particular area. Researchers can also search out reports by local authorities and government departments that touch on social policy and social work issues that are of interest to them.

The **internet** is obviously an important source for students and researchers collecting material for a literature review. It is host to a variety of different types of material – online journals, non-governmental organisation (NGO) and government reports, official websites, academics' home pages and so much more besides. There are also millions of websites of dubious nature that do not provide reliable information and should be used with caution.

Many databases and journals are now available online so searching the literature for articles and books in a particular field is likely to be carried out online. In addition, the Joseph Rowntree Foundation, Social Care Institute for Excellence (SCIE), Research in Practice, Making Research Count and other reputable bodies, local authorities, government departments and others, also have their own sites where reports and other information can be found. In addition, of course, researchers can always do a general search using a search engine such as Google or Yahoo.

However, researchers should be cautious about the material accumulated through this kind of search procedure, as some of it will be dubious in quality. By all means conduct such searches, but researchers should cultivate an attitude of scepticism towards them. While Google Scholar may be a useful search engine as this focuses more on academic sources, some of the articles, for example, may only be available via a payment or subscription. Researchers should not forget to keep good accurate records of all the references (see **Box 3b**) and sites that they have searched, and the key words used to access them.

Writing the literature review

When writing a literature review there are a number of points that are worth bearing in mind:

- *Be critical*. When reading the material that has been gathered, researchers should start to think about what the contribution of each item is to the area being investigated and about what its strengths and weaknesses are. A critical literature review should not be thought of as negative. It also entails sensitivity to the contribution that a book or article makes. These reflections should be used in the literature review.
- *Be sensitive* to the need to make distinctions between different sources of literature and their quality, as discussed above. As we have said, peer-reviewed journal articles are a more reliable source of evidence than, say, an anonymous item off the internet. When

compiling material for a literature review researchers will need to make judgements about what to include and what to exclude.

- *Adopt a narrative* when writing the literature review. This means not simply summarising each item, but showing how each item contributes to a story that the researcher is trying to construct about the literature in this area.
- *Do not try to include in your literature review everything* you read. This is very tempting, but is not a good strategy. Researchers should use the literature in such a way that it helps to build the narrative they are devising. This will almost certainly mean omitting some items that have been read.
- *Read some articles in academic journals* (or books) to see how the literature review is built up and how a narrative about the literature is constructed. **Box 3c** provides an example.
- Researchers should ensure that they keep *full and accurate details* of all the texts that they read. They may want to put these details on an electronic database (see **Box 3b**).
- Researchers will want to *link their literature reviews to their own research*, so it should be borne in mind that when writing the review they will need to adjust it later to take account of aspects of the findings that they may not have anticipated at the outset.
- It is important to think about *what kind of literature review is being done*. The idea of a 'systematic review' is discussed in Section 4.17. Systematic reviews have become the focus of a great deal of attention in recent years because for a certain kind of research question (particularly of the 'what works?' kind) they offer a robust and apparently dispassionate view of the literature. Systematic reviews are often contrasted with 'narrative reviews' that come much closer to the traditional type of review. The latter type of review can often appear haphazard in terms of both the literature search and how the review is presented. Commentators point out that systematic reviews are not suitable for all literature areas and that the technique tends to undermine the interpretive skill of the reviewer. However, the two types of review are in some ways getting less far apart. Increasingly, narrative reviewers are incorporating some systematic review procedures into their approach, such as: being explicit about the ways that the literature was searched including the keywords employed; assessing research for inclusion in terms of explicit quality criteria; and being explicit about how core themes extrapolated from the review were arrived at (see, for example, Glasby and Lester, 2005; Bryman, 2012; and see also Section 4.18 in this volume).

Questions for discussion

- What are the main functions of a literature review?
- Are some kinds of literature more important, and reliable, than others from the point of view of writing a literature review?

References

Bryman, A. (2012) *Social research methods* (4th edn), Oxford: Oxford University Press.
Glasby, J. and Lester, H. (2005) 'On the inside: a narrative review of mental health inpatient services', *British Journal of Social Work*, vol 35, no 6, pp 863-79.
Kemp, P.A. and Davidson, J. (2009) 'Gender differences among new claimants of incapacity benefit', *Journal of Social Policy*, vol 38, pp 589-606.

Further reading

Bryman, A. (2012) *Social research methods* (4th edn), Oxford: Oxford University Press, Chapter 5.

Hart, C. (1998) *Doing a literature review*, London: Sage Publications.

Hart, C. (2001) *Doing a literature search: A comprehensive guide for the social sciences*, London: Sage Publications.

Jesson, J., Matheson, L. and Lacey, F. (2011) *Doing your literature review: Traditional and systematic techniques*, London: Sage Publications.

Matthews, B. and Ross, L. (2010) *Research methods: A practical guide for the social sciences*, Harlow: Pearson Education Ltd, pp 92-109.

Website resources

Joseph Rowntree Foundation: www.jrf.org.uk

Making Research Count: www.uea.ac.uk/menu/acad_depts/swk/MRC_web/public_html

Research in Practice: www.rip.org.uk

Social Care Institute for Excellence (SCIE): www.scie.org.uk

Box 3c: Using the published literature to understand social policy and social work issues
Alan Bryman and Saul Becker

Kemp and Davidson (2009) take as their starting point government anxieties in Britain and elsewhere about the growth in the number of Incapacity Benefit claimants. They note that the number of claimants grew sharply between the late 1970s and the 1990s. The numbers of claimants have maintained a high level since the 1990s. Their actual research derives mainly from a survey of 1,843 new Incapacity Benefit claimants. The claimants constituted a random sample and were personally interviewed using a structured schedule. The article takes a number of different sources for the literature review:

- Government sources. They present evidence from a Green Paper that drew attention to the invisibility of women in discussions of Incapacity Benefit claiming.
- Academic commentary and research in academic books and journals concerning evidence in connection with patterns of Incapacity Benefit claiming.

The literature review is employed as a rationale and background to their survey and its findings. They note that the 'knowledge gap' concerning female Incapacity Benefit claimants is surprising, in light of the fact that they represent a large proportion of the population of claimants. They write:

This article seeks to address that knowledge gap. Drawing on empirical data from a national survey, it compares men and women aged under 60 who have recently claimed Incapacity Benefit (IB). In doing so, it sheds new light on the characteristics of male and female claimants and their routes onto IB. (Kemp and Davidson, 2009, p 590)

In this way, the literature is employed as a rationale and justification for conducting their own survey and as an indication of the reasons why the findings will be important.

In their conclusion, Kemp and Davidson return to the themes that drove and emerged from their literature review. They remind us that Incapacity Benefit claiming 'has been the focus of considerable scholarly attention', they note that 'research has been almost entirely focused on male claimants' in spite of women constituting 40% of claimants, and they point out again that 'very little research has examined their characteristics and circumstances or looked at differences that might exist between men and women in their routes onto IB' (Kemp and Davidson, 2009, pp 602-3). Reminding us of these deficits in the literature is important in the light of their survey research because it shows that 'there are indeed significant differences between male and female claimants of this benefit' (Kemp and Davidson, 2009, p 603). This is a strong conclusion that returns the reader to the issues spelled out in the literature review and relates these to the research findings. The issues of writing up research and relating findings to an established body of findings are further explored in Section 7.3 and *Box 7c*.

Reference

Kemp, P.A. and Davidson, J. (2009) 'Gender differences among new claimants of incapacity benefit', *Journal of Social Policy*, vol 38, pp 589-606.

3.4 The role of theory in social policy research

Robert Pinker

The **development and testing of theories** is an essential element in the conduct of social research. Theories set out explanatory and predictive propositions about the causal relationships between phenomena, such as, for example, the characteristics and incidence of poverty and the processes by which people become poor and escape from poverty. The question as to whether theory construction develops out of social research or, conversely, research develops out of theory, is part of a wider philosophical debate between *deductivists* and *inductivists* concerning the origins and status of human knowledge, and the nature of scientific enquiry itself.

Deductivists and inductivists hold differing views about the sequence in which scientific research should be conducted. **Deductivists** start by formulating a theory and then proceed from this general proposition to a consideration of particular cases in order to test their theory. **Inductivists** start by drawing inferences from particular cases from which they proceed towards the formulation of general theoretical conclusions.

The central assumption of the inductivist approach is that 'scientific knowledge grows out of simple unbiased statements reporting the evidence of the senses' (Medawar, 1984, p 98). 'In real life', however, as Peter Medawar suggests, 'discovery and justification are almost always different processes' and researchers seldom, if ever, start their enquiries with a clean sheet. They begin with a review of the relevant literature and some provisional ideas, or hypotheses, about the subject they wish to investigate (see, for example, Sections 3.2 and 3.3).

Medawar argues that the weakness in the inductivist approach is its 'failure to distinguish between the acts of the mind involved in discovery and proof'. Induction, he points out, is 'a logically mechanised process of thought which, starting from simple declarations of fact arising out of the evidence of the senses' purports to lead us on 'with certainty to the truths of general laws'. In Medawar's view, induction cannot fulfil these two functions of discovery and justification because 'it is not the *origin* but only the *acceptance* of hypotheses that depends on the authority of logic' (Medawar, 1984, p 33). For this reason, Medawar proposes that we 'abandon the idea of induction and draw a clear distinction between *having an idea* and *testing it* or *trying it out*'. We can then reconceptualise the relationship between the uses of imagination and sceptical criticism as the '*two* successive and complementary episodes of thought that occur in every advance of scientific understanding' (Medawar, 1984, p 33, original emphasis). The formulation of hypotheses requires an act of imagination. The testing of hypotheses requires the application of critical testing and experimentation.

Medawar's approach to the conduct of research shares much in common with that of Karl Popper. In Popper's **hypothetico–deductive method**, scientific enquiry starts with an imaginative conjecture, or 'hunch', which is set out in the form of a possible explanation of a causal relationship, a prediction or a solution to a problem. A conjecture is the first stage in the development of a scientific hypothesis that will give focus to the research and direction in the collection of relevant evidence. Scientific hypotheses, however, differ from conjectures insofar as they must be set out in forms that allow them to be tested and falsified by methods of observation and experiment. Scientific knowledge is distinguished from non-scientific knowledge insofar as it can be subjected to tests of falsifiability. Popper argues that we are never justified in deriving 'universal statements from singular ones, no matter how numerous' because such statements may turn out to be false (Popper, 1972, p 27). In this crucially important respect, scientific knowledge is always provisional and never proven in status. Hypotheses and theories should not, therefore, be treated as propositions to be defended but as propositions to be tested, revised and, if necessary, abandoned in response to countervailing evidence (see also Section 1.5).

In Popper's approach to scientific research we must rely 'upon the best tested of theories, which ... are the ones for which we have good rational reasons, not of course good reasons for believing them to be true, but for believing them to be the *best* available ... the best among competing theories, the best approximations to the truth' (Popper, 1978, p 95). On this basis, scientific knowledge will continue to advance through a 'method of bold conjectures and ingenious and severe attempts to refute them' (Popper, 1978, p 81). Popper's views have, in turn, been subjected to critical reappraisal by other philosophers. His claim that falsifiability is the hallmark of a scientific theory has been challenged on a number of grounds, as has his dismissal of inductivism. Not all scientific theories are predictive in character and it does not always follow that one negative finding invalidates a theory. It can also be argued that there are notably inductivist connotations to Popper's advice that we should rely on those theories that have, so far, stood up to rigorous testing. In this respect, Putnam reminds us that, in the real world of policy making, people do make inductions and draw inferences from available evidence without reaching unwarranted conclusions about the truth or falsity of their theories. Putman suggests that Popper draws an unnecessarily sharp distinction between the worlds of theory and practice. In doing so, he overlooks the fact that ideas are 'not just ends in themselves', but that they also 'guide practice' and 'structure whole forms of life' (Putnam, 1979, p 374).

There are, however, two good reasons why Popper's approach to scientific enquiry can improve the quality of social policy research. First, the ends and means of social policy are shaped by many *value judgements* that often conflict with each other. Policy researchers often hold strong political beliefs about the subjects they wish to investigate. Popper's injunction that theories are propositions to be tested is a useful corrective against value bias and partisanship in the conduct of research. Scholars test their propositions, ideologists defend them, if need be, against all countervailing evidence. Second, a Popperian approach leaves open the alternative possibilities that theory can generate research and research can generate theory since hypotheses can emerge at any point in either of these two interactive processes. ***Box 3d*** provides an illustration of this process, in the context of the role that theory played in relation to a major research programme on health inequalities.

Question for discussion

• Start thinking about a possible research topic and see how far you get before you begin formulating hypotheses.

References

Medawar, P. (1984) *Pluto's Republic*, Oxford: Oxford University Press.
Popper, K. (1972) *The logic of scientific discovery*, London: Hutchinson.
Popper, K. (1978) *Objective knowledge: An evolutionary approach*, Oxford: Clarendon Press.
Putnam, H. (1979) 'The "corroboration" of theories', in T. Honderich and M. Burnyeat (eds) *Philosophy as it is*, London: Penguin Books.

Further reading

Leisering, L. and Walker, R. (eds) (1998) *The dynamics of modern society: Poverty, policy and welfare*, Bristol: The Policy Press.
Lødemel, I. (1997) *The welfare paradox, income maintenance and personal social services in Norway and Britain, 1946-1966*, Oslo: Scandinavian University Press.
O'Brien, M. and Penna, S. (1998) *Theorising welfare: Enlightenment and modern society*, London: Sage Publications.

Box 3d: The role of theory in health inequalities research
Hilary Graham

In the UK, as in other societies, people living in more advantaged circumstances enjoy better health than those in poorer circumstances. These health differences are commonly referred to as health inequalities; in the US, the term 'health disparities' is preferred. Health inequalities typically take the form of a social gradient in which health improves steadily across the socioeconomic hierarchy. *Figure 3c* illustrates this staircase pattern.

Figure 3c: Proportion of adults aged 16 and over assessing their health as poor[a] by income quintile adjusted for household size and composition, England, 2003

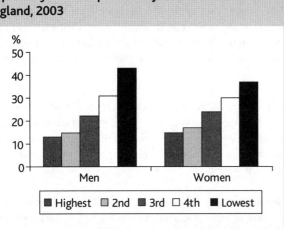

Note: [a] As fair, bad or very bad rather than as very good or good.
Source: Sproston and Primatesta (2004, Table 10.3)

Previous research has established that health-related social mobility cannot explain health inequalities. While healthier people are more likely to be upwardly mobile and those in poorer health are more likely to slip down the social class ladder, this explains only a small part of the social gradient in health. Other factors are clearly at work, and theory has been central to understanding them.

In recent decades, life course theories have been particularly influential. They start with evidence that health inequalities exist at all ages. There are health inequalities at birth and throughout childhood. In adulthood, social disadvantage is associated with higher risks of disease, disability and premature death. Building on this evidence, researchers have tested the theory that health is shaped across the course of people's lives, with past as well as current circumstances influencing physical and emotional health.

In support of this perspective, studies have found that the risk of poor health and premature death rises in line with duration of exposure to economic hardship. Those who enjoy good living conditions across their lives – both in childhood and adulthood – are less likely to die prematurely than people who, while living in advantaged circumstances now, had a poor start in life. Death rates are highest among those born into hardship and who never escape it.

While people's circumstances across their lives matter for their health, there is increasing evidence that childhood circumstances have particularly powerful effects. Studies suggest that these effects operate through a range of mechanisms.

First, a child's start in life influences their chances of doing well at school and getting a well-paid job; the chances are much higher for children born to better-off parents. This is particularly true in the UK, which is more unequal than many of its European neighbours.

Under this mechanism, childhood circumstances influence adult health indirectly, through their impact on future socioeconomic circumstances.

Second, childhood circumstances have direct health effects. For example, being born into a poor family increases the risk of lifelong health conditions and vulnerabilities. In addition, childhood disadvantage is associated with adolescent health behaviours like cigarette smoking; because such habits are hard to break, they often persist into adulthood and take a long-term toll on health.

In interpreting this evidence, it is important to be aware that childhood disadvantage does not inevitably lead to enduring disadvantage and poorer health. A higher risk of an adverse outcome means only that poorer children are more vulnerable than children in better-off families, not that they are doomed from birth. In rich countries, many adverse outcomes are uncommon even in the poorest groups.

Life course theories are helping to shed light on health inequalities. However, while there is extensive evidence to support them, research challenges remain. The UK's major longitudinal studies were established when Asian and African-Caribbean families made up a small proportion of the population. They, therefore, shed light on how childhood disadvantage can compromise future health among white children. However, they can say little about how children's cultural backgrounds and their exposure to, or protection from, racism influences their future lives and future health. Further, most of the evidence is quantitative. Inevitably, it reveals little about people's everyday experiences and their understandings of how social inequality affects their health. In addition, because surveys focus on individuals, they cannot capture the role of broader social institutions – such as the education system, the labour market and welfare agencies, for example – in social and health inequalities. For those drawn to life course perspectives on health inequalities, there are, therefore, many important questions to be explored!

Question for discussion
- How has research on the life course advanced understanding of socioeconomic inequalities in health?

Reference
Sproston, K. and Primatesta, P. (2004) *Health survey for England 2003, Volume 2, Risk factors for cardiovascular disease*, London: Office for National Statistics.

Further reading
Blas, E. and Sivasankara Kurup, A. (2010) *Equity, social determinants and public health programmes*, Geneva: World Health Organization.

Graham, H. (2007) *Unequal lives: Health and socioeconomic inequalities*, Buckingham: Open University Press.

Graham, H. (ed) (2009) *Understanding health inequalities* (2nd edn), Buckingham: Open University Press.

Website resources
UK data, research and policy
Department of Health (England): www.dh.gov.uk/en/index.htm
Department of Health, Social Services and Public Safety (Northern Ireland): www.dhsspsni.
    gov.uk
Health and Social Care, Welsh Assembly Government: http://wales.gov.uk/topics/
    health/?lang=en
Health Scotland: www.healthscotland.com
London Health Observatory: www.lho.org.uk
UN National Statistics: www.statistics.gov.uk/
The Poverty Site: www.poverty.org.uk/summary/uk.htm
Public Health Research Consortium: www.york.ac.uk/phrc/
Europe data, research and policy
European Commission (Public Health): http://ec.europa.eu/health/index_en.htm
World Health Organization Regional Office for Europe (WHO): www.euro.who.int
International data, research and policy
United Nations Development Programme (UNDP): http://hdr.undp.org/en/
World Health Organization (WHO) Commission on the social determinants of health: www.
    who.int/social_determinants/en/

3.5 The role of theory in social work research
Elaine Sharland

As Section 3.4 has shown, the relationship between theory and research is contested in social science because it is linked to debates about how we can know the social world and whether certain kinds of knowledge, evidence or ideas have more value than others. In social work it gets more complicated because there is a three-way relationship involved: between theory, research *and* practice.

At its broadest, theory can be understood as a set of interrelated concepts brought together to provide a plausible explanation of phenomena. Within this, we can identify different levels of theory. Both **grand theory**, concerned with societal level phenomena such as the 'risk society', and **middle range theory**, dealing with specific phenomena such as 'attachment', appear in social work research. We can also distinguish in content between **substantive theories**, concerning problems or situations, such as 'racial discrimination', and **practice or procedural theories**, such as 'anti-racist practice', intended to address these problems.

To look critically at the role that theory plays in social work research, the key characteristics to be considered are the **purposes** and **logic** of theory, and the **processes** through which it is generated and applied. To do this, it is helpful to distinguish between positivist, interpretivist and critical approaches to social work research (Trinder with Reynolds, 2000). Although the contrasts between them can be exaggerated, it is helpful to see how theory is differently configured within each.

Positivist research places its faith in objective evidence that can be measured in the social world, just as in nature. In social work, advocates for positivism tend to be associated with the 'evidence-based practice' movement, arguing for the 'appliance of science' in policy and practice (Sheldon, 1998; see also Section 1.6 and **Box 1d**). Here the purpose of theory is to explain relationships between discrete variables, usually between specific interventions and their outcomes. Theory is intended to be **nomothetic**, meaning to establish predictive laws that can be abstracted from specific contexts, based on statistically generalisable evidence. To achieve this, theory needs to be expressed in specific hypotheses that can be tested and falsified in the real world. Such **deductive** processes can also be complemented by **inductive** processes of theory building, where hunches and hypotheses are generated from existing evidence, and further tested. In social work this means that theory may be about practice, but is developed by expert researchers for application by practitioners and policy makers. It is mainly concerned with establishing whether certain types of intervention work, rather than how, where or why. Because this kind of theory predicts generally, it relies on the sort of comparable conditions and certainties that can be rare in social work, but are more often found in clinical disciplines such as psychology or health, from which social work research sometimes borrows.

Interpretive research aims not to reveal objective realities but to uncover the subjective experiences of people who make up the social world (Denzin and Lincoln, 1994). So the purpose of theory is not to establish laws of cause and effect, but to understand lived experience. For many in social work, where 'respect for persons' is a core value, and the everyday experience of vulnerable people is core business, this makes intuitive sense. Some interpretive approaches, such as 'grounded theory', explicitly emphasise the role of discovery through **induction** to generate middle range theory (Strauss and Corbin, 1994). Here theory is intended to be **idiographic**, meaning that although it is generated in one context, its helpfulness for understanding others can be explored, but its worth does not depend on whether it is proved right in all situations. Theory of this sort tends to be less popular with policy makers keen to know which interventions work best across the board. But it can be very helpful in bridging the gap between policy and the lived realities of practice, from professional and service user perspectives.

Critical research is an umbrella term describing several different approaches to social work research. They share the understanding that research is not an objective fact-finding process, but nor is a focus on subjective experience alone sufficient to capture social processes, structures or relationships of power. **Critical realist** approaches argue that if research is to be useful it must examine not just whether, but how, where and with whom interventions work (Pawson and Tilley, 1997). Theory should be developed through an **iterative** process of induction and deduction, to explain the underlying mechanisms of change through which interventions work in context. It is these theories of change, rather than the specifics of particular interventions, that should be ideographically **transferable** elsewhere.

Taking a different starting point, **standpoint or participative research** approaches hold that power is unequally distributed between gender, classes, ethnic groups, professionals and service users. So grand and middle range theories, about the relationship between power and knowledge, lie at the heart of this approach (Dominelli, 2005). Theory can also be refined through **logical** processes of induction and deduction, and through **dialogical** processes of exchange with research and practice. Here the main purpose of theory is for **praxis**, meaning its practical power to bring about change. So, the aim is not just to give voice to service users, carers or even practitioners who might otherwise be silenced, but also to empower them and transform the structural conditions that exclude or oppress them. **Post-modernist** approaches to social work research are similarly concerned with the relationship between knowledge and power, and with dialogue between theory, research and practice. But key to these is recognising that social work grapples with 'wicked problems' of uncertainty, complexity and ambiguity, which themselves are defining characteristics of post-modernity (Fook, 2002). Social work problems cannot be solved in any predictable or calculative way, and both positivist and structuralist standpoint approaches to the relationship between theory, research and practice epitomise the misunderstandings of modernity. Instead, some social work research has begun to draw on post-modern theories to help show, for example, how policy discourses seek to regulate service user identities and social work practice in the face of uncertainty, and how this might be resisted.

The distinctions drawn above are helpful for looking critically at the role of theory in social work research. But they probably present a more polarised picture than necessary, since social work research and theory are often more hybrid and pluralist than this. Very commonly there is a more fluid relationship between them, where theory is used as a **hermeneutic tool**, selected by researchers from a range of available theoretical ideas, to shed light on their question and findings. This is a good thing. Just as there is no single way of understanding any one complex problem, so the critical test of theory and research should be whether the approach taken to both is appropriate to the question(s) at hand. Also essential in social work is that research questions themselves reflect the concerns not just of policy makers, but practitioners and service users. Theoretical ideas that inform and emerge from research are likely to have most impact where they 'fit' with the issues encountered in everyday social work practice, and at the same time suggest alternative understandings and possibilities for change. *Box 3e* provides an illustration of how theory has been used by social work authors to think critically about the concept of 'risk'.

Question for discussion

• How can theory help you think about a social work question of your choice?

References

Denzin, N. and Lincoln, Y. (1994) *Handbook of qualitative research*, Thousand Oaks, CA: Sage Publications.

Dominelli, L. (2005) 'Social work research: contested knowledge for practice', in R. Adams, L. Dominelli and M. Payne (eds) *Social work futures: Crossing boundaries, transforming practice*, Basingstoke: Palgrave, pp 223-36.

Fook, J. (2002) *Social work, critical theory and practice*, London: Sage Publications.

Pawson, R. and Tilley, N. (1997) *Realistic evaluation*, London: Sage Publications.

Sheldon, B. (1998) 'Evidence-based social services: prospects and problems', *Research, Policy and Planning*, vol 16, no 2, pp 16-18.

Strauss, A. and Corbin, J. (1994) 'Grounded theory methodology: an overview', in N. Denzin and Y. Lincoln (eds) *Handbook of qualitative research*, Thousand Oaks, CA: Sage Publications, pp 273-85.

Trinder, E. with Reynolds, S. (2000) *Evidence based practice: A critical appraisal*, Oxford: Blackwell Science.

Further reading

Brodie, I. (2000) *Theory generation and qualitative research: School exclusion and children looked after*, ESRC 'Theorising Social Work Research' Seminar Series, 11 July, University of Luton (www.scie.org.uk/publications/misc/tswr/seminar6/brodie.asp).

Smith, D. (2000) *The limits of positivism revisited*, ESRC Theorising Social Work Research Seminar Series, 27 April (www.scie.org.uk/publications/misc/tswr/seminar5/smith.asp).

Box 3e: Using theory to think critically about social work and risk
Elaine Sharland

Risk is core business for social work policy and practice, but has been less critically researched or theorised in social work than in other disciplines. With this in mind, in 2010 the guest editors of a special issue of the *British Journal of Social Work* invited contributions on the theme of 'Social work and risk: critical perspectives'. The resulting collection of 15 papers demonstrates some of the diverse roles for theory in social work research, as the following four examples illustrate.

France et al (2010) note that there has been a range of interventions funded by the UK government, aimed at reducing the 'risk factors' that affect young people's lives. Some of these interventions have been evaluated, with their hypotheses tested deductively and successful outcomes shown. But France and colleagues criticise the assumptions that risk factors and their causes can be extracted from understanding their developmental pathways in social and cultural contexts. Instead, they present case study evidence supporting the holistic 'Pathways to prevention' model for promoting young people's well-being. The model and their appraisal of it are guided by theory, drawn from psychology and sociology, which places children's development and the risks they encounter in their environmental contexts. The authors elaborate this theory inductively, from the evidence they draw from practice.

Other authors also bring theory from related disciplines to inform their social work research and critique of risk-related policy and practice. Broadhurst et al (2010) draw on ethical philosophy, social and identity theories to argue that social work decision making about risk is a practical–moral activity that is situated, negotiated and complex. Using this frame of reference, they examine social workers' accounts of their own practice, concluding that the 'bureaucratic–instrumental' approach of risk management policy does not capture practice realities. Through dialogical exchange between theory and research evidence, they develop the concept of the 'informal logics of risk management', which in turn is ripe for further theorisation and research. Stanford (2010) explores similar territory, but begins with post-modern theories, about risk as the defining motif of contemporary society and the instrument of 'governmentality' regulating people's identities and behaviour. Working inductively from rich interview data, she develops a conceptual model of how social workers construct multiple, nuanced 'risk identities' for their clients and themselves. These enable social workers to resist the 'climate of conservatism' and take moral risks to do the right thing by their clients.

By contrast, Macdonald and Macdonald (2010) strongly support theory testing through rigorous empirical research as the basis for evidence-based practice. Their paper critiques policy assumptions that risk is calculable, and policy preoccupations with 'low-probability, high-cost' outcomes such as fatal child abuse. They draw on evidence and theory about decision making, judgement and error, to advocate for a 'return to uncertainty' as the route to 'intelligent risk management' in social work. But unlike other authors who also highlight uncertainty, they reject critical theories that replace the idea of 'scientific risk evaluation' with notions of 'situated judgement' or 'complexity'. Instead, they argue that social work resources should be concentrated on targeted, positive and rigorously evaluated interventions with wider populations than those thought to be highest risk. Their paper, and others, in contrast, illustrate what is most important and exciting about the relationship between theory, research and practice in social work: it can be controversial, it should be productive, and it is always a matter of judgement.

Question for discussion
• How have theories about risk helped research to shed light on social work practice?

References
Broadhurst, K., Hall, C., Wastell, D., White, S. and Pithouse, A. (2010) 'Risk, instrumentalism and the humane project in social work: identifying the informal logics of risk', *British Journal of Social Work*, vol 40, no 4, pp 1046-64.

France, A., Freiberg, K. and Homel, H. (2010) 'Towards a holistic prevention paradigm for children and young people', *British Journal of Social Work*, vol 40, no 4, pp 1192-210.

Macdonald, G. and Macdonald, K. (2010) 'Safeguarding: a case for intelligent risk management', *British Journal of Social Work*, vol 40, no 4, pp 1174-91.

Stanford, S. (2010) '"Speaking back" to fear: responding to the moral dilemmas of risk in social work practice', *British Journal of Social Work*, vol 40, no 4, pp 1065-80.

Further reading
Warner, J. and Sharland, E. (eds) (2010) 'Risk and social work: critical perspectives', *British Journal of Social Work Special Issue*, vol 40, no 4.

Webb, S. (2006) *Social work in a risk society: Social and political perspectives*, Basingstoke: Palgrave Macmillan.

Methodological issues and approaches

Detailed contents

4.1 Introduction

This chapter discusses key methodological issues, approaches and concerns that are related to, but which also transcend, quantitative and qualitative approaches to social policy and social work research. The chapter is divided into three parts.

Part One: Quantitative and qualitative research. In this introductory part of the chapter we examine the nature of, and debate about, *quantitative* and *qualitative* research, and how and why quantitative and qualitative methods may sometimes be combined (*integrated*), and *mixed methods* adopted.

Part Two: Approaches. In this part of the chapter we examine several *approaches* to social policy and social work research, including *feminist research, 'race' and ethnicity, user involvement in research, action research and cooperative inquiry, evaluation research, comparative research, post-structuralist perspectives, practitioner research, psychosocial research* and *unobtrusive methods*.

While the approaches have something in common, they each, nonetheless, offer a different stance on investigating and understanding the social world, and raise important issues and challenges for research in social policy and social work.

Part Three: Using existing research. Here we examine a number of uses of published research and data that already exist and which have usually been produced by other researchers. These include *secondary analysis, systematic reviews, reviewing and synthesising diverse evidence* and the *archiving* of data.

Throughout the chapter we illustrate these issues, approaches and themes by the use of a wide range of examples drawn from social work and social policy research.

PART ONE: QUANTITATIVE AND QUALITATIVE RESEARCH

4.2 The nature of quantitative and qualitative research

Alan Bryman and Saul Becker

The distinction between **quantitative** and **qualitative** research has had widespread currency in the social sciences for many years (particularly in sociology), but started to become a major area of debate and discussion in the late 1960s and early 1970s. Until then, *qualitative* research had occupied a position of near inferiority with respect to the far more pervasive and more revered *quantitative* methods. Qualitative methods were seen merely as different from quantitative ones, and rarely warranted more than a brief discussion in research methods textbooks of the time, wherein they were typically described in rather unfavourable terms.

What is significant about the growing use of the distinction between quantitative and qualitative research and the very considerable increase in discussion about the latter is that qualitative research came to be seen as a coherent alternative to quantitative research. Each can be seen as having a distinct cluster of concerns and preoccupations. Those associated with **quantitative** research can be viewed in the following terms (Bryman, 2012):

- *Measurement:* quantitative researchers seek to provide rigorous measures of the concepts that drive their research. Thus, there is often a great deal of concern in texts on quantitative research about how to *operationalise* concepts. The quantitative researcher searches for *indicators* to act as measures that can stand for or point towards the underlying concept. The very idea of a *variable* – an attribute on which people vary – which is so central to quantitative research, is indicative of this preoccupation with measurement. The emphasis on the measurement of prior concepts reflects a *deductive* approach to the relationship between theory and research (see also Sections 3.4 and 3.5).
- *Causality:* there is a concern to demonstrate causal relationships between variables, in other words, to show what factors influence people's behaviour, attitudes and beliefs. This preoccupation with causality can be seen in the widespread use of the terms *independent variable* and *dependent variable* to describe variables that, respectively, influence and are influenced by other variables.
- *Generalisation:* quantitative researchers invariably seek to establish that their findings apply more widely than the confines of their specific research context. Thus, there tends to be a concern to show that findings are representative of a wider population and this is responsible for the preoccupation in many research methods texts with *sampling* procedures that maximise the possibility of generating a representative sample (see also Chapter Five).
- *Replication:* one of the main ways in which the scientific orientation of quantitative research is most apparent is the frequent reference to the suggestion that the researcher

should follow clearly explicated procedures so that a study is reproducible. As in the natural sciences, it is believed to be important for a study to be capable of being checked by someone else, in case it was poorly conducted or the biases of the researcher were allowed to intrude into the results of the investigation.

Box 4a provides an illustration of these concerns in quantitative research, by focusing on one published study of the characteristics of Incapacity Benefit claimants and their routes into becoming recipients.

Box 4a: Quantitative research: an example
Alan Bryman and Saul Becker

The study covered here was first encountered in *Box 3c* (Section 3.3). In that box, Kemp and Davidson's (2009) use of the literature in connection with their article on gender differences in routes into Incapacity Benefit was examined. In a subsequent article (Kemp and Davidson, 2010), the authors report the results from the same research, and from follow-up interviews with a subsample of the original sample. The follow-up means that the study reported by Kemp and Davidson (2010) is a 'longitudinal' design, a type of research design discussed later in Section 5.3. The authors outline three research questions:

> First, who returned to work and what are the factors that were associated with that outcome? Second, among those recent claimants who did not return to work, what distinguished those who regarded themselves as being permanently off work due to sickness or disability from those who did not? Third, how employable are people who neither returned to work nor were permanently off sick, and did their employability get worse over time? (Kemp and Davidson, 2010, p 205)

In order to investigate these issues, a structured interview survey was conducted with 1,843 new Incapacity Benefit claimants. This sample constituted a stratified probability sample of new claimants. Claimants were stratified by region and by local authority unemployment rate. This stratification was meant to enhance the representativeness of the sample. The interviews were conducted by computer-assisted personal interview and a response rate of 56% was achieved. Six months after their participation in the survey (referred to by the authors as the 'baseline survey'), follow-up interviews were conducted by computer-assisted telephone interview with 74% of those claimants who had agreed in the baseline survey to be re-interviewed.

The authors developed a measure of 'work commitment' in order to help answer their research questions. This measure was made up of each claimant's degree of agreement with each of four statements. This style of questioning in surveys is known as Likert scaling (see Section 5.2). One of the statements was: 'Having a job is very important to me'. Interviewees had to indicate their degree of agreement with each statement on a five-point scale going from 'agree strongly' to 'disagree strongly'. The findings from this scale allowed the researchers to shed light on the first research question. For example, as Kemp and Davidson observe, it might be expected that one factor behind some claimants interviewed in the baseline survey returning to work by the time of the follow-up was that they had greater work commitment than those described by the authors as 'potential workers' and that the former have greater work commitment. In fact, that did not prove to be the case, and as the authors observe, 'this finding does question the policy assumption behind ESA [Employment and Support Allowance] about the lack of work aspirations among recent IB [Incapacity Benefit] claimants who have not returned to work but are not permanently sick or disabled' (Kemp and Davidson, 2010, p 212).

The authors examined the factors that were behind some claimants being in paid work by the time of the follow-up survey. Improvement in the health condition was a key factor for both men and women. This might seem obvious, but as Kemp and Davidson (2010) observe, not everyone whose condition had improved or who no longer had a condition had returned to work. The authors also found that 'closeness to the labour market was an important factor in who returned to work' (2010, p 218).

This study typified quantitative research in its preoccupation with *measurement* as a route to understanding. The authors generated measures of a wide range of variables. They developed indicators of concepts such as 'work commitment' to provide a scale to measure this concept. *Causality* is clearly in evidence in that the researchers were keen to establish why some people were in work by the time of the follow-up, whereas others were not. The researchers were also keen to establish a sample that would be representative of new claimants in Great Britain, and to this end used a stratified probability sampling approach of the kind described in Section 5.4. Finally, replication of this study would be reasonably straightforward since the procedures for conducting the research and the measurement of the main concepts is clearly outlined. However, if a replication were conducted, say, 10 years after the original study, it would be difficult to establish whether any differences in results between Kemp and Davidson's study and the replication were due to a problem with the original study or to such factors as changes in the policy context, or in the social context of claiming. In fact, it is likely that we would *expect* differences given the many changes that are likely to occur in policy and society at large.

References

Kemp, P.A. and Davidson, J. (2009) 'Gender differences among new claimants of incapacity benefit', *Journal of Social Policy*, vol 38, pp 589-606.

Kemp, P.A. and Davidson, J. (2010) 'Employability trajectories among new claimants of Incapacity Benefit', *Policy Studies*, vol 31, pp 203-21.

By contrast, **qualitative** research is seen as distinctive in the following respects:

- *Focus on actors' meanings:* qualitative researchers aim to understand the behaviour, values, beliefs, and so on of the people they study from the perspective of the subjects themselves. This tendency reflects a commitment that researchers should not impose their own understandings of what is going on.
- *Description and emphasis on context:* if you read an article or monograph based on qualitative research, it is difficult not to be struck by the attention to detail that is often revealed. There is frequently a rich account of the people and the environment. This is not to say that qualitative researchers are unconcerned with explanation, but that they provide detailed descriptions of the research setting. One of the chief reasons

for the detailed description of research settings is so that behaviour and beliefs can be understood in the specific context of the research setting. The meaning of events is, therefore, to be sought in the prevailing value system and structures that are possibly unique to the setting being studied.

- *Process:* there is a tendency for social life to be viewed in terms of unfolding processes so that events are depicted as interconnected over time and not as disparate.
- *Flexibility:* much qualitative research is relatively unstructured so that the researcher is more likely to uncover actors' meanings and interpretations rather than impose his or her own understandings. The lack of structure has the additional advantage that the general strategy is flexible, so that if the researcher encounters unexpected events that offer a promising line of enquiry, a new direction can be absorbed and followed up.
- *Emergent theory and concepts:* typically, concepts and the development of theory emerge out of the process of data collection rather than appearing at the outset of an investigation, which is what occurs in quantitative research. This preference for an *inductive approach* reflects the predilection among qualitative researchers for interpretation to take place in subjects' own terms.

Box 4b provides an illustration of these concerns in qualitative research, by focusing on a published study of social work practitioners' and managers' perspectives on the use of research to inform practice.

Box 4b: Qualitative research: an example
Harry Ferguson

A good example of qualitative research in social work and social policy is a New Zealand study by Liz Beddow (2011) of social workers' experiences of engaging in research and using research findings, or 'evidence', in their work, called 'Investing in the future: social workers talk about research'. The choice of this study is particularly appropriate here as it not only offers insights into why and how qualitative research is done, but also provides some interesting findings on how research is perceived and the factors influencing its adoption by practitioners and managers.

The article begins from a recognition that, internationally, there has been a strong emphasis in recent years 'on developing evidence-based or evidence-led practice in social work' (p 558). Increased demand for research-informed practice has stemmed from pressure on practitioners and policy makers to be more accountable by making explicit the knowledge on which their decisions are based. How to use scarce resources requires information or 'evidence' about 'what works' when intervening into the lives of service users and communities (see also Sections 1.5 and 1.6). The article points out that the notion of 'evidence' is contested in social work and social policy, as what counts as 'evidence', and how that knowledge is arrived at, is much debated. One view is that, for instance, a practitioner writing about his or her experience in one or more cases is a valid contribution to knowledge. Similarly, service users writing about their experience of services constitutes valid evidence for practice (see Sections 1.6 and 4.8). Another view is that it is only possible to produce reliable evidence through scientifically conducted research. Here, the emphasis tends to be on designing studies with control groups, for instance, where the actual impact of interventions and whether it 'works' can be measured (see Section 5.3). The article considers these debates, and focuses on the main aim of the study which was to explore the experiences and views of social work staff on evidence, and the extent to which research informs practice (on the debate about evidence, see also Webb, 2001; Gilgun, 2005; Berger, 2010; and Section 1.5 in this volume).

The research was based on one-to-one *interviews* with 17 'social workers, professional leaders and managers' (p 562), and group interviews (known as *focus groups*) with another 40 social work professionals. The one-to-one interviews were semi-structured, which means that the researcher had a list of pre-prepared questions that were framed in a manner most likely to produce data concerning the research question(s). This is often referred to as an *interview guide*. While the questions provide some structure and a list of topics to be covered, a flexible research process is followed which permits the interviewee to introduce information in whatever order best suits what they wish to say at times of their choosing (for a fuller discussion, see Section 6.8). Six focus groups took place. What such groups can add is the benefit of group interaction and the way in which a consensus emerges or debates tend to ensue (see Section 6.11). As would be expected from any well-written study, it provides detail on the make-up of the sample of participants: 80% were female ($n=33$), and, in age, 60% were aged between 30 and 50. Of these New Zealand-based social services employees, 80% are described as 'Pakeha (European)', followed by 10% ($n=4$), Pasifika (7%) and 2.4% ($n=1$) were Chinese. The fact that 2.4% amounts to just one participant shows how the point of using quantification in qualitative research is *not* to show statistical evidence but to provide for a profile of the sample and its possible implications in terms of the findings. The primary aim of working with relatively small samples of participants is to be able to explore in depth their experiences and the meanings they attach to them. Thus, a great deal of the study is devoted to quotations from the participants concerning the key themes identified. No effort was made to recruit a representative sample of social work staff. The participants were volunteers who responded to a general call for people to participate in the study. This is an appropriate way of doing research as long as the researcher is explicit about any possible biases or limitations that arise from the make-up of the sample. It means that the findings cannot be seen as generalisable to all social workers or agencies. In this instance, a researcher would speculate that those who volunteered may be especially interested in research, while those who did not put themselves forward may be indifferent to it. In reality, it may be that they do have an interest in research but felt that they just did not have time to get involved. Meanwhile, the cooperative participant may wish to be involved so that they can express critical views about the relevance of research, not necessarily because they wish to enthusiastically support it. In any event, what it is possible to claim from the findings is that the issues and patterns that emerge illuminate some aspects of some social workers' experiences under particular conditions.

The study found that there was general agreement among social services staff that they needed to be well informed, but often there was too little time to engage with research to update knowledge. This extended to barriers to social workers either conducting their own research or being allowed to grant researchers access to them to be part of research studies. Managers were so focused on service delivery goals that they did not regard social workers as having valid research activities to pursue. There was awareness among some participants of the need to make some form of inquiry into practice and evaluation a priority, and this was often linked to the need for raised expectations of social workers' skills and focus. The view here was that 'greater social worker participation and analysis of data were *investments* into the future' (p 564).

Most of the participants were aware of the arguments for measuring the outcomes of interventions based on a scientifically driven notion of 'evidence-based practice'. Some supported it, but more questioned it, due to 'their value driven desire for person-centred or participatory approaches to social inquiry' (p 566). Social workers were found to lack confidence and skills in research. Lack of time due to high caseloads and the absence of encouragement and support to engage in reading and writing were regarded as major impediments. There was insufficient 'thinking space', and rather than seeking knowledge to engage in critiques of their agency or practice, managers and practitioners mostly sought learning opportunities to meet immediate needs on the job and build their expertise. Scholarly activity was not regarded as an ethical imperative and was largely remote from the workplace: 'As a consequence, social work knowledge built from the ground up remains hidden. The desire to utilise the knowledge gained through experience and reflections on successes as well as failures was a feature of this study...' (p 568).

The qualitative nature of the study made it possible to go into some depth to establish front-line workers' and managers' experiences of, and relationships to, research. It provides some useful insights into the barriers and enablers that make a difference in whether research is utilised in practice. A key message to emerge is that being a research-informed practitioner is not simply a matter of individual choice and character. It is heavily influenced by how social workers 'largely lack the resources – time, money, access, skills and confidence – to ensure their work is underpinned by scholarship and research' (p 572). Strategies are needed to grow research confidence and capacity in the practitioner community, which need to include partnerships between them and research teams to encourage scholarly activity, and to grow a research agenda that is responsive to the concerns of practitioners and the needs of service users.

References

Beddow, L. (2011) 'Investing in the future: social workers talk about research', *British Journal of Social Work*, vol 41, pp 557-75.

Berger, R. (2010) 'EBP: practitioners in search of evidence', *Journal of Social Work*, vol 10, no 2, pp 175-91.

Gilgun, J.E. (2005) 'The four cornerstones of evidence-based practice in social work', *Research on Social Work Practice*, vol 15, no 1, pp 52-61.

Webb, S. (2001) 'Some considerations on the validity of evidence-based practice in social work', *British Journal of Social Work*, vol 31, no 1, pp 57-79.

Further reading

Butler, I. (2003) 'Doing good research and doing it well: ethical awareness and the production of social work research', *Social Work Education*, vol 22, no 1, pp 19-30.

Gilgun, J. and Abrams, L. (2002) 'The nature and usefulness of qualitative social work research: some thoughts and an invitation to dialogue', *Qualitative Social Work*, vol 1, no 1, pp 39-55.

Padgett, D. (2008) *Qualitative methods in social work research*, London: Sage Publications.

Shaw, I. (2011) *Evaluating in practice* (2nd edn), Aldershot: Ashgate.
Shaw, I. and Gould, N. (2001) *Qualitative research in social work*, London: Sage Publications.
The journal *Qualitative Social Work* is well worth consulting as it mostly carries articles
devoted, not surprisingly, to qualitative research in social work.

Question for discussion

• What are the main axes of difference between quantitative and qualitative research?

Reference

Bryman, A. (2012) *Social research methods* (4th edn), Oxford: Oxford University Press.

Further reading

Bryman, A. (2012) *Social research methods* (4th edn), Oxford: Oxford University Press, Chapters
1, 2, 7 and 17.
Hammersley, M. (1996) 'The relationship between qualitative and quantitative research:
paradigm loyalty versus methodological eclecticism', in J.T.E. Richardson (ed) *Handbook of
research methods for psychology and the social sciences*, Leicester: BPS Books, pp 159-74.

4.3 The debate about quantitative and qualitative research
Alan Bryman and Saul Becker

At one level, any discussion about the nature of quantitative and qualitative research
would seem to be about *technical* issues to do with the suitability or relevance of either
stance in relation to a research question. However, discussions about the two research
strategies have been bound up with debates about whether they reflect differing, even
divergent, *epistemological* assumptions and commitments. This kind of discussion reflects a
view that any research method is inextricably bound to a particular philosophy about how
the social world ought to be studied. Such ruminations tie quantitative research and its
associated research designs and research methods (such as experiments and questionnaire
surveys) to **positivism**, which posits that social life can, and should, be studied according
to the canons of the scientific method with its emphasis on directly observable entities.
Similarly, qualitative research with its associated research designs and research methods
(such as participant observation and intensive interviewing) is rooted in contrary views
about how social life should be studied, such as **phenomenology**, which implies that
the fact that people are capable of thought, self-reflection and language necessitates an
alternative framework that ascribes priority to the actor's perspective. This perception
of research methods can be seen very clearly in statements such as the following:

> ... the choice and adequacy of a method embodies a variety of assumptions
> regarding the nature of knowledge and the methods through which that
> knowledge can be obtained, as well as a root set of assumptions about the

nature of the phenomena to be investigated. (Morgan and Smircich, 1980, p 491)

According to such a view, the decision to engage in a research method, such as participant observation, represents not simply a choice of data-gathering technique but a commitment to an epistemological position that is antithetical to positivism, and that recognises the uniqueness of people and society as objects of study.

This kind of view of research methods has led some commentators to claim that *mixed methods research*, which combines quantitative and qualitative research (the focus of the next section), is not genuinely possible. A participant observer may collect questionnaire data to gain information about a slice of social life that is not amenable to participant observation, but this does not represent an integration of quantitative and qualitative research because the epistemological positions in which participant observation and questionnaires are grounded are incompatible views of how social reality should be studied. This position conceives of quantitative and qualitative research as paradigms (following Kuhn's [1970] analysis of revolutions in science) in which epistemological assumptions, values and methods are inextricably interwoven and are incompatible between paradigms (see, for example, Guba, 1985). Therefore, when a researcher combines the use of participant observation with a questionnaire, he or she is not really integrating quantitative and qualitative research, since they are incompatible: the integration is only at a superficial level and within a single paradigm. Smith and Heshusius, for example, decry the integration of research strategies because it disregards the assumptions underlying techniques and transforms 'qualitative inquiry into a procedural variation of quantitative inquiry' (1986, p 8).

One problem with this strapping together of epistemology and method is that it is not easy to sustain. Investigators who have attempted to explore connections between methods, on the one hand, and epistemological or theoretical positions, on the other, have often found that such supposed relationships are at best unclear and at worst simply wrong (see Bryman, 2012, for a review of this evidence). A classic participant observation study such as Whyte's (1943) *Street corner society* contains many characteristics of a supposedly positivist approach, such as an exploration of the connection between bowling scores and group social position.

Linking epistemology and method also implies that researchers approach research problems with a host of epistemological commitments which determine their data collection strategy, rather than in terms of the fit between the problem and method, the resources available to them and methodological exemplars. Such technical and practical considerations are likely to loom very large in the way in which a researcher tackles a problem, and authors of textbooks in social research methodology essentially advocate that this should be the case.

In other words, as several writers have argued (see, for example, Hammersley, 1992; Bryman, 2012), not only is it important not to exaggerate the differences between quantitative and qualitative research so that they appear to be warring positions, it is also important to recognise that research methods are not necessarily rooted to epistemological assumptions. Research methods can be far more free-floating than is generally appreciated. This recognition is crucial to the issue of combining quantitative and qualitative research, since it implies that the barriers to integrating the two research strategies are far less pronounced than is often suggested by writers who see methods as tied to particular epistemological positions. For many mixed methods researchers, particularly among those working in applied fields like evaluation research, one approach has been to adopt an essentially pragmatist position which entails suspending epistemological and ontological considerations, and using whichever tools – quantitative or qualitative – that will allow the study's research questions to be answered, although this pragmatist position has its critics too (see Greene and Hall, 2010).

Question for discussion

• To what extent are research methods inseparable from particular epistemological positions?

References

Bryman, A. (2012) *Social research methods* (4th edn), Oxford: Oxford University Press.

Greene, J.C. and Hall, J.N. (2010) 'Dialectics and pragmatism: being of consequence', in A. Tashakkori and C. Teddlie (eds) *SAGE handbook of mixed methods in social and behavioral research*, Los Angeles, CA: Sage Publications, pp 119-44.

Guba, E.G. (1985) 'The context of emergent paradigm research', in Y.S. Lincoln (ed) *Organization theory and inquiry: The paradigm revolution*, Beverley Hills, CA: Sage Publications, pp 79-104.

Hammersley, M. (1992) 'Deconstructing the qualitative-quantitative divide', in M. Hammersley (ed) *What's wrong with ethnography?*, London: Routledge, pp 159-73.

Kuhn, T.S. (1970) *The structure of scientific revolutions* (2nd edn), Chicago, IL: University of Chicago Press.

Morgan, G. and Smircich, L. (1980) 'The case for qualitative research', *Academy of Management Review*, vol 5, pp 491-500.

Smith, J.K. and Heshusius, L. (1986) 'Closing down the conversation: the end of the quantitative-qualitative debate among educational enquirers', *Educational Researcher*, vol 15, pp 4-12.

Whyte, W.F. (1943) *Street corner society*, Chicago, IL: Chicago University Press.

Further reading

Bryman, A. (1984) 'The debate about quantitative and qualitative research: a question of method or epistemology?', *British Journal of Sociology*, vol 35, pp 75-92.

Bryman, A. (2012) *Social research methods* (4th edn), Oxford: Oxford University Press, Chapter 26.

Greene, J.C. and Hall, J.N. (2010) 'Dialectics and pragmatism: being of consequence', in A. Tashakkori and C. Teddlie (eds) *SAGE handbook of mixed methods in social and behavioral research*, Los Angeles, CA: Sage Publications, pp 119-44.

Hammersley, M. (1992) 'Deconstructing the qualitative-quantitative divide', in M. Hammersley (ed) *What's wrong with ethnography?*, London: Routledge, pp 159-73.

4.4 Combining quantitative and qualitative research
Alan Bryman and Saul Becker

Writers and researchers who have been less wedded to the epistemological version of the debate about quantitative and qualitative research (see Section 4.3) have been very open to the possibility that the two research strategies can be fruitfully combined. Indeed, since the early 1990s, studies that combine the two have become quite numerous, whereas before then it was relatively unusual to find such work. In fact, the frequency with which **mixed methods research** (research that combines quantitative and qualitative approaches) occurs has even begun to cast doubt in some researchers' eyes about the credibility of the distinction.

There are a number of different ways in which mixed methods research is employed by social researchers (Bryman, 2006, 2012, Chapter 26). The discussion below only deals with some of the more prominent ways.

Triangulation: the idea behind triangulation is that the credibility of findings is greater when more than one source of data is employed to tackle an issue. The term was originally devised in connection with quantitative research, where it was argued that if a measure of a concept is devised and then cross-checked against another measure of the same concept, our faith in the findings will be greater. This notion has been extended into mixed methods research, where it is often suggested that if quantitative and qualitative studies can mutually confirm each other, we will have more robust findings in which we will have greater faith.

Qualitative research facilitates quantitative research: this second idea has been one of the most common justifications for combining the two research strategies, especially in the early years of mixed methods research. The most common way of thinking about it is to suggest that qualitative research, because it is relatively unstructured, can provide quantitative researchers with a steady stream of hypotheses. Moreover, since qualitative researchers rarely employ random sampling procedures of the kind discussed in Section 5.4, it is unlikely that we can generalise findings from it to populations. Also, it was sometimes suggested that since quantitative researchers generate 'hard' data (because the data are quantitative), we would get a better understanding of how much faith could be placed in the qualitative findings if they were treated as hypotheses that are subsequently confirmed by quantitative research. This kind of argument, which attaches a kind of epistemological priority to quantitative research, is less often encountered nowadays, since qualitative research is held in higher regard than was the case before the 1980s. Another way in which qualitative research is sometimes treated as being helpful in facilitating quantitative research is that it can provide quantitative researchers with ideas for structured interviews or questionnaire questions and the correct language that should be employed (see, for example, Nassar-McMillan and Borders, 2002).

Quantitative research facilitates qualitative research: the most common form of this context for mixed methods research is mentioned in ***Box 4c***, where an online survey was employed (among other uses) as a means of purposively sampling social policy academics for later qualitative semi-structured interviews. In this way, individuals can be selected in terms of characteristics that are relevant to the qualitative research.

Quantitative and qualitative research deal with different research questions or issues within a project: this fourth approach to combining quantitative and qualitative research is probably the one that occurs most frequently nowadays. This orientation to mixed methods research recognises that quantitative and qualitative research have different strengths and purposes, and that a better overall picture will often emerge when the two are combined. It can be seen in ***Box 4c*** where the two research strategies had different roles in relation to the investigation. Another interesting example is a study by Taylor-Gooby (2001) in which he takes up the idea of a 'risk society' that was a significant influence on New Labour thinking, and explores its implications for social welfare. As Taylor-Gooby observes, the implications of such thinking are substantial given their emphasis on a reduced role for government and greater individual responsibility. These issues were tackled in two ways. First, four focus groups made up of between eight and twelve participants were conducted. The discussions were concerned with 'how people thought about risk, uncertainty and security in their daily lives' (Taylor-Gooby, 2001, p 200). Taylor-Gooby then went on to analyse the first seven waves of data collected from the British Household Panel Survey (BHPS) (see **Box 5b** for a brief description of the BHPS) 'to examine the way in which some of the risks of modern social life affect particular groups' (Taylor-Gooby, 2001, p 200). He concludes:

> The focus groups produced suggestive evidence that individuals are aware of the new uncertainties associated with risk society, but that there are differences across social groups in people's confidence in their capacity to manage them and their potential need for state support.... The analysis of the BHPS shows that while most people regard the future with some optimism, many have difficulty in predicting their future circumstances accurately. (Taylor-Gooby, 2001, p 209)

In this way, through the use of mixed methods research, different aspects of the phenomenon being researched could be explored.

Qualitative research enhances quantitative research or vice versa: this fifth approach entails building on or augmenting qualitative findings with quantitative data or building on or augmenting quantitative findings with qualitative data. **Box 4c** provides an example of a research project in which the qualitative data allowed an elaboration or enhancement of the quantitative data gleaned from an online survey.

Box 4c: Mixed methods research: an illustration
Alan Bryman, Saul Becker and Joe Sempik

This box outlines the research methods employed in a study by Becker, Bryman and Sempik (2006; see also Bryman et al, 2008) of the criteria that social policy researchers employ in evaluating the quality of social policy research. The issue of quality criteria for quantitative research and for qualitative research is discussed later in Sections 5.2 and 6.2 respectively. The growth in the use of mixed methods research, which combines quantitative and qualitative research, has fostered interest in how the quality of such research should be appraised as well.

A web-based survey of social policy researchers was conducted. This was done by sending an email to members of a Social Policy discussion list and to members of the Social Policy Association (SPA) (the two memberships overlap considerably) notifying them of the questionnaire, how to find it and inviting people to answer it. A total of 251 social policy researchers completed the online questionnaire. A commercial online survey firm (Survey

Galaxy, www.surveygalaxy.com) provided the platform for the administration of the survey. (A discussion of web-based surveys can be found in Section 5.7.) One of the main ways in which social policy researchers' criteria for assessing the contribution of research were explored was to present respondents with 35 possible criteria, each of which they were asked to classify in terms of degree of importance. The findings are shown in *Table 4.1*.

Table 4.1: Rank order of quality criteria that social policy academics think are important when judging published research

Rank order		Respondents classifying criterion as 'Very Important'	
	(n = 251, except where otherwise stated)	Number	%
1	The research is written in ways that are accessible to the appropriate audiences	208	82.9
2	The research designed adopted clearly addresses the research question(s)	207	82.5
3	The ways in which data were collected and analysed are transparent (n=250)	197	78.8
4	An explicit account of the research process (design and method(s) and analysis of data is provided	192	76.5
5	The research makes a contribution to knowledge	173	68.9
6	The informed consent was given	167	66.5
7	The safety of participants has been assured (n=250)	166	66.1
8	The research conforms to appropriate ethical codes and protocols (eg SRA/BSA/ Research Governance Framework for Health and Social Care)	145	57.8
9	The safety of researchers has been assured	126	50.2
10	Data are stored and protected according to established protocols and legislation	116	46.2
11	The researcher has sought to be as objective as possible (n=247)	108	43.7
12	An explicit account of the ethics and governance of the research is provided	106	42.2
13	The research should help achieve better outcomes for 'service users' of social policy (n=246)	101	41.1
14	The research has the potential to develop the capacity of policy makers and/or practitioners to make informed and ethical decisions (n=249)	99	39.8
15	The research has potential value for policy makers (n=250)	96	38.4
16	The researcher provides a clear statement of his/her value position (n=249)	95	38.2
17	The research has the potential to develop the capacity of policy makers and/or practitioners to take appropriate actions (n=249)	91	36.5
18	The research has potential value for 'service users' (individuals or groups at the receiving end of social policy interventions) (n=250)	91	36.4
19	Research participants have been given the findings of the research study (n=250)	90	36.0
20	Details are provided about the funding body which commissioned the research	90	35.9
21	Service users have been consulted about the research aims and objectives (n=249)	89	35.7
22	The research has produced recommendations for policy and/or practice (n=247)	87	35.2
23	The research achieves an effective synthesis between theory and knowledge (n=248)	81	32.7
24	The research is informed by a theoretical position (n=249)	79	31.7
25	The research has potential value for practitioners (n=249)	77	30.9
26	The research should help to bring about change (n=247)	69	27.9
27	Service users have been involved appropriately in all stages of the research (n=249)	62	24.9
28	The research has the potential to empower 'service users' (n=248)	53	21.4
29	The research makes a contribution to theory (n=250)	39	15.6
30	The research is published in a prestigious refereed academic journal (n=250)	33	13.2
31	The research provides good value for money (n=250)	32	12.8
32	A randomised controlled design was used (n=243)	31	12.8
33	A publication deriving from the research is cited in prestigious refereed academic journals (n=249)	29	11.6
34	The research is published in a professional journal/magazine (n=249)	19	7.6
35	The research is published as a chapter in a book (n=248)	6	2.4

Source: Becker, Bryman and Sempik (2006)

In addition, semi-structured interviews were conducted by telephone with 28 of the survey respondents who had indicated that they were prepared to be interviewed. In fact, 90 respondents had agreed to be interviewed. Purposive sampling (see Section 6.6) was used to select the 28 interviewees. The criteria for selection were derived from the respondents' different orientations to research and quality in social policy research. The interview questions invited participants to elaborate in greater detail than was possible in the survey, on the quality criteria that they employed. In particular, a question was included in the interviews about quality criteria in mixed methods research as this was an issue that was explored in an open question in the e-survey but which did not produce a great deal of detail. The authors write:

> The semi-structured interviews were designed to allow a variety of issues to be explored in greater depth than was possible in the e-survey. In areas of methodology that have no or few agreed upon quality criteria, the ability to ask questions in an open manner is extremely valuable, as the questions are unlikely to lend themselves to the creation of fixed-choice options. Specifically in relation to the issues addressed in this article, the semi-structured interviews allowed for an enhancement of the survey findings. (Bryman et al, 2008, p 264; see also Bryman, 2006)

As regards the appraisal of the quality of mixed methods research in the social policy field, Bryman et al (2008) report that the e-survey revealed that social policy researchers want the quality of mixed methods research to be assessed using both quantitative and qualitative research criteria but that each component of a mixed methods study should be assessed using criteria appropriate to it. The semi-structured interviews were able to provide some information that complemented this finding. When asked to stipulate quality criteria for mixed methods research, three criteria stood out in interviewees' answers. First, the interviewees felt that the methods used should be appropriate to the research questions. This is consistent with the emphasis on research questions in Chapter Three. Second, they felt that the research methods should be transparent, so that it was clear how the research was conducted. The third criterion was that the quantitative and qualitative research elements should be integrated. It is sometimes argued that too often mixed methods researchers treat their quantitative and qualitative data as separate domains that are not brought together (see, for example, Bryman, 2006; O'Cathain et al, 2008). A failure to integrate quantitative and qualitative findings was clearly viewed negatively by the interviewees. In addition, a fourth criterion figured in some of the interviews but not as prominently as the other three: mixed methods researchers should provide a rationale for their use of both quantitative and qualitative research. In other words, it was felt that the justification for conducting both quantitative and qualitative research should not be presumed to be self-evident. Mixed methods researchers need to justify its use, just as they would with any other research strategy.

This, then, was a project that employed mixed methods research to examine aspects of judgements about the assessment of the quality of research in the social policy field. The semi-structured interviews allowed the researchers to provide more in-depth and detailed accounts of the assessment of quality than was feasible in the online questionnaire. Specifically in connection with the issue of the appraisal of research quality, while the e-survey findings provided information about researchers' views of the broad contours of the issue, even though open questions were asked as well as closed ones, greater depth was required to provide a more detailed understanding of the issues, and this was provided by the semi-structured telephone interviews.

References

Becker, S., Bryman, A. and Sempik, J. (2006) *Defining 'quality' in social policy research: Views, perceptions and a framework for discussion*, Lavenham: Social Policy Association (www.lboro.ac.uk/research/ccfr/Publications/Defining_quality_in_social_policy_research.pdf).

Bryman, A. (2006) 'Integrating quantitative and qualitative research: how is it done?', *Qualitative Research*, vol 6, pp 97-113.

Bryman, A., Becker, S. and Sempik, J. (2008) 'Quality criteria for quantitative, qualitative and mixed methods research: the view from social policy', *International Journal of Social Research Methodology*, vol 11, pp 261-76.

O'Cathain, A., Murphy, E. and Nicholl, J. (2008) 'The quality of mixed methods studies in health services research', *Journal of Health Services Research and Policy*, vol 19, pp 92-8.

Research that integrates quantitative and qualitative research has not only become more common and accepted but has also helped to bridge the gulf that has sometimes pitched quantitative and qualitative researchers against each other. However, as with all forms of research, it is still the responsibility of researchers to ensure that their research methods are tailored to their research questions. Mixed methods research does not provide a short cut around this necessity.

Question for discussion

- Do the supposed epistemological issues that relate to quantitative and qualitative research mean that they cannot be combined?

References

Bryman, A. (2006) 'Integrating quantitative and qualitative research: how is it done?', *Qualitative Research*, vol 6, pp 97-113.

Bryman, A. (2012) *Social research methods* (4th edn), Oxford: Oxford University Press.

Nassar-McMillan, S.C. and Borders, L.D. (2002) 'Use of focus groups in survey item development', *Qualitative Report*, vol 7, no 1 (www.nova.edu/ssss/QR/QR7-1/nassar.html).

Taylor-Gooby, P. (2001) 'Risk, contingency and the third way: evidence from the BHPS and qualitative studies', *Social Policy and Administration*, vol 35, pp 195-211.

Further reading

Bryman, A. (2012) *Social research methods* (4th edn), Oxford: Oxford University Press, Chapter 27.

4.5 Being prepared: managing particular research methods

Alan Bryman and Saul Becker

In the previous sections we have discussed the nature of, and differences between, quantitative and qualitative research, and some of the issues to be considered when they are combined in mixed methods studies.

Quantitative and qualitative research methods each bring with them a distinct cluster of issues to do with research conduct, organisation and management. It is not feasible to cover every possible kind of contingency that relates to every research method, but in this section we try to bring out some relevant points. Before conducting any piece of research, be it qualitative, quantitative or mixed methods, researchers must be aware of, and be prepared for, the key issues and challenges that are associated with that approach and the method(s) selected to answer the research questions.

For example, with *survey* research, based on structured interviews (face-to-face or telephone), or postal or online questionnaires, an important consideration, once the final sample has been selected, is keeping track of who replies and who does not. All surveys result in non-response. This is a problem for researchers because it means that even if they have sampled randomly, they are likely to end up with a sample that is less representative than it might otherwise have been because those who decline may differ from those who do not. If the level of non-response can be kept low, there is a greater chance that the sample's representativeness will be less adversely affected.

In the case of postal and online questionnaire surveys, response rates are often very low so it is especially important to boost responses as far as possible. One way of boosting the response rate is to follow up respondents who have not replied. To do this the researcher will need to have some kind of identifying code on the questionnaire that will allow them to identify who has replied (and by implication, who has not). Many survey researchers follow up non-respondents after two to three weeks and again two to three weeks after that. This all means that the researcher needs to keep good records of returns.

Surveys employing a *longitudinal design* pose particular management issues with regard to keeping respondent attrition to a minimum. With panel designs, people may become tired of being regularly interviewed and need to be persuaded to continue their participation (birthday and seasonal greetings cards can help in this regard), but also keeping track of new members (children and new partners) and departing members (due to death or marriage break-up) of households needs to be borne in mind. With cohort studies, where there may be several years between interviews, keeping track becomes especially crucial so that members of the cohort are not lost forever to the study when they move home or where other changes take place.

When survey research involves more than one interviewer, a further management issue is that of ensuring that interviewers ask exactly the same questions in exactly the same order, and that they write down precisely what is said to them. Getting across the significance of such requirements is likely to require some training. If there is divergence in the asking and recording of questions, the validity of the variables will be jeopardised. A similar issue that arises in relation to *content analysis* is to ensure that the coding of textual material is checked so that validity is not undermined. Similarly, with *structured observation* it is important that there are checks on the allocation of codes to observed behaviour. Failure to manage the consistency of interviewing, of coding text or of recording behaviour will result in measures of questionable validity.

A further issue with *quantitative* research is the necessity to think about issues of data analysis early on. It is tempting to leave this phase until all the data have been collected but researchers need to think about what kinds of data they are likely to end up with as a consequence of asking questions in a certain way, and what kinds of analysis can be performed on them. Also, researchers need to be familiar with the kinds of statistical tools they can use so that they don't have to learn them at the last minute – when deadlines are possibly tight. An issue related to this is that researchers need to be familiar with the statistical software that they are going to use before the data begin to come in. This point applies also to *qualitative* researchers who intend to use a computer-assisted qualitative data analysis package (see Section 6.16). It is not a good idea to have to learn new software at the last minute when the researcher may be in a rush.

With *qualitative* research methods such as *semi-structured* and *unstructured interviewing* and *focus groups*, the standard advice is to record interviews and transcribe them. Two points stand out here. First, an interviewer needs to make sure that the recording hardware is up to the task in terms of the quality of the microphone and the recording quality of the machine, the batteries and the possible intrusion of external noise. In this respect, it is always a good idea to test out the equipment first. Also, the researcher needs to be prepared for the possibility that one or two interviewees will decline to be recorded, so it is necessary to go prepared with a notepad to take notes. Second, researchers should not underestimate how long transcription takes and the volume of paper it generates. A rule of thumb is to allow six hours of transcription for one hour of interview. Ten one-hour interviews mean 60 hours of transcription. However, if an interview is of limited value, it may be wise to transcribe just portions of the interview. Because a large volume of paper is quickly built up by a lot of transcription, it is probably best to begin analysis (coding) of the data as soon as possible to offset the feeling of being overwhelmed by the data, and so that if the analysis suggests new leads, these can be followed up while the fieldwork is ongoing.

In the case of *ethnography*, it is crucial to keep a record, often referred to as *field notes*, concerning observations and conversations. These need to be written up as soon as possible, so that key points and reflections are not forgotten, but preferably not in a way that will draw attention to the researcher so that people begin to feel self-conscious about being observed or drawn into conversations. Field notes should be as comprehensive as possible since they are likely to be the ethnographer's main source of data and can even be submitted to analysis through a computer software program.

Question for discussion

- Identify some of the main elements that require preparation for, and management of, when conducting: (a) a large postal questionnaire survey; (b) research using semi-structured interviews.

PART TWO: APPROACHES

4.6 Feminist research

Lesley Hoggart

There is no single model of feminist research, methodology, epistemology or research methods, and how and why feminists should undertake research has long been a matter of dialogue and debate among feminist researchers. Indeed, feminist research in the new century has become more diversified, as well as increasingly advocating multiple understandings of what is viewed as a complex social world (Olesen, 2007). Nevertheless, within a diverse body of research it is possible to identify some generally recognised common concerns.

The ways in which feminist researchers define feminism influences their methodological choices. A broad definition of feminism – such as *a position with the political aim of challenging discrimination against women and/or promoting greater equality between the sexes* – offers a positive, non-prescriptive approach for feminist researchers. Within this framework, feminist research would aim to add to our knowledge of discriminatory and oppressive structures, and be concerned with transforming gender relations. What has emerged over years of debate is not a blueprint, but a broad consensus about some guiding principles of feminist research (*Figure 4a*).

Figure 4a: Some principles of feminist research

1. Feminists value the different experiences, concerns and opinions of women.
2. Feminist research acknowledges the active presence of the researcher in the process of knowledge production.
3. Feminists try to overcome the subject–object divide that places the researcher as the expert subject gathering data and generating knowledge, and the researched as merely the object of the research endeavour. This involves addressing power relationships and seeking to combine the knowledge and experience of researchers and researched.
4. Feminist research (which can include research on men and by men) is politically for women and seeks to improve women's lives in some way. An important part of this may be sharing results with women whom the findings will benefit, and with the institutions responsible for policies.

The **Women, Risk and AIDS Project** (WRAP), a study into the sexual practices and beliefs of young women, has often been cited as a good example of feminist research. In-depth interviews gave a voice to young women, and the power relationship between the researcher and researched was acknowledged. The researchers located themselves as 'fallible' and subjective within the research process, and made the process of data analysis transparent by exploring the relationship between the contributions of the young people and the interpretations of the researchers:

> Our conception of gendered power relations made it necessary for us to interpret the young people's accounts, rather than acting as a conduit through which they could simply speak for themselves. (Holland et al, 1998, p 29)

They are therefore open about how their theoretical framework of gendered power relations shaped the way in which they interpreted the young people's stories of heterosexuality. The project examined the exercise of power in existing gender relations, identifying heterosexuality as male-dominated, and arguing that young women are under pressure to comply with this construction through 'the male in the head'. Finally, the researchers developed, and disseminated, policy recommendations aimed at empowering young women to take control of their sexual lives (Holland and Ramazanoglu, 1994; Holland et al, 1998).

Within the broad principles outlined above (not all of which are necessarily applied to each piece of feminist research), there is room for a wide variety of approaches, as, indeed, different feminists have proposed. There is also room for a range of research methods that can include both qualitative and quantitative approaches. Although many feminists favour qualitative research methods (such as unstructured interviews; see Section 6.8) that facilitate open, in-depth expression of women's experiences and views, others have argued that '[f]eminists should use any and every means available for investigating the condition of women in sexist society' (Stanley, 1990, p 12). One prominent feminist, Ann Oakley, has consciously sought to maintain a feminist research consciousness while utilising the 'gold standard' of quantitative research – the randomised controlled trial (RCT) (Oakley, 2005; see also Section 5.3 in this volume).

Feminist methodologies originally developed as feminists began to expose what they understood to be a sexist bias in traditional social research, and by disputing positivism's claim to objectivity (Harding, 1987; Eichler, 1988). The 'myth' of value-free research was thereby challenged by research in which the researchers' values and interpretations were acknowledged as central to the research process: 'Feminism is in the first place an attempt to insist upon the experience and very existence of women. To this extent it is most importantly a feature of an ideological conflict, and does not of itself attempt an "un-biased" or "value-free" methodology' (Roberts, 1981, p 15). This was an important part of a broader trend within social research that criticised positivism, questioned the search for 'truth' and explored the role of the researcher in the production of knowledge. The feminist critique also encompassed many areas of social science. In social policy, for example, an early feminist concern was to explain the gendered nature of existing welfare provision (Wilson, 1977; Dale and Foster, 1986; Pascall, 1986).

An early, and continuing, debate centres on the issue of subjectivity versus objectivity. While objectivity assumes that there is an objective reality – or truth – that researchers can capture, subjectivity points to the importance of subjective (that is, the researcher's) opinions and values in their generation of knowledge. A feminist methodology can involve an open acknowledgement of subjectivity. This is defended by pointing out that no research can be value free, and that to admit this at the outset is in fact a step towards more honest research (Roberts, 1981; Finch, 1991). The further, distinct claim that feminist research may be more objective than androcentric traditional research (that privileges a masculine point of view) because it produces less distorted knowledge was proposed by Harding (1987). Harding claimed that knowledge grounded in women's experience of struggles against male domination can produce a more complete knowledge of gendered social lives than that based only on men's experiences. This is a central claim of Feminist Standpoint that sought to develop new feminist knowledge of gendered social lives through 'women speaking their truth' (see Hartsock, 1997). The argument was that this produced a more complete knowledge, that was, therefore, closer to 'reality'.

Critics of Feminist Standpoint have argued that feminists should privilege subjectivity over objectivity, emotionality over rationality and experience over experiments, and not seek to capture 'reality' (Stanley and Wise, 1993). One problem with such an approach is that privileging subjective knowledge involves viewing reality as a matter of competing interpretations (an approach strongly associated with *post-modernism*; see Section 4.12). This can become so removed from practical concerns that it undermines the value of social research. It is particularly problematic in social policy and social work research, in which feminists are often seeking to understand, and change, the social world. A more promising approach is to attack the binary thinking behind the subjective–objective, qualitative–quantitative dichotomy and acknowledge that no research can be wholly objective (Ramazanoglu with Holland, 2002). What feminists can do is to make their interpretations clear, and to recognise that there is no way of producing knowledge that is problem-free.

Other debates include those around difference and diversity, representing 'others' in research, and what it means to be reflexive. Feminists have long argued for reflexive research, which involves researchers being aware of, and making visible, their own experiences and presence in the research process (Roberts, 1981; Stanley, 1990). More recently, it has been argued that it is not enough for feminist researchers to reveal themselves, but that they should seek to uncover what might be hidden secrets and silences, thus openly reflecting on the significance of their own identities for their research, and indicating how this may have influenced their behaviour in the field (Ryan-Flood and Gill, 2010). One paper, for example, reflects on the academic process of critiquing 'thinness' while personally 'wanting to be thin' (Throsby and Gimlin, 2010). Feminist reflections on many of these issues – particularly those concerning the relationships between researchers, their research and research participants – are also clearly intrinsic to considerations of what constitutes ethical research (Edwards and Mauther, 2002).

The growth of a number of different approaches to feminist research follows from a focus on women's experiences, and an understanding of the diversity of these experiences. Feminist researchers have become ever more sensitive to differences among women, including differences in power. Lesbian research, post-modernist feminism, post-colonial feminist thought, research based on the experiences of disabled women, and many more, have all contributed to a view of feminist research in which 'contending models of thought jostle, divergent methodological and analytical approaches compete, once clear theoretical differences blur, and divisions deepen, even as rapprochement occurs' (Olesen, 2007, p 312). Notwithstanding such diversity, the distinctiveness of feminist methodology can be seen in the relationship between epistemology and feminist politics: '[f]eminist research is politically *for* women, feminist knowledge has some grounding in women's *experiences*, and in how it *feels* to live in unjust gendered relationships' (Ramazanoglu with Holland, 2002, p 16; original emphasis).

Box 4d: The critical study of men, masculinities and welfare
Harry Ferguson

A significant development in the social sciences over the past 20 years has been the emergence of research about men and masculinities. In the past, research tended to be all about men's lives – at work, sport, in wars etc – to the exclusion of women, and in many respects children. Section 4.6 shows the ways in which the women's movement and feminist research challenged the power of men, and the assumption that they were the 'natural' leaders and that 'mankind' could refer to the experience of women as well as men. Growing numbers of social science researchers have built on this by not simply taking 'men' and 'masculinity' for granted and as 'natural', but studying in new critical ways the power structures and relationships that characterise men's lives and masculinities. This is helping to reveal further the nature of male privileges. But it is also showing the differences between men and how these are sustained by relationships of power, as well as reciprocity and pleasure. For instance, given that being heterosexual is regarded (and imposed) as the norm of manhood, this means that gay men are positioned at the bottom of a hierarchy of what 'real' men are supposed to be and are victims of homophobia and persecution. The focus on masculinities (Connell, 2005), rather than a single 'masculinity' has also revealed the vulnerability of many men, and the need for social work and social policy to address these needs. Suicide rates among men are relatively high and life expectancy lower, in part due to men's neglect of their health and not seeking medical intervention soon enough. This has led, for instance, to important research on men's help-seeking behaviours and consideration of how welfare policy and practice can encourage earlier take up of health, social care and counselling services by men (O'Brien et al, 2005; Featherstone et al, 2007).

Fatherhood is another area gaining increased attention from researchers, for instance, in terms of how family policy does and does not provide opportunities for men to take paternity leave, and more generally, how professionals intervene with men to improve and support their caring capacities (Ferguson and Hogan, 2004; Featherstone, 2009). It is clear that men's behaviours are not reducible to biological differences between them and women, but are significantly shaped by socially constructed norms about masculinity, which are different to the social expectations placed on women and femininity.

Research has also given considerable attention to policy and practice responses by the police, criminal justice system and health and social care services to men who perpetrate various forms of violence against children and women. This includes a considerable amount of research into the effectiveness of group intervention programmes for men who perpetrate intimate abuse against their wives or partners (Gondolf, 2002).

Some social scientists argue that researching men's lives requires approaches that take account of the nature of masculinity. Because gender norms and socialisation mean that men generally are discouraged from being open about their lives and feelings, it is suggested that researchers need to take this into account in how they engage with men in interviews, focus groups and so on, and have strategies which acknowledge and try to get beyond any barriers (Schwalbe and Wolkomir, 2002).

Question for discussion
- How might researching men's lives and welfare issues differ from researching the lives of women?

References

Connell, R.W. (2005) *Masculinities*, Cambridge: Polity Press.

Featherstone, B. (2009) *Contemporary fathering: Theory, policy and practice*, Bristol: The Policy Press.

Featherstone, B., Rivett, M. and Scourfield, J. (2007) *Working with men in health and social care*, London: Sage Publications.

Ferguson, H. and Hogan, F. (2004) *Strengthening families through fathers: A study of families in need with particular reference to the development of policy and practice with vulnerable fathers*, Dublin: Department of Social Community and Family Affairs.

Gondolf, E.W. (2002) *Batterer intervention systems: Issues, outcomes and recommendations*, New York: Sage Publications.

O'Brien, P., Hunt, K. and Hart, G. (2005) "'It's caveman stuff but that is to a certain extent how guys still operate": men's accounts of masculinity and help seeking', *Social Science & Medicine*, vol 61, pp 503-16.

Schwalbe, M. and Wolkomir, M. (2002) 'Interviewing men', in J.F. Gubruim and J.A. Holstein (eds) *Handbook of interview research: Context and method*, Thousand Oaks, CA: Sage Publications, pp 203-19.

Question for discussion

- To what extent should methodological concerns associated with feminist research be considered in all research projects?

References

Dale, J. and Foster, P. (1986) *Feminists and state welfare*, London: Routledge.

Edwards, R. and Mauther, M. (2002) 'Ethics and feminist research: theory and practice', in M. Mauther, M. Birch, J. Jessop and T. Miller (eds) *Ethics in qualitative research*, London: Sage Publications, pp 14-31.

Eichler, M. (1988) *Nonsexist research methods: A practical guide*, London: Routledge.

Finch, J. (1991) 'Feminist research and social policy', in M. Maclean and D. Groves (eds) *Women's issues in social policy*, London: Routledge, pp 194-212.

Harding, S. (ed) (1987) *Feminism and methodology*, Milton Keynes: Open University Press.

Hartsock, N. (1997) 'Comment on Hekman's "truth and method: feminist standpoint theory revisited": truth or justice?', *Signs*, vol 22, no 21, pp 367-74.

Holland, J. and Ramazanoglu, C. (1994) 'Coming to conclusions: power and interpretation in researching young women's sexuality', in M. Maynard and J. Purvis (eds) *Researching women's lives from a feminist perspective*, London: Taylor & Francis, pp 125-48.

Holland, J., Ramazanoglu, C., Sharpe, S. and Thomson, R. (1998) *The male in the head: Young people, heterosexuality and power*, London: Tufnell Press.

Oakley, A. (2005) *The Ann Oakley reader: Gender, women and social science*, Bristol: The Policy Press.

Olesen, V. (2007) 'Early millennial feminist qualitative research: challenges and contours', in N. Denzin and Y. Lincoln (eds) *Landscape of qualitative research* (3rd edn), London: Sage Publications, pp 311-70.

Pascall, G. (1986) *Social policy: A feminist perspective*, London: Routledge.

Ramazanoglu, C. with Holland, J. (2002) *Feminist methodology: Challenges and choices*, London: Sage Publications.

Roberts, H. (ed) (1981) *Doing feminist research*, London: Routledge.

Ryan-Flood, R. and Gill, R. (2010) *Secrecy and silence in the research process: Feminist reflections*, London: Routledge.

Stanley, L. (1990) 'Introduction', in L. Stanley (ed) *Feminist praxis: Research, theory and epistemology in feminist sociology*, London: Routledge, pp 3-19.

Stanley, L. and Wise, S. (1993) *Breaking out: Feminist consciousness and feminist research* (revised edn), London: Routledge.

Throsby, K. and Gimlin, D. (2010) 'Critiquing thinness and wanting to be thin', in R. Ryan-Flood and R. Gill, *Secrecy and silence in the research process: Feminist reflections*, London: Routledge, pp 105-16.

Wilson, E. (1977) *Women and the welfare state*, London: Tavistock.

Further reading

Ramazanoglu, C. with Holland, J. (2002) *Feminist methodology: Challenges and choices*, London: Sage Publications.

Ribbens, J. and Edwards, R. (1998) *Feminist dilemmas in qualitative research: Public knowledge and private lives*, London: Sage Publications.

Ryan-Flood, R. and Gill, R. (2010) *Secrecy and silence in the research process: Feminist reflections*, London: Routledge.

4.7 'Race' and social policy research
Gary Craig and Savita Katbamna

Mainstream social policy texts, with few exceptions, have historically contained little discussion of 'race' and ethnicity. This has begun to change since the mid-1990s, although the situation is still uneven (Craig, 1999, 2007; Craig and Ahmad, 2002). It is arguable that this marginalisation has continued within the present volume where less than 1% of the total wordage is given over to discussions of 'race', in a context where black and minority (BME) people now constitute substantially more than 10% of the UK population.

In parallel with this, 'race' has also historically been the 'missing dimension' (Rai, 1995) in social research; again the situation has improved slightly, given further impetus by recent debates on 'race', including the consequences of the murder of Stephen Lawrence, discussion of asylum-seeking and migration and debates about the nature of multiculturalism. However, much social policy research still has an inadequate 'race' dimension. The recent comment by former Home Office Minister John Denham that 'we should move on from "race"' may legitimise this neglect. Evidence suggests that even in areas with a high concentration of BME people, inclusion of participants from these populations often occurs as an afterthought, as little consideration of issues of 'race' and ethnicity appear to have been given by either funders or researchers. The reasons for this derive in part from institutional and individual racism, but also from methodological limitations of many studies, regardless of their auspices, limitations shaping each stage of the research process, the formulation of research questions, the employment of researchers, the commissioning of research, data collection and analysis.

One difficulty is that most research organisations, including university units, do not incorporate a specialist 'race' dimension in their work. It is thus often left to individual researchers to include 'race' issues. These researchers may be of minority origin themselves and can feel marginalised within their own workplace; there are still disproportionately few senior BME researchers in a position to influence research agendas. Sometimes, funders or commissioners of research may specify consideration of 'race'-related issues in research studies. However, in a culture where research agendas are set by funding bodies in consultation with the research community, 'race', overall, tends often to occupy an invisible space. An absence of organisational policy, strategy or practice ethos to address the 'race' dimension inevitably then results in ad hoc and inconsistent practice patterns (Vickers et al, 2010). For example, bilingual interviewers are often recruited on a sessional basis and given minimal training to conduct interviews. Issues of cost are certainly important and these need to be faced early on in discussion with funders; for example, as *Box 4e* shows, employment of bilingual interviewers at the outset of studies may involve additional costs but can be crucial for ensuring that they have adequate training to enable them to assist with all stages of the research process, including the development of questionnaires, recruitment of participants, conducting interviews, interpretation and dissemination of results.

Box 4e: Attitudes to ageing and financial planning for care in old age in South Asian communities
Gary Craig and Savita Katbamna

Over the last two decades, the British minority ethnic population in Britain has undergone a major transformation. One of the most significant changes is an increase in the number of older people, as those who migrated to Britain in the late 1950s and 1960s approach retirement age (ONS, 2001).

The ageing of wider British society has prompted much debate about the roles of the individual, the family and the state in meeting the long-term care needs of older people. However, the issues affecting the care needs of minority ethnic older people have received relatively little attention. The small amount of evidence available remains largely tentative, mostly due to the under-representation in national and local surveys of minority ethnic respondents, particularly those who are non-English-speaking (Parker and Clarke, 1997; Deeming and Keen, 2000).

Katbamna et al's (2004) study explored how men and women from the East Midlands Gujarati and Bangladeshi communities thought about ageing and financial planning for care. A diverse group of 103 participants, aged 40-50 and 50-65, took part in a series of single-sex focus groups and in-depth interviews. Participants were recruited via telephone, information leaflets and personal visits to voluntary and community organisations, places of worship and colleges. The interviews were conducted by bilingual interviewers, and then tape-recorded, transcribed and translated.

The findings indicate that cultural norms also shaped participants' attitudes to ageing. In line with the majority population, Gujarati participants tended to see ageing in terms of chronological age; in contrast, Bangladeshi participants thought in terms of life stage – a 40-year-old grandparent would consider themselves 'old'.

Just as in the majority population, concerns about health and income were paramount, but with some significant attenuating factors. Almost all participants in the older age group reported poor health. Bangladeshi participants, in particular, were likely to be afflicted with chronic conditions and had low expectations of living long and healthy lives. This is confirmed by wider studies of health inequalities (Nazroo, 2001).

With the exception of Gujarati participants in the younger age group, a majority of participants were concerned about surviving on a low income. Many male Bangladeshi participants were either unemployed or in poorly paid jobs without adequate pension provision; the circumstances of women, most of whom were economically inactive, was even worse. Some women from the Bangladeshi community linked their financial insecurity to having an older spouse (Khanum, 2001), increasing the chance of early widowhood. Some feared being abandoned in the UK if their spouses returned to Bangladesh to retire. Given the sensitivity of the issues involved, funding was secured to employ two bilingual interviewers to assist from the outset with all aspects of the research. Without their cultural insight, many of these findings would not have been uncovered.

Although intergenerational obligation was regarded as a corner stone of family life (family was perceived to have a 'moral obligation' to provide care), there was considerable doubt about relatives' ability and willingness to help. Similar doubts were rarely expressed about the state, which many regarded as having a 'legal' duty to provide support in old age. Consequently, it is likely that increasing numbers of older people in these communities will look to the state for support – with clear implications for policy makers, planners and practitioners in health and social care services.

References

Deeming, C. and Keen, J. (2000) *Paying for old age?*, Interim research report from the King's Fund Long-Term Care Financing Project, London: King's Fund.

Katbamna, S., Bakht, S., Shah, J. and Barker, G. (2004) *Perspectives on ageing and attitudes towards financial planning for care in old age in the South Asian communities*, Leicester: Department of Health Sciences, University of Leicester.

Khanum, S. (2001) 'The household patterns of a "Bangladeshi village" in England', *Journal of Ethnic and Migration Studies*, vol 27, no 3, pp 489-504.

Nazroo, J. (2001) *Ethnicity, class and health*, London: Policy Studies Institute.

ONS (Office of National Statistics) (2001) *2001 Census: Standard area statistics (England and Wales)*, Manchester: Economic and Social Research Council (ESRC)/JISC Census Programme, Census Dissemination Unit, University of Manchester.

Parker, G. and Clarke, H. (1997) *Attitudes and behaviour towards financial planning for care in old age*, Leicester: Nuffield Community Care Studies Unit (NCCSU), University of Leicester.

The relatively small representation of minority communities in the UK population (over 10% overall but lower in most areas) is often used to justify their exclusion from general research intended to have wider applicability. The fact that the population is unevenly distributed across the country is also often used to justify their exclusion from studies. In qualitative research, it is believed that low numbers of members from minority communities in small sample sizes lead to meaningless data and results. Research that addresses minority communities is believed always to incur high costs – allegedly because of the collection of data in minority languages – and require complex research designs. The study in **Box 4e** used researchers matched for language and culture and did cost more, but the quality of the research was enhanced in each case as a result of taking these issues seriously (see also Phillimore et al, 2009).

In quantitative research, it is also argued that low numbers of potential respondents from minority communities lead to results that are difficult to interpret statistically. The use of 'booster samples' is often viewed as an unsatisfactory solution, on the grounds that these require complex research designs with complicated and costly analysis. However, having an adequately sized sample, often from boosting a sample, is critical to ensuring an effective 'race' dimension to research and need not be more expensive (Britton et al, 2002). Many researchers have reservations about using common sampling techniques for minority communities. They argue here that samples drawn only from densely populated 'minority' areas are not representative, and are biased against members of these communities who live elsewhere; given the concentration of these minorities in a relatively few areas, this seems a particularly inappropriate argument.

In Rai's (1995) groundbreaking study, many researchers were unsure how to address 'race' in research, citing uncertainty about which minority communities to include in particular research studies, and a lack of awareness of their specific cultural norms and social circumstances. A 'play safe' option was often, therefore, adopted, resulting in ignoring minority communities in research, often with the implicit or explicit collusion of policy organisations which themselves have not incorporated an effective 'race' dimension in their own policies and practices (see Craig, 2001, 2007).

Arguments for having a clear 'race' perspective within social research are, however, important. First, without it, research is racist and incomplete. Second, the minority population in the UK, already substantial, is growing – in some areas, minority ethnic groups are actually the *majority* population, or are a majority of children and younger people, and this will be increasingly the case, a result of demographic change. Third, the minority ethnic population, contrary to popular belief, is very diverse, a diversity reflected in significant differences which exist between, but also *within*, various subgroups – for example, as between Turks, Turkish Kurds and Turkish Cypriots – and which is increasingly regarded as superdiverse (Robinson and Reeve, 2008; Fanshawe and Sriskandarajah, 2010). These differences are a product of migration histories, settlement patterns, languages, religious and cultural traditions, socioeconomic circumstances and social support networks (Katbamna et al, 2004). The assumption of homogeneity, which influenced early research on minority ethnic groups, has had particularly unfortunate consequences for the development of appropriate and relevant policy to meet the needs of differing communities. Fourth, minority ethnic communities often face the severest social problems, with higher levels of unemployment and dependency on state benefits, poor housing and health, and having greater difficulty in accessing goods and services. These difficulties, again often the consequence of institutional racism (Craig, 2000, 2001, 2007; Katbamna, 2000; Craig and Ahmad, 2002; Katbamna et al, 2002; Vickers et al, 2010), lead to minority ethnic groups (including now many with refugee or asylum-seeker status) becoming 'invisibilised', particularly in areas with small minority populations (NYBSB, 2007). In terms of issues of citizenship and social cohesion, the consequences for policy and politics of ignoring the difficult and diverse experiences and views of minority ethnic groups are clear – for example, the disturbances in northern cities during 2001 and more recently in London, Birmingham and other parts of England in 2011, where issues raised in some areas had their origins in racial tensions.

However, although some minority ethnic groups – particularly those of Bangladeshi and Pakistani origin – experience higher levels of deprivation, this is not uniformly the case. Similarly, there are vast differences in the level of literacy in English, educational attainment and in the mother tongue. These differences are often strongly associated with gender, where a higher proportion of older women in all subgroups do not speak English (Modood et al, 1997). This requires special efforts to engage non-English speakers (by, for example, interviews in the language of choice, as in the example given) as well as other marginalised groups. Thus, an increasingly strong theme in social policy research must be to trace the varied social and economic trajectories of different minority ethnic groups, incorporating different methodological approaches in qualitative and quantitative research to overcome language and communication problems, and applying sensitivity about gender-related cultural issues.

This would help a move away from problematising minorities (which, by ignoring structural causes of their disadvantage, itself feeds racism) and towards seeing minorities as citizens with needs, rights and contributions to society. Important steps in this direction would be for all research-related agencies effectively to monitor 'race' issues both for employees and users – as many public agencies are now required to do under the terms of the Race Relations Amendment Act 2000 – and for research funders to insist on an appropriate 'race' dimension in all research they support.

Question for discussion

- What factors should funding bodies take into consideration to ensure that the 'race' and ethnic dimensions of research are appropriately addressed in work they fund?

References

Britton, L., Chatrik, B., Coles, B., Craig, G., Hylton, C. and Mumtaz, S. (2002) *Missing connexions?*, Bristol: The Policy Press.

Craig, G. (1999) '"Race", poverty and social security', in J. Ditch (ed) *An introduction to social security*, London: Routledge, pp 206-26.

Craig, G. (2000) '"Race" and welfare', Inaugural lecture as Professor of Social Justice, Hull: University of Hull.

Craig, G. (2001) '"Race" and New Labour', in G. Fimister (ed) *An end in sight?*, London: Child Poverty Action Group, pp 92-100.

Craig, G. (2007) 'Cunning, unprincipled, loathsome: the racist tail wags the welfare dog', *Journal of Social Policy*, vol 36, pp 605-23.

Craig, G. and Ahmad, W. (2002) '"Race" and social policy', in P. Alcock, A. Erskine and M. May (eds) *A student companion to social policy* (2nd edn), Oxford: Blackwell, pp 91-7.

Fanshawe, S. and Sriskandarajah, D. (2010) *'You can't put me in a box'. Super-diversity and the end of identity politics in Britain*, London: Institute for Public Policy Research.

Katbamna, S. (2000) *'Race' and childbirth*, Buckingham: Open University Press.

Katbamna, S., Bakhta, S., Shah, J. and Barker, G. (2004) *Perspectives on ageing and attitudes towards financial planning for care in old age in the South Asian communities*, Draft report, Leicester: Department of Health Sciences, University of Leicester.

Katbamna, S., Bhakta, P., Parker, G., Baker, R. and Ahmad, W. (2002) 'Supporting South Asian carers and those they care for: the role of the primary health care team', *British Journal of General Practice*, vol 52, pp 300-5.

Modood, T., Berthoud, R., Lakey, J., Nazroo, J., Smith, P., Virdee, S. and Belshon, S. (1997) *Ethnic minorities in Britain: Diversity and disadvantage*, London: Policy Studies Institute.

NYBSB (2007) *Ethnic minorities in rural areas*, London: Department for Environment, Food and Rural Affairs.

Phillimore, J., Goodson, L., Hennessy, D. and Ergun, E. (2009) *Empowering Birmingham's migrant and refugee community organisations*, York: Joseph Rowntree Foundation.

Rai, D.K. (1995) *In the margins: Social research amongst Asian communities*, Social Research Papers No 2, Hull: University of Humberside.

Robinson, D. and Reeve, K. (2008) *Experiences of new immigration at the neighbourhood level*, York: Joseph Rowntree Foundation.

Vickers, T., Craig, G. and Atkin, K. (2010) *Research with BME populations in social care*, London: National Institute for Health Research.

Further reading

Craig, G. (1999) '"Race", poverty and social security', in J. Ditch (ed) *An introduction to social security*, London: Routledge, pp 206-26.

Modood, T., Berthoud, R., Lakey, J., Nazroo, J., Smith, P., Virdee, S. and Belshon, S. (1997) *Ethnic minorities in Britain: Diversity and disadvantage*, London: Policy Studies Institute.

Rai, D.K. (1995) *In the margins: Social research amongst Asian communities*, Social Research Papers No 2, Hull: University of Humberside. [Part of the argument in Section 4.7 draws on this text.]

Website resources

The Race Equality Foundation researches and publishes a substantial volume of material, particularly about 'race' in housing and health but also in other welfare areas as well as providing training and consultancy: www.raceequalityfoundation.org.uk

Intute, the (former) Social Science Information Gateway, is a website which can be searched for useful information relevant to 'race' and ethnicity: www.intute.ac.uk/socialsciences

4.8 User involvement in research

Peter Beresford

Interest in user involvement in research has greatly increased in recent years. It has come to mean people on the receiving end of policy and professional practice – as service users, patients and citizens – having a say or role in what happens to them and in such policy and provision (Beresford and Croft, 1993). Three strands of research where there is such involvement can be identified. These are:

- *User involvement in research:* where involvement is added to existing research projects, initiatives, organisations and other arrangements.
- *Collaborative research:* where service users and/or their organisations and researchers and/or their organisations jointly initiate, undertake and are involved in the governance of research.
- *User-led or user-controlled research*, which is initiated, undertaken and controlled by service users and their organisations (Wallcraft et al, 2009).

Such 'user involvement research' has grown from two different sources. These are first from researchers, research-related organisations and broader pressures for participation that seem to follow from growing political and ideological interest in consumerism and 'the active citizen'. Second, and much earlier interest can be traced to the emergence of first the disabled people's and subsequently other 'service user' organisations and movements, which have worked to advance the rights and interests of people on the receiving end of health, social care and welfare policy, practice and provision (Beresford, 2003). These movements have often called existing research into question for perpetuating the status quo and their own disempowerment. They have argued, instead, for and developed 'user-controlled' research which:

- is concerned with changing and equalising research relationships between the researcher and the researched;
- seeks to advance the personal empowerment of participants and service users;
- prioritises making broader political and social change in line with the rights and interests of service users (Sweeney et al, 2009; Beresford and Croft, 2010).

User involvement in research can offer more or less involvement in all aspects of research structures, and also the research process, including:

- identifying the focus of research and research questions
- commissioning research
- seeking, obtaining and controlling research funding
- undertaking the research
- managing the research
- collating and analysing data
- producing findings
- writing up and producing publications
- developing and carrying out dissemination policies
- deciding and undertaking follow-up action (Beresford, 2003).

A range of benefits has been identified from involving service users in research. These include building trust, gaining a fuller picture and encouraging people to take part in research through employing service users as interviewers and researchers; opening up research agendas through gaining the ideas and insights of service users; and developing more social understandings and models to counter prevailing medicalised and individualising ones (Faulkner, 2009). *Boxes 4f, 4h* and *4i* illustrate user involvement in a number of social policy and social work research areas.

There is now a growing interest in the *impact* of user involvement in research – that is to say, what effects it actually has, what difference it can make. This interest has grown in both the research community and officially – on the part of government and funding organisations. This seems to have grown out of the view that the moral and ethical arguments for equalising research relationships, and including service users and their perspectives in research, are not sufficient justification for their involvement. In the context of user involvement research, impact has been taken to mean how involvement improves the quality and outcomes of research.

INVOLVE, the organisation set up by the government to advance public, patient and service user involvement in health, social care and public health research, undertook a review of impact in public involvement. A number of areas for possible impact were identified and explored in the literature. These were the impact on:

- research ethics
- people involved
- researchers
- research participants

- the wider community
- community organisations
- implementation and change.

INVOLVE did not focus specifically on the impact of user-controlled research, although it did highlight that such research did seem to focus on areas that did not get the attention of conventional researchers and policy makers (Staley, 2009, p 26). A systematic review of impact has highlighted the impact of user-led/controlled research for service users. This concluded that it was:

- more patient focused (with its concern with user-led outcomes);
- more empowering for service users than collaborative or consultative approaches to user involvement in research;
- involved service users in all stages of the research (Staniszewska et al, 2010).

While all research that includes user involvement has come in for some measure of questioning, user-controlled research has been the subject of particular methodological challenge (Rose, 2009; Sweeney et al, 2009). These criticisms do not necessarily surface formally. They are as likely to be part of informal and hidden discussions. Significantly, when the British Social Policy Association (SPA) surveyed its members, only 24.9% thought that it was 'very important' that service users were involved appropriately in all stages of research (Becker et al, 2010; see also *Box 4g* for a discussion of the SPA study).

User involvement research can both expect, and has already frequently experienced, challenges as being biased and lacking in rigour. Questions are raised about its relation with traditional positivist research values of 'objectivity', 'neutrality' and distance, even though, like other new paradigm research, it has made its own challenge to these (Hammersley, 2000; Beresford, 2003, 2007; Rose, 2009; Sweeney et al, 2009). Findings from such research can expect to be questioned as partial and partisan. Questions are raised about the problems which user-controlled research may pose because one sectional interest is seen to be dominant – that of service users. It is challenged in relation to criteria of 'validity' and 'reliability', yet all these questions may and should be raised of *all* research.

If user involvement is to prosper in research then a number of steps are likely to be needed. These include:

- systematically and comprehensively evaluating all forms of user involvement research;
- developing the theoretical base of user–controlled research;
- making training available for all stakeholders about user involvement research;
- reforming welfare benefits policy and practice to enable people on benefits to participate in research without risk or disadvantage;
- providing support for local user-controlled organisations to ensure a strong basis for supporting user involvement in research;
- addressing diversity to ensure that all groups have equal access to be involved in research, regardless of 'race', gender, sexuality, age, disability, class, culture and belief (Beresford and Croft, 2010).

Question for discussion

- What are the strengths and vulnerabilities of user involvement research?

References

Becker, S., Sempik, J. and Bryman, A. (2010) 'Advocates, agnostics and adversaries: perceptions of service user involvement in social policy research', *Social Policy and Society*, vol, 9, no 3, pp 355-66.

Beresford, P. (2003) 'User involvement in research: exploring the challenges', *Nursing Times Research*, vol 8, no 1, pp 36-46.

Beresford, P. (2007) 'User involvement, research and health inequalities: developing new directions', *Health and Social Care in the Community*, vol 15, no 4, pp 306-12.

Beresford, P. and Croft, S. (1993) *Citizen involvement: A practical guide for change*, Basingstoke: Macmillan.

Beresford, P. and Croft, S. (2010) *User controlled research: A review*, London: National Institute for Health Research (NIHR) College of Social Care Research.

Bryman, A. (2012) *Social research methods* (4th edn) Oxford: Oxford University Press.

Faulkner, A. (2009) 'Principles and motives', in J. Wallcraft, B. Schrank and M. Amering (eds) *Handbook of service user involvement in mental health research*, Chichester: Wiley-Blackwell, pp 13-24.

Hammersley, M. (2000) *Partisanship and bias in social research*, Buckingham: Open University Press.

Rose, D. (2009) 'Collaboration', in J. Wallcraft, B. Schrank and M. Amering (eds) *Handbook of service user involvement in mental health research*, Chichester: Wiley-Blackwell, pp 169-79.

Staley, K. (2009) *Exploring impact: Public involvement in NHS, public health and social care research*, Eastleigh: National Institute for Health Research (NIHR) INVOLVE.

Staniszewska, S., Brett, J., Herron-Marx, S., Seers, K., Bayliss, H. and Mockland, C. (2010) *Conceptualisation, measurement, impact and outcomes of patient and social care research: What is the evidence? A systematic review conducted by the School of Health and Social Studies, University of Warwick*, Coventry: University of Warwick.

Sweeney, A., Beresford, P., Faulkner, A., Nettle, M. and Rose, D. (eds) (2009) *This is survivor research*, Ross-on-Wye: PCSS Books.

Wallcraft, J., Schrank, B. and Amering, M. (eds) (2009) *Handbook of service user involvement in mental health research*, Chichester: World Psychiatric Association, Wiley-Blackwell.

Further reading

Beresford, P. (2003) *It's our lives: A short theory of knowledge, distance and experience*, London: Citizen Press in association with Shaping Our Lives.

Oliver, M. (2009) *Understanding disability: From theory to practice* (2nd edn), Basingstoke: Palgrave Macmillan.

Website resources

Centre for Disability Studies, University of Leeds, an interdisciplinary centre for research and education in the field of disability studies: www.leeds.ac.uk/disability-studies

INVOLVE, advisory body set up by the government to advance public, patient and user involvement in health, social care and public health research: www.invo.org.uk

Shaping Our Lives, a user-controlled organisation and network which carries out user involvement and user-controlled research: www.shapingourlives.org.uk and the networking website, SOLNET: www.solnetwork.org.uk

Folk.us, committed to involvement in health and social care research: www.folkus.org.uk

Joseph Rowntree Foundation, strongly committed to funding research with user involvement: www.jrf.org.uk

---

Box 4f: The Standards We Expect project: involving people in research about person-centred support
Peter Beresford

The Standards We Expect project was a three-year national research and development project supported by the Joseph Rowntree Foundation. It can be seen as an example of collaborative research, since it involved two university research centres, a voluntary organisation and a user-controlled organisation, Shaping Our Lives. At the same time, funding was held by the service user organisation and the project was committed to the values and principles of user-controlled research (Faulkner, 2010).

The focus of the project was 'personalisation', or as it described it, 'person-centred support'. 'Personalisation' emerged in the first decade of the 21st century as the new health and care buzz word (Glasby and Littlechild, 2009). First, it was used as a synonym for 'personal budgets', sums of money those eligible received to purchase their own system of support. Later, it was used to emphasise a broader 'person-centred' rather than service-led approach to social care and health policy and provision.

The project focused on three key questions:

- What does 'person-centred support' really mean?
- What are the main barriers to such person-centred support?
- How can these barriers be overcome?

In seeking to answer these questions, instead of drawing primarily on what politicians or policy makers, professionals or planners have to say, as is usually the case, it turned instead to the ideas and experience of the people support most directly affects: service users, their families and those who work directly with them – practitioners directly offering them support.

Service users were also centrally involved in initiating, planning, managing and carrying out the project. They not only carried out interviews and group discussions, but also provided 'empowerment' and other training for local service users and practitioners as part of the development part of the project. One problem that did inhibit the user-led principles of the project was the cumbersome and time-consuming ethical procedures that it had to go through. This meant that the original plan of involving local service users right at the start of the project had to be delayed until permissions had been obtained. The limitations of ethics procedures are a common problem getting in the way of user involvement and user-controlled research (Glasby and Beresford, 2007).

The Standards We Expect worked with a network of eight sites and an additional partnership of 12 organisations involving a wide range of services and service users, providing opportunities for them to meet, share experience, exchange and synthesise ideas and perspectives (Glynn et al, 2008).

The project's key concerns, in line with its commitment to goals of user-controlled research, including supporting people's empowerment and working for social change, was to increase opportunities for their involvement, and to seek to influence change through a coherent year-long 'influencing strategy' based on both 'top-down' and 'bottom-up' approaches to making change. A series of themes repeatedly emerged. These related to the values, funding, workforce, practice, nature, organisation, availability and accountability of social care.

Question for discussion
• What effects are involving people in research likely to have on the nature and purpose of that research?

References
Faulkner, A. (2010) *User controlled research: Some examples and themes arising*, Eastleigh: INVOLVE.

Glasby, J. and Beresford, P. (2007) 'In whose interests? Local research ethics committees and service user research', *Ethics and Social Welfare*, vol 1, no 3, pp 282-92.

Glasby, J. and Littlechild, R. (2009) *Direct payments and personal budgets: Putting personalisation into practice*, Bristol: The Policy Press.

Glynn, M., Beresford, P., Bewley, C., Branfield, F., Butt, J., Croft, S., Fleming, J., Patmore, C. and Postle, K. (2008) *Person-centred support: What service users and practitioners say*, York: Joseph Rowntree Foundation/York Publishing.

Further reading
Kemshall, H. and Littlechild, R. (2000) *User involvement and participation in social care: Research informing practice*, London: Jessica Kingsley Publishers

Box 4g: What do social policy academics think about service user involvement in research?
Joe Sempik

As Section 4.8 shows, there is a strengthening opinion among academics, policy makers and funding bodies that service users have an important role to play within research (see also Beresford, 2005, 2007). However, a study by Becker, Sempik and Bryman (2010) suggests that, when it comes to social policy academics and researchers, there are significant divisions on the issue. While many favour service user involvement, others are indifferent or even hostile to the notion. The 'advocates' see involvement as a partnership, between users who have experience of services and, therefore, understand their particular environment, and the researcher who is versed in the ways of the research community. Opponents question the value of involving service users in the research process and suggest that it is ideologically driven and tokenistic and at its worst it is exploitative.

The advocates believe that service users should be involved in all stages of the research process, from conceiving the research ideas through to the dissemination of findings. Becker et al (2010) identify seven main arguments that are put forward by the advocates who suggest that service user involvement:

- helps social policy research to be grounded in the everyday experiences of users;
- helps to ensure social policy research is relevant;
- helps in the formulation and design of the research and provides scrutiny of ethics and process;
- can help the researcher to gain access to research participants;
- can help the dissemination and implementation of findings;
- helps to make the research accessible and understandable;
- can improve the overall quality of social policy research.

There are an equal number of counter-arguments put forward by the opponents and those who are as yet undecided about the value of service user involvement (termed the 'adversaries' and 'agnostics' by Becker et al, 2010). Their arguments are that:

- service user involvement is a fad, driven by ideology rather than proven in value;
- service user involvement can be tokenistic in practice rather than a genuine exercise in involving other stakeholders. At its worst it can be exploitative;
- service users do not have the skills or knowledge to be involved, and may not have the abilities to engage with or conduct (or control) research;
- service users bring their own agendas to the research, and may seek to influence it in particular ways for their own purposes;
- service user involvement requires a 'representative' sample that may be difficult to assemble. A biased sample would lead to the promotion of a particular viewpoint or approach;
- service user involvement is costly and time consuming;
- the value of service user involvement is not proven, and it will not necessarily improve the overall quality of research findings.

While some social policy researchers see service user involvement as a de facto mark of quality, others argue that there is still no evidence to suggest that it, indeed, improves the quality of research.

Question for discussion
- Are ideological reasons sufficient for involving users in the research process or should it be based on evidence that shows it improves the quality of research?

References
Becker, S., Sempik, J. and Bryman, A. (2010) 'Advocates, agnostics and adversaries: researchers' perceptions of service user involvement in social policy research', *Social Policy and Society*, vol 9, no 3, pp 355-66.

Beresford, P. (2005) 'Theory and practice of user involvement in research: making the connection with public policy and practice', in L. Lowes and I. Hulat (eds) *Involving service users in health and social care research*, London: Routledge, pp 6-17.

Beresford, P. (2007) 'The role of service user research in generating knowledge-based health and social care: from conflict to contribution', *Critical Social Policy*, vol 3, no 3, pp 329-41.

Further reading
Beresford, P. (2007) 'User involvement, research and health inequalities: developing new directions', *Health and Social Care in the Community*, vol 15, no 4, pp 306-12.

Bryman, A. (2012) *Social research methods* (4th edn), Oxford: Oxford University Press.

Cotterell, P. (2008) 'Exploring the value of service user involvement in data analysis: "our interpretation is about what lies below the surface"', *Educational Action Research*, vol 16, no 1, pp 5-17.

Lowes, L. and Hulatt, I. (eds) (2005) *Involving service users in health and social care research*, London: Routledge.

Website resources
National Co-ordinating Centre for Public Engagement (NCCPE): www.publicengagement. ac.uk

See NCCPE page 'Methods of engaging the public': www.publicengagement.ac.uk/our-projects/involving-users-in-research-projects

See INVOLVE Resources page: www.invo.org.uk/Publications.asp

Box 4h: Involving learning disabled adults in research
Rachel Fyson

It has, for some time, been considered 'best practice' to involve adults with learning disabilities in research which is of direct relevance to their lives. This reflects a growing consensus that marginalised groups can, and should, be empowered through research, and that such empowerment means moving beyond being merely the passive 'objects' of research undertaken by others. Disability researchers have argued for an emancipatory research paradigm (Barnes, 1996; Oliver, 1997) in which research is developed, commissioned and the findings controlled by disabled user groups. However, within learning disability research, a model of participatory research is more commonly adopted (Stalker, 1998;

Chappell, 2000; Walmsley, 2001), in which learning disabled and non-disabled researchers work together as partners.

Participatory research requires careful planning and preparation, including full consideration of ethical issues. This is partly because of the need to support learning disabled adults to develop the skills to work as researchers (Burke et al, 2003), but it is also because of the ethical issues that arise from the dynamic between learning disabled and non-disabled researchers. What will happen after the participatory project ends needs to be explicitly considered from the start (Northway, 2000), including whether or not friendships may outlive the duration of the project. It may be difficult to reach mutually agreed endings when co-researching with people who are otherwise socially isolated (Atkinson, 2005). If the research subjects are also people with learning disabilities, further ethical sensitivities will arise around issues of informed consent (see also *Box 2b*). As a minimum, it is necessary to develop project information leaflets and consent forms in accessible formats. It is likewise vital that research findings are produced in accessible formats, so that not only academics and professionals, but also people with learning disabilities can make use of them.

Most participatory research undertaken to date has used qualitative methodologies. Some studies have been criticised for relying too heavily on the subjective experiences of learning disabled researchers, rather than attempting to adopt an objective stance as is the norm within traditional scientific approaches (McLaughlin, 2010). Questions have also been raised associated with the lack of transparency regarding the particular roles undertaken by learning disabled and non-disabled members of research teams (Walmsley, 2004; McClimens, 2008), and whether participatory approaches are able to include *all* adults with learning disabilities or merely the most able (Walmsley, 2001).

Despite these difficulties, however, participatory research has the potential to uncover 'truths' which would be inaccessible to non-disabled researchers. Given the right support and training, learning disabled researchers have proved to be better able to empathise with learning disabled research participants; they may also be able to put those in power (for example, politicians and service providers) on the spot by demanding straight answers. Participatory research has been particularly successful when it has tackled subjects that are of direct relevance to the learning disabled researchers themselves. Examples include not only social history (Rolph et al, 2005) but also projects exploring recent policy initiatives such as direct payments (Gramlich et al, 2002) and Learning Disability Partnership Boards (Fyson et al, 2004; Speaking Up, 2007), and work with the parents of adults with learning disabilities (Walmsley and Mannan, 2009).

Question for discussion
- What are the strengths and limitations of research that adopts a participatory approach to the involvement of adults with learning disabilities?

References
Atkinson, D. (2005) 'Research as social work: participatory research in learning disability', *British Journal of Social Work*, vol 35, no 4, pp 425-34.

Barnes, C. (1996) 'Disability and the myth of the independent researcher', *Disability & Society*, vol 11, no 1, pp 107-10.

Burke, A., Cummins, L., Forsyth, W., Fraser, A., McMillan, J., Thompson, A., McLellan, J., Snow, L., Fraser, M., Fulton, C., McCrindle, E., Gillies, L., LeFort, S., Miller, G., Whitehall, J., Wilson, J., Smith, J. and Wright, D. (2003) 'Setting up participatory research: a discussion of the initial stages', *British Journal of Learning Disabilities*, vol 31, no 2, pp 65-9.

Chappell, A. (2000) 'Emergence of participatory methodology in learning difficulty research: understanding the context', *British Journal of Learning Disabilities*, vol 28, no 1, pp 38-43.

Fyson, R., McBride, G. and Myers, B. (2004) 'Progress on participation? Self-advocate involvement in Learning Disability Partnership Boards', *Tizard Learning Disability Review*, vol 9, no 3, pp 27-36.

Gramlich, S., McBride, G., Snelham, N. and Myers, B. with Williams, V. and Simons, K. (2002) *Journey to independence: What self advocates tell us about direct payments*, Kidderminster: BILD.

McClimens, A. (2008) 'This is my truth, tell me yours: exploring the internal tensions within collaborative learning disability research', *British Journal of Learning Disabilities*, vol 36, no 4, pp 271-6.

McLaughlin, H. (2010) 'Keeping service user involvement in research honest', *British Journal of Social Work*, vol 40, no 5, pp 1591-608.

Northway, R. (2000) 'Ending participatory research?', *Journal of Learning Disabilities*, vol 4, no 1, pp 27-36.

Oliver, M. (1997) 'Emancipatory research, realistic goal or impossible dream?', in C. Barnes and G. Mercer (eds) *Doing disability research*, Leeds: The Disability Press, pp 15-31.

Rolph, S., Atkinson, D., Nind, M. and Welshman, J. (eds) (2005) *Witnesses to change: Families, learning difficulties and history*, Kidderminster: BILD.

Speaking Up (2007) *How well are Partnership Boards hearing the voices of people with learning difficulties and family carers?*, Cambridge/London: Speaking Up/Care Services Improvement Partnership and Valuing People Support Team.

Stalker, K. (1998) 'Some ethical and methodological issues in research with people with learning difficulties', *Disability & Society*, vol 13, no 1, pp 5-19.

Walmsley, J. (2001) 'Normalisation, emancipatory research and inclusive research in learning disability', *Disability & Society*, vol 16, no 2, pp 187-205.

Walmsley, J. (2004) 'Inclusive learning disability research: the (nondisabled) researcher's role', *British Journal of Learning Disabilities*, vol 32, no 2, pp 65-71.

Walmsley, J. and Mannan, H. (2009) 'Parents as co-researchers: a participatory action research initiative involving parents of people with intellectual disabilities in Ireland', *British Journal of Learning Disabilities*, vol 37, no 4, pp 271-6.

Further reading

Atkinson, D. (2005) 'Research as social work: participatory research in learning disability', *British Journal of Social Work*, vol 35, no 4, pp 425-34.

Lowes, L. and Hulatt, I. (2005) *Involving service users in health and social care research*, London: Routledge.

Walmsley, J. (2004) 'Inclusive learning disability research: the (nondisabled) researcher's role', *British Journal of Learning Disabilities*, vol 32, no 2, pp 65-71.

Website resources
BILD (British Institute of Learning Disabilities): www.bild.org.uk
Change: www.changepeople.co.uk
Foundation for People with Learning Disabilities: www.learningdisabilities.org.uk
Norah Fry Research Centre, University of Bristol: www.bristol.ac.uk/norahfry/

Box 4i: Involving looked after children in research
Sally Holland

When involving looked after children and young people in research there are ethical and legal issues that are shared with research with any children, and some that are unique. Here, these are briefly illustrated through a case study of a research project undertaken at Cardiff University called (Extra)ordinary Lives. This study was funded by the Economic and Social Research Council (ESRC) as a methodological project to explore the possibilities and limitations of participative research (Holland et al, 2010). Knowing that looked after children and young people's lives are subject to direct scrutiny under fixed categories, we decided to ask young people the following question: 'If you could research whatever area of your life you wished, using whatever means you choose, what would you do?'

We set up a fortnightly group session called 'Me, myself and I' and made available a range of materials and methods, including photography, video, drawing, diary keeping, peer or researcher interviewing, and much hanging around and playing games. Young people also generated materials at home between sessions and occasionally met up with a researcher to take them on a walking or driving tour of places that were significant to them. These are also known as mobile or 'go-along' interviews (Ross et al, 2009). Our dataset consisted of the material generated by and with the young people, and detailed ethnographic field notes written by the researchers and shared with any young people who were interested.

Ethically, key issues included access, consent and taking care of our participants (Renold et al, 2008). A voluntary sector advocacy group (Tros Gynnal) provided advice and premises for our project. We produced colourful information sheets and a short DVD. We needed consent from the local authority, young people, their social worker (if they were subject to a Care Order) and a birth parent (if they were accommodated on a voluntary basis under Section 20 of the Children Act 1989). Foster and kinship carers also had to be happy with the arrangement. It took several months to reach nine young people who were keen to take part. Eight of these worked with us for a year. Consent had to be ongoing. With a participative project no one can be clear at the outset exactly what the research will involve, so we explicitly reminded young people at regular intervals that they were part of a piece of research and could withdraw some, or all, of their data, while continuing to attend the 'club'. We developed strong relationships with the young people and decided to continue some involvement after the main project was completed. Over the next two years we met up with them for a Christmas skating reunion, for individual involvement in analysis, and to involve young people in disseminating the research at two ESRC social science festival events for young people.

This project was intensive and resource-heavy for the number of participants, but we believe that it allowed an in-depth exploration of these young people's everyday experiences, and because of the nature of participative research, in a way that might not have been possible with more conventional research methods.

Question for discussion

- Research into the lives of any children or young people raises ethical, legal and practical issues and dilemmas. What are the particular issues that arise in researching with looked after young people in foster, residential or kinship care?

References

Holland, S., Renold, E., Ross, N.J. and Hillman, A. (2010) 'Power, agency and participatory agendas: a critical exploration of young people's engagement in participative qualitative research', *Childhood*, vol 17, no 3, pp 360-75.

Renold, E., Holland, S., Ross, N.J. and Hillman, A. (2008) 'Becoming participant: problematising "informed consent" in participatory research with young people in care', *Qualitative Social Work*, vol 7, no 4, pp 427-47.

Ross, N.J., Renold, E., Holland, S. and Hillman, A. (2009) 'Moving stories: using mobile methods to explore the everyday lives of young people in public care', *Qualitative Research*, vol 9, no 5, pp 605-23.

Further reading

Gallagher, L. and Gallagher, M. (2008) 'Methodological immaturity in childhood research? Thinking through "participatory methods"', *Childhood*, vol 15, no 4, pp 499-516.

Holland, S. (2009) 'Listening to children in care: a review of methodological and theoretical approaches to understanding looked after children's perspectives', *Children & Society*, vol 23, no 3, pp 226-35.

Winter, K. (2010) 'The perspectives of young children in care and implications for social work practice', *Child & Family Social Work, vol* 15, no 2, pp 186-95.

Relevant organisations

Voices From Care is a user-led group based in Wales that has extensive experience of collaborating on research projects: www.voicesfromcarecymru.org.uk

The National Youth Advocacy Service (NYAS) has a wealth of experience in research, advocacy and legal matters concerning children and young people, including those who are looked after: www.nyas.net/index.html

4.9 The theory and practice of action research

Christopher Day and Patricia Thomson

The origin of action research is often traced to the work of social psychologists in Europe and America in the 1930s, in particular Kurt Lewin, whose early career in Berlin was associated with the Frankfurt School. Together with his students, Lewin carried out a series of quasi-experimental projects in factory and neighbourhood settings which aimed to show how the development of 'independence, equality and cooperation' through democratic participation in decision-making processes led to social action designed to redress exploitation and discrimination. Lewin stood against those who argued that economic and social gains could be achieved through the autocratic coercion associated with so-called 'scientific management' dominated by behavioural objectives (Lewin, 1946; Adelman, 1993). It was Lewin who developed the action research spiral – of planning, action, reflection and exploration of the effects of the planned actions – which is characteristic of all action research.

From this, we can see that:

- Action research is unique among research paradigms in that it sets out to achieve change through understanding the processes of change as well as the outcomes. It therefore espouses procedural principles of social justice.
- It is pragmatic and eclectic in its methods of systematic inquiry, no special training in the research methods being required.
- It is grounded in a belief in '... active participation by those who have to carry out the work in reflection on and exploration of problems that they identify and anticipate' (Adelman, 1993, p 9).
- It is the participants themselves who take decisions about the consequences of their inquiries. It is therefore potentially emancipatory.
- It is based on an epistemology in which theory is seen to reside in action. In effect, action research challenges the separation of research from action, the separation of the researchers from the researched, assumptions about the control of knowledge, and assumptions about the nature of educational reform (Grundy, 1994).
- It is often a collaborative enterprise and relies for its success, therefore, on social relationships within the group as a 'community of practice' (Wenger, 1998).

As Reason and Bradbury claim, then, action research is:

> ... a participatory, democratic process concerned with developing practical knowing in the pursuit of worthwhile human purposes, grounded in a participatory world view.... It seeks to bring together action and reflection, theory and practice, in participation with others, in the pursuit of practical solutions to issues of pressing concern to people, and more generally the flourishing of individual persons and their communities. (Reason and Bradbury, 2001, p 1)

There is a close association between action research and notions of reflective practice pioneered by John Dewey (1933) and later, Donald Schön (1973). Peter Grimmett (1989) provided one of the most useful of many commentaries about what exactly reflective practice means, identifying three variations:

1. *Instrumentally mediated action.* Here the purpose of enquiry is to resolve technical problems, for example, in the classroom or other social setting such as a community organisation, hospital or office, in order to increase efficiency, or to implement a policy generated outside the context of use. So, while this has the appearance of action research in its methods of inquiry, it does not illustrate principles of ownership and democratic participation that underpin Lewin's original notions.

2. *Deliberating among competing ends.* Here participants raise alternative ways of conducting their work through the action research in order to extend the choices that they can make about how to improve it. This variation is contextual, experientially based and often conducted within a community of practice. It adheres to Lewin's principles but does not necessarily explore the wider social or policy contexts in which the work occurs.

3. *Reconstructing experience.* This is aimed at transforming practice and, where appropriate, the organisational structures and cultures in which this takes place through 'restructuring any combination of personal experience, the situational context, image of self [as teacher, social worker, businesswoman, nurse etc] or assumptions held about professional practice' (Coombs, 2003, p 2).

From these variations it is a short step to identify how action research, since it is essentially about change (for the individual, organisation or society) through participation, is often associated with emancipatory and empowerment liberationist ideas. The advocacy of social and political change via participatory action research (PAR) was promulgated by progressive social movements of the 1960s and 1970s in education, social welfare and identity politics. These combined the earlier work by Lewin (1946) with other radical philosophies, for example, Freire (1970), Selener (1997) and Fals-Borda and Rahman (1991).

Herein lies a problem for those who are attracted to action research. Because it is about change, action researchers need to have knowledge not only of action research but also about change contexts and processes. In *first order* action research, action research is undertaken by participants and focuses on improving their own practices and their contexts through understanding them better. In *second order* action research, change leadership occurs where participants who seek to make changes are supported by action researchers.

To summarise, action research is a means of actively acknowledging the right of those close to practice – whether teachers, social workers or nurses, for example – to engage in systematic inquiry into their practices with a view to improving them, or even radically reforming them. In doing so, action researchers create new knowledge, and make the knowledge part of a renewed repertoire of practice which is then available for further action research. As Cochran-Smith and Lytle (2009) note, in relation to teacher inquiry as a stance:

> Neither interpretive nor process–product classroom research has foregrounded the teacher's role in the generation of knowledge about teaching. What is missing from the knowledge base for teaching, therefore, are the voices of teachers themselves, the questions teachers ask, the ways teachers use writing and intentional talk in their work lives, and the interpretive frames teachers use to understand and improve their own classroom practices. (Cochrane-Smith and Lytle, 1993, p 2)

The same message would apply to those in all human relating organisations. *Boxes 4j* and *4k* illustrate two action research projects.

Box 4j: Action research in action
Christopher Day and Patricia Thomson

Much action research takes place in social settings, whether these are in education, social services, health or other public services; and much of this is initiated as part of formal programmes that are supported by university tutors (for example, for academic awards). For this reason, we provide here an illustration of the nature of participant relationships in a sustained collaborative project operating within a hierarchical organisational structure, focusing on the challenges which university teachers faced in working to promote deep and sustained 'thinking and doing' among programme participants as they reflected on, and confronted, the challenges of personal, professional and organisational development. From this, we reflect on the kinds of qualities, competencies and knowledge needed by those 'second order' researchers who work in universities if they are to promote action research and support action researchers in settings that are not always readily open to change. We have chosen our experience of working with the whole of a newly established senior leadership team in a secondary school, but this might be any public service organisation. Like many contemporary public sector organisations, their goal was to produce demonstrable improvements in both their effectiveness and equity. We identify three change phases; these are not discrete but each contains a particular emphasis in the way we worked.

Phase 1
When this part-time programme began, not all the team were in place. Those who were in place were not all committed to an agreed direction for change, nor, indeed, the processes to be used. The first few meetings of the group focused, therefore, on establishing the integrity of the university tutors as change partners, and their commitment to supporting inquiries which were of personal and professional significance to both the individuals and the collective, rather than pursuing their own agenda or that of the headteacher and deputy. Recognising and working with tensions between individually and organisationally perceived needs was a key element in establishing trustworthiness. Such purposes are often unspoken in accounts, yet often form an important part of the agenda in the early phase of action research partnerships between universities, as external providers, and groups of staff who have to work alongside each other on a daily basis.

There was a second issue, also, in terms of our function as knowledge holders and knowledge brokers. The group didn't know what action research was and what it might mean for them. As trust and knowledge increased, so the capacity of the individuals to confront their own and each other's beliefs about the students and the community, and their own roles, responsibilities and practices as leaders of change grew. This period of gaining knowledge of action research, and different ways of seeing themselves and each other, was not always comfortable but was a key prelude to planning individual and collective reflection and inquiries.

Phase 2
Often ignored or underplayed in accounts of action research in organisations are the continuing powerful effects of practice cultures on staff. By these we mean the disposition to action and rapid problem solving that the contexts in which teachers and others work creates and reinforces a set of values that privilege practice over systematic inquiry

into practice. This is sometimes expressed through scepticism of the value of research. University tutors who engage in action research programmes need to have the ability to adopt pedagogies which challenge participants to think in new ways about their practices and the contexts in which they live, so that they may take knowledge-based decisions about whether or not to change and, if so, in what direction and at what pace. During this phase we focused on challenging existing orthodoxies of practice, indirectly through asking participants to read and interrogate existing published texts, and directly through Socratic dialogue. Participants needed to encounter multiple views and to develop ways of evaluating them as well as to recognise the necessity of questioning their taken-for-granted assumptions, and we identified this as the second (developmental) phase of engagement in planning action research. Had we not established trust, this difficult and ongoing phase of our work – which is needed also as a 'rite of passage' in accredited programmes – would have been impossible. Tutors who work with experienced professionals need to acknowledge the importance of the learning histories that they bring and, thus, that 'unlearning' may be part of the processes of new learning.

Phase 3

As we progressed through 60 hours of face-to-face meetings over a period of 12 months, initial cooperation turned to collaboration as the group matured in its relationship through its work together in the practice setting. This was complemented through working together as part of the action research planning programme. In a sense, the two merged as each session began by unpacking reflecting on practice as a means of considering the improvement of practice issues, particularly those directly concerned with the individual and collective leadership of others in processes of change. Because this was a leadership team, inevitably its planning was now focused on how it might influence others through the action research which it was planning. Yet, without the work in the first two phases, this would have been less rich. It was no accident that, whereas the first 30 hours had focused on self-reflection and knowledge of action research, this third phase focused on gaining knowledge about change in organisations, change leadership and change processes. Again, although there is much writing about action research as leading to change, there is little that considers change leadership.

At the end of two modules of course work, a three-tiered action research process was emerging, that of teachers examining their practice, that of the leadership team who were supporting them, and our own action research into pedagogical approaches to support change.

Further reading

Cochran-Smith, M. and Lytle, S. (2009) *Inquiry as stance: Practitioner research in the next generation*, New York: Teachers College Press.

Reason, P. and Bradbury, H. (eds) (2001) *The SAGE handbook of action research, participative inquiry and practice*, London: Sage Publications.

Box 4k: Using cooperative inquiry and participatory action research approaches to explore the nature of social work education
Reima Ana Maglajlic

As I studied social work during the 1991-95 war in Croatia, my induction into this profession was far from typical. Questions that remained long after I graduated echoed the ones posed by Torbert (1981): 'What ought education to do?' 'How might education do what it ought to do?' 'Which of their aims, strategies or behaviours would educators need to reform in order to educate more successfully?' I decided to explore these questions as part of my PhD. However, I didn't see myself as, or want to be, the sole 'expert' when exploring the answers to these questions. I wanted to do that with others who had relevant experience but were seldom asked to contribute their expertise throughout a research process – from setting the research questions (or, in this case, negotiating the ones asked above), deciding how to explore them (which methods to use), gathering further information from others who may have had relevant experiences/expertise (data collection), making sense of the information collected (data analysis or, in action research terms, reflection), applying them in practice (action) and/or sharing these actions and findings with others (dissemination of the findings). Hence, I chose to use a second-person action research strategy (see Section 4.9 for further details).

The people I wanted to do the inquiry with were people who use social care services, social work students and social work practitioners. I wanted to conduct this study with them as co-researchers as they represented those who were seldom asked to contribute their expertise, and yet each has a stake in the process and content of social work education. Because of that, a mixture of cooperative inquiry and participative action research (PAR) approaches seemed relevant, particularly due to a myriad of power issues that exist between the three groups noted above. In relation to cooperative inquiry, it can be seen as a 'counterpartal role inquiry' (Heron, 1996; Heron and Reason, 2001). This is a type of cooperative inquiry where the co-researchers have differential power roles and experiences, for example, an inquiry about a practitioner–service user relationship, conducted collaboratively by social work practitioners and service users themselves, in which power is complex and ever present.

As I have also lived and worked in both England and Bosnia and Herzegovina, I conducted two studies, one in each of these contexts. First, I initiated a research group in Cambridge, England, which had 20 members: six people who used or had used social care services, five social work practitioners and nine students. Two years later, a group was initiated in Sarajevo, Bosnia, where the group had 15 members: six students, five professionals and four people who used social care services. These are only some of their identities or experiences, but they are the ones relevant for the study in question.

Practitioner and student co-researchers were approached to take part in a variety of ways, but mainly through related social work programmes (involving current and former students). Members who use social care services were approached through local voluntary organisations run or led by people who use social care services. All volunteered to take part in the study, as co-researchers. The study questions were amended through the initial interviews with individual group members that also explored each co-researcher's expectations of the study process.

My role within the process was that of the group facilitator. The core of the study was the inquiry group meetings, held every two weeks (in Sarajevo) or four weeks (in Cambridge) where the group members reflected on their experiences to date and decided what actions to undertake between the meetings and outside their group. The length and timing of both meetings and the study itself was negotiated with all of the participants and was based on the time they wanted to commit to such a process. To aid their reflection, the group members decided to do a variety of things: in Cambridge, to review other research conducted on social work education to date. In Sarajevo, the group devised questionnaires on social work education and practice that were administered to the social work students and social work practitioners who worked in statutory social work services there. The Cambridge group produced a set of recommendations for social work education that were shared with the social work programme educators, while in Sarajevo the group initiated a set of workshops that were to run concurrently with the programme. In both settings, the group conclusions were that similar groups should be run within the social work programmes, with an emphasis on promoting community-based and critical approaches to social work knowledge and practice.

Question for discussion
- What considerations would lead researchers to adopt cooperative inquiry and participatory action research (PAR) approaches as opposed to other qualitative research methods?

References

Heron, J. (1996) *Co-operative inquiry: Research into the human condition*, London: Sage Publications.

Heron, J. and Reason, P. (2001) 'The practice of co-operative inquiry: research "with" rather than "on" people', in P. Reason and H. Bradbury (eds) *Handbook of action research: Participative inquiry and practice*, London: Sage Publications, pp 179-88.

Torbert, W.R. (1981) 'Why educational research has been so uneducational: the case for a new model of social science based on collaborative inquiry', in P. Reason and J. Rowan (eds) *Human inquiry: A handbook of new paradigm research*, Chichester: John Wiley & Sons, pp 141-51.

Further reading

Healy, K. (2001) 'Participatory action research and social work: a critical appraisal', *International Social Work*, vol 44, no 1, pp 93-105.

Maglajlic Holicek, R.A. (2009) *Towards collaborative social work education and practice: A counterpartal role inquiry with service users, practitioners and students in England and Bosnia and Herzegovina*, Saarbrucken: VDM Verlag.

Maglajlic Holicek, R.A. and Baldwin, M. (2009) 'From reflection to action within community social work: the role of action research as a method for social work education and practice', in V. Leskosek (ed) *Theories and methods of social work: Exploring different perspectives*, Ljubljana: University of Ljubljana, pp 61-80.

Website resources

Action research theses (an additional resource for students who are considering doing action research for their thesis): www.scu.edu.au/schools/gcm/ar/art/arthesis.html

International Journal of Action Research: www.hampp-verlag.de/hampp_e-journals_IJAR.htm
Pedagogy & Theatre of the Oppressed: www.ptoweb.org/
Refugees and Asylum Seekers Participatory Action Research (RAPAR): www.rapar.org.uk/

Question for discussion

* What is distinctive about action research and why is the participation in the research process of those being researched regarded as so important?

References

Adelman, C. (1993) 'Kurt Lewin and the origins of action research', *Educational Action Research*, vol 1, pp 7-24.

Cochran-Smith, M. and Lytle, S. (1993) *Inside outside: Teacher research and knowledge*, New York: Teachers College Press.

Cochran-Smith, M. and Lytle, S. (2009) *Inquiry as stance: Practitioner research in the next generation*, New York: Teachers College Press.

Coombs, C.P. (2003) 'Developing reflective habits of mind, values and ethics', *Educational Administration*, vol 1, no 4, pp 1-8.

Dewey, J. (1933) *How we think*, New York: Heath and Co.

Fals-Borda, O. and Rahman, M.A. (eds) (1991) *Action and knowledge: Breaking the monopoly with participatory action research*, New York: Apex Press.

Freire, P. (1970) *Pedagogy of the oppressed*, New York: Herder & Herder.

Grimmett, P.P. (1989) 'A commentary on Schön's view of reflection', *Journal of Curriculum and Supervision*, vol **5, no** 1, pp 19-28.

Grundy, S. (1994) 'Action research at the school level: possibilities and problems', *Educational Action Research*, vol 2, pp 23-38.

Lewin, K. (1946) 'Action research and minority problems', *Journal of Social Issues*, vol 2, pp 34-46.

Reason, P. and Bradbury, H. (eds) (2001) *The SAGE handbook of action research, participative inquiry and practice*, London: Sage Publications.

Schön, D.A. (1973) *Beyond the stable state. Public and private learning in a changing society*, Harmondsworth: Penguin.

Selener, D. (1997) *Participatory action research and social change*, Ithaca, NY: Cornell Participatory Action Research Network.

Wenger, E. (1998) *Communities of practice: Learning, meaning, and identity*, Cambridge: Cambridge University Press.

4.10 Evaluation research

Colin Robson

To state the obvious, evaluation research is both evaluation and research. The term is useful because, while evaluation is widespread in modern societies, much of what goes on is of dubious quality and unworthy of being labelled research. Evaluation is typically defined as *an attempt to assess the value or worth of something*. Both public services, and private businesses and other concerns, now work in a climate of accountability, efficiency, value for money, and so on, where managers and others press (or are pressed) towards some form of evaluation. The argument for evaluation research is that, by following the canons of social science research, you are likely to produce more trustworthy findings than you would get from simple informal evaluations.

Some researchers see a tension between the traditional tasks of research in describing, explaining and understanding, and evaluating. Also, evaluation research almost always has a clear political dimension. However, there is increasing recognition that both values (including the values of the researcher) and political considerations permeate all social policy and social work research. Evaluation research is simply an area where they are more obviously inescapable, and where the conventions and procedures of formal research provide particularly valuable checks and balances. Murtagh (2001) provides a useful brief review of the 'politics and practice of urban policy evaluation'. He discusses the issues involved in carrying out evaluation research in this context, providing a case study of evaluation of urban policy in Derry/Londonderry.

Newcomers to evaluation commonly assume that its purpose is self-evident. Is the policy effective in achieving its planned goals? A concern for *outcomes* is important and is commonly linked to the claim that RCTs (randomised controlled trials; see Section 5.3) are the 'gold standard' for evaluations, although this view is disputed (for example, Hough, 2010; see also **Box 1e** in Section 1.6 in this volume). Certainly evaluation can legitimately have many purposes, including finding out:

- if client needs are met;
- how a policy is operating;
- how it might be improved;
- how the costs involved compare with the benefits that it provides; and
- why it is working (or not working).

More than one purpose may be covered, with improvement almost always being of interest, even if not stated as the main purpose. Murtagh's (2001) example, referred to above, includes two very different approaches to evaluation, stressing different purposes.

Evaluation research is often commissioned research. Those commissioning the study may well not know what they need. A not uncommon request is to 'design a questionnaire to ...'. This is an example of the 'method of data collection' cart being put before the 'research design' horse (see also Sections 5.3 and 6.3). It calls for sensitive exploration by the researcher. What is going to be most useful for the commissioner of the research? Do they need to have hard outcome evidence by the end of the year? Or is there a suspicion that things might not be working out as envisaged, and the concern should be mainly on what is happening in practice? However, unintended consequences of social interventions are found widely, and policy makers have been known to fight shy of funding an evaluation that might reveal some unpleasant truths. Evaluation research calls for well-developed personal, social and communicative skills in the researcher, to navigate these tricky waters (Robson, 2011).

Murtagh's (2001) study was a large multilevel study (defined below), carried out by external evaluators. Evaluations can, of course, also be small-scale when they are much more likely to be carried out by 'insiders' (Robson, 2000). The fact that a study is an evaluation neither rules in nor rules out particular research designs or methods of collecting data. This is much more a question of the type of research question to which one is seeking answers (Robson, 2011), and of the purpose of the evaluation. Murtagh incorporates an impressive range of methods using both quantitative and qualitative methodologies. His two main approaches are 'community audit' and 'participatory action research' (PAR), and these illustrate the point that any approach has its strengths and limitations. Murtagh concludes that 'by focusing on local actors in [community audit] valid but silent interests can be missed and issues about ownership and control over action research can cause problems in the interpretation and use of data. However, combining a number of mutually supporting techniques within a single evaluation design might meet both the expectations of funders and funded' (2001, p 231). *Box 4l* provides details of a complex, consortium-led, national evaluation of a government programme to help people with disabilities and health difficulties into employment – the New Deal for Disabled People (NDDP).

An important outcome of the evaluation is a report. While sharing many characteristics with research reports in general, evaluation reports often differ in that they include *recommendations* for action arising from the findings. It is crucial that the report communicates with the intended audience(s). Different reports may be needed for different audiences (for example, funders or sponsors, professionals, clients, and so on; see also Section 7.3) and may need to be very different in style and length. A one-page 'executive summary' is almost always useful (see also Section 7.4 for further discussion about tailoring outputs for different audiences).

Box 4l: Evaluating policy: the New Deal for Disabled People
Bruce Stafford

After piloting in 1998, the New Deal for Disabled People (NDDP) was implemented nationally in 2001. It was a voluntary programme designed to help people with disabilities and health conditions secure (sustainable) employment. Its delivery was contracted out by the public employment service, Jobcentre Plus, to a national network of providers known as job brokers. The evaluation of NDDP is an example of a large-scale independent study commissioned by a government department, the Department for Work and Pensions (DWP). A UK–US consortium conducted the evaluation, and the organisations in the consortium at the end of the evaluation were: Abt Associates (US), National Centre for Social Research and the Universities of Loughborough, Nottingham, Oxford and York.

In summary, the aims of the evaluation were to:

- establish the experiences and views of a wide range of people involved in the NDDP;
- explore the operational effectiveness and management of the service; and

- establish the effectiveness of the NDDP including its net impact.

The evaluation had a mixed and multi-method design. Over the six years (July 2001-November 2006) covered by the evaluation there were surveys of the eligible population, employers, job brokers and programme participants. There was also qualitative research with key actors, including participants, job broker and Jobcentre Plus staff and employers. In addition, survey and administrative data were used in the impact and cost–benefit analyses. Underpinning these components was the DWP's administrative NDDP evaluation database. A key feature of the evaluation design was that many of the data collection components had a longitudinal dimension. As a consequence, different research elements captured changes in the programme as it evolved.

The formative evaluation, on how the programme worked and why, drew on the qualitative interviews and the surveys of participants and employers. The impact evaluation was originally conceived as a social experiment (or RCT; see Section 5.3 and *Box 5a*), but ministers subsequently rejected this design and a matched comparison methodology using administrative data was adopted instead. That is, the impact analysis entailed comparing benefit and employment outcomes for participants with a matched group of non-participants (the counterfactual). Each participant was matched to 10 non-participants using a number of demographic variables, such as age and sex, and benefit variables, such as duration, as well as type of disability.

Findings from surveys, administrative data and the impact analysis fed into a cost–benefit analysis, which was conducted from the perspectives of the participant, the government and society as a whole, the latter being the sum of the first two. Costs and benefits were estimates for each of these three perspectives.

The evaluation findings informed policy makers of the effectiveness of the programme (via impact and cost–benefit analyses), identified 'gainers' and 'losers', and analysed how and why the programme worked. For example, the research identified the factors associated with variations in the performance of job brokers, and associated with moves off benefit into employment. In addition, the findings informed and influenced wider policy debates within government, such as the then ongoing reforms to Incapacity Benefit and the design of the Pathways to Work pilots. Within the DWP, the findings also benefited policy analysts working on programmes for older people and the New Deal for 50 Plus. In addition to policy makers, findings were presented to those involved in actually delivering the programme.

The evaluation of NDDP is significant because of the number of participants on the programme – 260,330 between July 2001 and November 2006 (see Stafford et al, 2007; Stafford, 2011). The programme helped 110,950 (43%) find jobs by November 2006, and the cost–benefit analysis estimated a positive net social benefit of £2,915 to £3,163 for longer-term and £613 to £861 for more recent claimants.

The evaluation is in some respects a-typical of UK government-commissioned studies due to its scale, duration and that there were 19 published reports. Many government-commissioned evaluations cover only the very early years (even months) of an intervention and may focus on 'what works and why' and not include a systematic assessment of net impact. However, it is an example of some of the larger-scale evaluations that government have commissioned (such as those for some of the other New Deals, Pathways to Work and Educational Maintenance Allowance), of consortium working, and of the variety of research methods that can and are used in evaluations.

References

Stafford, B. (2011) 'Supporting moves into work: New Deal for disabled people findings', *Scandinavian Journal of Disability Research*. First published on 27 May 2011 (i First): www.tandfonline.com/doi/abs/10.1080/15017419.2011.558235

Stafford, B., Corden, A., Meah, A., Sainsbury, R. and Thornton P. (2007) *New Deal for Disabled People: Third synthesis report – Key findings from the evaluation*, DWP Research Report No 430, Leeds: Corporate Document Services.

Question for discussion

• How does evaluation research differ from other types of research?

References

Hough, M. (2010) 'Gold standard or fool's gold? The pursuit of certainty in experimental criminology', *Criminology and Criminal Justice*, vol 10, pp 11-22.

Murtagh. B. (2001) 'The politics and practice of urban policy evaluation', *Community Development Journal*, vol 36, pp 223-33.

Robson, C. (2000) *Small-scale evaluation: Principles and practice*, London: Sage Publications.

Robson, C. (2011) *Real world research: A resource for users of social research methods in applied settings* (3rd edn), Oxford: Wiley-Blackwell.

Further reading

Bamberger, M., Rugh, J. and Mabry, L. (2006) *Real world evaluation: Working under budget, time, data, and political constraints*, London: Sage Publications.

Hall, I.M. and Hall, D. (2004) *Evaluation and social research*, Basingstoke: Palgrave Macmillan.

Robson, C. (2000) *Small-scale evaluation: Principles and practice*, London: Sage Publications.

Website resources

American Evaluation Association: www.eval.org/resources.asp
European Evaluation Society: www.europeanevaluation.org

4.11 Comparative research methods

Emma Carmel

Comparison is part of the way in which we think about our everyday lives as well as part of social policy and social work research generally. **International comparative social research** refers to something more specific (the term is from Hantrais, 2009, pp 2-9): *the explanation of similarities and differences between socioeconomic and political phenomena* *in two or more countries.* These phenomena can be conceptualised on a large scale, like 'welfare states', or 'child poverty rates', or they can involve micro-level comparisons, of individual experiences and behaviour, like 'users' experiences of mental health services', or 'professional discretion in care for older people'.

There are several reasons why we undertake international comparisons, but in public policy studies, they commonly revolve around (Landman, 2002; Hantrais, 2009, p 11):

- specifying our understanding of particular phenomena by describing and analysing more cases of it;
- explaining policy outcomes and/or evaluating relative policy success and failure in different settings;
- using variations in cases to test or generate theories;
- learning lessons from different cases for policy and/or practice improvement – or to avoid mistakes.

In all such research, however, there is a tension, or even trade-off that must be addressed in the research design: how do we capture the complexity of our cases while also ensuring we can say something *comparatively* – about more than one case?

Defining the research problem

An important way to overcome comparability problems is to ensure that the concepts you use 'travel' from one country or language to another, without losing their meaning (Rose, 1991), so that they are focused enough to be precise, but general enough to be applied in different contexts (Sartori, 1973). Undertaking this task can be difficult, and has implications for the interpretation of research findings. For example, a concept can appear to apply in a range of settings, but not actually describe the same kind of institution, activity, policy or process in all cases (Mangen, 1999, pp 111-13). This poses significant problems of comparability across cases, especially for qualitative studies, where lack of attention to conceptualisation can result in misunderstanding or misinterpretation of data. It has been argued that this problem can be turned to an advantage in qualitative comparative research, so that comparing the meaning of concepts, such as 'care', or 'welfare', or 'well-being' in different countries can reveal insights about broader sociopolitical or institutional differences (Ferrari, 1990; Carmel, 1999).

In quantitative comparative research, the trade-off is not as acute, but conceptualising the research problem appropriately for comparison can still pose difficulties. For example, comparative evaluations of the extent and causes of welfare state reform in OECD (Organisation for Economic Co-operation and Development) countries have had to directly address the 'dependent variable problem'. This problem revolves around how we can define welfare state reform generally enough to compare the same phenomenon across many different cases, but specifically enough not to include every new social policy measure in its definition. This led to significant debate about how far particular conceptualisations (and their measurement) shape our findings and their interpretation (Clasen and Siegel, 2007).

Choosing cases

Comparative social policy traditionally compares policies or welfare systems, taking the national level as the unit of analysis, but it might be more appropriate for the research to compare cities or regions (Schunk, 1996), while the role of international organisations such as the European Union (EU), or The World Bank, means that policies are not only made at national level (Kennett, 2001; Yeates, 2008). The researcher must distinguish between local, regional, national and international policies and contexts very carefully when specifying their research question.

It is also necessary to decide whether to study a few ('small-*n*') or many ('large-*N*') cases (Peters, 1998, pp 58-78). If interested in detail and context, practical and resource issues usually dictate a *small-n* study, to focus on the nuances of the cases at hand. These studies often use *qualitative* research methods – the trade-off is made in favour of capturing complexity. In small-*n* studies, however, the choice of which cases to compare becomes analytically very significant, to ensure that findings are not merely a function of having selected particular cases to compare. *Large-N* studies facilitate the study of a wide range and variety of countries. These studies are usually *quantitative* and are best suited to searching for generalisable patterns in policies and outcomes, and for classifying a wide range of cases. Here, the trade-off is made in favour of simplicity and comparability, although it has more recently been strongly argued that in welfare state research this simplicity can be misleading (Ebbinghaus, 2005). A complementary approach has also been developed, which is gaining increasing interest in social policy studies: *fuzzy-set analysis*, which facilitates the comparison and categorisation of cases by their differences in degree and in kind, and permits the combination of quantitative and qualitative data (Ragin, 2000; see Kvist, 1999 for a pioneering application to comparative social policy).

Data collection and analysis

The final problem of comparability concerns data analysis. Regarding quantitative data, the main distinction is between harmonised and standardised data. **Harmonised data** are data which have been collected for particular purposes, and which are afterwards recalculated so that as far as possible the variables in different datasets measure the same thing, either to create a new dataset, such as the Luxembourg Income Study, or by the individual researcher combining different national secondary datasets. However, some differences in measurement and calculation across countries and data cannot be harmonised *post hoc*, and these data must be analysed with caution to avoid drawing false conclusions about comparability. The alternative approach is to use **standardised data**, which are collected by using a common questionnaire in a range of countries. Standardised data can also be created by asking national experts to complete questionnaires on their respective countries using a common format, or formulae for the calculation of benefits and services for a 'model' person or family. Standardised data ensure a much greater degree of comparability, but non-trivial problems of translation can still arise in questionnaire design, so that multi-language and multi-country teams of researchers are usually required. These kinds of data are much less available than harmonised data, due to their costs and scale.

For qualitative comparativists, language remains an issue for data collection and analysis, and the process of translation must be part of, rather than prior to, the process of interpreting data to prevent loss of meaning. It is also especially important to be familiar with the sociopolitical and institutional contexts of the research in order to avoid major errors of interpretation, and here again, multi-country teams of researchers can help limit such problems (Chamberlayne and King, 1996; Quilgars et al, 2009). *Box 4m* provides an illustration of some of the issues and challenges confronting researchers wanting to examine and understand poverty across countries.

Question for discussion

- What are the advantages and pitfalls of undertaking comparative research?

Box 4m: Comparative research on poverty
Jonathan Bradshaw

Since the 1990s, our capacity to analyse poverty comparatively has been greatly enhanced by the availability of new data. Thus, the Luxembourg Income Study (LIS) has included more countries, more sweeps and has become the vehicle for comparative analysis of poverty (UNICEF, 2005). The Organisation for Economic Co-operation and Development (OECD) regularly accumulates data from member countries and undertakes detailed analysis of poverty and inequality (OECD, 2008). Perhaps most exciting of all is the development by the EU of the Statistics on Income and Living Conditions (EU-SILC) which has become the main vehicle for producing the indicators of social inclusion which are designed to monitor the Lisbon Strategy using the Open Method of Coordination (OMC) (TÁRKI/Applica, 2010).

However, there are a number of problems:

- Studies using these datasets tend to define poverty as an arbitrary point on the general distribution of income. LIS and OECD tend to use 50% of the median and the EU uses 60% of the median.
- Income has to be adjusted to household size by using equivalence scales. These scales have no basis in science – the EU uses the modified OECD scale that the OECD has abandoned. The OECD uses the square root of the number of people in the household. The choice of equivalence scale influences the composition of the poor.
- Income is really only an indirect indicator of poverty – it is only a partial representation of deprivation, social exclusion, want or need.
- The results are sensitive to the general shape of the income distribution and the threshold is very different in different countries. Thus, for example, the relative poverty threshold in EU-SILC for a couple with two children in Latvia in 2007 was €615 and in the UK €1,989 in purchasing power parities per month. The at-risk of poverty rate in both countries was 19%. Yet the poor in Latvia, even taking into account differences in purchasing power, were living at much lower levels.

- They fail to take account of the distribution of income within families – especially problematic for those (southern EU) countries with significant minorities of people living in multi-family households.
- Most analyses report poverty rates, not poverty gaps – how far below the poverty line people are.
- The cross-sectional datasets do not allow an analysis of how often or how long people are in poverty, although some comparative data is emerging (OECD, 2008) and more may emerge from the cohort element in the EU-SILC.

Out of these criticisms there have been two important developments. First, more work has begun to use deprivation indicators (OECD, 2008; TÁRKI/Applica, 2010; Fusco et al, 2011), and indicators of deprivation have been added to the EU set (Guio, 2009). Second, broader multidimensional indices of material well-being have been developed (Bradshaw and Richardson, 2009; OECD, 2009).

Question for discussion
- What are the key problems in making comparisons of poverty between different countries?

References

Bradshaw, J. and Richardson, D. (2009) 'An index of child well-being in Europe', *Journal of Child Indicators Research*, vol 2, no 3, pp 319-51.

Fusco, A., Guio, A.-C. and Marlier, E. (2011) *Income poverty and material deprivation in European Countries*, Working Paper No 2011-04, Luxembourg: CEPS/INSTEAD Working Papers (www.ceps.lu/pdf/3/art/609.pdf).

Guio, A.-C. (2009) *What can be learned from deprivation indicators in Europe?*, Luxembourg: Eurostat (http://epp.eurostat.ec.europa.eu/cache/ITY_OFFPUB/KS-RA-09-007/EN/KS-RA-09-007-EN.PDF).

OECD (Organisation for Economic Co-operation and Development) (2008) *Growing unequal? Income distribution and poverty in OECD countries*, Paris: OECD.

OECD (2009) *Doing better for children*, Paris: OECD.

TÁRKI/Applica (2010) *Study on child poverty and child well-being in the European Union*, Budapest: TÁRKI Social Research Institute (www.tarki.hu/en/research/child poverty/index.html).

UNICEF (United Nations Children's Fund) (2005) *Child poverty in rich countries 2005*, Innocenti Report Card 5, Florence: UNICEF (www.unicef-irc.org/publications/pdf/repcardbe.pdf).

Further reading

Alcock, P. (2006) *Understanding poverty* (3rd edn), London: Palgrave Macmillan.

Marlier, E., Atkinson, T., Cantillon, B. and Nolan, B. (2007) *The EU and social inclusion: Facing the challenges*, Bristol: The Policy Press.

Website resources

European Union Income and Living Conditions (EU-SILC) database: http://epp.eurostat.ec.europa.eu/portal/page/portal/microdata/eu_silc

Organisation for Economic Co-operation and Development (OECD) poverty statistics: www.oecd.org/

Luxembourg Income Study (LIS): www.lisproject.org/

References

Carmel, E. (1999) 'Concepts, context and discourse in a comparative case study', *International Journal of Social Research Methodology*, vol 2, no 2, pp 141-50.

Chamberlayne, P. and King, A. (1996) 'Biographical approaches in comparative work', in L. Hantrais and S. Mangen (eds) *Cross-national research methods in the social sciences*, London: Pinter, pp 95-104.

Clasen, J. and Siegel, N. (2007) *Investigating welfare state change. The 'dependent variable problem' in comparative analysis*, Cheltenham: Edward Elgar.

Ebbinghaus, B. (2005) 'When less is more. Selection problems in large-*N* and small-*n* cross-national comparisons', *International Sociology*, vol 20, no 2, pp 133-52.

Ferrari, V. (1990) 'Socio-legal concepts and their comparison', in E. Øyen (ed) *Comparative methodology. Theory and practice in international social research*, London: Sage Publications, pp 63-80.

Hantrais, L. (2009) *International comparative research. Theory, methods, and practice*, Basingstoke: Palgrave.

Kennett, P. (2001) *Comparative social policy: A critical introduction*, Buckingham: Open University Press.

Kvist, J. (1999) 'Welfare reform in the Nordic countries in the 1990S: using fuzzy-set theory to assess conformity to ideal types', *Journal of European Social Policy*, vol 9, no 3, pp 231-52.

Landman, T. (2002) *Issues and methods in comparative politics: An introduction*, London: Routledge.

Mangen, S. (1999) 'Qualitative research methods in cross-national research settings', *International Journal of Social Research Methodology*, vol 2, no 2, pp 109-24.

Peters, B.G. (1998) *Comparative politics: Theory and methods*, London: Macmillan.

Quilgars, D., Elsinga, M., Jones, A., Toussaint, J., Ruonavaara, H. and Naumanen, P. (2009) 'Inside qualitative, cross-national research: making methods transparent in a EU housing study', *International Journal of Social Research Methodology*, vol 12, no 1, pp 19-31.

Ragin, C. (2000) *Fuzzy-set social science*, Chicago, IL: Chicago University Press.

Rose, R. (1991) 'Comparing forms of comparative analysis', *Political Studies*, vol 39, no 3, pp 446-62.

Sartori, G. (1973) 'Faulty concepts', in P.G. Lewis and D.C. Potter (eds) *The practice of comparative politics*, London: Longman/Open University Press, pp 356-91.

Schunk, M. (1996) 'Constructing models of the welfare mix: care options of frail elders', in L. Hantrais and S. Mangen (eds) *Cross-national research methods in the social sciences*, London: Pinter, pp 84-94.

Yeates, N. (2008) *Understanding global social policy*, Bristol: The Policy Press.

Further reading

Hantrais, L. (2009) *International comparative research. Theory, methods, and practice*, Basingstoke: Palgrave.

Kennett, P. (2001) *Comparative social policy: A critical introduction*, Buckingham: Open University Press.

Landman, T. (2002) *Issues and methods in comparative politics: An introduction*, London: Routledge.

Mahony, J. and Rueschmeyer, D. (eds) (2003) *Comparative historical analysis in the social sciences*, Cambridge: Cambridge University Press.

Sica, A. (ed) (2006) *Comparative methods in the social sciences* (vols 2-4), London: Sage Publications.

4.12 Post-structuralist perspectives
Carolyn Noble

While post-structuralism and post-modernity are often used interchangeably, there are important distinctions between these two cultural theories. *Post-modernism* is concerned with exploring theories of society, culture and history (Bauman, 1992). Reason and rationality, as representing the path to objectivity, to the truth of being, as leading social change and progress through grand political and social ideas and technological advances orchestrated through a welfare state and guided by a powerful and authoritative human actor, was to be jettisoned in favour of openness and tolerance (Bauman, 1992). This openness and tolerance was to be undertaken without reason and moral, political, social and cultural absolutes (Bauman, 1992; Chambon and Irving, 1994). Social structures (such as class, gender, ethnicity, governmentality, that is, prisons, schools, hospitals) are seen to oppress, exclude, alienate and discriminate and are to be challenged and their authority and legitimacy is to be questioned (Leonard, 1997; Foucault, 2001). The local activity is favoured over the global and difference and diversity are freed from invisibility and explored and appreciated (Leonard, 1997; Pease and Fook, 1999).

Post-structuralism's focus is on the symbolic, such as language, identity, the subjective, and sites and forms of power, and its analyses created new meanings and understandings in the symbolic realm. Post-structuralists, taking ideas from Derrida, Lacan and Foucault, are more concerned with notions around how language influences what is knowledge, who speaks from that knowledge base and what legitimacy and centrality is given to that knowledge (Foucault, 1982, 2001, 2009; Choat, 2010). Language practices are embedded with symbols and meaning which, when opened up (deconstructed), expose a multitude of meanings and speaking subjects (discourses) (Chambon et al, 1999). Not only are people positioned as having multiple speaking positions, these positions are constructed by the dominant discourses from science, economics, politics, law and welfare, which construct individuals to act in fixed and homogeneous ways (Irvine, 1999; Healy, 2000). Focusing on the post-structuralist discourse, the world is best understood as a mass of cultural groups, each with their own system of meanings, understandings, needs and purposes so that no group or literary text should have a privileged voice over the other (Noble, 2004). Moving away from the universal (and from the notion of the state) to focusing on the local communities and giving voice to the different and diverse social networks and social, political, cultural and language groupings in these communities, highlights the complexities of people and their everyday lives and their relation to the sociopolitical and cultural scripts. Social interaction, cohesiveness and stability depend on negotiated settlements between and among the many social and cultural grouping coexisting in any given society and any particular time (Leonard, 1997).

The concept of relativity takes hold. In this analysis, society is regarded as more discursive, fluid, changeable and ambiguous, and the human condition is open to many interpretations, meanings and many realities. Power resides in the many social discourses that inform our social position and our understanding of social issues and problems. The challenge is to unpack these meanings and realities in a way that frees new identities, knowledge, and opens up public discourses to new narratives associated with the social and human condition and its interaction with culture, politics, economics, language, power plays and ideas (Yeatman, 1994).

Shifting from an analysis of social structures to a study of social thought, these 'post' theories are transforming the social science discourse, resulting in a paradigm shift in social work, social policy and social research. These ideas give meaning to how welfare users (for example) have been constructed as either deserving, non-deserving, or as undeserving (and the resulting consequences that this construction elicits). Policy documents are seen as constructing a particular type of welfare subject such as 'single mother', 'unemployed youth', with its oppressive and discriminatory script and are now open to challenge and re-construction (Noble, 2004). An example that Healy (2000) gives when talking about service users from a social worker's perspective is that a 'violent offender' may also be seen as a 'survivor of sexual assault,' 'a loyal son' and 'protective father', 'a person battling addiction' and 'dedicated worker'. This example also highlights the way language can hide multiple identifies and multiple positions (or subjectivities). Governmentality is challenged as directing how its citizens think, act and behave through its institutions (hospitals, schools, prisons), and social work practice is seen as contributing to the control and surveillance of the very population it is trying to help/empower/rehabilitate (Noble, 2004; Healy, 2000).

The challenge of these 'post' theories is for social policies to broaden their concept of social rights, human need, individual freedom and common good to include different subjects previously submerged in the broad universal principles of traditional social policy practices (such as women, ethnic groups, people with disabilities, young and old people, indigenous peoples) (Jamrozik, 2001). Of course, such theories are not without criticism. The focus on the individual, subjectivity, identity and difference, shifts the focus away from structural inequalities of class, ethnicity, gender, ability, age and the wider social forces of global power and capital interests as *the* constraining factors in reaching human betterment (Fraser, 2008). If relativism is the central tenet, then how can social workers and policy makers act with any certainty and social researchers inform policy developments? Pease and Fook (1999) and Ife (1999) suggest a form of social work practice that values diversity and legitimates difference but holds onto the enlightenment ideals of emancipatory social justice and human rights as well as continuing to engage in political struggles against all forms of oppression.

Question for discussion

• In what ways do post-structuralist approaches seek to move social work and social policy analysis forward?

References

Bauman, Z. (1992) *Intimations of postmodernity*, London: Routledge.
Chambon, A. and Irving, A. (eds) (1994) *Essays on postmodernism and social work*, Toronto: Canadian Scholars' Press Inc.

Chambon, A., Irving, A. and Epstein, L. (eds) (1999) *Reading Foucault for social work*, New York: Columbia University Press.

Choat, S. (2010) *Marx through post structuralism: Lyotard, Derrida, Foucault, Deluze*, London: Continuum International Publishing Group.

Foucault, M. (1982) 'The subject and power', *Critical Inquiry*, no 8, pp 777-95.

Foucault, M. (2001) *Madness, civilization: A history of insanity in the age of reason*, London: Routledge.

Foucault, M. (2009) *Security, territory, population: Lectures at the Collège de France*, Basingstoke: Palgrave Macmillan.

Fraser, N. (2008) *Adding insult to injury: Nancy Fraser debates her critics* (edited by K. Olson), London: Verso.

Healy, K. (2000) *Social work practices: Contemporary perspectives on change*, London: Sage Publications.

Ife, J. (1999) 'Postmodernism, critical theory and social work', in B. Pease, and J. Fook (eds) *Transforming social work practice: Postmodern critical perspectives*, Melbourne: Allen & Unwin, pp 211-23.

Irving, A. (1999) 'Waiting for Foucault: social work and the multitudinous truth(s) of life', in A. Chambon, A. Irving and L. Epstein (eds) *Reading Foucault for social work*, New York: Columbia University Press, pp 211-23.

Jamrozik, A. (2001) *Social policy in the post-welfare state: Australia on the threshold of the 21st century*, Melbourne: Longman.

Leonard, P. (1997) *Postmodern welfare: Reconstructing an emancipatory project*, London: Sage Publications.

Noble, C. (2004) 'Postmodern thinking: where is it taking social work?', *Journal of Social Work*, vol 4, no 3, pp 289-304.

Pease, B. and Fook, J. (eds) (1999) *Transforming social work practice: Postmodern critical perspectives*, Melbourne: Allen & Unwin.

Yeatman, A. (1994) *Postmodern revisionings of the political*, New York: Routledge.

Further reading

Flynn, T.R. (2005) *Sartre, Foucault, and historical reason, 2: A post-structuralist mapping of history*, Chicago, IL: Chicago University Press.

Kelly, M.G. (2009) *The political philosophy of Michel Foucault*, New York: Routledge.

Lyotard, J.-F. (1991) *The postmodern condition: A report on knowledge*, Minneapolis, MN: University of Minnesota Press.

Midgley, J. (1999) 'Postmodernism and social development: implications for progress, intervention and ideology', *Social Development Issues*, vol 21, no 3, pp 5-13.

Mishra, R. (1999) *Globalisation and the welfare state*, Cheltenham: Edward Elgar.

Parton, N. (ed) (1996) *Social theory, social change and social work*, London: Routledge.

Parton, N. and O'Byrne, P. (2000) *Constructive social work: Towards a new practice*, Basingstoke: Palgrave.

Powell, F. (2001) *The politics of social work*, London: Sage Publications.

Williams, F. (1996) 'Postmodernism, feminism and the question of difference', in N. Parton (ed) *Social theory, social change and social work*, London: Routledge, pp 61-76.

4.13 Practitioner research
Ian F. Shaw

Practitioner research involves a practitioner or group of practitioners carrying out enquiry in order to better understand their own practice and/or to improve service effectiveness. While practitioner research may occur in fields as diverse as pharmacy, criminal justice and teaching, the emphasis in what follows is on social work and social care. Projects are typically small and localised and there is great variation in topic, design and methodology. Associated characteristics of practitioner research include direct collection or reflection on existing data; professionals setting research aims, which are usually for practical or immediate benefits; and a focus on the researcher's own practice and/or that of their peers.

A systematic review of published studies (Mitchell et al, 2010) identified several barriers to practitioner research:

Resources: including lack of time, research confidence and expertise and difficulties in arranging cover. Obtaining practical support and the reliance on external collaboration and support were also problematic.

Professional identity: social workers may view themselves as helpers rather than intellectuals, and question how research knowledge fits with other sorts of knowledge, including intuition, experience, authority and policy.

Organisational system and culture exacerbate difficulties faced around workload, role expectation and lack of support. Social workers in small, isolated agencies and settings are particularly disadvantaged.

The review identified possible success factors for undertaking practitioner research. These appear to include working in a close team environment (that is, small teams of practitioner researchers or forms of peer support) with group ownership and passion for the practice focus of their projects. Clear project milestones to address time management, forward planning and maintaining motivation, and the support of the employing organisation, also proved important facilitators. There have also been useful initiatives to facilitate the development of practitioner research networks. The evidence about practitioner research suggests that questions of research ethics are not given extended attention, although the ethical challenges of being an insider researcher call for sensitive handling.

The primary *substantive* focus of most practitioner research in social work has been on actual or potential service users, and the primary issue or *problem* focus has been on understanding or evaluating social work services and understanding/strengthening user involvement in social work, through partnership or empowerment. Two thirds of the studies reviewed by Mitchell et al (2010) focused on people as actual or potential services users. The great majority of studies adopted qualitative methodologies, usually unstructured or semi-structured interviews, but also focus groups. Very few involved quantitative methods.

Interesting and nicely balanced questions are posed by the activity of practitioner research, sharpened by the estimate that at any one time there are probably two to three times as many current practitioner researchers as academic researchers in the UK (Shaw, 2005).

Perhaps the question with the more far-reaching implications is how we understand the relationship between practitioner research and mainstream academic social research. There are three possible answers that, although apparently different, are not necessarily exclusive. First, practitioner research may be viewed as a small-scale and perhaps rudimentary form of academic research. For practitioners who aspire to an academic career, this may be a useful way of seeing the activity. Second, is practitioner research a form of social work practice? Social workers have sometimes preoccupied themselves asking if research in general is similar to or very different from practice. Indeed, a case has been made that social work research is distinguished by its practice agenda (SPRING, 2009). Third, should practitioner research best be understood as a distinctive form and culture of inquiry? Possibly so. It may not be helpful to envisage practitioner research as being either 'inside' or 'outside' practice or research. It seems best to depict the experience of practitioners, in their practitioner-as-researcher work, as possessing a sociality outside, or at least on the margins of, *both research and practice* – an uncomfortable but creative marginalisation marked by an identity that is neither research nor practice (Lunt et al, 2009).

If this is true, support and facilitation for practitioner research will not be simply about providing information on methods and techniques. A practice that has an intrinsic emergent quality to it cannot be reduced to a set of prior rules or textbook prescriptions. The problems of development of practitioner research are often framed in a 'deficit' way – that researchers lack skills, time, support and so on. These considerations may be true but must be counterbalanced by a recognition that the identity of practitioner research emerges in the process of doing it. It should be supported, where they emerge, by wider communities of practice. In doing so, we should note that practitioner researchers seem rarely to directly involve service users (see Section 4.8). The research foci are likely to differ – but users, carers and practitioners as researchers share a common risk of marginalisation from the academic mainstream that suggests grounds for active conversations between one another.

Question for discussion

- In what ways is practitioner research similar to or different from social research done by mainstream researchers? Why are those similarities and differences significant for social work practice?

References

Lunt, N., Shaw, I. and Mitchell, F. (2009) 'Practitioner research in CHILDREN 1st: cohorts, networks and systems' (www.iriss.org.uk/sites/default/files/iriss-practitioner-research-children1st-report-2009.pdf).

Mitchell, F., Lunt, N. and Shaw, I. (2010) 'Practitioner research in social work: a knowledge review', *Evidence & Policy*, vol 6, no 1, pp 7-31.

Shaw, I. (2005) 'Practitioner research: evidence or critique?', *British Journal of Social Work*, vol 35, no 8, pp 1231-48.

SPRING (Southampton Practice Research Initiative Network Group) (2009) 'The Salisbury Statement on Practice Research' (www.socsci.soton.ac.uk/spring/salisbury/).

Further reading

McLeod, J. (1994) *Practitioner research*, London: Sage Publications.
Rice, N. and Youdin, R. (2011) *Practitioner as researcher: Integrating research into professional practice*, New York: Pearson Publishers.

Relevant organisations

Knud Ramian has run the most sustained and significant series of practitioner research networks through The Evaluation Centre, Department of Psychiatry, County of Aarhus, 8200 Risskov, Denmark.

Website resources

Lunt, N. (2009) Podcast on 'Practitioner research: literature review': www.iriss.org.uk/resources/practitioner-research-programme-literature-review-neil-lunt
Shaw, I. (2009) Podcast on 'Practitioner research': www.iriss.org.uk/resources/practitioner-research-programme-literature-review-ian-shaw

4.14 Psychosocial research

Lynn Froggett

Googling 'psychosocial research' produces over 5,000,000 results, generally referring to social and psychological inquiry that relates to people's health or well-being. However, in the UK, an emergent arena of Psychosocial Studies is generating research that moves beyond the psyche/social dualism to think about the psychological and the social together (see, for example, Clarke and Hoggett, 2009; Day Sclater et al, 2009). Such research rejects the notion of an individual abstracted from society and sees subjectivity as inscribed in intra-psychic, interpersonal, institutional and societal relations (Froggett, 2002; Frosh et al, 2003; Froggett and Hollway, 2010). These dimensions mutually constitutive are sometimes in tension – for example, a social service user might feel supported by social workers but in conflict with the organisation – their entitlements are determined by moral/ideological policy discourses on rights and responsibilities which they may subscribe to in principle, yet feel oppressed by in practice.

The key features of psychosocial research can be summarised as follows.

Ontologically, what is commonly described as 'individual' (inner/intra-psychic) is already thoroughly social (interpersonal/cultural/societal), while the 'social' is imbued with the 'psychic' life of individuals. A key concern is the development of adequate accounts of the inextricably intertwined psyche/social relation. Hence psychosocial research on identity moved beyond positioning theory where identity is assimilated to social locatedness (gender/'race'/class etc), to ask how and why people invest in positions which are produced both projectively because they fulfil emotional functions and discursively (see Skeggs, 1997, on positioning theory; Hoggett, 2000, and Froggett, 2002, on the infusion of social and political life with emotions; and Hollway, 2008 for a critique of categorising research subjects discursively and demographically).

Epistemologically, the researcher's own mind and senses are regarded as key research instruments. The researcher's subjective response to participants and the societal–collective context informs data collection and analysis. Psychosocial researchers try to avoid imposing categories and frameworks and devise methodologies where, as far as possible, the object of knowing is allowed to reveal itself (Alford, 1989). However, recognition of researcher subjectivity does not preclude a critically realist stance where reality imposes limits on knowing and resists the omnipotent control of the researcher. Hence, alongside analytic social scientific inquiry there is interest in forms of attention developed in clinical settings, in which the person seeking knowledge maintains an open receptive state of mind and tries to avoid imposing their own preconceptions on the object of inquiry, for example, 'negative capability', where premature characterisation and interpretation are withheld as the object is beheld 'without memory or desire' (Bion, 1962, 1970), and 'reverie', which allows a syncretistic appreciation of the object (Bion, 1962, 1970; Ehrenzweig, 1967).

The idea of the psychosocial subject as a meeting point of inner and outer forces, something constructed and yet constructing, a power–using subject, which is also subject to power, is a difficult subject to theorise, and no one has yet worked it out. There is concern to develop methodologies which bring inquiry as close as possible to research participants' experience: 'A psycho-social approach towards social research is an attitude, or position towards the subject(s) of study rather than just another methodology' (Clarke and Hoggett, 2009, p 2). 'Experience near' and 'experience distant' methods of data generation and analysis (Geertz, 1974) may be used in combination: 'thick description' may be alternated with critical analysis. Recent debates on research into social work practice have focused on experiences at the practice interface as well as what practice achieves and its societal contextualisation; the terms 'practice near' and 'practice distant' describe alternative ways of apprehending practice processes and identifying practice outcomes (*Journal of Social Work Practice*, 2009).

The influence of psychoanalytic thinking is evident in how researchers and researched are regarded as emotional, conflicted, defended and not transparent to themselves. This means that in research, how things are said and what is not said and cannot be said are significant. Data generation therefore allows tacit, embodied and affective dimensions of experience to emerge; for example, in Tavistock models of infant and institutional observation (Hinschelwood and Skogstad, 2000; 2007 *Infant Observation* journal) or biographical narrative interviews structured to respect interviewees' habitual patterns of self-expression (Wengraf, 2001). Para-linguistic detail is included in transcripts; object-handling and visual media may be incorporated. Interpretations consider body language, omissions, silences and quality of interaction between research participants.

The concern with tacit and unconscious dimensions of experience demands hermeneutic interpretation; a common strategy is to analyse data fragments, hence provisional interpretation of data parts, such as observational instances or parts of an interview which seem worthy of special attention, perhaps because they are puzzling or paradoxical. Interpretations of these parts must make sense in relation to other parts, and to the whole before they are accepted as plausible. Reflexive strategies such as panels (Froggett and Wengraf, 2004) or reflective seminars (Hollway, 2008) are essential so that researchers can challenge one another's disposition to interpret data in particular ways, perhaps because of their own life experiences or commitments. Interview fragments must find iterative support within the whole. Interpretations filter through researcher subjectivity, aspects of which are opaque for ideological or biographical reasons, necessitating reflexive strategies such as panels or reflective seminars. Hoggett et al (2010) acknowledge that psychosocial research has been criticised for 'top-down' interpretation and advocate a dialogical approach to data collection and interpretation in dialogue with research participants.

Much psychosocial research uses psychoanalytic and social scientific concepts together to explore conscious and unconscious aspects of agency. Post-Kleinian thinking (Hoggett, 2000; Hollway and Jefferson, 2000; Clarke, 2006) tends to refer heuristically to 'inner world' (object relations) and 'outer world' (social relations). Even though inner/object relations and social relations are inextricably intertwined, they denote different registers of experience that may conflict and generate anxiety. The aim is to understand how people internalise the world they live in, and how they also produce it by enacting their own anxieties and desires, relations to people and how things are produced, internalised or defended against, and to recognise the desiring and divided nature of subjectivity. For example, in 'Becoming a mother' (ESRC-funded Identities and Social Action Programme) first-time mothers were interviewed and observed relating to their babies (Elliott et al, 2009). The researchers traced interactions between the mothers and babies, showing how the baby's demands activate the mother's sense of how she was cared for, and how this influences her own caregiving identifications of mothers with babies, and babies with mothers, showing the significance of separateness/separation in negotiating maternal identity, and how 'emotional and physical demands of the baby catalyse the mother's infantile experience and her own associations of being cared for' (Urwin, 2007, p 2; see also Hollway, 2010). By contrast, post-Lacanian thinking uses psychoanalytic concepts to explore the inscription of subjectivity in the sociocultural domain through discourse. In a project on young masculinities, Frosh et al (2003) conducted interviews and focus groups with teenage boys to understand which identity positions were available to them, and why particular boys took up specific positions.

This account has selectively identified contributions relevant to social work, counselling, psychotherapy and social policy. Psychosocial research is a varied, trans-disciplinary field (Stenner, 2008). It uses diverse theoretical resources to achieve non-dualistic approaches to a problem that is as old as social science: the individual/society relation. Influences include critical theory, post-structuralism and Bordieusian and Deleuzian approaches. Discursive psychology has been influential, so have the sociology of emotions and psychoanalysis.

Boxes 4n and **4o** provide two illustrations of the application of psychosocial methods, first in a restorative justice setting, and second with a focus on social workers' responsiveness to unaccompanied asylum-seeking children.

Question for discussion

- How does psychosocial research try to move approaches that treat the individual and society as though they are separate beyond dualistic views of the individual and society?

Box 4n: Psychosocial methods in action
Lynn Froggett

Two linked projects aimed to investigate the contribution of creative interventions in Restorative Justice programmes (Froggett, 2007; Froggett et al, 2007; Farrier et al, 2009). The projects generated a mixture of primary observational and verbal data: film footage of young offenders working with a range of artistic media in a restorative justice context and biographical interviews with them. Secondary data included professionally compiled information relating to assessment, offending history and life situation held on file. The orientation of the research was psychosocial in that it focused on various dimensions of restoration and reparation for the young people: as a state of mind, a mode of interpersonal relating, an internalisation of a relationship to a moral community and a relationship to the wider society mediated through the youth justice system.

Specific findings were that for some young offenders creative activities, in the context of personal or group relationships, could facilitate or contain creative or destructive states of mind; enable these to be symbolised in language and artwork; develop capacity to experience reparative wishes towards victims; and engage in community-based reparation programmes. By providing artwork as a 'third' focus of attention to facilitate self-expression (Froggett, 2008), the research used 'experience near' methods (Hollway, 2009) with the young people, who tended to find the binary structure of a conventional interview intimidating.

Implementing the practice and research programme required close collaboration with youth justice professionals, youth workers and community artists, and the methodology was 'practice near' in the sense that that the process of practice and inquiry were intertwined in the use of creative media to enable and record identity work and moral reflection. However, the research design also incorporated 'experience distant' and 'practice distant' strategies such as the analysis of data in standardised formats held on file and updated periodically by successive professionals as the young person moved through the youth justice system.

The use of film and other visual media allowed for interpretation that moved constantly back and forth between embodied and imaginative enactments of emotional states and verbal expression. Critical incidents were analysed with people from outside the research team (Farrier et al, 2010) and Biographical Narrative Interpretive panel analysis, in which panel members reflexively challenge one another's interpretations, was used to ensure researcher reflexivity (see Wengraf, 2001; Froggett and Wengraf, 2004). Pen portraits or vignettes – a form of writing that preserves the emotional vitality of the researcher's experience in the service of reflexive transparency – were also incorporated (Froggett and Hollway, 2010). The research demonstrated the value of a psychosocial approach in researching a form of practice (creative interventions in a youth justice context) and developing policy, in terms of promoting 'creative' rather than compensatory or punitive routes to community-based reparation.

References
Farrier, A., Froggett, L. and Poursanidou, K. (2009) 'Offender based restorative justice and poetry: reparation or wishful thinking?', *Youth Justice*, vol 9, no 1, pp 63-78.

Froggett, L. (2007) 'Arts based learning in restorative youth justice: embodied, moral and aesthetic', *Journal of Social Work Practice*, vol 21, no 2, pp 249-361.

Froggett, L. (2008) 'Artistic output as intersubjective third', in S. Clarke, H. Hahn and P. Hoggett (eds) *Object relations and social relations: The implications of the relational turn in psychoanalysis*, London: Karnac, pp 87-111.

Froggett, L. and Hollway, W. (2010) 'Psychosocial research analysis and scenic understanding', *Psychoanalysis, Culture and Society*, vol 15, no 3, pp 281-301.

Froggett, L. and Wengraf, T. (2004) 'Interpreting interviews in the light of research team dynamics', *Critical Psychology*, vol 10, pp 94-122.

Froggett, L., Farrier, A. and Poursanidou, K. (2007) 'Making sense of Tom: seeing the reparative in restorative justice', *Journal of Social Work Practice*, vol 2, no 1, pp 103-17.

Hollway, W. (2009) 'Applying the "experience-near principle" to research: psychoanalytically informed methods', *Journal of Social Work Practice*, vol 23, no 4, pp 461-74.

Wengraf, T. (2001) *Qualitative research interviewing: Biographic narrative and semi-structured methods*, London: Sage Publications.

Box 4o: Psychosocial research into social workers' responsiveness to unaccompanied asylum-seeking children

Ravi K.S. Kohli

Social work with refugee children requires an understanding by workers of many 'inner' and 'outer' worlds, within which facts and feelings co-exist (Schofield, 1998). Here, problem sorting and sense making take place together in relation to children's experiences as forced migrants, looking back at their past, anticipating the future and settling down to a daily routine in a new country. It is by working together on 'surface' and 'depth' issues (Howe, 1996) that psychosocial work can create a distinctive, helpful trajectory for their lives.

In my own study of social workers and their responsiveness to unaccompanied asylum-seeking children (Kohli, 2007), 29 social workers in four areas of the UK were interviewed about unaccompanied young people in their care. Half the practitioners worked in specialist unaccompanied asylum-seeking children's teams, and half in more generalist child and family social work teams. Entering the teams, and obtaining permission to carry out interviews about the politically and therapeutically sensitive subject (Lee, 1993) of caring for refugee children, was difficult. There were many borders of trust that needed to be safely negotiated before practitioners could talk openly. Overall, they needed to be accompanied in their story telling, and to have a sense that their story of the children's stories would not be 'audited' for effectiveness, and that they would not be criticised. Each of the social workers was asked, within an extensive semi-structured interview, to tell the story of one young person they were working with, taking into account the context of their own relationship with the young person, and their thoughts about working with unaccompanied children more generally.

The three main research areas regarding social work practice were:

• What social workers knew about the young people's past lives, current circumstances and future hopes and fears.

- How social workers described resettlement and the ways they helped unaccompanied minors to resettle.
- How social workers experienced the young people and what sense they made of their own relationships with them.

Each story was then analysed in relation to the ways in which it illuminated differing dimensions of their engagement with the young people's inner and outer worlds. The social workers' narratives encompassed three dimensions: doing practically helpful things, particularly in organising and coordinating formal networks of care and protection; being kind, and listening to stories of deep uncertainty and distress, particularly in evoking people who had died or disappeared, or in working with immigration uncertainties; and in longer-term work helping young people to have a sense of faithful companionship over time, in order to lessen loneliness.

Overall, despite the complexity of the work, practically and therapeutically, social workers explained how they tried to keep unaccompanied minors safe, how they helped them to grow friendship networks and recover kinship strands where possible, and how they expected (and planned for) the young people's talents and interests to lead to educational and employment success. Psychosocially, these aspects of safety, belonging and success were the ones that reached and bridged inner and outer worlds. The use of psychosocial research methods enabled the study to draw out these emotional as well as practical elements of the social workers' and young people's experiences.

Question for discussion
- How might a researcher be experienced as trustworthy within contexts that are politically, practically and psychologically complex?

References
Howe, D. (1996) 'Surface and depth in social work practice', in N. Parton (ed) *Social theory, social change, and social work*, London: Routledge, pp 77-97.
Kohli, R. (2007) *Social work with unaccompanied asylum seeking children*, Basingstoke: Palgrave Macmillan.
Lee, R.M. (1993) *Doing research on sensitive topics*, London: Sage Publications.
Schofield, G. (1998) 'Inner and outer worlds: a psychosocial framework for child and family social work', *Child & Family Social Work*, vol 3, pp 57-67.

Further reading
Ahern F.L. (ed) (2000) *Psychosocial wellness of refugees. Issues of qualitative and quantitative research*, New York: Berghahn Books.
Eastmond, M. (2007) 'Stories as lived experience: narratives in forced migration research', *Journal of Refugee Studies*, Special Issue: 'Methodologies of refugee research', vol 20, no 2, pp 248-64.

Relevant organisations
Children's Legal Centre Refugee and Asylum Seeking Children's Project: this is a registered charity and aims to help non-immigration specialist professionals working with asylum-seeking and refugee children find out about this group of children's rights and entitlements.

Their non-technical explanations of rights and entitlements is excellent and a good general resource, although each child will require specialist detailed advice in relation to their own precise circumstances: www.childrenslegalcentre.com/index.php?page=404_childrens_legal_centre

British Refugee Council Children's Services: the best known of the Refugee Council's services for children is the Children's Panel who work directly with separated children, as well as giving advice to those involved in their support (www.refugeecouncil.org.uk/howwehelp/directly/children). The Panel members work with separated children and young people seeking asylum who are under the age of 18 when they enter the UK and with asylum-seeking young people under 21 who, in the absence of a parent, are caring for younger brothers or sisters, to:

- assist the young people access legal representation;
- guide the young people through the asylum process;
- accompany the young people to asylum interviews, tribunal and appeal hearings, magistrates and crown court appointments;
- support the young people during appointments with GPs, hospitals, social services or other service providers.

Website resource

Forced Migration Online, Psychosocial Working Group: www.forcedmigration.org/psychosocial/

References

Alford, C.F. (1989) *Melanie Klein and critical social theory: An account of politics, art and reason based on her theory*, New Haven, CT and London: Yale University Press.

Bion, W.R. (1962) *Learning from experience*, London: Maresfield.

Bion, W.R. (1970) *Attention and interpretation*, London: Maresfield.

Clarke, S. (2006) 'Theory and practice: psychoanalytic sociology and psycho-social studies', *Sociology*, vol 40, no 6, pp 1153-69.

Clarke, S. and Hoggett, P. (2009) 'Researching beneath the surface: a psychosocial approach to research practice and method', in S. Clarke and P. Hoggett (eds) *Researching beneath the surface*, London: Karnac, pp 1-26.

Day Sclater, S., Jones, D.W., Price, H. and Yates, C. (eds) (2009) *Emotions: Psychosocial approaches*, Basingstoke: Palgrave.

Ehrenzweig, A. (1967) *The hidden order of art*, London: Paladin.

Elliott, H., Gunaratnam, Y., Hollway, W. and Phoenix, A. (2009) 'Practices, identification and identity change in the transition to motherhood', in M. Wetherall (ed) *Theorising identities and social action*, London: Palgrave Macmillan, pp 19-37.

Froggett, L. (2002) *Love, hate and welfare*, Bristol: The Policy Press.

Froggett, L. and Wengraf, T. (2004) 'Interpreting interviews in the light of research team dynamics', *Critical Psychology*, vol 10, pp 94-122.

Froggett, L. and Hollway, W. (2010) 'Psychosocial research analysis and scenic understanding', *Psychoanalysis, Culture and Society*, vol 15, no 3, pp 281-301.

Frosh, S., Phoenix, A. and Pattman, R. (2003) 'Taking a stand: using psychoanalysis to explore the positioning of subjects in discourse', *British Journal of Social Psychology*, vol 42, pp 39-53.

Geertz, C. (1974) 'From the native's point of view: on the nature of anthropological understanding', *Bulletin of the American Academy of Arts and Sciences*, vol 28, no 1, pp 26-45.

Hinschelwood, R.D. and Skogstad, W. (2000) *Observing organisations: Anxiety, defence and culture in health care*, London: Routledge.

Hoggett, P. (2000) *Emotional life and the politics of welfare*, London: Palgrave Macmillan.

Hoggett, P., Beedell, P., Jimenez, L., Mayo, M. and Miller, C. (2010) 'Working psycho-socially and dialogically in research', *Psychoanalysis, Culture and Society*, vol 15, pp 173-88.

Hollway, W. (2008) 'The importance of relational thinking in the practice of psycho-social research: ontology, epistemology, methodology, and ethics', in S. Clarke, H. Hahn and P. Hoggett (eds) *Object relations and social relations: The implications of the relational turn in psychoanalysis*, London: Karnac, pp 137-62.

Hollway, W. and Jefferson I. (2000) *Doing qualitative research differently*, London: Sage.

Infant Observation (2007) Special Issue on 'Becoming a mother: changing identities', edited by C. Urwin, *Infant Observation*, vol 10, no 3.

Journal of Social Work Practice (2009) Special Issue on 'Practice near research', edited by S. Briggs and L. Froggett, *Journal of Social work Practice*, vol 23, no 4.

Skeggs, B. (1997) *Formations of class and gender*, London: Sage Publications.

Urwin, C. (2007) 'Doing infant observation differently? Researching the formation of mothering identities in an inner London borough', *Infant Observation*, vol 10, no 3, pp 239-51.

Wengraf, T. (2001) *Qualitative research interviewing: Biographic narrative and semi-structured methods*, London: Sage Publications.

Further reading

Clarke, S. and Hoggett, P. (eds) (2009) *Researching beneath the surface*, London: Karnac.

Website resources

UK Psychosocial Studies Network: www.psychosocial-network.org/
The International Research Group for Psychosocietal Analysis: www.irgfpsa.org

4.15 Unobtrusive methods
Stewart Page

Traditionally, many social researchers have emphasised the formal, even pretentious, aspects of research – we thus have a multitude of solemn and rather non-user-friendly textbooks on statistics and rules for research procedures.

We seldom, however, acknowledge the incompleteness and naiveté of our approach. Much research implicitly assumes, for example, that research participants will simply 'respond', that is, will write or verbalise faithfully what they think or will do. By contrast, unobtrusive or 'indirect' methods neither seek nor depend on the obtaining of informed consent from participants. One such method, often used in absence of 'hypotheses' or focused expectations, is the use of hidden data-recording techniques, or periods of covert 'participant observation' (see, for example, Goffman, 1961; Rosenhan, 1973), that is, in which observed participants are unaware of being observed with the observer's research purposes in mind.

Attitudes, or other information about one's self, are frequently unreliable predictors of behaviour in real settings. Thus, a telling contrast exists between what individuals do when they realise or suspect that they are being observed, compared to when they assume their behaviour is unverifiable, anonymous or otherwise unknowable to others. This contrast appears frequently in studies comparing observable or 'public' with privately expressed behaviour, that is, when the 'chips are down'. Several studies, summarised in Page (2000), found, for example, that people referring subtly to past psychiatric treatment, homosexuality or to AIDS, were given information that was known independently to be inaccurate, in telephone rental enquiries concerning availability of advertised rooms or flats. Using various comparison conditions in these studies, for example, with callers making no mention of any of the above issues, landlords seldom reported accommodation as unavailable.

Put bluntly, individuals in real life situations do not 'behave' after giving *consent* to be observed. That is, they behave with spontaneity and, usually, essential self-interest. Moreover, the most reliable predictors of what X will do are often observations of past behaviours, that is, performed under the presumption of privacy. Some indirect methods, such as content analysis (see Section 5.8), gather observations from sources clearly not involving the issue of consent – such as magazines, newspapers, internet websites, media presentations or archival sources. Rathje and Murphy (1992) demonstrated how the tracking and analysis of human rubbish could be used as a means of research and investigation.

In referring to methods known as indirect or unobtrusive, we draw principally from the writings of Webb et al (1966, 1981) in which they mention the example of analysing the comparative popularity of museum exhibits by measuring wear and damage to floor tiles in front of each. Webb et al believed that social science research should be supplemented (not replaced completely) by unobtrusive procedures, whenever feasible. Lee (2000) has also provided a comprehensive and valuable summary of studies using these methods. As an illustration of how unobtrusive methods might be used to observe human behaviour, the famous US television series *Candid Camera* became notorious, although also respected by social scientists, for its effective studies of human behaviour under conditions of presumed privacy and freedom from evaluation by others. The series used unobtrusively filmed records of unknowing individuals – 'participants' – upon confronting a variety of contrived although apparently 'real' social situations. The individuals were thus free to 'be themselves', usually to their later embarrassment.

Darley and Latane (1970), using a similar approach, also studied the typical passivity and non-intervention of bystanders, when confronted with apparent (simulated) emergency situations, such as a victim experiencing an apparent heart attack or other emergency situation. 'Unobtrusive' means non-interfering, or unnoticed. Thus, our research lesson is that, whenever appropriate, we should consider the use of methods which do not themselves affect or render misleading the data being gathered. The term 'unobtrusive' thus refers not to specific statistical analyses or designs, but to a general class or type of method, and overall strategy for research. When we critique conventional research, we often note that a particular study seems to have omitted something important regarding generalisability, for example, a certain comparison or control group. An equally cogent criticism, from the perspective of unobtrusive methods, would be the question: 'What would those participants have done, had they been informed or known they were being observed?'.

Assessing the current status of unobtrusive methods involves the underlying matter of informed consent. For example, many research methods, prevalent at the time of Webb et al's first publication (1966), remain relatively popular today. Perhaps this reflects the much increased research emphasis today on the ethical matter of consent; that is, the methods remain popular not necessarily through any inherent guarantee of validity, but because it is usually not difficult to obtain and document participants' consent to take part in them (Page, 2000; see also Chapter Two in this volume). The increased sensitivity about informed consent in research also seems congruent with the rise of a broader epistemological view, indeed the very antithesis of unobtrusive measures, that research participants should be viewed not just as data providers or 'objects' to be observed, but as consenting and participating kindred spirits – even actively evaluating and collaborating in the research at hand, as other approaches discussed in this chapter show clearly. Even more generally, the increased concern with documenting informed consent for research participation may also reflect society's increased concerns with consumerism, openness, and redressing dyadic situations supposedly representing power differentials, for example, teacher and student, or researcher and participant.

Consequently then, unobtrusive methods, based on data gathered without the cooperation or knowledge of participants, do not seem strongly represented today within conventional methodology and epistemology of research (Lee, 2000; Graziano et al, 2009). Such methods do indeed involve ethical pitfalls, and in some cases their use may be legally precarious. By contrast, however, it is interesting that Webb et al did not view the methods as inherently unethical, and in fact, indeed contrary to the current preoccupation with informed consent, saw them as *enabling researchers to sleep better*, that is, as non-invasive means of protecting participants' privacy and avoiding disruption in their lives (Webb et al, 1966, p vii).

Historically, social research has attempted generally to appear systematic, quantitative and 'scientific', that is, in emulation of the natural sciences, with frequent adherence to direct, consented-to methods (see Friedman, 1967). This pattern of development, however, might have turned out differently. That is, had conventional methods not gained such entrenchment, or had they been questioned for their narrowness, and unobtrusive methods favoured instead, much social research might then have taken a different path. For example, Psychology, as one social science, might well have become a strong candidate to become known as the science whose unique identifying characteristic or 'microscope' was the deliberate and strategic use of unobtrusive approaches with which to observe and study behaviour occurring in the real world.

Questions for discussion

- Identify the advantages and disadvantages of using unobtrusive methods in social policy or social work research.
- How might you design or arrange a study to investigate attitudes towards a certain minority group or controversial topic? In terms of establishing the validity of your study, would you depend exclusively on responses to interviews, surveys, questionnaires or other methods where respondents usually want to 'look good', even though such methods are frequently used in research today? In the spirit of unobtrusive research methods, what are some

other ways to study these attitudes, that is, which do not depend on the active, knowing cooperation and consent of the participants?

References

Darley, J. and Latane, B. (1970) *The unresponsive bystander: Why doesn't he help?*, New York: Appleton Century Crofts.

Friedman, N. (1967) *The social nature of psychological research*, New York: Basic Books.

Goffman, E. (1961) *Asylums: Essays on the social situation of mental patients and other inmates*, New York: Anchor Books.

Graziano, A., Raulin, M. and Cramer, K. (2009) *Research methods: A process of inquiry*, Toronto, ON: Pearson Education Canada.

Lee, R. (2000) *Unobtrusive methods in social research*, Buckingham: Open University Press.

Page, S. (2000) 'The lost art of unobtrusive measures', *Journal of Applied Social Psychology*, vol 30, no 10, pp 2126-28.

Rathje, W. and Murphy, C. (1992) *Rubbish: The archaeology of garbage*, New York: HarperCollins.

Rosenhan, D. (1973) 'On being sane in insane places', *Science*, vol 179, pp 250-8.

Webb, E., Campbell, D., Schwartz, R. and Sechrest, L. (1966) *Unobtrusive measures: Nonreactive research in the social sciences*, Chicago, IL: Rand-McNally.

Webb, E., Campbell, D., Schwarz, R., Sechrest, L. and Grove, J. (1981) *Nonreactive measures in the social sciences*, Dallas, TX: Houghton Mifflin.

Further reading

Rosnow, R. and Rosenthal, R. (1997) *People studying people: Artifacts and ethics in behavioral research*, New York: Freeman.

Website resource

Compiled by William Trochin, a detailed and non-technical summary of indirect research methods and related issues: www.socialresearchmethods.net/kb/unobtrus.php

PART THREE: USING EXISTING RESEARCH

4.16 Secondary analysis
Karen Rowlingson

What is secondary analysis?

Secondary analysis is when a researcher analyses data that they themselves did not collect (see Bryman, 2012). For example, a researcher (secondary analyst) can analyse statistics on a range of issues including the numbers of births, marriages, deaths, criminal convictions and immigration. Government departments routinely collect these statistics, as well as many others (see Section 5.10). Government departments also carry out regular surveys to collect information on issues such as health, crime, income, employment, and so on. These data are then archived at the University of Essex Data Archive and can be analysed by other people outside government (see Section 4.19). This archive also has data from academically funded surveys, such as the British Household Panel Survey (BHPS) (see **Box 5b**) and the British Social Attitudes (BSA) Survey (see **Box 5d**). These too can be accessed and analysed.

On some occasions, secondary analysis is the analysis of data that the secondary analyst had collected in the past for a different purpose from the one that they now have. Perhaps they had been commissioned to collect some data on student debt and had carried out a survey of students and their finances. At a later date they decide to use these data to analyse student employment rates. This would also be secondary analysis.

Secondary analysis is usually thought of in terms of quantitative research but in recent years there have been attempts to encourage secondary analysis of qualitative data, for example, through the development of an archive for qualitative data at the University of Essex (Corti et al, 1995; see also Section 4.19). My focus here is on *quantitative* secondary analysis.

Advantages and disadvantages of doing secondary analysis

As a research method, secondary analysis has a number of **advantages** and disadvantages. It is a relatively cheap method as data from the University of Essex Archive can be provided free through the internet or sent through the post for a fee that may be nominal. The analyst does, of course, need a computer and appropriate software.

Secondary analysis is a relatively quick method of research as someone else has already been through the more time-consuming job of collecting the data. Having said this, it takes time for the analyst to get to know the data and to carry out the analysis, and sometimes it is easy to underestimate how time-consuming this method is.

Depending on the type of data used, analysts can gain access to surveys with massive sample sizes and there is therefore scope for considerable subgroup analysis (see *Figure 4b*).

Figure 4b: *Examples of major annual or continuous surveys*

Name (geographical area covered)	Effective sample size[a]	Response rate (%)[a]
British Crime Survey (England/Wales)	46,983	76
British Social Attitudes Survey (GB)	4,486	54
Citizenship Survey (England/Wales)	4,189 core	59
Family Resources Survey (GB)	43,173	58
General Household Survey (GB)	12,023	73
Health Survey for England (England)	14,250	64
International Passenger Survey (UK)	259,000	80
Labour Force Survey (UK)	52,000	53
Living Costs and Food Survey (UK)	10,397	51
Wealth and Assets Survey (GB)	30,595	55

Note: This draws on information in Social Trends 2010 (ONS, 2010). The effective sample sizes and response rates refer to the most recent survey included in Social Trends.

Another advantage of secondary analysis is that comparable data are increasingly available for other countries, enabling comparative analysis of secondary data (for example, through the European Community Household Panel). Data are also available over a number of years, enabling comparisons over time (for example, the General Household Survey started life in 1971, enabling three decades' worth of comparisons to be made).

In methodological terms, secondary analysis can be used for *triangulation* purposes. For example, some of the results of a smaller ad hoc survey can be compared with a much larger official survey to check the validity of the former. And secondary analysis of data can be replicated by another analyst to check on the reliability of the original research.

There are, however, **disadvantages** to the method. First of all, a certain degree of skill is needed in manipulating and analysing data that can often be large-scale and complex. For example, the BHPS 2008-09 includes 184 data files occupying 605 megabytes of disk space, and with over 200 files related to documentation. Secondary analysts therefore need a high level of skill in data handling and analysis and such skills are in relatively short supply in Britain. Other datasets, such as the BSA Survey, are, however, much less complex.

Another problem with secondary analysis is that the available data do not always perfectly fit the secondary analyst's research question for a number of reasons. Perhaps the population is slightly different. Or perhaps the sample is not large enough to enable certain types of subgroup analysis. Or perhaps some key questions were not asked, or at least were not asked in exactly the way the secondary analyst would have liked.

Most official quantitative data are archived at the University of Essex and so are easily accessible (see Section 4.19). The data also come with comprehensive information about how they were collected. But some ad hoc surveys, particularly those carried out by commercial companies, may never be archived and so access may be very difficult to obtain. Once the data have been obtained there may be very little information about them. For example, the full questionnaire may not be available and so it would be impossible to see how the questions were asked.

Nevertheless, despite all the disadvantages to this approach, there is an enormous amount of quantitative information just waiting to be analysed, and ***Box 4p*** gives one example of a secondary analysis project.

Box 4p: An example of secondary data analysis: the links between disability and family formation
Stephen McKay

The aim of this research project was to consider whether disabled people were more likely to experience divorce and family breakdown than the rest of the population – and if they had fewer opportunities to enter into partnerships in the first place. Evidence from smaller-scale studies suggested that disabled people might be facing such disadvantages (Clarke and McKay, 2008). However, there had been little systematic evidence or analysis on this matter for the UK, and so this research aimed at filling this important gap, by conducting new analysis of existing datasets. Funding came from the DWP and the Office for Disability Issues.

While a variety of different datasets were used, two were of particular importance – the 2001 Census and the British Household Panel Survey (BHPS). Individual-level data from the 2001 Census were obtained from the ESRC Census Programme, while the BHPS was available from the UK Data Archive (see 'Website resources' at the end of this section). We used data in SPSS format (a commonly used package in social science), but the datasets are also readily available in Stata and SAS. An important issue was that the different sources often used different definitions of disability, although each included aspects of an impairment that affected day-to-day living.

The 2001 Census made it possible to look at the overall relationship between disability and family status, without having to worry about non-response (the Census is compulsory) and with a very large number of people to analyse (the 'academic access' version of the Census micro-data contains 1.8 million people). This source enabled us to identify that disabled people had a higher rate of divorce and a lower rate of marriage, and were more likely to remain single. These points only became clear after controlling for differences in age group. Disabled people tended to be older than average, and age also had a strong link with marital status.

As a sample survey, the BHPS contained many fewer people (about 10,000 in each year), but had the important feature of following people over time. Our analysis looked at people's changing marital and disability status over the period from 1991 to 2005 (15 waves of BHPS data). Despite being much smaller than the Census, analysis of the BHPS presented greater technical challenges owing to its greater complexity, the result of a long questionnaire and of tracking people over time.

Use of the BHPS enabled us to tackle more of the more *causal* questions – did disability affect the rate of divorce, or might divorce (a stressful event) be leading to a higher incidence of disability? The research found that among those living alone and with a limiting health condition, some 4.7% found a partner each year, compared with 7.6% for those who were not disabled. Poor mental health tended to have a greater effect on changes in marital status than any physical disabilities. Overall, disabled people did face different chances of family breakdown compared with non-disabled people. These differences remained after taking account of differences in age, gender and other background variables.

Question for discussion
• What are the advantages and limitations of secondary data for analysing disability?

Reference
Clarke, H. and McKay, S. (2008) *Exploring disability, family formation and break-up: Reviewing the evidence*, DWP Research Report No 514, London: Department for Work and Pensions.

Further reading
Field, A. (2009) *Discovering statistics using SPSS* (3rd edn), London: Sage Publications.
Marsh, C. and Elliott, J. (2008) *Exploring data* (2nd edn), Cambridge: Polity Press.

Website resources
Economic and Social Data Service (ESDS): www.esds.ac.uk/
Economic and Social Research Council (ESRC) Census Programme www.census.ac.uk/
Office for Disability Issues: www.odi.gov.uk/
University of Essex Data Archive: www.data-archive.ac.uk

Questions for discussion

• What types of research project are best carried out by means of secondary analysis?
• Summarise the pros and cons of carrying out secondary analysis.

References

Bryman, A. (2012) *Social research methods* (4th edn), Oxford: Oxford University Press.
Corti, L., Foster, J. and Thompson, P. (1995) 'Archiving qualitative research data', *Social Research Update*, 10 (http://sru.soc.surrey.ac.uk/SRU10.html).
ONS (Office for National Statistics) (2010) *Social Trends 2010*, London: ONS (www.ons.gov.uk/ons/search/index.html?newquery=social+trends+2010 [go to pdf report Social Trends 40 Full Report]).

Further reading

Bryman, A. (2012) *Social research methods* (4th edn), Oxford: Oxford University Press.
Miller, R., Acton, C., Fullerton, D. and Maltby, J. (2002) *SPSS for social scientists*, Basingstoke: Macmillan.

Website resource

University of Essex Data Archive: www.data-archive.ac.uk

4.17 Systematic reviews
Mary Dixon-Woods

How best to conduct reviews of previous studies has become a focus of increasing interest and debate. One of the striking developments of recent years has been the emergence of *systematic review* as a distinct methodology. Systematic review methodology developed partly in response to criticisms that unstructured and poorly disciplined reviews of studies are likely to be flawed because, confronted with a large body of evidence, reviewers are susceptible to a range of heuristics, biases, prejudices and sloppy practices. Reviewers may, for example, focus on a small subset of studies but not describe how they selected them; be influenced by their own perspective and expert opinions; fail to assess the quality of studies they review; combine the findings of studies in inappropriate ways; not adequately account for publication bias (the problem that studies with positive findings are more likely to be published than those with negative findings); and marshal the evidence in support of their preferred theories.

The remedy has been seen to lie in the routinisation of processes of review through use of systematic techniques aimed at revealing to external scrutiny the basis of decisions about which studies have and have not been included in a review; making explicit and systematic the processes of summarising data across multiple studies; and, where appropriate, increasing the statistical power of estimates of effect. *Figure 4c* summarises the key characteristics.

Figure 4c: Characteristics of a systematic review

- Explicit study protocol.
- Address a formal, pre-specified, highly focused question.
- Define the eligibility criteria for studies to be included in the review in advance.
- Explicit about the methods used for searching for studies, including any efforts to track down unpublished work or studies published in foreign languages.
- Screen publications for inclusion in the review against a priori criteria.
- Conduct formalised appraisals to assess their scientific quality and otherwise limit the risk of bias.
- Use explicit methods to combine the findings of studies.

Systematic review has become established as a scientific research methodology in its own right, but it has also acquired political and social force as one of the cornerstones of the evidence-based practice and policy movement (see Section 1.6). However, it is not without controversy. A particular focus of criticism of early forms of systematic review methodology was that they offered little or no place for qualitative research (Dixon-Woods et al, 2001). Simply put, not everything we need to know about the world can be measured or counted, and other forms of data are often needed to form a comprehensive view or understanding of an area. The last decade has seen explicit acknowledgement of the relevance and utility of qualitative research in systematic reviews, and a number of methodological developments (*Figure 4d*) aimed at enabling qualitative research studies to be synthesised or summarised either on their own or with quantitative research findings.

Figure 4d: **Examples of methods that may be used in conducting a synthesis of qualitative studies**

Bayesian meta-analysis	Thematic analysis
Content analysis	Grounded theory
Case survey methods	Meta-ethnography
Case-by-case analysis	Realist synthesis
Qualitative comparative analysis	Critical interpretive synthesis
Narrative summary	Meta-narrative mapping

The critical determinant of a choice of method, when conducting a review of evidence, is the nature of the review question to be addressed. Just as primary research requires different methods and different theoretical perspectives depending on the purpose of the research, so too will reviews. It may help to distinguish heuristically the purpose of the review into being primarily *aggregative* or *interpretive*. *Aggregative syntheses* focus on *summarising data*, perhaps using techniques such as meta-analysis. Although sometimes (mis)appropriated (for example, the terms 'meta-analysis' and 'systematic review' are occasionally treated as synonymous), the term 'meta-analysis' is properly used in a circumscribed way to describe the quantitative pooling of study findings.

Interpretive syntheses are concerned with the development of concepts and the specification of theories that integrate those concepts. Interpretive synthesis involves processes similar to primary qualitative research, in which the concern is with *generating* concepts that have maximum explanatory value. This approach achieves synthesis through incorporating the concepts identified in the primary studies into a more subsuming theoretical structure.

Methods for conducting reviews of research evidence

A number of organisations now publish guidance on how to undertake systematic reviews of studies, including The Cochrane Collaboration, the Campbell Collaboration and the UK NHS Centre for Reviews and Dissemination (CRD). This guidance focuses primarily on reviews of the effects and effectiveness of specific interventions, and primarily (although not exclusively) on aggregative reviews of quantitative data.

Methods for conducting a review of evidence that includes qualitative studies remain at varying stages of development and evaluation. It is worth noting that there are now several approaches that are, practically, very similar, but have different names and slightly different variants; the same terms are sometimes used to describe quite different things ('meta-synthesis' being one of these); some publications claim to use particular methods, but on more detailed inspection turn out not to have done so, or to have done so very poorly; and, overall, confusion about terminology and defining features abound.

It is also worth being aware that some approaches to including qualitative research in systematic reviews represent 'new' methods specifically designed to tackle the issue of synthesis, or modifications of these methods; others are primary research methods that have been adapted for the purpose of review and synthesis. Some are firmly based on the conventional systematic review template; some involve hybrids of conventional systematic review methodology and more interpretive strategies; and some represent a more fundamental challenge to the idea, premises and methods of conventional systematic review. In part, these different forms arise because, as we outline below, there often is an uneasy fit between the frame offered by conventional systematic review methodology and the kinds of epistemological assumptions and research practices more usually associated with qualitative research (Dixon–Woods et al, 2006).

Defining the review question

Defining the review question is one of the principal tasks of conventional systematic review. The normal procedure is to specify a clear set of criteria focused around a specific question, defining the study designs to be included (for example, RCTs, case control studies, etc) as well as characteristics related to the question, including populations of interest and outcomes of interest.

If the question is one requiring an interpretive account of the literature, there are good reasons for adopting a position closer to that of primary qualitative research than to conventional systematic review. A more iterative approach to question specification might be used. This would treat the question and its parameters as fundamentally unsettled and open to critique: rather than something defined very precisely in advance, the precise terms of an interpretive review question might not be determined until closer to the end of a review.

Finding the studies

Conventional systematic review methodology strongly emphasises the importance of rigorous and systematic searching to identify the population of relevant material for the parameters of the review. The importance of having a clear account of how searching was conducted is strongly emphasised, and the development and evaluation of search strategies is itself a sub-field of systematic review methodology.

Where the aim is to apply such approaches to qualitative studies, a number of challenges arise. Identifying qualitative studies using formalised search strategies is often frustrating because of poor indexing of such studies on electronic databases. More fundamentally, where the review question and its parameters are not well defined from the outset, practical problems may arise in trying to use a formalised and easily audited search strategy. Highly protocolised forms of searching might also become frustrating and unhelpfully constraining.

Selection of material for inclusion

One of the important principles of conventional systematic review is that all possible data that might contribute to the synthesis should be identified, as exclusion of relevant data might affect estimates. A meta-analysis, for instance, is concerned with quantifying how successful a particular intervention is on average, and will therefore want to include all relevant data that might assist in estimating that average. As a check on the impact of including and excluding certain studies, quantitative syntheses use methods such as sensitivity analysis.

For an interpretive review, such an approach might be very challenging, as it may be difficult to identify all relevant studies while the boundaries of relevance remain unsettled. An alternative might involve some form of theoretical sampling, with the reviewer continuing until theoretical saturation is reached. However, it could be argued that once systematic reviews fail to be *explicit* and *reproducible*, and allowed to include (apparently) idiosyncratically chosen literatures, they are no longer systematic. It is difficult to identify the checks analogous to sensitivity that might be used to determine the effects of including or excluding particular studies in an interpretive synthesis.

Appraising studies for inclusion

Systematic appraisal of quality of evidence is undertaken by those conducting systematic reviews to reduce the possibility of bias. Broad inclusion criteria – for example, adequate randomisation for RCTs – may be used to determine whether a study is suitable for inclusion. More detailed assessments of papers that are included in the review may also be undertaken to identify specific defects, and techniques such as sensitivity analysis used to explore the effects of such defects on the synthesis.

Whether or how to make judgements of the quality of qualitative research reports has been much contested. No consensus has yet emerged. A decision to exclude qualitative studies from a review on the grounds of quality is not straightforward to execute. Because of the diversity of qualitative study designs and approaches, it is at present impossible to specify universally agreed a priori defects, equivalent to inadequate randomisation for RCTs, that would indicate that a qualitative study is fatally flawed. Checklist-style approaches to assessing quality of qualitative papers are problematic and do not necessarily lead to agreement between reviewers on quality of studies (Dixon-Woods et al, 2007). Moreover, precisely how 'weak' qualitative findings should be attenuated or excluded in any synthesis is not yet clear.

Conducting a synthesis

Choices about methods for summarising and/or synthesising bodies of evidence will be strongly influenced by the purpose of the review. The methods listed in *Figure 4d* vary in their degree of procedural specification and in the kinds of interpretive and aggregative work they require. Some require the conversion of one form of data into another. For example, Bayesian meta-analysis uses qualitative research to improve quantitative estimates. Other methods, such as meta-ethnography, proceduralise some aspects of the review process, but still rely on some level of interpretation by the reviewer. Some, such as realist synthesis, require a high level of creativity and critical interpretation on the part of reviewers; indeed, critical interpretive synthesis is in many (although not all) ways a codification and formalisation of the traditional authorial approach to reviewing.

In summary, conventional systematic review methodology has emerged in response to criticisms that informal reviews may be incomplete or misleading. It requires a priori specification of the review question, the methods of searching, methods of quality appraisal, and methods of synthesis. Methodological innovations aimed at including qualitative research in systematic reviews are increasingly appearing, but are still evolving.

Question for discussion

• What are the challenges when including qualitative research in systematic reviews?

References

Dixon-Woods, M., Fitzpatrick, R. and Roberts K. (2001) 'Including qualitative research in systematic reviews: opportunities and problems', *Journal of Evaluation in Clinical Practice*, vol 7, pp 125-33.

Dixon-Woods, M., Bonas, S., Booth, A., Jones, D.R., Miller, T., Sutton, A.J., Shaw, R.L., Smith, J.A. and Young, B. (2006) 'How can systematic reviews incorporate qualitative research? A critical perspective', *Qualitative Research*, vol 6, pp 27-44.

Dixon-Woods, M., Sutton, A., Shaw, R., Miller, T., Smith, J., Young, B., Bonas, S., Booth, A. and Jones, D. (2007) 'Appraising qualitative research for inclusion in systematic reviews: a quantitative and qualitative comparison of three methods', *Journal of Health Services Research and Policy*, vol 12, pp 42-7.

Further reading

Petticrew, M. and Roberts, H. (2005) *Systematic reviews in the social sciences: A practical guide*, London: Wiley-Blackwell.

Pope, C., Mays, N. and Popay, J. (2007) *Synthezising qualitative and quantitative health evidence: A guide to methods*, Maidenhead: Open University Press.

Sandelowski, M. and Barroso, J. (2007) *Handbook for synthesizing qualitative research*, New York: Springer Publishing Company.

Thomas, J. and Harden, A. (2008) 'Methods for the thematic synthesis of qualitative research in systematic reviews', *BMC Medical Research Methodology*, vol 8, p 45.

Website resources

Dixon-Woods, M., Agarwal, S., Young, B. et al (2004) *Integrative approaches to qualitative and quantitative evidence*, London: Health Development Agency (www.nice.org.uk/aboutnice/whoweare/aboutthehda/evidencebase/keypapers/papersthatinformandsupporttheevidencebase/integrative_approaches_to_qualitative_and_quantitative_evidence.jsp).

Evans, I., Thornton, H. and Chalmers, I. (2006) *Testing treatments: Better research for better healthcare*, London: British Library (www.jameslindlibrary.org/testing-treatments.html).

Higgins, J.P.T. and Green, S. (eds) (2009) *Cochrane handbook for systematic reviews of interventions*, Version 5.0.2, The Cochrane Collaboration (www.cochrane-handbook.org).

NHS CRD (Centre for Reviews and Dissemination) (2008) *Systematic reviews: Guidance for undertaking reviews in health care*, York: NHS CRD (www.york.ac.uk/inst/crd/pdf/Systematic_Reviews.pdf).

4.18 Reviewing and synthesising diverse evidence to inform policy and action

Jennie Popay, Catherine Pope and Nicholas Mays

As Section 4.17 has shown, there are increasing demands for evidence reviews to be more transparent and robust. Methods to achieve this are most developed in reviews of the effectiveness of interventions and/or policies – referred to here as Cochrane effectiveness reviews. In this section we consider methods developed to improve the transparency and robustness of reviews that answer different types of questions and hence incorporate qualitative and/or quantitative evidence, which we refer to as diverse evidence reviews (DERs) (more detail is provided in Mays et al, 2005; and Pope et al, 2007). The word 'review' refers to the whole process of collating evidence while 'synthesis' is when evidence in a review is combined in some way. There are debates about the legitimacy of combining diverse evidence (Harden and Thomas, 2005), but our starting point is that DERs are a logical extension of the use of mixed method research designs and illuminate important questions for research, policy and practice.

An overview of the evidence review process

There are two broad types of evidence reviews: 'knowledge support' reviews aiming to summarise evidence on a particular topic and 'decision support' reviews focusing on answering a particular question. The aims determine the review questions, the evidence to be included and hence the synthesis methods to be used. Whatever the method, all evidence reviews include the same basic elements (Pope et al, 2007, p 22). However, in Cochrane effectiveness reviews these form a linear staged process (see *Figure 4e*), regulated by strict rules to minimise bias, while in DERs the processes are iterative (see *Figure 4f*).

Questions should be specified clearly before a review begins in discussion with potential users of the review. However, in DERs they may be revised as the review proceeds. All reviews should have a protocol but for DERs these provide an enabling framework guiding the review rather than a straitjacket. Search strategies and study quality appraisal are not discussed in detail here, but in DERs these are also iterative processes. Relevant evidence may be identified through a comprehensive search or a sampling strategy (random or purposeful; see Sections 5.3 and 5.4) while methodological quality is not typically used to decide whether a study should be included but instead as part of a process of exploration and interpretation during the synthesis process (Spencer et al, 2003). Theory testing and development is an important but neglected element in all systematic reviews (Petticrew and Egan, 2006) but this can be a defining characteristic of quality in DERs, allowing them to move from a simple listing of recurring themes to more explanatory syntheses (Pawson and Bellamy, 2005; Popay, 2005).

Figure 4e: The generic elements and linear process involved in Cochrane effectiveness reviews

Figure 4f: The interactive nature of diverse evidence reviews

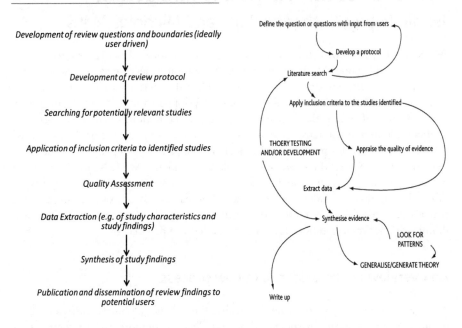

Approaches to synthesis in diverse evidence reviews

Synthesis of findings from multiple sources is the heart of any review. Synthesis methods can be located along a continuum from integrative approaches involving pooling of quantitative findings, for example, meta-analysis, to interpretative approaches involving qualitative evidence, for example, meta-ethnography (Dixon-Woods et al, 2004). Below, four types of methods are described: narrative, qualitative, quantitative and Bayesian. These can be used with qualitative and/or quantitative evidence and produce both integrative and interpretative syntheses.

Narrative approaches to synthesis

Traditional literature reviews can include any type of evidence. They typically use thematic analysis and findings are usually juxtaposed in their original form, with no attempt to transform them into a common metric. They are usually less systematic and transparent about how evidence was selected for inclusion or how findings are produced than the methods described below. However, because they are flexible and can handle a wide range of evidence they are likely to remain an important tool for research and policy.

Narrative synthesis (NS) is a systematic and transparent process using a narrative (as opposed to statistical) approach to combining study findings. It always involves the descriptive juxtaposition of findings from included studies but where the evidence allows, the final synthesis can be more integrative or interpretative and provide new knowledge. Guidance on NS produced by Popay and colleagues in 2005 highlights three situations in which it can be used: before undertaking a statistical meta-analysis; when a statistical meta-analysis isn't possible; and where the diversity of evidence included means a specialist approach to synthesis can't be used. The three elements of the NS described in this guidance and synthesis techniques it covers are shown in **Figure 4g**, which illustrates the synthesis process used in a review of evidence on 'barriers and enablers to the implementation of domestic smoke alarms' (Roen et al, 2006; see also Arai et al, 2005, 2007; Rodgers et al, 2009). The choice of specific techniques will depend on the evidence being reviewed. The diagram shows those techniques used and those rejected as not applicable in the smoke alarm review.

Realistic synthesis is another narrative approach (Pawson, 2006a). It focuses on impact/effectiveness but unlike Cochrane reviews it is a highly iterative, theory-driven process. The process draws on diverse evidence to test whether the theory or 'mechanism' underlying a programme/intervention works, for which groups and in what circumstances. If a preliminary analysis reveals that a programme works in certain ways for certain people, the reviewer develops an explanation or theory for why this happens. This explanation is then applied to a second programme underpinned by the same theory. If it performs as predicted, the theory is supported and/or expanded. If not, the theory is revised to take account of or explain any differences. Time and other resources determine how many comparisons are undertaken. An early realist synthesis (Pawson and Bellamy, 2005; Pawson, 2006b) focused on programmes that aimed to deter re-offending among child molesters by publicly 'naming and shaming' them, but there are few published examples of this approach and its generalisability has yet to be demonstrated.

Figure 4g: Synthesis process

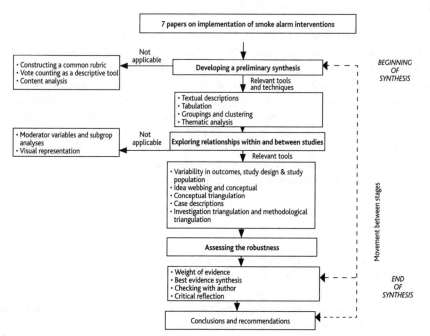

Source: Arai et al, 2007

Qualitative approaches to synthesis

These approaches involve converting all data into a qualitative form for synthesis. Meta-ethnography (Noblit and Hare, 1988; Doyle, 2003) aims to develop new theory to explain the range of research findings reported in multiple studies. Rona Campbell and colleagues have published demonstrations of meta-ethnography of evidence exploring questions concerned with people's use of medicines and experience of diabetes (Britten et al, 2002, 2010; Campbell et al, 2003). There is nothing, in principle, to stop its use for the synthesis of quantitative and qualitative findings, although it has not yet been used in this way. Cross-case analysis, which typically compare findings from different case studies using some sort of matrix or text-table format to juxtapose data, provide another method for qualitative synthesis (Ragin, 1993, 1997; Khan and van Wynsberghe, 2008).

Quantitative approaches

These approaches convert all data into quantitative (that is, numerical) form. The quantitative case survey method is a formal process for systematically coding quantitative and/or qualitative data across a number of independently conducted case studies to allow quantitative analysis (Yin and Heald, 1975; Larsson, 1993; Yin, 2003). A set of structured questions is used to extract data from each case study. Content analysis is used to transform the answers into a smaller number of categories based on explicit rules of coding, which can then be counted to identify dominant findings and make generalisations. These quantitative data may be subjected to statistical analysis.

Bayesian meta-analysis and decision analysis

This is another technique that can be used to convert any type of evidence into a quantitative form. The results are pooled for analysis and modelling. One advantage to this approach is that all relevant evidence can be brought to bear on questions of importance to policy/practice including expert judgements and public and/or stakeholder opinion. The analyses can include meta-analysis, quantitative modelling and simulations of effectiveness and cost-effectiveness. There are challenges involved in converting complex, implicit judgements into specific weights and probabilities but methods are available to do this. The Bayesian approach has been used to synthesise evidence from qualitative and quantitative research, for example, to assess the relative importance of a range of factors potentially affecting the uptake of childhood immunisations (Roberts et al, 2002).

Conclusion

The choice of a particular approach to the synthesis of diverse evidence will depend on the aim of the review, the questions to be addressed and the evidence included. Rigorous systematic reviews of diverse evidence are still at an early stage of development and so it is not possible to provide definitive quality criteria. On the other hand, it is possible to identify a set of questions that could usefully be used to check the quality of a review:

- Is the aim of the review clear – 'knowledge support' or 'decision support'?
- Are the review questions clearly specified?
- Are the methods described such that others could repeat the review using the same methods?
- Is each element in the synthesis justified?
- Do the questions posed and the type(s) of evidence reviewed 'fit' together'?
- Did the review team include the range of disciplines, skills, subject area knowledge and experience necessary to answer the question(s)?
- Where judgements are made on the basis of the synthesis, is the reasoning made clear, so that it can be discussed, if necessary, and revised, if found wanting?

Question for discussion

- Why do researchers choose to conduct diverse evidence reviews (DERs) and what kinds of research knowledge do they produce?

References

Arai, L., Popay, J., Roen, K. and Roberts, H. (2005) 'It might work in Oklahoma but will it work in Oakhampton? What does the effectiveness literature on domestic smoke detectors tell us about context and implementation?', *Injury Prevention*, vol 11, pp 148-51.

Arai, L., Britten, N., Popay, J., Roberts, H., Petticrew, M., Rogers, M. and Sowden, A. (2007) 'Testing methodological developments in the conduct of narrative synthesis: a demonstration review of research on the implementation of smoke alarm interventions', *Evidence & Policy*, vol 3, no 3, pp 361-83.

Britten, N., Riley, R. and Morgan, M. (2010) 'Resisting psychotropic medicines: a synthesis of qualitative studies of medicine taking', *Advances in Psychiatric Treatment*, vol 16, pp 207-18.

Britten, N., Campbell, R., Pope, C., Donovan, J., Morgan, M. and Pill, R. (2002) 'Using meta-ethnography to synthesise qualitative research: a worked example', *Journal of Health Services Research and Policy*, vol 7, pp 209-15.

Campbell, R., Pound, P., Pope, C., Britten, N., Pill, R., Morgan, M. and Donovan, J. (2003) 'Evaluating meta-ethnography: a synthesis of qualitative research on lay experiences of diabetes and diabetes care', *Social Science & Medicine*, vol 56, pp 671-84.

Dixon-Woods, M., Agarwal, S., Young, B., Jones, D. and Sutton, A. (2004) *Integrative approaches to qualitative and quantitative evidence*, London: NHS Health Development Agency (www.nice.org.uk/niceMedia/pdf/Integrative_approaches_evidence.pdf).

Doyle, L. (2003) 'Synthesis through meta-ethnography: paradoxes, enhancement and possibilities', *Qualitative Research*, vol 3, no 3, pp 321-44.

Harden, A. and Thomas, J. (2005) 'Methodological issues in combining diverse study types in systematic reviews', *International Journal of Social Research Methodology*, vol 8, no 3, pp 257-71.

Khan, S. and van Wynsberghe, R. (2008) 'Cultivating the under-mined: cross case analysis as knowledge mobilisation', *Forum Qualitative Social Research*, vol 9, no 1 (www.qualitative-research.net/index.php/fqs/article/view/334).

Larsson, R. (1993) 'Case survey methodology: quantitative analysis of patterns across case studies', *Academy of Management Journal*, vol 36, no 6, pp 1515-46.

Mays, N., Pope, C. and Popay, J. (2005) 'Systematically reviewing qualitative and quantitative evidence to inform management and policy-making in the health field', *Journal of Health Services Research and Policy*, vol 10, no 1, pp 1-15.

Noblit, G. and Hare, R. (1998) *Meta-ethnography: Synthesising qualitative studies*, Newbury Park, CA: Sage Publications.

Pawson, R. (2006a) *Evidence based policy: A realist perspective*, London: Sage Publications.

Pawson, R. (2006b) 'Digging for nuggets: how "bad" research can yield "good" evidence', *International Journal of Social Research Methodology*, vol 9, no 2, pp 127-42.

Pawson, R. and Bellamy, J.L. (2005) 'Realist synthesis: an explanatory focus for systematic review', in J. Popay (ed) *Putting effectiveness into context: Methodological issues in the synthesis of evidence from diverse study designs*, London: Health Development Agency, pp 83-93.

Petticrew, M. and Egan, M. (2006) 'Relevance, rigour and systematic reviews', in J. Popay (ed) (2006) *Moving beyond effectiveness: Methodological issues in the synthesis of diverse sources of evidence*, London: National Institute for Health and Clinical Excellence, pp 7-8.

Popay, J. (2005) 'Moving beyond floccinaucinihilipilification: enhancing the utility of systematic reviews', *Journal of Clinical Epidemiology*, vol 58, no 11, pp 1079-80.

Pope, C., Mays, N. and Popay, J. (2007) *Synthesising qualitative and quantitative health evidence: A guide to methods*, Maidenhead: Open University Press.

Pope, C., Mays, N. and Popay, J. (2006) 'Informing policy making and management in healthcare: the place for synthesis', *Health Care Policy*, vol 1, no 2, pp 43-8.

Ragin, C. (1993) 'Introduction to qualitative comparative analysis', in T. Janoski and A. Hicks (eds) *The comparative political economy of the welfare state*, New York: Cambridge University Press, pp 299-319.

Ragin, C. (1997) 'Turning the tables: how case-oriented research challenges variable-oriented research', *Comparative Social Research*, vol 16, pp 27-42.

Roberts, K.A., Dixon-Woods, M., Fitzpatrick, R., Abrams, K.R. and Jones, D.R. (2002) 'Factors affecting the uptake of childhood immunisation: a Bayesian synthesis of qualitative and quantitative evidence', *The Lancet*, vol 360, pp 1596-9.

Rodgers, M., Petticrew, M., Sowden, A., Arai, L., Britten, N., Popay, J. and Roberts, H. (2009) 'Testing the guidance on the conduct of narrative synthesis in systematic reviews: effectiveness of interventions to promote smoke alarm ownership and function', *Evaluation*, vol 15, no 1, pp 49-74.

Roen, K., Arai, L., Roberts, H. and Popay, J. (2006) 'Extending systematic reviews to include evidence on implementation: methodological work on a review of community-based initiatives to prevent injuries', *Social Science & Medicine*, vol 63, pp 1060-71.

Spencer, L., Ritchie, J., Lewis, J. and Dillon, L. (2003) *Quality in qualitative evaluation: A framework for assessing research evidence*, London: Government Chief Social Researcher's Office, Prime Minister's Strategy Unit, Cabinet Office.

Yin, R. (2003) *Applications of case study research* (2nd edn), Thousand Oaks, CA: Sage Publications.

Yin, R. and Heald, K. (1975) 'Using the case survey method to analyse policy studies', *Administrative Science Quarterly*, vol 20, no 3, pp 371-81.

4.19 Data archiving

Louise Corti

Data archiving refers to the long-term storage of data and methods. For the social sciences this usually means keeping outputs from research projects, and adding sufficient information to this material to enable future re-use. These days 'data' are mostly digital.

Archiving data conserves unique resources and ensures that their research potential can be fully exploited. Unless preserved and documented, data that have often been collected at significant expense, with substantial expertise and involving respondents' contributions, may later exist only in a small number of reports that analyse only a fraction of the research potential of the data. Within a very short space of time digital data are likely to become lost or obsolete as technology evolves.

Archiving digital data requires that data are preserved in formats that can be accessed by researchers, now and in the future. Data should be safely stored and be available under terms and conditions that are appropriate for any particular collection.

Where are data archived?

Social science data in digital form are typically housed in 'data archives', which are centres that actively acquire, store and disseminate data for re-use in research, teaching and learning. Collection in paper format may also reside in traditional university, national or regional archives.

The data archiving 'movement' began in the 1960s within a number of key social science departments in the US that stored original data from survey interviews. The movement spread across Europe, and in 1967 the National Research Council for the Social Sciences established the UK Data Archive. In the late 1970s archives joined wider professional organisations – the Council of European Social Science Data Archives (CESSDA) and the International Association for Social Science Information Services and Technology (IASSIST). These were established to promote cooperation on key archival strategies, procedures and technologies.

The first social science data archives collected data of specific interest to quantitative researchers, such as opinion polls, but the trend for large-scale surveys grew, and by the late 1970s archives such as the UK Data Archive began to acquire major government surveys and censuses. Because of their large sample sizes and the richness of the information collected, these national surveys represent major research resources for the social scientist. Examples of major British government series include the General Household Survey, the Labour Force Survey and the Health Survey for England. These series are used by government departments for planning, policy and monitoring purposes, and by other researchers to present a picture of households, families and people in Britain.

By the 1990s, the UK collection had grown to thousands of datasets spanning a wide range of data sources relating to society, both historical and contemporary. Micro-data from surveys, censuses, registers and aggregate statistics derived from academic, commercial and public sector sources are available to the secondary analyst. Well-established UK-based academic large-scale surveys include the British Social Attitudes (BSA) Survey, and the longitudinal and cohorts studies, the British Household Panel

Survey (BHPS), the National Child Development Study (NCDS) and the Millennium Cohort Study (MCS). In European countries similar studies are also available for research use, but access to survey data varies rather widely across Europe.

In the 1990s, the UK research community recognised the needs of qualitative researchers by supporting a qualitative data archive (Qualidata). A new culture of preserving and re-using qualitative data emerged, and research studies from Peter Townsend's career, such as *Poverty in the UK* (1979) and *The last refuge* (1962), are now preserved for researchers to consult.

Since the mid-2000s, many funders of research have recognised the value of keeping research data for future use and have set up data-sharing policies requiring researchers to document and share data from their own projects.

Preparing data for archiving

Research data are created in a wide variety of types and formats depending on the research method used. Survey data are generally stored as 'micro-data' that are numeric, while in-depth interviews are typically transcribed from audio-recordings and stored as word-processed documents.

A key concern for a data archive is to ensure that the materials they acquire are free from any legal or ethical constraints, are in an appropriate format, are documented to a minimum standard that enables informed use and cover topics that are anticipated to meet the demands of users. In order to smooth the transition from data collection, potential depositors of data should follow guidelines and standards on documenting their research, advocated by the data archiving community.

Data archives undertake 'data processing' activities. First, the dataset is checked and validated, for example, by examining numeric data values and by ensuring data are anonymised to ensure that the risk of identifying individuals is minimised. Second, contextual information is collated which will describe the study and its methods, and contain questionnaires and topic guides or anything that makes the data more usable. A catalogue record collates structured 'meta-data' to enable data to be found through searching (for example, on the internet) and covers the size and content of the data collection, its availability and terms and conditions of access.

Accessing and using data

Users typically request data from a data archive in a particular format, such as a statistical or word-processing package. These days, data can be accessed via web download facilities or can be dispatched on portable media. Users are typically required to be registered with an archive and sign an agreement to the effect that they will not attempt to identify individuals when carrying out secondary analyses. Online analysis tools are also available where users can directly explore data via a web browser, such as Nesstar (see below).

Data available from data archives can be used for a number of purposes. Secondary analysis strengthens scientific inquiry, it avoids duplication of data collection and opens up methods of data collection and measurement (see also Section 4.16). Archived data enable new users to: ask new questions of old data; undertake comparative research, replication or re-study; and inform research design and promote methodological advancement. Finally, they provide significant resources for training in research and substantive learning, such as the measurement of poverty.

Question for discussion

- What kinds of sources of data would be useful for a comparative investigation into inequalities in health in Britain from 2000 to 2010?

References

Townsend, P. (1962) *The last refuge: A survey of residential institutions and homes for the Aged in England and Wales*, London: Routledge.

Townsend, P. (1979) *Poverty in the UK: A survey of household resources and standards of living*, London: Penguin Books.

Further reading

Cole, K., Wathan, J. and Corti, L. (2008) 'The provision of access to quantitative data for secondary analysis', in N. Fielding, R. Lee and G. Blank (eds) *SAGE handbook of online research methods*, London: Sage Publications, pp 365-84.

Corti, L. (2007) 'Re-using archived qualitative data: where, how and why?', *Archival Science*, vol 7, no 1, pp 37-54.

Relevant organisations

The Office for National Statistics (ONS) is the UK government department that provides an up-to-date, comprehensive and meaningful description of the UK's economy and society compiled from government data sources. It carries out high quality survey research for government departments and other public bodies on a range of social issues to help develop government policies, inform public debate and monitor changes over time: www.ons.gov.uk/

The Economic and Social Data Service (ESDS) Qualidata at the University of Essex provides information about availability and access to qualitative research materials in the social sciences. It also provides advice on the archiving and re-use of qualitative data: www.esds. ac.uk/qualidata/about/introduction.asp

The UK Data Archive at the University of Essex hosts the largest collection of accessible digital data in the social sciences and humanities in the UK, standing at over 5,000 data collections. Data are acquired from many different sources including central government, academic researchers, opinion poll organisations and other data archives world-wide. Users can search the catalogue and indexes for data and order data in a variety of formats and media, subject to approval: www.data-archive.ac.uk

Website resources

The CESSDA (Council of European Social Science Data Archives) catalogue provides a seamless interface to datasets from social science data archives across Europe: www. cessda.org/accessing/catalogue/

Corti, L., Witzel, A. and Bishop, L. (2005) 'On the potentials and problems of secondary analysis. An introduction to the FQS special issue on secondary analysis of qualitative data', *Forum Qualitative Sozialforschung/Forum: Qualitative Social Research*, vol 6, no 1 (www.qualitative-research.net/index.php/fqs/article/view/498). This is a whole issue of the journal devoted to the sharing and re-use of qualitative data.

The ESDS website (2010) contains relevant and up-to-date information on the provision and re-use of a broad range of social science data resources in the UK: www.esds.ac.uk

ESDS catalogue record for study number 1671: Townsend, P. (1969) *Poverty in the UK: A survey of household resources and standards of living* (www.esds.ac.uk/findingData/snDescription.asp?sn=1671&key=townsend).

IASSIST (International Association for Social Science Information Services and Technology): www.iassistdata.org/

Nesstar is a web-based system for the dissemination of data. It can be used to view data, including tabular (cube) data, and meta-data that have been published using Nesstar: www.nesstar.com/software/webview.html

Quantitative research

Detailed contents

5.1 Introduction

In this chapter we address the main aspects of conducting quantitative research. The chapter is divided into three parts.

Part One: Fundamentals of quantitative research. This begins by addressing the nature of quantitative research and the importance of the criteria that are conventionally employed by practitioners to establish the quality of their investigations. It then moves on to discuss two dimensions of quantitative research that are fundamental aspects of social policy and social work research associated with this strategy: the different kinds of research design employed by quantitative researchers (including experimental, cross-sectional, longitudinal and case study designs) and the approaches to sampling that they use.

Part Two: Methods for collecting and coding quantitative data. This begins by noting the importance of coding to the processing of data. The significance of coding lies in the importance of generating data that can be quantified. The methods for the collection of quantitative data that are discussed are:

- structured interviews and questionnaires in survey research;
- internet surveys;
- content analysis;
- structured observation;
- time use diaries;
- official statistics.

Strictly speaking, two of these methods – content analysis and official statistics – are not methods for collecting data. The former is a method of handling unstructured data and information such as media reports; and official statistics are a source of data that already exist (such as claimant counts). However, they are important sources of quantitative data and as such are treated as similar to methods for the collection of data.

Part Three: The analysis of quantitative data. This final section deals with the basic elements of conducting an analysis of quantitative data.

PART ONE: FUNDAMENTALS OF QUANTITATIVE RESEARCH

5.2 Quantitative research
Alan Bryman and Saul Becker

We have already encountered quantitative research in Chapter Four as an approach to social policy and social work research that draws on principles associated with the natural sciences for its fundamental principles. The main concerns and preoccupations of quantitative researchers can be viewed as stemming from this commitment. The four main concerns and preoccupations were described as being: measurement; causality; generalisation; and replication. Therefore, although the term *quantitative* research seems to imply that quantification is the sole distinguishing characteristic of this research strategy, it is clear that there is more to quantitative research than the mere presence of numbers.

As Bryman (2012) points out, in addition to its epistemological roots in a natural science view of the research process, quantitative research tends to have two important features that further distinguish it from qualitative research. First, the approach taken by quantitative researchers typically involves a *deductive* approach to the relationship between theory and research. This term was encountered in Robert Pinker's discussion of the role of theory in social policy research in Section 3.4. A deductive approach involves the drawing of research questions from an established body of knowledge that are then tested for their soundness. As Pinker points out, according to Karl Popper, we are unlikely to be able to demonstrate a definitive truth through such a process, since all we can have is a temporarily confirmed knowledge.

Second, quantitative research adopts an **objectivist** position with respect to the nature of social reality. This means that social phenomena and social reality are generally construed as 'out there' for social actors, as entities that confront them as out of their scope of influence. Thus, something like a social network can be viewed as a thing that is independent of the people who participate in it and as such a sphere in which they can have limited impact. It is viewed as a collection of connections between individuals and groups and little more. A **constructionist** position, which tends to be associated with qualitative research, tends to challenge this standpoint by paying greater attention to the role that individuals play in constructing that network and having an influence over it. In thinking of social reality in an objectivist manner, quantitative researchers display their commitment to a natural science model of the research process since the natural order is frequently conceptualised as a pre-existing phenomenon awaiting the analytic tools of the natural scientist.

Quality criteria in quantitative research

One of the ways in which the natural science leanings of quantitative research are particularly evident is in the criteria that are employed for assessing the quality of research. Quantitative researchers have developed a well understood and clear set of criteria that influence the way research is done and written about. To a certain extent, these criteria will be unsurprising because they exhibit clear connections with the four concerns and preoccupations among quantitative researchers outlined in Chapter Four.

Reliability

Reliability has to do with the consistency or stability of findings. This issue is most clearly apparent in connection with matters of measurement. To have a reliable measure means having one that is consistent. There are two main aspects of this notion. First, a measure needs to be *externally reliable*, meaning that it should not fluctuate over time. To take a simple example: if we develop a measure of client satisfaction with a social service provider, we would not expect people's levels of client satisfaction to fluctuate other than due to changes in such things as their personal circumstances or the manner in which the service is provided. In order to assess external reliability, the researcher might administer a series of questions (let us say, 10) about the levels of client satisfaction in a sample. This series of questions might be designed to establish a scale so that respondents' replies can be aggregated to form a level of client satisfaction for each respondent, and indeed for the sample as a whole. The questions might take the form of what is known as **Likert scale** items such as:

Staff are always responsive to my needs

| Strongly agree | Agree | Neither agree nor disagree | Disagree | Strongly disagree |

I find the rules for getting the particular service I need difficult to understand

| Strongly agree | Agree | Neither agree nor disagree | Disagree | Strongly disagree |

With a Likert scale, the respondent is provided with a series of statements that are designed to establish his or her feelings about an issue by getting the respondent to indicate the degree of agreement with the statement as in the two 'items' above. Each answer is 'coded' (see Section 5.5 for a discussion of coding) so that answers can be aggregated. Let us say that we administer the scale to a sample of home care recipients to measure their degree of satisfaction with the service. We would find out each individual's level of client satisfaction. If we then administered the same measure again a month or two later, we would hope that unless something very significant has happened in the meantime (such as an influx of new staff or a new set of administrative procedures), there will be a good correspondence between people's answers over the two time periods. If there is *not* a good correspondence, the measure is externally *un*reliable.

Internal reliability is an issue that is predominantly to do with what are known as multiple-item scales such as a Likert scale. It asks the question: are all the items that make up the scale coherent? In other words, are they all connected to each other? If they are not, perhaps because one of the items is poorly related to the other items, it is not going to be an internally reliable measure. After all, it is unlikely that you would want a scale in which one of the constituent items is unrelated to the others. Internal reliability is often established using a check known as *split-half reliability*. In the case of our imaginary measure of client satisfaction, this would mean taking the 10 items and randomly dividing them into two groups of five and then examining whether respondents' scores on one half correlate well with their scores on the other five items.

Validity

Validity is concerned with the issue of whether a measure that has been devised, such as our imaginary measure of client satisfaction, really gauges the underlying concept that it is presumed to be tapping. In other words, if we devise a scale of client satisfaction, how do we know that it is measuring client satisfaction and not something else? For a start, the measure must be reliable. If a measure is either internally or externally unreliable it cannot be a valid measure. If a measure fluctuated without explanation over time or if one or two of its constituent items was inconsistent with the others, it could hardly be valid. However, establishing reliability is only a first step in ensuring that a measure is valid. Several other approaches to estimating the validity of a measure are often used, of which two are discussed below. Other validity tests are discussed in Bryman (2012).

At the very least, a measure should have *face validity*. This means that the researcher should determine that, as far as we can tell, the measure has a very good chance of tapping the underlying idea (client satisfaction). A close reading of the literature on client satisfaction will help to increase confidence since this should help to map out the main issues. In addition, face validity can be boosted by asking others to check the items that make up the measure. These people might include researchers in the field, a supervisor, practitioners and clients themselves. As regards the latter, it might be useful to use a group discussion to help devise questions and to hold another discussion to get feedback on the items that have been designed.

A further way of looking at validity is *concurrent validity*. Here, the researcher employs a criterion for establishing how far people differ on the measure in terms of the criterion. It may be that there is an external criterion that might be used, such as whether people have complained in the previous six months about the service. If it were possible to relate respondents' replies to whether they have launched a complaint, this would enable us to gauge concurrent validity. If clients who were dissatisfied with the service were more likely to have complained than those who were satisfied, our confidence in the validity of the measure would be enhanced.

In addition to the question of the validity of measurement, there is the issue of the validity of the findings from an investigation. In this connection, it is common to distinguish between *internal validity* and *external validity*, although other notions of validity exist (Bryman, 2012). Internal validity is to do with the issue of the robustness of the findings from a quantitative research investigation in terms of how sure we can be about the causal connections that we might infer from the research. In other words, if we find that income affects health, how sure can we be that it is income that affects health differentials and not something else? This issue will be dealt with in greater detail in Section 5.3, since the issue of how confident we can be in our causal findings is a major consideration and one in which the classical experimental design or randomised controlled trial (RCT) is frequently regarded as a 'gold standard'. External validity is concerned with the issue of generalisation – to what populations and groups can we generalise our findings? If a study is externally valid, then it is generalisable to a specific population. The issue of generalisation is the focus of the next section.

Generalisation

Quantitative researchers typically want to be able to generalise their findings beyond the scope of the specific group (for example, a sample of respondents) on which they have conducted their investigation. This emphasis is connected with the adoption of natural science principles, since the focus on generalisation can be seen as sharing a predilection for findings that have similar importance and features of scientific laws.

This emphasis on generalisation reveals itself particularly in the attention given to ways of maximising the chances of securing a representative sample (see Section 5.4). In this context, sampling procedures that adopt probability and random sampling principles are seen as crucial because they are most likely to produce a sample that is representative of the population from which the sample was selected. Convenience and purposive samples are often held in low esteem because they are not based on these principles and hence are likely to be of unknown representativeness.

Replication

Scientists are frequently concerned that their findings should be capable of being replicated so that another scientist could, if they wanted to, attempt to reproduce their investigations. The idea behind the faith in replication is that findings should be (and should be seen to be) independent of the person producing them. There is always the possibility that a scientist has distorted his or her findings or has not taken care to eliminate all possible contaminating factors that might have had an impact on the findings. Replication offers the opportunity to check those findings. This means that the scientist needs to spell out the procedures followed and instruments used, so that someone else can follow the same route that was taken.

This principle of being able to spell out the ways in which research was conducted, the instruments used and the procedures for analysing data has been absorbed into quantitative research, where the ability to conduct a replication is a valued feature of a research design. In the social sciences, the potentially contaminating effects of the values of the researcher are more likely to intrude than in the natural sciences, so that replication has potentially greater importance.

Honouring in the breach

To take a cue from *Hamlet* (I.iv.16), many of these principles, when it comes to research practice, are customs that are honoured more 'in the breach' than 'in the observance'. In other words, while they are widely regarded as important principles, they are not universally observed. External reliability testing is potentially time consuming and the findings deriving from it can be ambiguous (how do we know that intervening events have not had an impact in the period between the two periods of data collection?). Validity testing can be similarly extremely time consuming once we go beyond establishing face validity. Generalisation from representative samples is often difficult because in social policy and social work research certain populations may not lend themselves to the probability sampling principles outlined in Section 5.4. It may be hard to know what the population is like (for example, homeless people, informal carers). Finally, replications are rarely carried out in either the natural or the social sciences because replication is a relatively low status activity; instead, it is probably more accurate to say that it is the ability to replicate – *replicability* – that is regarded as an important quality criterion rather than replication as such.

Question for discussion

- What is the difference between reliability and validity and what is the importance of these two ideas?

Reference

Bryman, A. (2012) *Social research methods* (4th edn), Oxford: Oxford University Press.

Further reading

Bryman, A. (2012) *Social research methods* (4th edn), Oxford: Oxford University Press, Chapter 3.
Litwin, M.S. (1995) *How to measure survey reliability and validity*, Thousand Oaks, CA: Sage Publications.

5.3 Research design
Alan Bryman and Saul Becker

The terms *research design* and *research method* have a superficial similarity and are often used interchangeably if not synonymously. In this book, we draw a distinction between the two. A *research method* is a technique for gathering data, like a questionnaire, interview or observation. A *research design* is a structure or framework within which data are collected. As de Vaus (2001, p 9) points out: 'The function of a research design is to ensure that the evidence obtained enables us to answer the initial questions as unambiguously as possible'. Understanding the nature of research design and the differences between the various types of design outlined below is important because a research design provides the structure that will enable the research questions we start out with to be answered. A research design is selected for its capacity to answer the research questions that drive an investigation.

Research methods can serve different designs. In other words, a method of data collection such as a questionnaire can be employed in connection with all of the research designs delineated in this chapter. Decisions about appropriate research methods are, in a sense, subsidiary to decisions about an appropriate research design, since it is the research design that provides the framework for answering research questions. An important principle to appreciate is that there is no universally superior research design (or indeed research method) – they are only as good as their suitability to the research questions being asked. It is important, therefore, to wean yourself off a personal preference for a research design or method because it may be blinding you to alternative and possibly more suitable ways of answering research questions.

In this section, we cover the four major types of research design:

- experimental (including quasi–experimental)
- cross–sectional (including social survey)
- longitudinal
- case study.

Experimental design

The term *experiment* is often used vaguely, particularly in everyday speech. In social research methodology, however, it has a specific meaning as a type of research design whose strength lies in its ability to demonstrate relatively clear findings which demonstrate internal validity, that is, that one variable (the independent variable) really does have a causal impact on another (the dependent variable).

Imagine that we hypothesise that client satisfaction with Housing Benefit departments is affected by the type of training that staff have received, in particular, whether they have received training in anger management. We are expecting the independent variable (training) to affect the dependent variable (satisfaction). A true experiment could have the following elements:

- Manipulation – the experimental treatment (training).
- Two groups – an *experimental group* that receives the anger management training and a *control group* that does not.
- Equivalence – of the experimental and control groups. This means that staff in the experimental and control groups must be equivalent in terms of their personal characteristics. This is ideally achieved through random assignment. In this case, staff in a Housing Benefit department would need to be randomly assigned to the two conditions, so that one group would have the training and the other (the control group) would not.
- Time order – client satisfaction will be measured before (pre-test) *and* after (post-test) the experimental treatment.

Thus, the structure of the experiment takes the form of a specific design sometimes called a *classical experimental design* or *RCT*.

Figure 5a: **Experimental design for examining the impact of training in anger management on client satisfaction with service provision**

Pre-test	Experimental	Post-test	Experimental
Client	treatment	Client	group
satisfaction	Training	satisfaction	
Random			
assignment			
Pre-test	No treatment	Post-test	Control group
Client	No training	Client	
satisfaction		satisfaction	

In this experiment, the experimental treatment involves some staff attending training in anger management and others not attending the training (see *Figure 5a*). The two groups must be randomly assigned, otherwise any differences observed between the experimental and control groups could be attributed to differences in the memberships of the two groups (see *Box 5a* for an illustration of an RCT). If we find that client satisfaction increases in the experimental group whereas in the control group it does not, we have strong, internally valid evidence to suggest that training in anger management does indeed have an impact on client satisfaction because we are able to eliminate such alternative possible explanations as:

- Client satisfaction might have increased anyway. This can be discounted because if that were the case it would have shown up in the control group.
- The attitudes of research participants may have changed. Again, because of the control group this can be discounted.
- Differences between the two groups. Random assignment allows this possible factor to be discounted.

Moreover, there is no ambiguity about which variable influences which, a problem that does occur in connection with a cross-sectional design. However, whether it fares as well in connection with the issue of external validity may be a different matter. The benefit office where the research was conducted may not be typical, in part, because it is difficult to imagine what a 'typical' office is.

It is often the case that when researchers seek to conduct experiments, for various reasons they are not able to randomly assign participants to the experimental and control groups. Managers may be unwilling to allow researchers that much control since it may have an impact on the efficient running of the department. Therefore, researchers have to make do with what is known as a *quasi-experiment*, in which all of the features in *Figure 5a* and *Box 5a* are met other than random assignment.

Box 5a: Randomised controlled trials
Stephen Joseph

Imagine a new social policy initiative is introduced to help unemployed people find paid work. A group of people who were provided with the initiative are contacted six months later and 60% are now in employment. Is this evidence that the initiative worked?

Perhaps 60% would have been re-employed anyway. We cannot say that the result was due to the initiative. If, however, we could show that those who received the initiative were more likely to be re-employed than those who didn't, then we are in a stronger position to attribute change to the initiative itself. If only 30% of another group of people who did *not* receive the initiative were re-employed, it seems more likely that the initiative has worked.

But when we look closer we find out that both groups live in different areas of the city, one group is older on average than the other and the data from one group was collected in 2010, the other in 2008. Because of these extraneous factors we still cannot say for sure that the result was due to the initiative.

To be able to say with confidence that the initiative led to re-employment, both groups would need to be equivalent on all the other factors that might otherwise account for any difference. This is the solution provided by the research design called the randomised controlled trial (RCT).

The RCT provides the strongest source of evidence about cause and effect within the field of social sciences. The reason it is the strongest source of evidence is that this is a formal experimental approach to try to rule out the influence of extraneous factors, and therefore offers the possibility that a causal relationship can be identified. How this is achieved is through 'randomisation'. For example, if we wanted to test the effectiveness of the new re-employment programme, we might set up a trial in which 400 people seeking work are randomly allocated to either the new re-employment programme or to the existing programme. Two hundred people receive the new programme and 200 receive the old programme. Six months later, has one group done better than the other? The important aspect is that the groups are large enough so that any differences between them will be averaged out so that the two groups are effectively equivalent except for the fact of whether or not they received the old or the new programme. That is the purpose of randomisation – to try to rule out any bias by randomly allocating people to one group or the other. We want the groups to be equal in terms of gender, age, length of time unemployed, motivation to find work and whatever else we think might exert an influence on the results. If the members of each group were not allocated randomly there is a danger that bias would creep in – for example, perhaps for some reason the researcher tends, without being aware of it, to allocate the more motivated people or more employable to one group than the other.

Figure 5b: **Design of randomised controlled trials**

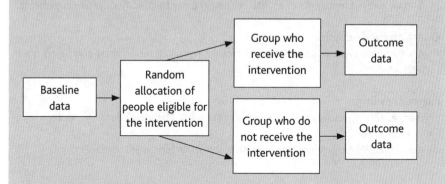

It is impossible to control for everything, which is why we rely on randomisation and large numbers to smooth away such variation. The larger the numbers, the more sure we can be that the differences between the groups are averaged out so that the only factor that might account for the difference is the experimental manipulation – in this case, the new re-employment programme.

The RCT is unique as a research design because it helps us to identify one particular variable as the cause of an observed difference. No other form of research design is able to do this.

As such the RCT deserves an important place in our research armoury. But this does require that we are able to make the case that all else is equivalent between the two groups. To evaluate an RCT one must look carefully at the groups to check for the possibility of unwanted sources of variation. RCT studies of high quality will provide data showing that the groups are equivalent on the other variables of possible interest.

RCTs are important because they are able to provide evidence of cause–effect relationships, but the complete removal of all but one source of influence is an impossible goal, particularly when RCTs are taken out of the laboratory into the real world. The best that can be expected is that we can say that the manipulation is the most likely source of change.

For this reason replication is important. Only when RCTs have been repeated with different research participants on a number of occasions and obtain the same results, can we be reasonably sure that a causal link between two variables has been identified.

Finally, it is important to remember that although RCTs are the most effective design for evaluating whether an intervention works, they do not necessarily tell us *why* the intervention works. We know that aspirin seems to cure headaches, but this does not imply that the lack of aspirin caused the headache in the first place. Interventions related to social policy and social work practice are often multifaceted, containing a variety of components, all of which are thought to lead to change, so knowing that an intervention is effective does not tell us what the key mechanisms are. This is illustrated in psychotherapy research, where it is well established from RCTs that psychotherapy 'works' but debate still continues about *how* psychotherapy works. As such, more sophisticated RCTs might use more than one experimental group in order to test for the relative effectiveness of several interventions, and to dismantle the components of an intervention in order to identify its active ingredients.

Question for discussion
- Are there interventions that cannot be evaluated using randomised controlled trials (RCTs)?

Further reading
Bryman, A. (2012) *Social research methods* (4th edn), Oxford: Oxford University Press, Chapter 3.
de Vaus, D. (2001) *Research design in social research*, London: Sage Publications.

Cross-sectional design

A cross-sectional design is typified by a social survey. Unlike an experimental design, there is no manipulation of a setting, almost always because the variables in which the researcher is interested are not capable of being manipulated for practical or ethical reasons. Examples of variables that are often regarded as independent variables but are not capable of being manipulated are gender, education, age, ethnicity, income and occupation. In the case of all of these variables, we cannot make research participants male or female, well or poorly educated, old or young, wealthy or poor, and so on. Also, there are some variables that, even if we could manipulate them, it would be ethically dubious or obnoxious to do so. We could hardly design an experiment to examine the effects of taking up smoking on relationships with partners, whereby some non-smokers were turned into smokers and others were not asked to smoke in order to examine the impact of taking up smoking. In view of what is known about the side effects of smoking, such an experimental design is inconceivable in ethical terms (see also Chapter Two).

The cross-sectional design contains the following features:

- It is based on existing differences between people rather than differences that are created by the experimenter.
- Data are usually collected on a large number of variables so that the connections among a wide range of variables can be studied.
- The design is usually based on the collection of data from a large number of cases, which may be people, organisations, newspapers, regions, etc.

The social survey in which the researcher collects a large amount of data from many people using a questionnaire or structured interview is one of the main ways in which the cross-sectional design appears in social policy and social work research.

There are two chief problems for the user of a cross-sectional design relative to an experimental design. First, the groups are not equivalent. For example, if we are interested in the relationship between age and client satisfaction, the people in different age bands are not equivalent to each other. Thus, 30- to 39-year-olds will differ from each other in terms of such factors as ethnicity, education, gender, income and occupation, all of which might have a connection with client satisfaction. Second, there is ambiguity about the direction of causality. If we are interested in whether client satisfaction and the reported demeanour of staff are related, if we do find a relationship it is difficult to know which way round the causal connection works. Does demeanour influence client satisfaction or does client satisfaction influence demeanour? As a result, it is sometimes suggested that cross-sectional designs are weak in terms of internal validity, although it is important not to exaggerate this point. Sometimes there is little ambiguity about the causal direction, for example, if we found that age and client satisfaction were related, it is impossible to imagine that client satisfaction affects age. Variables such as age, ethnicity and gender can be regarded as givens that are always independent variables. Further, statistical analysis can be used to remove some of the alternative explanatory variables that might contaminate relationships between variables when compared to the experimental design (see Bryman and Cramer, 2011, Chapter 10).

Longitudinal design

With a longitudinal design, there is no manipulation of variables (as in the cross-sectional design), but, unlike the cross-sectional design, data are collected on at least two occasions. Users of longitudinal designs are typically concerned to capture change over time, and also in many cases to deal with the time order problem that was outlined in the previous section as representing a problem for the cross-sectional design.

While there are several different types of longitudinal design, there is a crucial and basic distinction between the *panel design* and the *cohort design*. The **panel design** entails collection of data on the same group of people on at least two occasions. A major example of a panel design that has been used for addressing social policy research issues is the British Household Panel Survey (BHPS). This survey started in 1991: 10,000+

individuals in 5,000+ households based on probability sampling. Respondents are interviewed annually. See **Box 5b** for the use of this survey for social policy research.

Box 5b: The British Household Panel Survey: a longitudinal perspective on unpaid carers
Michael Hirst

Longitudinal studies are rich sources of data and analysis on key policy issues such as poverty, unemployment, family and household formation, educational outcomes and health inequalities. By gathering information about the same individuals on two or more occasions, longitudinal research highlights their changing outlooks and circumstances, enabling us to understand the dynamics of people's experiences – their duration, sequence and timing – and the processes at work. Longitudinal designs also help establish the temporal order of events, identify the factors associated with particular outcomes and increase confidence in the size and direction of causal associations (Menard, 1991).

The British Household Panel Survey (BHPS) began in 1991 with an initial sample of some 10,000 adults recruited in a design not unlike that of any cross-sectional household survey (Lynn, 2006). Since then, it has aimed to interview those same individuals every year, and their natural descendants on turning 16; other adults currently living with them are also interviewed. By including all household members, each wave is broadly representative of the population living in private households. In 2010, the BHPS sample was incorporated into Understanding Society, a new UK longitudinal household survey of the socioeconomic circumstances and attitudes of 100,000 individuals.

Many questions asked in the first round of the BHPS were repeated in subsequent waves, and by comparing individuals' responses year-on-year it is possible to build up a movie-like picture of their lives. What happens between waves may not be precisely known, and changing perceptions of social roles and identities may influence trends and outcomes. Loss of panel members who have died, moved overseas or cannot be traced further complicates longitudinal research, especially if those lost to follow-up differ in systematic ways from those who remain in the sample. Adjusting for panel attrition and non-response, by weighting the sample at the analysis stage, is an important consideration when measuring and explaining change.

By asking survey participants whether they looked after or helped a relative or friend who was ill, frail or disabled, the BHPS can be used to estimate trends and transitions in the provision of unpaid care (Hirst, 2001, 2002). Identifying the start of care episodes and key turning points in carers' lives is important for informing them of their rights, delivering benefits and services and preventing or alleviating adverse consequences (Aneshensel et al, 1995; Heaton et al, 1999; Carers UK, 2006; Cavaye, 2006). Taking on a caring role, especially one that involves a heavy or extended commitment over time, is associated with poor health, reduced social participation, limited employment prospects and financial hardship (Hirst and Hutton, 2001; Howard, 2001; Henz, 2004; Arksey et al, 2005; Hirst, 2005a; Becker, 2011).

The persistence of these adverse effects indicates a need for continuing support during the care episode and beyond (Hancock and Jarvis, 1994; McLaughlin and Ritchie, 1994; Chesson and Todd, 1996). The end of a protracted spell of care can be particularly difficult for carers when the cared-for person enters institutional care (Nolan and Dellasega, 2000), or dies (Boerner and Schulz, 2009; Corden et al, 2010). Thus, transitions into and out of a caring role identify points where assessment of carers' needs, and audit of service performance and professional practice, could be usefully focused.

The population of carers is continually changing as people stop providing care and others take on a caring role. As a result, more individuals are involved in caregiving across service planning, commissioning and budgeting cycles than are found in cross-sectional surveys. One implication is that the adequacy of resources for supporting carers depends on the frequency and duration of care episodes over time (Hirst, 2005b).

Longitudinal estimates show further that most people are involved in caregiving at some point in their lives, especially in late middle and early older age (Hirst, 2005a). However, the demand for care varies considerably across the life course, driven by changing healthcare needs within and between the generations. Caring relationships are, therefore, extremely diverse, as are carers' characteristics, family structures and household circumstances.

Policy action and practical interventions that take account of such diversity and changing circumstances are likely to be most effective in supporting carers. Such measures would benefit a large section of the population over time.

Question for discussion
- What are the strengths and weaknesses of a longitudinal household survey for investigating the formation of social roles, attitudes and identities?

References

Aneshensel, C., Pearlin, L., Mullan, J., Zarit, S. and Whitlatch, C. (1995) *Profiles of caring: The unexpected career*, London: Academic Press.

Arksey, H., Kemp, P., Glendinning, C., Kotchetkova, I. and Tozer, R. (2005) *Carers' aspirations and decisions around work and retirement*, DWP Report No 290, Leeds: Corporate Document Services.

Becker, S. (2011) 'Informal family carers', in K. Wilson, G. Ruch, M. Lymbery and A. Cooper (eds) *Social work: An introduction to contemporary practice* (2nd edn), Harlow: Pearson Education Ltd, pp 426-55.

Boerner, K. and Schulz, R. (2009) 'Caregiving, bereavement and complicated grief', *Bereavement Care*, vol 28, pp 10-13.

Carers UK (2006) *In the know: The importance of information for carers*, London: Carers UK.

Cavaye, J. (2006) *Hidden carers*, Edinburgh: Dunedin Academic Press.

Chesson, R. and Todd, C. (1996) 'Bereaved carers: recognising their needs', *Elderly Care*, vol 8, pp 16-18.

Corden, A., Hirst, M. and Nice, K. (2010) 'Death of a partner: financial implications and experience of loss', *Bereavement Care*, vol 29, pp 23-8.

Hancock, R. and Jarvis, C. (1994) *The long term effects of being a carer*, London: HMSO.

Heaton, J., Arksey, H. and Sloper, P. (1999) 'Carers' experiences of hospital discharge and continuing care in the community', *Health and Social Care in the Community*, vol 7, pp 91-9.

Henz, U. (2004) 'The effects of informal care on paid work participation in Great Britain: a life course perspective', *Ageing & Society*, vol 24, pp 851-80.

Hirst, M. (2001) 'Trends in informal care in Great Britain during the 1990s', *Health & Social Care in the Community*, vol 9, pp 348-57.

Hirst, M. (2002) 'Transitions to informal care in Great Britain during the 1990s', *Journal of Epidemiology and Community Health*, vol 56, pp 579-87.

Hirst, M. (2005a) 'Carer distress: a prospective, population-based study', *Social Science & Medicine*, vol 61, pp 697-708.

Hirst, M. (2005b) 'Estimating the prevalence of unpaid adult care over time', *Research, Policy and Planning*, vol 23, pp 1-16.

Hirst, M. and Hutton, S. (2001) *Informal care over time*, York: Social Policy Research Unit, University of York.

Howard, M. (2001) *Paying the price: Carers, poverty and social exclusion*, London: Child Poverty Action Group.

Lynn, P. (ed) (2006) *Quality profile: British Household Panel Survey Version 2.0. Waves 1 to 13: 1991-2003*, Colchester: Institute for Social and Economic Research, University of Essex.

McLaughlin, E. and Ritchie, J. (1994) 'Legacies of caring: the experiences and circumstances of ex-carers', *Health & Social Care in the Community*, vol 2, pp 241-53.

Menard, S. (1991) *Longitudinal research*, London: Sage Publications.

Nolan, M. and Dellasega, C. (2000) 'Supporting family carers during long-term care placement for elders', *Journal of Advanced Nursing*, vol 31, pp 759-67.

Further reading

Becker, S. (2011) 'Informal family carers', in K. Wilson, G. Ruch, M. Lymbery and A. Cooper (eds) *Social work: An introduction to contemporary practice* (2nd edn), Harlow: Pearson Education Ltd, pp 426-55.

Berthoud, R. and Gershuny, J. (eds) (2000) *Seven years in the lives of British families: Evidence on the dynamics of social change from the British Household Panel Survey*, Bristol: The Policy Press.

Fine, M. (2007) *A caring society? Care and the dilemmas of human service in the twenty-first century*, Basingstoke: Palgrave Macmillan.

Nocon, A. and Qureshi, H. (1996) *Outcomes of community care for users and carers*, Buckingham: Open University Press.

Nolan, M., Grant, G. and Keady, J. (1996) *Understanding family care: A multidimensional model of caring and coping*, Buckingham: Open University Press.

Twigg, J. and Atkin, K. (1994) *Carers perceived: Policy and practice in informal care*, Buckingham: Open University Press.

Relevant organisations

The Afiya Trust: www.afiyatrust.org.uk

Age UK: www.ageuk.org.uk

Carers UK: www.carersuk.org

Contact a Family: www.cafamily.org.uk

Counsel and Care: www.counselandcare.org.uk

The Princess Royal Trust for Carers: www.carers.org

Website resources

British Household Panel Survey (BHPS): www.iser.essex.ac.uk/survey/bhps

Government policy, services and other help for carers: www.direct.gov.uk/en/CaringForSomeone/index.htm

UK Data Archive: www.data-archive.ac.uk/

UK Longitudinal Studies Centre: www.iser.essex.ac.uk/survey/ulsc

Understanding Society: www.understandingsociety.org.uk/

By contrast, a **cohort design** takes everyone born in a particular period and follows them through at regular intervals. A major example of a cohort design that has been used for addressing social policy and social work research issues is the National Child Development Study (NCDS), which is based on 17,000 children born in Britain between 3-9 March 1958. The cohort has been followed up at ages 7, 11, 16, 23, 33, 41-2, 46 and 50-1.

All longitudinal designs suffer from the problem of attrition (drop-outs), whereby some people refuse or are unable to continue their participation. This can be a problem if the drop-outs differ systematically from those who remain. There is the related problem of knowing how to deal with the issue of people who move away from an area or country, die or leave a household, although this issue affects the panel rather than the cohort design. There is also a related issue of *addition*, namely, how to deal with people who might become candidates for later inclusion on grounds of maintaining representativeness of the sample. Examples of groups that might raise this issue are new household members or an influx of new migrants.

Given a suitable length of time, the panel design allows the researcher to distinguish between the effects of age on respondents and cohort effects (effects due to similarities among those born at a similar time, for example, 'baby boomers'), since members of the sample will have been born at different times. Because members of a cohort design will be of the same age, cohort effects cannot be targeted.

Case study

The case study is typically the detailed and intensive examination of one or a very small number of cases. But what is a case? A case might be an organisation, a person, a community, a household or even an event (for example, a decision and its effects, or the implementation of a policy). While the case study is typically associated with a single case, some case study research entails more than one case and is probably better described and thought of as a *multiple case study design*.

As the discussion of the case study in Section 6.4 suggests later, the case study is primarily associated with qualitative research and with ethnography in particular (on this point, see also Section 6.10). However, this association between the case study and qualitative research should not be exaggerated. Case studies can involve the collection of quantitative data, either exclusively or as part of a mixed methods strategy of the kind discussed earlier in Section 4.4.

With a case study, the researcher is not treating the case as a sample of one. The case study researcher does not claim that the chosen case is somehow representative and can therefore be generalised to a wider universe of cases. Instead, the arguments for case studies are largely to do with the ability to generate findings that are theoretically interesting and are capable of being taken up by other researchers for further elaboration. In this connection, Yin's (2009) use of the term *replication logic* is interesting. The term is used mainly in connection with multiple case study research. Yin argues that case studies using similar procedures on a research question will enhance our understanding. Also, any interesting differences in findings might be attributable in interesting ways to contrasts between the cases. The idea behind a replication logic, then, is that the researcher should aim to replicate findings using similar procedures across cases. This idea can be extended to suggest that when a researcher conducts a single case study, the findings may be taken up by another researcher to extend the findings (perhaps exploring some further implications) or to examine a somewhat contrasting case to see if the findings hold there.

Question for discussion

- To what extent is it legitimate to argue that only true experiments allow the researcher to establish cause and effect?

References

Bryman, A. and Cramer, D. (2011) *Quantitative data analysis with SPSS 10 for Windows: A guide for social scientists*, London: Routledge.

de Vaus, D. (2001) *Research design in social research*, London: Sage Publications.

Yin, R.K. (2009) *Case study research: Design and methods* (4th edn), Los Angeles, CA: Sage Publications.

Further reading

Bryman, A. (2012) *Social research methods* (4th edn), Oxford: Oxford University Press, Chapter 3.

de Vaus, D. (2001) *Research design in social research*, London: Sage Publications.

5.4 Sampling
Karl Ashworth

Why sample?

We select a sample either to say something about a particular class of units, or to compare two classes of units to see if they differ in certain ways. A sample is a selection of units from the collection of all such units, known as a population. The sample is a means to understanding the population.

It is seldom practical to collect information from all population members, and unnecessary when sampling offers a practical, cheaper and quicker option. Typically, the number of units sampled is substantially smaller than the total number of units in the population. We need to be confident that our sample is representative of the population. It is through an understanding of how the sample is drawn that we can address this question.

It is convenient to distinguish two broad sampling methods, probability and non-probability, each of which has various advantages and disadvantages that need to be weighed within the context of the research question and resources.

Probability sampling

The essence of probability sampling is that each member of the population has a (known, non-zero) chance of being included in the sample: it is an objective procedure, the selection process is unbiased and the precision of population estimates can be calculated.

Usually, a sample is used to estimate the value of some population characteristic, for example, the average height of adults in Britain. The more similar population members are to each other in this characteristic, the more likely it is that the sample mean will be close to the population mean. The variance typically is the statistic used to measure variability, and is also an important component of the equation to estimate the precision of the sample estimate of the population mean (the standard error of the mean). The formulae used to calculate the mean, variance and standard error of the mean are presented here (**Table 5.1**). These pertain to the case of simple random sampling, described below, but generalise to other more complex sampling schemes.

The formulae are given using two different notations to emphasise that we are using sample statistics to estimate population parameters. The population parameters typically are denoted in upper case to distinguish them from sample statistics (see, for example, Kish, 1965; Kalton, 1983). However, as is apparent from **Table 5.1**, the mechanics of the calculation are the same:

- n is the number of units in the sample
- N is the total number of units in the population
- y_i are the observations on unit i, in the sample and population.

Table 5.1: Formulae for calculating the sample and population mean and variance

	Sample statistic	Population parameter
Mean	$\hat{\bar{y}} = \sum_{i=1}^{n} y_i$	$\bar{Y} = \sum_{i=1}^{N} y_i$
Variance	$s^2 = \dfrac{\sum_{i=1}^{n}(y_i - \hat{\bar{y}})^2}{n-1}$	$\sigma^2 = \dfrac{\sum_{i=1}^{N}(y_i - \bar{Y})^2}{N}$
Standard error	$se_{\hat{\bar{y}}} = \dfrac{s}{\sqrt{n}}\sqrt{1-\left(\dfrac{n}{N}\right)}$	

It is important to realise that the idea behind the standard error of the mean arises from the notion of a *sampling distribution of means*. In other words, if we were to take the mean of each possible sample of size n from a population, we could arrange each sample mean as a frequency distribution and calculate the mean of the means. The resulting distribution is approximately normally distributed with a mean value equalling the population mean. As the mean of the sampling means equals the population mean, the sample mean is an unbiased estimator of the population mean. This does not guarantee that the mean arising from any one sample will be the same as the population mean; chance selections, arising from sampling variability, may result in different groups of units producing different sample means. However, using the standard error, we can estimate, with a given degree of confidence, the range within which the population mean will fall.

The confidence intervals are given by:

$$\hat{\bar{y}} \pm tse_{\hat{\bar{y}}}$$

Where $\hat{\bar{y}}$ is the estimated mean from the sample, $se_{\hat{\bar{y}}}$ is the estimated standard error of the mean and t is the value returned from the t-distribution corresponding to the desired confidence probability level.

For example, a hypothetical sample size of 196 students selected from a campus population of 2,000 had an average daily consumption of 5 units of alcohol, with a variance of 4 units. So, we can be 95% sure that in this hypothetical campus student population the average daily intake of alcoholic units was in the range of:

$$1.96 \times \frac{\sqrt{4}}{\sqrt{196}} \sqrt{1 - \left(\frac{196}{2000}\right)}$$

$$= 1.96 \times 0.14 \times 0.15 \qquad\qquad = 0.04$$

We can be 95% sure that the population mean falls between the following values:

$$4.73 < \bar{Y} < 5.27$$

The value of $1-n/N$, more commonly symbolised as $1-f$, is known as the *finite population correction* (fpc), and f is the *sampling fraction*. With a small sampling fraction, the fpc is close to unity and has little effect on the estimate of the standard error. The effect of ignoring the fpc is negligible with a large sample and small sampling fraction; when the sampling fraction is 5% or less the fpc can be ignored (Cochran, 1977).

It is apparent that the standard error of the mean is influenced by three factors. The fpc is one factor, typically with a small effect. A second is the population variance – a smaller variance enables more precise estimates. Finally, the critical factor is the sample size – larger samples give more precise results. It is worth reflecting on the fact that what is important is the actual size of the sample and not the size of the sampling fraction, as long as the sampling fraction remains small. In other words, provided the two populations have the same variance, we can get virtually as precise an estimate from a sample of 400 from a population of 500,000 as we can from a sample of 400 from a population of 50,000.

Sample designs

Simple random sampling

Simple random sampling (srs) is a scheme that requires each unit in the population to have an equal probability of selection (epsem). Typically, it requires a list (sampling frame) of the members of the population and the assignment of a unique number to each member. We then require a selection method that meets the epsem condition. One type of method is the urn-based approach, where a list of numbers is written, each on a separate piece of paper; these are then placed in an urn, thoroughly mixed and as many draws as required are made. The British National Lottery follows a machine equivalent procedure of randomly sampling six balls from 49. Other methods use random digit tables (for example, described in Kalton, 1983). Today, the easiest approach is to use a computer to generate the numbers. However, often srs is impractical and other approaches are used in practice.

Stratified sampling

Stratification is the process of splitting the sampling frame into separate subgroups (strata) that are defined using supplementary information on the sampling frame. The selection procedure is still random, because within each subgroup (stratum), elements are selected at random. A principal reason for stratification is that it can produce more precise variance estimates than srs, when the stratification factors are associated with the outcome(s) under investigation. However, stratification by factors that do not influence the research question does not result in any gain in precision. In addition, stratification can be used to ensure that certain groups are represented in the sample. For example, stratification by geographic region ensures that people from each region in the country are covered (see **Box 5c**).

Box 5c: The Living Costs and Food Survey: sampling
Karl Ashworth

The Living Costs and Food Survey (LCF), carried out by the Office for National Statistics (ONS), is an ongoing survey that reports on a quarterly and annual basis. Its main purpose is to collect data on the current spending patterns of UK households. It has many uses across various government departments and other research organisations but a primary use is as an input to the calculation of the retail and consumer prices indices (RPI/CPI).

The ONS carries out the sampling and data collection for the LCF in Great Britain, while NISRA (the Northern Ireland Statistics and Research Agency) undertakes sampling and data collection in Northern Ireland. The British component of the LCF uses the Royal Mail's

---

Postcode Address File (PAF) as the sampling frame. This is a list of delivery points (addresses) to which the Royal Mail delivers. In order to reduce the number of ineligible non-residential addresses, ONS uses the Small User PAF, which excludes those address delivery points which are flagged as an 'organisation'.

The LCF is an example of a stratified multi-stage survey. Stratification is achieved by ordering the PAF in such a way that addresses are sorted by postcodes, first by country and then within England by Government Regions. As a systematic selection procedure is used, the ordering of the frame ensures the sample is spread across the country in a way that reflects the population size of the region/country. This helps to ensure that data collection, by chance, is not skewed heavily in favour of one region at the expense of others.

The LCF includes in the frame the entire Scottish mainland, but not the islands. This is because few people live in these locations and data collection is expensive. This exclusion could induce a small bias in the estimates but this is anticipated to be negligible.

Postcodes on the frame are grouped into around 9,000 postcode sectors, which act as primary sampling units (PSUs) for the LCF. The first stage of sampling selects 638 PSUs using probability proportional to size (number of delivery points). The second stage of sampling selects 18 addresses from each selected PSU giving a total of 11,484 addresses that are issued to interviewers. This two-stage selection method is often employed to achieve a sample that has been selected with equal probability of selection (epsem). An epsem sample is desirable because, in the absence of any adjustments for non-response, it is self-weighting, and this reduces the size of the standard error of an estimator calculated from the sample. The important feature of this design that makes it epsem is selection with probability proportional to size at Stage 1 and the selection of a fixed number of addresses at Stage 2.

The LCF now also employs a further stage of selection in order to select a single household from an address. If an interviewer finds that a delivery point consists of more than one address, or there is more than one household at an address, then a doorstep random selection procedure is used to select one household. Consequently, the LCF design is not a true epsem design that makes population estimation slightly more complex and less precise than it would be under a true epsem design.

The LCF sample is selected annually and allocation of the addresses for fieldwork is done on the basis of that year's selection. It is important to ensure that fieldwork is balanced roughly evenly across the 12 months, and to ensure that all areas of Great Britain are covered in any one month, that is, there is a balance of interviews across space and time, to ensure we are comparing like with like. The principal aim is to get quarterly data that are roughly representative of Great Britain – although allocation is balanced on a monthly basis, interviewers may have to make many calls to get an interview, and can go outside of the calendar month to return their monthly quota.

Another reason for stratification might be to over-sample some comparatively rare subgroups of the population to ensure that sufficient numbers of them were available for robust analysis. Here, the sampling fractions vary between the strata, and weighting adjustments to correct for this must be made in the analysis.

Cluster and multi-stage sampling

Cluster sampling embodies the notion that the population units can be aggregated into meaningful higher order units and assigned exclusively to a higher order unit. For example, in Britain residential addresses can be aggregated to postcode sectors and districts.

Out of the approximately 9,600 postcode sectors, aggregated into around 9,000 primary sampling units (PSUs), a fixed number is chosen, and these are usually selected with probability proportionate to size (pps), that is, the number of addresses within the sector (see **Box 5c**). Its main attraction is that interviewers do not have to travel as far as they would if the sample was randomly spread across the country so fieldwork costs are lower.

A principal disadvantage of cluster sampling is that units within the cluster are likely to be correlated with each other, for example, people who live in the same neighbourhood tend to have more in common with their neighbours than with other randomly selected members of the general population. This has a number of consequences, particularly on the precision of the estimate. However, a design effect can be calculated which shows the loss of precision incurred relative to srs.

Multi-stage sampling is the repeated act of sampling lower units from higher order units and **Box 5c** demonstrates a three-stage process of drawing samples of PSUs, addresses and households.

Systematic sampling

Systematic sampling involves randomly choosing a starting position on the list and selecting every kth element from the starting point. It is a convenient procedure and is often employed in practice. The sampling fraction determines k, so that if we were to select 150 employers from a list of 1,200, k = 1,200/150 = 8, so we determine a starting point between 1 and 8 through selecting a random number between 1 and 8. If the number were 3, the 3rd, 11th, 19th and so on would be selected. This is similar to splitting the sampling frame into k strata and selecting one element from each stratum.

It is important to take any ordering into account that could exist on the list. Sometimes ordering can be used to our advantage. **Box 5c** shows how ordering can be used to ensure a geographic spread of a sample. In some cases ordering can produce a more precise sample than could be achieved through simple random sampling. However, some types of naturally occurring ordering in the list could potentially have a detrimental effect on the sample. For example, a list of employees might be ordered by department and level of pay, so that the kth element corresponded primarily to higher (or lower) earners because of the ordering in the list. This would be undesirable and the list should be re-ordered either to be random or, if possible, to achieve a gain in precision (see Cochran, 1977, Chapter 8).

Non-probability sampling

There are times when probability samples either cannot be used, for example, in the absence of a sampling frame, or when the cost is prohibitive. In these circumstances, other non-probability sampling procedures are available.

The essence of non-probability sampling is that a judgement is made about the specific units that are included in the sample. The process is not objective, all units do not have a known chance of inclusion and, strictly speaking, estimates of precision usually should not be calculated. The value of these methods very much depends on the objectives of the research.

Quota sampling

Quota sampling is particularly common in market research and in electoral polls. It is similar to stratified sampling in that the population is subdivided into groups in advance of selection, for example, controlling for sex and social class. A quota – the number of required interviews – is set within each control (stratum), for example 30 men and 30 women within each of social groups 1, 2 and 3. The underlying assumption is that the control variables account for systematic differences in the research variables of interest. In other words, once these control variables have been accounted for, the only difference between people within a control group is caused by random variation.

It is the method of selection that makes the procedure non-random because interviewers are allowed to select any people who meet these characteristics. This could lead to a whole range of potential biases. For example, if interviewing only took place on weekdays during the day, workers are likely to be under-represented. However, proponents argue that it is better able to guarantee a representative sample than are probability samples.

Haphazard/availability/convenience sampling

These approaches use units that happen to be available. This is relatively common in experimental social science. In circumstances where a high degree of similarity between units is likely, it can be useful. For example, among young healthy people, the impact of a stimulus on neuronal conductivity might not vary greatly. It would, therefore, be justifiable to allocate students randomly to an experimental or control group to test the impact of a stimulus. However, generalising the findings to the wider population of human beings assumes that only very minor random variation exists between individuals in the sample and population. Where a population estimate is required, generally, it is not a recommended approach.

Question for discussion

* What are the key elements of a 'good' sample?

References

Cochran, W.G. (1977) *Sampling techniques* (3rd edn), New York, NY: John Wiley & Sons.
Kalton, G. (1983) *Introduction to survey sampling*, Sage Publications University Paper Series: Quantitative Applications in the Social Sciences, no 35, Beverley Hills, CA: Sage Publications.
Kish, L. (1965) *Survey sampling*, New York: John Wiley & Sons.

Further reading

Kalton, G. (1983) *Introduction to survey sampling*, Sage Publications University Paper Series: Quantitative Applications in the Social Sciences, no 35, Beverley Hills, CA: Sage Publications.

PART TWO: METHODS FOR COLLECTING AND CODING QUANTITATIVE DATA

5.5 Overview of methods for collecting and coding quantitative data

Alan Bryman and Saul Becker

Six main approaches for collecting and coding quantitative data are considered in the sections that follow:

- structured interviews and questionnaires;
- using the internet for the collection of quantitative data;
- content analysis;
- structured observation;
- time use diaries;
- official statistics.

Each of these approaches to the collection and coding of data is underpinned by the preoccupations outlined in relation to quantitative research in Sections 5.2, 5.3 and 5.4. Content analysis is not a research method in the sense of a way of collecting data; it is an approach to the analysis of unstructured data so that the data can be quantified. The translation of unstructured data, such as newspaper articles, into quantitative data through coding is more or less its defining feature. However, at another level, content analysis does have features of a research method, in the sense that the distinctive coding practices that are involved essentially create data. Official statistics are also not so much a research method as sources of data that social policy and social work researchers seek to draw on in order to tailor to their research questions.

One feature that is also common to all of these methods is the need to 'code' the data that are collected. In their different ways, users of each of the methods must turn the material into a numerical form so that the kinds of statistical analysis covered in Section 5.11 can be implemented. Coding is at once a simple but potentially complex activity. Take, for example, the case of devising a Likert scale of the kind mentioned in Section 5.2. There, it was imagined that we wanted to construct a scale to measure levels of client satisfaction with a service provider. Let us look again at the two items that were presented as possible candidates for inclusion in the scale. Here is the first one:

Staff are always responsive to my needs

Strongly agree	Agree	Neither agree nor disagree	Disagree	Strongly disagree
5	4	3	2	1

A common way of coding items such as these is to allocate numbers to them as has been suggested. Everyone indicating agreement is given a score of 4 for their answers. But what about the next one?

I find the rules for getting the particular service I need difficult to understand
    Strongly   Agree   Neither agree   Disagree   Strongly
     agree   nor disagree   disagree

A score of 4 could be given to 'Agree' but this would be incorrect. If the direction of scoring is supposed to indicate that a higher score indicates satisfaction, giving a score of 4 for 'Agree' with the second question would be incorrect because someone choosing that answer is really indicating dissatisfaction. Consequently, for an item like this, the direction of scoring needs to be reversed and should go from 1 (Strongly agree) to 5 (Strongly disagree). Thus, although the process of allocating a coding scheme to questions is relatively straightforward, care is still necessary. Further, there is a recognised problem with Likert scales, whereby it is known that some respondents will answer all the constituent items in a scale in the same way. This kind of response bias can be addressed by varying the wording to guard against this effect.

Even greater care is necessary when coding materials that are unstructured. This issue commonly arises with the following kinds of data:

- *Answers to open questions.* With closed questions, such as the items in a Likert scale, coding is relatively simple, but with open questions, decisions have to be made about which category an answer belongs to before it can be coded. There is always the possibility that the coder will incorrectly allocate an answer to a category. This is a major reason why survey researchers invariably prefer closed questions.
- *Newspaper and magazine articles and television programmes.* The kinds of materials discussed in Section 5.8 are unstructured materials. While some items can be easily coded, such as whether certain words are used, coding in terms of themes requires interpretation and is therefore difficult and potentially prone to error.
- *Behaviour.* Which is the subject of the method covered in Section 5.9, similarly, has to be interpreted by the observer before it can be coded. Whether an instance of behaviour is assigned to the correct category also requires interpretation and is potentially a source of error.

Coding is a crucial stage in the processing of data before they can be analysed statistically, but it is one where there is considerable potential for error. In order to keep such errors to a minimum, the researcher needs to spell out the rules for allocating items to a category, and if possible to get others to check the allocations that are made. Failure to do so creates problems in the reliability and validity of the measures derived from the coding process.

5.6 Structured interviews and questionnaires in survey research
Alison Park

This section explores the range of tasks involved in survey design – from decisions about how a questionnaire will be administered and questionnaire design, to the coding and editing of the data collected.

Once a survey-based approach has been decided on, a choice needs to be made about the *mode* in which the survey will be carried out. The most important distinction that exists is between modes that involve an interviewer (who works through the questionnaire to record a respondent's answers) and 'self-completion' methods (where respondents work through the questionnaire themselves).

Interviewer-mediated surveys

There are two main types of interviewer-mediated surveys – *face-to-face* and *telephone* interviews. In both cases, the interviewer can either use a paper questionnaire or a computer-based questionnaire. The former is often referred to as PAPI interviewing (pen/pencil and paper interviewing) and the latter as CAPI (computer-assisted personal interviewing). See *Box 5d* for an example of the combined use of these two ways of administering a structured interview in a survey.

Box 5d: The British Social Attitudes Survey: data collection
Alison Park

The British Social Attitudes (BSA) Survey series was initiated in 1983 by Social and Community Planning Research (SCPR, now the National Centre for Social Research, NatCen) and has been carried out annually ever since. Its primary purpose is to monitor and interpret changing social values over time. Funding for the survey comes primarily from the main government departments, the Economic and Social Research Council (ESRC) and charitable trusts. All data are deposited at the ESRC Data Archive at the University of Essex (see Section 4.19).

The sample
Each year's sample comprises a national probability sample of adults aged 18 and over, living in private households in Great Britain. The sampling frame used is the Postcode Address File (PAF).

In 1994, 1998 and 2003, the BSA Survey was accompanied by a Young Persons' Social Attitudes survey. This involved interviewing all 12- to 19-year-olds living in the same household as an adult BSA respondent (Park, 2004).

From 1999 onwards, the survey has been accompanied by an annual sister survey in Scotland, known as Scottish Social Attitudes. This is because, although Scotland is included in the BSA sample, the number of respondents interviewed there is too small to permit anything but the most cursory analysis.

The questionnaire
The survey has covered a wide range of political, social and moral topics over its lifetime. Because the series is designed to examine change (or stasis) over time, many questions are repeated from one year to the next. However, new topics are regularly introduced and even topics that have been covered in the past are refreshed to ensure that their coverage of the

---

issues is as up-to-date as possible. The survey primarily focuses on people's attitudes, but also collects details of their behaviour patterns and household circumstances for analysis purposes.

Examples of topics covered by the series include:

- political trust
- voting behaviour
- marriage and cohabitation
- poverty
- sex
- racism
- the NHS
- education

- social security
- devolution
- transport
- the environment
- national identity
- social capital
- assisted dying
- social inequality

Fieldwork
Each BSA interview consists of a face-to-face interview using computer-assisted interviewing techniques (CAPI) and a self-completion questionnaire that can be completed by the respondent immediately after the CAPI interview or at a later date. The length of the face-to-face element of the questionnaire varies from year to year, but usually averages at around 60 minutes.

Between 3,500 and 4,500 interviews take place each year, most of which are carried out over the summer months. Prior to fieldwork all interviewers are personally briefed by a researcher. The response rate for the BSA in 2009 was 55%.

Analysis
By repeating questions included in previous rounds, the survey series has allowed analysts to build up increasingly detailed pictures of how British attitudes and values are developing over time and has also enabled the development of theoretical understanding about their implications for policy. Moreover, for any given year, the range of sociodemographic and socioeconomic questions included in the survey makes it possible to ascertain how far attitudes, expectations and views about particular issues vary between one section of society and another.

Each survey generates an edited book that examines and tries to explain movements in the British public's beliefs and values (Park et al, 2011). Contributions from a range of authors are included, and a variety of analytic techniques are used, from logistic and multiple regression to factor analysis.

International Social Survey Programme (ISSP)
This programme is organised by a group of research organisations, each of which agrees to field annually an agreed module of questions on a chosen topic area. Since 1985, an ISSP module has been included on each BSA Survey, always administered as part of a self-completion supplement. Modules are repeated at intervals in order to examine change over time as well as to permit comparison between countries.

References

Park, A. (2004) 'Has modern politics disenchanted the young?', in A. Park, J. Curtice, K. Thomson, C. Bromley and M. Philips (eds) *British social attitudes: The 21st report*, London: Sage Publications, pp 23-48.

Park, A., Curtice, J., Phillips, M. and Clery, E. (eds) (2011) *British social attitudes: The 27th report*, London: Sage Publications.

Website resources

Economic and Social Research Council (ESRC) UK Data Archive: www.data-archive.ac.uk

International Social Survey Programme (ISSP): www.issp.org

National Centre for Social Research (NatCen): www.natcen.ac.uk

Scottish Centre for Social Research: www.scotcen.ac.uk

One of the main disadvantages of interviewer-mediated surveys is the fact that they are expensive. Put simply, interviewers need to be paid. However, interviewer-mediated interviews also have considerable advantages over self-completion methods. In particular, the presence of an interviewer means that these surveys tend to achieve higher response rates than self-completion ones. Moreover, the fact that the interviewer is responsible for administering the questionnaire helps minimise error, particularly when compared with paper-based self-completion methods.

Face-to-face surveys are much more expensive than telephone surveys, but tend to achieve higher response rates, particularly when the sample is drawn from the general population rather than from specific groups. They also allow the use of visual aids such as showcards, which can help respondents to answer. Face-to-face interviews are usually more appropriate than telephone interviews if the interview is likely to last for a long time, as it is easier to hold a respondent's concentration in person than over the telephone. Consequently, some face-to-face interviews can last for well over an hour, while telephone interviews would rarely last this long.

However, telephone surveys do have their advantages. They are cheaper and are ideal when a long interview or visual aids are not required. They can be particularly invaluable when carrying out surveys of employees or employers.

Self-completion methods

Self-completion methods require respondents to work through and complete a questionnaire on their own. Some self-completion formats use paper questionnaires, although, increasingly, self-completion questionnaires are being completed on a computer, either as a program on a laptop computer or via the internet or email (see Section 5.7 on internet surveys).

Clearly, self-completion questionnaires can make use of visual cues (unlike telephone surveys). However, in their paper form they suffer from the fact that, as no interviewer is present, the format of the questionnaire must be as simple as possible. This is overcome when the questionnaire is administered via a computer, as the computer program can guide the respondent through the questionnaire (for example, by automatically taking the respondent to the next relevant question).

Self-completion questionnaires can reach their target respondent in a number of different ways. One common method is the postal survey, whereby paper self-completion questionnaires are mailed out to a sample of individuals or addresses. A principal advantage of this method is that it is cheap (particularly when compared with interviewer-mediated methods). However, levels of response to postal surveys tend to be much lower than with interviewer-mediated surveys, and the design of the questionnaire has to be sufficiently simple to allow respondents to work their way through it without assistance.

Other self-completion delivery methods include using interviewers to deliver and/or to collect questionnaires (which can boost response), and email. Some CAPI surveys can involve a self-completion element, whereby the respondent is given the interviewer's laptop and asked to work through a set of self-completion questions on the screen.

Identifying the information you want to collect

This stage sounds deceptively simple – identifying the information needed to fulfil the objectives of the research. However, although some information requirements will be very evident from the outset, others can be less so. For this reason, researchers often spend time considering existing material about the subject – carrying out a literature review, for example, and finding out about other quantitative and qualitative research that has been conducted.

If the subject matter for the research is particularly new or complex, questionnaire design is often preceded by detailed qualitative work which can help map out the main areas likely to be of interest.

When considering the information that a questionnaire will collect, researchers also have to consider the range of analyses they will want to carry out with the data. It is particularly important to consider the range of 'background' information required about respondents. If a researcher is interested in whether the views of men and women differ, the questionnaire will clearly need to record the sex of the respondent!

Question design

When designing questions, attention needs to be paid to the tendency of respondents to 'satisfice', that is, to respond in a way that requires the least effort but which they think will suffice (Krosnick and Alwin, 1987). This makes it important to minimise the difficulty of the task being set respondents, as the higher the burden of the task, the more likely respondents are to satisfice (Holbrook et al, 2003). This means, for example, questions should avoid asking people to recall events that happened a long time before, or to count the number of times they have done a common or relatively trivial task over an unrealistically long time period.

Different types of question

The questions used in questionnaires tend to be *closed* rather than *open*. Closed questions involve the interviewer allocating the respondent's answer to a category in a predetermined list. The following is an example of a closed question:

'How would you describe the wages or salary you are paid for the job you do – on the low side, reasonable, or on the high side. IF LOW: Very low or a bit low?'

This gives the respondent four different options to choose from, and the interviewer will record one of these as appropriate:

Very low
A bit low
Reasonable
On the high side

This same question could easily be turned into an open question:

'How would you describe the wages or salary you are paid for the job you do?'

In this case, no options are offered to the respondent and the interviewer would simply record what he or she said (usually verbatim). These questions will then need to be 'coded' before they can be analysed. Open questions tend to be used when it is not possible to predict the nature or range of responses that people will give to the question. Some closed questions will also include an open-ended option to record any responses that do not fit into the predetermined list.

Researchers often use showcards, which list the range of possible answer options to a closed question, in cases where the respondent has to choose between a number of possible answers. In general, it is most appropriate to use showcards when the question is long and there are many answer categories to choose from (Dillman and Christian, 2005).

Question wording

When designing questions the aim should be to arrive at a wording that will be interpreted by respondents in a similar way. Consequently, the language used should be as simple, clear and unambiguous as possible.

Questions should not be double-barrelled – that is, asking two questions at once. Consider, for example, the following statement:

'How much do you agree or disagree that buses in this area are unreliable and too expensive?'

This question conflates two distinct and very different aspects of public transport (reliability and cost), both making it hard for many respondents to answer, and hard for any researcher to interpret its results.

If a survey's findings are to be seen as credible, it is also important that questions are not leading – in other words, that they do not push respondents towards giving a particular answer. Consider, for example, the question:

'What is it that makes you proud to be British?'

This question, assuming it is not preceded by a question asking people *whether* they are proud to be British, is leading because it makes it difficult for those who are *not* proud to say so. A less leading version would be:

> 'What is it that makes you proud to be British, or are you not proud of being British at all?'

Sensitive questions

Tourangeau, Rips and Rasinski (2000) make a helpful distinction between three types of sensitive topic areas: those that are intrusive (for example, questions about sexuality or income), those subject to social desirability (voting, 'green' behaviour) or those that relate to fear of disclosure (admitting to a criminal act). However, it is worth remembering that often respondents are less awkward about answering such questions than researchers (or interviewers) are about asking them.

A number of different techniques are used in these sorts of circumstances. Some questions try to 'normalise' the less socially acceptable option by suggesting that this sort of behaviour is common or by asking respondents what 'most people' think about an issue before asking their own opinion. Other common methods include using self-completion methods during a face-to-face interview or giving the respondent a showcard with numbered options and asking them only to tell the interviewer the number. The setting within which an interview takes place can also matter; Brener et al (2006) found that school pupils reported higher rates of 'negative' behaviours when they were interviewed at school than they did when interviewed at home.

Question order and context

The order in which questions are asked during an interview is important. Not surprisingly, it is not advisable to begin an interview with particularly difficult or sensitive questions; these should be introduced once the respondent has got used to the interview and is feeling more comfortable.

It is also important to bear in mind that the context within which questions are asked can affect the responses that are given. Asking, for instance, how much a person gives to charity immediately after a series of questions about attitudes to charitable giving is probably not going to produce the most accurate reading possible.

Question filtering

Some questions are asked of all respondents; others are only asked of a subgroup, usually determined by their responses to previous questions. The instruction used to direct interviewers (or, in the case of self-completion surveys, respondents) to the next relevant question is called a **filter instruction**. In computer-assisted surveys (whether face to face, telephone or online), filtering can be programmed into the survey.

Pre-testing

It is good practice to pre-test new questions to check that they are as clear to respondents and interviewers as they are to researchers. A range of different methods are used, the most common being cognitive tests (which apply intensive qualitative techniques to a small number of questions) and pilot tests (which test out all, or part, of the questionnaire in a more quantitative manner).

Data collection

Once the questionnaire has been designed and tested, and various administrative procedures completed, data collection (or 'fieldwork') can begin.

Response rates – the number of successfully 'achieved' interviews as a proportion of the interviews 'possible' – need to be monitored throughout the fieldwork period in order to identify problems as early as possible and take remedial action.

Survey organisations are increasingly using respondent incentives to boost response rates. Incentives can range from vouchers for high street shops, to books of postage stamps, fridge magnets or pens! Incentives can be 'conditional', which means they are given only to those people who take part in the survey, or 'unconditional', which means they are given to everyone selected to take part, irrespective of whether or not they go on to participate. Some key patterns have been identified by a number of studies into the effects of incentives (Church, 1993; Singer et al, 1999). First, prepaid incentives are more effective than promised incentives, because they introduce a sense of 'reciprocity'. Second, monetary incentives are more effective than non-monetary incentives. And third, response rates increase with the value of the incentive but with diminishing returns. In other words, the impact of offering a £5 voucher over no incentive at all will be greater than the difference between offering a £10 voucher over a £5 one.

If interviewers are being used to carry out data collection, it is important that they all have a clear, and similar, understanding as to the purpose of the survey and the mechanics that they should follow in carrying out their interviews. For this reason, it is common practice to have interviewer 'briefings' at which the survey and its various administrative requirements are introduced. Briefings can also play an important role in boosting interviewer morale and helping to ensure that a good response rate is achieved (Campanelli et al, 1997).

Data preparation

Once a questionnaire has been completed and returned, the data can enter the next stage of the survey process – data preparation. The two main features of data preparation are *editing* and *coding*.

If paper questionnaires have been used, the results will have to be keyed or scanned so that it is in electronic form.

Editing

Data editing involves checking the quality of the data and, where possible, correcting any errors. This process is usually more laborious when the data were collected using PAPI techniques; with CAPI or CATI (computer-assisted telephone interviewing) methods, the scope for errors in data entry can be limited by the computer program.

A number of common editing checks are usually made. These include: checking that questions have been asked only of those who should have been asked them (*filter checks*); checking that responses lie within an appropriate range – for example, that people do not have 30 children (*range checks*); and checks to ensure logical consistency between different answers (*logic checks*). In all cases, the editing process can only correct identifiable errors where there is a clear clue as to their resolution.

Coding

Most survey questions are 'closed', that is, respondents and interviewers choose from a range of specified options. Otherwise a respondent's answer has to be recorded, and the information collected then has to be reduced to a numeric form before it can be analysed. To do this, the researcher examines a number of responses to the question and develops a 'code frame' that lists a number of possible answers and allocates a numeric code to each. This code frame is then used to code all subsequent responses to this question.

Question for discussion

- What are the main advantages of face-to-face surveys over other modes of survey administration?

References

Brener, N.D., Eaton, D.K., Kann, L., Grunbaum, J.A., Gross, L.A., Kyle, T.M. et al (2006) 'The association of survey setting and mode with self-reported health risk behaviours among high school students', *Public Opinion Quarterly*, vol 70, pp 354-74.

Campanelli, P., Sturgis, P. and Purdon, S. (1997) *Can you hear me knocking? An investigation into the impact of interviewers on survey response rates*, London: National Centre for Social Research.

Church, A.H. (1993) 'Estimating the effect of incentives on mail survey response rates: a meta-analysis', *Public Opinion Quarterly*, vol 57, pp 62-79.

Dillman, D.A. and Christian, L.M. (2005) 'Survey modes as a source of instability in responses across surveys', *Field Methods*, vol 17, pp 30-51.

Holbrook, A., Green, M. and Krosnick, J.A. (2003) 'Telephone versus face-to-face interviewing of national probability samples with long questionnaires: comparisons of respondent satisficing and social desirability response bias', *Public Opinion Quarterly*, vol 67, pp 79-125.

Krosnick, J.A. and Alwin, D. (1987) 'An evaluation of cognitive theory of response order effects in survey measurement', *Public Opinion Quarterly*, vol 51, pp 201-19.

Singer, E., Gebler, N., Raghunathan, T., van Hoewyk, J. and McGonagle, K. (1999) 'The effect of incentives in interviewer-mediated surveys', *Journal of Official Statistics*, vol 15, pp 217-30.

Tourangeau, R., Rips, L.J. and Rasinski, K. (2000) *The psychology of survey response*, Cambridge: Cambridge University Press.

Further reading

Bradburn, N., Sudman, S. and Wansink, B. (2004) *Asking questions: The definitive guide to questionnaire design*, San Francisco, CA: Jossey-Bass.
Park, A., Curtice, J., Phillips, M., and Clery, E. (eds) (2011) *British social attitudes: The 27th report*, London: Sage Publications.

Website resources

National Centre for Social Research (NatCen): www.natcen.ac.uk
Office for National Statistics: www.ons.gov.uk/ons/index.html
Scottish Centre for Social Research: www.scotcen.org.uk

5.7 Internet surveys
David de Vaus

Survey research has been transformed by the use of computer-assisted interviewing (CAI). Computer-based interviewing is well established in telephone surveys and since the mid-1990s has been used to administer interviews using the internet. The role of internet surveys has grown rapidly with vastly improved computer access and speeds, mobile devices (for example, smart phones, iPad, wireless), greater standardisation and simple-to-use software.

Web surveys

While early internet surveys involved distributing electronic questionnaires as email attachments, email is now mainly used to recruit and follow up samples and for pointing respondents to a URL at which to complete the survey instrument. Respondents complete the survey instrument online either in one sitting or by returning several times. Once completed, responses are automatically returned to a web server and collated for statistical analysis. These online questionnaires can be interactive, whereby the questions are tailored on the basis of respondent characteristics and responses to earlier questions. Among other things, web-based questionnaires can:

- automatically skip questions, depending on answers to earlier questions as well as give modules of questions to selected individuals;
- create dynamic questionnaires in which questions are created 'on the fly' based on earlier responses;
- check for errors and prompt respondents to check answers;
- ensure that instructions are followed;
- ensure that questions are answered in the intended order;
- automatically code and compile responses;
- automatically conduct preliminary analysis and provide feedback to respondents.

Web surveys can be implemented quickly and at lower cost than some alternatives. Once the questionnaire has been developed, increasing the sample size is simple and cheap. Where sample members are invited using emails, the task of following up non-responders is simple, quick and inexpensive.

Internet samples

Samples for internet surveys are constructed in a number of ways. These include:

- *advertising* for volunteers on specific websites, listservers and chat groups;
- *pop-up web page questionnaires* to be answered by visitors to a specific web page;
- *commercial internet panels* that provide samples of cases with specific characteristics.

These samples are of no value for generalising results beyond the specific group of respondents. However, some internet sampling strategies have been developed to obtain more representative samples. These methods include:

- recruiting a representative sample using normal random sampling methods, and then *paying to connect all sample members to the internet* in return for their participation in surveys for a set period (see Knowledge Networks website listed below);
- *using quota internet samples* to make a sample representative of a population in specific respects;
- *weighting internet samples* to reflect the population in specific respects.

Problems with internet samples

While internet surveys can collect information from large numbers of people relatively quickly and cheaply, the quality of the samples on which they rely is a major focus of criticism. These samples encounter three main difficulties.

First, they *lack a sampling frame*. Probability samples require an unbiased sampling frame that contains all the elements of the population from which the sample is to be drawn. Since there is no list of internet users, it is very difficult to obtain general population samples for internet surveys. Second, they encounter *coverage bias*. Although internet access is rapidly increasing, internet users continue to over-represent particular groups (for example, younger and affluent). Third, internet samples are subject to *response bias* due to their generally low response rates.

Internet surveys also face other practical difficulties, including low response rates that may stem from sources such as a fear of viruses, privacy concerns and slow internet connections. In the past, internet surveys have also encountered software and hardware compatibility difficulties. However, faster connections and better integration with internet browsers is reducing the extent of these problems.

While the absence of sampling frames is a problem for implementing internet surveys for general population surveys, this is not a problem for many well-defined and internet-connected populations. Internet surveys can be well suited for members of particular organisations (for example, all staff and students in a university, trades union members or staff in a business) or client groups (for example, customers, patients in a hospital).

Internet surveys can also be part of a multi-modal strategy. Some large national panel surveys that track people at regular intervals have recruited samples in the traditional way but provide a variety of ways (including internet questionnaires) to respond to the follow-up questionnaires. Some national census agencies such as the Australian Bureau of Statistics are employing internet-based census returns among the alternative ways of participating in the Census.

Setting up a web survey

Apart from recruiting a sample, an internet survey involves developing and distributing an electronic questionnaire, receiving electronic responses and compiling these for analysis. This process has been simplified by dedicated software for producing and deploying internet surveys. One fully featured package is Survey Crafter. A listing and reviews of this and other software is available on the Meaning Consulting Services website (see below).

As internet speeds have increased, many web surveys are now designed, distributed, returned and analysed entirely online. All the work for fully online surveys is conducted on an internet server. The 'Online survey sites' (see below) list some sites on which to create and administer fully online web surveys.

An alternative way of setting up a web survey is to use a *mixture of online and offline* stages. Using special software such as Survey Crafter, you can develop an electronic questionnaire on your own computer for web deployment. This questionnaire is then uploaded to an internet server and made available to the sample. Responses are then electronically returned to the server for downloading to your local computer for analysis, either by the internet survey software or with specialist statistical software such as SPSS.

Question for discussion

- What are the main advantages and sampling problems when using the internet to conduct a survey?

Further reading

Couper, M.P. (2000) 'Web surveys: a review of issues and approaches', *Public Opinion Quarterly*, vol 64, pp 464-94.
Couper, M.P. (2008) *Designing effective web surveys*, New York: Cambridge University Press.
Dillman, D.A. (2000) *Mail and internet surveys: The total design method*, New York: Wiley.
Fricker, R.D. and Schonlau, M. (2002) 'Advantages and disadvantages of internet surveys: evidence from the literature', *Field Methods*, vol 14, no 4, pp 347-67.

Website resources

Knowledge Networks (representative internet sampling methods, password required): www.knowledgenetworks.com/knpanel/index.html
Web Survey Methodology: www.websm.org
Web survey software – Meaning Consulting Services: www.meaning.uk.com/your-resources/software-database

Online survey sites

Survey Crafter: www.surveycrafter.com
Survey Monkey: www.surveymonkey.com
Response-O-Matic: www.response-o-matic.com
Instant Survey: www.instantsurvey.com/
SurveyTracker: www.surveytracker.com/
Zoomerang: www.zoomerang.com/
SurveyWriter: www.surveywriter.com/site/index.html
Survey Galaxy: www.surveygalaxy.com

5.8 Content analysis
David Deacon

Content analysis is used to quantify the manifest features of texts. In the past, some practitioners have claimed that it represents an objective form of textual analysis, but these sorts of claims need to be treated sceptically. As such, it can provide insights into issues such as how the media (or others) report homelessness or domestic violence. Such information can be useful to contextualise the ways in which policy issues surface and become discussed.

There are various stages involved in deploying this method and these are outlined below. An example of its application is set out in ***Box 5e***. Before applying the method, researchers need to consider whether it is appropriate for their research objectives. Content analysis is a method that aims to produce 'a big picture': delineating manifest trends, patterns and absences over large aggregations of texts. But by looking at meaning making *across* texts, the method skates over complex processes of meaning making *within* texts: the latent levels of form and meaning.

Sampling

Sampling considerations in relation to content analysis are essentially the same as those that concern any attempt to generate a representative sample. Researchers first need to identify their research population (which is determined by the research objectives) and then decide on a sampling strategy that will produce an adequate representation of that population (see Section 5.4). As a general rule, the bigger the sample is, the better. Issues regarding representativeness operate in two ways: *horizontally* – how far backwards or forwards in time should sampling extend the sampling period? And *vertically* – how extensively should researchers sample across the component elements of their 'population'? For example, if researchers are interested in examining media representations of disability, should they concentrate on news reporting or extend their analysis to include fictional and actuality forms?

Box 5e: Media reporting of the voluntary sector
David Deacon

This illustration is based on a study by Deacon (1999).

Sampling
Horizontal dimensions
A composite sample of four weeks' British local and national broadcast and press coverage was analysed. Sampling began on Monday, 26 October 1992 and from that date every eighth day was sampled, for 27 further days.

Vertical dimensions (national media)
All national daily and Sunday newspapers for each sample day were analysed. For the national broadcast sample, recording on each sample day began at 9.00am and concluded at 12.00pm, and included all actuality coverage on BBC1, BBC2, ITV, Channel 4 and BBC Radio 4 that could be categorised as one of the following: news, current affairs, entertainment, general information or social action programming. BBC Radio 2's 'Jimmy Young' show and BBC Radio 1's 'News '92/3' were also added to the sample.

Vertical dimensions (local media)
Four counties were purposively selected for their regional and demographic variation. All newspapers published in these areas on the sampling days were analysed. The local television sample comprised the main early evening regional news programmes broadcast in each of the local sample areas, for both BBC1 and ITV, on each of the sample weekdays. Local radio was not sampled due to logistical difficulties.

Sampling unit
In the main, the sampling units were individual items within programmes and newspapers (that is, separate news and feature items). Where broadcast programmes were not segmented, the entire programme was taken as the sampling unit.

What was counted?
Up to five 'voluntary sector' organisations could be coded per item (more, if the sample unit was an entire programme). These codes indicated the area of activity of each organisation, the nature of its presentation and the role it fulfilled in the item. These roles were organised under two broad categories: 'Doing' (for example, fundraising, providing services, and so on) and 'Commenting' (for example, criticising other organisations, highlighting issues, and so on). Each voluntary sector source could be assigned up to two roles per item (if appropriate). Assorted other descriptive details related to each item were also coded (for example, length of item, its location and position).

Qualifying criteria
An item or programme was deemed relevant if it either mentioned any organisation that was (1) non-profit making; (2) non-statutory; (3) non-party political; (4) not affiliated to a professional group; and (5) had a formal structure; or (6) referred to broader issues concerning the voluntary sector.

Coding and analysis

More than 4,500 items and programmes were included in the analysis. Coverage was found to cluster around general and non-contentious areas of voluntary activity (for example, children, animals and health) and neglected organisations working in minority or contentious issue domains. Voluntary organisations received more coverage for their deeds (fundraising, doing good works, and so on) than for their political interventions (raising topics, adjudicating on the views or actions of others). When voluntary sector sources were included as commentators, their most common role was a 'signalling' one: highlighting issues and concern for public debate rather than directly engaging in the cut and thrust of political argument. Instances of direct media criticism of voluntary agencies were rare, but scant attention was paid to the broader political questions raised by the expanding role and importance of the voluntary sector in Britain.

Reference

Deacon, D. (1999) 'Charitable images: the construction of voluntary sector news', in B. Franklin (ed) *Social policy, the media and misrepresentation*, London: Routledge, pp 51-68.

Researchers also need to decide on the sampling unit. Some content analysis studies have a very precise focus, taking individual words as their sampling units to explore 'the lexical contents and/or syntactic structures of documents' (Beardsworth, 1980, p 375). Other studies provide a more generalised analysis that involves coding themes and features in texts. The second form is the most widely adopted in social research and the basic sampling unit tends to be an entire text (for example, a television programme) or clearly identifiable component elements of a text (for example, separate news items within a television programme). Once chosen, the selected sampling unit becomes the 'host' to all textual elements that are subsequently quantified.

What to count?

What is counted is determined by the research objectives and these decisions require the production of:

- *a coding schedule*, which lists the variables of the researcher's analysis;
- *a coding manual*, which sets out the coding values for each of the variables.

Their design requires a lot of careful deliberation, as some things are easier to categorise than others. Piloting is essential at this stage, to discern how readily the variables and values can be operationalised, and to gain some sense of their comprehensiveness. As a general rule, content analysis works most reliably in the coding of manifest features of texts.

Qualifying criteria

Researchers need to define what criteria will be used to decide which sample units fall within their study's remit. Sometimes this is quite straightforward. Imagine you wanted to conduct an analysis of media reporting of a specific social policy or social work initiative. For this study, your qualifying criteria could simply be any explicit reference made to the policy in a sampled item or programme. Other topics are more problematic. For example, the case study in **Box 5e** describes a content analysis of media coverage of the voluntary sector (Deacon, 1999). As there is no consensus as to how to define the voluntary sector, careful thought needs to be given to identifying 'when a voluntary sector item is a voluntary sector item'. Should the study include items that mention trades unions and political parties, or solely focus on registered charities? In the case described, neither strategy was adopted – in the former instance, because it would have made the study too inclusive (in Britain, the voluntary sector is generally seen as separate from unions and political parties); in the latter, because it would have been too restrictive (many voluntary organisations do not have charitable status).

Coding

The key principle in coding is to be very systematic in applying the research instruments. Even with well-piloted coding schedules and manuals, examples may be encountered that do not fit neatly within the researcher's categories. Once the researcher has decided on a coding solution, the decision should be noted down, and repeated studiously for similar cases.

The issue of consistency is particularly important when more than one person is involved in the coding, as there may be inconsistencies *between* the interpretations of coders. Various statistical procedures can be used to test for inter-coder reliability.

Analysis

In data analysis researchers need both to describe the findings and interpret their significance. The first task is straightforward, but the second requires considerably more imagination and reflexivity. Researchers should be directive in their analysis of the results at the start, avoiding the temptation of indiscriminately trawling for numbers, as this is a recipe for confusion.

New directions: 'Push Button' content analysis

Media content is now routinely stored in various digital formats and these archives can be searched using keywords to identify and quantify coverage on specific topics. Deacon (2007) argues that the methodological implications of this trend have not been discussed and identifies several validity and reliability concerns.

Validity

1. By relying on keywords to identify relevant content, this method of analysis is better at analysis of tangible 'things' (people, events, organisations etc) than more abstract 'themes'.

2. The most commonly used sources of digital news content are text-only, which precludes analysis of the visual dimensions of news content.
3. In text databases, items are removed from the context in which they initially appeared, which prevents consideration of relational links between items.
4. Many digital news databases have a limited historical reach, which restricts the opportunity for historical analysis.

Reliability

Deacon's (2007) study assessed Lexis Nexis, the most widely used digital newspaper archive in contemporary media analysis, and identified several reliability concerns:

1. Inconsistent counts produced by identical keyword searches conducted in Lexis Nexis and another major digital news archives.
2. Some internally inconsistent results produced by searches conducted within Lexis Nexis.
3. Examples of duplicated content.
4. Examples of missing content.
5. Inconsistent unitisation (that is, occasions where separate items were bundled together as one item).

These validity and reliability concerns do not mean that digital news archives should never be used for media analysis, but highlight the need for caution:

1. 'False positives' should always be weeded out. These are occasions where a keyword may have several meanings and the resulting search identifies content that is not related to the focus of the research.
2. Researchers should recognise the dangers of being too precise in the key words used as this can create a problem of 'false negatives'. This is a situation where much relevant material is inadvertently excluded from the search because the terms of the search are too constricted.
3. Item lists should always be checked for duplicated material.
4. Individual items should be scrutinised to check for any inconsistencies in the unitisation of the content.
5. As a preliminary exercise, keyword searches should be conducted using very general terms for the titles and periods being analysed. This is to check that there are no significant, structural omissions in the archive coverage for the sample period.

Conclusion

Content analysis provides an extensive rather than intensive analysis of texts and only offers answers to the questions posed. It requires care and rigour in design and implementation and does not offer much opportunity to explore textual aspects to develop new insights. Nor can it be said to provide an 'objective', value-free perspective. Arbitrary decisions are involved in all stages of the research process: what you count, how much you sample, how you categorise, and so on; and all of these decisions ultimately depend on the researcher's judgement of what is significant. Therefore, findings produced by this method do not represent incontrovertible facts. They are 'constructs', and when presenting them researchers must be open about the construction process.

Question for discussion

- Is the coding process both central to content analysis and its defining feature?

References

Beardsworth, A. (1980) 'Analyzing press content: some technical and methodological issues', in H. Christian (ed) *The sociology of journalism and the press*, Keele: Keele University, pp 371-95.

Deacon, D. (1999) 'Charitable images: the construction of voluntary sector news', in B. Franklin (ed) *Social policy, the media and misrepresentation*, London: Routledge, pp 51-68.

Deacon, D. (2007) 'Yesterday's papers and today's technology: digital newspaper archives and 'Push Button' content analysis', *European Journal of Communication*, vol 22, no 1, pp **5-25**.

Further reading

Weber, R. (1990) *Basic content analysis*, London: Sage Publications.

5.9 Structured observation
Alan Bryman and Saul Becker

Structured observation is a somewhat underutilised method for gathering data on people's behaviour. Unlike the kind of participant observation in which ethnographers engage, the observer is typically on the sidelines of the aspect of social life he or she is studying.

The idea is to use an *observation schedule*, which is similar to a structured interview schedule of the kind used in survey research, to observe people and their behaviour in terms of already established categories. The researcher will usually be interested in several variables and for each variable there will be at least two categories in terms of which behaviour needs to be coded. Imagine that we are interested in the way social security claimants are treated by social security staff. An observer might want to categorise the behaviour of both claimants and the member of staff concerned. Regarding the member of staff, the focus of interest may be issues such as: 'Does the member of staff greet the claimant?' 'How long does he or she spend checking through the claimant's application form?' 'Does the member of staff provide help with any aspects of the form that have not been fully completed?' Many of these issues are relatively straightforward for an observer to assess. More difficult to code, because they require some interpretation on the part of the observer, might be more impressionistic issues in which the researcher might be interested, such as whether the member of staff is friendly, whether he or she is helpful, whether he or she becomes aggressive towards a claimant, and so on. In order to devise indicators of such issues, the researcher needs to make the observation schedule as straightforward as possible so that the observer has very little interpretation to do. The problem with interpretation of what is going on (such as whether the member of staff is being friendly) is that observers may not be consistent in their application of criteria and if there is more than one observer, they may not be consistent with each other.

A further issue that requires consideration in connection with structured observation is the issue of sampling. Bearing in mind that there may be several members of staff helping claimants at any one time, is each member of staff continuously observed over several days, or is there some attempt to sample members of staff and the times they are observed? Observing all members of staff continuously would require a large research team and would be very wearing for the members of staff. Accordingly, a researcher might want to observe just one or two members of staff at any one time. Alternatively, one may want to video-record interactions. But this still leaves open the questions: how are they chosen and when are they observed? A random sampling approach is the most desirable strategy, but with structured observation further issues arise. Should each staff member be observed for a whole day? If the answer is that this is undesirable because it might be exhausting for them, when should they be observed? This issue is important since we should not always observe a particular member of staff at the same time each day, because his or her behaviour may vary considerably over the course of the day and this would not be captured if, for example, he or she was always observed between 9.00am and mid-morning. In the morning, members of staff may feel friendlier and more helpful than later in the day when they may have experienced some difficult situations. Consequently, it is likely to be necessary to ensure that the observation of members of staff takes place at different times of the day. Other sampling techniques that are fairly specific to structured observation are discussed in Bryman (2012, Chapter 12).

A US study of meetings between family care staff and parents of children with emotional and behavioural disorders illustrates the use of an observation schedule to examine the degree to which the family care team were family-friendly (Singh et al, 1997). This meant assessing whether each of several things happened in the meeting, such as:

- a statement is made to the parent that all information will be kept confidential;
- the parent is asked what treatments or interventions he/she felt worked/didn't work in the past;
- the parent's ideas are elicited about the types of service he/she would prefer;
- the parent is involved in designing the service plan.

In each case, the item could be recorded by observers on a yes/no/not applicable basis. The foregoing items are all relatively straightforward to record but one requiring more interpretation was:

- family members are attended to in a courteous fashion at all times.

A total of 79 meetings were observed, although we are not told how they were sampled. A crucial issue for research of this kind is obtaining consent, and in this case we are told that permission was obtained from all those involved in the meetings, including children. This point is very important since structured observation is a rather invasive technique, especially in emotionally charged situations of this kind. In fact, the research shows that the family-friendliness of the meetings was variable, although, overall, the authors described it as reasonably good.

The main advantage of structured observation is that it allows the researcher to study behaviour directly rather than indirectly by asking people about their own behaviour through a questionnaire or interview. ***Box 5f*** provides an illustration of a research instrument designed to capture how social workers spend their time at work. Rather than observe the behaviour of social workers in a structured way, the researchers in this example devised a self-completion form for social workers themselves to record how they spent their day, in 15-minute blocks. The example outlines some of the issues involved in designing and preparing this self-completion time diary. Of course, asking people questions about their own behaviour is vulnerable to such things as misrepresentation, inaccurate reporting and recall error. On the other hand, with structured observation there is always the risk that people adjust their behaviour to the observer's presence. However, it is extremely difficult to determine how far and in what ways behaviour is affected by being observed.

Box 5f: The use of time diaries
Mary Baginsky

This box explores the key issues for assembling the instrument used in a study where a time diary methodology was applied to the collection of information on social workers' workloads (Baginsky et al, 2010). The data that resulted informed the Social Work Task Force's recommendations (Social Work Task Force, 2009). The remit of the Task Force covered social workers in whatever setting or agency they worked and ideally these should have been represented proportionally. As with many of the decisions, the timescales challenged our ability to be able to do this. The solution that we adopted was to sample 30 local authorities and approach both adult and children's services to seek their cooperation. We also engaged with the private and the voluntary sectors as far as children were concerned, but failed to gain the collaboration of those working with adults in these sectors. While most diaries were completed during the same week, we did allow departments to choose from two other weeks if they had a specific circumstance such as an inspection, although we made sure to avoid 'odd' weeks such as those with bank holidays.

We knew that the best response rates for diary surveys are achieved when respondents are recruited personally, but again the time constraints around the project ruled this out. In the event, nearly 1,200 social workers completed the diary exercise, but this could have been much higher if we had been able to engage with potential respondents directly.

A great deal of time and attention was given to developing the activities list and the team consulted widely with practitioners and academics. As the social workers completing the diary would be working with adults and children in a range of settings, the activities had to be described to reflect this. There has been considerable concern in recent years about the amount of time that social workers are spending on feeding the bureaucratic machine rather than in face-to-face contact with clients. But it also has to be recognised that social workers are applying their professional skills to the reports they write and assessments that they make. So we wanted to encompass all client-related work – broken down into contact and non-contact time as well as other professional and non-professional activities. We also devised a questionnaire that sat alongside the diary to capture background information on the respondents, as well as their views on issues impacting on the social work profession.

It was important to the team that we designed an instrument that was relatively easy to complete in hard copy or electronically – we had feedback from another team about the difficulties they had encountered when using a web-based instrument, so that format was not considered – and we employed a graphic designer to construct the final instrument. We also provided a clear set of instructions on how to complete, where to seek help and how to return the completed instrument. Perfection is an elusive quality, but we were confident that we had arrived at something that was definitely fit for purpose, although it is only fair to acknowledge that the irony of imposing a burden to measure burden was not lost on the researchers or on the social workers.

The period over which a diary is kept needs to be sufficient to capture usable data, but not too long to risk boredom or indifference. It was thought that a working week would be acceptable. We also needed to arrive at appropriate time intervals for recording activities. While we wanted to achieve a seamless view of their days, we had to recognise the effort which social workers were devoting to this – so we made a guess. We judged five minutes would annoy, 30 minutes would risk too much data loss and so we decided on 15-minute intervals. Both the 'week' and the '15 minutes' worked well at pilot and study stages. However, the diary did not allow simultaneous activities to be recorded. We could have created 'compound activities' (see Nordhaus, 1999) but this would have made the activities list very long so we arrived at the simple solution of asking people to make a judgement as to which they considered to be the main activity, and if they undertook two activities at the same time, over, say, half an hour, to allocate the time proportionately. One of the complaints about time diaries has been that they underestimate activities which are completed quickly but which may be significant (Juster, 1985), and while we recognised this as a risk, it was one we had to accept. Other charges against them have been that respondents may be selective over what they record or enter their data retrospectively rather than in the required intervals and increase the risk of recall error. We thought the latter was very likely to happen with most social workers choosing to complete at lunchtime or at the end of the day. Nevertheless, diary methods have been shown to produce reliable accounts of time use at the aggregate level (see, for example, Robinson and Bostrom, 1994). Validity tests have been conducted on time diaries which have included contacting respondents randomly throughout the day and asking them what they were doing, shadowing and other observational techniques (Pentland et al, 1999).

In this study time diaries made it possible to collect data on the workloads and work patterns of social workers that, it is hoped, will strengthen policy decisions around the profession. It is also hoped that the lessons learned from this exercise will feed into a larger-scale survey. In that event, time spent preparing the ground will be repaid in abundance.

Question for discussion
- What types of research questions are diary methods best equipped to answer?

References

Baginsky, M., Moriarty, J., Manthorpe, J., Stevens, M., MacInnes, T. and Nagendran, T. (2010) *Social workers' workload survey. Messages from the frontline. Findings from the 2009 survey and interviews with senior managers*, London: Department for Children, Schools and Families and Department of Health.

Juster, F.T. (1985) 'Preferences for work and leisure', in F.T. Juster and F.P. Stafford (eds) *Time, goods, and well-being*, Ann Arbor, MI: Institute for Social Research.

Nordhaus, W. (1999) *Measurement of time with multiple activities: Discussion notes*, Discussion presented at the Workshop on Measurement of and Research on Time Use, 27-28 May, convened by the Committee on National Statistics of the National Research Council, US.

Pentland, W.E., Harvey, A.S. and McColl, M.A. (1999) *Time use research in the social sciences*, New York: Kluwer Academic Publishing Group.

Robinson, J.P. and Bostrom, A. (1994) 'The overestimated workweek? What time diary measures suggest', *Monthly Labor Market Review*, August, pp 11-23.

Social Work Task Force (2009) *Building a safer, stronger future: The final report of the Social Work Task Force*, London: Department for Children, Schools and Families and Department of Health.

Further reading

Alaszewski, A. (2006) *Using diaries for social research*, London: Sage Publications.

Bolger, N., Davis, A. and Rafaeli, E. (2003) 'Diary methods: capturing life as it is lived', *Annual Review of Psychology*, vol 54, pp 579-616.

Larson, R. (1989) 'Beeping children and adolescents: a method for studying time use and daily experience', *Journal of Youth and Adolescence*, vol 18, no 6, pp 511-30.

Question for discussion

- For what kinds of research questions might structured observation be a useful research method in social policy and social work research?

References

Bryman, A. (2012) *Social research methods* (4th edn), Oxford: Oxford University Press.

Singh, N.N., Curtis, W.J., Wechsler, H.A., Ellis, C.R. and Cohen, R. (1997) 'Family friendliness of community-based services for children and adolescents with emotional and behavioural disorders and their families: an observational study', *Journal of Emotional and Behavioural Disorders*, vol 5, no 2, pp 82-92.

Further reading

McCall, G.J. (1984) 'Systematic field observation', *Annual Review of Sociology*, vol 10, pp 263-82.

5.10 Official statistics

David Gordon

In the original sense of the word, "Statistics" was the science of Statecraft: to the political arithmetician of the eighteenth century, its function was to be the eyes and ears of the central government. (Sir Roland Fisher, cited in Gaither and Cavazos-Gaither, 1996, p 243)

The word statistics is derived from the Italian word for *state*. Therefore, all *statistics* were originally 'official statistics' as they were literally information collected for and by the state. However, in modern societies statistics are collected and published by a wide range of organisations, including governmental organisations. Nevertheless, it is always important to remember that no statistics can be considered to be 'objective facts'; they are all paid for and collected by some organisation for a specific purpose (often a policy purpose).

Many textbooks claim that statistics were first described by John Graunt of London, a 'haberdasher of small wares' in a tiny book called *Natural and political observations made upon the Bills of Mortality*, published in 1672. However, policy-relevant statistics collected during population and housing censuses have a much longer history than this, with records dating back to early Babylonian, Egyptian and Chinese civilisations. These innovative early Asian and African censuses were undertaken primarily for military, tax and land allocation purposes (Nissel, 2001). The first censuses in Europe were conducted by the Roman Empire, usually on a quinquennial basis (the word *census* is Latin in origin) but, after the empire's collapse, census taking declined with only a few sporadic and usually incomplete, population counts occurring until the 1800s (for example, the Gaelic *Senchus fer n'Alba* in 7th-century England, the *Doomsday Book* in 1086 and the 'Hearth Tax' counts in 14th-century France). Censuses in Quebec in 1666, in Iceland in 1703, in China in 1711 and in Sweden in 1749 were influential in promoting the idea of 'modern' census taking and by the beginning of the 19th century many countries had instituted a regular national census programme (Rees et al, 2002).

National census information plays a central part in any assessment of social conditions in the world. They are the only source of reliable and comprehensive data on the sociodemographic and economic situation of the world's populations. For example, only census data provide high quality estimates of such basic factors as the number of children and the number of families and households. They are similarly the only high quality source of basic employment information, such as employment status, occupation, industry, place of work, current activity status, and so on. It cannot be overemphasised that census data are always much more reliable than survey-based data and should always be used in preference to survey data when they are available for the time frame in question. The main problem with census data is that they are only collected every 10 years in most countries (some countries carry out a census every five years), and only a limited amount of basic information is collected.

Apart from the National Census, there are two other main sources of 'official' statistics: *sample survey data* and *administrative statistics*. In the UK, most of these government statistics are catalogued in the Office for National Statistics (ONS) *Guide to official statistics* (www. ons.gov.uk/ons/index.html), additionally, Jones and Elias (2006) provide an audit of administrative data sources.

A lot of statistical data are available free of charge from the ONS website (www.statistics.gov.uk) at both national and small area level (see neighbourhood statistics at www.neighbourhood.statistics.gov.uk/ and also from the national Economic and Social Data Service [ESDS] www.esds.ac.uk/). Statistics about Northern Ireland are available from the Northern Ireland Statistics and Research Agency (NISRA) (www.nisra.gov.uk/). Statistics about Scotland are available from the Scottish Government (www.scotland.gov.uk/Topics/Statistics) and statistics about Wales from the Welsh Government (www.wales.gov.uk/topics/statistics/?lang=en).

Most of the data described in the *Guide to official statistics* are administrative statistics relating to the specific functioning of national and local government departments. Many are very specialised (for example, the Turkey Census, Ship Arrivals, General Ophthalmic Services – Vouchers, and so on) and of limited interest to most social policy and social work researchers. However, some, like the unemployment claimant count and accidents at work, are of both considerable academic and political interest and sometimes a subject of controversy. During the 1980s, 30 changes were made to the way the unemployment count was measured, many of which resulted in a reported reduction in the number of unemployed. These changes, during a period of high unemployment, led to a widespread belief that the unemployment statistics were being 'fiddled' (Taylor, 1990; Royal Statistical Society, 1995; Levitas, 1996).

The UK government typically commissions 10-20 social surveys each year, including a range of one-off issue-specific surveys that vary in content from year to year (for example, the Psychiatric Morbidity Survey). Recently, five major government surveys have been merged into the Integrated Household Survey (IHS) that collects information on about 450,000 people. The IHS consists of a core question set and separate question modules incorporating the, General Lifestyle Survey, Living Costs and Food Survey, English Housing Survey, Annual Population Survey and Life Opportunities Survey.

Similar surveys are also carried out in Northern Ireland, as are a range of country-specific surveys, for example, the Health Survey for England, Welsh Health Survey and the Scottish Household Survey. Academic researchers can obtain the raw data from all these (and many other) surveys from the ESRC UK Data Archive (www.data-archive.ac.uk/). Most datasets can be downloaded via the internet once the relevant forms have been completed.

Finally, information about a wide range of longitudinal cohort studies can be found on the Our Changing Lives website (www.ourchanginglives.net/).

International statistics

Until the 1990s, virtually all official statistics produced by international organisations were simple compilations of data collected from the countries' national statistical offices. However, the end of the 20th century witnessed a revolution in the collection and availability of high quality statistical information, particularly from countries in the developing world (see **Box 5g** for an examination of the comparison of such statistics in Europe). Data from four main harmonised surveys are now available:

1. Demographic and Health Surveys (DHS): since the mid-1980s, the DHS programme has assisted countries in conducting national surveys on fertility, family planning and maternal and child health. Since 1997, DHS micro-data from over 200 surveys in over

75 countries has been made available, free of charge via the web (www.measuredhs. com).

2. Living Standards Measurement Study (LSMS): since 1985, over 265 LSMS and other similar national sample surveys have been conducted in 83 countries (Grosh and Muñoz, 1996; Chen and Ravallion, 2000; http://iresearch.worldbank.org/ lsms/lsmssurveyFinder.htm). Currently micro-data from 89 surveys are available to researchers.

3. Multiple indicator cluster surveys (MICS): these household surveys are specifically designed to help countries accurately assess progress for children in relation to the 1990 *World Summit for Children* goals. Currently, micro-data is available from 85 MICS survey (www.childinfo.org/mics.html).

4. World Health Survey (WHS): in 2003 over 90 countries participated in the WHS and micro-data are available to researchers (www.who.int/healthinfo/survey/whsresults/ en/index.html).

Box 5g: International statistical comparisons in Europe
David Gordon

Many researchers want to compare statistical information about different countries. However, statistics are social constructs that were developed for specific historical and cultural purposes. Since countries have had different cultural and economic histories, it is unsurprising that there are many differences between their social statistics. This is not problematic for analysis within countries but it raises substantial problems when trying to compare countries (see also Section 4.11).

Although there are United Nations (UN) and European Union (EU) conventions regarding the collection of social statistics and the calculation of indices, there are no international agreements on sociodemographic data comparable, for example, to the International Classification of Causes of Death developed by the World Health Organization (WHO), according to the rules of which most countries now report their mortality data (Colman, 1999). International compilations of social indicators, therefore, either have to take as read the differences in definition and usage employed by participating countries, and present them with appropriate warnings, as does the Council of Europe and the Organisation for Economic Co-operation and Development (OECD), or instead, attempt to harmonise them by re-computing indices from raw data, as Eurostat (European Statistical Office) does for EU member states. Harmonisation by Eurostat improves comparability but after such processing, some data will no longer be identical to that reported by the national statistics offices in question.

For example, results from the same Labour Force Survey produced by Eurostat, the Luxembourg Employment Study and the national statistical office of an EU member state may often differ, even though the same dataset is being analysed. It is important, therefore, to make clear which source is being used in any report (for example, Labour Force Survey [LFS] unemployment rate according to Eurostat or the national statistical office).

The major problem with many comparative studies that make use of social statistics is that many simple concepts appear to be unambiguous and not open to the possibility of measurement differences (see also Section 4.11). This is an illusion; there is not a single social indicator that is measured in the same way in every country even within the EU. For example, anthropological studies indicate that all societies have a concept of 'age' and the concept of age seems simple and not open to definitional differences. Unfortunately, this is not the case: two definitions of 'age' are in use in different countries of the EU. The first is 'age in completed years' (in other words, a given birthday having been reached). The second is 'age achieved during the calendar year in question', even when the birthday has not been reached. For every one year of birth there are two years of completed age, and vice versa. With classification by completed years, events at a given age apply to people on average half a year older compared with age reached during the year. That makes a difference to statistics on mean age of the workforces, mean age of mother at first birth, and so on.

Harmonised statistics produced by Eurostat

Eurostat produces a range of statistical analyses from member states which are mainly based on the:

- Labour Force Surveys (LFS), required by the Treaty of Rome
- Household Budget Surveys (HBS), needed to produce the UN System of National Accounts, particularly inflation estimates.

More recently, Eurostat has funded the harmonisation of Time Use Survey (TSU) data from member states (www.h2.scb.se/tus/tus/default.htm). Unfortunately, it is very difficult for academic researchers to gain access to the Eurostat harmonised datasets. Consequently, a much more limited set of member states' HBS and LFS data have been extensively analysed by the Luxembourg Income Study (LIS) and Luxembourg Employment Study (LES) (see www.lisproject.org).

In 2000, a list of 17 core 'variables' for use in the EU was first agreed. These core social variables were subsequently revised (Eurostat, 2007) as follows:

Core variables

Demographic information
- Sex
- Age in completed years
- Country of birth
- Country of citizenship at time of data collection
- Legal marital status
- De facto marital status (consensual union)
- Household composition

Geographic information
- Country of residence
- Region of residence
- Degree of urbanisation

Socioeconomic information
- Self-declared labour status
- Status in employment
- Occupation in employment
- Economic sector in employment
- Highest level of education completed
- Net monthly income of the household

In addition to the harmonised variables from existing data collected by countries, official statistical information in Europe is available from six main EU-wide surveys:

- Adult Education Survey (AES): www.epp.eurostat.ec.europa.eu/portal/page/portal/microdata/adult_education_survey

- European Health Interview Survey (EHIS): www.ec.europa.eu/health/data_collection/tools/mechanisms/index_en.htm#fragment0
- European Union Survey of Income and Living Conditions (EU-SILC): www.epp.eurostat.ec.europa.eu/portal/page/portal/microdata/eu_silc
- European Working Conditions Surveys (EWCS): www.eurofound.europa.eu/ewco/surveys/index.htm
- European Quality of Life Survey (EQLS): www.eurofound.europa.eu/areas/qualityoflife/eqls/index.htm
- Eurobarometer: www.europa.eu.int/comm/public_opinion/

The EU-SILC replaced the longitudinal European Community Household Panel (ECHP) survey in 2003.

Meta-data and high quality information sources

One of the major problems with trying to compare employment statistics in different EU member states is where to find the necessary meta-data on definitions, concepts and survey methods; for example, does the LFS in Portugal and Finland use the same concept of a household?

Fortunately, the University of Mannheim has for many years provided help with these issues via their excellent website for the Eurodata Research Archive (www.mzes.uni-mannheim.de/eurodata/index.html).

Conclusion

Comparative studies and social policies have often failed to achieve their aims due to inadequate knowledge of the contexts in which state intervention and statistical measurement have taken place, and due to inadequate comparative data to aid policy development. Out of necessity, policy decisions at European level have often been based on simplistic assumptions concerning the disappearance of national differences and the belief that European integration will emerge quite naturally from the harmonisation of social policies (Affichard et al, 1998). Social policy and social work researchers in the 21st century need a greater awareness of these theoretical and statistical problems, if the promise of effective international social policy and social work development is to be realised.

References

Affichard, J. with Hantrais, L., Letablier, M.-T. and Schultheis, F. (1998) *Social situation in member states of the European Union: The relevance of quantitative indicators in social policy analysis*, Dublin: European Foundation for the Improvement of Living and Working Conditions.

Colman, D. (1999) 'Demographic data for Europe: a review of sources', *Population Trends*, vol 98, pp 42-52.

Eurostat (2007) *Task Force on core social variables: Final report*, Luxembourg: European Commission.

Additionally, individual-level census data are available to download from the Integrated Public Use Microdata Series (IPUMS), and harmonised micro-data are available from

159 national censuses in 55 countries, which include 326 million personal records (www.international.ipums.org/international/). It is now possible to download over the internet and analyse comparable social survey and census micro-data from almost every country in the world. Few global analyses have yet been produced but high quality statistical data are now readily available to social policy and other researchers for the first time in history (Gordon et al, 2003).

Question for discussion

• Are official statistics 'objective' facts about the world?

References

Chen, S. and Ravallion, M. (2000) *How did the world's poorest fare in the 1990s?*, World Bank Occasional Paper, New York: The World Bank.

Gaither, C.C. and Cavazos-Gaither, A.E. (1996) *Statistically speaking: A dictionary of quotations*, Bristol: Institute of Physics Publishing.

Gordon, D., Nandy, S., Pantazis, C., Pemberton, S. and Townsend, P. (2003) *Child poverty in the developing world*, Bristol: The Policy Press.

Grosh, M.E. and Muñoz, J. (1996) *A manual for planning and implementing the Living Standards Measurement Study Survey*, Living Standards Measurement Study Working Paper no 126, Washington, DC: The World Bank.

Jones, P. and Elias, P. (2006) *Administrative data as a research resource: A selected audit*, London: National Data Strategy.

Levitas, R. (1996) 'Fiddling while Britain burns? The "measurement" of unemployment', in R. Levitas and W. Guy (eds) *Interpreting official statistics*, London: Routledge, pp 45-65.

Nissel, M. (2001) '200 years of the Census of Population', *Social Trends*, no 31, London: The Stationery Office.

Rees, P., Martin, D. and Williamson, P. (2002) *The census data system*, London: John Wiley & Sons.

Royal Statistical Society (1995) 'The measurement of unemployment in the UK', *Journal of the Royal Statistical Society A*, vol 158, pp 363-417.

Taylor, D. (1990) *Creative counting*, London: Unemployment Unit.

Further reading

Dorling, D. and Simpson, L. (1998) *Statistics in society*, London: Arnold.

Kerrison, S. and Macfarlane, A. (eds) (2000) *Official health statistics: An unofficial guide*, London: Arnold.

Levitas, R. and Guy, W. (eds) (1996) *Interpreting official statistics*, London: Routledge.

Website resources

Demographic and Health Surveys: www.measuredhs.com
Economic and Social Data Service (ESDS) www.esds.ac.uk/
Economic and Social Research Council (ESRC) Data Archive: www.data-archive.ac.uk/
Integrated Public Use Microdata Series (IPUMS): www.international.ipums.org/international/
Multiple indicator cluster surveys: www.childinfo.org/mics.html
Office for National Statistics (ONS): www.ons.gov.uk/ons/index.html

PART THREE: THE ANALYSIS OF QUANTITATIVE DATA

5.11 Analysing data
Duncan Cramer

Qualitative and quantitative variables

When analysing numerical data statistically, it is necessary to make a distinction between two kinds of variable that the data may represent because the appropriate procedures for analysing these two kinds of variable differ. A variable is a quality that consists of two or more categories. For example, the variable of biological sex generally consists of the two categories of female and male. The variable of marital status may comprise the five categories of the never married, the married, the separated, the divorced and the widowed. The categories that make up these variables are qualitatively distinct. Females differ from males in various ways. The never married may differ from the married in numerous ways. Variables consisting of qualitatively distinct categories are variously known as qualitative, categorical or nominal variables. Numbers may be used to name or to represent these qualitative categories. For example, females may be coded as 1 and males as 2. The never married may be coded as 1, the married as 2, the separated as 3, and so on. Numbers are simply used to indicate a particular category but do not reflect any other characteristic of that quality. Other qualitative variables include whether someone is employed, holds a particular religious belief, belongs to a particular ethnic group, has a particular occupation, and so on.

Qualitative variables need to be distinguished from quantitative variables in which the categories are quantitative and represent increasing size. For example, the quantitative variable of age may consist of categories that refer to whole years. Someone who is 40 is older than someone who is less than 40. In other words, the categories can be ordered in terms of their size. Attitudes towards issues, such as mothers working outside their home, are considered to be quantitative variables in that higher scores on the attitude scale may represent a more positive attitude to that issue. Similarly, the rank ordering of possibilities, such as from whom one is likely to seek help, is a quantitative variable in which smaller numbers such as 1 and 2 generally indicate a higher ranking.

Having made this distinction between qualitative and quantitative variables, and at the risk of inviting some confusion, it is important to point out that some variables may be treated as either a qualitative or a quantitative variable. For example, the variable of biological sex may be viewed as a quantitative variable in that females may be seen as having more 'femaleness' than males. To the extent that the categories of a variable can be ordered in this way, these variables can be treated as if they were quantitative. The variable of social class is one that can be dealt with as either a qualitative variable in which the classes are seen as being qualitatively distinct or a quantitative variable in which higher social classes are viewed as representing greater social status.

Descriptive statistics

Tables and charts

In order to make sense of the data collected in a study it is usually necessary to summarise the results for the main variables. Such summaries are often referred to as descriptive statistics, in that they simply describe the main features of the results and no attempt is made to draw any inferences from them as is the case with inferential statistics. The only way of summarising qualitative variables is to count the number of cases that fall into a particular category and to present these frequencies as they are or as a percentage of the total number of cases. These figures may be displayed in the form of a table such as that shown in **Table 5.2**. This table presents the number and percentage of cases in five categories of employment status for a sample of 140 people. The percentages have been rounded to a whole figure following the usual rounding convention. The number is rounded up by one if the first decimal place is 0.5 or more (for example, 40/140 x 100 = 28.57 = 29) and is left as it is if the first decimal place is less than 0.5 (for example, 10/140 x 100 = 7.14 = 7). This procedure results in this instance in the total percentage being slightly greater than 100.

Table 5.2: Frequency of employment status

Employment status	Number (n)	Percentage (%)
Full-time paid work	50	36
Part-time paid work	40	29
Unemployed, looking for work	15	11
Looking after the home	25	18
Other	10	7
Total	140	101

These frequencies may be broken down with respect to further qualitative variables such as biological sex. A table showing the frequency of cases broken down in terms of two or more qualitative variables is known as a contingency table in that the frequency of cases in the category of one variable (for example, employment status) is dependent or contingent on the category of the other variable (for example, sex). It is also known as a cross-tabulation, in that one variable (for example, employment status) is tabulated across the other variable (for example, sex). A contingency table of employment status in women and men is presented in **Table 5.3**. Where the number of cases in the categories of the second variable is not the same, as in this example, the relative sizes of the categories are easier to grasp if percentages rather than the number of cases is used. For example, although the number of women and men who are unemployed is the same at 10, because the sample of women is almost twice as big as that of men, the percentage of unemployed women (11) is almost twice as small as that of unemployed men (20).

Table 5.3: Frequency of employment status in women and men

Employment status	Women		Men	
	n	%	n	%
Full-time paid work	20	22	30	60
Part-time paid work	30	33	5	10
Unemployed, looking for work	10	11	10	20
Looking after the home	25	28	0	0
Other	5	6	5	10
Total	90	100	50	100

The figures in tables may be turned into diagrams in order to provide further information about the relative size of the groups, thereby making it easier for some people to understand what is being conveyed. For example, the contingency table in **Table 5.3** can be converted into the clustered bar chart in **Figure 5c** where the height of the bar corresponds to the percentage and where the bars for women and men are clustered together to make their comparison easier.

Figure 5c: The employment status of women and men

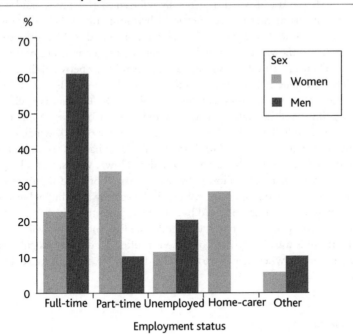

Measures of central tendency

Quantitative variables, such as the number of children a woman has, may also be presented in terms of a frequency table. **Table 5.4** shows the number of children that a sample of 10 women have. For instance two women have no children, three women have one child and so on. Quantitative variables are not usually presented as frequency tables for two main reasons. First, these tables would take up considerable space, particularly the more categories and variables there are. And second, there are useful descriptive statistics that can summarise in a few numbers the main characteristics of the distribution of the values in these categories.

Table 5.4: Number of children per woman

Number of children	Number of women
0	2
1	3
2	2
3	1
4	1
5	0
6	1

In describing a distribution of values such as those in **Table 5.4**, it is useful to know what value characterises the centre or central tendency of the distribution of values. There are three main measures of central tendency. These are the mode, the median and the arithmetic mean (*M*), the last of which is generally referred to as the mean and which differs from other means such as the geometric or harmonic mean. The mode is the most common value that in this case is 1. 'Women with one child' is the most frequent category. The median is the value that divides the values arranged in order of size into two equal halves. There are 10 values. So the median lies midway between the 5th and the 6th value. The 5th value is 1 and the 6th value is 2 so the median is 1.50. Fifty per cent of the women have two or more children and 50% have less than two children. The mean is the sum of all the values divided by the number of cases (*N*). The total number of children is 20 (0 + 0 + 1 + 1 + 1 + 2 + 2 + 3 + 4 + 6 = 20) which divided by 10 gives a mean of 2.00 (20/10 = 2.00). Women on average have 2.00 children each.

When the distribution of values is bunched towards the lower values, as it is here, the mode will be the lowest value (1) followed by the median (1.50) and then the mean (2.00). Conversely, when the distribution of values is skewed towards the higher values, the lowest value will be the mean, followed by the median and then the mode . When the distribution of scores is symmetrical, the mode, median and mean will have the same value. The mean is usually reported because it is often used in the calculation of other statistics particularly when values are normally distributed. A normal distribution is bell-shaped.

Measures of dispersion

Statistical measures of central tendency do not provide any information about the spread or dispersion of the values in the distribution. It is useful to know how much the values vary. The simplest measure is the range of values that is the difference between the highest and the lowest value. The range in the number of children per woman in this sample is 6 (6 − 0 = 6). A more complicated and widely used measure of dispersion is the standard deviation (*SD*). There are three main reasons for its popularity. First, unlike the range, which is based on only the extreme values of the distribution, every value in the distribution contributes to the calculation of the standard deviation. Second, when the distribution of values is normally distributed, the standard deviation together with the mean provides information about the percentage of values that fall between various values of the distribution. For example, about 34% of the values will fall between the mean and one standard deviation either above or below the mean. And third, the standard deviation is used in calculating many other useful statistics.

The standard deviation is the square root of the variance. The variance is the mean of the sum of the squared deviations or differences between each value and the mean of the values. In other words, the variance is the mean squared deviation. Unsquaring the variance (or mean squared deviation) by taking its square root gives the standard deviation that is similar to but not exactly the same as the mean deviation. There are two kinds of standard deviation and variance. One is sometimes known as the sample standard deviation or variance because this describes the standard deviation and variance for the sample. In this measure the sum of squared deviations is divided by the number of cases that is 10 in our example.

The other measure is often referred to as the estimated population standard deviation and variance. In this measure the sum of squared deviations is divided by the degrees of freedom (*df*) that for this statistic is the number of cases minus 1 ($N-1$). This slight adjustment provides an unbiased estimate of the population standard deviation and variance. It has the effect of making the standard deviation and variance larger. This effect will be greater for small samples. The estimated population standard deviation and variance is used in calculating other kinds of statistics and so is more widely used than the sample standard deviation and variance. The calculation of the standard deviation and variance is shown in *Table 5.5*.

Table 5.5: Calculations for the variance and standard deviation

Values		Mean – values	Squared deviations
0		2–0 = 2	$2^2 = 4$
0		2–0 = 2	$2^2 = 4$
1		2–1 = 1	$1^2 = 1$
1		2–1 = 1	$1^2 = 1$
1		2–1 = 1	$1^2 = 1$
2		2–2 = 0	$0^2 = 0$
2		2–2 = 0	$0^2 = 0$
3		2–3 = –1	$-1^2 = 1$
4		2–4 –2	$-2^2 = 4$
6		2–6 = –4	$-4^2 = 16$
Sum	20		32
N	10		
Mean	2		
Variance		Sample	32/10 = 3.20
		Estimate	32/(10–1) = 3.56
Standard		Sample	$\sqrt{3.20} = 1.79$
deviation		Estimate	$\sqrt{3.56} = 1.89$

Correlation

The straight-line or linear relationship between two quantitative variables may be expressed as a Pearson correlation coefficient (*r*). For example, we could use Pearson's correlation to see whether families with bigger household incomes generally have fewer children. A Pearson's correlation has two characteristics. The first characteristic is the sign of the correlation, which can be positive or negative. A positive correlation means that high values on one variable (for example, household income) go with high values on the other variable (for example, number of children). A negative correlation means that high scores on one variable (for example, household income) go with low values on the other variable (for example, number of children). If we thought that families with bigger incomes had fewer children we would expect a negative correlation. Negative values and correlations have a negative sign whereas positive values and correlations usually have no sign.

The second characteristic of a correlation is its size or value that can vary from 0 to +1. A correlation of 0 or close to 0 means that there is no linear relationship between the two variables but there may be a non-linear relationship between them. A correlation of +1 means that there is a perfect relationship between the two variables. The bigger the correlation, the stronger the linear relationship is between the two variables. The size of a correlation may be described verbally as follows: 0.19 or less is very low (small or weak); 0.20 to 0.39 is low; 0.40 to 0.69 is moderate; 0.70 to 0.89 is high (big or strong); and 0.90 or more is very high. These ranges are approximate and not definitive. The proportion of the variance that is shared between two variables is given by squaring the correlation. So, a correlation of 0.50 means that 0.25 ($0.50^2 = 0.25$) or 25% (0.25 x 100 = 25) of the variance is common to the two variables. The squared correlation is known as the coefficient of determination.

The estimated population standard deviation (*SD*) or variance of the two variables can be used to calculate Pearson's correlation as shown in the following two formulae.

$$r = \frac{\text{covariance estimate of variables A and B}}{\sqrt{\text{variance estimate of A}} \times \sqrt{\text{variance estimate of B}}}$$

$$= \frac{\text{covariance estimate of variables A and B}}{SD \text{ estimate of A} \times SD \text{ estimate of B}}$$

This is one example of the usefulness of these two measures of dispersion.

Tests of statistical significance

When collecting data we usually want to know the extent to which we can generalise the findings from our sample to the population in which we are interested. For example, we may wish to know to what extent the correlation we have found in our sample is likely to be true of the population from which we have drawn our sample. To do this, we need to ideally select a sample at random from the population of values although it is not always possible to do this. We then need to test the statistical significance of our finding that is based on the probability of it occurring by chance. Findings that have a probability of occurring 1 or fewer times out of 20 are considered not to have happened by chance and are called 'statistically significant'. Findings that have a probability of occurring more than 1 time out of 20 are judged to have happened by chance and are referred to as being 'statistically non-significant'.

This probability level is usually expressed as the proportion 0.05 (1/20 = 0.05) but may also be referred to as the percentage 5 (0.05 x 100 = 5). Findings are more likely to be statistically significant the bigger the sample. For instance, a weak correlation of 0.10, which is very small, is statistically significant at the 0.05 level with a sample of 385 or more when there are no sound reasons for predicting the direction of the correlation. Much of statistical analysis in the social sciences is concerned with establishing the size and statistical significance of findings.

Computer analysis

Carrying out data analysis through handwritten calculations can be very time-consuming and prone to error, both of which increase the greater the dataset. For those who intend, or have, to conduct several statistical analyses of data, it is generally advisable to learn how to use one of a number of computer packages of programs that have been developed for these purposes. One of the most widely available and used packages is called, since 2008, PASW Statistics. PASW is the abbreviation for Predictive Analytic Software. Prior to 2008 it was called SPSS. This package was first produced in 1965 and is regularly revised. The latest version at the time of writing is PASW Statistics 19.

Question for discussion

- What is the difference between a qualitative and a quantitative variable?

Further reading

Bryman, A. and Cramer, D. (2011) *Quantitative data analysis with IBM SPSS 17, 18 and 19: A guide for social scientists*, Hove: Psychology Press.
Howitt, D. and Cramer, D. (2010) *An introduction to statistics in psychology* (5th edn), Harlow: Pearson.
Howitt, D. and Cramer, D. (2011) *An introduction to PASW Statistics (SPSS) in psychology: For version 19 and earlier* (5th edn), Harlow: Pearson.

Qualitative research

Detailed contents

6.1 Introduction

In this chapter we address the main aspects of conducting qualitative research. The chapter is divided into three parts.

Part One: Fundamentals of qualitative research: this section begins by addressing the nature of qualitative research and the quest among some practitioners for alternative criteria of quality from those employed by quantitative researchers (described in Section 5.2). It then moves on to discuss two aspects of quantitative research that are fundamental aspects of social policy and social work research associated with this strategy: the different kinds of research design employed by quantitative researchers (including cross-sectional, longitudinal and case study designs) and the approaches to sampling that they use.

Part Two: Qualitative research methods and sources of qualitative data: this section explores the main methods for the collection of qualitative data and covers:

- semi–structured and unstructured interviewing;
- telephone interviewing;
- ethnography;
- focus groups;
- biographical method;
- documents; and
- the use of the internet for collecting qualitative data.

Part Three: The analysis of qualitative data: this final section deals with the basic elements of conducting an analysis of qualitative data. Several important approaches are covered:

- grounded theory and analytic induction (this section also addresses the way in which qualitative researchers typically code their data);
- computer–assisted analysis;
- discourse analysis;
- conversation analysis; and
- narrative analysis.

Finally, we consider some of the issues involved in the selection of 'verbatim quotes' for use in the reporting of qualitative findings.

PART ONE: FUNDAMENTALS OF QUALITATIVE RESEARCH

6.2 Qualitative research
Alan Bryman and Saul Becker

We have already encountered qualitative research in Chapter Four as an approach to social policy and social work research that employs principles that are not only different from those operating in the natural sciences but that also in many respects entail a rejection of those principles. The main concerns and preoccupations of qualitative researchers can be viewed as stemming from this commitment to alternative criteria. The four main concerns and preoccupations were described as being: a focus on actors' meanings and description, along with an emphasis on context, process and flexibility. Therefore, although the term *qualitative* research seems to imply that the absence of quantification is the chief distinguishing characteristic of this research strategy, it is clear that there is more to it than the mere lack of numbers.

As Bryman (2012) points out, in addition to its epistemological roots in a view of the research process that seeks out an alternative to a natural scientific approach, qualitative research tends to have two important features that further distinguish it from quantitative research. First, the approach taken by qualitative researchers typically involves an *inductive* approach to the relationship between theory and research. This term was encountered in Robert Pinker's discussion of the role of theory in social policy research in Section 3.4. An inductive approach entails generating concepts and theory out of data rather than the quantitative research approach in which concepts and theoretical ideas guide the collection of data.

Second, qualitative research adopts a *constructionist* position with respect to the nature of social reality. This means that social phenomena and social reality generally are taken as created out of the actions and interpretations of people during their social interactions. To take the example of a social network suggested first in Section 5.2, a constructionist position would pay greater attention to the role that individuals play in constructing a network and having an influence over it. In treating social reality in a constructionist mode, qualitative researchers are inclined to treat it not as something that exists beyond the reach and influence of people, but as something that they are in a continuous process of forming and revising.

Quality criteria in qualitative research

One of the ways in which the tendency of qualitative researchers to associate themselves with principles that are different from those of the natural scientist (and indeed the quantitative researcher) is in their discussions of the criteria that are employed for assessing the quality of research. Whereas quantitative researchers have developed a well understood and clear set of criteria that influence the way research is done and written about (see Section 5.2), in qualitative research no such generally agreed criteria exist.

Two basic stances exist with regard to the suitability and relevance of the four criteria outlined in Section 5.2, which we call *adaptation* and *replacement* stances. An **adaptation stance** essentially argues that the conventional criteria (validity, reliability, generalisability and replication) are relevant but need to be adapted to the nature and orientation of qualitative research. One reason for this preference is that to suggest that criteria such as validity and reliability are not relevant could be taken to imply that qualitative research is *in*valid and *un*reliable, or at least that qualitative researchers are not concerned about the possibility that they might be invalid and unreliable. This may not be a sound public relations strategy so some writers on qualitative research criteria have preferred to adapt the quantitative research criteria.

Adaptation position

An example of an adaptation position has been provided by LeCompte and Goetz (1982), who propose the following criteria:

- *External reliability:* can the study be replicated? This is difficult to achieve because it is difficult to freeze a situation so that different researchers can approach the same situation in the same way. High profile re-studies of small-scale societies by ethnographers often give rise to very contrasting findings (Bryman, 1994). In particular, there is the problem of alternative reasons for differences, such as the gender, age and social position of the qualitative researcher (for example, whether accompanied by a spouse), whether exactly the same kind of context is being studied and the significance of different time periods for the findings. However, as with the quantitative research criterion of replication, it is possibly the *ability* to replicate, so that procedures are fully set out, that is crucial, rather than whether a replication takes place and what its findings are.
- *Internal reliability:* do different researchers in a team agree over their observations and what they are told? This is an interesting criterion but holds little relevance to lone researchers, although some might wish to seek confirmation from others of their interpretations.
- *Internal validity:* is there a good match between researchers' observations and their theoretical ideas? This is a great strength of qualitative research because concepts and theories emerge inductively out of the data, so that there is likely to be a good correspondence between the data and concepts unless the researcher draws unwarranted inferences from the data. However, it is difficult to come up with clear-cut standards to assess this feature.
- *External validity:* can findings be generalised to other settings/populations? This criterion is often regarded as a problem for qualitative research because it does not usually draw on probability and random sampling procedures for selecting research participants and often employs a case study research design that does not readily permit generalisation to a wider population. On the other hand, for qualitative researchers, the goal is not to generalise to populations but to provide a theoretical understanding that can be taken up by other researchers. Williams (2002, p 131) takes a somewhat different position when he argues that in qualitative research, generalisations frequently take the form of *moderatum* generalisations whereby aspects of a situation 'can be seen to be instances of a broader recognizable set of features'. In fact, Williams suggests, it

is not that he is recommending that qualitative researchers should seek to forge such generalisations, but that they frequently do so anyway, but do not recognise that this is what they are doing.

Replacement position

As an example of a replacement position, there is the work of Lincoln and Guba (1985), who propose four criteria that are analogous to, but different from, quantitative research criteria. The criteria are concerned with whether findings are *trustworthy*. To a large extent, their work reflects a concern about whether it is ever possible to arrive at a single, definitive account of social reality. This is often referred to as an *anti-realist* position that has strong affinities with the post-modernist standpoint described in Section 4.2. In many respects, their criteria are to do with making research *appear* trustworthy rather than with whether following their suggestions will actually make it trustworthy. By contrast, criteria such as reliability and validity assume a realist position, which assumes that there is an external reality that can be described and represented by the social policy researcher.

Figure 6a: **Lincoln and Guba's alternative criteria and their equivalent conventional criteria terms**

Alternative criteria	Quantitative research criteria
Credibility	Internal validity
Transferability	External validity
Dependability	Reliability
Confirmability	Objectivity

Figure 6a presents Lincoln and Guba's alternative criteria (1985) and what they take to be the equivalent terms associated with the conventional criteria employed in quantitative research. While their ideas are controversial, and by no means have the hold that conventional criteria have among quantitative researchers, their ideas are interesting. *Credibility* is concerned with the question of whether a set of findings is believable. Lincoln and Guba stipulate a variety of activities and practices that can enhance the believability of findings. These include: triangulation (see Section 4.4); negative case analysis, whereby the researcher seeks out cases that go against the grain of an emerging finding, so that the findings may be revised in the light of the new information (a strategy associated with analytic induction; see Section 6.16); and what they call 'member checks'. Member checks, often also called *respondent validation* and *member validation*, is an increasingly commonly used procedure whereby the researcher provides research participants with some of his or her research materials and asks them to comment on them. Different kinds of materials might be, and have been, used by researchers, such as: transcripts or summaries of interviews; short reports of findings; and drafts of articles or chapters. The idea is to make the research findings more credible by being able to state that aspects of them have been verified by the very people on whom the research was conducted. For researchers of a less anti-realist persuasion than Lincoln and Guba, member checks are often a useful way of increasing the accuracy of their findings.

Transferability is concerned with the issue of whether a set of findings is relevant to settings other than the one or ones in which it was conducted. In order to enhance transferability, Lincoln and Guba recommend detailed accounts of research settings (often referred to as *thick descriptions*). Such accounts allow other researchers to establish whether findings hold up in other contexts. For Lincoln and Guba, whether a set of findings is transferable to other contexts is entirely an empirical question and not something that is intrinsic to an investigation. What the qualitative researcher can do is to provide someone wishing to consider the generalisability of findings with the material that are required for determining whether findings apply to another context. There are affinities here with Yin's (2009) notion of a *replication logic*, discussed in Section 5.3, and Williams' (2002) idea of *moderatum* generalisations (see the discussion above).

Dependability is concerned with the question of how far we can rely on a set of findings. To this end, Lincoln and Guba advocate an auditing approach using an 'audit trail'. This means that records must be kept of all stages of the research process, including minutes of meetings and details of decision making during each phase of a project, so that questions such as the following can be addressed: 'Have correct procedures been followed?' 'Have records been kept of how people were sampled?' 'Were they properly briefed in terms of ethics?' 'Do the data warrant the conclusions generated?' This is potentially very demanding for the auditors who are likely to be peers. Such a procedure would involve going through transcripts of interviews, field notes, minutes of meetings, draft reports, and so on in order to establish dependability. It is not surprising, therefore, that there are very few examples of an audit trail approach being used in practice (Bryman, 2012).

Confirmability is concerned with issues such as whether the researcher allowed personal values to intrude excessively or in an unwarranted way. To assess confirmability, Lincoln and Guba advocate an audit trail approach for this criterion as well. A puzzling feature of this criterion is its use of objectivity as a parallel criterion in quantitative research. In fact, it is not entirely clear that quantitative researchers nowadays typically accept this as a criterion. Most recognise that values and biases intrude into the research process, but take the view that the crucial issue is to keep these to a minimum, although some writers, working from the vantage point of specific commitments, argue that the social researcher should *not* attempt to be value-free (Temple, 1997). As Seale (1999, p 45) suggests, in juxtaposing confirmability against objectivity, Lincoln and Guba have set up a somewhat overdrawn contrast.

In adopting a position that largely depicts qualitative researchers as engaged in a game of persuading readers and others that their version of an aspect of social reality is more credible and authoritative than other possible accounts, Lincoln and Guba are at variance with quantitative research *and* with much qualitative research. By no means would all qualitative researchers subscribe to Lincoln and Guba's implicit view that there can be many different versions of reality, and that the key feature for a researcher is that of persuading others of his or her version. Indeed, there has been some evidence of a return to traditional ways of thinking about issues such as validity and reliability in qualitative research (see, for example, Armstrong et al, 1997) while some writers have preferred, like LeCompte and Goetz (1982), not to reject the terms validity and reliability and to cast them in a manner more acceptable to qualitative researchers (for example, Mason, 2002).

Further, there has been an increase in the number of schemes outlining criteria for assessing the quality of qualitative research (for example, Tracy, 2010). One of the most comprehensive sets of criteria is that of Spencer et al (2003), which has 18 quality dimensions of quality in qualitative research with specific criteria for each dimension. Their scheme builds on several existing schemes and on interviews and focus groups with social researchers. In addition, Stige et al (2009) have proposed that the notion of quality criteria should be reconceptualised as an agenda for dialogue. Nonetheless, Lincoln and Guba's suggestions are interesting and some of their ideas about features such as an auditing approach are intriguing if difficult to implement.

Question for discussion

• Why do quality criteria in qualitative research appear to be so controversial?

References

Armstrong, D., Gosling, A., Weinman, J. and Marteau, T. (1997) 'The place of inter-rater reliability in qualitative research: an empirical study', *Sociology*, vol 31, pp 597-606.

Bryman, A. (1994) 'The Mead/Freeman controversy: some implications for qualitative researchers', in R.G. Burgess (ed) *Studies in qualitative methodology*, vol 4, Greenwich, CN: JAI Press, pp 1-27.

Bryman, A. (2012) *Social research methods* (4th edn), Oxford: Oxford University Press.

LeCompte, M.P. and Goetz, J.P. (1982) 'Problems of reliability and validity in qualitative research', *Review of Educational Research*, vol 52, pp 31-60.

Lincoln, Y. and Guba, E. (1985) *Naturalistic inquiry*, Beverley Hills, CA: Sage Publications.

Mason, J. (2002) *Qualitative researching* (2nd edn), London: Sage Publications.

Seale, C. (1999) *The quality of qualitative research*, London: Sage Publications.

Spencer, L., Ritchie, J., Lewis, J. and Dillon, L. (2003) *Quality in qualitative evaluation: A framework for assessing research evidence*, London: Government Chief Social Researcher's Office (www.civilservice.gov.uk/wp-content/uploads/2011/09/a_quality_framework_tcm6-7314.pdf).

Stige, B., Malterud, K. and Midtgarden, T. (2009) 'Toward an agenda for evaluation of qualitative research', *Qualitative Health Research*, vol 19, pp 1504-16.

Temple, B. (1997) '"Collegial authority" and bias: the solution or the problem?', *Sociological Research Online*, vol 2 (www.socresonline.org.uk/2/4/8.html).

Tracy, S.J. (2010) 'Qualitative quality: eight "big tent" criteria for excellent qualitative research', *Qualitative Inquiry*, vol 16, pp 837-51.

Williams, M. (2002) 'Generalisation in interpretive research', in T. May (ed) *Qualitative research in action*, London: Sage Publications, pp 125-43.

Yin, R.K. (2009) *Case study research: Design and methods* (4th edn), Los Angeles, CA: Sage Publications.

Further reading

Lincoln, Y. and Guba, E. (1985) *Naturalistic inquiry*, Beverley Hills, CA: Sage Publications.

Seale, C. (1999) *The quality of qualitative research*, London: Sage Publications.

6.3 Research design: an overview

In Section 5.3, a research design was referred to as a structure or framework within which data are collected. This notion, which was framed within the context of quantitative research, is equally applicable to qualitative research. As with quantitative research, a research design is a *mechanism for linking research questions and evidence*. Understanding the principles of research design is therefore as important for qualitative researchers as it is for quantitative researchers. Moreover, the basic forms of research design introduced in Section 5.3 are equally applicable to a qualitative research strategy, although the experimental design is rarely, if ever, found in such a context. The next two sections discuss the three research designs that were introduced – the *case study*, which is frequently extended into a multiple case study approach (Eisenhardt, 1989), *cross-sectional design* and *longitudinal design*. While the implementation of these designs in qualitative research differs somewhat from their use in quantitative research, the methodological issues involved are fundamentally the same.

Reference

Eisenhardt, K.M. (1989) 'Building theories from case study research', *Academy of Management Review*, vol 14, no 4, pp 532-50.

6.4 Case study
Martyn Hammersley

The term *case study* is not used in a standard way in the methodological literature, and at face value it can be misleading, since there is a sense in which all social science research involves cases. Nevertheless, we can identify a core meaning of the term as referring to research that investigates a small number of cases, possibly even just one, in considerable depth (Hammersley, 1992, Chapter 11).

Case study is often contrasted with two other influential kinds of research design: the *social survey* and the *experiment*. The contrast with the survey relates to dimensions already mentioned: the number of cases investigated, and the amount of detailed information the researcher collects about each case studied. Other things being equal, the less cases investigated the more information can be collected about each of them. *Social surveys* study a large number of cases but usually gather only a relatively small amount of data about each one, focusing on a small range of features relating to what are taken to be key variables (cases here are usually, although not always, individual respondents). By contrast, in case study, large amounts of information are collected about one or a few cases, across a wide range of features. Here the case may be an individual (as in life history work), an event, an institution, or even a whole national society or geographical region. Case study can also be contrasted with *experimental research*. While the latter also often involves investigation of a small number of cases compared to survey research, what distinguishes it from case study is the fact that it involves direct control of variables. In experiments, the researcher creates the case(s) studied, whereas case study researchers identify cases out of naturally occurring social phenomena.

The term 'case study' is also often taken to carry implications for the *kind* of data that are collected, and perhaps also for *how these are analysed*. Frequently, but not always, it implies the collection of unstructured data, and qualitative analysis of those data. Moreover, this relates to a more fundamental issue about the purpose of the research. It is sometimes argued that the aim of case study research should be to capture cases in their uniqueness, rather than to use them as a basis for wider empirical or theoretical conclusions. This is partly a matter of emphasis: it does not necessarily rule out an interest in coming to general conclusions, but it does imply that these are to be reached by means of inferences from what is found in particular cases, rather than through the cases being selected in order to test a hypothesis. In line with this, it is frequently argued that case study adopts an inductive or an abductive orientation. However, by no means all advocates of case study take these positions.

Another question that arises in relation to case study concerns objectivity, in at least one sense of that term. Is the aim to produce an account of each case from an external or research point of view, one that may contradict the views of the people involved? Or is it solely to portray the character of each case 'in its own terms'? This contrast is most obvious where the cases are people, so that the aim may be to 'give voice' to them rather than to use them as respondents or even as informants. However, this distinction is not clear-cut. Where multiple participants are involved in a case, they may have different views. And even the same person may present different views on different occasions. Furthermore, there are complexities involved in determining whether what is presented can ever 'capture' participant views rather than presenting an 'external' gloss on them. But there is also a question about what sort of description of cases, and of the perspectives of those involved in them, is required for research purposes.

Some commentators point out that a case is always a 'case of something', so that an interest in some general category on the part of the researcher is built in from the beginning, even though definition of that category may change over the course of the research. In line with this, there are approaches to case study inquiry that draw on the comparative method in order to develop and refine theoretical categories. Examples include analytic induction (Cressey, 1953), grounded theorising (Glaser and Strauss, 1967), historical approaches employing John Stuart Mill's methods of agreement and difference (see Skocpol, 1979) and case-based or configurational approaches (Byrne and Ragin, 2009; Rihoux and Ragin, 2009), including qualitative comparative analysis (Ragin, 1987, 2008).

Another area of disagreement concerns whether case study is a method – one with advantages and disadvantages that is to be used as and when appropriate, depending on the problem under investigation – or a paradigmatic approach that one simply chooses or rejects on philosophical or political grounds. Even when viewed simply as a method, there can be variation in the specific form that case studies take, in:

- the number of cases investigated;
- whether there is comparison, and, if there is, as regards the character it has and the role it plays;
- how detailed the case studies are;
- the size of the case(s) dealt with;
- what researchers treat as the context of the case, how they identify it and how much of it they seek to document;
- the extent to which case study researchers restrict themselves to description, explanation and/or theory, or engage in evaluation and/or prescription.

Variation in these respects depends, to some extent, on the purpose that the case study is intended to serve. Where it is designed to test or illustrate a theoretical point, then it will deal with the case as an instance of a type, this being described in terms of a particular theoretical framework (implicit or explicit). Where case study is concerned with developing theoretical ideas, it is likely to be more detailed and open-ended in character. The same is true where the concern is with describing and/or explaining what is going on in a particular situation for its own sake. Where the interest is in some problem in the situation investigated, then the discussion will be geared to diagnosing the problem, identifying its sources and perhaps outlining what can be done about it.

Many commentators, however, regard case study as more than just a method – they see it as involving quite different assumptions about how the social world can and should be studied from those underlying other approaches (see, for example, Hamilton, 1980; Simons, 1996, 2009). Sometimes, this is formulated in terms of a contrast between positivism, on the one hand, and naturalism, interpretivism or constructionism, on the other. In some forms, case study is viewed as more akin to the kind of portrayal of the social world that is characteristic of novelists, short story writers and even poets. Those who see case study in this way may regard any comparison of it with other methods in terms of advantages and disadvantages as fundamentally misconceived. Others view the idea that case study is an arts-based paradigm as a symptom of a misguided anti-scientism, and as signalling abandonment of a proper commitment to social science.

Question for discussion

• What are the arguments for and against case study as a methodological approach? Is it just one method among others?

References

Byrne, D. and Ragin, C. (eds) (2009) *The SAGE handbook of case-based methods*, London: Sage Publications.

Cressey, D. (1953) *Other people's money*, Glencoe, IL: Free Press.

Glaser, B.G. and Strauss, A. (1967) *The discovery of grounded theory*, Chicago, IL: Aldine.

Hamilton, D. (1980) 'Some contrasting assumptions about case study research and survey analysis', in H. Simons (ed) *Towards a science of the singular: Essays about case study in educational research and evaluation*, Norwich: Centre for Applied Research in Education, University of East Anglia, pp 78-92.

Hammersley, M. (1992) *What's wrong with ethnography?*, London: Routledge.

Ragin, C. (1987) *The comparative method*, Berkeley, CA: University of California Press.

Ragin, C. (2008) *Redesigning social inquiry: Fuzzy sets and beyond*, Chicago, IL: University of Chicago Press.

Rihoux, B. and Ragin, C. (eds) (2009) *Configurational comparative methods: Qualitative comparative analysis (QCA) and related techniques*, Thousand Oaks, CA: Sage Publications.

Simons, H. (1996) 'The paradox of case study', *Cambridge Journal of Education*, vol 26, no 2, pp 225-40.

Simons, H. (2009) *Case study research in practice*, London: Sage Publications.

Skocpol, T. (1979) *States and social revolutions: A comparative analysis of France, Russia, and China*, Cambridge: Cambridge University Press.

Further reading

George, A. and Bennett, A. (2005) *Case studies and theory development in the social sciences*, Cambridge, MA: MIT Press.

Gerring, J. (2006) *Case study research: Principles and practices,* Cambridge: Cambridge University Press.

Gomm, R., Hammersley, M. and Foster, P. (eds) (2000) *Case study method,* London: Sage Publications.

Stake, R. (1995) *The art of case study research,* Thousand Oaks, CA: Sage Publications.

Yin, R. (2008) *Case study research* (4th edn), Thousand Oaks, CA: Sage Publications.

6.5 Cross-sectional design and longitudinal design

Alan Bryman and Saul Becker

Cross-sectional and longitudinal design, introduced in Section 5.3, in the context of quantitative research, are equally relevant to qualitative research. The first of these two designs is most frequently employed in connection with qualitative research using semi-structured interviewing and unstructured interviewing. In these cases, the researcher interviews a cross-section of people at a particular moment in time. Of course, they can never be interviewed at precisely the same point in time, any more than the interviewees in a social survey, conducted by a structured interview, can be interviewed simultaneously. What the researcher attempts to do is to interview a variety of people within the time frame of his or her investigation.

It is not common to write about qualitative researchers as users of a cross-sectional design, but that is essentially what is involved in most qualitative interview studies. For example, in an article discussing her research on pension planning, Karen Rowlingson (2002, p 632) writes that, '41 people were interviewed in depth from a cross-section of the public. Quotas were set to ensure a reasonable mix of: men and women; different employment/social class groups; and different life-cycle/age groups'. There is next to nothing to distinguish this design from one that a survey researcher using a structured interview or postal questionnaire might use to examine the same kind of issue. Because she did not sample randomly, Rowlingson was unable to generalise from her sample of 41 to a wider population. However, the same point could be made of many surveys in social policy or social work research that are not based on random sampling or even quota sampling (see Section 5.4).

Similarly, Dean and Shah (2002) report the results of a qualitative investigation using semi-structured interviews with 47 recipients of Family Credit. The research was conducted in September 1999, one month before Family Credit was due to be replaced by Working Families Tax Credit. The sample was compiled through three sources: the then Department of Social Security, snowball sampling and advertisements for interviewees. Once again, this would appear to be a cross-sectional design which allows the authors, in much the same way as Rowlingson, to glean 'a much richer understanding of processes, motivations, beliefs and attitudes than can be gleaned from quantitative research' (Rowlingson, 2002, p 632).

Unsurprisingly, the cross-sectional design can be extended into a longitudinal design. Extending a cross-sectional design into a longitudinal design is particularly valuable for charting changes in experiences and views following a change of some sort. For example, Arksey's (2002) research on the support needs of informal carers was conducted in four social services departments in the North of England. These were chosen to reflect a 'cross-section of authorities'. In addition to interviewing a senior manager in each authority and some practitioners, Arksey interviewed 51 carers. She writes:

> Semi-structured interviews with carers were held at two points in time: as soon as possible after they had been assessed under the Carers Act … and six months after the first interview…. The first interview focused on the process and form of assessment, and any associated service provision. The second interview concentrated on changes during the six-month interval, and the perceived outcome of assessment for carers. (Arksey, 2002, p 85)

Box 6a provides a more detailed illustration of the way in which a longitudinal design can be employed in relation to qualitative research.

Box 6a: Qualitative longitudinal research
Bren Neale

The past decade has seen a significant growth in qualitative methods for tracking individuals or groups over time. This reflects the growing need to understand the lived experience of change and continuity in the social world, the processes by which change occurs and the agency of individuals in shaping or accommodating these processes (Neale and Flowerdew, 2003). Understanding how and why change is created, lived and experienced is important in policy contexts where individuals or organisations are required to change their behaviour (Corden and Millar, 2007). Designs and strategies for working through time are flexible and creative but two approaches are commonly used. *Prospective designs* involve tracking individuals or groups through life course or policy transitions as they occur. Working flexibly, each wave of data collection is used to inform the next. The timeframes vary; tracking may be done intensively for those undergoing a particular turning point or policy intervention (see, for example, Corden and Nice, 2006), or extensively to discern changes over the life course (see, for example, Laub and Sampson, 2003). *Repeat cross-sectional designs*, in contrast, may or may not involve the same individuals. These are commonly used to 're-visit' classic studies in order to uncover historical processes of change within particular communities or organisations (see, for example, Johnson et al, 2010).

Whatever the design, qualitative longitudinal (QL) research enables an exploration of complex timescapes or flows of time – for example, the pace of change; the nature of turning points in an unpredictable life journey; the intersection of time and space to locate and contextualise experiences; and reflections of past and future at each new fieldwork encounter. Prospective designs can be combined with retrospective life history accounts to enable the causes and consequences of change to be understood 'backwards,' from the vantage point of the present (Laub and Sampson, 2003). Likewise, capturing imaginary futures at each follow-up is a powerful way to understand the changing aspirations of individuals, and how and why their life chances are forged, enabled or constrained over time (Adam and Groves, 2007).

Mixed longitudinal designs that bring QL and survey data into conversation with each other are also increasingly evident. Combining the depth of QL analysis with the breadth of survey analysis can produce more robust evidence for policy, although the extent to which these different forms of data can be integrated remains unclear (Laub and Sampson, 2003). Further challenges include the management and multidimensional analysis of large, complex datasets, ethical issues of intrusion and disclosure for participants, sample maintenance and the ethics of secondary use of QL datasets. However, the method yields compelling data with significant explanatory power.

Ridge and Millar (2011) studied the complex dynamics of work, benefits and family lives among 50 lone mothers and their children, against a backdrop of tenuous employment environments and state policies that require lone mothers to work. Starting from a baseline where the mothers left Income Support and started paid work, they conducted three waves of in-depth interviews with both generations over four to five years. Gathering retrospective data on the employment histories of the mothers, and data on their future aspirations, for example, for housing, security and pensions, they examined the impact of employment on family life and living standards and explored the challenges of sustaining low-income employment over time. Their findings – that income security is not easily achieved or maintained – have implications for the well-being of low-paid families over time and the level and nature of state financial support available to them.

Timescapes is a QL initiative run by a consortium of researchers from the Universities of Leeds, London South Bank, Cardiff, Edinburgh and The Open University. Funded for five years (2017-12) by the Economic and Social Research Council (ESRC), Timescapes is advancing QL research, building resources of QL data (the Timescapes Archive) for sharing and re-use and faciliating secondary analysis of QL datasets. The core projects explore personal relationships and identities across the life course. An affiliation scheme is in operation to support new and existing QL researchers, and to facilitate the sharing of QL datasets through the archive. Further details of the core projects, affiliation scheme and resources for QL methods, archiving and secondary analysis are available through the Timescapes website (see below).

Question for discussion
• What are the particular gains and challenges of working qualitatively through time?

References

Adam, B. and Groves, C. (2007) *Future matters: Action, knowledge, ethics*, Leiden: Brill.

Corden, A. and Millar, J. (2007) 'Introduction', in J. Millar (ed) 'Qualitative longitudinal research for social policy', Themed section of *Social Policy and Society*, vol 6, no 4, pp 529-32.

Corden, A. and Nice, K. (2006) *Pathways to work: Findings from the final cohort in the QL panel of incapacity benefits recipients*, Research Report no 398, London: Department for Work and Pensions.

Johnson, J., Rolph, S. and Smith, R. (2010) *Residential care transformed: Revisiting Townsend's 'The last refuge'*, London: Palgrave Macmillan.

Laub, J. and Sampson, R. (2003) *Shared beginnings, divergent lives: Delinquent boys to age 70*, Cambridge, MA: Harvard University Press.

Neale, B. and Flowerdew, J. (2003) 'Time, texture and childhood: the contours of longitudinal qualitative research', *International Journal of Social Research Methodology*, vol 6, no 3, pp 189-99.

Ridge, T. and Millar, J. (2011) 'Following fathers: working lone mother families and their children', *Social Policy & Administration*, vol 45, no 1, pp 85-97.

Further reading

McCleod, J. and Thomson, R. (2009) *Researching social change*, London: Sage Publications.

Millar, J. (ed) (2007) 'Qualitative longitudinal research for social policy', Themed section of *Social Policy and Society*, vol 6, no 4, pp 529-95.

Saldaña, J. (2003) *Longitudinal qualitative research: Analyzing change through time*, Walnut Creek, CA: AltaMira Press.

Relevant organisation

Timescapes, an ESRC Qualitative Longitudinal Study initiative: www.timescapes.leeds.ac.uk

These examples help to underline the point made in Section 5.3, that research designs can be associated with different research methods. Where qualitative research in the areas of social policy and social work may differ from the use of cross-sectional design and longitudinal design in quantitative research is in respect of the range of interviews involved. In the case of Arksey's research, it is not just the carers who were interviewed, since, as noted above, she also interviewed a small number of senior managers and front-line practitioners. Quantitative researchers often compare samples of respondents, for example, samples of both practitioners and clients of social services departments, but they would not normally interview very small numbers of senior managers, as Arksey did, because they would not constitute a big enough sample. Purposive sampling of the kind frequently practised by qualitative researchers (see Section 6.6) sometimes results in very small numbers of people in a particular category that would not form the basis for a sample in a survey. However, the basic point being made in this section is that cross-sectional designs and longitudinal designs form viable frameworks for the collection of qualitative data, especially in interview-based research.

Question for discussion

- How similar is the cross-sectional design in qualitative research to the cross-sectional design in quantitative research?

References

Arksey, H. (2002) 'Rationed care: assessing the support needs of informal carers in English social service authorities', *Journal of Social Policy*, vol 31, pp 81-101.

Dean, H. and Shah, A. (2002) 'Insecure families and low-paying labour markets: comments on the British experience', *Journal of Social Policy*, vol 31, pp 61-80.

Rowlingson, K. (2002) 'Private pension planning: the rhetoric of responsibility, the reality of insecurity', *Journal of Social Policy*, vol 31, pp 623-42.

Further reading

de Vaus, D. (2001) *Research design in social research*, London: Sage Publications.

6.6 Sampling in qualitative research
Clive Seale

Qualitative researchers are often interested in generalising their findings to other settings in much the same way as researchers who use quantitative methods. Because of this, all of the considerations outlined in Section 5.4 with regard to the principles of probability sampling, quota sampling and the rest are also relevant for qualitative designs. This can get forgotten if qualitative researchers become excessively attached to the notion of difference between their own approaches and those of their quantitatively minded colleagues. Nevertheless, there are some sampling techniques developed to further the particular aims of qualitative researchers, the application of which may involve dispensing with quantitative sampling logic on certain qualitative projects, and these are outlined in this section.

One of the characteristics of much qualitative research is that it is devoted to discovering, in the words of John Lofland, 'what kinds of things are happening, rather than to determine the frequency of predetermined kinds of things that the researcher already believes can happen' (1971, p 76). Thus, instead of seeking to describe how many red, or black, or oval pebbles there are on a beach, the qualitative researcher may be searching for the pebble that stands out from the rest. This can require looking in unusual places, perhaps using geological knowledge and quantitative data about the existing distribution of shapes and colours to direct the search to the most likely spot. Thus, theory and ongoing data analysis – in short, brain work – may direct the hunt. Once found, the new phenomenon is studied intensively because it is likely to change current theories of how pebbles are formed. Thus, qualitative sampling may concentrate on the search for theoretically rich examples, so that many have said its purpose is to create *theoretical generalisations* rather than the *empirical generalisations* of quantitative researchers (Mitchell, 1983).

Sampling in qualitative research, then, may take forms that are unpredictable, being close in character to the operations used by the scholar in an archive wishing to select which file to investigate next. This will depend in part on what was found in the last file, in part on the investigator's own perspective of the relevant literature on his or her subject, and on the emerging shape of the project which will usually take the form of a story that the investigator wishes to tell. Perhaps the best attempt at conveying this spirit of open-ended, yet intellectually directed, inquiry is the account of 'theoretical sampling' given by Glaser and Strauss, arising from their observational study of hospital wards in the 1960s (see **Box 6b** for a full example). Here, the researcher's emerging theory influences sampling decisions.

> ## Box 6b: Theoretical sampling
> Clive Seale
>
> Theoretical sampling, proposed originally by Glaser and Strauss (1967), involves a researcher sampling to extend and broaden the scope of an emerging theory. Cases, settings or people are chosen to study with a view to finding things that might challenge and extend the limitations of the existing theory, which may not incorporate sufficiently the range of phenomena that can occur:

> Theoretical sampling is the process of data collection for generating theory whereby the analyst jointly collects, codes, and analyzes his data and decides what data to collect next and where to find them, in order to develop his theory as it emerges. This process of data collection is *controlled* by the emerging theory.... The basic question in theoretical sampling ... is: *what* groups or subgroups does one turn to *next* in data collection? And for *what* theoretical purpose? In short, how does the sociologist select multiple comparison groups? The possibility of multiple comparisons are infinite, and so groups must be chosen according to theoretical criteria. (1967, pp 45-7)

Glaser and Strauss illustrate theoretical sampling from their own work among dying people, in which the concepts of 'awareness contexts' and 'dying trajectories' were developed:

> Visits to the various medical services were scheduled as follows: I wished first to look at services that minimized patient awareness (and so first looked at a premature baby service and then a neurosurgical service where patients were frequently comatose). I wished then to look at dying in a situation where expectancy of staff and often of patients was great and dying was quick, so I observed on an Intensive Care Unit. Then I wished to observe on a service where staff expectations of terminality were great but where the patient's might or might not be, and where dying tended to be slow. So I looked next at a cancer service. I wished then to look at conditions where death was unexpected and rapid, and so looked at an emergency service. While we were looking at some different types of services, we also observed the above types of service at other types of hospitals. So our scheduling of types of service was directed by a general conceptual scheme – which included hypotheses about awareness, expectedness and rate of dying – as well as by a developing conceptual structure including matters not at first envisioned. Sometimes we returned to services after the initial two or three or four weeks of continuous observation, in order to check upon items, which needed checking or had been missed in the initial period. (1967, p 59)

Unlike a statistical sample whose size is limited by setting the degree of confidence with which the researcher wishes to generalise from sample to population, theoretical sampling is potentially endless, since the researcher can never be certain that a further case will exhibit properties that force some further changes in a theory. Glaser and Strauss propose a pragmatic solution to this in their idea of 'theoretical saturation'. This point is said to be reached when new data generate no further theory development, with categories and their properties therefore appearing fully developed. Of course, the researcher must try very hard to seek out diverse groups and settings before concluding that a theory is saturated. This means that rather different criteria apply in judging a statistical versus a theoretical sample. The statistical sample is judged adequate according to underlying laws of probability, on the basis of which the likelihood of sample results holding true in the population is estimated. The theoretical sample is judged adequate if no obvious exceptions to the theory are evident to the critical reader, who may use human judgement and imagination to make this assessment, and deem a theory empirically 'thin' or unconvincing if the existence of plausible exceptions has not been investigated.

Reference
Glaser, B.G. and Strauss, A.L. (1967) *The discovery of grounded theory: Strategies for qualitative research*, Chicago, IL: Aldine.

While **Box 6b** suggests a continuing interaction between data collection and analysis throughout the life of a project, it is also the case that sampling decisions made at the outset of a study, and then more or less followed through regardless of what emerges, can be theoretically informed. Thus, a researcher may seek to maximise the chances of generating insights by choosing comparison groups carefully. Qualitative studies quite often begin by wishing to explore the unique position of a particular group of people (for example, women, or a group with a self-defined sexual, ethnic or religious identity). The case for uniqueness, however, may be hard to prove in the absence of a comparison group (for example, men, or those with a different sexual, ethnic or religious self-identification). This was demonstrated in a study of breast cancer narratives in newspapers (Seale, 2002). Previous studies (see, for example, Lupton, 1994) had focused on the portrayal of women, arguing that their responses to cancer were shown in ways likely to intimidate and disadvantage women readers with the disease. Seale's study compared portrayals of men with cancer as well as women, showing that stereotypes of masculinity were also present, and pointing to both differences and similarities in the way each gender was depicted.

An essential conceptual tool for the researcher interested in sampling for theoretical richness is the idea that sampling ought to be devoted, in part, to searching for a 'negative instance' or 'deviant case' that, by contradicting an emerging theory, may in the end extend or deepen it. In quantitative research such instances are conceived of as threats to a study's validity, and the attempt to rule out alternative explanations (for example, spurious variables) can lead to some very creative approaches to research design and analysis (see, for example, Campbell and Stanley, 1966). In qualitative research the deviant case may be actively sought out, because it is likely to generate a more robust theory. Thus, Dingwall and Murray (1983) extended the sampling of an earlier study of hospital casualty departments so that children as well as adults were sampled. Although children sometimes came to casualty with mild problems, or having self-inflicted injuries, they were not stigmatised for this, in contrast to adults. The initial theory that staff stigmatised people for doing these things had to be modified to state that staff, before doing this, assessed how free patients were to make choices. Children were deemed not to be free, so were not blamed for their acts, and a few adults were eventually found who fulfilled this criterion as well, thus making for a better theory.

Snowball, volunteer and convenience sampling are also methods used by qualitative researchers. A sampling frame is not always available, and some members of the relevant group may be hard to approach. In the *snowball approach*, the researcher asks each interviewee who else might be relevant and willing to be interviewed, so that a network of contacts is built up. *Volunteers* may be recruited through advertisements in a variety of sites – newspapers, the internet, notice boards or word of mouth. Or the research may simply begin with whoever is *conveniently available* – a friend or a passer-by – and continue that way until sufficient insights are judged to have been generated. These methods, of course, may be somewhat theoretically informed, and may in practice be applied in a mixed fashion, the research using elements of each on any one project. But these methods are unlikely to result in samples that represent a defined population, since volunteers are usually different from non-volunteers, people who are conveniently available are likely to be different from those who are not, and people who are part of social networks are likely to be different from the socially marginalised. None of this may matter if the aim of the project is solely to generate theoretical insights rather than to generalise empirically. In practice, however, it is rare for qualitative researchers to maintain exclusive focus on theoretical generalisation, and they very frequently slip into statements that require consideration of how representative their samples may be of a particular population.

Carrying out checks to become more aware of how accidents of sampling may have influenced results is often advisable. Sieber (1979) gives an example of this and shows, incidentally, that numbers also have a role to play in qualitative research. He was concerned, in the course of his study of school districts, that he had interacted more with education officials than rank and file teachers, thus distorting his estimates of job satisfaction. He conducted a small survey of randomly sampled teachers, asking them fixed-choice questions about their levels of satisfaction. Beforehand, he had tried to predict what results he would get, using his knowledge derived from the qualitative case study material he had collected. He found that his predictions of satisfaction were too optimistic when compared with the survey results, and concluded that he had 'fallen prey to … elite bias, despite recent training in the dangers of giving greater weight to prestigious figures as informants' (1979, p 1353). Sieber suggests that such checking exercises can be done during fieldwork so that sampling can be adjusted if need be. More examples showing the use of quantitative data to check the representativeness of qualitative samples can be found in Seale (1999).

Sampling in qualitative research, then, is quite various, and sometimes has a different purpose from sampling in statistical studies where representation of a population is a priority. It is important to be aware of the different consequences that sampling decisions may have for the kind of arguments one wishes to sustain. In this respect, sampling in both quantitative and qualitative research is exactly the same.

Questions for discussion

- When is it appropriate to sample without regard to representativeness?
- What sampling methods are appropriate for researching 'hidden' populations (that is, groups concerned to hide their activities from official surveillance)?
- Why might random sampling from a list of a population be relevant in a research project involving qualitative data and analysis that you are planning? How would you go about achieving this?

References

Campbell, D.T. and Stanley, J.C. (1966) *Experimental and quasi-experimental design for research*, Chicago, IL: Rand McNally.

Dingwall, R. and Murray, T. (1983) 'Categorisation in accident departments: "good" patients, "bad" patients and children', *Sociology of Health and Illness*, vol 5, no 2, pp 121-48.

Lofland, J. (1971) *Analysing social settings: A guide to qualitative observation*, Belmont, CA: Wadsworth.

Lupton, D. (1994) 'Femininity, responsibility, and the technological imperative: discourses on breast cancer in the Australian press', *International Journal of Health Services*, vol 24, no 1, pp 73-89.

Mitchell, J.C. (1983) 'Case and situational analysis', *Sociological Review*, vol 31, no 2, pp 187-211.

Seale, C.F. (1999) *The quality of qualitative research*, London: Sage Publications.

Seale, C.F. (2002) 'Cancer heroics: a study of news reports with particular reference to gender', *Sociology*, vol 36, no 1, pp 107-26.

Sieber, S. (1979) 'The integration of fieldwork and survey methods', *American Journal of Sociology*, vol 78, no 6, pp 1135-59.

Further reading

Glaser, B.G. and Strauss, A.L. (1967) *The discovery of grounded theory: Strategies for qualitative research*, Chicago, IL: Aldine.
Seale, C.F. (1999) *The quality of qualitative research*, London: Sage Publications, Chapter 7.
Strauss, A.L. and Corbin, J. (1990) *Basics of qualitative research: Grounded theory procedures and techniques*, Newbury Park, CA: Sage Publications.

Website resources

Grounded Theory Online: www.groundedtheoryonline.com/
Qualitative Research Guidelines Project: www.qualres.org/HomeSamp-3702.html
Research Methods Knowledge Base: www.socialresearchmethods.net/kb/sampling.php

PART TWO: QUALITATIVE RESEARCH METHODS AND SOURCES OF QUALITATIVE DATA

6.7 Overview of the main research methods and sources of data in qualitative social policy and social work research

Alan Bryman and Saul Becker

In this section, the main methods for collecting qualitative data are examined. Six main research methods and sources of data are examined:

- unstructured interviews and semi-structured interviewing;
- ethnography;
- focus groups;
- biographical method;
- documents – historical and contemporary, as well as those which are web-based and those which are not; and
- using the internet for the collection of qualitative data.

Each of these methods and approaches to the collection of data is underpinned by the preoccupations outlined in relation to qualitative research in Sections 6.2 and 6.3.

Some of the analytic styles that appear in the sections on the analysis of qualitative data are difficult to distinguish from methods of data collection. This point applies to *discourse analysis* (Section 6.17), *conversation analysis* (Section 6.18) and *narrative analysis* (Section 6.19). In each case, while they represent styles of analysis, they are not exclusively that because the data have to be prepared in such a way as to enable the analysis to take place. With conversation analysis, for example, the analyst records conversations and transcribes in precise detail (including such things as the length of pauses in conversation) in order to enable the analysis to take place. Similarly, narrative analysis can be thought of as an approach to the analysis of qualitative data that takes the uncovering of narratives in people's interview replies as its central feature. However, increasingly those researchers adopting the approach carry out interviews that are specifically designed to elicit narratives.

In qualitative research, therefore, there is less of a sharp distinction between research methods and sources of data, on the one hand, and analysis on the other. In grounded theory, for example, the collection and analysis of data are depicted as intertwined and constantly revised in the light of each other.

The rise of the internet as a platform or springboard for conducting qualitative research will be evident in this chapter. In Section 5.7, it was noted that the internet is increasingly being used as a means of conducting surveys; in qualitative research, the rise of web-based methods of data collection is just as evident, as can be seen in Section 6.14 and in the section on ethnography (6.10), where the notion of virtual ethnography is introduced. Also, web-based documents are increasingly a focus of interest (see **Box 6f**).

6.8 Semi-structured and unstructured interviewing

Annie Irvine

Interviewing is a primary mode of data collection in qualitative research; 'semi-structured' and 'unstructured' interviews are labels used to describe two types of interview. Many other terms will be encountered, including, among others: *in-depth, qualitative, focused, non-directive, narrative* and *biographical*. While some authors specify what distinguishes their particular approach from others, these names are sometimes used interchangeably, which can be confusing. However, what these approaches share is a commitment to flexibility and to letting interviewees 'speak for themselves' in their own words. As such, qualitative interviews are used in studies that seek to understand personal experiences, perspectives and meanings (Mason, 2002a; Rubin and Rubin, 2005; Kvale and Brinkmann, 2009). Here, we take the terms 'semi-structured' and 'unstructured' to describe two examples within the range of qualitative interview approaches.

Some researchers argue that there is no such thing as an unstructured interview – every social interaction is structured in a number of ways (Jones, 1985; Collins, 1998; Mason, 2002b). However, for present purposes, 'structure' can be thought of as the degree to which the topics for discussion, the wording and the ordering of questions are *pre-specified* by the researcher and the extent to which there is *flexibility* to change or adapt these aspects in the course of the interview. The difference between semi-structured and unstructured interviews is really one of degree, and it is reasonable to think of these approaches as on a continuum (Bryman, 2012). Both employ open, non-directive questions but vary in the extent to which themes are pre-determined and the amount of latitude given to interviewer and interviewee in the way that questions and responses are formulated.

In a *semi-structured interview*, the interviewer uses an interview guide organised around key areas of interest. A number of questions are devised in advance and the aim is to cover all main topics during the interview. However, there is freedom to make on-the-spot adjustments to the guide, to follow the flow of the interviewee's responses. This might mean: modifying the order in which questions are asked; changing the wording of questions; clarifying the meaning of questions; adding or omitting questions according to their relevance to the particular interviewee; or varying the amount of time given to particular topics.

In comparison, an *unstructured interview* is shaped far more by the interviewee. The researcher may start out with just one very open initial question, or a small number of broad themes to explore (Bryman, 2012). Subsequent probes will emerge out of the story that unfolds. The interviewee is invited to play a more active role in shaping the direction of the discussion and can introduce topics as they see relevant. However, some interviewees may find an interview approach that has very little structure or focus somewhat confusing or disconcerting (Jones, 1985; Holt, 2010). A less structured interview is also likely to result in less structured data, which may therefore be more challenging and time-consuming to analyse (Tighe, 2001).

Semi-structured interviews are used to explore a range of topics in social policy and social work research (see, for example, Nice et al, 2008; Glendinning et al, 2009; Corden et al, 2010a). Studies that describe the interview approach as 'unstructured' seem to be rather less common, but examples include Connolly (2004), Durham (2002) and Irwin (2008).

Semi-structured and unstructured interviews are challenging. They are time-consuming, require stamina and high levels of concentration, and demand a range of practical, social and communicative skills, which improve only with experience. Although some have argued against the use of prescriptive guidelines for qualitative interviewing (see, for example, Jones, 1985; Rapley, 2004), there are a number of aspects that are useful to consider.

Establishing rapport: rapport refers to the degree of understanding, trust, respect and comfort that develops between the interviewer and the interviewee (Arksey and Knight, 1999). The time to start creating these ties is as soon as the relationship begins, which may be over the telephone when negotiating and arranging access. Every interview is a unique social encounter and the kind of relationship that seems appropriate will differ depending on the interviewee (Jones, 1985). Opinions differ on the extent to which research relationships can or should be reciprocal, and the issue of 'power' is a perennial concern (Oakley, 1981; Ribbens, 1989; Cotterill, 1992). Essentially, however, in any research encounter the interviewer should aim to be personable, polite and interested. During the interview, they should listen attentively and avoid conveying a sense of urgency or impatience (although it should be remembered that the interviewee may be short on time!). The interviewer should let people know that their views and opinions are valuable and after the interview write to thank them for taking part in the study.

Asking questions and eliciting information: the interviewer should try to ask open rather than leading questions, using words that are understandable and appropriate for the person who is being interviewed. If interviewees use terminology that is unfamiliar, they should be asked to explain what they mean, rather than the interviewer guessing. The interviewer should summarise or recap to check they have got the story right.

Even if they think they have understood, a useful strategy may be to 'play the innocent' (Hermanowicz, 2002) in order to elicit more detailed explanations from interviewees. Prompts can be used if necessary, but people should be given time to think and to reflect; the interviewer should not intervene too quickly. Introducing photographs, documents or visual tasks to the interview can be other useful ways to encourage deeper discussion (see, for example, Wilson et al, 2007; Bagnoli, 2009; Guenette and Marshall, 2009). Although the interview guide should be used flexibly, it is important to be familiar with the overall set of questions or themes to be covered. The better interviewers are able to hold the main questions in their heads, the more free-flowing the conversation can be.

Listening: interviewers must be competent active listeners. This involves attentive listening, both to the words being spoken by the interviewee, but also to how they are being said, for instance the emphases and emotional tone used. Although some interviewees will be less talkative than others, as a general rule interviewers should make sure that they do more listening than speaking. By listening carefully, they may become aware of additional questions to ask and will know when to probe or prompt for more detailed responses, specific examples or clarification. Wengraf (2001) describes the 'double attention' that is necessary when conducting semi-structured interviews, focusing simultaneously on what the interviewee is saying and on monitoring how the interviewer is progressing through the topics. This is no easy task and takes practice! It can be useful to note down key points as they are raised, to provide reminders of items the interviewer may want to come back to later in the conversation. However, interviewers should avoid focusing on note taking at the expense of engaging visually with the interviewee.

Emotions and well-being: while participation in a research interview can be a positive experience, there are also potential harms, including undue intrusion into private and personal spheres, embarrassment, distress or fatigue. Throughout interviews, it is important to be alert to verbal and non-verbal signs of how the interviewee is responding to the research encounter. While some topics are more obviously sensitive, emotions can emerge unexpectedly in any interview. It is useful for interviewers to think in advance about how they would respond if an interviewee became upset or distressed and also how they would take care of their own emotional well-being (Kavanaugh and Ayres, 1998; Goodrum and Keys, 2007; Mitchell and Irvine, 2008).

Recording and transcription: it is essential to have a comprehensive record of the interview and in studies that use semi-structured or unstructured interviews, an audio recording is almost always made. A digital recorder (rather than cassettes) provide higher quality audio that is more easily navigated when listening back. Before the interview, interviewers should practice using their equipment and always take spare batteries. They should explain to interviewees why recording is important and ask their permission. Experience suggests that refusal is rare, but this should always be respected. In any case, it is important to make brief notes during the interview just in case the recording fails. After the interview, it is useful to make additional notes, for example, how the interviewer felt the interview went, non-verbal aspects of the interaction and details of the wider context/setting. Ideally, audio recordings should be transcribed in full, but bear in mind that transcription is very time-consuming and can be costly if paying for it to be done professionally (for more on transcription, see Poland, 2002).

In addition to these practical and ethical considerations, there is also a more theoretical debate going on about the use and usefulness of interviews in qualitative research (Mason, 2002b; Holstein and Gubrium, 2004; Potter and Hepburn, 2005; Silverman, 2006; Hammersley, 2008). It is worth engaging with these debates as they can help us to think more reflectively about what we can aim or claim to achieve through the use of interviews. However, for most social researchers, interviews are considered a practical and effective way to generate rich and insightful data. **Box 6c** provides an example of how semi–structured interviews were used in a recent study.

Box 6c: An example of semi and unstructured interviews
Annie Irvine

Disability Living Allowance (DLA) and Attendance Allowance (AA) are monetary benefits designed to meet the additional costs of disability relating to personal care or mobility needs. In 2009, the Department for Work and Pensions (DWP) commissioned research that would contribute to greater understanding of the use and impact of DLA and AA (Corden et al, 2010a, 2010b). A key aim of the research was to find out *what difference* these benefits make to people's lives. This is a complex issue to address as people have different understandings and levels of awareness about the benefits they receive. Therefore, a qualitative approach using semi-structured interviews was appropriate.

To understand how people conceptualised DLA/AA and how these benefits fitted into overall household budgets, the interview guide was designed to be used in stages. First, there were open questions and prompts about people's health condition or disability and how this had an impact on their daily living (for example, shopping, cooking and housework); then there were questions about the ways that people addressed these needs; and then questions about how they were able to afford to pay for any practical or material supports. This approach meant that the researchers needed to retain information from responses to earlier questions about additional needs in order to go back through each of these points when asking how people were able to afford to pay for things. Therefore, during the earlier part of interviews, researchers made notes (on a notepad or on the interview guide itself) and used these as prompts to return to.

Specific questions about the use and impact of DLA/AA were embedded at points throughout the interview guide. However, given the flexible nature of semi-structured interviews, if participants began to talk at other stages in the interview about their use of DLA/AA or what difference they felt these benefits had made to their lives, researchers were responsive to this and allowed people to continue. Valuable information about the difference made by DLA/AA was thus gathered through a combination of direct questions, non-directive prompts about meeting the costs of daily living and participants' spontaneous comments.

Interviews were conducted with parents whose child received DLA, working-age recipients of DLA and older people receiving AA. A 'family' of interview guides was developed, each following the same format but with some questions altered to be appropriate to the specific group. For example, older people who had retired were not asked about employment. Three researchers carried out the interviews. All interviews were conducted face to face, usually in people's homes, and were audio-recorded with participants' permission. Sometimes

---

other people, including partners, siblings or children, were present and contributed to the discussion.

Some participants needed to take breaks during the interview to rest or take medication and interviews were sometimes paused while a nurse or carer called in. The researcher's visit was also a welcome social occasion for some participants. So, although the interview was designed to last 60-90 minutes, visits often lasted up to two hours overall.

References

Corden, A., Sainsbury, R., Irvine, A. and Clarke, S. (2010a) *The impact of Disability Living Allowance and Attendance Allowance: Findings from exploratory qualitative research*, DWP Research Report, No 649, Norwich: The Stationery Office.

Corden, A., Sainsbury, R., Irvine, A. and Clarke, S. (2010b) *Appendices to the impact of Disability Living Allowance and Attendance Allowance: Findings from exploratory qualitative research*, DWP Research Report, No 649, Norwich: The Stationery Office.

Question for discussion

- What are the strengths, limitations and challenging aspects of conducting semi-structured and unstructured interviews?

References

Arksey, H. and Knight, P. (1999) *Interviewing for social scientists: An introductory resource with examples*, London: Sage Publications.

Bagnoli, A. (2009) 'Beyond the standard interview: the use of graphic elicitation and arts-based methods', *Qualitative Research*, vol 9, no 5, pp 547-70.

Bryman, A. (2012) *Social research methods* (4th edn), Oxford: Oxford University Press.

Collins, P. (1998) 'Negotiating selves: reflections on "unstructured" interviewing', *Sociological Research Online*, vol 3, no 3 (www.socresonline.org.uk/3/3/2.html).

Connolly, M. (2004) 'Developmental trajectories and sexual offending: an analysis of the pathways model', *Qualitative Social Work*, vol 3, pp 39-59.

Corden, A., Sainsbury, R., Irvine, A. and Clarke, S. (2010a) *The impact of Disability Living Allowance and Attendance Allowance: Findings from exploratory qualitative research*, DWP Research Report, No 649, Norwich: The Stationery Office.

Corden, A., Sainsbury, R., Irvine, A. and Clarke, S. (2010b) *Appendices to the impact of Disability Living Allowance and Attendance Allowance: Findings from exploratory qualitative research*, DWP Research Report, No 649, Norwich: The Stationery Office.

Cotterill, P. (1992) 'Interviewing women: issues of friendship, vulnerability and power', *Women's Studies International Forum*, vol 15, no 5/6, pp 593-606.

Durham, A. (2002) 'Developing a sensitive practitioner research methodology for studying the impact of child sexual abuse', *British Journal of Social Work*, vol 32, pp 429-42.

Glendinning, C., Arksey, H., Jones, K., Moran, N., Netten, A. and Rabiee, P. (2009) *Individual budgets: Impacts and outcomes for carers*, Research Findings, York: Social Policy Research Unit, University of York.

Goodrum, S. and Keys, J. (2007) 'Reflections on two studies of emotionally sensitive topics: bereavement from murder and abortion', *International Journal of Social Research Methodology*, vol 10, pp 249-58.

Guenette, F. and Marshall, A. (2009) 'Time line drawings: enhancing participant voice in narrative interviews on sensitive topics', *International Journal of Qualitative Methods*, vol 8, no 1, pp 85-92.

Hammersley, M. (2008) *Questioning qualitative inquiry*, London: Sage Publications.

Hermanowicz, J.C. (2002) 'The great interview: 25 strategies for studying people in bed', *Qualitative Sociology*, vol 25, no 4, pp 479-99.

Holstein, J.A. and Gubrium, J.F. (2004) 'The active interview', in D. Silverman (ed) *Qualitative research: Theory, method and practice*, London: Sage Publications, pp 140-61.

Holt, A. (2010) 'Using the telephone for narrative interviewing: a research note', *Qualitative Research*, vol 10, no 1, pp 113-21.

Irwin, J. (2008) '(Dis)counted stories: domestic violence and lesbians', *Qualitative Social Work*, vol 7, pp 199-215.

Jones, S. (1985) 'Depth interviewing', in R. Walker (ed) *Applied qualitative research*, Aldershot: Gower Publishing Company, pp 45-55.

Kavanaugh, K. and Ayres, L. (1998) '"Not as bad as it could have been": assessing and mitigating hard during research interviews on sensitive topics', *Research in Nursing and Health*, vol 21, pp 91-7.

Kvale, S. and Brinkmann, S. (2009) *InterViews: Learning the craft of qualitative research interviewing* (2nd edn), Thousand Oaks, CA: Sage Publications.

Mason, J. (2002a) *Qualitative researching* (2nd edn), London: Sage Publications.

Mason, J. (2002b) 'Qualitative interviewing: asking, listening and interpreting', in T. May (ed) *Qualitative research in action*, London: Sage Publications, pp 225-41.

Mitchell, W. and Irvine, A. (2008) '"I'm okay, you're okay?" Reflections on the well-being and ethical requirements of researchers and research participants in conducting qualitative fieldwork interviews', *International Journal of Qualitative Methods*, vol 7, no 4 (http://ejournals. library.ualberta.ca/index.php/IJQM/article/view/4053).

Nice, K., Irvine, A. and Sainsbury, R. (2008) *Pathways to Work from Incapacity Benefits: A study of experience and use of the Job Preparation Premium*, DWP Research Report, No 474, Leeds: Corporate Document Services.

Oakley, A. (1981) 'Interviewing women: a contradiction in terms', in H. Roberts (ed) *Doing feminist research*, London: Routledge and Kegan Paul, pp 30-61.

Poland, B.D. (2002) 'Transcription quality', in J.F. Gubrium, and J.A. Holstein (eds) *Handbook of interview research: Context and method*, London: Sage Publications, pp 629-49.

Potter, J. and Hepburn, A. (2005) 'Qualitative interviews in psychology: problems and possibilities', *Qualitative research in Psychology*, vol 2, pp 281-307.

Rapley, T. (2004) 'Interviews', in C. Seale, G. Gobo, J. Gubrium and D. Silverman, (eds) *Qualitative research practice*, London: Sage Publications, pp 15-33.

Ribbens, J. (1989) 'Interviewing: an "unnatural situation?"', *Women's Studies International Forum*, vol 12, no 6, pp 579-92.

Rubin, H.J. and Rubin, I.S. (2005) *Qualitative interviewing: The art of hearing data* (2nd edn), Thousand Oaks, CA: Sage Publications.

Silverman, D. (2006) *Interpreting qualitative data* (3rd edn), London: Sage Publications. [See Chapter 4 'Interviews', pp 109-52.]

Tighe, C.A. (2001) '"Working at disability": a qualitative study of the meaning of health and disability for women with physical impairments', *Disability & Society*, vol 16, no 4, pp 511-29.

Wengraf, T. (2001) *Qualitative research interviewing*, London: Sage Publications.

Wilson, S., Cunningham-Burley, S., Bancroft, A., Backett-Milburn, K. and Masters, H. (2007) 'Young people, biographical narratives and the life grid: young people's accounts of parental substance use', *Qualitative Research*, vol 7, pp 135-51.

Further reading

Arksey, H. and Knight, P. (1999) *Interviewing for social scientists: An introductory resource with examples*, London: Sage Publications.

Gubrium, J.F. and Holstein, J.A. (eds) (2002) *Handbook of interview research: Context and method*, London: Sage Publications.

Kvale, S. and Brinkmann, S. (2009) *InterViews: Learning the craft of qualitative research interviewing* (2nd edn), Thousand Oaks, CA: Sage Publications.

Relevant organisations

Introductory training courses on qualitative interviewing are offered periodically by:
The Social Research Association: www.the-sra.org.uk/training.htm
National Centre for Social Research (NatCen): www.natcen.ac.uk/events-and-training
University of Surrey: www.fahs.surrey.ac.uk/daycourses

Website resource

A guide to different types of interview approach, with example transcripts, is available from the Economic and Social Data Service (ESDS) Qualidata, led by the UK Data Archive at the University of Essex: www.esds.ac.uk/qualidata/support/interviews

6.9 Telephone interviewing in qualitative research

Annie Irvine

Methodological textbooks have traditionally advised that the telephone mode is not well suited to the task of qualitative interviewing (Rubin and Rubin, 1995; Legard et al, 2003; Gillham, 2005). In particular, the lack of face-to-face contact is said to restrict the development of rapport and a 'natural' encounter, elements that are often considered to be important for generating good qualitative data. It is also said that depth and nuance of meaning may be lost in a telephone interview. However, there are potential advantages of using the telephone for research interviews, for example, savings in time and travel costs and greater anonymity around sensitive topics. Therefore, it is not uncommon to find qualitative studies in various fields of applied social science research that have conducted some or all interviews by telephone. Recent examples include Glendinning et al (2009), Owen et al (2008) and Becker et al (2010). This chapter summarises some of the main considerations when thinking about whether to use telephone interviews in a qualitative study.

Resources and convenience: because they do not involve travel, telephone interviews are cheaper to conduct than face-to-face interviews and take less time overall to complete. Although the interview itself may not necessarily be shorter, a telephone interview may feel less intrusive on the participant's schedule and may demand less time in meeting, greeting and generally 'hosting' a researcher. If the interview has to be rescheduled at short notice, you will be less inconvenienced if you have not made a journey and there are no travel plans to rearrange. For these reasons, offering a telephone interview may be a particularly useful strategy when trying to secure an interview with busy professionals. In contrast, some people may enjoy the more social encounter that accompanies a face-to-face interview.

Telephone interviews were used for pragmatic reasons in a recent study that considered people's experiences of managing mental health and employment (Irvine, 2008). The original intention had been to conduct all interviews face to face. However, recruitment rates to the study were higher than anticipated and so the telephone was used for some interviews so that all volunteers could be included in the study while remaining within planned budgets and timescales.

Accessibility and inclusion: telephone interviews make it possible to include participants who are located in places that would be impractical or impossible to access. Using telephone interviews, studies can include the views of a research population that is widely dispersed, individual participants who are geographically distant from the researcher, or people in restricted environments which may be inaccessible to a researcher (for example, prisons). There may also be factors that restrict the researcher's ability to travel, for example, physical disability or caring responsibilities. Thus, telephone interviews may also enhance inclusion and diversity among researchers themselves.

However, a minority of people do not have access to a telephone and some people have physical or sensory impairments that make this mode of communication difficult (Wenger, 2002; Ison, 2009). Chapple (1999) suggests that it may be inappropriate to use telephone interviews where there are language barriers that could increase the likelihood of misunderstandings.

An example from my own experience, which particularly highlights the value of considering telephone interviews, occurred in a study of mental health and incapacity benefits (Sainsbury et al, 2008). One participant had repeatedly cancelled or failed to show up at our arranged meeting place. On my final attempt to rearrange the interview, she told me that she experienced agoraphobia, which explained her difficulties in keeping our appointment. I suggested that we could conduct the interview by telephone instead, which the participant agreed would be fine. This interview generated very interesting and valuable perspectives, which it would have been a great shame to miss.

Ethics and safety: research participants may prefer a telephone interview if they are concerned about anonymity or if the research topic is of a very sensitive nature (Kavanaugh and Ayres, 1998; Chapple, 1999; Sturges and Hanrahan, 2004). Participants may feel that telephone interviews are less intrusive and carry less risk than either letting a researcher into their home or travelling elsewhere to meet a researcher in person (Langford, 2000; Sweet, 2002; Ruane, 2005). Safety may also be a consideration for the researcher, for example, if participants are located in dangerous settings or are perceived as posing a 'high risk' (Sturges and Hanrahan, 2004).

Physical context and practicalities: telephone interviews will not be appropriate if understanding and experiencing the participants' environment is important to your research questions. For ethnographic studies, immersion in the participants' environment is fundamental to the methodology, and so telephone interviews are unlikely to be compatible (Sweet, 2002). On the other hand, for different types of research topic, 'loss of contextual data may not always undermine the quality of qualitative findings' (Novick, 2008, p 395). If using telephone interviews, there will be constraints on the extent to which visual materials can be shared. Any reference documents to be used during the interview will have to be sent to participants in advance (Dicker and Gilbert, 1988). Finally, it is important to have a good quality telephone connection and suitable equipment that is practical to use if you wish to audio-record and/or take notes during the discussion.

Interactional considerations: in a face-to-face interview, researchers have access to non-verbal signals of participants' confusion, reticence, discomfort or distress that may be provoked by a particular question or their ongoing involvement in the research encounter. Although such emotions might be perceptible through tone of voice or hesitation, they may be harder to pick up on in a telephone interview. It has also been suggested that nuances of meaning may be lost in a telephone interview because communication takes place through facial expression and 'body language' as well as speech (Gillham, 2005; Fielding and Thomas, 2008). The participant also has more limited access to any non-verbal indications of how the researcher is responding to what they are saying. In the absence of visual signals (such as nods, smiles or quizzical looks), researchers may need to use more explicit vocalised indications of understanding or requests for clarification (Dicker and Gilbert, 1988; Stephens, 2007).

A common perception is that it is harder to develop rapport and conduct a 'natural' conversation over the telephone (Shuy, 2003; Gillham, 2005). In telephone interviews, the absence of visual information may also lead to more interruption or talking over one another, leading to difficulties in hearing one another (Dicker and Gilbert, 1988; Stephens, 2007). Extended pauses in the conversation may seem more awkward over the telephone and it may be unclear what is happening if the interviewee falls silent (Sweet, 2002). Telephone interviews may also feel more tiring and it may seem more difficult to suspend the conversation if the participant becomes upset or requires a comfort break.

Empirical research on qualitative telephone interviews

Perhaps as a result of the above factors, it has been said that telephone interviews are shorter, that detailed probing is more difficult and that topics and questions need to be less complex (Gillham, 2005; Ruane, 2005; Gray et al, 2007). However, the empirical evidence base on telephone interviews is currently underdeveloped, particularly when it comes to the types of interactional consideration outlined above (Novick, 2008). Useful contributions on qualitative telephone interviewing have been made by Holt (2010), Rose (1998), Stephens (2007), Sturges and Hanrahan (2004) and Sweet (2002). The overall conclusion of these authors is that telephone interviews can be used effectively in qualitative research, generating useful data and good rapport. However, few studies have considered in detail the differences in the spoken interaction that might emerge through the use of telephone interviews as compared with face-to-face interviews.

A recent exploratory study (Irvine et al, 2010) has made an initial contribution to filling this gap in knowledge. Using techniques drawn from conversation analysis, the study compared a small set of qualitative semi-structured telephone and face-to-face interviews. Key findings included that: participants in telephone interviews generally spoke less than in face-to-face interviews and so telephone interviews tended to be shorter overall; the researcher gave less frequent vocalised responses (such as 'mm hm' or 'right') in telephone interviews; there were more instances of speaker overlap on the telephone; participants asked for clarification slightly more often during telephone interviews; and telephone participants seemed somewhat less confident that what they were saying was relevant or useful for the researcher. However, a comparable range of substantive themes was covered.

Conclusion

Telephone interviews are increasingly being used in qualitative research and many researchers consider them to be an effective way of generating data. However, their appropriateness will vary depending on the topic of inquiry, the type of information sought, the characteristics of the participants interviewed and the method used to analyse the data. For some studies, the practical and ethical advantages of telephone interviews may outweigh perceived interactional shortcomings. However, for certain research topics or methodologies, a face-to-face encounter may be essential.

Question for discussion

- If, for practical or ethical reasons, you decide to use telephone interviews in a research project, how might this affect the spoken interaction and how might you want to adapt your interviewing style?

References

Becker, S., Sempik, J. and Bryman, A. (2010) 'Advocates, agnostics and adversaries: researchers' perceptions of service user involvement in social policy research', *Social Policy and Society*, vol 9, no 3, pp 355-66.

Chapple, A. (1999) 'The use of telephone interviewing for qualitative research', *Nurse Researcher*, vol 6, no 3, 85-93.

Dicker, R. and Gilbert, J. (1988) 'The role of the telephone in educational research', *British Educational Research Journal*, vol 14, pp 65-72.

Fielding, N. and Thomas, H. (2008) 'Qualitative interviewing', in N. Gilbert (ed) *Researching social life* (3rd edn), London: Sage Publications, pp 245-65.

Gillham, B. (2005) *Research interviewing: The range of techniques*, Buckingham: Open University Press.

Glendinning, C., Arksey, H., Jones, K., Moran, N., Netten, A. and Rabiee, P. (2009) *Individual budgets pilot projects: Impact and outcomes for carers*, York: Social Policy Research Unit, University of York.

Gray, P.S., Williamson, J.B., Karp, D.A. and Dalphin, J.R. (2007) *The research imagination. An introduction to qualitative and quantitative methods*, Cambridge: Cambridge University Press.

Holt, A. (2010) 'Using the telephone for narrative interviewing: a research note', *Qualitative Research*, vol 10, no 1, pp 113-21.

Irvine, A. (2008) *Managing mental health and employment*, DWP Research Report, No 537, Leeds: Corporate Document Services.

Irvine, A., Drew, P. and Sainsbury, R. (2010) *Mode effects in qualitative interviews: A comparison of semi-structured face-to-face and telephone interviews using conversation analysis*, Research Works, 2010-03, York: Social Policy Research Unit, University of York.

Ison, N.L. (2009) 'Having their say: email interviews for research data collection with people who have verbal communication impairment', *International Journal of Social Research Methodology*, vol 12, no 2, pp 161-72.

Kavanaugh, K. and Ayres, L. (1998) '"Not as bad as it could have been": assessing and mitigating hard during research interviews on sensitive topics', *Research in Nursing and Health*, vol 21, pp 91-7.

Langford, D.R. (2000) 'Developing a safety protocol in qualitative research involving battered women', *Qualitative Health Research*, vol 10, no 1, pp 133-42.

Legard, R., Keegan, J. and Ward, K. (2003) 'In-depth interviews', in J. Ritchie and J. Lewis (eds) *Qualitative research practice: A guide for social science students and researchers*, London: Sage Publications, pp 138-69.

Novick, G. (2008) 'Is there a bias against telephone interviews in qualitative research?', *Research in Nursing and Health*, vol 31, pp 391-8.

Owen, J., Higginbottom, G.M.A., Kirkham, M., Mathers, N. and Marsh, P. (2008) 'Ethnicity, policy and teenage parenthood in England: findings from a qualitative study', *Social Policy and Society*, vol 7, no 3, pp 293-305.

Rose, K.E. (1998) 'The telephone as a data collection instrument in a qualitative study of informal carers of terminally ill cancer patients,' *European Journal of Oncology Nursing*, vol 2, no 1, pp 59-61.

Ruane, J.M. (2005) *Essentials of research methods: A guide to social science research*, Oxford: Blackwell Publishing.

Rubin, H.J. and Rubin, I.S. (2005) *Qualitative interviewing: The art of hearing data* (2nd edn), Thousand Oaks, CA: Sage Publications.

Sainsbury, R., Irvine, A., Aston, J., Wilson, S., Williams, C. and Sinclair, A. (2008) *Mental health and employment*, DWP Research Report, No 513, Leeds: Corporate Document Services.

Shuy, R.W. (2003) 'In-person versus telephone interviewing', in J.A. Holstein and J.F. Gubrium (eds) *Inside interviewing: New lenses, new concerns*, Thousand Oaks, CA: Sage Publications, pp 175-93.

Stephens, N. (2007) 'Collecting data from elites and ultra elites: telephone and face-to-face interviews with macroeconomists', *Qualitative Research*, vol 7, no 2, pp 203-16.

Sturges, J.E. and Hanrahan, K.J. (2004) 'Comparing telephone and face-to-face qualitative interviewing: a research note', *Qualitative Research*, vol 4, no 1, pp 107-18.

Sweet, L. (2002) 'Telephone interviewing: is it compatible with interpretive phenomenological research?', *Contemporary Nurse*, vol 12, no 1, pp 58-63.

Wenger, G.C. (2002) 'Interviewing older people', in J.F. Gubrium and J.A. Holstein (eds) *Handbook of interview research: Context and method*, Thousand Oaks, CA: Sage Publications, pp 259-78.

Further reading

Novick, G. (2008) 'Is there a bias against telephone interviews in qualitative research?', *Research in Nursing and Health*, vol 31, pp 391-8.

Shuy, R.W. (2003) 'In-person versus telephone interviewing', in J.A. Holstein and J.F. Gubrium (eds) *Inside interviewing: New lenses, new concerns*, Thousand Oaks, CA: Sage Publications, pp 175-93.

Sturges, J.E. and Hanrahan, K.J. (2004) 'Comparing telephone and face-to-face qualitative interviewing: a research note', *Qualitative Research*, vol 4, no 1, pp 107-18.

Website resource

Realities, part of the Economic and Social Research Council (ESRC) National Centre for Research Methods: www.socialsciences.manchester.ac.uk/realities/resources/toolkits/phone-interviews/index.html

6.10 Ethnography
John D. Brewer

Ethnography is a style of research rather than a single method and can be defined as: 'the study of people in naturally occurring settings or "fields" by means of methods which capture their social meanings and ordinary activities, involving the researcher participating directly in the setting, if not also the activities, in order to collect data in a systematic manner but without meaning being imposed on them externally' (Brewer, 2000, p 10). It is commonly confused with participant observation, but ethnography does not necessarily require participation and its repertoire of techniques also includes in-depth interviews, discourse analysis, personal documents and vignettes. Visual methods, like video, photography and film, are now also popular, giving us the sub-field of 'visual ethnography' (Pink, 2001; and see also *Box 6e* in this chapter). The use of web-based material, garnered, for example, through online interviews or blogs, and which gives us 'virtual ethnography' (Hine, 2000) or, as it is sometimes called, 'digital ethnography' (Murthy, 2008), has risen in popularity with the popularity of the internet, although internet communication carries significant dangers for the ethnographer (Mann and Stewart, 2000). All these methods are used in other research as well, but what distinguishes their application in ethnography is that they are employed to meet the objectives that distinguish this style of research; namely, the exploration of the social meanings of people by close involvement in the field.

Ethnography has endless application. There are few topics after all that cannot be approached in terms of the social meanings and behaviours of the participants involved, although the boundaries of every topic are not necessarily always satisfactorily covered this way. The focus on social meanings ensures that ethnographic research is based on *case studies* (see Travers, 2001). The case can comprise single individuals or a group, particular events or situations, a specific organisation or cluster of organisations (see Cassell and Symon, 2004), a social institution, neighbourhood, national society or global process (see Burawoy et al, 2000), but what distinguishes an ethnographic approach is that the case permits detailed, rich and in-depth study. This often restricts ethnography to a specific locality or small number of localities, although it is possible to examine variations within a case or across cases in space and time, thereby engaging in comparative research and generalisations.

The increasingly trans-local nature of ethnography encourages both 'team ethnography', that is, multiple researchers, and 'mobile ethnography', that is, both multiple sites and mobile processes and people (see O' Reilly, 2009). Proper sampling of cases, primarily through non-probabilistic forms of sampling, extends the possibility of making generalisations (on generalisation from case studies, see Gomm et al, 2000). Its critics usually present ethnography as being very unsystematic, but rigorous practice has been introduced through the development of qualitative forms of sampling, computer-assisted qualitative data analysis packages, team-based ethnographies that permit geographical spread, and close attention to research practice in the field, among other things. There is now also a burgeoning field in secondary analysis of ethnographic data as part of the encouragement to re-work existing qualitative data (see Heaton, 2004). The Economic and Social Data Service (ESDS) has made available online several pioneering British qualitative studies for this purpose (www.esds.ac.uk/qualidata).

Two features of contemporary ethnographic practice are worth stressing here. The first is angst over methodology; the second, the development of applied ethnography. Method and methodology are interpolated in ethnography in a problematic manner. Ethnography became closely associated with a particular methodology, known as *naturalism*, within which it was privileged as the principal method and its weaknesses overlooked. Critics of naturalism meanwhile rejected ethnography outright. This has prevented ethnography from assuming the dominant mantle in post-positivist social research, and allowed hoary complaints to re-surface. Goldthorpe attacked ethnography for failing the 'logic of inference' in social science, which demands that the social world exists independently of our ideas about it and information about it permits inferences beyond the data at hand (2000, p 67). While this reifies one approach to research – and suggests that the ethnographic perspective could usefully be applied to quantitative researchers' notions of science – it rules out the possibility of ethnography except with probabilistic samples. Unfortunately, whatever defence ethnography might mount is undermined by the 'principled irrationalism' of post-modernism (Goldthorpe, 2000, p 69), which so bedevils ethnography.

It was inevitable that ethnography would be a battleground on which post-structuralists and post-modernists fought the conflict against the Enlightenment ethos of rational social science. Ethnography had such a tenuous link to this ethos anyway, often being presented as an alternative to more scientific models of social research, that ethnography was always susceptible to criticisms of its methodological foundation and the technical reliability of its practice. What was surprising was that it should be ethnographers themselves who potentially undermined their own practice. First, in social and cultural anthropology in the 1980s, and then, in sociology, ethnographers themselves criticised ethnographic representations of social reality and queried the criteria by which ethnographic data could be evaluated. Denzin and Lincoln (1998, pp 21-2) famously described such doubts as ethnography's dual crises, and no substantive ethnographic study or methodological account was free from agonising about the status of the method, the data, the text and the author's presence and voice.

The 'crisis of representation' challenges that ethnography can produce universally valid knowledge by accurately capturing the nature of the social world 'as it is' – a view described as 'naive realism' by Hammersley (1990, 1992). All accounts are constructions and the whole issue of which account more accurately represents social reality is meaningless (see Denzin, 1992). In as much as ethnographic descriptions are partial, selective, even autobiographical, in that they are tied to the particular ethnographer and the contingencies under which the data were collected, the traditional criteria for evaluating ethnography become problematic, as terms like 'validity', 'reliability' and 'generalisability' lose their authority, hence the 'crisis of legitimation'. These crises have implications for how we understand ethnographic accounts: ethnography does not neutrally represent the social world (but then, in this view, nor does anything else). There are implications for the claims ethnographers are able to make about their account: ethnography is no longer a privileged description of the social world from the inside (once called 'thick description' in order to emphasise its richness and depth). And there are implications for the written text, for ethnographers should no longer make foolish authority claims in order to validate the account as an accurate representation of reality.

However, many have tried to rescue ethnography from the worst excesses of post-modernism. Sets of guidelines exist by which the practice of ethnography is codified (Silverman, 1989, 2001; Hammersley, 1990, 1992; Stanley, 1990; Brewer, 2000). What one might call 'post post-modern ethnography', advocates the possibility and desirability of systematic ethnography and remains rooted in realism, albeit weaker versions. Hammersley's account of subtle realism (1990, 1992), for example, makes clear that he believes in independent truth claims that can be judged by their correspondence to an independent reality. 'Post post-modern ethnography' contends that while no knowledge is certain, there are phenomena that exist independent of us as researchers, and knowledge claims about them can be judged reasonably accurately in terms of their likely truth. This shares with realism the idea that research investigates independently knowable phenomena but breaks with it in denying that we have direct access to these phenomena. It shares with anti-realism recognition that all knowledge is based on assumptions and human constructions, but rejects that we have to abandon the idea of truth itself. A similar argument has been mounted to enable us to persevere with the idea of bias as a way of distinguishing good and bad research (Hammersley, 2000).

Another motif of contemporary ethnographic practice is its growing application to policy making in areas such as social work, law, education and healthcare (see **Box 6d** for a social work example). There are textbooks directed towards the practice of applied qualitative research (Walker, 1985) and other programmatic claims (see Bulmer, 1982; Finch, 1986; Rist, 1981; Wenger, 1987). The popularity of applied ethnography among ethnographers and policy makers conceals a tension between ethnographic research designed with the express purpose of addressing policy, and that whose findings are used coincidentally as part of a body of knowledge drawn on to inform policy decisions. The former is genuinely 'applied' research; the latter is 'pure' or 'basic' research that has an intended or unintended policy effect. In either respect, ethnography can offer the following to policy makers (taken from Brewer, 2000, p 164). It can:

- help provide the world view and social meanings of those affected by some policy or intervention strategy;
- help provide the views of those thought to be part of the problem that the policy or intervention strategy is intended to address;
- be used to evaluate the effects of a policy or intervention strategy as these effects are perceived and experienced by the people concerned;
- be used to identify the unintended consequences of policy initiatives and strategies as they manifest in the experiences of people;
- be used to provide cumulative evidence that supplies policy makers with a body of knowledge that is used to inform decision making;

• be used to supplement narrow quantitative information and add flesh to some of the statistical correlations and factual data used to inform decision making.

Box 6d: An example of social work practice ethnography
Jeffrey Longhofer and Jerry Floersch

Opportunities to use practice ethnography include naturalistic settings where practitioners and clients interact. The primary aim is to explore the context, actions, thoughts and feelings generated by the structured relationships among practitioners and clients. Topics for investigation are broad, including child welfare (de Montigny, 1995; Aarre, 1998), homelessness (Wagner, 1993; Desjarlais, 1997; Connolly, 2000), substance abuse treatment (Summerson-Carr, 2010), rural poverty (Christensen et al, 1998) and the effects of deinstitutionalisation on people with mental health problems (Rhodes, 1991; Townsend, 1998; Weinberg, 2005). Data collection and theoretical and philosophical components underlie the method. Data collection refers to how the researcher participates in and observes day-to-day practice interactions and how the researcher records information, for example, audio, video and/or extensive note taking. When researchers analyse data, they necessarily invoke theory and philosophical assumptions regarding the nature of social reality (that is, ontology) and the rules and criteria for making knowledge claims (that is, epistemology). In short, researcher assumptions are closely entwined with how they (re)present ethnographic data; therefore, identifying these are necessary for interpreting conclusions (for an illustration of how philosophical and research techniques produce specific interpretations, see Floersch, 2002, pp 215-20).

Floersch (2002) and Longhofer, Kubek and Floersch (2010) used practice ethnography to study social workers (that is, case managers) and their clients who live with severe mental illnesses. These studies explored the practice language, theory and situated knowledge that workers used when helping clients live in communities. Case managers and clients were followed for several years as they went about the work of case management. Researchers collected experience-near vignettes of actual case management and, regardless of the practice theory workers were trained in, researchers asked: 'How do social workers conduct work with theory or practical wisdom?'. This question fits the method's focus on in-vivo, or naturalistic, interaction. Among all participants involved in a given client's treatment or service plan (that is, providers, family, peers and social welfare workers), field researchers recorded the actual practice conversations (that is, their theoretical and practical language), examined written case notes, and queried case managers and clients about their experience.

A central aim of practice ethnography is to compare the actual in-vivo explanations of workers and clients with alternative perspectives for representing worker and client conceptualisations of problems, solutions, strengths and progress. For example, Floersch (2002) discovered a practitioner practical or situated knowledge: 'doing for', 'doing with', 'gets it' and 'low and high functioning'. These complemented the strengths of case management theory and were derived from the interaction between the practical (that is, learning by doing) and the theoretical (that is, education, training or supervision). Often, when theory did not work, managers used everyday experience (that is, practical wisdom or situated knowledge) to make up the difference. In *On being and having a case manager*, Longhofer, Kubek, and Floersch (2010) conducted an ethnographic study to show how a practical language of 'doing for', 'doing with', 'stand by to support' and 'letting go' could be mapped over established clinical theories; here, practice ethnography was employed to illustrate how social workers performed different kinds of work with different types of knowledge; findings were used to inform an alternative practice perspective and method: relational case management.

Practice ethnography investigates interactions in open systems. It is a method to understand interactions over time and is radically different from the experimental method, which operates in a closed system, where the variables can sometimes be controlled and manipulated. In the above examples, each encounter between case manager and client had a stated or unstated objective that was often mandated by regulatory and governmental agencies. And practices were driven by theories or models (for example, strengths, empowerment, cognitive-behavioural and psychodynamic). The distance travelled (the case manager and client) between the stated aim and the actual practice can be represented as an experiential space where meaning (that is, *being* and *having* a case manager) is produced. This space, or gap, is where practitioner and client experience is lived. In short, practice derives its meanings and resistances through in-vivo experience across time. Thus, the goal of practice ethnography is to discover how treatment, service or intervention 'meanings' emerge from the potentials and liabilities of ongoing practitioner and client relationships.

Question for discussion
- Identify a gap between what a practice theory presupposes about a particular social work field and the clients served, and what the actual practice experience is. How do workers and clients attempt to close the gap? Consider how ethnography might be used to explore this gap.

References

Aarre, K. (1998) 'The child welfare debate in Portugal: a case study of a children's home', in I.R. Edgar and A. Russell (eds) *The anthropology of welfare*, London: Routledge, pp 57-72.

Christensen, P., Hockey, J. and James, A. (1998) '"You just get on with it": questioning models of welfare in a rural community', in I.R. Edgar and A. Russell (eds) *The anthropology of welfare*, London: Routledge, pp 16-32.

Connolly, D.R. (2000) *Homeless mothers: Face to face with women and poverty*, Minneapolis, MN: University of Minnesota Press.

de Montigny, G. (1995) *Social working: An ethnography of front-line practice*, Toronto, ON: University of Toronto Press.

Desjarlais, R. (1997) *Shelter blues: Sanity and selfhood among the homeless*, Philadelphia, PA: University of Philadelphia Press.

Floersch, J. (2002) *Meds, money, and manners: The case management of severe mental illness*, New York: Columbia University Press.

Longhofer, J., Kubek P. and Floersch, J. (2010) *On being and having a case manager: A relational approach to recovery in mental health*, New York: Columbia University Press.

Rhodes, L. (1991) *Emptying beds: The work of an emergency psychiatric unit*, Berkeley, CA: University of California Press.

Summerson Carr, E. (2010) *Scripting addiction: The politics of therapeutic talk and American sobriety*, Princeton, NJ: Princeton University Press.

Townsend, E. (1998) *Good intentions overruled: A critique of empowerment in the routine organization of mental health services*, Toronto, ON: University of Toronto Press.

Wagner, D. (1993) *Checkerboard square: Culture and resistance in a homeless community*, Boulder, CO: Westview Press.

Weinberg, D. (2005) *Of others inside: Insanity, addiction and belonging in America*, Philadelphia, PA: Temple University Press.

Further reading

Floersch, J. (2000) 'Reading the case record: the oral and written narratives of social workers', *Social Service Review*, vol 74, no 2, pp 169-91.

Floersch, J. (2004) 'Ethnography: a case study of invented clinical knowledge', in D.K. Padgett (ed) *The qualitative research experience*, Belmont, CA: Wadsworth/Thomson Learning.

Floersch, J. (2004) 'A method for investigating practitioner use of theory in practice', *Qualitative Social Work*, vol 3, no 2, pp 161-77.

Floersch J., Longhofer, J. and Nordquest M. (2008) 'Ethnography', in M. Gray and S. Webb (eds) *Social work theories and methods*, Thousand Oaks, CA: Sage Publications, pp 152-60.

Website resources

A website that describes an interdisciplinary study of families in everyday life: www.celf.ucla.edu

A website describing the practice of ethnographic research and findings of a study of case managers: www.relationalcasemanager.com/

Box 6e: Visual ethnography
Samantha Warren

Photographs, film, drawing and media images are at the heart of visual research. What makes visual research ethnographic is taking a grounded approach to exploring research participants' everyday lives (Pink, 2006). There are two broad approaches to visual ethnography:

- involving research participants in making, or selecting, images about their lives; and
- emphasising the researcher's view of participants' lives.

Both approaches are concerned with bringing the research context to the fore. Of course, context is not only visual, and spans the whole range of embodied, emotional and sensory engagement with research environments. However, images – especially photographs – evoke more than recognition of the scene depicted and, as such, using images has much to offer ethnographic researchers interested in accessing deeper levels of emotional and sensory meaning. Nonetheless, visual ethnographers need to take care not to regard images as 'truth' or evidence that 'proves' the existence of something (Warren, 2002). Even if images are not edited, airbrushed or otherwise enhanced, they are still selected from many other possible options, through the photographer's choice of scene, subject and framing; or through the actual selection of images from a media text, such as a report, or magazine, for example. These considerations should not be seen as disadvantageous, however, since incorporating reflections about these issues enriches the data by further understanding the image-maker's culture.

Participant-led approach

A collaborative methodology, sometimes referred to as 'photo-voice', involves asking participants to take photographs or to collect images that in some way capture the theme under study (Wang and Burris, 1997). The resulting images are then discussed during a semi-structured interview with the researcher. This method is particularly useful for research with vulnerable groups, such as children or people with mental health problems, or for those who are unable to express themselves articulately in language; for example, Booth and Booth (2003) used this method to research learning difficulties among mothers, and Herssens and Heylighen (2009) asked congenitally blind children to take photographs to help them explain their everyday experiences to a sighted researcher.

Photo-voice also empowers participants, as they are free to select the aspects of their experiences they wish to share (Warren, 2005). It is important to remember that the data in a photo-voice study are generated during the interview discussions that centre on the photograph. Studying the images alone would not generate appropriate data since it is usually impossible for the researcher to guess the significance of the photograph to the participant. However, analysis of the interview transcripts is also not sufficient by itself, since, in a photo-voice study, images and text stand in relation to one another, as what Mitchell (1994) calls 'image-text'. Collier (2000) puts forward a useful framework for analysing data of these kind.

Researcher-driven approach

Sometimes it is not appropriate for participants to photograph their own practice because of the demands of their role, for example, in a classroom or clinical setting. It may also be that the participant is not best placed to reflect on their own practice, or that something they do not consider important is actually of great interest to the researcher. In these cases visual ethnography may involve the researcher generating still images or video recordings themselves. Visual ethnography, here, takes the form of 'documentary photography' whereby the researcher captures 'visual field notes', usually to augment a written diary. An example of this from educational research is Prosser and Schwartz's (1998) analysis of pupil–teacher interaction. This is also a particularly useful method to use where complex social scenes are being researched, since the camera can record a 'cultural inventory' of everything taking place in front of it (Collier and Collier, 1986). However, the introductory caveat that images do not represent a single 'truth' is particularly important here, and the researcher must acknowledge their own reflexivity in producing the photographs and film. This can be further acknowledged if the researcher records images from the 'field', and shows them to participants during interviews in much the same way as for 'photo-voice' above. This method was used to good effect in a study of organisational change in a hospital setting by Buchanan (2001), who showed photographs he had taken of mundane activities to a group of healthcare workers.

Recent developments in 'visual autoethnography' include the bringing together of these two approaches in a sharing of both researcher and participant-generated photographs during extended interviews. Scarles' (2010) work on the effects of tourist photography on host communities is pioneering this approach.

References

Booth, T. and Booth, W. (2003) 'In the frame: photo-voice and mothers with learning difficulties', *Disability & Society*, vol 18, no 4, pp 431-42.

Buchanan, D. (2001) 'The role of photography in organizational research: a reengineering case illustration', *Journal of Management Inquiry*, vol 10, no 2, pp 151-64.

Collier, J. (2000) 'Approaches to analysis in visual anthropology', in T. van Leeuwen and C. Jewitt (eds) *Handbook of visual analysis*, London: Sage Publications, pp 35-60.

Collier, J. and Collier, M. (1986) *Visual anthropology: Photography as research method*, Albuquerque, NM: University of New Mexico Press.

Herssens, J. and Heylighen, A. (2009) 'A lens into the haptic world', Paper presented at 'Include: International Conference on Inclusive Design', Royal College of Art, London, April.

Mitchell, J. (1994) *Picture theory*, Chicago, IL: University of Chicago Press.

Pink, S. (2006) *Doing visual ethnography*, London: Sage Publications.

Prosser, J. and Schwartz, D. (1998) 'Photographs within sociological research', in J. Prosser (ed) *Image based research: A sourcebook for qualitative researchers*, London: Falmer Press, pp 101-15.

Scarles, C. (2010) 'Where words fail, visuals ignite: opportunities for visual autoethnography in tourism research', *Annals of Tourism Research*, vol 37, no 4, pp 905-26.

Wang, C. and Burris, M.A. (1997) 'Photovoice: concept, methodology and use for participatory needs assessment', *Health and Behaviour*, vol 24, no 3, pp 369-87.

Warren, S. (2002) 'Show me how it feels to work here: using photography to research organizational aesthetics', *Ephemera: Theory and Politics in Organizations*, vol 2, no 3, pp 224-45.

Warren, S. (2005) 'Photography and voice in critical qualitative management research', *Accounting, Auditing and Accountability Journal*, vol 18, no 6, pp 861-82.

Further reading

Hurworth, R. (2003) 'Photo-interviewing for research', *Social Research Update*, vol 40, University of Surrey.

Pink, S. (2006) *Doing visual ethnography*, London: Sage Publications.

Website resources

inVisio, International Network for Visual Studies in Organizations: www.in-visio.org

PhotoVoice: www.photovoice.org

Ethnography has long been recognised as complementing survey research, but the use of ethnography as the principal source of evidence is appropriate given certain research topics or subjects (taken from Brewer, 2000, pp 164-5), when:

- the information is new and unfamiliar and 'closed questions' in surveys cannot be formulated;
- the information requested is too subtle or complex to be elicited by questionnaires and other quantitative techniques;
- actors' social meanings are required in order to illuminate the causal explanations derived from statistical explanations;
- a longitudinal element is required in order to study social processes over time;

- the subjects of the research are not amenable to study by quantitative means because they are inarticulate, elite, resistant or sensitive to research, small in number or difficult to locate geographically.

Question for discussion

- How concerned should practising ethnographers be about methodological issues and disputes?

References

Brewer, J.D. (2000) *Ethnography*, Buckingham: Open University Press.

Bulmer, M. (1982) *The uses of social research*, London: Allen & Unwin.

Burawoy, M., Blum, J., George, S., Gille, Z., Gowan, T., Haney, L., Klawiter, M., Lopez, S., O'Riain, S. and Thayer, M. (2000) *Global ethnography*, Berkeley, CA: University of California Press.

Cassell, S. and Symon, G. (2004) *Essential guide to qualitative methods in organizational research*, London: Sage Publications.

Denzin. N. (1992) 'Whose cornerville is it anyway?', *Journal of Contemporary Ethnography*, vol 21, pp 120-32.

Denzin, N. and Lincoln, Y. (1998) 'Entering the field of qualitative research', in N. Denzin and Y. Lincoln (eds) *Collecting and interpreting qualitative materials*, London: Sage Publications, pp 1-34.

Finch. J. (1986) *Research and policy*, Brighton: Falmer Press.

Goldthorpe, J. (2000) 'Sociological ethnography today: problems and possibilities', in J. Goldthorpe, *On Sociology*, Oxford: Oxford University Press, pp 65-93.

Gomm, R., Hammersley, M. and Foster, P. (2000) *Case study method*, London: Sage Publications.

Hammersley, M. (1990) *Reading ethnographic research*, London: Longman.

Hammersley, M. (1992) *What's wrong with ethnography?*, London: Routledge.

Hammersley, M. (2000) *Taking sides in social research*, London: Routledge.

Heaton, J. (2004) *Reworking qualitative data*, London: Sage Publications.

Hine, C. (2000) *Virtual ethnography*, London: Sage Publications.

Mann, C. and Stewart, F. (2000) *Internet communication and qualitative research*, London: Sage Publications.

Murthy, D. (2008) 'Digital ethnography: an examination of the use of new technologies in social research', *Sociology*, vol 42, pp 837-55.

Pink, S. (2001) *Doing visual ethnography*, London: Sage Publications.

Rist, R. (1981) 'On the utility of ethnographic research for the policy process', *Urban Education*, vol 15, pp 48-70.

Silverman, D. (1989) 'Six rules of qualitative research: a post-Romantic argument', *Symbolic Interaction*, vol 12, pp 215-30.

Silverman, D. (2001) 'The potential for qualitative research: eight reminders', in D. Silverman, *Interpreting qualitative data*, London: Sage Publications, pp 285-302.

Stanley, L. (1990) 'Doing ethnography, writing ethnography: a comment on Hammersley', *Sociology*, vol 24, pp 617-28.

Travers, M. (2001) *Qualitative research through case studies*, Thousand Oaks, CA: Sage Publications.

Walker, R. (1985) *Applied qualitative research*, Aldershot: Gower.

Wenger, C. (1987) *The research relationship: Practice and politics in social policy research*, London: Allen & Unwin.

Further reading

Atkinson, P., Coffey, A., Delamont, S., Lofland, J. and Lofland, L. (2001) *Handbook of ethnography*, London, Sage Publications.
Brewer, J.D. (2000) *Ethnography*, Buckingham: Open University Press.
Hammersley, M. and Atkinson, P. (2007) *Ethnography: Principles in practice* (3rd edn), Abingdon: Routledge.
O'Reilly, K. (2005) *Ethnographic methods*, Abingdon: Routledge.
O'Reilly, K. (2009) *Key concepts in ethnography*, London: Sage Publications.

Website resources

Economic and Social Research Council (ESRC), Economic and Social Data Service (ESDS) Qualidata, qualitative data archive, University of Essex: www.essex.ac.uk/qualidata
Economic and Social Data Service, Pioneers of Qualitative Research, ESDS Qualidata:www.esds.ac.uk/qualidata/access/pioneers.asp
CAQDAS Network, University of Surrey: www.surrey.ac.uk/sociology/research/researchcentres/caqdas/

6.11 Focus groups
Janet Smithson

A focus group is a group of usually 6–12 participants, with a moderator asking questions about a particular topic or set of issues, and involving some kind of collective activity. Interactions between participants are a distinctive characteristic of focus group methodology, differentiating it from other group interviewing techniques (Kreuger, 1998). Practical advantages to using focus groups include the chance to collect a lot of data on a topic over a short time (Bloor et al, 2001). Group discussions are intended to generate rich data as respondents rise to challenges and defend views. Focus groups provide researchers with direct access to the language and concepts that participants use to structure their experiences and to think and talk about a designated topic.

However, there are often problems with organising groups. In practice, groups tend to be based on availability rather than sample representativeness, which highlights the need for rigorous recruitment procedures to avoid such bias. Moderating focus groups can be complex, requiring training and experience, and the data obtained can be difficult to transcribe and analyse (Pini, 2002).

When are focus groups appropriate?

Focus groups are suitable for collecting group opinions, sounding out complexities around issues, for studying group interactions and for researching people who may feel more comfortable in a group setting. Focus groups with children have been shown to be very effective for collecting data in a setting which children feel comfortable with (Ronen et al, 2001). Certain topics are commonly understood to be unsuitable for the focus group context and are better left for other methods. These may include personal or sensitive topics, people's personal experiences or life histories, sexuality, infertility or financial status (see *Figure 6b*). What is viewed as private varies with age and gender, and between different cultural groups (Smithson, 2007).

Figure 6b: Topics too sensitive or personal for a focus group

In a study of parenthood and paid work, we asked about the right stage to have a child, and got bland responses with minimal discussion.

Extract 1: New parents in organisational study

1. Mod   Now we're going to talk in general about ... sort of British attitudes towards having children and when to have a child. And what, would you say there was a right time to have a child? Not just you but ... everyone?
2. Ann   It's everybody's own choice, isn't it? Everybody's ... different, aren't they?
3. Mod   [pause] Mhmm. [pause]
4. David I think everyone has to take a view as to when's the right time.
5. Mod   So there's not a particular right time?

This general question elicited socially acceptable responses. It is likely that the individuals in the group hold stronger views than this. This question was asked at the start of the focus group. It may have elicited a different response if asked later on when people were more comfortable with the group.

Conducting focus groups

In focus group handbooks (Greenbaum, 1998; Morgan and Kreuger, 1998; Kreuger and Casey, 2008), groups of 8-12 participants are generally recommended. Barbour and Kitzinger (1999) advocate fewer participants, but stress that the nature of the topics to be discussed should determine the size of the group. Smaller groups give more space for all participants to talk and explore themes in detail (Brannen et al, 2002). The number of focus groups to be conducted should reflect the type and number of any subgroups included in the study (Bloor et al, 2001). Time and money are also crucial factors, as recruiting, hosting, transcribing and analysing focus groups can be expensive.

Focus groups should last between one and two hours, with discussion following a semi-structured topic guide (Vaughn et al, 1986; see also Section 6.8 in this volume). Morgan and Bottorff (2010) point out that there is 'no single right way to conduct focus group research. Instead, researchers must understand both the possible ways of doing focus groups that are relevant for their goals and how to choose a set of methods that can meet those goals' (2010, p 581). Market research focus groups tend to have less interaction between group members, while other research focuses on the participants' agendas and is less tied to a topic guide. Data collected from focus groups can include note taking, audio-transcription and video recording. Ethical concerns of how to deal with confidentiality in a group setting need to be made explicit from the start.

Focus groups are typically homogeneous – for example, a group with a similar medical condition, or from a shared cultural background (see ***Figure 6c***). Hughes and DuMont (1993, p 776) argue that 'Within-group homogeneity prompts focus group participants to elaborate stories and themes that help researchers understand how participants structure and organize their social world'.

Figure 6c: Highlighting shared cultural norms

Extract 2: A group of British Asian male students, moderated by a British Asian woman.

1. Mod   Would you settle down with somebody without being married?
2. All   No.
3. Mod   Would you live with somebody?
4. All   No.
5. Asim We don't believe in that.
6. Mod   Is that because of your religion?
7. All   Yeah, yeah.
8. Asim Yeah, religion.

The extract shows a shared understanding of social norms in this group, and the participants talked about this collectively (Asim, line 5, 'We don't believe in that'). Homogeneous focus groups can highlight cultural and other variations by providing a 'voice' to particular groups.

Analysis of focus groups

Groups, rather than individuals within groups, are usually viewed as the unit of analysis, and focus group analyses are often criticised for treating the data as identical to individual interview data, by presenting individual quotes lifted out of the group discussion context (Wilkinson, 1998). Conversations between participants may help them to clarify for themselves what their opinion is, and people's views may change during the discussion process (Morgan and Krueger, 1993). Analysis of focus group data should consider how opinions are jointly constructed in this particular group context, rather than presenting opinions or attitudes as individual, static statements (***Figure 6d***).

Figure 6d: Jointly making sense of experiences

Extract 3: Expectant and new mothers in an organisational focus group share experiences of isolation on maternity leave.

1. Rachel   I'm going to every single coffee morning that they say you know.
2. Wendy   ... and especially if you're on maternity you sort of lose contact with your work mates, don't you?
3. Rachel   You forget how to have a conversation....
4. Wendy   And then you're not, unless you can go to things like that....

5. Rachel   Yes.
6. Wendy   Otherwise you're totally on your own.

Analysis of these views would make less sense if the group collaboration was ignored.

The role and impact of focus group participants on each other and on the perspectives that emerge have been considered in a variety of articles on interactions within focus groups, often drawing on conversation analysis or discourse analysis (see, for example, Myers, 1998, 2006; Kitzinger and Frith, 1999; Puchta and Potter, 1999, 2002; Stokoe and Smithson, 2002; Wilkinson, 2004).

However, Morgan (2010) suggested that the unit of analysis depends on the researcher's interpretative framework; if the research has a practical purpose, individual quotes may be sufficient. Duggleby (2005) outlined three distinct types of focus group data: individual data, group data and group interaction data, and Onwuegbuzie et al (2009) built on this to produce a framework of analysis techniques appropriate for each type. Whichever analytical techniques and approaches are chosen, the analysis needs to take into account the social context of the talk, for instance, the moderator's impact as a gendered and embodied being, and the tendency to produce socially appropriate answers.

New ways of using focus groups

The growing popularity of online and telephone focus group methods is partly due to cost and time savings, but there are methodological and ethical reasons for choosing them (Gaiser, 2008). Frazier et al (2010) used telephone and face-to-face focus groups to include people in remote areas and people with health problems, and concluded that the quality of the data was equivalent to equally lively conversations. An online focus group method can similarly bring together geographically distant participants (Bloor et al, 2001), and people with disabilities or illnesses (Kralik et al, 2006), as well as enabling people to discuss sensitive issues anonymously. Ways of regulating participation to limit possible misuse include making contact individually with participants before the online group occurs, and having clear moderating rules.

Conclusion

The focus group method enables a wide variety of opinions to be given and considered, and interactive techniques observed. A strength of focus group methodology is the possibility for research participants to develop ideas collectively, bringing forward their own priorities and perspectives, to create theory grounded in the participants' experience and language. Limitations of focus groups are that they can be difficult in practice both at the recruitment stage and the transcription and analysis stages, and they are unsuitable for some topics and research questions. The key to using focus groups successfully is in ensuring that their use is consistent with the objectives and purpose of the research.

Question for discussion

- What are the ethical and practical considerations that researchers need to be aware of when planning to conduct focus groups around sensitive or personal issues?

References

Barbour, R.S. and Kitzinger, J. (1999) *Developing focus group research: Politics, theory and practice*, London: Sage Publications.

Bloor, M., Frankland, J., Thomas, M. and Robson, K. (2001) *Focus groups in social research*, London: Sage Publications.

Brannen, J., Lewis, S., Nilsen, A. and Smithson, J. (eds) (2002) *Young Europeans, work and family: Futures in transition*, London: Routledge.

Duggleby, W. (2005) 'What about focus group interaction data?', *Qualitative Health Research*, vol 15, pp 832-40.

Frazier, L.M, Miller, V.A., Horbelt, D.V., Delmore, J.E., Miller, B.E. and Paschal, A.M. (2010) 'Comparison of focus groups on cancer and employment conducted face to face or by telephone', *Qualitative Health Research*, vol 20, no 5, pp 617-27.

Gaiser, T.J. (2008) 'Online focus groups', in N. Fielding, R.M. Lee and G. Blank (eds) *The SAGE handbook of online research methods*, London: Sage Publications, pp 290-306.

Greenbaum, T. (1998) *The handbook for focus group research*, London: Sage Publications.

Hughes, D. and DuMont, K. (1993) 'Using focus groups to facilitate culturally anchored research', *American Journal of Community Psychology*, vol 21, no 6, pp 775-806.

Kitzinger, C. and Frith, H. (1999) 'Just say no? The use of conversation analysis in developing a feminist perspective on sexual refusal', *Discourse and Society*, vol 10, no 3, pp 293-316.

Kralik, D., Price, K., Warren, J. and Koch, T. (2006) 'Issues in data generation using email group conversations for nursing research', *Journal of Advanced Nursing*, vol 53, no 2, pp 213-20.

Kreuger, R.A. (1998) *Analyzing and reporting focus group results. Focus group kit, Volume 6*, Los Angeles, CA: Sage Publications.

Kreuger, R.A. and Casey, M.A. (2008) *Focus groups: A practical guide for applied research*, Thousand Oaks, CA: Sage Publications.

Morgan, D.L. (2010) 'Reconsidering the role of interaction in analyzing and reporting focus groups', *Qualitative Health Research*, vol 20, no 5, pp 718-22.

Morgan, D.L. and Bottorff, J.L. (2010) 'Advancing our craft: focus group methods and practice', *Qualitative Health Research*, vol 20, no 5, pp 579-81.

Morgan, D.L. and Kreuger, R.A. (1993) 'When to use focus groups and why', in D.L. Morgan (ed) *Successful focus groups*, London: Sage Publications, pp 1-19.

Morgan, D.L. and Kreuger, R.A. (1998) *The focus group kit*, Los Angeles, CA: Sage Publications.

Myers, G. (1998) 'Displaying opinions: topics and disagreement in focus groups', *Language in Society*, vol 27, pp 85-111.

Myers, G. (2006) '"Where are you from?" Identifying place', *Journal of Sociolinguistics*, vol 10, pp 320-43.

Onwuegbuzie, A.J., Dickinson, W.B., Leech, N.L. and Zoran, A.G. (2009) 'A qualitative framework for collecting and analyzing data in focus group research', *International Journal of Qualitative Methods*, vol 8, no 3, pp 1-21.

Pini, B. (2002) 'Focus groups, feminist research and farm women: opportunities for empowerment in rural social research', *Journal of Rural Studies*, vol 18, no 3, pp 339-51.

Puchta, C. and Potter, J. (1999) 'Asking elaborate questions: focus groups and the management of spontaneity', *Journal of Sociolinguistics*, vol 3, pp 314-35.

Puchta, C. and Potter, J. (2002) 'Manufacturing individual opinions: market research focus groups and the discursive psychology of attitudes', *British Journal of Social Psychology*, vol 41, pp 345-63.

Ronen, G.M., Rosenbaum, P., Law, M. and Streiner, D.L. (2001) 'Health-related quality of life in childhood disorders: a modified focus group technique to involve children', *Quality of Life Research*, vol 10, no 1, pp 71-9.

Smithson, J. (2007) 'Using focus groups in social research', in P. Alasuurtari, L. Bickman, and J. Brannen (eds) *The SAGE handbook of social research methods*, London: Sage Publications, pp 356-71.

Stokoe, E.H. and Smithson, J. (2002) 'Gender and sexuality in talk-in-interaction: considering conversation analytic perspectives', in P. McIlvenny (ed) *Talking gender and sexuality*, Amsterdam: John Benjamins, pp 79-110.

Vaughn, S., Shay Schumm, J. and Sinagub, J. (1996) *Focus group interviews in education and psychology*, Thousand Oaks, CA: Sage Publications.

Wilkinson, S. (1998) 'Focus group methodology: a review', *International Journal of Social Research Methodology, Theory and Practice*, vol 1, no 3, pp 181-204.

Wilkinson, S. (2004). 'Focus group research', in D. Silverman (ed) *Qualitative research: Theory, method, and practice*, Thousand Oaks, CA: Sage Publications, pp 177-99.

Further reading

Bloor, M., Frankland, J., Thomas, M. and Robson, K. (2001) *Focus groups in social research*, London: Sage Publications.

Kreuger, R.A. and Casey, M.A. (2008) *Focus groups: A practical guide for applied research*, Thousand Oaks, CA: Sage Publications.

Morgan, D. (ed) (2010) *Qualitative Health Research*, Special Issue on Focus Groups, May, vol 20, no 5.

Website resources

Forum for Qualitative Social Research (FQS): www.qualitative-research.net/fqs/fqs-eng.htm
The Social Research Association: www.the-sra.org.uk
Online Qualitative Data Analysis: onlineqda.hud.ac.uk

6.12 Biographical method
Joanna Bornat

The term 'biographical method' is used in relation to a wide range of approaches, auto/biography, life writing, narrative, biographical interpretive, ethnographic, oral history and personal documents, as Roberts (2002) has shown. Although each has its own particular history and usage, and some have had longer periods of evolution than others, in social science research they share certain characteristics. These include the eliciting of a personal account and the valuing of subjectivity; a concern for accuracy and sensitivity in representation; engagement with the complexities of transcription; explorations of levels of meaning; and identifying the dynamics of biographical construction, all while grasping the significance of temporality for researched and researcher. Together, biographical methods are generative of rich data and engaging methodological debate, hence their popularity in social science investigations.

The use of biographical methods has a continuity within the history of sociology which proponents point to when justifying the approach. C. Wright Mills argues this with his mid-20th-century critique of the polarities of 'grand theory' and detailed 'abstracted' empiricism in US social science, which, he argued, had come to neglect the vision of the founders, Durkheim, Weber and Mannheim. He called for a 'sociological imagination' that '… enables us to grasp history and biography and the relations between the two in society' (Mills, 1959, p 6). From this, he argued, it is possible to understand society in terms of the variety of the individuals whose actions create it and in turn to understand how societies and their histories determine the lives of those individuals. At the turn of the century, Ken Plummer made the same argument, highlighting Mills' 'Marxist inspired' plea (Plummer, 2001, p 6) to centre the human subject in social science research. In doing so he traces social science methods back to the work of the Chicago School and their recording of the voices of people in the streets, neighbourhoods and working and family life, for investigations of poverty, delinquency and organisations, precursors of 'a style which now constitutes a large and growing underbelly of social science research' (Plummer, 2001, p 2).

From the many variants, three are presented here: narrative, oral history and the biographical interpretive method. Each represents a different tradition and approach to data elicitation, interpretation and analysis. All place great emphasis on securing the confidence of an interviewee in an interview situation that guarantees support and consent. All rely on a range of sampling techniques, ranging from single interview case studies to theoretical or structured samples drawn from defined populations, often augmented by snowballing techniques. In what follows, distinguishing features of each of the three methods are outlined.

Narrative methods

Proponents of narrative methods make links directly to the Chicago School; however, they move beyond the simple telling of a story of events, situations or relationships to interpretations that are indicative of language use, cultural symbols and understandings of the self. Although narrative methods encompass a range of approaches, what is shared among them is 'attention to sequences of actions' relating to individual actors (Riessman, 2008, p 11). To take a narrative approach is to identify within accounts how stories are constructed, culturally and socially, and to read the text for what might be unspoken or against the grain of what has been articulated. With a late 20th-century post-modern interdisciplinary eclectism, proponents draw on phenomenological, semiotic and discourse and conversational analysis to inform their engagement with texts, seeking out themes, turning points and considering truth and validity in what is presented (Andrews et al, 2008).

Such approaches to analysis require an interview style that is conversational rather than directive, more ethnographic than focused, with a search for detail and particularity. Narratives elicited may come in a range of forms, from the concisely told story of an incident or an event, to the more general and discursively constructed account covering a transition or a whole lifetime.

Drawing on traditions in linguistic analysis, Riessman advocates a 'structural narrative' approach, focusing on forms within spoken and written text which provide clues to intention and meaning as tellers make use of emotions, reasoning and performance in their communications. Forms of analysis vary, given the range of research contexts in which narrative approaches have been used, for example, in medicine (Greenhalgh and Hurwitz, 1998), anthropology (Skultans, 1998), psychology (Sarbin, 1986; Crossley, 2000), media studies (Ryan, 2004), feminist studies (Personal Narratives Group, 1989), linguistics (Bamberg, 1997), organisation studies (Denning, 2005), history (Roberts, 2001) and literature (Hawthorn, 1985). These suggest a plethora of possible analytical opportunities.

Oral history

Oral history, with its combining of methods drawn from history and sociology, places much emphasis on the significance of temporal context and memory, with the recorded spoken word as the main source. Debates about the validity of memory developed from arguments establishing realist credentials for oral history (Thompson, 2000), to positions where the interview is viewed as an object in itself, with a shape and totality determined by an individual's life events and the social relationship of the interview. As Portelli, the leading Italian oral historian argues, the oral history interview '... tells us less about *events* than about their *meaning*' (original emphases), and that 'the unique and precious element which oral sources possess in equal measure is the speaker's subjectivity' (1981, p 67).

Oral history in its early and subsequent development has drawn on sociology for methods of structuring data collection. While some studies rest on only a handful of interviewees (see, for example, Thomson, 1994; Portelli, 1997), others have found ways to representivity with theoretical sampling, with opportunistic recruitment or snowballing (see, for example, Bertaux and Bertaux-Wiame, 1981; Lummis, 1987; Thompson, 2000; Bornat, 2002; Hammerton and Thomson, 2005; Thompson and Bauer, 2006; Bornat et al, 2009). Typically, the interview schedule will take a life history approach with particular aspects or topics given emphasis depending on the focus of the study. As for data analysis, a range of approaches, some more familiar to historians and some to sociologists, is typically followed (see, for example, Cándida Smith, 2002). In the main these would be recognisable as thematic in approach, drawing directly or indirectly on the type of constant comparative analysis and theme searching typical in grounded theory (Glaser and Strauss, 1968).

An early commitment to a form of history making which seeks to give expression to marginalised voices in studies of ageing, ethnicity, class, gender, colonialism, tradition, displacement, resistance and exclusion (Perks and Thomson, 2006; Abrams, 2010), and which emphasises the importance of language, emotions and the qualities of orality, presents something of an ethical challenge, as Thompson and others have pointed out (Borland, 1991; Portelli, 1997; Thompson, 2000; Bornat and Diamond, 2007). The tension lies in the commitment to the ownership rights of interviewees in their spoken words while seeking ways to interpret without creating distance with the resulting output, be this a book, aural, visual or online publication (Frisch, 1990).

Biographical interpretive method

The main features of the biographical interpretive method developed from the work of Schütze, writing in 1980s Germany, who was greatly influenced by Anselm Strauss, Howard Becker, Erving Goffman and others. The use of an in–depth interview method and its subsequent analysis that Schütze developed and which has been further refined by Gabriele Rosenthal (2004), requires the separating out of the chronological story from the experiences and meanings which interviewees provide. The process depends on an understanding that what is told will be a product of conscious consideration as well as unconscious cultural and social processes. At its heart it requires a psychosocial approach to generating and interpreting data, with methods elaborated by Tom Wengraf (2001), and Prue Chamberlayne and colleagues (2000, 2004; see also Section 4.14 in this volume).

At the heart of the method is an approach to interviewing which is dependent on the generation of an open narrative, in which the interviewer plays a minor role. Typically the interview begins with a single opening invitation to speak. This is followed by more focused questioning informed by the interview and research questions. Analysis involves the elaborate codification of the interview in such a way as to identify themes, having separated out the 'lived life' from the 'told story' in the transcribed interview (Wengraf, 2001, p 231). Text segments are then labelled as to whether they are descriptive, argumentative, reporting, narrative or evaluative biographical. In this way, biographical interpretive analysis addresses the data with hypotheses that draw on significant segments of text. Wengraf (2001) details the procedure for interpreting biographical data, showing how hypotheses and counter-hypotheses are drawn up and explored, preferably by groups of people working together, as to their likely effect on someone's life. This phenomenological approach to understanding biographical data focuses on the individual's perspective within an observable and knowable historical and structural context, and what it is like to be the person describing their lives and the various decisions, turns and patterns of that life (Wengraf, 2001, pp 305-6).

Question for discussion

- What are the main methodological challenges presented by a biographical approach and what are the rewards?

References

Abrams, L. (2010) *Oral history theory*, London: Routledge.

Andrews, M., Squires, C. and Tamboukou, M. (eds) (2008) *Doing narrative research*, London: Sage Publications.

Bamberg, M. (ed) (1997) *Oral versions of personal experience: Three decades of narrative analysis: A special issue of the* Journal of Narrative and Life History, Mahwah, NJ: Lawrence Erlbaum.

Bertaux, D. and Bertaux-Wiame, I. (1981) 'Life stories in the baker's trade', in D. Bertaux (ed) *Biography and society*, London: Sage Publications, pp 169-89.

Borland, K. (1991) '"That's not what I said": interpretive conflict in oral narrative research', in S.B. Gluck and D. Patai (eds) *Women's words: The feminist practice of oral history*, London: Routledge, pp 63-75.

Bornat, J. (2002) 'Doing life history research', in A. Jamieson and C. Victor (eds) *Researching ageing and later life*, Buckingham: Open University Press, pp 117-34.

Bornat, J. and Diamond, H. (2007) 'Women's history and oral history: developments and debates', *Women's History Review*, vol 16, no 1, pp 19-39.

Bornat, J., Henry, L. and Raghuram, L. (2009) '"Don't mix race with the specialty": interviewing South Asian geriatricians', *Oral History*, vol 38, no 1, pp 74-84.

Cándida Smith, R. (2002) 'Analytical strategies for oral historians', in J.F. Gubrium and J.A. Holstein (eds) *Handbook of interview research: Context and method*, London: Sage Publications, pp 711-31.

Chamberlayne, P., Bornat, J. and Apitzsch, U. (eds) (2004) *Biographical methods and professional practice*, Bristol: The Policy Press.

Chamberlayne, P., Bornat, J. and Wengraf, T. (eds) (2000) *The turn to biographical methods in social science*, London: Routledge.

Crossley, M.L. (2000) *Introducing narrative psychology: Self, trauma and the construction of meaning*, Buckingham: Open University Press.

Denning, S. (2005) 'Transformational innovation: a journey by narrative', *Strategy & Leadership*, vol 33, no 3, pp 11-16.

Frisch, M. (1990) *A shared authority: Essays on the craft and meaning of oral and public history*, Albany, NY: State University of New York Press.

Glaser, B. and Strauss, A. (1968) *The discovery of grounded theory*, London: Weidenfeld & Nicholson.

Greenhalgh, T. and Hurwitz, B. (1998) *Narrative based medicine: Dialogue and discourse in clinical practice*, London: BMJ Books.

Hammerton, A.J. and Thompson, P. (2005) *'Ten Pound Poms': Australia's invisible migrants*, Manchester: Manchester University Press.

Hawthorn, J. (1985) *Narrative: From memory to motion pictures*, London: Edward Arnold.

Lummis, T. (1987) *Listening to history*, London: Hutchinson.

Mills, C.W. (1959) *The sociological imagination*, Oxford: Oxford University Press.

Perks, R. and Thomson, A. (2006) *The oral history reader* (2nd edn), London: Routledge.

Personal Narratives Group (1989) *Interpreting women's lives: Feminist theory and personal narratives*, Bloomington, IN: Indiana University Press.

Portelli, A. (1981) 'What makes oral history different?', *History Workshop*, vol 12, pp 96-107.

Portelli, A. (1997) 'The massacre at Civitella val di Chiani (Tuscany, June 29, 1944): myth and politics, mourning and common sense', in A. Portelli (ed) *The battle of Valle Giulia: Oral history and the art of dialogue*, Madison, WI: University of Wisconsin Press, pp 140-60.

Plummer, K. (2001) *Documents of life 2*, London: Sage Publications.

Riessman, C. (2008) *Narrative methods for the human sciences*, London: Sage Publications.

Roberts, B. (2002) *Biographical research*, Buckingham: Open University Press.

Roberts, G. (ed) (2001) *The history and narrative reader*, London: Routledge.

Rosenthal, G. (2004) 'Biographical research', in C. Seale, G. Gobo and J. Gubrium (eds) *Qualitative research practice*, London: Sage Publications, pp 48-64.

Ryan, M.-L. (ed) (2004) *Narrative across media the languages of storytelling*, Lincoln, NE: University of Nebraska Press.

Sarbin, T.R. (1986) 'The narrative as a root metaphor for psychology', in T.R. Sarbin (ed) *Narrative psychology: The storied nature of human conduct*, New York: Praeger, pp 3-21.

Skultans, V. (1998) 'Anthropology and narrative', in T. Greenhalgh and B. Hurwitz (eds) *Narrative based medicine: Dialogue and discourse in clinical practice*, London: BMJ Books, pp 225-33.

Thompson, P. (2000) *The voice of the past* (3rd edn), Oxford: Oxford University Press.
Thompson, P. and Bauer, E. (2006) *Jamaican hands across the Atlantic*, Kingston: Ian Randle Publishers.
Thomson, A. (1994) *Anzac memories: Living with the legend*, Melbourne: Oxford University Press.
Wengraf, T. (2001) *Qualitative research interviewing*, London: Sage Publications.

Further reading

Abrams, L. (2010) *Oral history theory*, London: Routledge.
Riessman, C. (2008) *Narrative methods for the human sciences*, London: Sage Publications.
Wengraf, T. (2001) *Qualitative research interviewing*, London: Sage Publications.

Relevant organisations

The Centre for Narrative Research: www.uel.ac.uk/cnr/
Oral History Society: www.ohs.org.uk

6.13 Documents in qualitative research
Jane Lewis

Documentary sources are possibly the most taken-for-granted in any research project; after all, we can all read a document and take notes. However, most first-year undergraduates are familiar with the problem of what to take notes on, and the danger of ending up with a sheaf of notes that approaches book-length. This problem often re-emerges at the beginning of a piece of original research, and much depends on approaching documents with good research questions.

Documents take many forms and many researchers do not get beyond published sources, in the form of books or government reports and policy papers, together with press comment, which gives an indication as to how a policy was received and debated. Diaries and memoirs of political figures can also be useful for understanding the debates and position of actors. Personal documents also exist for ordinary people, which may sometimes give an idea as to how policies were received. However, these are relatively rare and difficult to trace. The Mass Observation Archive at the University of Sussex has collected written observations from a large number of people for the whole of the post-war period. These are unpublished, archival sources. The unpublished records of government departments exist in The National Archives (for a guide to these, see Land et al, 1992; Bridgen and Lowe, 1998). There is, usually, a '30-year rule' on these documents, meaning that they only become publicly available after 30 years have elapsed.

It is also important to think about the order in which to read documentary materials: for example, newspapers before or after government documents? There are no rules to be followed here and a lot depends on how much knowledge the researcher has about the subject. It is often a good idea to begin with source materials that are more generally focused and that therefore provide more context (thus, newspapers before government documents). But, if the research is relatively small and tightly focused, it may be better to plunge into policy documents that are precisely related to the topic, establish which ones are particularly important, and then read 'around' those in particular to get more of an idea of how they have been received (thus, documents before newspapers). Given that researchers are likely to begin many investigations with some form of documentary research (it is always necessary to acquire a good substantive knowledge of the topic before interviewing, for example), it is also important to keep detailed references. This is crucial for footnoting and endnoting, but also, as interpretations of the material mature, it is inevitable that notes on a particular point will have to be re-checked.

Historical documents

Historical documents are by no means easy to define. Most historians believe that it is not possible to write good history without the perspective that comes only with a certain amount of distance from the events. Those interested in social policy and social work issues rarely venture beyond the point at which archival sources cease to become available. The main archival sources for social policies are the records of government departments, in the form of memoranda, correspondence, minutes of meetings and the like, which in the UK are held at The National Archives. Local record offices, which may hold personal papers as well as local government archival materials, operate a similar rule. Researchers may also want to pursue the records of important actors. Voluntary organisations, for example, may keep their own archival records, or may have deposited them elsewhere (for example, the records of the Family Planning Association are kept by the Wellcome Library for the History of Medicine; see Cook et al, 1984, for a guide to post-war historical documents).

Archival records provide very detailed data and are usually very time consuming to use. Nevertheless, they provide close insights into policy making. Printed and published documents may provide a variety of competing explanations for the introduction of a particular policy. The records of the government department involved will usually contain documents and correspondence (including reference to major actors outside government) that discuss the various options and enable the researcher to see how a decision was reached. Thus, John Macnicol (1980) was able to conclude that the introduction of Family Allowances in 1944 had much more to do with the aim of keeping down wages than with any desire to do something about the falling birth rate, child poverty or rewarding women's domestic work (all issues in the preceding debate). To work with this level of data is very different from working with a Green or White Paper. It is easy to become submerged in the detail, and once again, the researcher needs to keep a firm grasp of both the research questions and the larger picture. Unless the research topic is explicitly historical, it is unlikely that the researcher will be able to explore every avenue offered by archival sources or extensively cross-check what is said by one government department with another.

There are also what are often referred to as *primary printed documents*. Historians often divide their bibliographies into 'primary' and 'secondary' sources. While secondary sources provide a commentary on a particular historical event and usually offer an interpretation of it, a primary source is something written by a contemporary and published at the time. It is important to put such source material, which may take the form of books, pamphlets or articles published in newspapers and magazines, alongside the archival material; wherever possible evidence should be 'triangulated', that is, examined using three different types of source material.

Finally, it is important that the researcher is clear about why it is necessary to look at historical documents. Many doctoral theses in social policy and some in social work have an 'historical chapter', in which the author traces the evolution of a particular policy, usually in the post-war period. If the researcher is working with the idea of *path dependence*, for example, which stresses the importance of the role that historical experience plays in forming mutually consistent expectations on the part of actors in the absence of central guidance, then history (and institutions) obviously 'matters'. But all too often there is no clear justification for the historical chapter, and at worst it is implied that somehow, knowing about the past will explain the present. However, mere chronology cannot explain. The researcher must have a particular reason for investigating the past. Thus, Bridgen and Lewis (1999) sought to investigate how the boundary between health and social care, which is particularly striking in the UK context, had been constructed over time; archival documents revealed the extent to which this had been a struggle over the respective responsibilities of health and local authorities.

Contemporary documents

Contemporary documents may appear somewhat easier to deal with; at least the researcher does not have to pay so much attention to the different levels of data and how to integrate them. However, there may be greater problems to do with selection and decisions about the weight to attach to a particular document. The interrogation of contemporary material also presents particular challenges in respect of meaning and context. It will be rare that a document that is agreed by several key actors to be important has not already been analysed by an academic or policy analyst. However, a researcher pursuing an original piece of research must go back to the original document because his or her research questions will in all likelihood be different to those informing existing commentaries.

Any government document must first be located in terms of the debates giving rise to it, inside and outside Parliament and the civil service. Thus, for example, a researcher investigating family policies under the Labour governments of 1997-2010 and reaching first for what appears to be the earliest relevant document – the 1998 Home Office's Green Paper, *Supporting families* – has to know something about the debates about family change before he or she can even begin to appreciate the significance of the title, with its reference to 'families' rather than 'the family'. The researcher will come to the document with particular research questions, but he or she also needs to be able to assess the document on its own terms: what is included and excluded, where the emphasis falls and why, what it reveals about the role of the state in this difficult policy arena. *Grey literature* – that is, ephemeral pamphlet material from 'think tanks' and campaign groups, now often available on the internet – will help to elucidate the position adopted by key actors, just as Parliamentary Debates will help to refine the researcher's understanding of the position of politicians active in the debate. Thus, if the document *Supporting families* proves material in answering the questions the researcher has about family policies, reading it is only to begin the process of understanding what it contains. If the researcher wanted to look at family policies in the early and mid-1990s, there would be no such explicitly titled document to go to. But this does not mean that there were no family policies. Indeed, the researcher interested in early 21st-century family policies would miss much of the most important material if his or her attention were to be confined to the 1998 Home Office document. An exploration of social policy development must pay attention to the process of problem definition and to the theoretical literature on the way in which policy gets made (Ham and Hill, 1997; Stone, 1997; Sabatier, 1999; see also Chapter One, this volume) if the researcher is to be successful in tracking down documents that might be relevant.

Researchers are likely to face an overwhelming amount of documentary evidence, including the possibilities opened up through the internet (see **Box 6f**). Finding an entry point, a logical way of proceeding and reaching a judgement about how to weigh the evidence, is crucial. In respect of the latter, a basic appreciation of who is speaking (and why that person or organisation), when they are speaking (and why then), how they are defining the problem and where they are looking for solutions (and why) will always serve the researcher well in terms of placing the text and evaluating its claims.

Question for discussion

• What kinds of documents are useful for the study of social policy and why?

References

Bridgen, P. and Lewis, J. (1999) *Elderly people and the boundary between health and social care 1946-1991*, London: Nuffield Trust.

Bridgen, P. and Lowe, R. (1998) *Welfare policy under the Conservatives, 1951-1964: A guide to documents in the Public Record Office*, London: Public Record Office.

Cook, C., Waller, D., Leonard, J. and Leese, P. (1984) *The Longman guide to sources in contemporary British history*, London: Longman.

Ham, C. and Hill, M. (1997) *The policy process in the modern state* (3rd edn), London: Prentice Hall.

Home Office (1998) *Supporting families*, London: Home Office.

Land, A., Lowe, R. and Whiteside, N. (1992) *The development of the welfare state 1939-51: A guide to documents in the public record office*, London: Public Record Office.

Macnicol, J. (1980) *The movement for family allowances 1918-45*, London: Heinemann.

Sabatier, P.A. (1999) *Theories of the policy process*, Boulder, CO: Westview Press.

Stone, D. (1997) *Policy paradox: The art of political decision-making*, New York: W.W. Norton.

Further reading

Scott, J. (1990) *A matter of record*, Cambridge: Polity Press.

Website resource

The National Archives: www.nationalarchives.gov.uk

Box 6f: Documents in qualitative research: web analysis
Patrick Carmichael

The development of internet technologies, and the World Wide Web in particular, has had significant impacts in many fields of human activity, and research is no exception. The sheer volume of data and range of material now available online has allowed a wider audience for documents which were previously only accessible by a few. It has allowed the development of 'virtual' museums and archives whose original content is scattered across the world, and promoted new computer-aided research methods. Recent initiatives such as the development of secure digital repositories (Lavoie and Dempsey, 2004), moves towards 'open' publishing of public data and standards like the Data Documentation Initiative (Blank and Rasmussen, 2004) are providing researchers with new opportunities to preserve, publish, exchange, find and re-use qualitative data.

Documents available online range from digitised versions of those originally on paper or other materials (scanned images of historical documents, for example) through to those which have been published online but which parallel or replicate conventional formats (such as government reports published both as web pages and downloadable files to be printed out), to those 'born digital', some of which challenge conventional notions of what a 'document' is. These may consist of hypertexts (sets of linked pages connected to each other and to external resources by 'anchors' and 'references'), but may also incorporate media other than text: images, audio, video, embedded animations, visualisations and simulations. The emerging technologies of the 'semantic web' (Feigenbaum et al, 2007) allow the production of much richer hypertexts than the web pages with which we are now familiar, and allow the generation of documents 'on the fly' from sources across the internet, evolving as data sources themselves change.

These possibilities have led to new forms of representation, which blur the distinction between data, document, production and even performance. Daniel's (2007) acclaimed interactive 'project' (the term deliberately chosen for this very reason), published in the online journal *Vectors*, consists of accounts of life in a Californian women's prison presented in a way that is, like the accounts themselves, fluid and fragmented. An interactive web interface allows the reader to choose a path through the project, skimming the surface or 'drilling down' through the hypertext to explore a particular narrative or theme in detail. In other cases, online documents can be annotated with contextual information, interpretations or translations, which can be displayed according to the preferences of the reader. These resources are typically the products of collaborations between technologists and archivists, curators or researchers, and represent only a small proportion of the documents available online.

In contrast, the group of technologies characterised as 'Web 2.0' allows the rapid production of textual content and new forms of publishing and interaction. Particularly significant are the self-published 'blogs', which range from collections of governmental or corporate press releases to personal commentaries, diaries, testimonies and 'citizen journalism'; and wikis, which allow collaborative writing and editing through a web interface, usually, but not always, with attribution of contributions. Unlike conventional documents, these forms of text may change rapidly and are subject to highly variable editorial practices. As such, they have become important means by which established checks and constraints (peer review, editorial control, censorship, injunctions) can be circumvented (see Hendler, 2010, for a discussion of the emerging role of wikis as sites for 'whistleblowers'). For the researcher, wikis and blogs can be valuable 'documents' if the primary concern is to gauge opinion or to explore particular perspectives, but the partiality and transience of many such resources should always be taken into account.

Internet technologies allow not only innovative forms of document and new models of authorship; they also support and enable new research practices. Online collaboration environments allow document sharing and collaborative analysis, with original documents, analyses and researchers potentially being widely dispersed. Similarly, both the publication online of existing documents, and the ease with which contemporary researchers can archive documents, open up new possibilities for secondary analysis, longitudinal analysis of sets of related documents and the revisiting of 'classic studies' (Savage, 2005).

Questions for discussion
- With the advent of web technologies, does it make sense to still talk about 'documents'?
- What are the potential benefits and pitfalls of using 'Web 2.0' sources such as wikis and blogs as sources in research?
- How does the availability of documents online impact on ethical considerations such as informed consent, confidentiality and attribution?

References
Blank, G. and Rasmussen, K.B. (2004) 'The data documentation initiative: the value and significance of a worldwide standard,' *Social Science Computer Review*, vol 22, no 3, pp 307-18.

Daniel, S. with Loyer, E. (2007) 'Public secrets', *Vectors*, vol 2, no 2 (www.vectorsjournal.org/projects/index.php?project=57).

Feigenbaum, L., Herman, I., Hongsermeier, T., Neumann, E. and Stephens, S. (2007) 'The semantic web in action', *Scientific American*, vol 297, no 12, pp 90-7.

Hendler, C. (2010) 'The story behind the publication of the WikiLeaks's Afghanistan logs', *Columbia Journalism Review*, July 28 (www.cjr.org/campaign_desk/the_story_behind_the_publicati.php).

Lavoie, B. and Dempsey, L. (2004) 'Thirteen ways of looking at ... digital preservation', *D-Lib Magazine*, vol 10, nos 7-8 (www.dlib.org/dlib/july04/lavoie/07lavoie.html).

Savage, M. (2005) 'Revisiting classic qualitative studies', *Forum: Qualitative Sozialforschung*, vol 6, no 1, Art 31 (www.nbn-resolving.de/urn:nbn:de:0114-fqs0501312).

Further reading
Blank, G., Fielding, N. and Lee, R. (eds) (2008) *The SAGE handbook of online research methods*, London: Sage Publications.

Hine, C. (ed) (2005) *Virtual methods: Issues in social research on the internet*, Oxford: Berg.

Website resources
The British Library is the national Library of the UK and has large (and increasing) collections of digital materials: www.bl.uk

The CAQDAS Networking Project at the University of Surrey provides support in all aspects of qualitative data analysis, including working with online sources, collaborative analysis and web-based analysis tools: www.surrey.ac.uk/sociology/research/researchcentres/caqdas/

The ESRC Economic and Social Data Service (ESDS) provides support to both data providers and researchers who want to use online data, including advice on citation, analysis and ethical issues. They also host a number of significant collections of qualitative data: www.esds.ac.uk

The International Data Documentation Initiative (which is mainly of interest to data providers) provides some interesting insights into future possibilities for online research: www.ddialliance.org

The UK National Archives is the UK government's official archive, containing records ranging from digitised versions of historically significant documents to specialised collections of text, images, audio and video: www.nationalarchives.gov.uk/

The University of Southern California's *Vectors* journal mentioned above is 'open access': www.vectorsjournal.org/

In the US, the Library of Congress fulfils a similar role to the British Library: www.loc.gov

6.14 Using the internet for the collection of qualitative data

Henrietta O'Connor and Clare Madge

The methodological potential offered by online research methods for those engaged in social research is now widely acknowledged. The internet presents researchers with a myriad of opportunity for interacting with participants in innovative ways and generating both quantitative data (Dillman, 2007; Dillman et al, 2009; see also Section 5.7), and conducting qualitative research (Mann and Stewart, 2000; James and Busher, 2009). Indeed, 'Internet-based data collection is now part of the mainstream canon of methodological choices' (Stewart and Williams, 2005, p 395). In particular, online methods are increasingly being used by researchers with an interest in issues relating to the fields of social policy and social work, such as health issues (Stewart and Williams, 2005; Ayling and Mewse, 2009) and research with young people (Fox et al, 2007). Qualitative research techniques such as participant observation, discourse analysis and ethnographic research have been used in a virtual setting to study online communities and specialised websites (Hine, 2000; Domínguez et al, 2007; Rybas and Gajalla, 2007). The suitability of cyberspace as an interview venue has also been explored and it is asynchronous interviews, characterised by the fact that they do not take place in 'real time', which have received the most attention to date (Bampton and Cowton, 2002; Orgad, 2005, 2006; James and Busher, 2006). Synchronous or 'real time' online interviewing has received less attention (Gaiser, 1997; Chen and Hinton, 1999; Mann and Stewart, 2000; O'Connor and Madge, 2001) but is nonetheless a valuable way of using the internet to collect qualitative data and is an increasingly accessible method given innovations in online communication technologies such as instant messaging (Stieger and Goritz, 2006).

An example of a pioneering internet-based research project, 'Cyber-parents' (O'Connor and Madge, 2001), is discussed below to highlight some of the issues involved when collecting data through virtual synchronous interviewing. For this particular project, which was initiated to examine how new parents use the internet as an information source and as a form of social support, data were collected using online synchronous interviews. During the interview process a number of interesting differences emerged between online and offline interviews, raising a series of questions about this methodological approach: 'Does the electronic interviewer require different skills to engage the interviewees and build up rapport than the "real world" interviewer?' 'What impact does the virtual setting have on the researcher's role in the research process?' 'Does the disembodying quality of online research alter the interview process?' It is to this final question we now turn (see Madge and O'Connor, 2002, for a discussion of the other questions).

The online interview is a process that usually removes the tangible presence of the researcher (unless a webcam is used), so bodily presence (age, gender, hairstyle, clothes) become invisible. According to Chen and Hinton (1999, para 13.2), this results in the potential of the virtual interview to become the 'great equaliser', with the interviewer having less control over the interview process. This, we feel, is a rather utopian vision. In our case we posted photographs of ourselves on our dedicated project web pages and shared our background interests with the female interviewees, both important processes in creating rapport and breaking down the researcher–researched relationship, giving 'clues' to our bodily identities. This may have influenced the interview process, making the white, technologically proficient, 30-something, women feel more comfortable in talking to us. Additionally, in the situation of a virtual interview, the speed of typing dominates the interaction rather than the most vocal personality, which, although having the potential to disrupt power relations among groups, has the possibility of marginalising people with poor or slow keyboard skills. Moreover, the 'equaliser' argument glosses over the structural power hierarchies that enable researchers to set the agenda, to ask the questions and to benefit from the results of the interview process.

Nevertheless, we must acknowledge that for the interviewees, the ability to mask their identity changed some accepted norms of behaviour and probably allowed them a more active voice in shaping the tone and atmosphere of the interview. Despite Gaiser's (1997, p 142) warning that virtual interview discussion may be '… superficial and playful', with interviewers finding it more difficult to persuade participants to '… reconceptualise their behaviour … to participate in substantive discussion', we found that a relaxed and informal atmosphere was created which provided a platform for successful interviewing. Indeed, as is common in conventional situations when women interview other women, the interviews all provided high levels of self-consciousness, reflexivity and interactivity. Whether this was owing to the nature of the interviewees (self-selected, motivated, frequent online users), or owing to the nature of the subject matter, clearly being very close to the hearts of the women involved, it is difficult to judge. In our virtual interviews we did not encounter the much written about '… aura of suspicion' surrounding '… stranger-to-stranger communication in cyberspace' (Smith, 1997, p 40). From this research example, it is clear that the advantages of conducting synchronous online interviews in an environment without the temporal or spatial restrictions of 'real world' interaction are many. For example, the internet offers the potential for interfacing with groups of people who are widely geographically distributed or those difficult to reach via conventional research approaches (Mann and Stewart, 2000; Reeves, 2000; Pendergrass et al, 2001). The indicative data gained from online research may also be useful for research on population subgroups and for exploratory analysis (Lamp and Howard, 1999; Burrows et al, 2000). Savings of time and money, for example, the elimination of costs associated with the transcription process, are also to be recommended. As Ayling and Mewse (2009, p 575) have recently argued: 'Online qualitative research is valuable in its own right, and ... the advantages considerably outweigh the difficulties, particularly in accessing individuals who might not present to other research settings to discuss experiences that would otherwise be too difficult to talk about'.

Although online research methods are no longer in their infancy, many of their potentials and limitations are still to be discovered and evaluated. Moreover, it is actually unlikely that there will be a radical transformation of social policy and social work research through ICT (information and communication technology), but rather it offers some interesting new potentials in terms of making visible '... arenas of social life previously distant and concealed' (Crang et al, 1999, p 11). However, Phippen (2007, p 1) argues that 'while there is a significant body of social research that considers the online world, the methods used to research such things are what one might describe as traditional in nature'. He argues that the vast majority of research methods used to explore the virtual world to date have been 'conventional' in nature, and have involved a translation of on-site methods (including focus groups, surveys and interviews) to the online environment. He suggests that there is now the need to explore more novel methods that might be used to examine the virtual world. This call, especially to examine Web 2.0 technologies, has been mirrored by Beer and Burrows (2007). The exciting potential offered by such Web 2.0 technologies for collecting data are yet to be explored fully: for example, the potential of using blogs as research diaries, social networking sites as locations of virtual interviews, and digital story telling for performative social science. Indeed, the fast pace of change of technological innovation means that new technological developments are likely to continue to shape innovative methodological approaches in the future.

Question for discussion

- What are the potentials and limitations of online synchronous interviews for social policy research?

References

Ayling, R. and Mewse, A.J. (2009) 'Evaluating internet interviews with gay men', *Qualitative Health Research*, vol 19, no 1, pp 566-76.

Bampton, R. and Cowton, C.J. (2002) 'The e-interview', *Forum Qualitative Sozialforschung/ Forum: Qualitative Social Research*, vol 3, no 2 (www.qualitative-research.net/index.php/fqs/article/view/848).

Beer, D. and Burrows, R. (2007) 'Sociology and, of and in Web 2.0: some initial considerations', *Sociological Research Online*, vol 12, no 5 (www.socresonline.org.uk/12/5/17.html).

Burrows, R., Nettleton, S., Please, N., Loader, B. and Muncer, S. (2000) 'Virtual community care? Social policy and the emergence of computer mediated social support', *Information, Communication and Society*, no 3, pp 1-16.

Chen, P. and Hinton, S.M. (1999) 'Realtime interviewing using the World Wide Web', *Sociological Research Online*, vol 4, no 3 (www.socresonline.org.uk/4/3/chen.html).

Crang, M., Crang, P. and May, J. (1999) *Virtual geographies*, London: Routledge.

Dillman, D.A. (2007) *Mail and internet surveys: The tailored design*, 2nd edn, Hoboken, NJ: John Wiley.

Dillman, D.A., Phelps, G., Tortora, R., Swift, K., Kohrell, J., Berck, J. and Messer, B. L. (2009) 'Response rate and measurement differences in mixed-mode surveys using mail, telephone, interactive voice response (IVR) and the internet', *Social Science Research*, vol 38, pp 1-18.

Domínguez, D., Beaulieu, A., Estalella, A., Gómez, E., Schnettler, B., and Read, R. (2007) 'Virtual ethnography', *Forum Qualitative Sozialforschung/Forum: Qualitative Social Research*, vol 8, no 3 (www.qualitative-research.net/fqs-texte/3-07/07-3-E1-e.htm).

Fox, F., Morris, M. and Rumsey, N. (2007) 'Doing synchronous online focus groups with young people: methodological reflections', *Qualitative Health Research*, vol 17, no 4, pp 539-47.

Gaiser, T. (1997) 'Conducting online focus groups: a methodological discussion', *Social Science Computer Review*, vol 15, no 2, pp 135-44.

Hine, C. (2000) *Virtual ethnography*, London: Sage Publications.

James, N. and Busher, H. (2006) 'Credibility, authenticity and voice: dilemmas in online interviewing', *Qualitative Research*, vol 6, no 3, pp 403-20.

James, N. and Busher, H. (2009) *Online interviewing*, London: Sage Publications.

Lamp, J.M. and Howard, P.A. (1999) 'Guiding parent's use of the internet for newborn education', *Maternal-Child Nursing Journal*, no 24, pp 33-6.

Madge, C. and O'Connor, H. (2002) 'On-line with e-mums: exploring the internet as a medium for research', *Area*, no 34, pp 92-102.

Mann, C. and Stewart, F. (2000) *Internet communication and qualitative research*, London: Sage Publications.

O'Connor, H. and Madge, C. (2001) 'Cyber-mothers: online synchronous interviewing using conferencing software', *Sociological Research Online*, vol 5, no 4 (www.socresonline.org.uk/5/4/o'connor.html).

Orgad, S. (2005) 'From online to offline and back: moving from online to offline relationships with research informants', in C. Hine (ed) *Virtual methods: Issues in social research on the internet*, Oxford: Berg, pp 51-65.

Orgad, S. (2006). 'The cultural dimensions of online communication: a study of breast cancer patients' Internet spaces', *New Media & Society*, vol 8, no 6, pp 877-99.

Pendergrass, S., Nosek, M.A. and Holcomb, J.D. (2001) 'Design and evaluation of an internet site to educate women with disabilities on reproductive health care', *Sexuality and Disability*, no 19, pp 71-83.

Phippen, A. (2007) 'How virtual are virtual methods?', *Methodological Innovations Online*, vol 2, no 1 (http://erdt.plymouth.ac.uk/mionline/public_html/viewarticle.php?id=43&layout=html).

Reeves, P.M. (2000) 'Coping in cyberspace: the impact of internet use on the ability of HIV-positive individuals to deal with their illness', *Journal of Health Communication*, no 5, pp 47-59.

Rybas, N. and Gajjala, R. (2007) 'Developing cyberethnographic research methods for understanding digitally mediated identities', *Forum Qualitative Sozialforschung/Forum: Qualitative Social Research*, vol 8, no 3 (www.qualitative-research.net/index.php/fqs/article/view/282/620).

Smith, C. (1997) 'Casting the net: surveying an internet population', *Journal of Computer Mediated Communication*, vol 3, no 1 (http://jcmc.indiana.edu/vol3/issue1/smith.html).

Stewart, K. and Williams, M. (2005) 'Researching online populations: the use of online focus groups for social research', *Qualitative Research*, vol 5, no 4, pp 395-416.

Stieger, S. and Göritz, A.S. (2006) 'Using instant messaging for internet-based interviews', *CyberPsychology and Behavior*, vol 9, no 5, pp 552-9.

Further reading

Ess, C. (2009) *Digital media ethics*, Cambridge: Polity Press.

Fielding, N., Lee, R.M. and Blank, G. (eds) (2008) *The SAGE handbook of online research methods*, London: Sage Publications.

Hewson, C., Yule, P., Laurent, D. and Vogel, C. (2003) *Internet research methods*, London: Sage Publications.

James, N. and Busher, H. (2009) *Online interviewing*, London: Sage Publications.

Mann, C. and Stewart, F. (2000) *Internet communication and qualitative research*, London: Sage Publications.

Website resources

Centre for Research into Innovation, Culture and Technology at Brunel University: www.brunel.ac.uk/depts/crict/vmesrc.htm

Cyber-parents research project: www.geog.le.ac.uk/baby/

ESRC Research Programme: Virtual society? The social science of electronic technologies (home page): http://virtualsociety.sbs.ox.ac.uk/

Exploring online methods in a virtual training environment: www.geog.le.ac.uk/orm/

Mapping Cyberspace: www.MappingCyberspace.com

Study Site for Online Interviews in Real Time: www.sagepub.com/salmonsstudy/default.htm

PART THREE: THE ANALYSIS OF QUALITATIVE DATA

6.15 Analysing qualitative data: an overview
Alan Bryman and Saul Becker

The next four sections address different approaches to the analysis of qualitative data. Sometimes, *content analysis* (see Section 5.8) is considered to be an approach to the analysis of qualitative data. It does indeed do this, in that the technique can be employed to analyse unstructured data such as newspaper articles, semi-structured interview transcripts, diaries and novels. However, content analysis draws on a quantitative research strategy in order to analyse such data.

The approaches to qualitative data analysis covered in this section are:

* grounded theory
* discourse analysis
* conversation analysis
* narrative analysis.

Unlike content analysis, each of these approaches to analysing qualitative data seeks to preserve the nature of the data, albeit in different ways and degrees. That is to say, they aim for an analytic approach that is consistent with the underlying principles of qualitative research. Grounded theory is best thought of as a general strategy that can be applied to a wide range of qualitative data. Narrative analysis is typically employed as a means of unpacking the underlying themes that run through such sources of data as interview transcripts. The search for themes often underpins grounded theory as well as other approaches to qualitative data analysis. Uncovering themes is a feature of many accounts, such as when Irvine (2011) writes in relation to her research on people suffering mental health problems who were in employment:

> Interviews were audio recorded (with participants' permission) and transcribed verbatim. Data were then summarized under a set of thematic headings and managed using the qualitative data analysis programme MaxQDA. Analysis involved detailed examination of the data for emerging themes and categories within each of the study's research questions. Analysis and reporting remaining grounded in the narratives and language of the study participants. (Irvine, 2011, p 757)

The search for underlying themes is also apparent in the 'Framework' approach discussed in **Box 6g**. Discourse analysis and conversation analysis take the detailed examination of language use as their point of departure. For the social policy and social work researcher these two approaches offer alternative ways of understanding interactions and pose new challenges. For example, discourse analysts and conversation analysts might analyse the transactions between a benefit claimant and personal adviser, or between a social worker and someone requiring an assessment of their needs. Here, the focus of analysis is not on the content specifically, but on the ways in which talk is used to construct the interaction and to confer roles on each party. Understanding the process of these and similar interactions adds an additional dimension to an appreciation of what goes on in the delivery and implementation of social policy and social work.

Section 6.16 also covers coding and computer-assisted qualitative data analysis. Coding was also encountered in the previous chapter, but, as Section 6.16 shows, the goals of coding in qualitative data analysis are somewhat different in that the links between data and concepts are somewhat less fixed and more fluid there than they are in connection with quantitative data (see Chapter Five). In qualitative research, codes are often revised and are a way of leading to concepts rather than being quantitative markers of pre-existing concepts. Whereas the quantitative researcher typically devises a number of categories for each variable and each category is then allocated a code in terms of which the researcher then allocates people, newspapers, behaviour or whatever, in qualitative research the codes are gradually built up out of the data. Indeed, in some approaches to analysing qualitative data, there is a very flexible relationship between data collection and analysis, as in grounded theory, where data are often analysed in the course of data collection to give the researcher ideas about which cases or contexts should be focused on in later stages of the enquiry. Coding in this kind of context needs to be flexible to accommodate changes in the direction of the research that might be suggested by further data collection. **Box 6g** describes such an approach that draws on standard techniques like coding and brings them together into a coherent analytic strategy.

Coding is sometimes a controversial activity in qualitative data analysis: narrative analysts, for example, sometimes argue that it undermines the underlying coherence of what people say in interviews. However, it is a common way of handling qualitative data and beginning the process of qualitative data analysis, and moreover, it is increasingly conducted using computer software, although as Potter and Hepburn observe in Section 6.17, the use of such software tends to be eschewed in discourse analysis. This development and some of the issues involved in coding and its implementation with the aid of computer software is also covered in Section 6.16.

A further issue that qualitative researchers have to consider is the use of quotations from interviews and conversations with the people they study. The use of verbatim quotations to provide evidence of themes that are extracted from the data is widespread. Thus, in her study of mental health and employment, Irvine writes: 'Quotations are in participants' own words, but have been edited for anonymity, brevity and clarity in some cases' (Irvine, 2011). Thus, she provides evidence of one theme referred to as 'motivation to return from absence – the role of sick pay' by summarising the meaning of the theme for her participants and by providing illustrative quotations as evidence, such as:

> 'To be brutally honest, I came back because I was gonna go down to half pay by six months, so there was a sort of pressure thing there.... I wasn't particularly compos mentis when I came back, I don't think.' (male, 40s)

> 'After about four months I said "I've got to get back into work" because you only get six months on full pay, which is a big incentive.' (male, 50s) (both quoted in Irvine, 2011, p 760)

The use of quotations such as these is an issue that has been given scant attention over the years, but in Section 6.20, Corden and Sainsbury provide a discussion of researchers' approaches to the use of such verbatim quotations.

Reference

Irvine, A. (2011: in press) 'Fit for work? The influence of sick pay and job flexibility on sickness absence and implications for presenteeism', *Social Policy & Administration*, vol 45.

Box 6g: Critical qualitative theory and 'Framework' analysis
Matt Barnard

Over the last 25 years, the National Centre for Social Research (NatCen) has been one of the most prominent organisations arguing for the importance of using qualitative research within policy-orientated research. Over that period, the approaches to qualitative research used by NatCen have developed organically, drawing on a wide range of schools of thought but also responding to the needs of an applied context. Within this context NatCen has become most associated with a tool for data management called 'Framework' (see below), but this tool in fact implies and is nested within a range of assumptions and principles that form a coherent and distinct approach to qualitative research and qualitative data analysis. Many of these assumptions and principles were set out explicitly and implicitly in NatCen's book *Qualitative research practice* (edited by Jane Ritchie and Jane Lewis, 2003) along with other related publications (see Ritchie and Spencer, 1994; Given, 2008). However, there has never been a document that has brought together the ideas contained in these documents into a single account of the approach. This gap has recently been filled by the development of a new concept, 'critical qualitative theory' (CQT), and a set of **six key tenets** that can be used to identify and define the approach developed by NatCen.

As its name suggests, CQT is firmly placed within the philosophical school of thought known as 'critical realism'. This means that ontologically, reality is seen as something that exists independently of those who observe it (in opposition to social constructionism), but epistemologically, that reality is only accessible through the perceptions of people and is therefore necessarily affected by their interpretations (in opposition to positivism) (Archer et al, 1998). Within this context, the aim of CQT is to explore both people's individual perceptions but also what those perceptions tell us about the social world more broadly. This philosophical base leads directly to the **first tenet** of CQT, which is a belief in the methodological and practical compatibility of qualitative and quantitative methods. Many of NatCen's studies combine both approaches, and this is seen as appropriate and desirable, based on the belief that both methodologies can be viewed as existing within the same philosophical paradigm (critical realism) but are used to answer different kinds of research question (see also Section 4.4 on mixed methods research).

The philosophical basis for CQT also leads directly to a **second tenet** of the approach, which is to maintain an inductive–deductive balance during the research process. It does this in a 'U-shaped' way: at the start, existing research and theory is used to design and plan a study; in the field and during early analysis the focus is on understanding and exploring participants' views and experiences from their point of view; then, towards the end of the analysis, the findings of the research are put back into the context of theory and existing research. However, throughout the process meta-concepts, such as foundations', 'trigger', 'mechanism' and 'impact', are used to help make sense of the data.

The **third tenet** of CQT, which has profound implications for the analysis of qualitative data, is that qualitative research is generalisable in terms of the range and diversity of the findings although not the prevalence. As such, its aim is to produce findings that are meaningful without enumeration. This does not mean that it is not possible or desirable to do further (quantitative) research to determine the prevalence of views or impacts. Instead, it is argued that the aim of qualitative research is to produce findings that do not *need* enumerating to be meaningful and that it is not *possible* to enumerate these findings using a purely qualitative approach.

The **fourth tenet** of CQT is that the process of data collection provides the bedrock for the formal analytical stage. The aim of an interview within CQT is to map the full range of views and experiences of an individual and to probe fully to gain a rich understanding of a participant's perspective. Unlike some other approaches, within CQT there is a strong requirement for interpretation to be heavily grounded in and supported by the data. It should also be noted that reflecting its roots in critical realism, within CQT efforts are made to be 'objective' during data collection.

The **fifth tenet** of CQT is that it is possible to distinguish conceptually data management and interpretation. Data management is a process of coding that involves using pre-defined conceptual boxes that are then applied to the data. Interpretation involves using the data to create meaningful categories based on judgements of the 'essence' and 'similarity' of individual aspects of the data. This leads on to the **sixth tenet** of CQT, which is that it is possible and desirable to do both thematic and case-based analysis. That is, the process of analysis should involve looking at themes that are common across the dataset but also looking within individual cases and comparing cases to each other to search for typologies and higher order explanations. As such, the importance of Framework as an approach to data management becomes clear. In order to do both thematic and case-based analysis, a data management tool is required that facilitates the comparison between particular aspects of accounts, but also preserves the individual accounts as a whole. However, a CQT approach can use other data management tools and approaches, and equally Framework can be used by approaches to qualitative research other than CQT.

The Framework tool for data management

Framework is a case-and-theme-based tool for managing qualitative data that was developed by Jane Ritche and Liz Spencer in the 1980s while they were at NatCen and is now widely used in social policy research (Pope et al, 2006). The data are displayed within a matrix format, with each row assigned to an individual case (often, a single participant) and each column assigned a theme. The matrix is not unlike the kind of spreadsheet that is used in statistical software programs such as SPSS, which has cases going across (as rows) and variables going down (as columns), but instead of numbers or fixed codes, the cells contain data that need to be interpreted. The column headings or themes are chosen after a process of familiarisation with the dataset and a good Framework will have themes that feel logical and match the way participants talk about things, meaning that it is easy to know where to place data and where to find it when the interpretation stage begins. It will also have themes that are relevant to most participants in the study. Although there will always be some empty cells in the matrix, a well-managed dataset will not have too many as this would make it hard to compare themes across cases. On the other hand, none of the cells should be too large, which means that a theme should be specific enough that the analyst is not trying to cram too much data into each cell.

Another key element of the Framework tool is that the material that is put into the cells is not verbatim text but a summary. There are two reasons for this. The first is that a key advantage of Framework is that the analyst can physically look down and across cells; in other words, that the data are displayed in a very accessible way. This means it is much easier to get an overall sense of what people are saying. But in order to do this the cells cannot be too large, and it is only possible to control the size easily by summarising the data. If verbatim data are used, very large chunks need to be included otherwise the extracts become so decontextualised that it is difficult to understand what is going on.

The other reason for summarising is for the very reason that it abstracts from, or reduces, the verbatim text, and so moves the analysis on a small step. Eventually, all the data will have to be abstracted to the level of concepts and categories, as that is the fundamental aim of qualitative data analysis. Framework enables this to be done in a series of small steps, rather than one big jump, and summarisation begins this process. This is not to say that the analyst will never go back to the verbatim text. It does mean, however, that the process of managing data also involves some interpretation. This is not seen as a negative feature, because in order to analyse it the data have to be interpreted at some point.

Framework is a conceptual tool that can be operationalised in a number of ways. Originally, it was done on A3 sheets of paper, using a ruler and a pencil. For a long time NatCen used Excel to create the matrix, but recently it has developed and launched a bespoke piece of software called FrameWork, which permits the display of summarised data in a matrix output, but has the additional advantage of the summaries being hyperlinked to the verbatim text.

Questions for discussion
- What are the implications of using a critical qualitative theory (CQT) approach for qualitative analysis rather than another approach such as grounded theory?
- What implications does the data management approach that the analyst chooses have for the kind of analysis they can do?

References

Archer, M., Bhaskar, R., Collier, A., Lawson, T., and Norrie, A. (1998) *Critical realism*, London: Routledge.

Given, M. (2008) *The SAGE encyclopaedia of qualitative research methods*, London: Sage Publications.

Pope, C., Ziebland, S. and Mays, N. (2006) 'Analysing qualitative data', in C. Pope and N. Mays (eds) *Qualitative research in health care*, Blackwell Publishing: BMJ books, pp 63-81.

Ritchie, J. and Lewis, J. (2003) *Qualitative research practice: A guide for social science students and researchers*, London: Sage Publications.

Ritche, J. and Spencer, L. (1994) 'Qualitative data analysis for applied policy research', in A. Bryman and B. Burgess (eds) *Analyzing qualitative data*, London: Routledge, pp 172-94.

Relevant organisation
National Centre for Social Research (NatCen): www.natcen.ac.uk

6.16 Grounded theory, coding and computer-assisted analysis

Graham R. Gibbs

Much qualitative research analysis of social reality requires that we understand the 'symbolic world' of those we study, that is, the meanings and interpretations that people apply to their experiences. The researcher may start with some understanding of a phenomenon, even before finishing the collection of data, but this understanding expands during the course of the project by continually checking data against interpretations until we are satisfied we have a full grasp of the phenomenon. The procedures most researchers use to manage and prepare data for such analysis are quite straightforward although time consuming. These involve:

- Compiling the corpus of data (field notes, transcripts, images, audio and video recordings). Despite the growing popularity of images, audio and video data in research, most researchers still transcribe their interviews and observations as they find this form of textual data much easier to use in the subsequent stages of analysis.
- Detailed reading of the transcripts (or listening to the recordings, or looking at the video and images), both to gain an impression of their content as a whole and to begin to generate ideas, hunches, categories and themes that interpret the phenomenon. At this point many researchers find it helpful to write a précis of each case.
- Explicitly searching for categories and patterns in the data, marking the data with category (or 'code') labels. In this process of coding the researcher marks passages of text (or parts of images) as being examples of things represented by the code names.
- Constructing thematic outlines using the codes to lay out the sequence in which topics will be considered.

In the past, these procedures involved the physical manipulation of data (literally cutting up transcripts and sorting the cuttings into sets of associated extracts kept in folders or files), but nowadays the process can be conducted using software (although some still prefer 'manual' methods, especially for small-scale studies). Whatever approach is used, good data management is key. Qualitative data are voluminous – Miles and Huberman's (1994) evaluation of innovation in a school system produced over 3,000 pages of field notes. It is vital that the analysis is not partial (leaving out significant data or giving more weight to some data) and is comprehensive (does not omit key phenomena), but above all is worked up from the data rather than reflecting a pre-existing idea supported by highly selective examples. The danger of what Silverman (2001, pp 222-3) refers to as anecdotalism is rife as there is always a temptation to give undue weight to particularly colourful, surprising or intriguing examples in the data even if they are not actually common, typical or theoretically significant (see also Section 6.20 in this volume).

Grounded theory

The most commonly used analytic approach which also most closely reflects the emphasis on working 'up from the data' is Glaser and Strauss' (1967) *grounded theory*. In the 1960s many researchers undertook qualitative research by using their reading of the literature and theory and their prior experience in the field to construct an a priori list of categories that they would then use to mark up the data. Glaser and Strauss rejected this. For them, not only should the researcher maintain an open mind in order to find new phenomena in the data (the process of *open coding*), but far from 'testing' existing ideas (or hypotheses) the analyst should take an *inductive* approach, that is, be concerned with constructing analytic codes and categories from the data and discovering new theory. For Glaser and Strauss it was important to maintain *theoretical sensitivity* by immersing oneself in the data and staying open to new ideas, interpretations and ultimately theories which would be grounded in the data. This sensitivity enables the researcher to generate or discover ways of categorising the data.

The principal way of ensuring that the coding is thorough and consistent is the *constant comparative method*. The researcher begins by examining 'incidents' recorded in fieldwork or mentioned in interviews, incidents being discrete acts or the expression of an attitude by respondents (Becker and Geer, 1960). Each is coded into as many theoretical categories as possible (open coding). Categories may be derived from terms used by participants (characterising aspects of their work, for example), from interpretations developed by the analyst and sometimes from existing analytic constructs (found, for example, in the literature). Before assigning a code to a passage of text or other data, the method requires that we re-examine all incidents or passages previously coded using the same category. This recursive approach ensures that theoretical properties of categories are fleshed out as analysis proceeds. It helps identify different categories and the relationship between categories. Thus, conceptualisation emerges during coding and this is aided and recorded by the writing of 'analytic memos' on the meaning and significance of the code or category. Such memos specify the properties of the codes, define relationships between categories and identify gaps, such as potential related codes.

There is a tendency for initial coding approaches to produce very descriptive codes, coded passages that are decontextualised (devoid of meaning because they are removed from their context) and, above all, too many codes. Therefore, most grounded theorists and researchers adopting similar coding approaches describe different levels or forms of coding at different stages of the analysis and recommend that the analyst moves from descriptive codes to more conceptual or theoretical codes while at the same time reducing the number of key codes being used. Glaser (1978) and Charmaz (2006) refer to two stages, initial, open or substantive coding and later, theoretical coding. Strauss and Corbin (1998), who describe three stages, open coding, axial coding and selective coding, have developed a range of hints, suggestions and heuristics about how the codes may be refined from stage to stage. Glaser (1992) has criticised this for being too mechanistic and for forcing theories onto the data rather than allowing them to emerge, but most researchers find steps and heuristics very helpful for guiding their own practice. One procedure that most grounded theorists agree on is that of dimensionalising codes – recognising that they have properties or dimensions. Open coding often develops a number of related codes that can be gathered together as types, forms, occurrences, consequences, causes or settings for other, more abstract, analytic and theoretical codes. Such grouping reduces the number of codes and creates more theoretical categories. In the later stages of analysis the researcher concentrates on clarification, simplification and 'reduction' of the theory to limit the number of categories germane to the emerging theory. Ongoing analysis can now focus just on those categories and they become 'theoretically saturated', that is, the dimensions and properties of the category include all the variations found in the data. It becomes immediately apparent whether a subsequent incident requires modification of the category. Where it does, the category is coded and compared to existing categories; if not, the incident need not be coded.

Over the years there has developed a range of distinct accounts of grounded theory, typified by the disagreements between the originators Glaser and Strauss. Such differences may account for the fact that, while the majority of qualitative researchers claim adherence to grounded theory, inquiry into their working practices reveals substantial variation and deviation from the steps laid down in the canonical texts (Fielding and Lee, 1998). As long as the research is based on thorough and exhaustive analysis, this probably does not matter much, but as Seale (2001, pp 658-9) notes, it all too often leads to a superficial 'pattern analysis' that simply reports major themes without any attempt to develop theory or investigate more subtle relationships and processes. A key recent development has been the proposal by Charmaz (2006) of a constructivist grounded theory. She has argued, *pace* Denzin and Lincoln (1994), that the essential principles of grounded theory are compatible with the view that theory rather than simply being discovered is actually constructed by the analyst during analysis by engaging, interacting and interpreting the respondent.

Other analytic approaches

The popularity of the coding method can be gauged by the fact that several other approaches to qualitative analysis have embraced many of the key ideas of grounded theory. Thus the *template analysis* approach (Crabtee and Miller, 1992; King, 2004) and *interpretative phenomenological analysis* (Smith et al, 2009) borrow many procedures from grounded theory. In addition, both take a more explicit case-by-case approach that owes much to another, earlier approach, *analytic induction*. According to this method, developed by Znaniecki (1934), following the initial identification of a phenomenon and the inductive generation of a hypothesis about it that should apply to all the cases, the researcher engages in repeated rounds of checking each case against the hypothesis. When a case does not fit, either the hypothesis is tweaked to make it fit, or if that is not possible, the researcher revises the definition of the phenomenon to which the hypothesis applied. Analytic induction has not been much used in recent decades, partly because of the recognition of its logical flaws (Hicks, 1994) but also because it was overtaken by the popularity of coding approaches. Nevertheless, although template analysis and interpretative phenomenological analysis use coding, they have retained a case-by-case iterative development of initial coding as a key mechanism for the evolution of analysis.

There has been a revival of interest in pure case-by-case approaches prompted by Ragin's (1987) 'qualitative comparative analysis'. The method compares outcomes across multiple cases. It uses mathematics to systematically identify 'universal conditions' which are always present in particular combinations when the phenomenon occurs. Much of this is now done with the assistance of dedicated software programs, and recent developments have allowed for the inclusion of fuzzy sets that encompass outcomes that are present only to a certain degree.

Computer-assisted qualitative data analysis

Many qualitative researchers now use dedicated, computer-assisted qualitative data analysis software (CAQDAS) to assist their analysis. Most such software supports the coding approach to analysis by including facilities to code and revise the coding of data, organise the coding scheme and retrieve coded data. Data that may be analysed include text (including tables and pdf documents), images, audio or video recordings. **Box 6h** provides an example of the use of CAQDAS.

The programs support the annotation of data and the writing and linking of analytic memos. Many now include a range of text retrieval or textual analysis functions that range from sophisticated text searching (multiple terms, searching for similar words or words with the same root, and searching in defined passages) through to concordance, word frequencies, keyword in context and linked cluster diagrams. Most also support the integration of variable-based data (also called attributes or families), such as quantitative and categorical data about cases, respondents or settings which can be linked to the qualitative data. Several programs now support the integration of GIS (geographical information systems) data.

Box 6h: An illustration of the use of computer-assisted qualitative data analysis in social policy research
Graham R. Gibbs

The COPING Project (2010) is a large, EU-funded, mixed methods, multinational study of the resilience of young children who have a parent in prison. It consists of various stages that included a large-scale quantitative survey of the children of prisoners and their families, and semi-structured interviews with a subset of these. Over 300 interviews were held across four countries, Germany, Romania, Sweden and the UK.

The research team decided to undertake a thematic analysis of the interviews, based broadly on grounded theory principles, and to use QSR NVivo software to record this analysis, integrate it with quantitative data and manage the data and analysis across the four countries. Some team members had experience of the software, and others had used other packages that supported thematic coding and retrieval in similar ways. It was also judged that NVivo had the best support for integrating the quantitative data the research team already had with the qualitative analysis.

The research team established a standardised project for each country to use with three main parts: standardised file naming, standardised attributes and an initial coding scheme. Standardised file naming avoided duplicate files and meant the team could identify interviews from the same family from the file name. These names were also used for the cases in NVivo so that case data (essentially the interviews) could be linked with case attribute data. The latter comprised a subset of variables from the quantitative survey carried out in the first stage of the project, and a few scale-like questions included in the semi-structured interviews. Using standard names, these survey data were easily imported into the project using a spreadsheet file and the attributes created were used in analytic queries to investigate the relationship of attributes, like ethnicity and loneliness, with the codes created in the qualitative analysis.

An initial coding scheme was developed from three sources: the interview schedule, a small number of initial interviews undertaken by members of the UK team and the joint previous experience and analytical knowledge of the team. It was discussed and agreed on at a multinational team meeting. While this meant it was only partly grounded in the data, it did enable each country team to start from a common perspective. Each code was accompanied by a short explanation, which was often also a set of ideas for subcodes. For example:

Resilience
Covers indicators/signs of resilience or stress. Indicators: courage/bravery/heroism. Stress factors, for example, isolation withdrawal/low mood/behavioural problems. Sleep habits/ sleep patterns. Undisturbed sleep/nightmares/night terrors.

The research team fully expected this frame to be modified, and indeed it was. Modifications took two forms. First, in coding the interviews in the standard grounded way, researchers came across new ideas and phenomena not envisaged at the start of the project. Second, analytic teams needed to include extra codes to cover some of the issues that were specific to their country, reflecting cultural differences, legal particularities and differences in social and professional practice.

Website resource
The COPING Project: www.coping-project.eu/

A key function in most programs is a sophisticated retrieval facility for coded passages, images etc. At its simplest this means the researcher can quickly retrieve all the data coded in a particular way – the equivalent of the paper-based researcher looking through all the data collected in one folder or file. But the programs go much further than this in allowing searches for both Boolean and non-Boolean combinations of codes, and codes and variables. Boolean searches use terms such as 'and', 'or' and 'not' so one can undertake a search for and retrieve data that is coded at one code 'or' at another code, or data at one code 'and' which is in a case that has a certain attribute or variable value. Non-Boolean searches allow for the combining of codes using terms like 'near' or 'overlapping'. Such retrievals are very quick and easy to do and allow the analyst to undertake a rapid investigation of a wide range of relationships between codes and between codes and variables to investigate things like gender and age variations or the coincidence in the data of several ideas and concepts or talk about those ideas. Using software does not guarantee good quality analysis, but at least it provides the tools so that researchers can undertake well-organised, thorough, well-documented and grounded analyses.

Question for discussion

- In what ways can a coding scheme be developed and how can the researcher tell when codes are theoretically saturated?

References

Becker, H. and Geer, B. (1960) 'Participant observation: the analysis of qualitative field data', in R.N. Adams and J. Preiss (eds) *Human organisation research*, Homewood, IL: Dorsey Press, pp 267-89.

Charmaz, K. (2006) *Constructing grounded theory: A practical guide through qualitative analysis*, London: Sage Publications.

Crabtree, B.F. and Miller, W.L. (eds) (1992) *Doing qualitative research*, London: Sage Publications.

Denzin, N.K. and Lincoln, Y.S. (eds) (1994) *Handbook of qualitative research*, London: Sage Publications.

Fielding, N. and Lee, R.M. (1998) *Computer analysis and qualitative research*, London: Sage Publications.

Glaser, B. (1978) *Theoretical sensitivity*, Mill Valley, CA: Sociology Press.

Glaser, B. (1992) *Emergence vs forcing: Basics of grounded theory analysis*, Mill Valley, CA: Sociology Press.

Glaser, B. and Strauss, A. (1967) *The discovery of grounded theory*, Chicago, IL: Aldine.

Hicks, A. (1994) 'Qualitative comparative analysis and analytic induction: the case for the emergence of the social security state', *Sociological Methods and Research*, vol 23, pp 86-113.

King, N. (2004) 'Using templates in the thematic analysis of text', in C. Cassell and G. Symon (eds) *Essential guide to qualitative methods in organizational research*, London: Sage Publications, pp 256-70.

Miles, M. and Huberman, A. (1994) *Qualitative data analysis: An expanded sourcebook*, Beverley Hills, CA: Sage Publications.

Ragin, C. (1987) *The comparative method: Moving beyond qualitative and quantitative strategies*, Berkeley, CA: University of California Press.

Seale, C.F. (2001) 'Computer-assisted analysis of qualitative interview data', in J.F. Gubrium and J.A. Holstein (eds) *Handbook of interview research: Context and method*, Thousand Oaks, CA: Sage Publications, pp 651-70.

Silverman, D. (2001) *Interpreting qualitative data. Methods for analysing talk, text and interaction*, London: Sage Publications.

Smith, J.A., Flowers, P. and Larkin, M. (2009) *Interpretative phenomenological analysis: Theory, method and research*, London: Sage Publications.

Strauss, A.L. and Corbin, J.M. (1998) *Basics of qualitative research: Techniques and procedures for developing grounded theory*, Thousand Oaks, CA: Sage Publications.

Znaniecki, F. (1934) *The method of sociology*, New York: Farrar and Rinehart.

Further reading

On qualitative software and its relationship to qualitative analysis:

di Gregorio, S. and Davidson, J. (2008) *Qualitative research design for software users*, Maidenhead: Open University Press, McGraw-Hill.

Lewins, A. and Silver, C. (2007) *Using software in qualitative research: A step-by-step guide*, London: Sage Publications.
On the procedures of qualitative data analysis:
Bernard, H.R. and Ryan, G.W. (2010) *Analyzing qualitative data: Systematic approaches*, Los Angeles, CA: Sage Publications.
Boeije, H. (2010) *Analysis in qualitative research*, Los Angeles, CA: Sage Publications.
Bryant, A. and Charmaz, K. (eds) (2010) *The SAGE handbook of grounded theory*, Los Angeles, CA: Sage Publications.
Gibbs, G.R. (2007) *Analyzing qualitative data*, London: Sage Publications.

Website resources

For those interested in qualitative software, see: www.surrey.ac.uk/sociology/research/researchcentres/caqdas/
For those interested in qualitative analysis, see: onlineqda.hud.ac.uk/

6.17 Discourse analysis
Jonathan Potter and Alexa Hepburn

Discourse analysis refers to a cluster of methods and approaches, including continental discourse analysis, critical discourse analysis (see ***Box 6j***), discursive psychology and conversation analysis (see Section 6.18 and ***Box 6k***), that focus on the role of *talk* and *texts* in social life. Different forms of discourse analysis place different emphasis on specific practices of interaction and the broader discursive resources that underpin that interaction. With an emphasis on practices, Anssi Peräkylä (1995) studied the different features that come to make up AIDS counselling (the way questions are asked, dreaded matters broached, advice delivered, and so on). This was within the conversation analytic tradition of Harvey Sacks and Emanuel Schegloff. With an emphasis on resources, Margaret Wetherell and Jonathan Potter (1992) studied the various symbolic systems (or 'interpretative repertoires') that white majority group members draw on to justify ethnic inequalities and to undermine moves towards social change. This is within the critical discourse analytic tradition, and is influenced by the ideas of Michel Foucault.

Discourse research varies in its methodological procedures and assumptions. The following stages are common in many discourse studies:

1 *Question formulation*. Discourse research typically asks questions of the form 'What is an X?' or 'How is X done?'. What is a complaint, say, and how do complaints get done, get resisted or break down? These kinds of questions contrast to common social science questions such as 'What is the effect of X on Y?'.
2 *Data collection*. Although they traditionally focused on open-ended interviews, discourse analysts have increasingly concentrated on audio or video records of actual interaction in everyday or institutional settings. Studies have worked with data collected therapy and counselling, 911 calls, police interrogations, food talk at family mealtimes, mediation and so on.
3 *Data management*. Digital audio and video allows instant access, easy searching filing and categorising, as well as providing a flexible environment for transcription. Unlike

grounded theorists or ethnographers, discourse researchers have rarely used qualitative analysis software such as NVivo. Rather, the first move is often transcription. If there is a small amount of data, this will be transcribed directly using a system developed by the conversation analyst Gail Jefferson (see Hepburn and Bolden, in press). For larger datasets, it may be first transcribed in a coarser manner to allow preliminary searching, filing and categorising.

4 *Developing a corpus.* Discourse research is intensive. It requires the researcher to engage with the specifics of a set of materials. Depending on the question, this will typically involve the development of a specific corpus of examples. Once a corpus has been produced it will be transcribed to a higher level of accuracy. The associated audio or video passages can be edited into a collection so the researcher can work with both recording and transcript in parallel.

5 *Analysis.* The precise nature of the analysis will depend to some extent on the question being addressed. It will typically involve working with the corpus to identify some phenomenon or social practice, to describe its form and regularity. This is an iterative procedure with examples being dropped from the corpus and added to the corpus as the research ideas are refined (see Hutchby and Wooffitt, 1998).

6 *Validation.* Four considerations are central to the justification of analytic findings. First, the analysis should work with, and be sensitive to, the orientations of the participants themselves, which are most powerfully shown in the turn-by-turn unfolding of interaction. Second, the analysis should be able to deal with deviant cases. Departures from standard patterns are highly informative, either showing that a generalisation is suspect, or highlighting its robustness. Third, analysis will build on and mesh with earlier research; if it clashes with earlier work it will need to account for that clash. Fourth, discourse work is validated by readers being able to compare claims and interpretations with materials reproduced in the research report – it is a public and transparent process.

Box 6i: Child-centred counselling in Kids Helpline
Jonathan Potter and Alexa Hepburn

One of the aims of discursive research is to explicate the nature of interaction in institutional settings. We have been working with a team of Australian researchers on calls to Kids Helpline, which is a national Australian service that offers telephone counselling to children and young people. The research was focused on various aspects of how the helpline does its work. One topic of particular interest was how it achieves its mission of empowering children and developing child-centred practice while at the same time avoiding advice giving. For example, the study identified a practice that was highly suited to delivering such empowerment. This involved the counsellors using interrogatives that implicated advice. Callers were asked about actions that they had made, or would make in the future, that were relevant to resolving their problems. The virtue of working in this way is that callers are able to draw their own conclusions on the basis of their own superior knowledge of their situation and their own capacities within it. Using an interrogative form softens the normative pressures and knowledge asymmetry that are characteristic of advice (Heritage and Sefi, 1992).

Take the illustrative (and analytically simplified) example below. A client has called and reported that a friend has threatened to 'bash her' unless she gives her US$15 for losing her eyeliner. Note the way the counsellor builds the interrogative, focusing on possible future courses of action on lines 15-17:

9.1.8 Give me some advice

```
01 Caller:      >An er< s:sh:she reckons that <I owe her fifteen> dollar:s,
02              because the eyeliner (0.4) costed (0.2) fifteen dollar:s,
03              [          (1.0)    ]
04 Caller:      [((Chewing noises))] and (1.4) uh:m (0.3) tk now she
05              reckons tha' she's gunna put me in hospital?=like bash me
06              up?
07              (0.7)
08 Couns:       Ao:h:.=o:ka:y,
09              [          (1.0)    ]
10 Caller:      [((Chewing noises))]
11 Couns:       HHhh e-She's really a:ngry isn't she.
12 Caller:      Yeh ah know. An ah don't know what to do.
13 Couns:       N:y:eah::.
14              (0.2)
15 Couns:       .Hhh (0.7) Is there any way that- (0.7) dthat you can:
16              uhm: maybe replace it with an eyeliner th't (.) you
17              can affor:d?
18              (0.7)
19 Caller:      I doh' have any money.
20              (0.2)
```

The client's assertion that they do not know what to do is hearable, and heard by the counsellor, as an appeal for help. With the interrogative on 15-17 she identifies a possible course of action that might manage the problem. Note that this form of delivery softens the normative force of advice – there is no 'You *should* do X'. Note also that the interrogative form counters the standard epistemic asymmetry in advice sequences by treating the caller as knowing more (for example, about what they can afford, what the contingencies effecting this course of action might be).

The client's claim that she does not 'know what to do' (line 12) works as an appeal for help from the counsellor as to how she might address her problem. The counsellor's subsequent interrogative (lines 15-17) can be heard sequentially, and substantively, as responsive to this request for help, as advice. With the interrogative, the counsellor forwards a particular course of action that the client might take to address her problem – replacing the eyeliner with one the client 'can afford'. A question that enquires about the client's capacities is thus used as a vehicle to propose a specific course of future action for the client and, in this respect, is 'doing a suggestion' but with less of the prescriptive force of standard advice forms. The client can respond from her own perspective and lifeworld, working with her understanding of her own capacities.

The wider point here is that the analysis captures a recurrent pattern in practices of advice giving – the way client-centred counselling is delivered – and makes sense of what otherwise seems a somewhat odd injunction for the helpline counsellors to avoid giving advice. Butler and colleagues (2010) hope that this will be an important resource for training and quality control. Crucially, it is a resource that is based in an explication of the actual practices taking place in the setting itself, rather than the normative assumptions that are common in the counselling literature, or findings garnered through simulation or role acting.

Question for discussion
- What advantages does an interrogative or questioning form have for the delivery of advice?

References
Butler, C., Potter, J., Danby, S., Emisson, M. and Hepburn, A. (2010) 'Advice implicative interrogatives: building "client centred" support in a children's helpline', *Social Psychology Quarterly*, vol 73, pp 265-87.
Heritage, J. and Sefi, S. (1992) 'Dilemmas of advice: aspects of the delivery and reception of advice in interactions between health visitors and first time mothers', in P. Drew and J. Heritage (eds) *Talk at work*, Cambridge: Cambridge University Press, pp 359-419.

Further reading
Heritage, J.C. and Clayman, S. (2010) *Talk in action: Interactions, identities and institutions*, London: Wiley-Blackwell.
Potter, J. (2010) 'Discursive psychology and the study of naturally occurring talk', in D. Silverman (ed) *Qualitative analysis: Issues of theory and method* (3rd edn), London: Sage Publications, pp 187-207.
Silverman, D. (1997) *Discourses of counselling: HIV counselling as social interaction*, London: Sage Publications.

Website resources
Kids Helpline: www.kidshelp.com.au/

Box 6j: Critical discourse analysis: an example
Ruth Wodak

All forms of critical discourse analysis (CDA) have manifold roots including: rhetoric, text linguistics, anthropology, philosophy, socio-psychology, cognitive science, literary studies, pragmatics and sociolinguistics (Wodak and Meyer, 2009). In order to address complex social problems (such as discrimination, power in organisations or identity politics), CDA is inherently problem-oriented and interdisciplinary. The term 'critical' is rooted in 'critical theory' and implies to take nothing for granted and open up all kinds of meaning productions to multiple readings. Furthermore, self-reflection of the researchers is continuously expected (Chilton et al, 2010).

The discourse-historical approach (DHA) in CDA enables analysis of the historical (that is, intertextual) dimension of discursive actions by exploring the ways in which particular discourses are subject to change through time, and by integrating social theories to explain context. The DHA has already been used in various organisational contexts (for courtroom interactions, crisis intervention centres, hospitals and schools; see Wodak, 1996). Moreover, all empirical events are investigated across four heuristic 'levels of context' (Wodak, 2009a, 2009b):

- the immediate text of the communicative event in question (for example, the transcript of part of a management team meeting);
- the intertextual and interdiscursive relationship between utterances, texts, genres and discourses (for example, transcripts of interviews with team members related to meeting minutes, interaction dynamics and agendas of meetings);
- the extralinguistic social (for example, physical gestures, facial expressions) and institutional frames (for example, formal hierarchical structure, informal power relations and organisational imperatives) of a specific 'context of situation';
- the broader sociopolitical and historical context within which discursive practices are embedded (for example, knowledge derived from ethnography of the organisation, aspects of the broader social and cultural macro-environment).

Understanding the empirical phenomenon as having hierarchical levels of context allows an unpacking of the relationship between the motivations of organisational actors and their actions. This relationship between intent and action can be understood through the concepts of 'discursive strategies' and 'linguistic devices'. The term 'strategy' implies a more or less intentional plan of practices (including discursive practices) adopted to achieve a particular goal.

The DHA involves *four stages of analysis*: an identification of a relevant issue and the refinement of research questions; the systematic collection of data linked to the research questions; the analysis and drawing of conclusions from the data; and the formulation of critique and application of the results (Reisigl and Wodak, 2009).

As in other forms of CDA, DHA assigns texts to *genres* (such as a meeting). A 'genre' may be characterised as 'a socially ratified way of using language in connection with a particular type of social activity' (Fairclough, 1995, p 14). The DHA considers *intertextual* and *interdiscursive relationships* between utterances, texts, genres and discourses, as well as extra-linguistic social/sociological variables, the history of an organisation or institution, and situational frames. Intertextuality allows the researcher to deconstruct the immediate and long-term history of topics, genres and discussions (Kwon et al, 2009). As with all forms of CDA, the application of the results can be made accessible to wider audiences so that they can be used to affect practical change by better understanding the dynamics of strategic discussion.

Question for discussion
- Which are the most important stages in any critical discourse analysis (CDA) and how do these stages differ from other approaches to discourse analysis?

References

Chilton, P., Tian, H. and Wodak, R. (2010) 'Reflections on discourse and critique in China and the West', *Journal of Language and Politics*, vol 9, no 4, pp 489-507.

Fairclough, N. (1995) *Critical discourse analysis: The critical study of language*, London: Longman.

Kwon, W., Clarke, I. and Wodak, R. (2009) 'Organizational decision-making, discourse, and power: integrating across contexts and scales', *Discourse and Communication*, vol 3, no 3, pp 273-302.

Reisigl, M. and Wodak, R. (2009) 'The discourse-historical approach (DHA)', in R. Wodak and M. Meyer (eds) *Methods for critical discourse analysis* (2nd revised edn), London: Sage Publications, pp 87-121.

Wodak, R. (1996) *Disorders of discourse*, London: Longman.

Wodak, R. (2009a) *The discourse of politics in action: 'Politics as usual'*, Basingstoke: Palgrave Macmillan.

Wodak, R. (2009b) 'The semiotics of racism – a critical discourse-historical analysis', in J. Renkema (ed) *Discourse, of course*, Amsterdam: John Benjamins, pp 311-26.

Further reading

Titscher, S., Meyer, M., Wodak, R. and Vetter, E. (2000) *Methods of text and discourse analysis*, London: Sage Publications.

Wodak, R. and Krzyżanowski, M. (eds) (2008) *Qualitative discourse analysis for the social sciences*, Basingstoke: Palgrave.

Wodak, R. and Meyer, M. (eds) (2009) *Methods of critical discourse analysis* (2nd revised edn), London: Sage Publications.

Question for discussion

• What considerations are relevant in the validating of discourse analytic studies?

References

Hepburn, A. and Bolden, G. (in press) 'Transcription for conversation analysis', in J. Sidnell and T. Stivers (eds) *Blackwell handbook of conversation analysis*, Oxford: Blackwell.

Hutchby, I. and Wooffitt, R. (1998) *Conversation analysis*, Cambridge: Polity Press.

Peräkylä, A. (1995) *AIDS counselling: Institutional interaction and clinical practice*, Cambridge: Cambridge University Press.

Wetherell, M. and Potter, J. (1992) *Mapping the language of racism: Discourse and the legitimation of exploitation*, Brighton and New York: Harvester Wheatsheaf and Columbia University Press.

Further reading

Potter, J. (in press) 'Discourse analysis and discursive psychology', in P. Camic (ed) *The handbook of research methods in psychology*, Washington, DC: American Psychological Association Press.

Wetherell, M., Taylor, S. and Yates, S.J. (eds) (2001) *Discourse as data: A guide for analysis*, London: Sage Publications.

Wooffitt, R. (2005) *Conversation analysis and discourse analysis: A comparative and critical introduction*, London: Sage Publications.

Website resources

Ethno/CA news: www.paultenhave.nl/

Loughborough Discourse and Rhetoric Group: www.lboro.ac.uk/departments/ss/centres/darg/dargindex.htm

6.18 Conversation analysis
Charles Antaki

At first sight, conversation analysis (CA) looks unpromising to the researcher in social policy or social work. CA's insistence on working with the fine detail of talk, its curious notational symbols and its resistance to talking about people's motivations and private feelings all seem to confine it to the linguist's laboratory. But CA started out as a way of understanding something as applied and urgent as telephone calls to an emergency psychiatric helpline, and has a long tradition of working on routine social trouble including sites of social policy and social work interest, like the doctor's surgery, the police interrogation, the interview between claimant and personal adviser, the social worker's assessment of a disabled person or family carer, to name but a few.

The basic idea is that in any of these situations – like life anywhere – the business is transacted through talk. Six minutes' interaction between person A and person B comes out as a 'doctor's consultation' only because one person is offering symptoms and complaints, and the other one is asking questions, offering a diagnosis and prescribing some course of action. Props may well be used, and posture, gaze and movement all make their contributions, but if we start out with looking at the talk, we will have got the essence of the interaction in our sights. Once we do, we can ask important questions which cannot be asked on any other basis. We cannot satisfactorily ask doctors or patients how they do what they do on the basis of their recollections, since we know that recollections are partial, faulty and, in any case, likely to be moulded by the question being asked. With a video or audio record, however, we have some reasonably faithful capture of what happened, and we can start very carefully and soberly seeing what was done, and how it was done.

The 'pure' conversation analyst will be satisfied with that, as giving them another chapter in their understanding of the social world; but the 'applied' conversation analyst can go a step further. Remembering that official events like police interrogations and social work assessments have an official set of prescriptions, they can ask: how does what actually happened compare with the official account of what should happen? They can also ask: how does what actually happened, as analysed with the benefit of the video and audio tape, compare with the version that appears on the official record as written in the official file? *Box 6k* provides an illustration of this.

Box 6k: The management of 'choice'
Charles Antaki

One of the most powerful illustrations of CA's contribution to applied social policy and social work is its cool appraisal of what can actually happen in encounters between professionals and service users.

A vivid illustration of this comes from a project researching everyday life in a residence for people with learning disabilities. The care staff had, among other things, a commitment to offering the residents 'choice' whenever they could, as part of their mission to empower the residents and put them more in control of their everyday lives. Often, however, the staff's actual means of offering choice had counter-productive effects, simply because of the way they put the question. In the extract below, the staff member ('Tim') offers the resident a 'choice' of what to do in preparing food. However, such checks may have the unwanted consequence of inducing the resident to change their answer. After all, what seems to be the re-issue of a question may indicate that there was something wrong with the answer. That danger is revealed in this simple episode. Staff member Tim and resident 'Alec' are in the kitchen preparing food. Tim is asking Alec which potato peeler he wants to use:

Extract 1. VC-08; 04:12. Potato peeler.
1 Tim: Which one do you wanna use (0.2) thi:s one or
2   [this one
3→   Alec: [That one that one   ]
4   [((*points toward one of the peelers, out of shot*))   ]
5 Tim: °Go on°
6→   Alec: ((*picks up one of two peelers now in shot*))
7 Tim: [Are you gonna use that one   ]
8   [((*points toward peeler Alec is holding*))]
9   [or this one   ]
10   [((*points to different peeler on the worktop*))]
11   (.3)
12→   Alec: >That one< ((*puts down his peeler and picks up the*
13   *peeler on the worktop*))
14 Tim: ((*turns away*)) (°well y'go on°)

At line 3, the resident seems clearly to favour one potato peeler over another. One might wonder why it is that the staff member, at lines 7-9, requires confirmation of what looks to be a simple and decisive choice. Perhaps Tim interprets Alec's inspection of the first peeler as some doubt or reluctance, which needs checking; or it may be that he has some ulterior motive (in fact, it turns out that the peelers are not equally good, and the second peeler is easier to use). One way or another, the effect is that Alec, taking the hint that his answer was wrong, 'changes his mind' – we put the term in scare quotes – about his decision. He drops the one he first chose, and follows Tim's implied preference.

We can collect more evidence to see if this is a general pattern, and speculate on why it might suit staff members to ask repeat questions. It seems to be a way of negotiating the routine problem anyone has, who needs to look out for the interests of others: the dilemma of allowing free choice (and being true to the ideals of empowerment), or of making sure that the 'right' choice is made (and preventing harm, or keeping to what is institutionally convenient) (see Antaki et al, 2009). Care staff can manage the dilemma by repeating their question, seemingly to confirm the resident's choice, but, at the same time, implying that it is not the right one, so getting the resident to change it. CA identifies the practice, and turns it over to the applied community for any action that it might see as appropriate.

To do this kind of thing one has to collect as good a record of what happened as possible, and then go through it, line by line, making as full a transcription as possible, and analysing it bearing in mind one's knowledge of conversational sequences and structures. Then one will see what the speakers are up to, and, as in this case, how the professional's institutional demands interact with their conversational imperatives. Whatever one will find will be based on the strong evidence of first-hand data, analysed by a set of well-developed theoretical tools.

A note on notation
Why all the squiggles? Simply to try and reproduce at least some of the music of ordinary speech. The printed sentence is an artificial, cleaned-up fiction that leaves out a great deal of what makes spoken language work. A pause, for example, between two words can be ... well, significant. And different pauses have different significances, hence the convention of measuring pauses in tenths of a second, as in (.4) or, when it is the briefest of hearable pauses, a simple (.). And to go through some other features of talk that probably carry some weight of meaning: speed (words between > and < are rapidly spoken); intonation (an up ↑ or down ↓ arrow signals that the next sound is higher or lower than the surrounding talk); emphasis (an underlined sound is louder than what surrounds it). The last feature that appears in the extract is the overlap between two speakers' words, or between words and actions: that is signalled by the square brackets and the matching indentation of the lines. The point always is to try to approximate exactly what happened. True, we can never notate sounds or gestures perfectly, but even an approximation can help.

Question for discussion
* Suppose you were training social workers in how to interview clients about sensitive matters. How would it help to work with a video record, and a transcript, of their efforts?

Reference
Antaki, C., Finlay, W.M.L. and Walton, C. (2009) 'Choice for people with an intellectual impairment in official discourse and in practice', *Journal of Policy and Practice in Intellectual Disabilities*, vol 6, no 4, pp 260-6.

Further reading
Clayman, S. and Gill, V.T. (2004) 'Conversation analysis', in M. Hardy and A. Bryman (eds) *Handbook of data analysis*, London: Sage Publications, pp 589-606.
Hutchby, I. and Woofitt, R. (2008) *Conversation analysis* (2nd edn), Cambridge: Polity Press.

Website resource
An introduction to conversation analysis can be found at: www-staff.lboro.ac.uk/~ssca1/sitemenu.htm

To set about understanding what happens in an interaction, the analyst has to start a long way back. It is no good approaching such complicated data as talk-in-interaction without a set of tools up to the job. Ordinary common sense is tempting, but will leave the analyst utterly unprepared for the sheer complexity of organisation of talk. Fortunately, CA has now built up – after about 40 years of effort since the pioneering work of the sociologist Harvey Sacks (his fascinating lectures have been reproduced as Sacks, 1992) – a collection of structures that we can identify in talk. The most basic, and the most revealing for the whole principle of CA's illumination of talk, is what is called the *adjacency pair*. The notion is that a speaker will, by launching something that very strongly projects a certain class of response (a question projects an answer, a request an acceptance), show the next speaker what they are both doing at the moment, and directing (or limiting) what the next speaker can do next. The next speaker is at liberty to respond appropriately or not; but if they do not (and that will be marked by hesitation, a pause and perhaps something like 'well ...') then they will suffer – or exploit – the implications of doing so. Hence answering the question 'Can you lend me that book?' with a brief pause and a 'well ...' will mark the answer as not the expected one, and so economically signal that the answer is no.

Basic as that is, it shows up CA's principle of looking very closely at talk, even down to the pauses and the hesitations. People do not use language carelessly, since it is the best way we have to make our business known to others, and we know that others will take what we say (and how we say it) as significant. That simple fact opens up a rich seam of social research. The business of social life is done in talk, and recording it and analysing it in detail will reveal the detail of how that business is conducted.

Question for discussion

- Give an example of the kind of systematic regularity that conversation analysis has identified in talk. What would happen if someone flouted this regularity in an actual interaction?

Reference

Sacks, H. (1992) *Lectures on conversation*, vols I and II, edited by G. Jefferson, Oxford: Basil Blackwell.

6.19 Narrative analysis
Cassandra Phoenix

We organise our experiences through, and into, narratives, and assign meaning to them through storytelling. Narratives help guide action, and are a psycho-socio-cultural shared resource that give substance and texture to people's lives. Narratives are also a way of telling, and a means of knowing about our lives (Richardson, 2000). If we are constructed by stories, or are storytellers by nature, or perhaps both, then narrative must, surely, be a prime concern of researchers working within social work and social policy.

Smith and Sparkes (2006, 2008), and Sparkes and Smith (2008), point out that narrative scholarship is a varied, ongoing and contested enterprise rather than a singular, ossified one. Thus, while no singular definition can be expected (or desired), they emphasise numerous points of contact that exist between the different understandings of what a narrative inquiry is. These include the following:

- *Philosophical assumptions:* a grounding in interpretivism (see Smith, 1989), or, more recently termed 'non-foundationalism' (Smith and Deemer, 2000). From this perspective, narratives are not understood as a transparent window into people's lives, but rather as an ongoing and constitutive part of reality (Gubrium and Holstein, 1998; Bruner, 2002).
- *Identity:* a commitment to viewing identities as constituted through narratives.

- *Human relationships:* an emphasis on humans as relational beings, and the storied nature of our lives and lived experiences as they unfold in time (Randall and Phoenix, 2009).
- *Social action:* an understanding of narratives and interview accounts as examples of social action.

Elaborating on this final point, Atkinson, Coffey and Delamont (2003) explain how people use biographical accounts to construct their own lives and those of others. These accounts are not private, but are drawn from a culturally mediated repertoire of broader narratives. Accordingly, the accounts that people give of their lives need to be analysed in terms of the cultural resources that are used to construct them (for example, broader stories of health), the kinds of interpersonal or organisational functions they fulfil (for example, who does/doesn't benefit from health stories) and the socially distributed forms that they take (for example, who is [un]able to tell and live certain health stories).

Narrative analysis should be thought of not in the singular, but instead in the plural (Elliot, 2005). It refers to a family of methods for interpreting texts (for example, oral, written and visual) that have in common a storied form. Narrative analysis can be described as a technique that seeks to interpret the ways in which people perceive reality, make sense of their worlds and perform social actions. The purpose, notes Riessman (1993), is to see how respondents in various settings, such as interviews, impose order on the flow of experience to make sense of events and actions in their lives. It points, therefore, to the 'in-process' nature of interpretations and resists offering the final word on people's lives (Frank, 2004).

For Gubrium and Holstein (1998), on one side of narrative analysis we may focus 'on how a story is being told', while on the other side, we may have a 'concern for the various *whats* that are involved – for example, the substance, structure, or plot of the story' (p 165). Understanding both *what* stories describe, and *how*, is an important goal of narrative analysis.

There are no formulae for the 'best' way to analyse the stories we elicit and collect. Rather, a strength of thinking about our data as narrative is that it opens up the possibilities for a variety of analytic strategies (Coffey and Atkinson, 1996). Aspiring to make sense of different techniques and approaches currently operating under the broad umbrella term of 'narrative analysis', Phoenix, Smith and Sparkes (2010) developed a narrative typology. In this, they identified a range of analytical strategies that stem from two standpoints towards analysing narratives (see, for example, Polkinghorne, 1995; Lieblich et al, 1998; Richardson, 2000; Atkinson and Delamont, 2006; Smith and Sparkes, 2006; Riessman, 2008). These are termed *story analyst* and *storyteller*. A story analytic technique collects, invites and generates stories, and then conducts an analysis *of them* (see, for example, Phoenix and Sparkes, 2006, 2009). *Storytellers* often collect, invite and generate stories. Their analysis *is the story* (Bochner, 2001; Ellis, 2004). Stories, it is argued, do the work of analysis and theorising. This is because a good story itself is theoretical (Ellis and Bochner, 2006). Developing an awareness of the multiple forms of narrative analysis – and what they can offer as a way of knowing – can enable social scientists to make informed choices in their research.

Box 6l: Narrative analysis in action: 'being Fred'
Cassandra Phoenix

Phoenix and Sparkes (2009) examined data generated during a series of interactive interviews with a 70-year-old physically active man named 'Fred'. According to Ellis et al (1997, p 121), 'Interactive interviewing requires considerable time, multiple interview sessions, and attention to communication and emotions. It may also involve participating in shared activities outside the formal interview situation'. This form of interview is especially useful when gathering and analysing 'big stories' and 'small stories'.

Big stories are those told within a formal interview setting. *Small stories*, however, are usually told in fleeting moments of interactions and subsequently are often disregarded as data. Previously, narrative scholars have tended to analyse big *or* small stories. However, Phoenix and Sparkes (2009) argue that rather than be any better or 'truer', each type of story tells about different but interconnected regions of experience. They are, therefore, both equally salient in terms of narrative inquiry.

Demonstrating theory in action, Phoenix and Sparkes' analysis of Fred's story shows the ways in which he constructed the identities of *being fit and healthy* and *being leisurely* in older age through his use of big and small stories. For example, the authors recount the following *big story* that Fred told about his lifestyle during the interview context:

> I do think that the cross section of probably cycling, swimming and running or even walking, if you can't run then walk. Walking is excellent. It is excellent exercise but I do think you need this cross section of different exercises to keep really fit. (quoted in Phoenix and Sparkes, 2009, p 229)

By describing his physical activity beliefs (in greater detail than presented here), Fred performs the identity of *being fit and healthy*. Moreover, this was repeatedly confirmed via numerous *small stories* regarding his body, health and well-being. Small stories were recorded as field notes:

Field notes – 04/01/07
> Fred is driving and we are on our way to the café for a late breakfast. We are talking about Christmas, and Fred tells me that his daughter has renewed his subscription to *Men's Health* as a Christmas present.... "I like *Runners World* too" he continues. (Phoenix and Sparkes, 2009, p 228)

Using big and small stories as an analytical framework, Phoenix and Sparkes demonstrate how Fred is able to accomplish a personal story about positive ageing by constructing specific identities. These big and small stories were drawn from a variety of narrative resources ranging from the media, friends and Fred's experiences of his physical body. The accessibility of such resources allowed him to successfully perform an overarching storyline to give meaning to his life. The plotline of this was encapsulated by the phrase 'Life is what you make it'. They propose that Fred artfully crafts a coherent narrative of positive self-ageing that stands in opposition to prevailing western notions of negative ageing.

Their analysis illustrates the dynamic work involved in accomplishing a positive ageing identity through the use of both big and small stories. It also reinforces the notion that narratives are embodied, lived, socially shaped and central to the process of meaning making.

References
Ellis, C., Kiesinger, C. and Tillmann-Healy, L. (1997) 'Interactive Interviewing, talking about emotional experience', in R. Hertz (ed) *Reflexivity and voice*, London: SAGE, pp 119-49.
Phoenix, C. and Sparkes, A.C. (2009) 'Being Fred: big stories, small stories and the accomplishment of a positive ageing identity', *Qualitative Research*, vol 9, no 2, pp 83-99.

Question for discussion

- How important are 'stories' or 'the telling of stories' for improving relationships between different generational groups?

References

Atkinson, P. and Delamont, S. (2006) 'Rescuing narrative from qualitative research', *Narrative Inquiry*, vol 16, pp 164-72.

Atkinson, P., Coffey, A. and Delamont, S. (2003) *Key themes in qualitative research*, Oxford: AltaMira Press.

Bochner, A. (2001) 'Narratives virtues', *Qualitative Inquiry*, vol 7, pp 131-57.

Bruner, J. (2002) *Making stories*, Cambridge, MA: Harvard University Press.

Coffey, A. and Atkinson, P. (1996) *Making sense of qualitative data*, London: Sage Publications.

Elliot, J. (2005) *Using narrative in social research*, London: Sage Publications.

Ellis, C. (2004) *The ethnographic I*, Oxford: AltaMira Press.

Ellis, C. and Bochner, A. (2006) 'Analysing analytic autoethnography: an autopsy', *Journal of Contemporary Ethnography*, vol 35, no 4, pp 429-49.

Frank, A. (2004) *The renewal of generosity*, Chicago, IL: The University of Chicago Press.

Gubrium, J. and Holstein, J. (1998) 'Narrative practice and the coherence of personal stories', *The Sociological Quarterly*, vol 39, no 1, pp 163-87.

Lieblich, A., Tuval-Mashiach, R. and Zilber, T. (1998) *Narrative research*, London: Sage Publications.

Phoenix, C., Smith, B.M. and Sparkes, A.C. (2010) 'Narrative analysis in aging studies: a typology for consideration', *Journal of Aging Studies*, vol 24, pp 1-11.

Phoenix, C. and Sparkes, A.C. (2006) 'Young athletic bodies and narrative maps of ageing', *Journal of Aging Studies*, vol 20, no 2, pp 107-21.

Phoenix, C. and Sparkes, A.C. (2009) 'Being Fred: big stories, small stories and the accomplishment of a positive ageing identity', *Qualitative Research*, vol 2, no 9, pp 83-99.

Polkinghorne, D. (1995) 'Narrative configuration in qualitative analysis', in R. Wisniewski (ed) *Life history and narrative*, London: Falmer Press, pp 5-24.

Richardson, L. (2000) 'Writing: a method of inquiry', in N. Denzin and Y. Lincoln (eds) *Handbook of qualitative research*, London: Sage Publications, pp 923-48.

Randall, W. and Phoenix, C. (2009) 'The problem with truth in qualitative interviews: reflections from a narrative perspective', *Qualitative Research in Sport and Exercise*, vol 1, no 2, pp 125-40.

Riessman, C. (1993) *Narrative analysis*, London: Sage Publications.

Riessman, C. (2008) *Narrative methods for the human sciences*, London: Sage Publications.

Smith, B. and Sparkes, A.C. (2006) 'Narrative inquiry in psychology: exploring the tensions within', *Qualitative Research in Psychology*, vol 3, no 3, pp 169-92.

Smith, B. and Sparkes, A.C. (2008) 'Contrasting perspectives on narrating selves and identities: an invitation to dialogue', *Qualitative Research*, vol 8, pp 5-35.

Smith, J. (1989) *The nature of social and educational inquiry: Empiricism versus interpretation*, New York: Ablex Publishing Corporation.

Smith, J. and Deemer, D. (2000) 'The problem of criteria in the age of relativism', in N. Denzin and Y. Lincoln (eds) *Handbook of qualitative research* (2nd edn), London: Sage Publications, pp 877-96.

Sparkes, A.C. and Smith, B. (2008) 'Narrative constructionist inquiry', in J.A. Holstein and J.F. Gubrium (eds) *Handbook of constructionist research*, London: Guilford Press, pp 295-314.

Further reading

Lieblich, A., Tuval-Mashiach, R. and Zilber, T. (1998) *Narrative research*, London: Sage Publications.

Phoenix, C., Smith, B.M. and Sparkes, A.C. (2010) 'Narrative analysis in aging studies: a typology for consideration', *Journal of Aging Studies*, vol 24, pp 1-11.

Riessman, C. (2008) *Narrative methods for the human sciences*, London: Sage Publications.

6.20 Using verbatim quotations in writing up applied qualitative research

Anne Corden and Roy Sainsbury

Reports and articles presenting findings from qualitative research, based on interviews and group discussions, almost always include some verbatim quotations from people who took part. This is such common practice that it can be easy, both in writing up research and in reading the reports, to assume that everyone is working to a common set of rules and that everyone understands and accepts these. However, this is almost certainly not the case, as we found when we carried out an ESRC-funded project to explore the theory, practice and impact of using verbatim quotations in written research reports.

From an initial literature review we found rather limited discussion about the use of quotations in existing methodological texts. Among the authors who do engage with this in more detail, some argue that verbatim quotations provide powerful evidence in the arguments being made (see Beck, 1993). Sandelowski (2003) also emphasises their use in establishing validity of findings. Different kinds of arguments are that quotations make reports more interesting by introducing textual diversity (see Alasuutari, 1995; Holloway and Wheeler, 1996), and that more lively and interesting writing may be more likely to be read, or have a greater impact. Another reason for presenting spoken words is that this enables people who take part in research to speak for themselves (Beresford et al, 1999).

We then reviewed 56 publications (Corden, 2007) reporting qualitative research across different areas of social policy, suggested by experts in the fields of social care, family policy, health, employment, education, income maintenance and criminal justice. In addition to the reasons mentioned above it appeared that some authors were also using quotations to illustrate an author's point, or to show how participants expressed views and explained feelings. However, in many of the publications, authors gave *no explanation* of the theoretical or philosophical approach within which their work was located, underpinning their use of the quotations. We also found a wide range of style in length, number, editing conventions and the categories and attributed identities of the speakers, and often with no explanation for the approaches adopted. If you looked at even a small selection of qualitative research reports you would notice this diversity. Some reports will include a large number of quotations; others will use them very sparingly. There will be quotations of a single line and quotations of one or more pages. Some quotations will attempt to capture accents and dialects; some will be seemingly transcribed into BBC English. You will notice quotations full of 'ers' and 'ums', false starts and corrections; others will give the impression that the speaker was an expert grammarian.

To investigate the impact of verbatim quotations we sought the views of a sample of policy makers, analysts and research managers within government departments and third sector organisations (Corden and Sainsbury, 2006). This component of the research design provides challenging findings for authors of reports. There were sharp differences of opinion about the usefulness of verbatim quotations. Some said they liked having quotations, and verbatim words could be helpful in increasing understanding and encouraging confidence in findings. Some senior policy makers said they relied mainly on reading summaries and conclusions, and would only look at quotations if they needed to go into the main body of the report. They shared concerns about selection of the words that authors chose to use, and the images of participants that might be portrayed. For some research users, quotations were disliked and a source of irritation and might not be read at all.

Finally, we investigated the views of people who took part in research interviews, whose spoken words appear in researchers' reports. We did this by carrying out a small qualitative study to explore the views and experiences of a group of people taking part in a scheme to enhance employability through volunteering and then showing our written report to them (Corden and Sainsbury, 2005). Again, there were differences in opinions, but strong feelings were expressed. Some people thought the contrast between their words as spoken and the researchers' written Standard English, with correct punctuation, cast them in negative light. Others wanted their speech 'tidied up', so that it would be taken seriously. Nobody liked the idea of having synonyms, and some did not want to be described as belonging to groups that they thought did not reflect well on themselves, including 'lone mother'. What was important in the way their words were used was that they did not stand out as different in a way that invited judgement or criticism, even though they knew other readers would not recognise them individually.

The overall conclusions from our study were that it would be wrong to look for the definitive 'set of rules' about using quotations. Researchers use them for different purposes, and readers and speakers have different views. Essentially, all researchers are faced with a series of choices about how they present their qualitative data. The important thing is that researchers make *justifiable* choices, which are made transparent within the report or article. Researchers need to consider whose views count when they select verbatim quotations for inclusion within their own writing, and make clear what they have decided.

So, when you next write up a piece of qualitative research you could try asking yourself the following questions:

• What is my approach to the selection of verbatim quotations to use? What is my justification for this?

- What am I trying to do in using quotations? What is my purpose and intention?
- What impact will the quotations have on my readership? What impact am I trying to achieve? Does it matter if my selected quotations are not read, or whether readers look mainly at these and skim my own text?
- Have I addressed ethical issues sufficiently, including maintaining confidentiality and anonymity for the people I am reporting, and not casting them in a negative light?
- Have I taken into account the views of those who spoke the words?

And when you have answered all these questions to your own satisfaction, then tell us in your report.

Question for discussion

- Read two articles reporting findings deriving from research based on semi-structured interviews. What are the different approaches to the presentation of verbatim quotations employed by the authors concerned?

References

Alasuutari, P. (1995) *Researching culture: Qualitative method and cultural studies*, London: Sage Publications.

Beck, C.T. (1993) 'Qualitative research: the evaluation of its credibility, fittingness and auditability', *Western Journal of Nursing Research*, vol 15, no 2, pp 263-6.

Beresford, P., Green, D., Lister, R. and Woodward, K. (1999) *Poverty first hand: Poor people speak for themselves*, London: Child Poverty Action Group.

Corden, A. (2007) *Using verbatim quotations in reporting qualitative social research: A review of selected publications*, ESRC 2226, York: Social Policy Research Unit, University of York.

Corden, A. and Sainsbury, R. (2005) *Research participants' views on use of verbatim quotations*, ESRC 2094, York: Social Policy Research Unit, University of York.

Corden, A. and Sainsbury, R. (2006) *Using verbatim quotations in reporting qualitative social research: The views of research users*, ESRC 2187, York: Social Policy Research Unit, University of York.

Holloway, I. and Wheeler, S. (1996) *Qualitative research in nursing*, Oxford: Blackwell Science.

Sandelowski, M. (2003) 'Tables or tableaux? The challenges of writing and reading mixed methods studies', in A. Tashakkori and C. Teddlie (eds) *Handbook of mixed methods in social and behavioural research*, Thousand Oaks, CA: Sage Publications, pp 331-50.

Website resource

All publications from the study on the theory, practice and impact of using verbatim quotations can be found on the project page on the Social Policy Research Unit website: php.york.ac.uk/inst/spru/research/summs/verbquot.php

seven

Dissemination, knowledge transfer and making an impact

Detailed contents

7.1 Introduction

Dissemination and knowledge transfer (KT) is concerned with communicating to relevant audiences in appropriate ways the knowledge and information learned from research enquiry. This is an integral part of the research process. Whether research then has an 'impact' on social policy or social work practice requires us to examine the processes by which research is adopted and utilised by policy makers and professionals (see Sections 1.6 and 1.7). These are some of the concerns for this chapter.

In this chapter we examine and discuss:

- what is meant by *dissemination*, *KT* and *impact*, and how this phase of research 'fits' with the other stages of the research cycle;
- the main vehicle for research dissemination – the *written report* – and we offer practical guidance on how to make reports accessible and well structured, and how to relate research findings to an established body of knowledge;
- 10 key issues that need to be addressed when considering a *dissemination and KT strategy* for any piece of social policy or social work research;
- how research can *make an impact* and contribute in some way to evidence-based policy and practice.

7.2 Dissemination and knowledge transfer as part of the research process
Saul Becker and Alan Bryman

Defining dissemination, knowledge transfer and impact

The dictionary defines *dissemination* as: 'To spread (information, ideas, etc) widely' (Collins, 2001, p 227). Other terms closely associated with dissemination include 'broadcast, circulate, diffuse, disperse, distribute, propagate, publish, scatter, sow, spread' (Collins, 1996, p 174). In the context of social policy and social work research, dissemination is thus concerned with *communicating information, evidence and knowledge gained from research to relevant audiences*. This dissemination can include the communication of information about research findings, about messages from research, implications for policy and practice, policy or practice recommendations, knowledge about the research methodologies employed, and so on.

In the last few years there has been increasing use of the term 'knowledge transfer' (KT) to refer to the *activities* and *process* of dissemination of research and other evidence to inform and impact on policy and practice. Specifically, KT activities in social policy and social work may include consultancy, conference papers, conference and other networking activities in relevant communities of interest, external speaking and presentations, public engagement, blogs, informal advice to various stakeholders, advisory board membership, and so on.

Sometimes the term 'knowledge exchange' is used to infer that the process is not simply a 'one-way street' (academics 'transferring' knowledge *to* others), but that knowledge is 'exchanged', mediated and developed *between* academics and others, with all parties learning and benefiting from the knowledge, expertise and contribution of others, and with greater intention that the knowledge gained will be *used* in some way to inform or influence policy or practice (see, for example, **Box 7b**).

A further distinction may also be helpful at this stage. The term 'research utilisation' is used in this volume and elsewhere to refer to the *take-up* and *use* or *application* of research, directly to *determine* or *inform* policy or practice (see also **Figure 1l** in Chapter One). While there are differences in terminology and meaning around phrases such as 'KT' and 'knowledge exchange', in this chapter we refer to dissemination and KT while recognising that all stakeholders, including service users ('experts through experience') have much to contribute to the process of knowledge creation, transfer and evidence-informed policy and practice. At its core, however, without dissemination and KT activities, there is little likelihood, or chance, that research will be taken up and used (research utilisation).

When research *is* used, it is often referred to as 'having an impact'. The London School of Economics (LSE) Public Policy Group (PPG) (2011, p 5) defines a 'research impact' as a 'recorded or otherwise auditable occasion of influence from academic research on another actor or organization'. It distinguishes between *academic* and *external* impacts:

a. *Academic impacts* from research are influences upon actors in academia or universities, eg as measured by citations in other academic authors' work.
b. *External impacts* are influences on actors *outside* higher education, that is, in business, government or civil society, eg as measured by references in the trade press or in government documents, or by coverage in mass media. (LSE PPG, 2011, p 5)

In this chapter, our interest in research impact is concerned more with *external* impact rather than academic impact – in other words, the impact of research on policy and practice.

For any piece of research it is important for the researchers, in discussion with their funders and other involved parties, to identify the appropriate and relevant audiences for dissemination and KT. The relevant audiences might include policy makers, social work and other professionals and practitioners, service users, government and non-governmental organisations (NGOs), research funders themselves, academics, and potentially the public as a whole. **Box 7a** illustrates the types of issues, concerns and requirements that research funders have when they are commissioning research or awarding a grant. These concerns need to be understood by researchers from the outset, and they will affect the ways that researchers *think* about their work throughout the research process, from initial ideas and who should be involved in articulating these, through to the ways in which research is *conducted*, to the kinds of *output* and *dissemination* strategies required. Some funders have an explicit aim to commission research that can 'make an impact' while others are more concerned to develop theoretical and conceptual knowledge.

Dissemination and KT will also include letting research participants know about the findings, and in some cases this can act as an important test of validity for the study as a whole. Different audiences will need to know about different aspects; for example, some may need to know specifically about the findings, others may be more interested in knowing about the application of methods or research designs, while some may simply want to know what *they* should do as reflective practitioners. We return to these issues later in Section 7.4.

Box 7a: Understanding and managing funders' requirements
Sharon Witherspoon

Understandably, researchers often experience funders' rules and requirements as 'constraints'. But most constraints arise rather fundamentally from what different funders, and different types of funders, are trying to achieve by funding research, and understanding these aims may be helpful.

There are a number of dimensions along which funders will vary, including:

- Priorities given to *applied* as compared to *non-applied* work. Most funders with programmes in social work or social policy are interested to some extent in the *implications* for policy or practice (the Nuffield Foundation, the Joseph Rowntree Foundation, various government departments), although important fundamental research may be accepted in some areas by these funders or by funders such as the Economic and Social Research Council (ESRC) and The Leverhulme Trust.
- Priorities given to *descriptive* as compared to *explanatory* research. Are funders trying to describe how things are, or to understand underlying causes?
- Linked but not reducible to this: priorities given to understanding *outcomes* as compared to *processes*. Again, many funders are concerned with both, but government departments or funders who seek to improve policy or practice are likely to care about outcomes or about comparing outcomes of different interventions.
- Views about the role of research in *policy engagement*. Does the funder expect researchers to be involved or to produce a body of work that others may use?
- Finally, whether the money comes from *public funding* or *private or endowment funding*. This affects not only the timescale of the funders' interest, but also the different accountability – and hence accounting – regimes constraining the research.

An important principle is for researchers to look carefully at what a particular funder is looking for *before* deciding to apply. Research is usually better when researchers and funders have a clear and shared view about where a particular project fits into the research landscape. Nowadays most funders use the web to say what they are trying to achieve; transparency about these issues is constructive.

Researchers often experience research application procedures as another constraint. Different funders use different processes or a mix of them, according to their goals. Processes may vary according to whether:

- Procurement rules or a funder's underlying aims suggest a *competitive tendering process*, or *direct commissioning*, or *grant making of a more or less proactive type*. Tendering usually comes with clear procedural rules; The Social Research Association provides excellent information on good practice in tendering on its website and argues that budgetary constraints should be clearly communicated. Funders may commission directly when they know what research they wish to do and/or who they might ask to do it. In the case of grants, some funders make very clear statements about their substantive interests, while others are less prescriptive.

- Funders have views on the degree of precision they are seeking about the *research design and methodology*. Some funders (such as the National Lottery) may not be directly concerned with design issues while others will be very concerned that the methodology is robust and appropriate to the research question(s).
- Funders have capacity to offer *substantive guidance*. Many funders use an outline procedure to select applications for the final stage, and this short-listing usually involves judging both relevance to the funder's own interests and methodology and robustness. Even with projects initiated by researchers, some funders provide substantive feedback rather than passively saying yes or no, and these suggestions may sometimes be useful improvements.
- Funders use *peer review* involving other researchers, policy makers, practitioners or service beneficiaries.
- Funders expect longer-term engagement with researchers in *communicating research findings* or expect research to influence their own decision making. Public bodies should always allow research findings to be made public in some way.

Two particular issues warrant further discussion. First, there is some evidence that less research has been done on the *outcomes* of social work or social policy interventions (using experimental designs including, but not restricted to, randomised controlled trials [RCTs]) than would be desired by some practitioners and users (Stevens et al, 2009), and that there is a shortage of *quantitative* research skills in this area (Sharland, 2009). These two issues are analytically separable but empirically linked: if there were more quantitative research capacity in this area, we might have better information about the outcomes of policy and practice changes or about the effects of different interventions, as assessment of these requires at least some quantitative work. Research capacity is an obvious constraint on the research agenda; for the longer-term health of social policy and social work research, funding for capacity building remains a priority (MacInnes, 2009).

A second issue for much social work/social care research is how to ensure appropriate involvement of users and beneficiaries. Different funders, researchers and users have a range of views on this, and there is variation too according to the specific issue being examined and the methodology required. Most funders in the area of social work and social care wish to see evidence that the service users and beneficiaries have some input into the research agenda, and make an appropriate contribution to research projects, including dissemination and KT activities. Funders may vary in their judgements of what is appropriate. Some seek to involve users as researchers while others use an advisory group model to ensure appropriate input. Some funders put more stress on specialist research skills and the need for objectivity than others, as activist users may have their own positions on issues being researched. Researchers may want to think about whether a single model of user engagement is appropriate for different funders and different types of research.

Question for discussion
- How can an individual funder's aims and rules affect dissemination and knowledge transfer (KT) activities?

References

MacInnes, J. (2009) *Final report: Strategic adviser for quantitative methods: Proposals to support and improve the teaching of quantitative research methods at undergraduate level in the UK* (www.esrc.ac.uk/_images/Undergraduate_quantitative_research_methods_tcm8-2722.pdf).

Sharland, E. (2009) *Strategic adviser for social work and social care research: Main report to the ESRC training and development board* (www.esrc.ac.uk/_images/Main_report_SW_and_SC_tcm8-4647.pdf).

Stevens, M., Liabo, K., Witherspoon, S. and Roberts, H. (2009) 'What do practitioners want from research, what do funders fund and what needs to be done to know more about what works in the new world of children's services?', *Evidence & Policy*, vol 5, no 3, pp 281-94.

Further reading

Ebrahim, A. and Ross, C. (2010) 'The Robin Hood Foundation', Harvard Business School Case 310-031, Boston, MA: Harvard Business School.

Oakley, A. (1998) 'Experimentation and social interventions: a forgotten but important history', *British Medical Journal*, vol 317, no 7167, p 1239.

Tuan, M. (2008) *Measuring and/or estimating social value creation: Insights into eight integrated cost approaches*, Seattle, WA: Bill & Melinda Gates Foundation (www.gatesfoundation.org).

Relevant organisations

British Academy: www.britac.ac.uk

Economic and Social Research Council (ESRC): www.esrc.ac.uk

Joseph Rowntree Foundation: www.jrf.org.uk/

The Leverhulme Trust: www.leverhulme.ac.uk/

Nuffield Foundation: www.nuffieldfoundation.org/

Sage Publishing: www.sagepub.com/

Social Care Institute for Excellence (SCIE): www.scie.org.uk/

Society for Prevention Research: www.preventionscience.org/

Social Work Policy Institute evidence-based practice initiative: www.socialworkpolicy.org/research/evidence-based-practice-2.html

Locating dissemination and knowledge transfer in the research cycle

Figure 1m in Chapter One shows that dissemination and KT is a distinct phase of a dynamic research cycle. The dissemination of research findings to relevant audiences, and the promotion of the findings as research evidence, follow a *cognitive phase* and the *doing research phase*, all of which need to be managed effectively if the research process is to be rigorous and the findings are to be trustworthy. As we have said, the *dissemination and KT phase* is concerned with *communicating* information, evidence and knowledge gained from the other stages of the research cycle, particularly the findings, to relevant audiences through various (KT) activities. In the context of *evidence-based policy and practice* (see Section 1.6), dissemination and KT activity becomes especially important. Put simply, unless policy makers and practitioners have the information and knowledge gained from research, there is little chance that research will either *determine, inform* or *influence* their policy and practice (see Section 1.6 and *Figure 1l*). *Box 7b* illustrates how

KT and knowledge exchange is being managed strategically and actively by one research centre that seeks to disseminate research evidence on the third sector and to make an impact on policy and practice.

Box 7b: Knowledge exchange and impact: the Third Sector Research Centre

Pete Alcock

The Third Sector Research Centre (TSRC) was established in 2008 to carry out research on the third sector in the UK. It has received funding for five years, initially by the ESRC, the Office for Civil Society (OCS) and the Barrow Cadbury Trust (BCT), and is managed by the ESRC as one of their research centres. It is based at the University of Birmingham, and is a collaborative venture with the University of Southampton. The collaborative nature of the funding for TSRC means that a commitment to developing and delivering academic research which can inform policy and practice is built into the aims and structure of the Centre, and it is a leading example of ESRC commitment to ensuring that their research makes an impact on the policy process. This does not change the commitment of TSRC to ensuring that its research is robust and independent. However, it does mean that the Centre has developed active measures for ensuring that its work is developed in close engagement with those who might use and benefit from it.

Central to the TSRC mission to engage with its research users has been the establishment of the Centre's Knowledge and Exchange Team (KET). The team consists of two full-time staff who, although employed by the universities, work out of the National Council for Voluntary Organisations (NCVO) offices in London. This was arranged to give the team a London base, given the large number of leading policy and practice agencies based in the capital; but also (and more importantly) to provide them with access to the experience and networks of the NCVO within the third sector. KET work alongside the research team at NCVO, and have also developed close links with the policy and research sections of all of the other major third sector agencies.

These agencies are represented on an Advisory Board for the Centre, and KET work closely with this Board and with a range of other stakeholder groups that TSRC have established to ensure that regular contact is maintained with representatives of research users in the sector. Many of these groups, and the OCS itself, are in practice English agencies. TSRC is a UK research centre and has also developed advisory groups and networks with practitioners and policy makers in Scotland, Wales and Northern Ireland.

The primary function of KET is to provide a bridge between the academic research of the Centre and the research users in policy and practice across the nation. This is about much more than just publication and dissemination of research findings, although this is a key commitment. Engagement with users and stakeholders has been developed across the research process through advice and consultation on research questions, gathering of data and recruitment of respondents, commentary and feedback on emerging findings, and production of user-friendly versions of conclusions and recommendations. Not all research centres and projects will be able to afford dedicated knowledge exchange teams, of course, but the principle of building user engagement into research planning is one that all those interested in policy relevant and social work research need to consider and implement.

Question for discussion
- Should policy makers and practitioners expect researchers to translate all research findings into accessible forms and make them available through non-academic outlets?

Website resource
The Centre has a dedicated website, maintained by KET, where examples of user engagement can be explored and all publications from TSRC accessed: www.tsrc.ac.uk

Given the concern in much social policy and social work research, both to understand and to improve policy making and practice (see Sections 1.3 and 1.4), it is possible to identify five underlying principles which might guide any approach to dissemination and KT. These are shown in *Figure 7a*.

Figure 7a: Five principles for dissemination and knowledge transfer in social policy and social work research

1 Dissemination and KT activities need to be seen as an integral part of the research process, not as an optional extra or 'luxury'.
2 The essence of dissemination is *communication*. This requires clarity of expression and the use of appropriate vehicles of communication that are relevant to particular and specific audiences. Thus, dissemination and KT is about making research and research findings accessible, understandable, useful and relevant to a range of specialist, lay and user audiences, including 'end users' of services and 'research users', as well as the public itself, which has ultimately been responsible for much of the (public) funding of social research. Clear communication requires clarity in written and verbal expression, experience and other qualities.
3 Dissemination and KT of research is about generating, transferring, sharing and exchanging information and evidence, for knowledge, for meaningful and informed dialogue, for understanding, for power and, where appropriate, for change.
4 Dissemination and KT is essential if research is to determine, inform or to influence policy and practice.
5 Dissemination and KT is an integral aspect of the researcher's task. Notwithstanding the importance of points 1-4 above, dissemination and KT helps to get researchers' work better known and develops their own profile; it contributes to their publication list and academic credibility (the number and quality of publications are ways in which researchers are often 'judged' by the academic community); and it can give them a sense of value, purpose and satisfaction that their work is known and may be utilised, and have an impact.

Question for discussion

- What is dissemination and knowledge transfer (KT) and why is it important?

References

Collins (1996) *Collins paperback dictionary and thesaurus*, Glasgow: HarperCollins Publishers.

Collins (2001) *Collins paperback English dictionary*, Glasgow: HarperCollins Publishers.

LSE (London School of Economics) PPG (Public Policy Group) (2011) *Maximising the impact of your research: A handbook for social scientists*, London: LSE PPG (http://blogs.lse.ac.uk/impactofsocialsciences/).

7.3 How to write up research

Stephen Potter

Before any piece of research can be disseminated, there needs to be an 'output', a *vehicle for communicating the research to relevant audiences*. In most cases, this will be a *written report* that contains, not least, the findings as well as broader discussions of methodology, conclusions and recommendations. In this section we focus on the written report and in particular the *process of writing up research*. We offer *practical suggestions and guidance* on how to write up research so that it can be *accessible* and *relevant* for different audiences – key principles for dissemination and KT identified in **Figure 7a**.

Guidance for writing up research

There are dangers in the term *writing up research*. First, it implies that writing is something you do separately at the *end* of a research project – little more than an add-on to the 'real' work of doing the research itself. But until your research is written up in some form or other, nobody will know of it. A second danger in the idea that writing is only done at the end of a project is that this undermines the need to write *throughout* the project. This is for several reasons. First, writing on the project proposal and intended research can act as a vehicle for both obtaining feedback on a proposed investigation and stimulates self-reflection (having to produce a paper to explain a project helps you to reflect on its design and conceptual basis). A paper, conference or workshop presentation at the *start* of a project can be very helpful. There are also pilot studies or work-in-progress reports that provide that all-so-necessary feedback and reflection as a project progresses. Take these as real opportunities to develop and hone your writing skills and style.

Organising research writing

Reporting research can take many forms, from conference papers, blogs, wikis or reports through to a dissertation or thesis. Particularly for a large work, such as a report or dissertation, it is useful to start by putting together an outline structure. This initial planning stage ensures that you do not waste time and effort in writing up sections that you later need to discard or substantially modify. List the section headings, indicate what each of these will contain and how they will develop the work's 'storyline' (in other words, where things will be at the beginning of the section and where they will be at the end). One useful way to develop a structure for each section or chapter can be to develop it as a PowerPoint presentation or some other 'storyboard' format. Once you find a basic flow and sequence that works, you can then fill in the detail. This approach works particularly well if the time you have for writing is broken up into a series of short slots. This technique breaks the writing process down into manageable chunks.

For a *thesis, research report* or *major article*, the structure could involve:

- *Analysing the research question you are addressing:* explain the questions or issues involved. Defining the research question or questions you are answering is vital to understanding your research, yet this is often skimped on, leading to considerable problems.
- *Reviewing what others have done:* in any type of research paper you have to show that you know where your research fits with what others have done on your subject (see also Section 3.3 and **Box 7c**). Structure this review of existing knowledge into arguments and themes. Do the ideas of others make sense to you? Are there conflicts or contradictions, or do you detect undue bias? If so, is there a reason (for example, do writers approach the subject from the viewpoint of different stakeholders)? Do these ideas relate to the 'real world' of social practice that you know? Work towards an end point that shows your research is about something that needs investigating.
- *Your research project and method:* explain your project, choice of method and how the methods chosen were used to gather and analyse data. Do not forget to report the logic behind the research method used. Particularly in social policy and social work, it is crucial to explain why you researched an issue in the way you did (methodology discussion) as well how your chosen methods were used.
- *Reporting your research results:* a 'classic' approach in writing up research is first to report results and then to have a separate section on discussion and conclusions. This can work well, but particularly in subjects such as social policy and social work, researchers develop a 'storyline' that takes their reader into an exploration of what they have discovered. For example, if there is a key argument that someone else has put forward, the new findings are structured around this, showing if the new information supports or contradicts viewpoints within this debate.
- *Analysis, discussion, conclusions and recommendations:* this is the most important part of your writing. Whatever you do, do not just say 'the facts speak for themselves' and leave it at that. The whole thing about research writing is demonstrating your ability to analyse, discuss and contribute to social policy and social work's community of knowledge (see **Box 7c**). If you have integrated discussion and evaluation as you reported your results, the boundary between reporting and this section could seem arbitrary. However, it is here that you might pull together observations and basic analysis that took place while reporting results and draw a bigger picture. You might also want to discuss the weaknesses and limitations of your research.

A project proposal discussion paper would obviously be structured differently, concentrating on the first two points above, leading on to a discussion intended to identify the issues on which you want feedback, for example, the appropriateness of the research method, access to participants/data or choice of analysis method.

Flow and comprehension

Structuring a piece of research work, particularly a large work, is not an easy job. You should allow time for development and revision. Guiding your reader through your work is very important; sometimes you make connections in your mind rather than stating clearly how your points link up. At places where your writing reaches a key point or changes direction, it is important to include 'signposts' to help, for example:

- At the start of each section or chapter of a report, say *what the section contains* and its *purpose*. That will prepare the reader for the contents and the sequence in which they are tackled.
- In larger works, it is useful to have a *summary* at the end of the sections, pulling together the key issues in those sections and indicating how these will be followed up in the next.
- *'Pulling together' summary points* should feature where your writing takes any new direction. You might say 'This is what I have discovered, the implications are these, and so we need to explore the following to develop our understanding further'.

Also, you should make sure that your work answers the question(s) you posed at the start. You should not drift off the subject. However, it may be that the question you started with was the wrong one or was more complex than you first thought. If so, make this shift in focus clear.

Writing style

As well as the structure of your writing, there is the detailed question of style. Look at some social policy or social work research articles or reports. First, consider for *whom* they are written. Is it for practitioners, policy makers or academics? Is it a specialist or more general audience? The audience determines the writing style you should use. Academic writing is not (or *should* not be) about writing convoluted sentences full of jargon. It needs to be clear and appropriate for your audience, even if technical terms do feature. You should try to find a style of writing that you find comfortable but equally works academically. Seek to find your 'own voice' within the style of your discipline and one that is appropriate for the audience you are addressing.

For any audience, there are issues of style and grammar that can make all the difference in how your writing is received, quite aside from the research and arguments it contains. One way to explore this issue is to analyse social policy and social work articles and reports that you have read. Devise a list of things that make it difficult for you to understand these (see *Figure 7b*).

Figure 7b: **Things that can make social policy and social work publications difficult to understand**

- Over-complex and long sentences.
- Undefined jargon and technical terms.

- Very 'dense' writing: saying a lot in a few words that need to be read several times to get the meaning.
- Simply presenting a list of 'facts' that may, or may not, have some links.
- Shifting from one subject of discussion to another with no explanation as to why one follows on from another.
- Conclusions that are not backed up by evidence.

Go back and check that you have not included in your writing any of the stylistic traits that annoy you! And finally, it is very useful to get someone else to read your draft for style, flow and comprehension. Often you cannot spot where you have lost your reader.

Box 7c: Relating findings to the established body of knowledge
Stephen Potter

Section 7.3 considers 'structure' when writing up research and provides some outline guidance on relating your findings to existing knowledge. This is a crucial part of your research; through it you will show the relationship of your findings to those of your colleagues in the field. The foundations of this relationship should have been set when you reviewed and evaluated your topic area (covered in Chapter Three). Indeed, before you even start reporting your findings, you should return to your topic or literature review and particularly to your evaluation of issues, debates and choice of method that informed the design of your own research project.

Once you have your results, it is useful to think through the strategic ways your own research relates to existing knowledge. Is your research:

1 *An extension of the existing way of understanding and researching this topic?* For example, a study of health inequality that has applied an established theory and research approach to a new group of people or a new situation (see also *Box 3d*).
2 *Comparing or challenging the results of other studies?* For example, you may have found that important factors were missing in other studies and you have sought to fill that data gap.
3 *Comparing or challenging the method of measurement or evaluation indicators used?* This is not just about adding new information, but questioning the form of the information. For example, you may say that, as a measure of 'success', your research has shown that a particular indicator is misleading.
4 *Challenging the research method used?* This is further on from challenging a measure used, saying that a different method is needed. For example, using a qualitative approach assessing residents' perceptions of road safety rather than a quantitative approach.
5 *Challenging a theoretical approach to the subject?* Your research may throw doubts on a particular theoretical approach, or provide evidence to support one theory rather than another.
6 *Challenging a policy or practice response?* The above points will inevitably have policy and practice implications, but research can focus on policy formulation and implementation itself. However, it is important to explain the research justifications (such as data, method and theory) behind a policy or practice recommendation.

You may find it useful to make a list of the ways in which your research relates to existing knowledge. The list above is not exhaustive, so use it as a starting point. You could use the presentation headings technique suggested above to structure this section of your work as it is important to establish a sequence or structure in relating your results to existing knowledge. You may start by comparing your research at the level of the data and information it contains, and then move on to how that relates to measurement and meaning, which could go on to a discussion of method and possibly theory. So, having made a list of the strategic ways your research relates to existing knowledge, see if you can then structure this into a sequence that allows you to make comparisons to existing knowledge at different levels – from data, to indicators, to techniques, to method, to theory (or any other level that you identify yourself). Policy and practice implications may be picked up at any of these levels.

Of course, in structuring your discussion, you are not starting from scratch. Your topic or literature review should have started to set up the broad approach of your research and this will have informed your research project design. You could return to that and pick up the discussion and debate where you left off. Equally, in reporting your results, you may have started to make some initial comparisons to existing knowledge. This is most likely at the level of comparing data, such as to existing studies, and you may have already pointed out some areas where there are similarities and differences. You might also have provided some comments on some implications of the results.

Seek to build up a picture that relates your findings to what others have done in your subject area. Think through a 'storyline' that will guide your reader. You could start by summarising what were the crucial issues that had resulted in you undertaking the research in the first place. In undertaking the research you may have changed your understanding and modified the information that you sought to gather. Explain this, and why. You can then pick up key results (particularly if you had highlighted them already when reporting your results) and work your way towards what you see as your most strategic findings. Invite your reader to join you in your research journey, and share with them how you have built up a picture of your discoveries. As mentioned above, one useful way to scope out your structure may be to put it together as a presentation.

Question for discussion
- Starting with the six numbered categories above, make a list of the ways in which *your* research relates to existing knowledge.

Further reading
Potter, S. (ed) (2006) *Doing postgraduate research*, London: Sage Publications.

Questions for discussion

- Take an article or piece of written work that you have had to read for your studies:
  - What sections did you find most difficult to understand and why? Did anything annoy you?
  - Does the written piece have a clear 'storyline' or argument that develops through it? What 'signposts' have been used?
  - Are the conclusions or recommendations clear and justified by the evidence presented?

- Were there any bits you simply did not understand at all? (Could you rewrite this to make it understandable?)
- What part did you find most enjoyable to read? Why was this?
- Would you have inserted a summary at any point?
- Would you have reordered the material?

Critiquing someone else's written work should help you to think through these issues for your own writing. Go now and follow your own advice!

Further reading

Dunleavy, P. (2003) *Authoring a PhD: How to plan, draft, write and finish a doctoral thesis or dissertation*, Basingstoke: Palgrave Macmillan.
Ward, A. (2006) 'The writing process', in S. Potter (ed) *Doing postgraduate research*, London: Sage Publications, pp 71-109.

7.4 Ten questions to inform dissemination and knowledge transfer
Saul Becker and Alan Bryman

As researchers embark on the dissemination and KT phase of the research cycle (see Section 7.2), they need to consider a range of strategic and practical issues. In this section we identify 10 questions that should be considered both *before* and *during* the dissemination and KT phase for any piece of social policy and social work research.

1. Who 'owns' the research and who is responsible for dissemination and KT? For example, is it the researchers, the funding agency, the university or research unit – or others? This issue needs to be transparent and resolved *before* the research commences, as it may mean that in some cases researchers may have little ownership of the data and little control over whether or not the results can ever be made public. Matters of ownership and responsibility for dissemination and KT activities can be resolved by agreeing these issues in advance and by identifying these responsibilities as distinct clauses in any research *contract* or *agreement*.

2. What type of 'output' do the researchers, funders or other stakeholders want and expect? Is there a need for:

- a report (brief or detailed)?
- an executive summary?
- a short article (in a professional or academic journal)?
- a video, audio tape, blog?
- a presentation (seminar, conference paper, presentation to participants, to professionals)?
- a book?
- or a combination of these and other possible outputs?

It is important to have a clear view of the output(s) required from the earliest opportunity – at the research design stage if possible. Section 7.3 focused on *published outputs*, particularly on how to write up research. *Box 7a* considered some of the requirements of funders, and how these might affect outputs and dissemination.

3. What 'style' of dissemination and KT needs to be pursued? What does the funder want (see *Box 7a*)? Should there be *active* (proactive) dissemination and KT, whereby those responsible for these activities actively pursue the promotion of the research output(s), perhaps using multimedia, or more *passive* (reactive or 'low key') dissemination? Is low-key dissemination or a high profile launch or campaign required? Much research is published in report or monograph form and is rarely disseminated widely. Some large publicly funded research studies never see the light of day or have little, if any, impact. For example, *Box 7d* illustrates two cases where robust research evidence on social security and employment was 'ignored' or 'rendered irrelevant' by government departments, for a number of reasons. *Box 7f* also cites research that was 'neutralised' by the commissioning government department that 'was unhappy with the findings and declined to publish the report, instead writing their own version, which attributed the problems to local implementation issues and user resistance'.

Box 7d: How policy can ignore research: two cautionary tales
Roy Sainsbury

In an episode of the 1980s satirical series *Yes, Minister*, the naive and hapless Minister for Administrative Affairs, Jim Hacker, is faced with a piece of research which apparently shows conclusively a failure of government policy. While this alarms the Minister, his Permanent Secretary, Sir Humphrey, remains unruffled, advising Hacker that he can deploy one or more of a range of responses to unwelcome research findings, such as 'it's out of date', 'the sample on which it was based was too small', 'the policy has changed since the research was carried out' and 'the issues raised have already been dealt with'. Whatever riposte is chosen, and whether or not it is true, the effect is the same: the research can be happily dismissed and ignored.

Not every researcher will have been the victim of cynical and manipulative policy makers, but anyone who has carried out work intended to have an impact on government policy will probably have a story or two about how their rigorous and comprehensive piece of work ended up gathering dust. The general reason for this is that research, when completed or even while still in progress, is part of a wider, messier world of politics and policy making where rationality and logic are often trumped by other considerations and where bigger forces can easily relegate the role of research to a bit player (or no player at all). A couple of examples from the world of social security and employment research will serve here as illustrations. I have chosen these from work carried out from my research unit as I hesitate to suggest anyone else's research has been sidelined.

In the early 1990s, research funded by the then Department of Social Security (DSS) was carried out at the Social Policy Research Unit at the University of York into the arrangements for hearing appeals on Housing Benefit decisions made by local authorities (Sainsbury and Eardley, 1991). The main conclusion was reached that the system of using a board of local councillors to decide appeals failed at so many levels (it lacked independence, decisions were poor and claimants were effectively denied their appeal rights) that the case for transferring responsibility to the independent Social Security Appeal Tribunal system of the time was 'compelling'. But nothing happened. Why? As it was explained to us some years later by a departmental official, the argument was indeed seen as compelling but foundered on the twin rocks of local authority opposition and Treasury resistance. Local authorities did not want to relinquish any of their powers to central government, and the Treasury would not countenance increased expenditure, so plans for reform were dropped. Later in the 1990s, and without the aid of further research, government officials assessing the implications of the European Convention on Human Rights for domestic legislation concluded that Housing Benefit appeals contravened Article 6 of the Convention guaranteeing citizens an independent hearing in appeals against state agencies. The outcome was that, from April 2001, Housing Benefit appeals were to be transferred from local authorities to the independent appeals system. Power of research: 0; Realpolitik: 1.

Being ignored is one unpleasant fate, but being rendered irrelevant is perhaps worse. In 1998, the DSS established a number of pilot schemes under the umbrella of the New Deal for Disabled People in which disabled people were assigned a 'personal adviser' to help them move from Incapacity Benefit towards and into paid work. The aim was to find out 'what worked' for the many and diverse sick and disabled people who were known from previous research to be disadvantaged in the labour market. An elaborate and expensive research project, involving a number of research organisations, was designed and started. Within six months of the two-year project, a new minister had changed the basis of the pilots. Finding out how to get people into work was no longer a priority; rather, getting as many people as possible into work was. The research methodology was therefore no longer the most appropriate. Furthermore, within a year, policy makers had already decided the basic design of a national scheme to supersede the pilots, well before the research findings became available. Hence, when the research report appeared in 2001 (Loumidis et al, 2001), its utility to policy makers was hard to see. Power of research: 0; Realpolitik: 2.

This is not intended to be a Jeremiah version of research; there is much to be positive about, as this volume will demonstrate. However, these examples do show that research did not play the part in the policy process that researchers expected. The message to remember is that, in our enthusiasm for social research, we should not overestimate or assume its role in the policy process. Research can be in the right place at the right time but it probably is not as much as we would like to think. And even if it is, the Hackers and Sir Humphreys might get you anyway.

Question for discussion
- Why does research not always play a prominent role in the policy process?

References
Loumidis, J., Stafford, B., Youngs, R., Green, A., Arthur, S., Legard, R., Lessof, C., Lewis, J., Walker, R., Corden, A., Thornton, P. and Sainsbury, R. (2001) *Evaluation of the New Deal for Disabled People personal adviser service pilot*, DSS Research Report, No 144, Leeds: Corporate Document Services.

Sainsbury, R. and Eardley, T. (1991) *Housing Benefit reviews*, DSS Research Report, No 3, London: HMSO.

Website resource
The Department for Work and Pensions (DWP) website that makes available (free of charge) all DWP research project reports: http://research.dwp.gov.uk/asd/asd5/rrs-index.asp

Some research (including small–scale studies) manages to get high profile reporting and makes a significant impact on policy or practice. Sometimes this is by accident; most often it is a careful strategy of active dissemination with careful use of 'launches' and the media alongside other KT activities. ***Boxes 7e*** and ***7f*** provide examples of social policy and social work research which have made a significant impact on both policy and practice, utilising an active and multifaceted KT strategy, including formal launches, use of the media, different forms of presentation, consultancy, informal advice, networking, speeches, and so on.

Box 7e: Making an impact: the case of young adult carers in the UK
Fiona Becker

For the past 20 years or so in the UK, policy, law and professional practice on 'young carers' (children up to 18 years of age who have an unpaid caring role for another family member) have evolved and developed in a symbiotic relationship with the growing research literature which first described and then explained the experiences, circumstances and needs of this group of children (for a summary, see Becker, 2011). However, until very recently, there had not been a parallel development in terms of research, policy or practice for 'young adult carers'. These are people aged 18-24 years who provide care, assistance or support to another family member on an unpaid basis. Essentially, they have remained 'hidden' until recently, too old to be regarded as 'children' and 'young carers', and too young to be regarded as 'adult' carers.

The rationale and motivation for doing research about the experiences and needs of young adult carers stemmed from an emerging recognition that transitions from 'childhood' to 'adulthood' were becoming increasingly complex, difficult and risky, particularly for those facing poor housing, homelessness, substance misuse, mental health issues, poor education and long-term unemployment (Social Exclusion Unit, 2006). In addition, those providing services and interventions were increasingly concerned that support for young carers ceased when they turned 18 because of the demarcation in the provision of children's and adult services, leaving young adult carers without appropriate support at a time when they faced major decisions and life challenges concerning their own futures. Furthermore, the evidence base in the UK concerning young adult carers was weak, with only one previously published major study (Dearden and Becker, 2000), some secondary analysis of 2001 Census data in terms of training and employment opportunities for carers (Yeandle and Buckner, 2007), and some unpublished grey literature produced by local service providers.

In 2007/08 The Princess Royal Trust for Carers commissioned a study to explore the needs, experiences and service responses for young adult carers aged 16-24 in Britain (Becker and Becker, 2008). It included 16- to 17-year-olds because it wanted to capture the 'older' young carers of this age, to understand the transition issues that they faced as well as those of 18- to 24-year-olds. The mixed methods research used secondary analysis of 2001 Census data combined with in-depth interviews, focus groups and postal surveys. Interview transcripts were carefully reviewed utilising a Framework approach to qualitative data analysis and data management (see also *Box 6h* in this volume).

The *secondary analysis* identified that there were 290,000 carers aged 18-24 in the UK, with a quarter providing care for more than 20 hours per week. The report showed (through *surveys*, *interviews* and *focus groups*) that the extent and nature of caring often increases and becomes more complicated, demanding and time consuming as carers get older and are able to assume more responsibility. Although caring produces positive outcomes for some, such as enhanced coping skills, empathy and positive self-worth, the study found that young adult carers were often facing a range of adversities such as impaired or restricted education, unemployment, reduced opportunities for friendships, leisure and independence, poor mental health, and so on.

The research findings had implications for both carers' service providers and for policy makers within local authorities and other public sector bodies such as health, social care, education and social security. The report included boxed *case studies*, an *executive summary* (also published and distributed separately), simple to understand *statistics*, clear *recommendations* for policy and practice, as well as other attractive design features to make the report as accessible and as useful as possible (it can be downloaded free from www.saulbecker.co.uk).

Prior to the publication of the research report, the research team were asked to share early findings with the government in order to inform some of the thinking behind the National Carers Strategy (HM Government, 2008). Support for the study was also forthcoming from Dr Philippa Russell, chair of the government's Standing Commission for Carers, who prepared the foreword to the report. The credibility and reputation of the research team meant that access to ministers and civil servants was possible, indeed invited, and this increased the power to influence and inform policy thinking and policy making among a wide range of stakeholder groups.

An active and multifaceted dissemination and KT strategy was devised (see Section 7.4) in partnership with The Princess Royal Trust for Carers, and this enabled the findings to become widely available to policy makers and practitioners within a very short timeframe. A list of key people who should receive the report was drawn up by the authors and the Trust, and a free copy was sent to each of them with a covering letter outlining very briefly why the report was important for them to know about. The launch of the research report in 2009 included press releases and resulting national television and radio interviews, coverage in professional journals (for example, in *Community Care*) and presentations at national conferences and seminars for policy makers and professionals across the UK and in Australia, where professionals have also utilised the findings. The report was made available as a free download from the website of the then Department for Children, Schools and Families (now the Department for Education) as well as on the Trust's site. The findings were also presented at an invited seminar to specifically launch the National Young Carers Coalition in the Houses of Parliament in 2010, attended by members of both Houses, ministers, senior policy makers, service providers and young adult carers themselves, who also shared the platform with the authors. Each invitee was given a free copy. The government used the event for a ministerial announcement of a new national funding initiative for young carers and young adult carers.

The research has had a very immediate impact on policy making and service development. This is partly because of its *originality* and *significance* and the way in which the report was written and designed (see *Figure 7d*), as well as the long-established reputation for the *quality* and *rigour* of the research team. The *timing* of the publication was also very significant as it coincided with what professionals were already recognising but where they lacked a sound evidence base. In 2010, the Scottish Government used the research to inform the development of their carers' strategy and adopted its recommendations, which were included in its published strategy. Meanwhile, some English local authorities have developed strategic plans to address the needs of this group of carers for the first time and in so doing are drawing on the research evidence base provided by the report and are consulting with the authors for advice about ways forward. The Princess Royal Trust for Carers administered Comic Relief grant funding of £1.5 million in 2010 and as a consequence of the research extended the eligible age group to 24 years in order to encourage service providers to develop new services for carers up to this (older) age. Across the UK, local service providers (including local authorities, carers centres and third sector organisations) are citing the research as the evidence base for attracting new funding in order to develop services for young adult carers. New services are emerging across the UK to deliver support and advice to young adult carers with the intention of improving outcomes for them and their families. The effectiveness of these new services will need to be evaluated robustly in order to aid our understanding of 'what works', why, for whom and when.

Question for discussion
- Identify the key factors that helped this research to have an impact on policy and service development for young adult carers in the UK. How would you rank their importance?

References
Becker, F. and Becker, S. (2008) *Young adult carers in the UK: Experiences, needs and services for carers aged 16-24*, London: The Princess Royal Trust for Carers.

Becker, S. (2011) 'Informal family carers', in K. Wilson, G. Ruch, M. Lymbery and A. Cooper (eds) *Social work: An introduction to contemporary practice* (2nd edn), London: Pearson Longman, pp 426-55.

Dearden, C. and Becker, S. (2000) *Growing up caring: Vulnerability and transition to adulthood – Young carers' experiences*, Leicester: Joseph Rowntree Foundation.

HM Government (2008) *Carers at the heart of the 21st-century families and communities*, London: Department of Health.

Social Exclusion Unit (2006) *Transitions: Young adults with complex lives – A Social Exclusion Unit final report*, London: Office of the Deputy Prime Minister.

Yeandle, S. and Buckner, L. (2007) *Carers, employment and services: Time for a new social contract?*, Report No 6, Leeds and London: University of Leeds and Carers UK.

Further reading

Becker, F. and Becker, S. (2008) *Young adult carers in the UK: Experiences, needs and services for carers aged 16-24*, London: The Princess Royal Trust for Carers.

Becker, S. and Becker, F. (2009) *Service needs and delivery following the onset of caring among children and young adults: Evidence base review*, Cheltenham: Commission for Rural Communities.

Relevant organisations

Carers UK: www.carersuk.org

Crossroads Care: www.crossroads.org.uk

Department for Education: www.education.gov.uk/

NHS Carers Direct: www.NHS.uk/carersdirect

The Children's Society Include Programme: www.youngcarer.com

The Princess Royal Trust for Carers: www.carers.org

Website resource

For articles and reports freely available on young carers and young adult carers, including both recommended 'Further reading' texts, visit: www.saulbecker.co.uk

4. What are the (perceived) costs and benefits of each strategy? An active dissemination and KT strategy requires considerable time, resources and effort. Have you time to do many or just a few of the kinds of KT activities referred to above? Are there the resources to handle specialist, academic, practitioner, political or media enquiries? Do you want the attention? How will the commitment required for these KT activities affect your other ongoing work and responsibilities?

5. Who should receive the research output(s), and why? What do you want your audiences to do with it? (It's always worth letting them know in a covering letter or other communication.) Different target audiences will require different types of output because their own needs 'to know', and what you want from them, are likely to be different. For example, in typical hierarchical organisations (such as social services/work and health departments) different layers of the organisational structure have different needs for information. This is because people have different responsibilities, duties and information requirements:

- top managers will most often require *strategic* information to allow them to plan and evaluate service direction and effectiveness from year to year;
- middle managers will require more *tactical* information, on similar issues, but to enable operation from month to month;
- first line managers will require *operational* information – often for day-to-day management;
- front-line staff such as social workers most often require the *facts* – raw data – on which they can make immediate informed decisions.

This is not to say that front-line practitioners (or *street-level bureaucrats*; see Section 1.6) should not have access to other strategic information, or that top or middle managers should not have access to the facts, but that their immediate information needs are for useful, understandable and relevant information – requiring those responsible for dissemination and KT to target and refine the output(s) *according to who is to receive it,* and *why* they need to know. This will increase the likelihood of 'research utilisation'.

Linked to this are the different emphasis and focus needs of diverse audiences. Some will only be concerned with a particular part of the research or research findings because their concerns are more specialist or narrow. This may require researchers to use different language for different audiences, as well as a different form of presentation (for example, audio-visual or PowerPoint rather than written) or of communication (speech, consultancy, training, etc).

In some instances those responsible for dissemination and KT activities may need to reframe the findings into a style and manner relevant to a specific audience. In some cases it will be necessary to present only the main findings and 'messages' from research (messages for *that* particular audience); others might need 'recommendations' and an executive summary of just a few pages. In other instances it may be necessary to present the information in more diagrammatic form, using key charts or tables, or even as a 'clinical guideline'. Additionally, it may be important to undertake other complementary KT activities, including networking, external presentations, consultancy, blogs, etc.

It is usually helpful to seize, or create, opportunities to frame the findings in a popular discussion or concern that is timely. For example, if the research includes some information on a theme that is of popular interest, then it may be particularly attractive to the wider media. Sometimes, researchers will want to reach a highly specialist audience – part of a particular academic or other community of interest. Again, these targets can be identified and use made of *their* appropriate vehicles of communication (such as specialist journals, newsletters, magazines, discussion lists, radio shows, blogs, twitter, and so on). **Boxes 7e** and **7f** illustrate how some researchers engaged with different audiences to maximise impact.

Box 7f: Making an impact on the Integrated Children's System
Sue White

From 2007 to 2009, I led a research team investigating the impact of performance management on everyday practice in children's social care. The study was funded by the ESRC, and was thus independent of government. This proved very important in ensuring the maximum impact of the research. So overwhelming were the negative effects of the Integrated Children's System (ICS) on social workers' practice that it became a key focus of the study.

The ICS had been centrally prescribed and rolled out nationally, and was proclaimed as a veritable magic bullet which would inoculate social work against all manner of sloppy professional practices. Through detailed observations in five local authority sites, it became clear to us that, by attempting to micro-manage work through a rigid performance management regime and a centrally prescribed practice model, the ICS actually disrupted the professional task, engendering a range of unsafe practices (Broadhurst et al, 2010, 2011; Wastell et al, 2010; White et al, 2010). Yet, after searching the internet for information on the roll-out of the ICS, there were only accounts from senior managers and civil servants proclaiming its time-saving virtues, which were entirely discrepant with our findings.

We had earlier discovered that a research team at the Universities of Southampton and York (Shaw et al, 2009) had found similar effects in their government-funded evaluation of the ICS, concluded in 2006, before national roll-out. However, the Department for Children, Schools and Families (as it was then known) was unhappy with the findings and declined to publish the report, instead writing their own version, which attributed the problems to local implementation issues and user resistance. A member of our team, Professor David Wastell of The University of Nottingham Business School, was an expert in information systems design and we were clear that the problems with the ICS were fundamental design flaws, exacerbated by a cumbersome practice model and rigid performance regime.

In late 2008, media reporting of the brutal death of (Baby) Peter Connelly prompted the government to ask Lord Laming to review a range of reforms implemented following his report into the death of Victoria Climbié in 2000 (Laming, 2003). At this point, fearing more of the same kind of top-down command-and-control policy making, we wrote a short, punchy piece for *The Guardian* explaining some of the vicissitudes of the ICS. This prompted many practitioners to contact us, and at the same time various organisations such as the trades unions were articulating more forcefully the effects the ICS was having on social workers. This provoked more media attention, and a number of well-respected journalists from the press, radio and television began to cite our work and ask for interviews. This initially caused us some anxiety, but proved essential in keeping up the momentum. We sent written evidence to Lord Laming, sent papers to the ministers, shadow ministers and the chair of the Select Committee for Children, Schools and Families. We worked hard as a team to ensure rapid dissemination in academic journals with one paper (Broadhurst et al, 2010) fast-tracked in the *British Journal of Social Work*, resulting in 6,300 downloads of the advance access version between January and October 2009.

I was also contacted at this time by many of the software companies supplying the ICS who told of top-down interference in the design process and their own frustrations with the rigid specification drawn up by government, albeit with the best of intentions. We have continued to advise and support some companies in redesigning their systems.

In January 2009, I was contacted by a civil servant working for the Laming Review and asked if I would be agreeable to serving on the Social Work Task Force charged with undertaking a root-and-branch review of social work in England from 2009-10. This was subsequently confirmed and one of the first recommendations of the Task Force was a fundamental and wide-ranging review of the ICS. I am currently serving on the Munro Review that is aimed at reducing the administrative and bureaucratic burden on practice, and I have been given the lead on the information technology strand.

If you want your research to have an impact, first you must passionately believe that it needs to do so. You must be willing to put your head above the parapet, secure in the knowledge that your findings are robust. You must be prepared to publish outside of the academic mainstream, and to contact key individuals directly, even if at first they seem to be taking no notice.

Question for discussion
- How will you ensure your work reaches an audience beyond the academic community?

References

Broadhurst, K., Hall, C., Pithouse, A., Peckover, S., White, S. and Wastell, D. (2010) 'Risk, instrumentalism and the humane project – identifying the informal logics of risk management in children's statutory services', *British Journal of Social Work*, vol 140, pp 1046-64.

Broadhurst, K., Wastell, D., White, S., Hall, C., Peckover, S., Thompson, K., Pithouse, A. and Davey, D. (2010) 'Performing "initial assessment": identifying the latent conditions for error at the front-door of local authority children's services', *British Journal of Social Work*, vol 40, no 2, pp 352-70.

Laming, Lord (2003) *The Victoria Climbié Inquiry: Report of an inquiry by Lord Laming*, Norwich: The Stationery Office.

Shaw, I., Bell, M., Sinclair, I., Sloper, P., Mitchell, W., Dyson, P., Clayden, J. and Rafferty, J. (2009) 'An exemplary scheme? An evaluation of the Integrated Children's System', *British Journal of Social Work*, vol 39, no 4, pp 613-26.

Wastell, D., White, S., Broadhurst, K., Hall, C., Peckover, S. and Pithouse, A. (2010) 'Children's services in the iron cage of performance management: street level bureaucracy and the spectre of Švejkism', *International Journal of Social Welfare*, vol 19, pp 310-20.

White, S., Wastell, D., Broadhurst, K. and Hall, C. (2010) 'When policy o'erleaps itself: the tragic tale of the Integrated Children's System', *Critical Social Policy*, vol 30, pp 405-29.

It is also important to ensure that the research is communicated effectively to *all* relevant groups. Researchers should also make use of 'minority' publications and outlets where appropriate. Material should be tailored for particular readerships and needs. For example, sometimes this will require research findings to be translated into other languages or to be put into an audio format where, for instance, an audience has a visual impairment. At other times it will require findings to be written or presented in ways that are accessible, meaningful and understandable to people with other communication, sensory or learning difficulties.

6. When should information or findings be communicated? Here we need to consider *when* we want to disseminate material, not just *how*. Are dissemination and KT activities something that happens at the end of a project or at other stages (as well)? This will depend to a large extent on *why* those responsible for dissemination and KT actually *want* to communicate research findings and what kind of research it is. For example, the findings of theoretical research can only be disseminated when there is sufficient evidence to enable theoretical development – this will generally follow a lengthy period of research, reflection and peer review, and attempts at verification and falsification (see Section 1.5). Researchers concerned more with action research or practitioner research are more likely to disseminate material as they go along. Some of this will be in the form of tentative findings and interpretations, 'in progress' research reports or as working papers. If those responsible for KT want to have an impact on policy or practice, or are concerned with wider social change, then they must weigh up whether ongoing dissemination and KT activities will be more effective for these purposes than solely 'end-of-project' activities (see also point 10, below).

The timing will also depend on what and who researchers want to influence. To achieve 'maximum' impact researchers need to ensure that their outputs are, for example, released when the local authority or health authority are planning/reviewing the policy or practice, or when Parliament is sitting and not in recess, or when there is a growing political, professional or public awareness that action needs to be taken on a particular issue, as in the illustration provided in *Box 7e*. Making an impact requires considerable forward planning, strategy, as well as good timing and some luck. The LSE PPG (2011) has published a useful online guide to maximising the impacts of research.

7. Who else is working on this or a similar issue? Having 'allies' or access to other 'research mediators' can be very useful in helping to get research 'noticed' by policy makers and practitioners, and ultimately, in helping it to be utilised and have an impact. Are there, for example, think tanks or NGOs that are working in similar fields that could be allies in dissemination and KT? Could the dissemination of the research coincide with the publication or dissemination of the work of these research mediators? Is it possible to work together, or make use of any other topical issue, to promote the research? *Box 7e* shows how the launch of a research report on young adult carers deliberately coincided with the launch of a national coalition of NGOs at the same event in the Palace of Westminster, thus increasing the audience for both, and developing new networks of influence.

8. Can, or should, the media be used? Media work requires its own knowledge and skills, far too many to be discussed in this volume. Those responsible for dissemination and KT need to be prepared to seek advice about how best to use the popular and professional media, including news releases, radio and television interviews, blogs, and so on. They need to make the media work for them, rather than ending up working for the media. The illustrations in *Boxes 7e* and *7f* show how the media can help researchers to disseminate their studies to wider public and specialist audiences.

9. What should research participants be told about the findings? A 'user-conscious' dissemination and KT strategy will consider the research participants' 'needs to know' at an early stage, and will decide the appropriate forms, and timing, of dissemination and KT so that participants (and other service users) can be informed of findings and possible developments. Many participants are never given the results of the research in which they were involved (the same applies to many professionals as well as service users who take part in research). This is a source of constant criticism and gives social research a bad name. At the very least, participants should be given some form of accessible summary of the findings so that they can see how *their* contribution to the study was used and interpreted; for many respondents this may be a valuable source of information on a topic or issue that interested them enough for them to become research participants in the first place. It may also help to validate their own experiences and give them a sense of empowerment to see that they are 'not alone'.

For some forms of research, particularly qualitative approaches such as participant observation, providing the findings to respondents (in summary or more elaborate form) can act as an important source of validation of the findings and interpretations, and for the project as a whole, particularly where respondents are able to contribute to or influence the final output or report.

Finally, communicating findings to a wider population of *service users* (not just the service users who were the respondents for the research study itself) will enable users and the public to make informed judgements and choices based, to some extent, on research evidence. This will sometimes require communication of research in languages other than English, and/or using specialist forms of communication, where, for example, service users may have physical or mental impairments, or where there are learning or other difficulties.

10. Is the KT strategy aimed at informing or influencing policy and professional practice? If an aim of communicating research to relevant audiences is explicitly to have some *impact* then it will be important for researchers to address many of the issues outlined in the earlier discussion of evidence-based policy and practice (see Section 1.6). There we discussed in detail the issues, strengths, critiques and limitations of using research as evidence to *determine, inform* or *influence* policy and practice (what we referred to in *Figure 1l* as 'three levels of evidence-based policy and practice'), and the interested reader should revisit that earlier discussion. Here, we want to add just a few points about the *communication* of research evidence to make an impact. It must be emphasised, however, that dissemination of results on its own will not produce change in policy and practice (see, for example, *Box 7d*). For change to occur, there is a need for a detailed KT strategy whereby findings must be understood, trusted, adopted *and* utilised by policy makers and practitioners – a theme we return to in Section 7.5.

Gomm and Davies (2000) identify a number of reasons why poor communication of research helps to maintain a gap between research evidence and its utilisation by professionals (*Figure 7c*).

Figure 7c: How poor communication of research helps to maintain the research–practice gap

---

- Research findings tend to be published in 'academic' or 'obscure' journals which are read by some academics rather than by many practitioners. Many journals now report their 'impact/citation factors' which indicate that some of these articles are rarely cited or used by other academics.
- Many healthcare professionals and the majority of social workers have poor access to specialist libraries and sources of information.
- Where practitioners work in semi-isolation (in the community or primary care), there is less chance of messages from new research being disseminated by person-to-person communication.
- Information overload – the sheer weight of new information being produced.
- When research findings reach and are read by practitioners they are not sufficiently accessible to be understood and valued.

Source: Gomm and Davies (2000, p 135)

Gomm and Davies (2000) suggest that many practitioners express a preference for easy-to-read summaries with clear messages about implications for practice. This is confirmed by research conducted in local authorities examining how research can bring about change (Percy-Smith et al, 2002). The researchers found that the way in which research is *presented* affects the likelihood of it being read, disseminated further within an organisation and to other professionals, and whether the findings will be acted on.

Figure 7d lists the factors that contribute to good presentation of research and which thus increase the likelihood of findings being used to inform policy and practice (see also the guidance in Section 7.3 on how to write up research).

Figure 7d: Factors contributing to effective presentation of research

- A concise summary of research findings.
- Inclusion of recommendations, action points or checklists.
- Clearly presented data, case studies or examples.
- Orientation towards practitioners.
- Limited use of academic references, footnotes and so on.
- Clear identification of the key issues, why the research is important.
- Awareness of the multiple audiences for research, and who should read this particular document.
- Relevance and timeliness.

Source: Percy-Smith et al (2002, p 29)

Box 7e illustrates how 'timely' research on young adult carers utilised a number of approaches to dissemination and KT which are outlined in **Figure 7d**, and which helped the study to make an impact. The dissemination and KT activities included the publication of a full report (with policy and practice recommendations, and powerful case studies), a freely downloadable pdf of the full report, clear figures and statistics explained simply, a separately published (short) executive summary, media coverage, publications in practitioner and other journals, separate presentations to academics, practitioner and political audiences, and so on.

This approach to dissemination and KT, of *making research accessible, meaningful and relevant for different audiences, so that it can inform or influence policy and practice*, has manifested itself in a range of strategic national initiatives in the last few years, particularly in the health and social care spheres:

- The *National Institute for Health and Clinical Excellence* (NICE), the *NHS Centre for Reviews and Dissemination* (CRD), and the *Social Care Institute for Excellence* (SCIE) aim to make the best research evidence available to policy makers and professionals in medicine, healthcare and in social care respectively. The dissemination of best evidence by NICE and CRD most often involves the use of systematic reviews and meta-analysis (see also Section 1.6 and Section 4.17), and *clinical guidelines*. SCIE's remit is broader, to develop and promote knowledge about what works best in social care. Its mission is 'to identify and spread knowledge about good practice to the large and diverse social care workforce and support the delivery of transformed, personalised social care services. We aim to reach and influence practitioners...'. This includes not only the dissemination of reviews of evidence from research, but also disseminating knowledge from other sources, including users of services, those who deliver services and other stakeholders.

- *The Cochrane Collaboration* and the *Campbell Collaboration* are concerned with the preparation, maintenance and dissemination of systematic reviews of studies of interventions in the medical and health spheres (Cochrane), and in the social, behavioural and educational arenas (Campbell). Both have extensive libraries and databases of relevant studies.
- *Research in Practice* and *Making Research Count* are two national network organisations comprising universities, local and health authorities, third sector organisations and other agencies, aimed at disseminating the findings of research to relevant audiences to inform policy making and professional practice in health and social care. Both produce research-based reports, newsletters and other publications, and provide conferences, seminars and other events for members.
- Some research funders disseminate research findings directly to relevant audiences with an explicit intention of making an impact. The Joseph Rowntree Foundation, for example, publishes research and produces summaries and reviews of evidence, with a clear intention to bring about change.

Question for discussion

- What are the main issues that need to be taken into account when deciding a dissemination and knowledge transfer (KT) strategy for any piece of social research?

References

Gomm, R. and Davies, C. (2000) *Using evidence in health and social care*, London: Sage Publications.

LSE (London School of Economics) PPG (Public Policy Group) (2011) *Maximising the impact of your research: A handbook for social scientists*, London: LSE PPG (http://blogs.lse.ac.uk/impactofsocialsciences/).

Percy-Smith, J. with Burden, T., Darlow, A., Dowson, L., Hawtin, M. and Ladi, S. (2002) *Promoting change through research: The impact of research in local government*, York: Joseph Rowntree Foundation.

Further reading

Bogenschneider, K. and Corbett, T.J. (2010) *Evidence-based policymaking: Insights from policy-minded researchers and research-minded policymakers*, New York: Routledge.

Nutley, S.M., Walter, I. and Davies, H.T.O. (2007) *Using evidence: How can research inform public services?*, Bristol: The Policy Press.

Pawson, R. (2006) *Evidence-based policy: A realist perspective*, London: Sage Publications.

Website resources

The Campbell Collaboration: www.campbellcollaboration.org
Centre for Reviews and Dissemination (CRD): www.york.ac.uk/inst/crd/

Joseph Rowntree Foundation: www.jrf.org.uk/
Making Research Count: www.uea.ac.uk/menu/acad depts/swk/MRC web/public html/
National Institute for Health and Clinical Excellence (NICE): www.nice.org.uk/
Research in Practice: www.rip.org.uk
Social Care Institute for Excellence (SCIE): www.scie.org.uk
The Impact of Social Sciences Project: http://blogs.lse.ac.uk/impactofsocialsciences/
UK Cochrane Centre: http://ukcc.cochrane.org/

7.5 Making an impact
Saul Becker and Alan Bryman

Adoption, utilisation and change

In the final phase of the research cycle (see *Figure 1m* in Chapter One) we are concerned specifically with the *utilisation* of research evidence and its *application*, to *influence, inform, determine*, or where appropriate, to *change policy and practice*. This phase is closely linked with the dissemination and KT phase. Adoption, and the utilisation of research, cannot lead to change in policy and practice without adequate dissemination and KT, and any such strategy requires the 10 issues outlined in Section 7.4 to be considered from an early stage in the research itself.

In *Figure 1m* we identified the circumstances that are favourable to research having an impact on both policy and practice. So, for example, research is more likely to influence policy and practice where the researcher is trusted and authoritative, and where the methodology is relatively uncontested. These factors will help increase the adoption of research by policy makers and professionals (see *Boxes 7e* and *7f* for examples). It is also important to be aware that the 'loudest' research voice will not necessarily lead to the greatest adoption and utilisation of research, or to the largest change in policy and practice. Targeted dissemination and KT, on a softly-softly basis, can be as effective, if not more so, than, for example, attempts to embarrass a government, an organisation, aa agency or especially a person. *Box 7f*, for example, illustrates how research on the ICS led to changes in government policy.

All researchers will have their own personal goals and values in doing and disseminating research. All will be concerned to contribute to knowledge; otherwise there would be no point in conducting research in the first place. Some, especially those in social policy and social work, will want to disseminate findings to inform or change the practice of a specified group of people – perhaps, for example, social workers, care managers, benefits advisers or government policy makers. Others will be concerned to influence organisations, at a micro or macro-level. Others may wish to inform or change public attitudes through the process of adding to knowledge on a particular issue, social problem or concern. Yet others will be concerned to contribute to a movement for wider social (and political) change. These considerations will affect the style, manner, timing and forms of dissemination and KT activities (see Section 7.4).

Dissemination can also be an empowering force for research *participants*, other users of welfare and social services, their carers and for the wider public. Research evidence can highlight the circumstances and experiences of particular groups, and may help to enable a transfer (or redistribution) of resources to them. Where service users and carers are involved directly in the design, management, implementation and dissemination of research, this process may be particularly effective and empowering (see also Section 4.8). For research to have any impact on policy, actions or practices, however, we need to be clear about *what contributes to utilisation and change* in these spheres of activity. So, for example, do people need information and knowledge to change their policies or practices, or can they be *instructed* to change? Should information and knowledge be provided through training and professional development, or through policy, organisational and cultural change?

If an aim of social research is to impact on policy and practice, the dissemination and KT process needs to be used (and devised) in a purposeful and strategic way so as to maximise the potential for research utilisation and change. In some instances this will require a concentration on inappropriate attitudes and to try and highlight 'myths' in people's thinking; in other circumstances it will require close working between researchers and trainers to develop training materials based on messages from research; in other instances it will require the concentration of findings and messages on crucial *change agents* within an organisation – those who can go on to change the service, people or organisation itself. Those responsible for dissemination and KT will need to engage with many other actors, stakeholders and networks of interest if individual or organisational change is to be an outcome of the research process. *Figure 7e* identifies some issues that need to be considered where it is a goal for dissemination and KT to make an impact and to bring about change.

Figure 7e: Making an impact: some issues to consider

1 *What* do you want to change, and *why*? Are you concerned with professional knowledge, attitudes, culture, practice, behaviour, organisational structure, organisational culture, policy or wider social change? Be specific and precise. Identify and list the key 'targets' for change. Each may require their own strategy of engagement.

2 *Who* do you want to change? Can you identify specific groups or individuals? Are there 10 key people who should be targeted with research findings/messages and who could play a strategic role in bringing about these changes? How can you engage them directly?

3 In what *direction* do you want change to occur? What are the *outcomes* that you want from any change? For whose benefit is this change to occur? Who are the 'winners' and who are the 'losers'?

4 How can you bring about and secure change? What needs to happen to 'X' before 'Y' will change? What happens to 'Z' as a direct or indirect consequence?

5 What is your timescale? Can you identify and list clear and measurable targets or indicators of change in the short, medium and long term?

6 How will you know when something has changed? How can you monitor change and evaluate whether it has been successful or not?

7 How do you know that it was *your* research that was utilised to bring about change? What is the evidence? How can you systematically collect and collate that evidence?

With change, one round of the research cycle identified in *Figure 1m* becomes complete. The original 'seeing' of a social issue or social problem has, with some research and KT skill, and a little luck, led to changes in policy and/or practice and, hopefully, an improvement in whatever aspect of social life, social welfare, health, development or well-being that has been the subject of the research focus. However, the research *cycle* does not end here – it is dynamic and ongoing, with the monitoring and evaluation of new policies and practices.

As we have shown in this volume, this cycle of research, dissemination, KT and change does not take place in a vacuum. What can be understood through research, what can be achieved by it, and the types of change that can be brought about, are all influenced by the many factors which we have considered throughout this volume, including the political and ideological climate at the time, whether research is accepted as an evidence base for policy and practice, the quality and trustworthiness of the research, and so much more.

Research has the potential to make an impact and to inform, influence or deliver change, but it is a time-consuming and a difficult process, with no guarantee that policy or practice will actually change. Sometimes the best executed research changes nothing, is misrepresented or ignored, as we have seen in *Box 7d*. At other times, a small study can have an effect on policy that few would have thought possible, especially when an active and targeted KT strategy is in place, as we have seen in *Boxes 7e* and *7f*. This is *not* a lottery. Developing the expertise in conducting and managing social policy and social work research, and in disseminating research to relevant audiences, will maximise the *potential* for research to form a trustworthy evidence base for policy and practice. It can contribute to evidence-based policy and practice in diverse ways and at different levels.

As one *way of knowing* (see *Figure 1d* in Chapter One), research is the *only* foundation for policy and practice that allows self-correction through further research – which can check, verify or refute the knowledge base. The most important thing to remember is that research must be of the *highest quality*, and be rigorous and trustworthy. These quality requirements are essential; otherwise evidence-informed policy and practice, and impact, may be built on unreliable and precarious foundations.

Question for discussion

- List the advantages and disadvantages of using research as the evidence base for trying to bring about change in policy or practice.

Further reading

Bogenschneider, K. and Corbett, T.J. (2010) *Evidence-based policymaking: Insights from policy-minded researchers and research-minded policymakers*, New York: Routledge.

LSE (London School of Economics) PPG (Public Policy Group) (2011) *Maximising the impact of your research: A handbook for social scientists*, London: LSE PPG (http://blogs.lse.ac.uk/impactofsocialsciences/).

Rose, C. (2010) *How to win campaigns: Communications for change*, London: Earthscan.

Wilson, D. (1984) *Pressure: The A to Z of campaigning in Britain*, London: Heinemann.

Glossary

Note: All glossary items have been compiled by the contributors and editors.

Accessible: Materials or environments designed or adapted to be easily used/understood by people with a disability, people with learning disabilities or others.

Accessible information: Information provided in formats that can be understood by people with learning disabilities. As a minimum, this requires using simple words and pictures; it can also include providing information in audio or video formats.

Action orientation: The way people's talk or **Text** is designed to perform actions in particular settings.

Action research: An orientation to inquiry rather than a **Methodology**. Action research is a participatory, democratic process concerned with developing practical knowing in the pursuit of worthwhile human purposes and grounded in a participatory worldview. Action research seeks to bring together action and reflection, **Theory** and practice, in participation with others, in the pursuit of practical solutions to issues of pressing concern to people, and more generally the flourishing of individual persons and their communities.

Adoption (of research): The use made of research to understand, inform or to change policy and practice.

Advisory groups: These are often set up by funders of research to support a project in various ways. Members of such groups are usually people with particular knowledge of the issues, including policy makers and practitioners, or knowledge of the approach being adopted (for example, qualitative methods). Advisory groups have no executive authority in relation to projects and simply offer advice and support. Some **Steering groups**, particularly those set up by some government departments, can take a more active role in specifying the work to be done or taking part in decisions that can change the project's work.

Aggregate data: Statistics that relate to broad classes, groups or categories, so that it is not possible to distinguish the properties of individuals within those classes, groups or categories. Examples are population statistics on gender or national estimates compiled from regional data sources.

Analytic induction: An account of the process of scientific inquiry that has been appealed to by some qualitative researchers. It assumes that research begins with investigation of instances of the phenomenon to be explained, and leads into the formulation and testing of explanatory **Hypotheses**. Initially, the hypotheses will usually fail to fit the cases studied, and this will lead to their modification or abandonment, and/or to a reformulation of the nature of the phenomenon to be explained. Only when investigation of further cases throws up no exceptions can a hypothetical explanation be accepted as true, and only then provisionally – contradictory evidence may arise in the future, stimulating a resumption of the inquiry process. Those who developed analytic induction contrasted it with statistical method, in which hypotheses are accepted so long as the bulk of cases investigated do not contradict them.

Analytic memo: In **Grounded theory**, a short document, written by and for the analyst that discusses meaning and wider theoretical significance of codes. More generally, a document used in analysis containing the researcher's commentary on the primary data or codes of the project.

Anonymity: Ensuring anonymity means not revealing the identity of individuals, organisations or locations that are involved in a research study. This is slightly different from *confidentiality*, which means that the information that people provide will not be shared with others.

Anti-realism: This is an approach to knowledge that attacks realism by disputing its central tenets. It therefore denies that there is an externally knowable world that can be accurately and objectively represented and studied.

'Art versus science': A metaphor for contrasting approaches to *understanding* and *undertaking* social work.

Asylum: One of the words used to mean 'refuge' in accordance with the criteria set out in the United Nations (UN) Convention Relating to the Status of Refugees 1951.

Asylum seeker: A person who has applied to the government of a country other than their own for protection or refuge ('asylum') because they are unable or unwilling to seek the protection of their own government.

Asymmetry: Differences between different parties to an interaction in terms of their power, knowledge, institutional identities and so on.

Asynchronous/non-real time: Communication that takes place at different times, for example, email communication which is not simultaneous and does not require users to be online at the same time.

Bar chart: A graphical display of qualitative data in which each category is represented by a bar or rectangle and where the height of the bar indicates the number of cases.

Bias: A measure of the difference between the average estimate (from the **Sampling distribution of the means**) and the true population **Parameter**. It arises when some population members have unequal selection probabilities.

Biographical interpretive method: In-depth phenomenological interviewing and analysis.

Biography: An account of a person's life written by another individual; the practice of writing about another person.

Blog: A conflation of the words 'web log', a blog is a website where the main navigational framework is chronological, usually composed of news stories or online diary entries. Most blogs are primarily textual, although some use visual images or video ('vlogs') either as enhanced diaries or as electronic portfolios. Many blogs allow visitors to leave comments and it is this interactivity that distinguishes them as a **Web 2.0** technology.

Boolean search: Named after the mathematician, Boole, this is a search in which the items being searched for are combined by Boolean connectors such as 'and', 'or' and 'not'. For instance, one may search for text that matches the words 'luck' or 'chance'.

Booster sample: Sampling for **Surveys** usually involves taking a representative or random sample of the whole population or obtaining a stratified sample to make sure that all target groups are proportionately represented within the final sample population. However, in some cases, for example, where the overall population of minorities may be very low compared with the population as a whole, it may be necessary to boost – that is, deliberately increase – the sample of minorities to ensure that the sample is large enough to provide adequate good quality data. This is called booster sampling. The more formal term for this is 'disproportionate stratification'.

Budget: (a) A plan of expenditure; (b) an allocation of financial resources within which a particular research project is to be undertaken.

Campbell Collaboration: Analogous to **The Cochrane Collaboration** (see later), but is concerned with the preparation, maintenance and **Dissemination** of **Systematic reviews** of studies of interventions in the social, behavioural and educational arenas.

Canonical cases: Standard or expected cases which are characteristic of a practice; for example, 'fine thanks' in response to a 'howareyou' greeting.

Case study: A case can be defined as any phenomenon located in space and time about which data are collected and analysed, and can comprise single individuals or a group, particular events or situations, a specific organisation, a social institution, neighbourhood, national society or global process. Case studies can address the micro-situation of a single person in everyday life or the macro-situation of a nation state in the global world.

Category: The group or set of things, people or actions classified together because of common characteristics. In **Grounded theory**, the term is used interchangeably with 'code'.

Clinical guideline: A statement of how clinical professionals should act in respect of treatment or diagnosis in specified circumstances. Such guidelines may be more or less specific and may or may not be in some sense 'evidence-based'.

Closed questions: These are questions that supply the answers from which **Respondents** are asked to select and are commonly used in **Survey** research with questionnaires. Sometimes they include an open-ended option (for example, 'other') at the end.

Cluster sampling: A sampling technique that aggregates population members into groups (clusters) and it is these groups that are initially randomly selected.

Cochrane Collaboration: A well-established international network of specialists developing the evidence base for medical practice on an open and responsive basis with regular updating of **Systematic reviews** posted on the Collaboration's website.

Code: A term that represents an idea, **Theme**, **Theory**, dimension, characteristic etc of the data. Passages of **Text**, images etc in a qualitative analysis study can be linked to the same code to show that they represent the same idea, theme, characteristic etc.

Code of ethics: A formal set of guidelines intended to influence the behaviour of researchers in a way that is consistent with ethically acceptable practices.

Cohort design: A continuing research study that collects data over time about a group of individuals born in the same time period, and which may be conducted prospectively or retrospectively. A *prospective cohort study* involves a systematic follow-up for a defined period of time or until the occurrence of a specified event (for example, onset of illness, retirement or death). For a *retrospective cohort study*, data on the group's background, experience or **Life history** are already available.

Comparative method: A very general term referring to the fundamental approach of most scientific inquiry, in which cases are compared in order to try to identify the causes which bring about some type of phenomenon. **Experiments**, **Survey** analysis, grounded theorising and analytic induction all employ the comparative method.

Comparative research: Research which aims to identify and explain similarities and differences between social phenomena – events, processes, actors, social groups – in two or more contexts. It can involve comparisons of phenomena within one country, but more usually it refers to comparisons of socioeconomic and political phenomena in two or more countries, which is also known as 'cross-national research'.

Computer-assisted interviewing (CAI): The use of computers to assist in conducting interviews. The most common form of CAI is to use pre-programmed questionnaires and administering the **Questionnaire** either personally (CAPI), over the telephone

(CATI) or allowing the **Respondent** to self-administer the questionnaire (CASI). Self-administration may be conducted in a variety of ways including via email or the internet. These computer-assisted forms of data collection contrast with surveys that use paper questionnaires (commonly known as PAPI [pen/pencil-assisted personal interviewing]).

Computer–assisted qualitative data analysis (CAQDAS): Note: computers only assist. The software does not analyse. Term introduced by Fielding and Lee in 1991.

Confidence intervals: The upper and lower bounds of an estimate that describe the range within which the population **Parameter** will fall, with a given degree of probability, set by the researcher.

Conjecture: The first stage in the development of a scientific hypothesis that will give focus to the research and direction in the collection of relevant data.

Constant comparative method: A recursive approach to coding whereby as a passage is coded the analyst re-examines all incidents or passages previously coded the same way. This ensures that the theoretical properties of codes are fleshed out as analysis proceeds.

Constructionism: This is a theoretical approach within the social sciences that emphasises that social phenomena are constructed by people in and through their actions, rather than existing independently of those actions. In this respect, it contrasts with those approaches that emphasise the way in which people and their actions are shaped by external social structures and institutions. Constructionism takes its most radical forms when it is applied to people's understandings of the world, and even to social scientists' own research reports. Here it involves a rejection of the idea that accounts, even scientific accounts, represent the world. Rather, emphasis is given to the functions which accounts are designed to serve and their role in constructing the reality they purport merely to represent.

Content analysis: A term mainly used to describe the statistical analysis of content. Quantitative content analysis mainly focuses on the manifest features of texts, and requires the development of a coding frame that identifies which aspects should be counted, and in what way.

Context: A concept that is an inherent part of **Discourse analysis** and contributes significantly to how systematically it can be applied as part of interdisciplinary approaches. In the course of investigating complex **Social problems** it is necessary to draw on multiple theoretical approaches to analyse given contexts and relate these to texts. Thus contexts are, on the one hand, structural constraints and norms, time and space; on the other hand, cognitive perceptions of a given situation by speakers, viewers and listeners: whether 'context' is included in linguistic analysis and the definition of 'context' per se is dependent on prior theoretical decisions.

Contingency table: A table showing the frequencies of cases in the categories of two or more variables.

Convenience sampling: A type of sampling where the researcher uses cases that are most convenient or available. The sample is made up of whoever is willing and available to participate. This is a non-probability method of sampling.

Conversation analysis: A way of understanding the joint production of everyday life through a labour-intensive (qualitative) analysis of conversation. It promises an empirically grounded basis for understanding how issues in social policy are actually realised in interaction.

Correlation, Pearson's (r): An index of the strength and direction of the linear relationship between two **Quantitative variables**.

Counterpartal role inquiry: A type of cooperative inquiry where the co-researchers have differential power roles and experiences (for example, cooperative inquiry conducted by patients and doctors researching their experiences of working in or using healthcare services).

Credibility: The question of whether a set of findings is believable.

Critical qualitative theory: An approach to qualitative research that is grounded in a critical realist philosophy and that emphasises **Generalisability**, the use of existing theories and research, and analysis that is strongly rooted in the original data, and case-and-theme-based **Data management**.

Critical realism: A philosophical approach that combines an ontological belief in the existence of a reality independent of those that observe it with an epistemological approach that reality is only accessible through the perceptions of people and is therefore necessarily affected by their interpretations.

Critical research: Umbrella term describing diverse research approaches that consider research to be non-neutral, and are concerned with individual and social experiences, processes, structures and relationships of power.

Critique: 'Critique' carries many different meanings: some adhere to the Frankfurt School, others to a notion of literary criticism, some to Marxist notions. Adhering to a 'critical' stance should be understood as gaining distance from the data (despite the fact that critique is mostly 'situated critique'), embedding the data in the social context, clarifying the political positioning of discourse participants and having a focus on continuous self-reflection while undertaking research. Moreover, the application of results is aspired to, be it in practical seminars for teachers, doctors and bureaucrats, in the writing of expert opinions or in the production of school books.

Cross-sectional survey designs: Research design in which data are collected for all cases and all variables that apply to a single period in time.

Data: Social science data are the raw material out of which social and economic statistics and other research **Outputs** are produced. Social science data originate from social research methodologies or administrative records, while statistics can be produced from data. Data are the information collected and stored at the level at which the unit of analysis was observed, such as an individual or household. Data are processed to enable them to be analysed, such as with statistical or qualitative data software, which read the raw data from computer files, or data can be analysed using one or more other techniques, such as **Grounded theory**, **Discourse analysis**, and so on.

Data archives: Resource centres that acquire, store and disseminate digital data for **Secondary analysis** in research and teaching.

Data archiving: A method of conserving expensive data resources and ensuring that their research potential is fully exploited by researchers and others.

Data editing: Process of checking the quality of data and, where possible, correcting any errors.

Data management: The strategies, procedures and practices used to manage research data at any stage of a research project – from planning **Research design** and data collection to sharing data post-project. Strategies includes gaining adequate consent, assessing copyright, using appropriate data collection tools, choosing the longer-term data formats and controlling access. Well organised, well documented and safely stored data can aid the initial inquiry as well as any further uses in years to come.

Dataset: A collection of data records, such as numerical responses to a **Survey** or texts transcribed from **Qualitative interviews**, associated with a particular study. A dataset can be a file or group of files associated with one part of a study.

Deductive approach: The research process is conducted with reference to pre-existing theoretical ideas and concepts. Deductivists start by formulating a **Theory** and then proceed from this general proposition to a consideration of particular cases in order to test their theory. This approach contrasts with inductivists who start by drawing inferences from particular cases from which they proceed towards the formulation of general theoretical conclusions.

Deductive theory testing: Proceeds from general propositions to testing and/or falsifying specific **Hypotheses**.

Degrees of freedom (*df*): The number of values in a statistic that are free to vary.

Dependability: The question of how far we can rely on a set of findings.

Deviant case: Sometimes also known as 'negative instance', this is a term from **Qualitative data** analysis to describe an instance in which data do not fit, or initially appear to contradict, an emerging generalisation or theoretical proposition. Frequently such instances can extend or deepen a **Theory** by requiring its reformulation to take account of the anomaly.

Deviant case analysis: Exploration of exceptional examples as part of the validation of analytic claims.

Dichotomous variable: A variable that only has two categories or values.

Dimensionalising: Recognising the multiple properties or aspects that a code may have. For example, a code about activities may have a list of the several different kinds of activity as one of its dimensions. Duration, actors, settings etc may constitute other dimensions.

Directly allocated costs: These are usually seen as shared costs, for example, for an investigator who may be fully funded from other sources or a lab technician. Estate costs also fall under this heading and could include building and premises costs, services and utilities, insurance, maintenance and cleaning etc.

Discourse: Texts and talk in social practices.

Discourse analysis: A cluster of methods and approaches (including continental discourse analysis, critical discourse analysis, discursive psychology and **Conversation analysis**) that focus on the role of talk and texts in social life. Different forms of discourse analysis place different emphasis on specific practices of interaction and the broader discursive resources that underpin that interaction.

Discourse-historical approach: Approach to critical discourse analysis developed by Ruth Wodak in the late 1980s at the University of Vienna, to study complex social phenomena and their development in specific contexts, systematically, from different disciplinary angles, and in as much linguistic detail as possible. More specifically, **Text** and **Context** are focused on, and the development of certain topics, arguments, genres and discourses is traced in relationship to sociopolitical events. This implies that the study of (oral, written, visual) language necessarily remains only a part of the whole enterprise – hence discourse–historical approach research must be interdisciplinary. Moreover, in order to analyse, understand and explain the complexity of the objects under investigation, many different and accessible sources of data from various analytical perspectives are considered. The *principle of triangulation*, which implies taking a whole range of empirical observations, theories and methods as well as background information into account, is salient.

Dissemination: The communication to relevant audiences of information and knowledge gained from research.

Domain: The term used to refer to the broad practice contexts and also forms of service delivery within which social work research often takes place.

Economic and Social Research Council (ESRC): a UK funder of research on economic and social issues (see www.esrc.ac.uk).

Emancipatory research: Research which adopts an explicitly political and emancipatory **Paradigm**, in which a disempowered group are in full control of research about their lives or issues which affect their lives. Disability activists coined the term, but the approach may also be a useful way of thinking about research concerning any group of people who are disempowered by mainstream society.

Epistemological: Refers to a concern with what should be regarded and accepted as legitimate knowledge.

Epistemology: A set of assumptions about what should be regarded as acceptable knowledge.

Epsem (equal probability of selection method): A technique that ensures that each subset of size *n* population members has an equal chance of selection into the study.

Equivalence scale: A scale used to adjust household income so that it takes into account the number of people who have to live on that income and economies of scale.

Ethics: Is about human/animal/planetary welfare or flourishing – matters of right and wrong conduct, good and bad qualities of character and responsibilities attached to relationships. The term can be used in the singular to refer to a subject area ('Jane is studying ethics as part of her philosophy degree'), and in the plural to refer to norms, principles or character traits ('Jane's ethics are rather dubious').

Ethnography: A style of research rather than a single method. The study of people in naturally occurring settings or 'fields' by means of methods which capture their social meanings and ordinary activities, involving the researcher participating directly in the setting, if not also the activities, in order to collect data in a systematic manner but without meaning being imposed on them externally.

Evaluation research: Research that seeks to assess the worth or value of an innovation, intervention, programme, policy or service.

Evidence: (a) Means of proving an unknown or disputed fact; (b) support for a belief; (c) an indication; (d) information in a law case; (e) testimony; (f) witness or witnesses collectively; (g) the results or findings of systematic, robust and trustworthy empirical enquiry.

Evidence-based medicine (EBM): The integration of best research evidence with clinical expertise and patient values.

Evidence-based policy and practice: The formulation and implementation of policy and practice based on the best evidence available, including research evidence and evidence from other sources such as 'service users', professionals and other stakeholders.

Experiment: Often seen as the most fundamental modern scientific method. It can be contrasted most sharply with observation of naturally occurring events. It involves active intervention on the part of the researcher to set up a situation in which what is taken to be a key causal factor is varied and the effects of other relevant causal factors are minimised or maintained at the same level. The aim is to identify the independent effect of the key **Variable**: to discover whether it has the effects hypothesised, or whether these are a product of other factors.

Feminism: A position with the political aim of challenging discrimination against women and/or promoting greater equality between the sexes. It involves some sense of women having common interests as a result of unjust gender relations. There are, however, a great variety of different feminist theories and corresponding political strategies for change.

Feminist research: Challenges the 'myth' of objective, value-free research and acknowledges the centrality of the researchers' values and interpretations. It values the experiences and opinions of women, is politically *for* women and seeks to improve women's lives in some way.

Field notes: A record of field observation. Usually divided into three types: mental 'notes', jotted notes (prepared in the field) and full field notes (a detailed description of the round of observation).

Files: A discrete set of data held in computer software, for example, the complete transcript of a single interview.

Finding aids: Inventories, registers, indexes or guides to collections held by archives and manuscript repositories, libraries and museums. Finding aids provide detailed descriptions of collections, their intellectual organisation and sometimes of individual items in the collections.

Finite population correction (*fpc*): An adjustment made in simple random sampling to reflect the fact that samples are drawn from a finite population, compared to the infinite populations that are used in theoretical procedures.

Focus groups: Group discussions that are organised to explore a specific set of issues and involve some kind of collective activity. What is important in the focus group is the emphasis on interaction within the group based on topics that are of interest to the researcher.

Framework: A case-and-theme based approach to **Data management** that uses a matrix to display summarised data as an aid to analysis.

FrameWork: A **Computer-assisted qualitative data analysis software** (CAQDAS) package specifically designed to support the Framework approach to **Data management**.

Frequency distribution: A table that shows the number of cases in each category of a **Variable**.

Funnelling: A technique used in **Questionnaire** design to introduce sensitive questions. Questions begin broadly and increasingly narrow down to the point where the revelation of sensitive, personal or intimate information appears less sudden or surprising.

Generalisability: This means the applicability of the data to other like cases (also sometimes called 'external validity').

Genre: The conventionalised, more or less schematically fixed use of language associated with a particular activity and with particular functions for a specified speech community – as a socially accepted and conventionalised way of using language in connection with a particular type of social activity.

Governance: The study of governance focuses on the exercise of political power and the patterns of power in the relationships between different actors – state, civil society, public and private sectors, citizens and communities.

Governmentality: The study of governmentality is concerned with the sorts of knowledge, ideas and beliefs about aspects of society that contribute to the ways in which issues are problematised, and the strategies and tactics that governments use to deal with these.

Grand theory: Concerns societal level phenomena.

Grounded theory: A collection of (largely qualitative) data gathering and data analysis procedures in which the objective is to generate theories from data. Grounded theories can be of two types: 'substantive' (applicable to the setting studied) or 'formal' (applicable to a range of similar settings).

Haphazard sampling: A method of selecting sample members without conscious choice, but one that is still subject to unconscious effects and is still therefore subjective and likely to be biased.

Harmonised data: Data that have been collected for particular purposes, and which are afterwards adjusted so that as far as possible the variables in different **Datasets** measure the same thing, such as the number of hours that constitute part-time employment in different countries.

Hermeneutic tool: Helps to interpret, understand or explain.

Hypertext: Text displayed on a computer or other electronic device with references (hyperlinks) to other text that the reader can immediately access (usually by a mouse click or other command). The most familiar hypertext for most people is the network of linked web pages of the World Wide Web.

Hypotheses: A kind of research question, namely, one that postulates a possible relationship between two or more variables. Scientific hypotheses must be set out in ways that allow them to be tested and falsified by methods of observation and **Experiment**. See also **Conjecture**.

Idiographic generalisation: Understandings from specific contexts may be adapted to shed light on others.

Indicator: A measure that is used to represent a concept, such as 'occupation', as an indicator of social class.

Indirect costs: These are non-specific costs charged across all projects and could include general office and laboratory consumables, local administrative support as well as centrally provided services such as human resources, finance, computing and the library.

Inductive orientation: A contrast is sometimes drawn between two views of scientific method: inductive and deductive. The inductive view argues that science ought to start with the collection and analysis of data, from which theoretical ideas will then emerge. These may then be tested against further data.

Inductive theory building: Draws inference from particular cases and proceeds towards formulating **Theory**.

Informal carers: People who provide unpaid care to other family members or friends who need personal help, practical assistance or watching over because of frailty, physical impairment, learning disability or ill health, including mental illness. Some informal carers can be children or young people ('young carers' and 'young adult carers').

Informant: A term referring to an interviewee, especially where what the interviewee provides is information not accessible to the researcher by means of direct observation, for example, because the events described occurred in the past or took place in settings to which the researcher did not have access. The role of informants is particularly important in ethnographic research, especially in anthropology. The interviewee as informant is sometimes contrasted with the interviewee as **Respondent**.

Informed consent: A knowing agreement to take part in research.

Institutional interaction: The talk in institutional settings that performs and constitutes the nature of that institution.

Interdiscursivity: Indicates that discourses are linked to each other in various ways. If we define discourse as primarily topic-related, that is, a discourse on X, then this discourse might refer to topics or subtopics of other discourses Y and Z.

Internet server: Individuals connect to the internet by attaching to a server (computer) that has links to numerous other servers that form the internet. As well as providing access to the internet, servers store web pages and associated files. Files such as electronic questionnaires can be stored on a server and made available to all users of the internet or may be configured to allow restricted access based on passwords or some other identifier.

Interpretative repertoires: An organised cluster of terms; metaphors that are a resource for constructing versions of actions and events.

Interpretivism: A term sometimes used to refer to an approach in social research that emphasises the role of interpretation on the part of both those studied and the researcher. Interpretivists reject those views of human behaviour which portray it as a mechanical product of causes, whether biological, psychological, social structural or cultural. Instead, human action is treated as following a contingent course as a result of a process of interpretation by which actors make sense of the situations they face, and of their own concerns and goals in light of that situation. Moreover, it is taken to follow from this that any attempt on the part of researchers to understand the social world must rely on their ability to interpret the behaviour of those they are studying: scientific understanding of social life cannot take the form simply of following some abstract scientific method; it relies on a cultural capacity to make sense of other people's behaviour in the same way that they do themselves.

Interpretivist research: See **Interpretivism**.

Intertextuality: This refers to the fact that all texts are linked to other texts, both in the past and in the present. Such links can be established in different ways: through continued reference to a topic or main actors; through reference to the same events; or by the transfer of main arguments from one text into the next.

Interview mode: The manner in which an interview is carried out. The most common modes are face-to-face or telephone.

Knowledge and Exchange Team (KET): Based at the **Third Sector Research Centre** (TSRC).

Learning difficulty/disability (also intellectual impairment): People with an intellectual disability, formerly described as a 'mental handicap' (now regarded as a derogatory label).

Life history: Life history interviewing is one of the methods used by social scientists. It involves in-depth questioning of a person, or a small number of people, about their lives, often over several interview sessions. The usual rationale for this method is the argument that we can only understand a person's actions properly if we can see what they do or have done in the context of their life as a whole. However, life history work is also sometimes motivated by an interest in how people's lives develop, or in the experiences of a particular historical generation.

Likert scale: Widely used technique for measuring attitudes. Consists of a set of statements that respondents have to rate. Each respondent's replies are then scored and aggregated.

Linguistic realisation: The many ways certain goals and aims of speakers are realised in language-specific ways, depending on the context and functions of the utterance.

Longitudinal design: A **Research design** in which data are gathered from a selected group of individuals at intervals over a period of time. The two main types are **Cohort designs** and **Panel designs**. Examples of panel studies include the British Household Panel Study (BHPS) and ONS Longitudinal Study based on the census and vital event data (births, cancers, deaths) routinely collected for 1% of the population of England and Wales.

Longitudinal qualitative research: Repeat observations of, ideally, the same research subjects over time, using **Qualitative data** collection techniques, and focused on change at an individual rather than group level.

Mean, arithmetic (*M*): The sum of values divided by the number of values.

Meaning: This describes the beliefs, feelings, moods, perceptions and interpretations of people. The study of these meanings is normally associated with the idea that the social world is partly (or wholly) constructed and reconstructed by people on the basis of these meanings, which is a defining element of **Naturalism**.

Measures of central tendency: Indices such as the mean that describe the central or typical value of a set of values.

Measures of dispersion: Indices that describe the dispersion or spread of values in a set of values such as the **Standard deviation**.

Median: The value of the mid-point of a set of values ordered in size.

Memo: A succinct statement of the meaning of an analytic category or the definition of a code applied to the data.

Mental health service user/survivor: Someone who uses, or has used, mental health services.

Meta-analysis: A method of combining the findings of several research studies so as to reach an overall conclusion. In the context of healthcare, meta-analysis normally employs statistical techniques to pool the results of studies that in some cases may be too small to provide convincing conclusions.

Meta-data: Defined as 'data about data', such as the information contained in a library or data archive catalogue. For social science data, meta-data include information about the data file, the research study, such as describing the sample from which the data were drawn, the time period covered, and at a finer level, definitions of survey codes in a file, such as their description and values.

Method: Procedure for collecting research data.

Methodology: (a) The broad theoretical and philosophical framework within which methods operate and that give them their intellectual authority and legitimacy; (b) the study of methods.

Micro-data: Data collected from **Surveys** or compiled from other sources, at the level of the individual or group, rather than at the aggregate level. An example is a census or survey that has collected information about behaviour and the surrounding social and economic environment. Typically, certain information is removed to protect the confidentiality of the **Respondent**.

Middle range theory: Deals with specific social, interpersonal and individual phenomena.

Mixed methods: Research that combines quantitative and qualitative research.

Mode: The most frequently occurring value in a set of values.

Modernity: The social organisation of industrialising and industrialised societies of the West characterised by separations of church and state, art and science, the public sphere of work and politics from the private sphere of home, by the institution of economic, political and social rights attached to citizenship which serve to distinguish between nationalities, men and women, disabled and 'able-bodied', and so on. It involves the rise of new institutions, such as education and welfare, which organise people into categories, and become key sites for the acting out of collective norms and values. Rational and bureaucratic selection and allocation processes, backed up by scientific theories, are seen to provide a break with old forms of patronage and preferential distribution.

Moral concerns: In carrying out research with **Vulnerable people**, researchers need to be morally responsible for their lives and well-being in ways that do not increase their vulnerability.

Multi-stage sampling: Repeated drawing of sub-units from higher order units, for example, at Stage 1 drawing a sample of postcode sectors from all postcode sectors and at Stage 2 drawing a sample of addresses from the postcode sectors selected at Stage 1.

Narrative analysis: The collection and interpretation of life accounts in interview or other forms with reference to **Story** (and **Plot**) construction and attention to the teller's temporal ordering of events, use of descriptive or explanatory devices such as metaphor, and experiences.

Narrative methods: Searching for meaning in individual accounts by identifying elements of **Story**.

National Council for Voluntary Organisations (NCVO): see www.ncvo-vol.org. uk/ for more information.

Naturalism: This is an orientation concerned with the study of social life in real, naturally occurring settings; the experiencing, observing, describing, understanding and analysing of the features of social life in concrete situations as they occur independently of scientific manipulation. These naturally occurring situations are also sometimes called 'face-to-face' situations, mundane interaction, micro-interaction or everyday life.

Naturalistic records: Video or audio recordings of people interacting in everyday or institutional settings (not set up by the researcher).

Navigate: To move around a database held in a software package.

Negative case: A case that does not work as proposed in a hypothetical universal statement.

Neo-positivist: An approach influenced by **Positivism** in social science – the application of the scientific method to social life, including deductive reasoning and hypothesis testing, the collection of 'empirical data' and the use of scientific findings to make social changes.

Nomothetic generalisation: Can be applied to all contexts, based on statistically generalisable evidence.

Normative: Concerned with how society *should* be organised, rather than describing how it *is* organised, or trying to provide an explanation for *why* it is organised as it is.

Objectivity: A term that has a variety of meanings, and can therefore generate confusion and spurious disagreement. The most prominent meaning of 'objectivity' refers to a process of inquiry. Inquiry is objective if it follows the most rational course in seeking to produce knowledge; in other words, if it is not deflected from that course by prior assumptions, personal preferences, and so on. Here, the opposite of objectivity is bias: systematic error caused by features of the researcher.

Office for Civil Society (OCS): created in the Cabinet Office in May 2010 (for more information see www.cabinetoffice.gov.uk/resource-library/office-civil-society-structure-finalised).

Open coding: Initial qualitative coding in which the analyst keeps an open mind and looks for codes that reflect the respondents' interpretations of their actions and their world rather than codes that reflect pre-existing theories.

Open system: Referencing the multiple determinants that may or may not affect processes as they occur in the natural environment and everyday life. Such systems can be contrasted with the relatively closed system of laboratory environments.

Operationalisation: The process of generating one or more indicators of a concept.

Opt-in: To agree to participate in a research project by formally responding to a letter of invitation.

Opt-out: To be deemed to have given consent to be approached by a research team by not having formally refused or declined within a given timescale.

Oral history: Researching individual and collective experience through memory.

Output: A vehicle for communicating research to relevant audiences, such as a report, presentation and so on.

Panel attrition: Refers to the cumulative loss of respondents in successive waves of data collection through refusal, non-contact, moving overseas, being out-of-scope or death.

Panel designs: Collect comparable data about the same individuals on two or more occasions. The British Household Panel Survey (BHPS) is a prospective panel design, following up the same individuals over time.

Paradigm: A distinctive worldview or perspective that provides a unifying framework for thought and action among those who subscribe to its principles.

Parameter: A **Population** value of a distribution (such as the mean or **Variance**).

Participant observation: A method in which observers participate in the daily life of people under study.

Participatory research: Research which actively involves people with learning or other disabilities as co-researchers working on an equal footing to non-disabled researcher colleagues.

PASW Statistics: Since 2008, the new name of a widely used statistics software known previously as **SPSS**.

Percentage: The **Proportion** multiplied by 100.

Phenomenology: A philosophical position concerned with how we comprehend the world around us and with the ways in which that process of comprehension might be studied. The position places an emphasis on the bracketing of the analyst's experience.

Photo-elicitation: The use of photographs to elicit information in interviews.

Plot: A term used in narrative analysis. A length of time – the time limits of start and end – within which selected events are given meaning and connected as part of a specific storied outcome.

Policy implementation: The business of translating decisions into events, of 'getting things done'. Implementation relates to 'specified objectives', the translation into practice of the policies that emerge from the process of decision making.

Policy research: Research designed to *inform* or to *understand* one or more aspects of the public and **Social policy** process, including decision making and policy formulation, implementation and evaluation. Policy research also aims to provide answers and evidence that can contribute to the improvement of 'policy' and policy making, can lead to better practice and interventions, the reduction of **Social problems** and social distress, and the promotion of welfare and well-being. Policy research draws from the full range of research designs, methods and approaches outlined in this volume.

Population: The term given to all units that are defined by particular characteristics.

Positivism: A methodological position that believes in the application of natural science methods and procedures to the study of social life, which involves the notion that the social sciences address similar problems to the natural sciences, that social scientists confront a social world similar in most respects to the natural world, can focus on causal explanations and use deduction.

Positivist research: Seeks to explain and predict relationships, often causal, between objectively verifiable phenomena.

Post-modernism: This is a set of theories that in relation to knowledge argue that objective truth is unattainable. The search for objective truth is deconstructed and shown to dissolve into various language games about 'truth'. Knowledge is therefore relative, and people should thus be sceptical about truth claims. Post-modernism thus encourages us to examine the contingent social processes that affect research and which undermine the **Objectivity** and truthfulness of the knowledge.

Post-modernity: This term is more problematic than both **Post-structuralism** and **Post-modernism**, for it presupposes that society has broken from **Modernity** and now exists within a new epoch. Most social theorists do not go that far, recognising that some aspects of modernity still coexist with some significant changes. Thus, Giddens talks of 'reflexive modernisation' as the period we are now in, marked by globalisation, a post-traditional social order (where class, gender, sexuality, age and ethnicity are far more fluid and less fixed) and '**reflexivity**', where people do not follow fixed biographies, but are engaged in continual negotiation of the courses of their lives.

Post-structuralism: The body of theory to emerge in the 1960s from French philosophers, Foucault, Derrida and Lacan, as a **Critique** of Enlightenment thinking. It thus involves the rejection of the 'grand narrative', of the human subject as powerful, unitary and self-consciously political, of the necessity of progress, the belief in universal truths and unquestionable or scientific facts. Post-structuralists resist the construction of the world into oppositional categories: man/woman; ruling class/working class; civilised/uncivilised; culture/nature; tradition/reason. Instead, they focus on fragmented and changing subjectivities, on the way 'truths' about phenomena are constituted through the way people speak about them. Power and knowledge are thus interconnected, for discourses (sets of linked utterances or texts) are the vehicles that hold domination in place (for example, the power of medical discourses to define a person as 'disabled' or 'mad'), but also provide opportunities for contestation.

Practice validity: Criteria of utility that knowledge which is to be of use to practitioners must meet if it is to be relevant to practice scenarios, and which vary according to setting, knowledge source and paradigmatic affiliation.

Praxis: The practical power of theory and research to bring about change.

Precision: The extent to which an estimate lies close to the population **Parameter**.

Probability proportionate to size (PPS): Adjusts the probability of a higher order unit (cluster) being selected to be in proportion to the number of units in that cluster.

Problem–orientation: All approaches in critical discourse analysis (like all critical social sciences) investigate complex social phenomena and thus do not solely focus on a linguistic unit.

Proportion: The frequency of cases in a particular category or categories divided by the total number of cases in all categories.

Protocol: A plan of action, giving details of all the steps that will be followed in an investigation, and adopted as the key procedure for **Systematic reviews** in medical and social science.

Qualitative comparative analysis (QCA): A systematic analysis of the various configurations of cases, including ordinal variables called 'fuzzy sets'. Data can be interpreted qualitatively while causality between the variables can be examined.

Qualitative data: Qualitative data are collected using qualitative research methodology and techniques across the range of social science disciplines. Strategies often encompass a diversity of methods and tools rather than a single one and the types of data collected depend on the aims of the study, the nature of the sample and the discipline. As a result, data types extend to: in-depth or unstructured, individual or group discussion interviews, field and observation notes, unstructured diaries, observational recordings, personal documents and photographs.

Qualitative interview: The term 'qualitative interview' encompasses a wide range of interview techniques. These techniques share a commitment to exploring personal experiences and meanings in participants' own terms. However, there is much theoretical and methodological diversity within the range of qualitative interview techniques.

Qualitative variable: A variable in which the categories have no numerical relationship to one another.

Quantitative data: Quantitative data are collected using quantitative research methodologies and techniques across the range of social science disciplines. Strategies often encompass a diversity of methods and tools rather than a single one, and the types of data collected depend on the aims of the study, the nature of the sample and the discipline. As a result, data types extend to: structured interviews, questionnaires, behavioural data from structured observation and data deriving from **Content analysis**.

Quantitative variable: A variable in which the categories have a numerical relationship to one another and can be ordered in terms of size.

Questionnaire: The instrument used to collect information from a **Respondent**. It can either be completed by an interviewer interviewing the respondent or by the respondent him/herself (in which case it is referred to as a self-completion questionnaire).

Quota: A set number of interviews.

Quota control: The specification of particular characteristics of units that are to be selected.

'Race': A term introduced into anthropological discussion of the differences between people of differing ethnic groupings, to denote innate biological-physiological or intellectual and cultural differences between people. The term was part of a wider discourse that justified prejudicial, discriminatory and oppressive practices by those with power against those without. These practices are now generally brought together under the term 'racism' but, in the period of slavery, for example, these allegedly inherent racial differences were used to justify economic, political and physical exploitation of weaker ethnic groups by stronger ones.

Random selection: A method of selecting a sample that is objective; in other words, it does not allow any subjective influence over which units are included in the sample.

Randomised controlled trial (RCT): A research study in which subjects are randomly allocated between treatment and control or comparison groups. Sometimes regarded as the 'gold standard' in medical and health research.

Range: The difference between the highest and lowest value in a distribution of values.

Rapport: In a research context, this refers to the relationship that is built up between the researcher and participants in a study. A good rapport generally involves feelings of mutual trust, respect, safety and comfort during the research encounter.

Realism: This reflects a methodological position which advances two claims: that there is an external world independent of people's perceptions of it (so that there is more to find out about the social world than people's meanings); and that it is possible to obtain direct access to, and 'objective' knowledge about, this world. It permeates positivism to the point where the two terms are used interchangeably. However, the second principle is also a feature of **Naturalism**.

Reciprocity: An act of giving something to the participants in return for receiving information. This can reduce the power inequality between the researcher and the researched.

Recontextualisation: By taking an argument and restating it in a new context, we first observe the process of decontextualisation, and then, when the respective element is implemented in a new context, of recontextualisation. The element then acquires a new meaning because meanings are formed in use.

Reflexivity: Involves reflection by researchers on the social processes that impinge on and influence data. It requires a critical attitude towards data, and recognition of the influence on the research of such factors as the location of the setting, the sensitivity of the topic and the nature of the social interaction between the researcher and the researched. In the absence of reflexivity, the strengths of the data are exaggerated and/or the weaknesses underemphasised.

Refugee: A former **Asylum seeker** who has been *recognised* by the government as meeting the definition of a refugee set out in the United Nations (UN) Convention Relating to the Status of Refugees 1951. On being recognised by the government as a refugee, the person is conferred with 'refugee status'. In the UK, recognition as a refugee leads to 'indefinite leave to remain' (ILR) and attracts other rights, for example, family reunion and the issue of a refugee travel document.

Reliability: This describes the extent to which measurements are consistent when repeating a study using the same instruments under the same conditions.

Representativeness: The requirement that the structure and characteristics of the sample reflect those of the population.

Research costs: Funds for research are usually broken down into different categories. 'Direct costs' are those that are incurred only if the work goes ahead, for example, the salary of the researcher and the fieldwork costs. **Indirect costs** are those incurred by the organisation employing the researcher, for example, the accommodation costs or those of central services that have to be paid for, whether or not the particular project goes ahead. If a piece of work is funded there will be a number of indirect costs that are then attributed to the project. 'Overheads' is sometimes the term used instead of 'indirect costs' and they are usually calculated as a **Percentage** of the direct costs. There are often disputes about exactly what constitutes a direct or indirect cost, for example, the costs of senior staff who help to support and manage the project. Those funders who pay indirect costs (and not all do) will usually prefer to pay specific amounts for particular things, for example, accommodation, rather than a percentage of the direct costs.

Research design: A structure or framework within which data are collected. A research design is selected for its capacity to answer the research questions that drive an investigation.

Research Ethics Committees: Committees responsible for assessing whether proposals for research meet key standards in terms of ethics.

Research governance: The regulations, safeguards and standards that surround the research process. More specifically, it refers to the Department of Health's *Research governance framework for health and social care*.

Research synthesis: A broader term than **Systematic review**, more inclusive in scope, and referring to a wider range of techniques for collating and assessing research evidence. Arguably research synthesis is more closely tailored to the pluralism of **Social policy** and social work research.

Respondent: A term used to refer to a person whose responses to questions are collected and analysed, usually with a view to documenting the person's attitudes or opinions, rather than using him or her as a source of direct information about the world.

Response bias: Where the final sample of respondents is unrepresentative of the population because some types of selected sample members fail to respond at a greater rate than other types of selected sample members.

Response rate: The **Percentage** of a sample from which information is successfully obtained. Response rates are calculated differently depending on the method of questionnaire administration.

Responsive mode: Research proposals where the ideas for the piece of work come from the individual researcher, so that the funder is 'responding' to the application submitted, rather than seeking a project on a specific topic.

Retrieval (of coded passages): The act of bringing together for examination all the data coded at the same code. This is done so the data may be examined for patterns, correlations and differences.

Sample: A subset of a population.

Sampling: To sample means to select the case or cases for study from the basic unit of study where it is impossible to cover all instances of the unit. In probability sampling, each instance of the unit has the same probability of being included in the sample; in non-probability sampling, there is no way of estimating this probability or even any certainty that every instance has some chance.

Sampling distribution of the means: A hypothetical distribution that occurs through repeatedly sampling (with replacement) a fixed number of units from the same population, under the same conditions.

Sampling error (variability): The difference between an estimate and **Parameter** that arises randomly through the chance inclusion of the particular set of population members realised in a particular sample.

Sampling fraction: The number of units selected relative to the total number of population units.

Sampling frame: A list of population members that are numbered in such a way that their numbering corresponds to numbers randomly generated for selection from that list.

Sampling interval: The distance between two numbers on a list defined by the sampling fraction (see **Systematic sampling**).

Secondary analysis: Method used when a researcher analyses data that they themselves did not collect. Secondary analysis is also the method used when a researcher analyses data that they had collected in the past for a different purpose from the one that they now have. It is most often assumed to involve **Quantitative data** but can also involve qualitative data.

Self-completion methods: Methods that require respondents to work through and complete a questionnaire on their own, for example, a paper or electronic questionnaire.

Semantic web: As originally envisaged, describes methods and technologies to allow machines to understand the 'semantics' of information on the web in order to replicate human reasoning. While this ambitious project has not yet been realised, semantic *technologies* are increasingly used across the World Wide Web to enhance search tools, allow aggregation of diverse resources and construct interactive and dynamic websites.

Semi-structured interview: A research conversation that is shaped around an interview guide that has been pre-prepared by the interviewer, although there is flexibility to modify the sequence or wording of questions.

Sensitive research: Research that has potential implications for society or key social groups, and is potentially threatening to the researcher or subjects in bringing economic, social, political or physical costs.

Situated knowledge: Refers to the tacit, contextual or intuitive theories of practitioners; knowledge that is derived from particular practice events or activities.

Snowball sampling: Choosing respondents on the basis of previous respondents' recommendations or relationship networks, so that the eventual sample is likely to be a single or several networks of people. This is a non-probability method of **Sampling**.

Social policy: (a) An academic subject concerned with how and why policies have developed and how they operate in the social world; (b) the practice of social intervention and action aimed at securing social change to promote the welfare and well-being of citizens.

Social problems: Those conditions that are perceived as a collective rather than individual source of concern and which can be remedied or ameliorated by social action. There are competing explanations as to why certain social conditions or behaviours come to be regarded as social problems.

Socio-cognition: Discourse analytic approach that takes cognition as being the 'mediating link' between discourse/text and society/social groups. Hence, for example, there is the assumption that everybody has specific expectations about, and models of, contexts that help organise our language and communication in specific situations in culturally and socially adequate ways.

SPSS: An abbreviation for a package of computer programs called the Statistical Package for the Social Sciences and the name of the company that is responsible for it.

Standard deviation (SD): A measure of dispersion that is the square root of the **Variance** or mean squared deviations.

Standard error: The standard deviation of the **Sampling distribution of the means**. It provides a measure of imprecision in the estimate.

Statistical significance: The probability of a finding being due to chance or **Sampling error**.

Steering groups: See **Advisory groups**.

Story: A term used in **Narrative analysis**. Stories attempt to give coherence to lives by joining elements of experience together by use of a **Plot** and expressed through written, oral and visual means in autobiographies, biographies and related forms.

Stratification: The division of the population elements into groups defined by particular characteristics.

Stratified sampling: The **Random selection** of units within each **Stratum** defined by the stratification procedure, in advance of sampling.

Stratum: Particular groups defined by the process of **Stratification**.

Substantive theory: Theory whose content concerns problems or situations.

Survey: A **Research design** in which a sample of subjects is drawn from a population and studied (usually interviewed) to make inferences about the population. Surveys typically investigate social behaviour, family and life events, and public opinion or attitudes.

Synchronous/real time: Communication or 'chat' which takes place simultaneously, that is, messages are written and read at the same time by those online in different locations.

Systematic reviews: Reviews that draw together the results from a number of different research studies that are selected according to clear criteria, and which summarise these studies using standard **Protocols**.

Systematic sampling: A process that uses a randomly selected starting point between 1 and k, then chooses every kth member on the list, where k is defined as the overall **Sampling fraction**.

Telephone interview: A research interview conducted via the telephone. In the past, telephone interviews have tended to be used mainly for structured **Survey** research but, increasingly, the telephone mode is being used in social research to conduct various forms of **Qualitative interview**.

Text: 'Texts' are parts of discourses. They make speech acts durable over time and thus bridge two dilated speech situations, that is, the situation of speech production and the situation of speech reception. In other words, texts – be they visualised and written or oral – objectify linguistic actions.

Theme: A group of data related by subject matter that can make up part of a case but also be common across cases (for example, the theme of 'experiences of Ofsted inspections').

Theoretical sampling: A procedure involved in grounded theorising, requiring a researcher to sample in order to extend and broaden the scope of an emerging **Theory**. Cases, settings or people are chosen to study with a view to finding things that might challenge and extend the limitations of the existing theory.

Theoretical saturation: A procedure involved in grounded theorising, said to be reached when new data generate no further **Theory** development, with categories and their properties therefore appearing fully developed.

Theoretical sensitivity: Staying open to new ideas, interpretations and ultimately theories while immersing oneself in the data.

Theory: Refers to our existing knowledge and understanding surrounding an issue – what we know about the issue. Theories set out explanatory and predictive propositions about the causal relationships between phenomena.

Third party payment: In the context of healthcare systems, an arrangement by which individuals make financial contributions to a pool of resources against which they may subsequently claim the provision of healthcare. Such systems may be based on taxation, on social insurance or on private insurance.

Third Sector Research Centre (TSRC): Offers third sector organisations and policy makers access and input into robust research, aiming to bridge the gap between research and the third sector (see www.tsrc.ac.uk/About/tabid/347/Default.aspx for more information).

Transcription: The process of transferring audio or video recordings of speech or hand-written notes into a typed or word-processed form. In some cases special characters may be used to indicate aspects of how words were spoken.

Transferability: Whether a set of findings is relevant to settings other than the one or ones in which it was conducted.

Triangulation: Traditionally defined as the use of more than one method or more than one source of data to investigate the same research question. Its primary aim is to provide a check on the **Validity** and **Reliability** of the research. More recently, the definition of triangulation has expanded to encompass the combination of methods to answer different research questions within the same overarching study.

Unbiased sampling frame: A sampling frame is the list of elements of a population from which a sample will be drawn. This list is unbiased if it is a complete list of population elements or, if incomplete, the omitted elements are randomly rather than systematically missing.

Unobtrusive methods: Data collection techniques that do not involve direct elicitation from **Respondents** so that the information is obtained without the subject's prior knowledge, thus avoiding the 'reactive effect'.

Unstructured data: Data that are not structured in terms of categories relevant to the research at the point of collection.

Unstructured interview: A research conversation that is very much led by the interviewee. The researcher will be interested in a broad theme, but will have very few pre-prepared questions, and the direction of the discussion will vary according to topics raised by the interviewee.

User participatory research: Research in which users are active participants in the process of commissioning, designing and/or carrying out individual research projects or programmes.

Utilisation (of research): (a) Instrumental utilisation, when there is evidence of policy makers or practitioners acting on the findings of specific research studies; (b) conceptual utilisation, where research influences how policy makers and practitioners interpret and think about a social issue or problem.

Validity: Extent to which the data accurately reflect the phenomena under study.

Variable: An attribute in relation to which people (or any other units of analysis) differ.

Variance: A measure of dispersion that is the sum of squared deviations divided by the number of cases (sample variance) or the degrees of freedom (estimated population variance).

Vignette: A term with a double meaning. In one sense it describes a data collection technique, in which researchers present subjects with a hypothetical situation or scenario and ask them to write down how they or a third person would respond to it. It is particularly useful in dealing with very sensitive material. Its other meaning relates to the presentation of data where some aspect of the data are extracted and given special close analysis or description to act as an exemplar of a broader process.

Visual ethnography: Ethnographic research in which the visual forms a part.

Volunteer sampling: Sampling by asking for volunteers to take part in a study. This is a non-probability method of sampling.

Vulnerable people: Individuals who are marginalised and discriminated against in society due to their social positions, based on class, ethnicity, gender, age, illness, disability and sexual preferences. They are often difficult to reach and require special consideration to try to involve them in research. The term is also used to refer to people who are difficult to access in societies, and to those whose autonomy is impaired in some ways.

Web 2.0: A term applied to the range of web applications that allow interactive information sharing, interoperability and collaboration; this 'many-to-many' interaction contrasts with the typically 'one-to-many' nature of 'Web 1.0'. Web 2.0 technologies include **Wikis**, **Blogs**, collaborative bookmarking and 'social networking' sites.

Weighting: The procedure used to adjust samples so that the sample characteristics resemble those of the population. Sample weighting results in some individuals counting as less than one case while others may contribute more than one case.

Wiki: A wiki is a software application that allows the creation and editing of interlinked web pages via a web browser using a simplified mark-up language. Making web pages editable allows multiple authors to contribute to a single text or to edit or comment on others' work.

Index

Page references for the glossary are in **bold**.